P9-DUS-066

Mastering Payroll II

—From benefits and business expenses to sick pay and workers' compensation

by Debera J. Salam, CPP
Director
Payroll Information and Process Services

Debera J. Salam, CPP, has over 30 years' experience in payroll management and consulting on compliance issues. She is the author of *Principles of Payroll Administration* and *The Payroll Practitioner's Compliance Handbook: Year-End and Quarterly Reporting,* managing editor of the Ernst & Young *Payroll Perspectives Library* and contributing editor of *The General Ledger.* As one of the country's leading authors on payroll, Ms. Salam serves on the advisory board of the American Institute of Professional Bookkeepers. She provides U.S. payroll consulting, thought leadership, and training to businesses and organizations throughout the world.

© AIPB, Inc., 2021
ISBN 978-1-938741-15-9

All rights reserved. No part of this publication may be reproduced in any form or by any means without the prior written permission of the publisher.

This publication is designed to provide accurate and authoritative information regarding the subject matter covered. It is sold with the understanding that the publisher and author are not engaged in rendering legal, accounting or other professional services. If legal advice or other expert assistance is required, the services of a competent professional person should be sought.—From a Declaration of Principles jointly adopted by a Committee of the American Bar Association and a Committee of Publishers and Associations.

INTRODUCTION

Mastering Payroll II provides the practical knowledge needed to improve your skills and advance your career. The course comprises 12 sections and an optional "Final Examination." Upon completing this course, you should be able to:

1. Know how to handle different kinds of tax-free, tax-deferred or partially or fully taxable benefits, how to calculate the value of these benefits, impute them to wages, and collect and report taxes on the appropriate federal forms.

2. Understand the rules that apply to expenses, disability payments and sick pay, and how to calculate and collect taxes where appropriate, how to report taxes and use the appropriate forms, and how to understand the basics of workers' compensation insurance.

3. Choose the best method for withholding federal income tax from wages and be able to make correct deductions for garnishments and levies.

Note: Timely material, such as FICA (Social Security and Medicare) tax rates and limits, is based on 2021 information.

To get the most out of the course, this is the procedure we recommend:

1. Read the concise narrative that begins each section.

2. Read each section narrative twice. The second time, cover the solution to each illustrative problem and try to figure it out. *Actually write it out.* Regardless of how easy or difficult it may seem, simply *trying* to solve it and checking your answer against the correct solution will help you learn a great deal.

3. Take Quiz #1 at the end of each section to see what you have learned and need to review.

4. Take Quiz #2 at the end of each section to master any points previously missed.

At the end of the course, there is an optional, open-book *Final Examination*. A separate *Final Examination Answer Sheet* is provided on page 391 to fill in your answers. If you wish to receive an AIPB *Certificate of Completion*, you must achieve a grade of at least 70. Complete and return the *Final Examination Answer Sheet* to: AIPB Continuing Education, Suite 500, 6001 Montrose Road, Rockville, MD 20852.

Certified Bookkeepers who pass the Final Examination are eligible to register seven (7) CPECs.

Finally, please take a moment to fill out and send in the brief "Course Evaluation" at the back of your workbook (whether or not you take the final). It will help AIPB to improve this and other courses.

AIPB recommends the excellent reference material listed in the "Bibliography" on page 192.

AIPB wants to thank the people whose hard work contributed to this course, including Supervisory Editor (Ret.), L.G. Schloss, Department of Accounting and Law, Iona College, New Rochelle, New York; Technical Editor, Lisa Miedich, Employment Tax Specialist, Colorado Springs, Colorado; Carolee Brady and Joanne Brodsky for proofreading; and Carol Lovelady, Lovelady Consulting, Olive Branch, Mississippi for typesetting.

Thank you, enjoy the course and congratulations on taking a major step toward advancing your professional knowledge and career.

An Important Note About COVID-19 Federal Tax Programs

In response to COVID-19's impact on employers and employees, new laws were enacted, including the Families First Coronavirus Response Act (FFCRA) and Coronavirus Aid, Relief, and Economic Security Act (CARES). These laws extended paid leave to certain employees, enhanced unemployment insurance benefits and enhanced cash flow to employers through tax credits, deferred Social Security tax payments and forgivable loans under the Paycheck Protection Program (PPP).

Some states and localities enacted similar programs, including expanded paid leave, temporarily cancelled reporting requirements and extended due dates for payroll tax returns or payments, or both.

But all these laws and programs are of such complexity and of such short duration, they do not belong in a course that trains you to do payroll long-term, and so are not included in this workbook.

If you would like details on these programs, see Ernst & Young LLP, COVID-19 Employer Requirements and Considerations (go to *https://www.ey.com/en_us/tax/employment-tax-advisory-services/covid-19-employer-requirements-and-considerations*), co-authored by Debera Salam.

CONTENTS

WITHHOLDING FEDERAL INCOME TAX FROM WAGES

Introduction

There are three standard methods of withholding federal income tax from wages: the wage-bracket method, which is simpler but provides only approximately the same withholding amount as a computerized system; the percentage withholding method, which is more complicated but more closely approximates the same withholding amount as a computerized system; and the optional supplemental tax rate for withholding (22% effective 2018 through 2025). The mandatory rate that applies to supplemental wages in excess of $1 million in the year is 37% effective 2018 through 2025.

Federal Income Tax Withholding (FITW)

As explained in *Mastering Payroll*, an employee's federal income tax withholding (FITW) generally is based on seven factors:

1. **Employer pay period.** A pay period may be daily, weekly, biweekly, semimonthly, monthly, annual, or any period the employer chooses.

2. **Employee marital status.** Withholding rates are different for single, married and, effective January 1, 2020, head of household employees.

3. **For Forms W-4 provided before 2020, employee personal allowances.** The number of allowances the employee claims on the W-4 affects federal income tax withholding for each period.

4. **For Forms W-4 provided on and after January 1, 2020**, adjustments claimed to income or deductions in Steps 2, 3 and 4.

5. **All Forms W-4.** Additional income tax withholding requested.

6. **Employee federal taxable wages for the period.** All wages, overtime, bonuses, and other payments for the period are federal taxable wages and subject to federal income tax.

7. **Supplemental Wages.** Payments meeting the definition of supplemental wages are optionally taxed at 22% (effective for 2018 through 2025), and when they exceed $1 million in the tax year are mandatorily subject to a

---

flat rate of 37% (effective for 2018 through 2025) without regard to the W-4, including a Form W-4 claiming exemption from withholding.

To determine each employee's FITW, the employer applies factors 1 through 6 to the federal withholding tables in the current year IRS Publication 15-T *Federal Income Tax Withholding Methods*.

Federal Income Tax Withholding Tables

Effective January 1, 2020, there are five withholding tables in Publication 15-T—

Table 1: *Percentage Method Tables for Automated Payroll Systems*

Table 2: *Wage Bracket Method Tables for Manual Payroll Systems With Forms W-4 From 2020 or Later*

Table 3: *Wage Bracket Method Tables for Manual Payroll Systems With Forms W-4 From 2019 or Earlier*

Table 4: *Percentage Method Tables for Manual Payroll Systems With Forms W-4 From 2020 or Later*

Table 5: *Percentage Method Tables for Manual Payroll Systems With Forms W-4 From 2019 or Earlier*

Using this information, the employer locates the correct FITW amount depending on if the Form W-4 is older than January 1, 2020 or if it is a Form W-4 from 2020 and later. The tables for 2021 are reprinted, in part, on pages 3–5.

The Wage-Bracket Method

This method is easier and faster for those who prepare paychecks manually.

To recap the method described in *Mastering Payroll I*:

1. Using Table 3 for Forms W-4 From 2019 or Earlier or Table 2 for Forms W-4 From 2020 or later, pages 3–5, locate the wage-bracket table that describes the year of the Form W-4 (2019 or earlier, 2020 or later), employee's marital status ("Single Persons" or "Married Persons") and the pay period by which the employee is paid—"Weekly," "Biweekly," etc.

2. Go to the left-hand column and find the wage range in which the employee's gross wages fall.

Table 2: 2021 Wage Bracket Method Tables for Manual Payroll Systems With Forms W-4 From 2020 or Later

2021 Wage Bracket Method Tables for Manual Payroll Systems with Forms W-4 From 2020 or Later
WEEKLY Payroll Period

If the Adjusted Wage Amount (line 1h) is		Married Filing Jointly		Head of Household		Single or Married Filing Separately	
		Standard withholding	Form W-4, Step 2, Checkbox withholding	Standard withholding	Form W-4, Step 2, Checkbox withholding	Standard withholding	Form W-4, Step 2, Checkbox withholding
At least	But less than	The Tentative Withholding Amount is:					
$1,415	$1,425	$105	$178	$123	$226	$178	$254
$1,425	$1,435	$106	$180	$125	$228	$180	$257
$1,435	$1,445	$107	$182	$128	$231	$182	$259
$1,445	$1,455	$108	$184	$130	$233	$184	$262
$1,455	$1,465	$110	$186	$132	$236	$186	$264
$1,465	$1,475	$111	$189	$134	$238	$189	$266
$1,475	$1,485	$112	$191	$136	$240	$191	$269
$1,485	$1,495	$113	$193	$139	$243	$193	$271
$1,495	$1,505	$114	$195	$141	$245	$195	$274
$1,505	$1,515	$116	$197	$143	$248	$197	$276
$1,515	$1,525	$117	$200	$145	$250	$200	$278
$1,525	$1,535	$118	$202	$147	$252	$202	$281
$1,535	$1,545	$119	$204	$150	$255	$204	$283
$1,545	$1,555	$120	$206	$152	$257	$206	$286
$1,555	$1,565	$122	$208	$154	$260	$208	$288
$1,565	$1,575	$123	$211	$156	$262	$211	$290
$1,575	$1,585	$124	$213	$158	$264	$213	$293
$1,585	$1,595	$125	$215	$161	$267	$215	$295
$1,595	$1,605	$126	$217	$163	$269	$217	$298
$1,605	$1,615	$128	$219	$165	$272	$219	$300
$1,615	$1,625	$129	$222	$167	$274	$222	$302
$1,625	$1,635	$130	$224	$169	$276	$224	$305
$1,635	$1,645	$131	$226	$172	$279	$226	$307
$1,645	$1,655	$132	$228	$174	$281	$228	$310
$1,655	$1,665	$134	$230	$176	$284	$230	$312
$1,665	$1,675	$135	$233	$178	$286	$233	$314
$1,675	$1,685	$136	$235	$180	$288	$235	$317
$1,685	$1,695	$137	$237	$183	$291	$237	$319
$1,695	$1,705	$138	$239	$185	$293	$239	$322
$1,705	$1,715	$140	$241	$187	$296	$241	$324
$1,715	$1,725	$141	$244	$189	$298	$244	$327
$1,725	$1,735	$142	$246	$191	$300	$246	$331
$1,735	$1,745	$143	$248	$194	$303	$248	$334
$1,745	$1,755	$144	$250	$196	$305	$250	$337
$1,755	$1,765	$146	$252	$198	$308	$252	$340
$1,765	$1,775	$147	$255	$200	$310	$255	$343
$1,775	$1,785	$148	$257	$202	$313	$257	$347
$1,785	$1,795	$149	$259	$205	$317	$259	$350
$1,795	$1,805	$150	$261	$207	$320	$261	$353
$1,805	$1,815	$152	$263	$209	$323	$263	$356
$1,815	$1,825	$153	$266	$211	$326	$266	$359
$1,825	$1,835	$154	$268	$213	$329	$268	$363
$1,835	$1,845	$155	$270	$216	$333	$270	$366
$1,845	$1,855	$156	$272	$218	$336	$272	$369
$1,855	$1,865	$158	$274	$220	$339	$274	$372
$1,865	$1,875	$159	$277	$222	$342	$277	$375
$1,875	$1,885	$160	$279	$224	$345	$279	$379
$1,885	$1,895	$161	$281	$227	$349	$281	$382
$1,895	$1,905	$162	$283	$229	$352	$283	$385
$1,905	$1,915	$164	$285	$231	$355	$285	$388
$1,915	$1,925	$165	$288	$233	$358	$288	$391

Table 3: 2021 Wage Bracket Method Tables for Manual Payroll Systems With Forms W-4 From 2019 or Earlier (Weekly, married persons)

2021 Wage Bracket Method Tables for Manual Payroll Systems With Forms W-4 From 2019 or Earlier
WEEKLY Payroll Period

If the Wage Amount (line 1a) is		MARRIED Persons And the number of allowances is:										
At least	But less than	0	1	2	3	4	5	6	7	8	9	10
		The Tentative Withholding Amount is:										
$0	$235	$0	$0	$0	$0	$0	$0	$0	$0	$0	$0	$0
$235	$245	$1	$0	$0	$0	$0	$0	$0	$0	$0	$0	$0
$245	$255	$2	$0	$0	$0	$0	$0	$0	$0	$0	$0	$0
$255	$265	$3	$0	$0	$0	$0	$0	$0	$0	$0	$0	$0
$265	$275	$4	$0	$0	$0	$0	$0	$0	$0	$0	$0	$0
$275	$285	$5	$0	$0	$0	$0	$0	$0	$0	$0	$0	$0
$285	$295	$6	$0	$0	$0	$0	$0	$0	$0	$0	$0	$0
$295	$305	$7	$0	$0	$0	$0	$0	$0	$0	$0	$0	$0
$305	$315	$8	$0	$0	$0	$0	$0	$0	$0	$0	$0	$0
$315	$325	$9	$0	$0	$0	$0	$0	$0	$0	$0	$0	$0
$325	$335	$10	$1	$0	$0	$0	$0	$0	$0	$0	$0	$0
$335	$345	$11	$2	$0	$0	$0	$0	$0	$0	$0	$0	$0
$345	$355	$12	$3	$0	$0	$0	$0	$0	$0	$0	$0	$0
$355	$365	$13	$4	$0	$0	$0	$0	$0	$0	$0	$0	$0
$365	$375	$14	$5	$0	$0	$0	$0	$0	$0	$0	$0	$0
$375	$385	$15	$6	$0	$0	$0	$0	$0	$0	$0	$0	$0
$385	$395	$16	$7	$0	$0	$0	$0	$0	$0	$0	$0	$0
$395	$405	$17	$8	$0	$0	$0	$0	$0	$0	$0	$0	$0
$405	$415	$18	$9	$1	$0	$0	$0	$0	$0	$0	$0	$0
$415	$425	$19	$10	$2	$0	$0	$0	$0	$0	$0	$0	$0
$425	$435	$20	$11	$3	$0	$0	$0	$0	$0	$0	$0	$0
$435	$445	$21	$12	$4	$0	$0	$0	$0	$0	$0	$0	$0
$445	$455	$22	$13	$5	$0	$0	$0	$0	$0	$0	$0	$0
$455	$465	$23	$14	$6	$0	$0	$0	$0	$0	$0	$0	$0
$465	$475	$24	$15	$7	$0	$0	$0	$0	$0	$0	$0	$0
$475	$485	$25	$16	$8	$0	$0	$0	$0	$0	$0	$0	$0
$485	$495	$26	$17	$9	$1	$0	$0	$0	$0	$0	$0	$0
$495	$505	$27	$18	$10	$2	$0	$0	$0	$0	$0	$0	$0
$505	$515	$28	$19	$11	$3	$0	$0	$0	$0	$0	$0	$0
$515	$525	$29	$20	$12	$4	$0	$0	$0	$0	$0	$0	$0
$525	$535	$30	$21	$13	$5	$0	$0	$0	$0	$0	$0	$0
$535	$545	$31	$22	$14	$6	$0	$0	$0	$0	$0	$0	$0
$545	$555	$32	$23	$15	$7	$0	$0	$0	$0	$0	$0	$0
$555	$565	$33	$24	$16	$8	$0	$0	$0	$0	$0	$0	$0
$565	$575	$34	$25	$17	$9	$0	$0	$0	$0	$0	$0	$0
$575	$585	$35	$26	$18	$10	$1	$0	$0	$0	$0	$0	$0
$585	$595	$36	$27	$19	$11	$2	$0	$0	$0	$0	$0	$0
$595	$605	$37	$28	$20	$12	$3	$0	$0	$0	$0	$0	$0
$605	$615	$38	$29	$21	$13	$4	$0	$0	$0	$0	$0	$0
$615	$625	$39	$30	$22	$14	$5	$0	$0	$0	$0	$0	$0
$625	$640	$40	$32	$23	$15	$7	$0	$0	$0	$0	$0	$0
$640	$655	$42	$33	$25	$16	$8	$0	$0	$0	$0	$0	$0
$655	$670	$44	$35	$26	$18	$10	$1	$0	$0	$0	$0	$0
$670	$685	$45	$36	$28	$19	$11	$3	$0	$0	$0	$0	$0
$685	$700	$47	$38	$29	$21	$13	$4	$0	$0	$0	$0	$0
$700	$715	$49	$39	$31	$22	$14	$6	$0	$0	$0	$0	$0
$715	$730	$51	$41	$32	$24	$16	$7	$0	$0	$0	$0	$0
$730	$745	$53	$43	$34	$25	$17	$9	$1	$0	$0	$0	$0
$745	$760	$54	$45	$35	$27	$19	$10	$2	$0	$0	$0	$0
$760	$775	$56	$46	$37	$28	$20	$12	$4	$0	$0	$0	$0
$775	$790	$58	$48	$38	$30	$22	$13	$5	$0	$0	$0	$0

Table 3: 2021 Wage Bracket Method Tables for Manual Payroll Systems With Forms W-4 From 2019 or Earlier (Weekly, single person)

2021 Wage Bracket Method Tables for Manual Payroll Systems With Forms W-4 From 2019 or Earlier
WEEKLY Payroll Period

If the Wage Amount (line 1a) is		SINGLE Persons										
		And the number of allowances is:										
At least	But less than	0	1	2	3	4	5	6	7	8	9	10
		The Tentative Withholding Amount is:										
$0	$80	$0	$0	$0	$0	$0	$0	$0	$0	$0	$0	$0
$80	$90	$1	$0	$0	$0	$0	$0	$0	$0	$0	$0	$0
$90	$100	$2	$0	$0	$0	$0	$0	$0	$0	$0	$0	$0
$100	$110	$3	$0	$0	$0	$0	$0	$0	$0	$0	$0	$0
$110	$120	$4	$0	$0	$0	$0	$0	$0	$0	$0	$0	$0
$120	$130	$5	$0	$0	$0	$0	$0	$0	$0	$0	$0	$0
$130	$140	$6	$0	$0	$0	$0	$0	$0	$0	$0	$0	$0
$140	$150	$7	$0	$0	$0	$0	$0	$0	$0	$0	$0	$0
$150	$160	$8	$0	$0	$0	$0	$0	$0	$0	$0	$0	$0
$160	$170	$9	$1	$0	$0	$0	$0	$0	$0	$0	$0	$0
$170	$180	$10	$2	$0	$0	$0	$0	$0	$0	$0	$0	$0
$180	$190	$11	$3	$0	$0	$0	$0	$0	$0	$0	$0	$0
$190	$200	$12	$4	$0	$0	$0	$0	$0	$0	$0	$0	$0
$200	$210	$13	$5	$0	$0	$0	$0	$0	$0	$0	$0	$0
$210	$220	$14	$6	$0	$0	$0	$0	$0	$0	$0	$0	$0
$220	$230	$15	$7	$0	$0	$0	$0	$0	$0	$0	$0	$0
$230	$240	$16	$8	$0	$0	$0	$0	$0	$0	$0	$0	$0
$240	$250	$17	$9	$0	$0	$0	$0	$0	$0	$0	$0	$0
$250	$260	$18	$10	$1	$0	$0	$0	$0	$0	$0	$0	$0
$260	$270	$19	$11	$2	$0	$0	$0	$0	$0	$0	$0	$0
$270	$285	$20	$12	$4	$0	$0	$0	$0	$0	$0	$0	$0
$285	$300	$22	$13	$5	$0	$0	$0	$0	$0	$0	$0	$0
$300	$315	$24	$15	$7	$0	$0	$0	$0	$0	$0	$0	$0
$315	$330	$26	$16	$8	$0	$0	$0	$0	$0	$0	$0	$0
$330	$345	$28	$18	$10	$1	$0	$0	$0	$0	$0	$0	$0
$345	$360	$29	$19	$11	$3	$0	$0	$0	$0	$0	$0	$0
$360	$375	$31	$21	$13	$4	$0	$0	$0	$0	$0	$0	$0
$375	$390	$33	$23	$14	$6	$0	$0	$0	$0	$0	$0	$0
$390	$405	$35	$25	$16	$7	$0	$0	$0	$0	$0	$0	$0
$405	$420	$37	$27	$17	$9	$1	$0	$0	$0	$0	$0	$0
$420	$435	$38	$28	$19	$10	$2	$0	$0	$0	$0	$0	$0
$435	$450	$40	$30	$20	$12	$4	$0	$0	$0	$0	$0	$0
$450	$465	$42	$32	$22	$13	$5	$0	$0	$0	$0	$0	$0
$465	$480	$44	$34	$24	$15	$7	$0	$0	$0	$0	$0	$0
$480	$495	$46	$36	$26	$16	$8	$0	$0	$0	$0	$0	$0
$495	$510	$47	$37	$28	$18	$10	$1	$0	$0	$0	$0	$0
$510	$525	$49	$39	$29	$19	$11	$3	$0	$0	$0	$0	$0
$525	$540	$51	$41	$31	$21	$13	$4	$0	$0	$0	$0	$0
$540	$555	$53	$43	$33	$23	$14	$6	$0	$0	$0	$0	$0
$555	$570	$55	$45	$35	$25	$16	$7	$0	$0	$0	$0	$0
$570	$585	$56	$46	$37	$27	$17	$9	$1	$0	$0	$0	$0
$585	$600	$58	$48	$38	$28	$19	$10	$2	$0	$0	$0	$0
$600	$615	$60	$50	$40	$30	$20	$12	$4	$0	$0	$0	$0
$615	$630	$62	$52	$42	$32	$22	$13	$5	$0	$0	$0	$0
$630	$645	$64	$54	$44	$34	$24	$15	$7	$0	$0	$0	$0
$645	$660	$65	$55	$46	$36	$26	$16	$8	$0	$0	$0	$0
$660	$675	$67	$57	$47	$37	$27	$18	$10	$1	$0	$0	$0
$675	$690	$69	$59	$49	$39	$29	$19	$11	$3	$0	$0	$0
$690	$705	$71	$61	$51	$41	$31	$21	$13	$4	$0	$0	$0
$705	$720	$73	$63	$53	$43	$33	$23	$14	$6	$0	$0	$0
$720	$735	$74	$64	$55	$45	$35	$25	$16	$7	$0	$0	$0

3. For Forms W-4 from 2019 or earlier, go to the top of the page and locate the column with the same number of withholding allowances claimed by the employee on the W-4.

4. The point at which the wage-range line and the withholding allowance column intersect represents the correct amount of FITW.

> **PROBLEM 1:** Jeff is paid $660 each weekly period. On his 2019 W-4, he has claimed married with 2 allowances. How much federal income tax should be withheld from his paycheck?
>
> **SOLUTION 1:** $26 FITW. Here is the procedure for finding Jeff's FITW:
>
> 1. Go to Table 3 for "Married Persons—Weekly Payroll Period" (page 4).
>
> 2. Locate in the left-hand column the wage range for Jeff's gross taxable wages ($655–$670).
>
> 3. Near the top of the table, find the column for 2 allowances.
>
> 4. The point at which the wage-range line and allowance column intersect shows the correct amount of federal income tax to withhold from Jeff's paycheck: $26.

Employees who claim more than 10 allowances (applies only to Forms W-4 from 2019 and earlier). Prior to 2020, it was not unusual for employees with substantial deductible expenses such as mortgage interest or medical bills to claim more than 10 allowances on their W-4. When an employee claims more than 10 allowances, both the wage-bracket table (Table 3) and the percentage method withholding table (Tables 4–5) may be used, as follows:

1. Subtract 10 allowances from the total allowances claimed by the employee to yield the number of "excess allowances."

2. Using the "Percentage Method Income Tax Withholding Table for 2021" (Figure 1-2, page 8), find the correct dollars-per-allowance for the employer's pay period.

3. Multiply the number of excess allowances (result obtained in Line 1) by the dollars-per-allowance.

4. Subtract the result obtained in Line 3 from gross wages to get the employee's net taxable wages.

5. Locate the correct wage-bracket table (for Forms W-4 from 2019 or earlier Table 3, pages 4–5) for the employee's marital status and pay period (weekly, biweekly, etc.).

6. In the left-hand column of the wage-bracket table (Table 3), find the wage range that applies to the result obtained in Line 4.

7. Select the column at the top of the table for "10" withholding allowances.

8. The point at which the wage-range line and the allowance column intersect shows the correct FITW.

9. In lieu of #1–8, withhold as though the employee claimed only 10 allowances.

> **PROBLEM 2:** Jenna is paid $720 each weekly period. On her 2018 W-4, she has claimed single with 11 allowances. How much federal income tax should be withheld from her paycheck in 2021?
>
> **SOLUTION 2:** $0 FITW. To calculate:
>
> | | | |
> |---|---:|---:|
> | 1. Total wages | | $720.00 |
> | 2. Each allowance: | $83.00 | |
> | 3. Times excess allowance | × 1 | |
> | 4. Less: allowance amount | | (83.00) |
> | 5. Net taxable wages | | $637.00 |
> | 6. For wage-range single, weekly $630–$645 with 10 allowances, FITW is (Table 3, single, page 5), | | $ 0.00 |
>
> OR:
>
> 7. $0.00 ($720–$735, Table 3, single, page 5)

The Percentage Method of Withholding

Most computerized payroll systems use the percentage method (or a similar method) to calculate FITW. This method also may be used for manual payroll systems by following this procedure:

1. For Forms W-4 from 2019 or earlier, refer to Figure 1-2 below for the correct dollars-per-allowance for the employer's pay period and Table 5 (page 14). For Forms W-4 for 2020 and later, you will use Table 4 (page 13).

2. For Forms W-4 from 2019 and earlier, multiply the per-allowance dollar amount by the total number of withholding allowances claimed on the employee's W-4 and subtract the result from Line 2 from the employee's taxable wages for the period.

Figure 1-2
Percentage Method Income Tax
Withholding Table for 2021
(Dollars-per-allowance by Employer Pay Period)

Value of Payroll period	1 allowance
Daily or Miscellaneous	$ 17.00
Weekly	83.00
Biweekly	165.00
Semimonthly	179.00
Monthly	358.00
Quarterly	1,075.00
Semiannually	2,150.00
Annually	4,300.00

3. Find the marital status claimed on the employee's W-4 and the employee's pay period in the "Percentage Method Tables for Income Tax Withholding" (Table 3 [pages 4–5], or Tables 4–5 [pages 12–14]). Then find the wage range that includes the result on Line 3. (Note: We have provided only a portion of Tables 3, 4, and 5 for illustrative purposes.)

4. Calculate the amount to withhold.

> **PROBLEM 3:** Max is paid $1,000 in each weekly period. On his 2019 W-4 he claimed married with 2 allowances. How much federal income tax should be withheld from Max's regular pay using the percentage withholding method in 2021?
>
> **SOLUTION 3:** $64.24. To calculate using the percentage withholding method:
>
> Gross wages are $1,000 each weekly pay period.
>
> 1. Select from Figure 1-2 the correct dollars-per-allowance for a weekly pay period: $83.00.
>
> 2. Multiply the dollars-per-allowance by the number of allowances that Max claimed on his W-4: $83.00 × 2 = $166.00.
>
> 3. Subtract the result in Line 2 from the employee's taxable wages to yield net taxable wages subject to withholding: $1,000 – $166.00 = $834.00.

4. Use the "Percentage Method Tables for Income Tax Withholding" (Table 5, page 14). Table 5 shows that a "Married Person" paid taxable income of $834.00 weekly is taxed at the rate of 12% of wages in excess of $617.00 plus $38.20. To calculate:

$834.00 – $617.00 ($217.00) × 12% ($26.04) + $38.20 = $64.24 FITW

PROBLEM 4: Dina is paid $450 each weekly period. On her 2019 W-4 she claimed single with 2 allowances. What is her FITW using the percentage withholding method in 2021?

SOLUTION 4: $21.14. Here's the procedure for finding her FITW using the percentage withholding method:

1. Total wages	$450.00
2. Allowances claimed on W-4: ($83.00 × 2 = $166.60)	(166.00)
3. Amount subject to withholding (Line 1–Line 2)	284.00
4. Less: excess in Table 5 (single person)	(267.00)
5. Net taxable income	$ 17.00
6. Tax on $17.00 from Table 5 (single), ($17.00 × 12%)	$ 2.04
7. Plus $19.10 (Table 5, single) = Total Withholding	$ 21.14

NOTE: The IRS offers an Excel spreadsheet for easier calculation of income tax withholding using the percentage method. The spreadsheet is available at *https://www.irs.gov/businesses/small-businesses-self-employed/income-tax-withholding-assistant-for-employers.*

Supplemental Wages and the Alternative Withholding Tax Rate

Employers may optionally use a flat *supplemental withholding tax rate* for "supplemental wages"—payments in addition to regular wages that include commissions, bonuses, vacation pay in lieu of vacation, vacation pay given at termination, tips, awards, prizes, back pay, third-party sick pay, fringe benefits, taxable business expense reimbursements, severance pay, retroactive increases, taxable stock transactions, and overtime pay. The supplemental rate of withholding is 22% (for 2018 through 2025). The supplemental withholding tax rate may be used only under the following conditions:

1. When supplemental wages are paid separately from regular wages—or, if paid with regular wages, are clearly indicated as a separate amount.

2. When federal income tax was withheld from regular wages in the current or previous tax year (employees who earn very low wages or who claim many allowances may have had no FITW withheld).

   If an employer has not withheld federal income tax from regular wages in the current or previous tax year, the supplemental withholding tax rate *cannot* be used. For example, if an employee is paid only commissions and no regular wages, the supplemental withholding rate of 22% cannot be used. (However, should the supplemental wages in the year exceed $1 million, the 37% rate of withholding must be used on supplemental wages in excess of $1 million without regard to the employee's Form W-4 claiming exemption from FITW.) See IRS *Publication 15-A* for allowable withholding methods.

Supplemental Wages in Excess of $1 Million in a Calendar Year

When an employee's supplemental wages exceed $1 million for the year, federal income tax must be withheld at 37% (for 2018 through 2025), regardless of the employee's W-4 (even if the employee claimed exempt) and regardless of whether the employer withheld at the supplemental rate on any previous $1 million in supplemental wages.

The 37% rate, however, applies only to the amount *over* $1 million. For example, if a payment of $1,000 results in supplemental wages for the year of $1,000,050—$50 over the $1 million threshold—only $50 is subject to the 37% rate. The remaining $950 may be taxed at the supplemental withholding rate of 22% (if all requirements have been met) for 2021 or the aggregate method may be used.

> **PROBLEM 5:** John is to receive a final paycheck of $1,000 in 2021 comprising vacation and severance pay. If his employer uses the supplemental withholding tax rate for supplemental wages of less than $1 million, what will be his FITW?
>
> **SOLUTION 5:** $220 FITW. To calculate:
>
> $$\$1,000 \times 22\% \ [0.22] = \$220$$

PROBLEM 6: Sean is paid $510 a week. He claims married with 4 allowances on his 2019 Form W-4. In 2020, no federal income tax was withheld from Sean's pay. In 2021, his first payroll check includes a production bonus of $150. How should federal income tax be withheld from the bonus using the wage-bracket method?

SOLUTION 6: $10. Because no federal income tax was withheld from wages in the current or previous tax year, the supplemental withholding rate cannot be used. The employer must add Sean's $150 bonus to his regular wages of $510 (total $660). The FITW on $660 for a married employee with 4 allowances is $10. (See Table 3, 2019 and earlier for married persons, page 4, wage bracket $655 to $670.)

Table 4: 2021 Percentage Method Tables for Manual Payroll Systems with Forms W-4 from 2020 or Later (Weekly)

2021 Percentage Method Tables for Manual Payroll Systems With Forms W-4 from 2020 or Later
WEEKLY Payroll Period

STANDARD Withholding Rate Schedules (Use these if the box in Step 2 of Form W-4 is **NOT** checked)					Form W-4, Step 2, Checkbox, Withholding Rate Schedules (Use these if the box in Step 2 of Form W-4 **IS** checked)				
If the Adjusted Wage Amount (line 1h) is:		The tentative amount to withhold is:	Plus this percentage—	of the amount that the Adjusted Wage exceeds—	If the Adjusted Wage Amount (line 1h) is:		The tentative amount to withhold is:	Plus this percentage—	of the amount that the Adjusted Wage exceeds—
At least—	But less than—				At least—	But less than—			
A	B	C	D	E	A	B	C	D	E
Married Filing Jointly					**Married Filing Jointly**				
$0	$483	$0.00	0%	$0	$0	$241	$0.00	0%	$0
$483	$865	$0.00	10%	$483	$241	$433	$0.00	10%	$241
$865	$2,041	$38.20	12%	$865	$433	$1,021	$19.20	12%	$433
$2,041	$3,805	$179.32	22%	$2,041	$1,021	$1,902	$89.76	22%	$1,021
$3,805	$6,826	$567.40	24%	$3,805	$1,902	$3,413	$283.58	24%	$1,902
$6,826	$8,538	$1,292.44	32%	$6,826	$3,413	$4,269	$646.22	32%	$3,413
$8,538	$12,565	$1,840.28	35%	$8,538	$4,269	$6,283	$920.14	35%	$4,269
$12,565		$3,249.73	37%	$12,565	$6,283		$1,625.04	37%	$6,283
Single or Married Filing Separately					**Single or Married Filing Separately**				
$0	$241	$0.00	0%	$0	$0	$121	$0.00	0%	$0
$241	$433	$0.00	10%	$241	$121	$216	$0.00	10%	$121
$433	$1,021	$19.20	12%	$433	$216	$510	$9.50	12%	$216
$1,021	$1,902	$89.76	22%	$1,021	$510	$951	$44.78	22%	$510
$1,902	$3,413	$283.58	24%	$1,902	$951	$1,706	$141.80	24%	$951
$3,413	$4,269	$646.22	32%	$3,413	$1,706	$2,134	$323.00	32%	$1,706
$4,269	$10,311	$920.14	35%	$4,269	$2,134	$5,155	$459.96	35%	$2,134
$10,311		$3,034.84	37%	$10,311	$5,155		$1,517.31	37%	$5,155
Head of Household					**Head of Household**				
$0	$362	$0.00	0%	$0	$0	$181	$0.00	0%	$0
$362	$635	$0.00	10%	$362	$181	$317	$0.00	10%	$181
$635	$1,404	$27.30	12%	$635	$317	$702	$13.60	12%	$317
$1,404	$2,022	$119.58	22%	$1,404	$702	$1,011	$59.80	22%	$702
$2,022	$3,533	$255.54	24%	$2,022	$1,011	$1,766	$127.78	24%	$1,011
$3,533	$4,388	$618.18	32%	$3,533	$1,766	$2,194	$308.98	32%	$1,766
$4,388	$10,431	$891.78	35%	$4,388	$2,194	$5,215	$445.94	35%	$2,194
$10,431		$3,006.83	37%	$10,431	$5,215		$1,503.29	37%	$5,215

Table 4: 2021 Percentage Method Tables for Manual Payroll Systems with Forms W-4 From 2020 or Later (Biweekly)

2021 Percentage Method Tables for Manual Payroll Systems With Forms W-4 from 2020 or Later
BIWEEKLY Payroll Period

STANDARD Withholding Rate Schedules (Use these if the box in Step 2 of Form W-4 is **NOT** checked)					Form W-4, Step 2, Checkbox, Withholding Rate Schedules (Use these if the box in Step 2 of Form W-4 **IS** checked)				
If the Adjusted Wage Amount (line 1h) is:		The tentative amount to withhold is:	Plus this percentage—	of the amount that the Adjusted Wage exceeds—	If the Adjusted Wage Amount (line 1h) is:		The tentative amount to withhold is:	Plus this percentage—	of the amount that the Adjusted Wage exceeds—
At least—	But less than—				At least—	But less than—			
A	B	C	D	E	A	B	C	D	E
Married Filing Jointly					**Married Filing Jointly**				
$0	$965	$0.00	0%	$0	$0	$483	$0.00	0%	$0
$965	$1,731	$0.00	10%	$965	$483	$865	$0.00	10%	$483
$1,731	$4,083	$76.60	12%	$1,731	$865	$2,041	$38.20	12%	$865
$4,083	$7,610	$358.84	22%	$4,083	$2,041	$3,805	$179.32	22%	$2,041
$7,610	$13,652	$1,134.78	24%	$7,610	$3,805	$6,826	$567.40	24%	$3,805
$13,652	$17,075	$2,584.86	32%	$13,652	$6,826	$8,538	$1,292.44	32%	$6,826
$17,075	$25,131	$3,680.22	35%	$17,075	$8,538	$12,565	$1,840.28	35%	$8,538
$25,131		$6,499.82	37%	$25,131	$12,565		$3,249.73	37%	$12,565
Single or Married Filing Separately					**Single or Married Filing Separately**				
$0	$483	$0.00	0%	$0	$0	$241	$0.00	0%	$0
$483	$865	$0.00	10%	$483	$241	$433	$0.00	10%	$241
$865	$2,041	$38.20	12%	$865	$433	$1,021	$19.20	12%	$433
$2,041	$3,805	$179.32	22%	$2,041	$1,021	$1,902	$89.76	22%	$1,021
$3,805	$6,826	$567.40	24%	$3,805	$1,902	$3,413	$283.58	24%	$1,902
$6,826	$8,538	$1,292.44	32%	$6,826	$3,413	$4,269	$646.22	32%	$3,413
$8,538	$20,621	$1,840.28	35%	$8,538	$4,269	$10,311	$920.14	35%	$4,269
$20,621		$6,069.33	37%	$20,621	$10,311		$3,034.84	37%	$10,311
Head of Household					**Head of Household**				
$0	$723	$0.00	0%	$0	$0	$362	$0.00	0%	$0
$723	$1,269	$0.00	10%	$723	$362	$635	$0.00	10%	$362
$1,269	$2,808	$54.60	12%	$1,269	$635	$1,404	$27.30	12%	$635
$2,808	$4,044	$239.28	22%	$2,808	$1,404	$2,022	$119.58	22%	$1,404
$4,044	$7,065	$511.20	24%	$4,044	$2,022	$3,533	$255.54	24%	$2,022
$7,065	$8,777	$1,236.24	32%	$7,065	$3,533	$4,388	$618.18	32%	$3,533
$8,777	$20,862	$1,784.08	35%	$8,777	$4,388	$10,431	$891.78	35%	$4,388
$20,862		$6,013.83	37%	$20,862	$10,431		$3,006.83	37%	$10,431

Table 5: 2021 Percentage Method Tables for Manual Payroll Systems with Forms W-4 From 2019 or Earlier (Weekly)

2021 Percentage Method Tables for Manual Payroll Systems With Forms W-4 From 2019 or Earlier

WEEKLY Payroll Period

MARRIED Persons					SINGLE Persons				
If the Adjusted Wage Amount (line 1d) is		The tentative amount to withhold is...	Plus this percentage ...	of the amount that the wage exceeds...	If the Adjusted Wage Amount (line 1d) is		The tentative amount to withhold is...	Plus this percentage ...	of the amount that the wage exceeds...
at least...	But less than...				at least...	But less than...			
A	B	C	D	E	A	B	C	D	E
$0	$235	$0.00	0%	$0	$0	$76	$0.00	0%	$0
$235	$617	$0.00	10%	$235	$76	$267	$0.00	10%	$76
$617	$1,793	$38.20	12%	$617	$267	$855	$19.10	12%	$267
$1,793	$3,557	$179.32	22%	$1,793	$855	$1,737	$89.66	22%	$855
$3,557	$6,578	$567.40	24%	$3,557	$1,737	$3,248	$283.70	24%	$1,737
$6,578	$8,289	$1,292.44	32%	$6,578	$3,248	$4,103	$646.34	32%	$3,248
$8,289	$12,317	$1,839.96	35%	$8,289	$4,103	$10,145	$919.94	35%	$4,103
$12,317		$3,249.76	37%	$12,317	$10,145		$3,034.64	37%	$10,145

BIWEEKLY Payroll Period

MARRIED Persons					SINGLE Persons				
If the Adjusted Wage Amount (line 1d) is		The tentative amount to withhold is...	Plus this percentage ...	of the amount that the wage exceeds...	If the Adjusted Wage Amount (line 1d) is		The tentative amount to withhold is...	Plus this percentage ...	of the amount that the wage exceeds...
at least...	But less than...				at least...	But less than...			
A	B	C	D	E	A	B	C	D	E
$0	$469	$0.00	0%	$0	$0	$152	$0.00	0%	$0
$469	$1,235	$0.00	10%	$469	$152	$535	$0.00	10%	$152
$1,235	$3,587	$76.60	12%	$1,235	$535	$1,711	$38.30	12%	$535
$3,587	$7,113	$358.84	22%	$3,587	$1,711	$3,474	$179.42	22%	$1,711
$7,113	$13,156	$1,134.56	24%	$7,113	$3,474	$6,495	$567.28	24%	$3,474
$13,156	$16,579	$2,584.88	32%	$13,156	$6,495	$8,207	$1,292.32	32%	$6,495
$16,579	$24,635	$3,680.24	35%	$16,579	$8,207	$20,290	$1,840.16	35%	$8,207
$24,635		$6,499.84	37%	$24,635	$20,290		$6,069.21	37%	$20,290

SEMIMONTHLY Payroll Period

MARRIED Persons					SINGLE Persons				
If the Adjusted Wage Amount (line 1d) is		The tentative amount to withhold is...	Plus this percentage ...	of the amount that the wage exceeds...	If the Adjusted Wage Amount (line 1d) is		The tentative amount to withhold is...	Plus this percentage ...	of the amount that the wage exceeds...
at least...	But less than...				at least...	But less than...			
A	B	C	D	E	A	B	C	D	E
$0	$508	$0.00	0%	$0	$0	$165	$0.00	0%	$0
$508	$1,338	$0.00	10%	$508	$165	$579	$0.00	10%	$165
$1,338	$3,885	$83.00	12%	$1,338	$579	$1,853	$41.40	12%	$579
$3,885	$7,706	$388.64	22%	$3,885	$1,853	$3,764	$194.28	22%	$1,853
$7,706	$14,252	$1,229.26	24%	$7,706	$3,764	$7,036	$614.70	24%	$3,764
$14,252	$17,960	$2,800.30	32%	$14,252	$7,036	$8,891	$1,399.98	32%	$7,036
$17,960	$26,688	$3,986.86	35%	$17,960	$8,891	$21,981	$1,993.58	35%	$8,891
$26,688		$7,041.66	37%	$26,688	$21,981		$6,575.08	37%	$21,981

QUIZ 1   WITHHOLDING FEDERAL INCOME TAX FROM WAGES

Problem I.

For each of the following examples, determine net taxable wages (gross wages less allowances) subject to FITW using the percentage withholding method for Forms W-4 from 2019 and earlier. (Use the "Percentage Method Tables for Income Tax Withholding for 2021" in Figure 1-2, page 8.)

1. Employee with 2 allowances is paid $500 each weekly period.
   $_____

2. Employee with 3 allowances is paid $2,500 each monthly period.
   $_____

3. Employee with 1 allowance is paid $800 each semimonthly period.
   $_____

4. Employee with 0 allowances is paid $450 each weekly period.
   $_____

5. Employee with 4 allowances is paid $780 each biweekly period.
   $_____

Problem II.

Calculate the 2021 FITW for each of the following.

1. Susan's gross pay for the week of December 7, 2021, is $235; her FITW is $8.00. On December 21, she receives a Christmas bonus of $50. Susan has claimed single with 1 allowance on her 2019 Form W-4. Her employer uses the wage-bracket method. What is the FITW on her bonus?
   $_____

2. George is paid $1,000 each weekly period in 2021. He has claimed married with 8 allowances on his 2019 Form W-4. His employer uses the percentage withholding method.
   $_____

3. James is paid $650 each weekly period in 2021. He has claimed single with 1 allowance on his 2019 Form W-4. His employer uses the wage-bracket method.
   $_____

4. In September 2021, Mary receives severance pay of $1,500 at termination. Federal income tax was withheld from her regular wages paid during 2020 and 2021. Her employer wants to use the supplemental withholding tax rate.

   $_____

5. Ralphina is paid $685 each weekly period in 2021. She has claimed single with 11 allowances on her 2019 Form W-4. Her employer uses the wage-bracket method.

   $_____

Problem III.

Fill in the blanks.

1. In 2021, a 22% withholding tax rate is allowed for _____ wages.

2. The supplemental withholding tax rate may be used when supplemental wages are paid _____ from regular wages or, if combined with regular wages, are clearly indicated as a separate amount.

3. The _____ method of withholding most closely approximates the tax withheld by automated payroll systems.

4. The _____ - _____ method of withholding is an easier and faster way to calculate FITW when you don't have a payroll system to compute the tax.

5. If supplemental wages exceed $1 million for 2021, the rate of FITW is _____%.

QUIZ 1 *Solutions and Explanations*

Problem I.

1. $334.00
To calculate:

$83.00 per allowance for a weekly payroll period × 2 allowances = $166.00 amount to subtract from gross wages

$500 gross wages − $166.00 = $334.00 net taxable wages

2. $1,426.00
To calculate:

$358.00 per allowance for a monthly payroll period × 3 allowances = $1,074.00 amount to subtract from gross wages

$2,500 gross wages − $1,074.00 = $1,426.00 net taxable wages

3. $621.00
To calculate:

$800 gross wages − $179.00 per allowance for a semimonthly payroll period = $621.00 net taxable wages.

4. $450
Because there are no allowances, full gross wages are subject to FITW.

5. $120.00
To calculate:

$165.00 per allowance for a biweekly payroll period × 4 allowances = $660.00 amount to subtract from gross wages

$780 gross wages − $660.00 = $120.00 net taxable wages

Problem II.

1. $11.00
Because federal income tax of $8.00 was withheld in the tax year, the employer may use the supplemental flat tax rate of 22%. To calculate:

$50 × 22% [0.22] = $11.00

2. $10.10
To calculate:

1. Total wages	$1,000.00
2. Allowances claimed on W-4: ($83.00 per allowance* × 8 = $664.00)	(664.00)
3. Amount subject to withholding (Line 1 – Line 2)	336.00
4. Less: amount exempt on Table 5, married**	(235.00)
5. Net taxable income	101.00
6. Tax on $101.00 from Table 5** ($101.00 × 10%)	10.10

  *Figure 1-2, page 8.
**Table 5, married persons, page 14.

3. $54.00
To calculate:

1. Use single weekly table (Table 3, single, page 5)

2. Where the wage-range line of $630 – $645 meets the column for 1 allowance: $54 FITW.

4. $330.00

   Because FITW was deducted in the previous and current tax year, the employer may use the supplemental withholding tax rate of 22%: $1,500 × .22 (22%) = $330.00.

5. $0

   To calculate:

Total wages		$685.00
Each allowance (Figure 1-2, p. 8)	$83.00	
Times allowances over 10 (11 – 10)	× 1	
Less: allowance amount		(83.00)
Net taxable wages		$602.00
FITW for wage-range of $600 – $615 with 10 allowances (Table 3, single, page 5)		$0

   OR
   $0 ($675–$690 with 10 allowances)

Problem III.

1. supplemental

2. separately

3. percentage

4. wage-bracket

5. 37%

QUIZ 2   WITHHOLDING FEDERAL INCOME TAX FROM WAGES

Problem I.

For each of the following examples, determine net taxable wages (gross wages less personal allowances) subject to FITW using the percentage withholding method for Forms W-4 from 2019 and earlier. (Use the "Percentage Method Tables for Income Tax Withholding for 2021" in Figure 1-2, page 8.)

1. Employee with 4 allowances is paid $900 each biweekly period.
   $_____

2. Employee with 2 allowances is paid $600 each weekly period.
   $_____

3. Employee with 0 allowances is paid $3,500 each monthly period.
   $_____

4. Employee with 1 allowance is paid $1,800 each semimonthly period.
   $_____

5. Employee with 3 allowances is paid $2,800 each monthly period.
   $_____

Problem II.

Calculate the 2021 FITW for each of the following:

1. Carl is paid $725 each weekly period. He has claimed single with 7 allowances on his 2019 Form W-4. His employer uses the percentage withholding method.
   $_____

2. On October 12, 2021, Jane is paid $450 in regular wages for the weekly period ending October 8, 2021. She claimed married with 2 allowances on her 2019 Form W-4. Jane received no other pay in the year. On October 12, 2021, she also receives $200 in commissions. Her employer uses the wage-bracket method. What is FITW on her commission? $_____

3. Frank is paid $650 each weekly period. He claimed single with 2 allowances on his 2019 Form W-4. His employer uses the wage-bracket method.
   $_____

4. Leslie is paid a bonus of $3,500 in June 2021. Federal income tax was withheld from regular wages paid to her in 2020 and 2021. Her employer wants to use the supplemental withholding tax rate.

$_____

5. Jake is paid $800 each weekly period. He has claimed married with 12 allowances on his 2019 Form W-4. His employer uses the wage-bracket method.

$_____

Problem III.

Fill in the blanks.

1. Bonuses, commissions and overtime pay are all examples of

_____ _____.

2. The supplemental federal income tax withholding rate for 2021 is _____%.

3. If federal income tax has not been withheld from regular wages in the current or previous tax year, the employer may not use the

_____ _____ _____ rate for

supplemental wages payments.

4. Both the percentage method and the wage-bracket method withholding tables are published each year in the IRS publication _____

_____.

5. For 2021, supplemental wages in excess of $_____ are subject to a flat FITW rate of 37%.

QUIZ 2   *Solutions and Explanations*

> *Problem I.*
>
> **1.** $240.00
> To calculate:
>
> $165.00 per allowance for biweekly payroll period × 4 allowances = $660.00 amount to subtract from gross wages
>
> $900 gross wages – $660.00 = $240.00 net taxable wages
>
> **2.** $434.00
> To calculate:
>
> $83.00 per allowance for a weekly payroll period × 2 allowances = $166.00 amount to subtract from gross wages
>
> $600 gross wages – $166.00 = $434.00 net taxable wages
>
> **3.** $3,500
> Because there are no allowances, full gross wages are subject to FITW.
>
> **4.** $1,621.00
> To calculate:
>
> $1,800.00 gross wages – $179.00 per allowance for a semimonthly payroll period = $1,621.00 net taxable wages
>
> **5.** $1,726.00
> To calculate:
>
> $358.00 per allowance for a monthly payroll period × 3 allowances = $1,074.00 amount to subtract from gross wages
>
> $2,800 gross wages – $1,074.00 = $1,726.00 net taxable wages

Problem II.

1. $6.80
To calculate:

1. Total wages	$725.00
2. Allowances claimed on W-4: ($83.00 per allowance* × 7 = $581.00)	(581.00)
3. Amount subject to withholding (Line 1 − Line 2)	144.00
4. Less: amount exempt in Table 5, weekly, single**	(76.00)
5. Net taxable income	$ 68.00
6. Tax on $68.00 from Table 5** ($68.00 × 10% = $7.10)	$ 6.80

 *Figure 1-2, page 8.
**Table 5, weekly, single, page 14.

2. $25.00
Because federal income tax was not withheld in the current or previous tax year the commission was added to her most recent regular wage payment to determine taxes due ($450 gross + $200 commission = $650 taxable wages). Use the Table 3, weekly married persons, page 4. Where the wage-range line of $640–$655 meets the column for 2 allowances, FITW is $25.00.

3. $46
To calculate:

1. Use the Table 3, Weekly, Single, page 5.

2. Where the wage-range line of $645–$660 meets the column for 2 allowances, FITW is $46.

4. $770
To calculate:

$3,500 bonus × 0.22 (22% supplemental withholding tax rate) = $770 FITW

5. $0
To calculate:

Total wages		$800.00
Each allowance (Figure 1-2, p. 12)	$83.00	
Times allowances over 10 (12–10)	× 2	
Less: allowance amount		(166.00)
Net taxable wages		$634.00
FITW for wage-range of $625–$640 with 10 allowances (Table 3, Weekly, Married, page 4)		$ 0.00

Problem III.

1. supplemental wages

2. 22

3. supplemental withholding tax

4. Publication 15-T, *Federal Income Tax Withholding Methods.*

5. $1,000,000

TAXABLE AND NONTAXABLE BENEFITS

Many employees receive benefits (or "perks") such as employer-paid health insurance, complimentary coffee and donuts, free use of company vehicles, even all-expense-paid vacations. Some fringe benefits are partly or wholly taxable; others are completely tax-free. For more information on fringe benefits see IRS Publication 15-B, *Employer's Tax Guide to Fringe Benefits*.

Exempt Benefits

The following six categories of benefits generally are exempt from the federal taxation and reporting requirements:

1. **De minimis fringe benefits.** These benefits are not taxable because their value is so small ("de minimis") that accounting for them would be unreasonable or impractical. **Exception:** A cash payment (including gift cards or certificates), no matter how small, never qualifies as a de minimis fringe benefit (except for overtime meal money and transportation fare). *Note:* Even de minimis benefits in excess of $25 can be tax-free. The IRS has established no dollar value at which items fail to meet the de minimis definition.

Examples of benefits that may qualify as de minimis include *occasional* and *sporadic*:

- personal local calls made on the employer's phone

- employer-sponsored picnics or parties

- holiday gifts of tangible property such as a turkey, ham, cheese, or fruit basket

- occasional tickets to the theater or sporting events (not season passes)

- occasional personal use of a company copy machine (85% of usage must be for business)

- occasional meals furnished by the employer

- flowers, fruit baskets and books for special occasions such as an illness, birth, or death of a family member

- personal use of cell phone if the employer pays for cell phone services for a noncompensatory business reason

    PROBLEM 1: Raul receives a cash bonus of $25 that he uses to buy a ticket to a baseball game. Is this bonus taxable?

    SOLUTION 1: Yes, the bonus is taxable. Had the employer given Raul a ticket to the baseball game instead of cash, it would probably have qualified as a de minimis tax-free fringe benefit even if the value of the ticket exceeded $25.

2. **Working condition fringe benefits.** Reimbursements for work-related expenses or benefits are known as "working condition fringes." The following requirements must be met before a working condition fringe benefit qualifies as tax-free:

1. The expense must be directly related to the employer's trade or business.

2. In the case of a business-expense allowance, advance or reimbursement, the employee is required to substantiate the time, place, amount, and business purpose of expenses incurred and return monies not used for business expenses in a reasonable and specified period of time. Receipts are not required for expenses of $75 or less.

3. The employee must furnish to the employer records that show the amount that was incurred for the business expense—for example, employee expense statements, travel logs, trip sheets, and receipts.

Examples of working condition fringes other than business travel reimbursements include:

- memberships in professional associations

- subscriptions to professional publications

- paid education (seminars or "refresher" classes) directly related to the employee's current position

- materials and supplies furnished by employers to employees to perform their job duties

- license fees where the licensing is required for the employer's trade or business.

- cell phone or tablet usage charges (but not device itself) provided this benefit is provided primarily for non-compensatory business reasons.

3. **No-additional-cost benefits.** No-additional-cost benefits are those that are provided to the general public by the employer and offered to employees at no charge. Examples of no-additional-cost benefits include:

- free air travel for airline employees

- free use of an amusement park by park employees

- free lodging for employees of employer-owned hotels and motels

To qualify as tax-free, the employer may not incur substantial additional costs (including labor) in providing the service to employees, and the service must be one primarily offered to customers. For instance, free air travel for a retailer's employees would not qualify as tax-free; but may be tax-free to airline employees. If substantial costs are incurred by the employer, the service is no longer tax-free.

4. **Qualified employee discounts.** Some employers offer discounts to employees on goods or services sold by the employer. To qualify as tax-free, the percentage of discount on goods may not exceed the percentage of gross profit. In other words, employees must pay an amount at least equal to the cost of the merchandise. For services, the discount may not exceed 20% of the price customers normally pay. To be eligible for the discount the employee must be employed in the same line of business that produces the goods or provides the services to the general public.

PROBLEM 2: Rose is a receptionist for TaxCo. A TaxCo tax preparer spends an average of 5 hours to complete a return and is paid $10 per hour. The average customer pays $200 to have a return prepared. Does free tax preparation qualify as a tax-free benefit for Rose?

SOLUTION 2: No, it is not a qualified employee discount because providing the service to Rose costs her employer $50 (for 5 hours of labor). The service discount is 100%—much greater than the maximum 20% permitted. The maximum tax-free discount her employer can give her is $40 ($200 normal customer price × 20% = $40 discount).

PROBLEM 3: PlumbCo offers its employees a discount on plumbing services. Customers normally pay $75 per hour for its services. What is the maximum tax-free discount that PlumbCo can give to its employees?

SOLUTION 3: $15 per hour off the normal rate is the maximum tax-free discount PlumbCo can offer to its employees. To calculate:

$75 (normal price for customers) × 20% (maximum discount) = $15 (maximum employee discount)

5. **Medical and health care benefits.** Generally, employer payments for medical, dental and other health insurance are nontaxable to employees, their spouse, and their dependents. (The exemption also applies to COBRA premium payments paid on behalf of a former employee and his/her family members.) Complicated exceptions apply to health benefits provided under self-insured plans, if these plans disproportionately favor highly compensated employees.

Cash payments given to employees to purchase health insurance are treated as wages and subject to FIT, FITW, FICA, and FUTA unless the employee substantiates that the amount was used to purchase health insurance. Note also that cash payments to employees to pay for their own purchase of health insurance may result in hefty penalties to the employer under the Affordable Care Act's requirement to offer minimum affordable health insurance to their full-time employees.

Exception: Health insurance provided to 2% or more shareholder employees of S corporations must be reported as federal taxable income subject to federal income tax withholding. The amount of the benefit is exempt from Social Security, Medicare, and federal unemployment tax—but only if the health insurance is offered to all employees or a class or group of employees (e.g., only full-time workers) other than the 2% or more shareholder employees (IRC §3121(a)(2); IRS Announcement 92-14).

Employers are required to report the value of employer-provided health care benefits on Form W-2 box 12, Code DD. Employers that filed fewer than 250 Forms W-2 in the previous tax year are exempt from this reporting requirement. Also, a federal tax credit is available to eligible small employers—including tax-exempt organizations— that make non-elective contributions toward the cost of their employees' health insurance premiums. See IRS Publication 334 for more information about the small-employer tax credit.

The Affordable Care Act also changed the definition of a covered child. The value of these medical and health plans are exempt from FIT, FITW, FICA, and FUTA until the end of the calendar year in which the child turns 26. (Note that this revised definition of covered child doesn't apply to a Health Savings Account [HSA]).

> **Example:** Employee Jane's son, Raymond, turned 26 on April 1, 2021. The value of Raymond's health benefits are excluded from Jane's taxable wages through December 31, 2021.

Finally, businesses with 50 or more full-time employees must provide affordable, minimally essential health insurance to their full-time employees or be subject to an excise tax. Covered businesses also must meet additional employee and IRS reporting requirements. For more information, visit *https://www.irs.gov/affordable-care-act*.

6. **Athletic facilities on company premises.** If an employer sponsors an athletic facility on the premises or other property owned or leased by the employer, the employees' use of the facility is generally tax-free as long as it is not used primarily by the employer's customers. A facility available to all tenants of an office building qualifies as employer-operated. Reimbursements to employees for athletic facility memberships are taxable and subject to FIT, FITW, FICA, and FUTA.

7. **Identity theft protection services.** Identity theft protection services are excluded from wages subject to FIT, FITW, FICA and FUTA when provided to customers, employees or other individuals whose personal information may or could be compromised in a data breach. This exclusion from taxable wages doesn't apply to cash in lieu of identity protection services or when identity protection services are provided for reasons other than protecting employees in the event of a data breach (e.g., given in connection with an employee's compensation benefit package).

Identity theft protection services include (1) credit reporting and monitoring services, (2) identity theft insurance, (3) identity restoration services, and (4) other similar services.

Limited Exempt Benefits

Some fringe benefits are only partially tax-free. These include:

Adoption assistance. Effective January 1, 2021, employer payments or reimbursements of qualified adoption expenses up to $14,440 ($14,300 effective in 2020) per qualifying adoption provided under an adoption assistance program are not subject to federal income tax withholding. However, these amounts are subject to FICA, FUTA, and railroad retirement tax.

Qualified reimbursed expenses include reasonable and necessary adoption fees, court costs, attorney's fees, traveling expenses while away from home including meals and lodging, and other expenses directly related to, and of which the principal purpose is, the legal adoption of an eligible child by the taxpayer.

For employer payments or reimbursements to be nontaxable, the employer must have a written plan and employees must receive notification of the plan. The IRS does not have to approve the plan, but the following requirements must be met:

(1) all employees eligible to participate must be given reasonable notice of the terms and availability of the plan;

(2) benefits are offered to employees in general and do not discriminate in favor of highly compensated employees or their dependents;

(3) shareholders or owners or their spouses or dependents receive no more than 5% of all adoption assistance reimbursements or employer-paid expenses during the year. A shareholder or owner is someone who owns more than 5% of the stock, capital or profits on any one day of the year; and

(4) employees who receive adoption assistance provide reasonable substantiation that payments or reimbursements were made for qualified adoption expenses.

The IRS permits qualified adoption assistance plans to be made under a cafeteria plan, meaning that employees can pay for their adoption costs with pre-tax dollars up to the specified annual limit.

Important: All employer payments and pretax deductions for qualified adoption assistance expenses, including payments in excess of the nontaxable dollar limits for the year, must be reported on the W-2 in Box 12 preceded by Code "T."

Educational assistance. Employer-provided nonjob-related educational assistance benefits of up to $5,250 per year are nontaxable. The $5,250 exclusion applies to both graduate-level and undergraduate-level education.

A "graduate-level" course is one taken by an employee who has a bachelor's degree or is receiving credit toward an advanced degree if the course can be taken for credit by anyone in a program leading to a law, business, medical, or other advanced academic or professional degree.

Nonjob-related educational assistance benefits provided to retired, disabled or laid-off employees are nontaxable up to $5,250 when provided as the result of the employment relationship.

Dependent care assistance. The value of employer-provided child care, or the total reimbursement for child care under an employer's qualified plan*, is tax-free up to $5,000 per employee per year (reduced to $2,500 for married employees filing separate returns). Note that for 2021 only, the annual limit on dependent care assistance is $10,500 ($5,250 for single and married filing separately). Flexible spending accounts, where the employee is allowed to make pretax contributions toward the cost of their dependent care assistance, are allowed only under a qualified cafeteria plan.

Group-term life insurance. The value of employer-provided group-term life insurance is tax-free up to the first $50,000 value of monthly coverage. (See Section 8 for details.)

Length-of-service/safety achievement awards. If provided under a qualified plan, length-of-service and/or safety achievement awards received by all employees during the year are tax-free if they do not exceed an average of $400 per recipient. A tax-free award given to any one employee during the year may not exceed $1,600. In the absence of a qualified plan, the maximum annual tax-free award that any recipient may receive is $400. To qualify as a qualified length-of-service/safety achievement award, the item provided to the employee must be intangible property (e.g. a watch or lapel pin) and cannot be cash or a cash equivalent, such as a gift card.

> **PROBLEM 4:** Under DelCo's qualified plan, 4 of its 5 employees receive non-cash safety awards of $100 each and 1 employee receives $1,200. Are these awards tax-free to DelCo's employees?
>
> **SOLUTION 4:** Yes, all 5 non-cash awards are tax-free to employees because the average award is $320 per recipient for the year ($100 + $100 + $100 + $100 + $1,200 = $1,600 ÷ 5 = $320). Because the average non-cash award is less than $400, no employee received more than $1,600, and the employer has a qualified plan, all 5 non-cash awards are tax-free.

---

* For details on "qualified" plans, consult your tax advisor or benefits consultant.

PROBLEM 5: DelCo discontinues its qualified plan for safety achievement awards. The following year, the same 5 employees receive the same non-cash awards—4 get $100 each and 1 gets $1,200. Are these awards still tax-free?

SOLUTION 5: The 4 awards of $100 are tax-free; however, because there is no qualified plan, each employee is now allowed a maximum tax-free award of up to $400. For the employee who received the $1,200 non-cash award, DelCo is required to report taxable income of $800 ($1,200 award − $400 maximum = $800 taxable income).

Transportation Fringe Benefits

Public transit subsidies. Effective January 1, 2021 the first $270 per month of employer-provided transportation is tax-free. Partners and more than 2% shareholder employees of S corporations are excluded from the tax-free provision.

EXAMPLE: Employee Becky is provided with $280 per month in fare cards to travel to and from work. Effective January 1, 2021, the first $270 per month of the transportation fringe benefit is tax-free. The excess, or $10 per month, is taxable income subject to FIT, FITW, FICA, and FUTA.

Employer-provided transportation includes:

1. **Transportation to and from work in a commuter highway vehicle provided by the employer (i.e., van pool).** A vehicle meets the definition of a "commuter highway vehicle" if it has the capacity to seat at least six adults (not including the driver). It must be reasonable to expect that at least 80% of the vehicle's mileage will be used in transporting employees between home and work, and at least half of the adult seating capacity (excluding the driver) will be used to transport employees. To determine the fair market value (FMV) of employer-provided transportation fringe benefits, the employer may use actual cost or the safe-harbor valuation method of $1.50 for each one-way trip or $3.00 for each round-trip commute.

2. **Transit subsidies.** Tax-free employer-provided transportation also may include public transportation subsidies such as passes, tokens, fare cards, vouchers, or similar items provided to employees to reduce their costs for travel to and from work.

Partners and 2% or more shareholders of S corporations. When transit benefits are provided to partners and 2% or more shareholders of S corporations tokens or fare cards (not including privately operated van pools) are excluded from gross income only if the value of the tokens and fare cards in any one month does not exceed $21 [IRS Reg. 1.132-6(d)(1)]. If the value of the public transportation subsidy provided to partners or S Corporation shareholders exceeds $21 dollars in a month, the full value of the transportation subsidy is included in gross income and subject to FIT, FITW, FICA, and FUTA. The $21 is not adjusted for inflation.

3. **Employer-provided parking.** For calendar year 2021, the first $270 per month of employer-provided parking is tax-free. The employer can provide either parking or cash reimbursements based on adequate substantiation for the cost of parking.

"Qualified parking" includes:

a. parking at or near the employer's business premises; or

b. parking at a location from which the employee commutes to and from work by mass transit, a qualified commuter van highway vehicle, a car pool, or a van pool. [IRC §132(f)(5)(C)] Qualified parking does not include parking that is located at or near the employee's residence.

Fair market value (FMV) of employer-provided parking. Generally, the FMV of employer-provided parking is based on the cost (including taxes or other added fees) that an employee would pay in an arm's length transaction for the same parking space. If the employer is unable to determine this cost, then the value of the employee's parking is based on the cost that the employee would incur in an arm's length transaction for a parking space in the same parking lot or a comparable lot in the same general location and under the same or similar circumstances.

If an employer provides free parking primarily to its customers, and employees also receive their parking free of charge, then the parking provided to employees has no taxable value, and employees recognize no taxable income for their parking spaces.

> **EXAMPLE:** WeldCo operates an industrial plant in a rural area in which no commercial parking is available. WeldCo provides adequate parking spaces for its employees on its business premises at no cost to its employees. The parking spaces provided by WeldCo have no taxable value to its employees because an individual, other than an employee, would not pay to park in its lot. Thus, the parking provided by WeldCo is tax-free to its employees.

This rule does not apply, however, if an employer maintains *preferential* reserved spaces for employees. A reserved space is *preferential* if it is more favorably located to the business premises than the parking spaces available to the employer's customers. However, if preferential reserved parking is provided in an area such as the parking lot of a shopping center, and no shopping center or other parking lot in the geographical area charges for parking, then it appears that employees with preferential reserved parking need not recognize taxable income for the value of their parking spaces.

> **EXAMPLE 1:** ShopCo is located in a rural shopping center. Ample free parking is available to ShopCo's customers and employees in the shopping center parking lot. Parking spaces are not reserved for employees. The parking provided to ShopCo's employees has no taxable value, and taxable income need not be recognized for the parking spaces provided to employees.

> **EXAMPLE 2:** DrugCo is a pharmacy located in a downtown shopping mall. Ample free parking is provided primarily to customers in the mall's parking lot. Parking spaces reserved for employees are no closer to the mall than the spaces available to its customers. The parking spaces reserved for employees have no taxable value because the parking spaces are not preferential reserved spaces. The employees of DrugCo need not recognize taxable income for their parking spaces.

> **EXAMPLE 3:** BrassCo is a retailer of musical instruments and is located in a downtown shopping mall. BrassCo provides ample free parking to its customers and a separate parking lot near the entrance of the store for its store managers. Its customers are not permitted to park in the employees' lot, but may park in the customer lot across an access road from its business premises. The parking spaces provided to BrassCo's employees in the separate parking lot are preferential reserved parking. If individuals in other shopping malls or parking lots in the same geographic area are required to pay for parking, and if the average cost of this parking space is, say, $275 per month in 2021, the employees of BrassCo that park in the reserved parking spaces must recognize taxable income of $5 per month ($275 – $270). This income is subject to FIT, FITW, FICA, and FUTA.

The value of employer-provided parking is based on the employee's right to access the parking space on any given day and not the employee's actual use of the parking space. In addition, the value of one parking space cannot be allocated to more than one employee.

EXAMPLE: Rosemary, a store manager of BrassCo, has unlimited access to her preferential reserved parking space. During the month of March, Rosemary used the parking space only 5 days because she was away on business travel for one week and took vacation for 2 weeks. Because Rosemary had access to the parking space for the entire month, the amount includable in her gross income (and subject to FIT, FITW, FICA, and FUTA) is the FMV of the free parking that in 2021 exceeds $270 per month.

Qualified transportation fringe benefits may be provided only by employers to their employees. "Employee" includes common-law employees and other statutory employees such as officers of corporations. Self-employed individuals are not employees for purposes of the transportation fringe benefit and parking benefit exclusions. Therefore, partners, 2% or more shareholders of S Corporations, sole proprietors, and other independent contractors are not employees for purposes of the partial tax-free exclusion for parking. An individual who is both a 2% or more shareholder of an S Corporation and an officer of that S Corporation is not considered an employee for purposes of the tax exemption.

If a partner, self-employed individual or 2% shareholder employee would be able to deduct the cost of parking as a trade or business expense, the value of free or reduced parking is excludable from income as a working condition fringe benefit [IRS Reg. 1.132-5(a)(1) and 1.132-1(b)(2)].

Cash allowances for parking. An employer-provided cash allowance for employee parking meets the requirements of a tax-favored transportation or parking benefit, but only if employees meet an employer's requirements for substantiation. For example, if in 2021 an employer provides employees with a $270 per month cash allowance for parking and employees are required to submit their parking receipts at the end of the month, then the substantiation requirements are met, and the parking allowance is exempt from FIT, FITW, FICA, and FUTA. On the other hand, if an employee is given a cash allowance for parking and is not required to provide proof that the allowance was used to pay for a qualified transportation fringe benefit, the allowance is considered income subject to FIT, FITW, FICA, and FUTA.

Employer-provided cash allowances for mass transit passes. Cash reimbursements for transit system vouchers are FIT, FITW, FICA, and FUTA taxable if there is a transit voucher system within the employee's metropolitan area that *is readily available for direct distribution* to employees by the employer or by a voucher or fare-media provider. Cash reimbursements are nontaxable only if:

1. A *transit system voucher* is not acceptable to a train, subway or bus system as fare or in exchange for a ticket or other fare media.

2. The employer cannot purchase the voucher directly from the transit system or from *a voucher or fare-media provider*. Vouchers purchased by a third-party, such as an employee benefits administrator do not qualify if the employer could have obtained the vouchers directly from a voucher provider.

3. A voucher or similar item is not *readily available for direct distribution* by the employer to employees, which means that:

   The *fare media charges,* the fees voucher providers charge, are higher than the cost individual employees would pay on their own and cannot be too high. Whether fees are too high is determined on a case-by-case basis. If an employer can choose among transit system vouchers, it must use the one with the lowest fee when deciding if the fee is too high. If an employee must use more than one transit system, i.e., more than one voucher, the employer can average the fees to decide if the fees are too high.

   There are *other restrictions* that prevent the vouchers from being readily available to employees. *Other restrictions* include:

   - unreasonable *advance purchase requirements,* such as making vouchers available only once a year or failing to provide vouchers within a reasonable time of receiving payment. An example of a reasonable requirement would be monthly advance purchase.

   - *quantity requirements,* such as a $2,580.00 minimum for an employer seeking to purchase only $230 in vouchers.

   - *limited voucher denominations*, such as monthly vouchers for employees who do not use up the monthly limit. Lower denominations, such as those in $5 increments, can be used by almost all employees.

Employers concerned about the taxability of cash reimbursements for fare media should consult a CPA or other qualified consultant.

Discrimination tests and flexible benefit plans. Qualified transportation benefits maintain their tax-free status even if offered only to highly-compensated employees. Transportation fringe benefits may be offered to employees on a pretax basis (see Section 7); however, these benefits cannot be offered under a cafeteria plan. If an employee opts for cash in lieu of transportation fringes, the cash amount is wages subject to FIT, FITW, FICA, and FUTA.

Business deduction for transportation fringe benefits. Under the Tax Cuts and Jobs Act of 2017 (TCJA and effective January 1, 2018), employers cannot claim an expense deduction on their federal business income tax return for the cost of transportation fringe benefits. An employee's pretax contribution for transportation fringe benefits is considered an employer cost.

EXAMPLE 1: In 2021 WedgeCo employees are allowed to contribute up to $270 per month for the purchase of transit passes. WedgeCo contributes nothing towards the cost of the transit passes. Employee Tyrone is paid $2,000 per month and makes a pretax $270 contribution for transit passes. WedgeCo can claim a deduction on its federal business income tax return of only $1,730 ($2,000 – $270) for salary expense because a deduction is not allowed for the pretax transit contribution of $270.

EXAMPLE 2: Assume the same facts as Example 1, except that WedgeCo pays the cost of up to $270 in transit benefits, nothing is deducted from employees' wages. WedgeCo may claim a salary expense deduction on the federal business income tax return of $2,000, but no deduction can be claimed for the $270 it paid for Tyrone's transit passes because the $2,000 salary expense deduction includes the $270.

Note in the examples above that there is no effect on the federal payroll tax treatment of Tyrone's transit passes. His transit benefits, whether paid directly by WedgeCo or deducted on a pretax basis, continue to be excluded from his FIT, FITW, FICA, and FUTA taxable wages.

Rules for State Taxes

Some benefits that are exempt from federal income tax are not exempt from state income or local taxes. Contact your state or local taxing authorities for details.

QUIZ 1   TAXABLE AND NONTAXABLE BENEFITS

Problem I.

Categorize each benefit as one of the following:

transportation fringe benefit   *de minimis fringe*
qualified employee discount   *employer-provided medical insurance*
no-additional-cost service   *working condition fringe*

1. Personal use of the company photocopy machine. _____

2. Reimbursement of fees for a tax seminar for the company accountant. _____

3. Free personal use of health club facilities for health club employees. _____

4. $5 off eye examinations for Eye-Care Center employees. _____

5. Employer-provided vision care. _____

6. Reimbursement for cost of "park and ride" parking. _____

Problem II.

Fill in the blanks.

1. Employer-paid memberships in professional associations and subscriptions to professional publications are examples of _____ _____ fringe benefits.

2. To meet the requirements of a working condition fringe such as employer-paid travel, the benefit must be directly related to the _____ trade or business, and the _____ must substantiate the amount, time, place, and business purpose of the expense.

3. An employee discount on services is tax-free as long as the discount does not exceed _____% of the amount that customers normally pay for the service.

4. Employer-provided dependent care assistance is tax-free up to _____ per employee per year.

5. For 2021, employer-provided adoption assistance is tax-free up to _____ per child.

Problem III.

Multiple choice. Circle the correct answer.

1. If the cost of a widget is $30 and it retails for $50, the maximum tax-free discount an employee can receive is:

    a. $10   b. $20   c. $30   d. $50

2. Reimbursements for nonjob-related graduate-level education made through a qualified educational assistance plan is tax-free up to how much per employee per year?

    a. $10,000   b. $5,000   c. $0   d. $5,250

3. Which of the following is tax-free as a de minimis fringe benefit?

    a. a ticket to a theater event
    b. season tickets to sporting events
    c. $30 merchandise discount
    d. $10 cash bonus

4. Which of the following is a tax-free working condition fringe?

    a. personal long-distance calls made on the employer's phone
    b. reimbursement for medical school for the company treasurer
    c. professional licensing fee for employee plumbers
    d. employer-paid legal fees for the drafting of a will

5. Under a qualified plan, the average length-of-service award for all recipients for the year is tax-free up to:

    a. $800   b. $1,200   c. $400   d. $1,600

6. The monthly tax-free limit for employer-provided parking for 2021 is:

    a. $130   b. $21   c. $270   d. $265

QUIZ 1 Solutions and Explanations

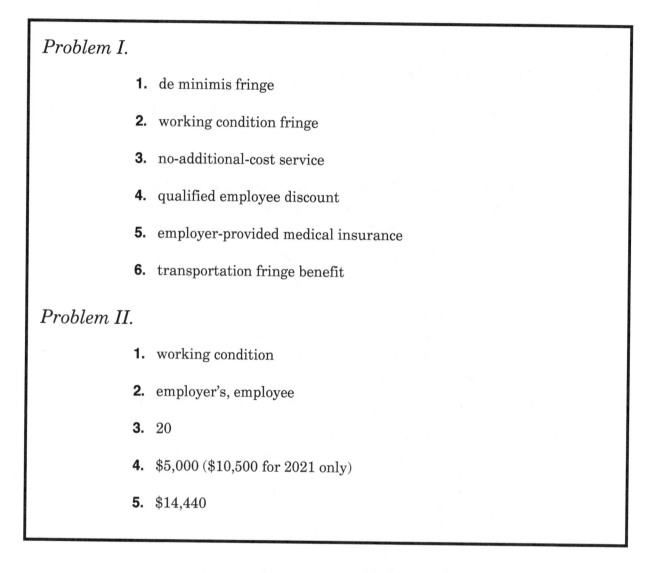

Problem I.

1. de minimis fringe

2. working condition fringe

3. no-additional-cost service

4. qualified employee discount

5. employer-provided medical insurance

6. transportation fringe benefit

Problem II.

1. working condition

2. employer's, employee

3. 20

4. $5,000 ($10,500 for 2021 only)

5. $14,440

Problem III.

1. b

   For a qualified employee discount to remain tax-free, the discount cannot exceed the profit margin, in this case, $50 – $30 = $20.

2. d

3. a

   No cash bonus ever qualifies as a de minimis benefit.

4. c

5. c

6. c

QUIZ 2   TAXABLE AND NONTAXABLE BENEFITS

Problem I.

Categorize each benefit as one of the following:

transportation fringe benefit	*de minimis fringe*
qualified employee discount	*employer-provided medical insurance*
no-additional-cost service	*working condition fringe*

1. A carpentry shop's reimbursement to an employee carpenter for carpentry tools. _____

2. Employer-provided dental insurance. _____

3. An employer-sponsored retirement party. _____

4. Employer-provided subway tokens. _____

5. A 15% discount on store merchandise for a retailer's employees. _____

6. Free train fare for railroad employees. _____

Problem II.

Fill in the blanks.

1. For 2021, reimbursements for nonjob-related undergraduate education made through a qualified educational assistance plan are tax-free up to $_____.

2. Length-of-service and safety achievement awards paid under a nonqualified plan are tax-free up to a maximum of $_____ per employee per year.

3. Employee discounts on merchandise are tax-free as long as the employee pays an amount at least equal to the _____ of the item.

4. Effective January 1, 2021, the monthly tax-free limit for employer-provided transit subsidies for 2% or more shareholder employees is $_____.

5. The age through which an employee's adult child's health coverage is nontaxable for federal tax purposes is _____.

Problem III.

Multiple choice. Circle the correct answer.

1. Dependent-care assistance benefits are tax-free up to what amount per employee per year?

    a. $50,000   b. $1,600   c. $5,250   d. $5,000

2. The average customer of CarpetCo pays $60 per hour for carpet cleaning services. What is the maximum tax-free discount CarpetCo's employees may receive?

    a. $ 9 per hour
    b. $12 per hour
    c. $60 per hour
    d. $30 per hour

3. Under a qualified plan, the maximum tax-free length-of-service award to any one employee per year is:

    a. $5,000   b. $1,400   c. $1,600   d. $400

4. The office manager of BuildCo is reimbursed his educational expenses for his undergraduate degree in business administration. What kind of benefit is this?

    a. working condition fringe
    b. educational assistance
    c. length-of-service award
    d. de minimis fringe

5. An employee's occasional personal local calls made on the employer's telephone are tax-free as a:

    a. working condition fringe
    b. de minimis fringe
    c. no-additional-cost service
    d. qualified employee discount

6. Effective January 1, 2021, employer-provided transportation subsidies to rank-and-file employees are tax-free up to what amount per month?

    a. $270   b. $21   c. $265   d. $130

QUIZ 2   Solutions and Explanations

Problem I.

1. working condition fringe

2. employer-provided medical insurance

3. de minimis fringe

4. transportation fringe benefit

5. qualified employee discount

6. no-additional-cost service

Problem II.

1. $5,250

2. $400

3. cost

4. $21

5. 26

Problem III.

1. d

2. b
To remain tax-free, employee discounts on employer services may not exceed 20% of the price that customers normally pay.

3. c
However, to be tax-free, the average award per recipient under a qualified plan may not exceed $400 per year.

4. b
This education is not related to the office manager's current job.

5. b

6. a

Section 3
REPORTING FOR FRINGE BENEFITS

Introduction

Fringe benefits are considered to be wages and are covered by tax and reporting requirements. Laws seeking to limit the tax exemption of various benefits have made their taxation and reporting highly complex.

When to Tax and Report Fringe Benefits

Employers are required to recognize income and withhold applicable taxes on all taxable fringe benefits at the time they are paid. However, an employer may withhold and report taxes on taxable noncash fringe benefits (i.e., personal use of a company-owned car or plane, transportation fringe benefits, group-term life, and nonqualified deferred compensation) at any other frequency it chooses—weekly, biweekly, monthly, quarterly, or any other period provided they are taxed and reported by the end of the year. Employers need not notify employees or the IRS of their election. Moreover, this frequency may be changed throughout the year and need not be consistent from pay period to pay period.

> **EXAMPLE:** TruckCo's sales representatives drive company-owned vehicles for personal use all year. Tax on the value of this personal use is withheld and reported only at the end of the year. The company is in compliance with IRS rules.

> **EXAMPLE:** RaCo provides group-term life insurance to all of its employees. Although the value of this benefit accrues monthly, the company withholds and reports FICA on the taxable portion of the benefit quarterly. The company is in compliance with IRS rules.

The Special Accounting Rule

Determining the value of certain noncash fringe benefits, such as the personal use of a company-owned vehicle, requires time-consuming calculations that can be burdensome at year-end. To make it easier for employers, the IRS allows employers to use the "special accounting rule"—an option that permits employers to treat certain noncash fringe benefits provided in the last two months of the year as having been received in the following year. In other words, benefits earned in November and December 2021 need not be reported or taxed until December 2022.

To use the special accounting rule, employers must meet two requirements:

1. Employees affected by the rule must be notified of its use at some time between receipt of their last paycheck of the year and receipt of their W-2s (no later than January 31). However, because the special accounting rule affects tax planning for employees who itemize (where state deductions continue to appy), many companies notify employees of this election as early in the year as possible.

2. The special accounting rule must be used for all employees who receive the same type of benefit.

   EXAMPLE: Peter uses his company vehicle for personal use each month during 2021. If his employer elects to use the special accounting rule, it may treat the portion of this benefit received by the employee in November and December 2021 as having been received in 2022— provided that it does the same for all employees using company vehicles for personal use.

   PROBLEM 1: In October 2021, ACME elects to use the special accounting rule for employees who drive company trucks. Employee Forms W-2 will be distributed on January 31, 2022. What is the latest date ACME may notify employees of its election?

   SOLUTION 1: No later than January 31, 2022.

Reporting Fringe Benefits on the W-2 for 2021

Fringe benefits are reported on the W-2 in Boxes 10, 12, 13, and 14.

Box 12: Each entry must include both the special letter code that the IRS has assigned to the benefit and its dollar value. The dollar values are expressed, with decimal points, but *without* dollar signs or commas. For example, contributions of $1,500 to a Section* 401(k) plan would be shown as:

D 1500.00 [IRS letter code . . . space . . . amount]

---

* The word "Section" refers to those sections of the tax code that address the tax treatment of certain benefits. They are provided here for reference. Some benefits are nicknamed after the section of the tax code that covers them, such as a "401(k) plan."

The letter codes are as follows:

Code

A Total Social Security tax not withheld from tips. (*DO NOT* report this amount in Box 4.)

B Total Medicare tax not withheld from tips. (*DO NOT* report this amount in Box 6.)

C Value of group-term life over $50,000. This amount also is included in Boxes 1, 3 (up to the Social Security wage limit of $142,800 for 2021) and 5. (No Medicare limit applies.)

Codes D-H, S, Y, AA, BB, and EE are used to report employee pretax contributions to a deferred compensation plan or salary reduction agreement. Check Box 13 ("Retirement Plan") when reporting amounts using these codes.

D Cash or deferred compensation arrangement [Section 401(k)]. Check "Retirement Plan" in Box 13.

E Salary reduction used to purchase an annuity contract [Section 403(b)]. Check "Retirement Plan" in Box 13.

F Salary reduction for a Simplified Employee Pension Plan (SEP) [Section 408(k)(6)]. Check "Retirement Plan" in Box 13.

G Deferred compensation plan for state or local government employees [Section 457(b)]. Check "Retirement Plan" in Box 13.

H Deferred compensation plan for a tax-exempt organization [Section 501(c)(18)(D)]. Check "Retirement Plan" in Box 13.

J Nontaxable third-party sick pay.

K 20% excise tax on excess "golden parachute" payments. (A golden parachute payment is a guaranteed payment made to top executives in the event that a company is sold or the employee's position is eliminated.) Excise taxes also are reported in Box 2.

L Substantiated expense reimbursements—the amount equal to the government rate.

M Social Security tax not withheld from a former employee on the value of taxable group-term life insurance over $50,000. (*DO NOT* report in Box 4.)

N Medicare tax not withheld from a former employee on the value of taxable group-term life insurance over $50,000. Do not show uncollected additional Medicare tax (0.9% on wages over $200,000.) (DO NOT report in Box 6.)

P Through December 31, 2017, this box was used to report tax-free moving expense reimbursements made directly to the employee. (Do not report tax-free reimbursements made directly to a third party such as a moving company.) Effective January 1, 2018 and through December 31, 2025, all moving expenses paid or reimbursed by employers are included in wages subject to FIT, FITW, FICA, and FUTA, unless incurred by *members* of the US Armed Forces who move under a military order to a permanent change of station. Accordingly, effective January 1, 2018, Code P does not apply, except for the US Armed Forces.

Q Nontaxable combat pay (for military employers only).

R For employer contributions to an employee's medical savings account (MSA).

S For employee contributions to a Savings and Incentive Match Plan for Employees of Small Employers (SIMPLE) Individual Retirement Account (IRA). Also check "Retirement Plan" in Box 13.

T For employer payments or reimbursements for qualified adoption expenses under an adoption assistance plan. Report total payments and reimbursements, including those in excess of the $14,440 nontaxable limit for 2021.

V Show the amount that is equal to the difference between the fair market value of the nonstatutory stock over the exercise price of nonstatutory stock option(s) granted to your employee with respect to that stock from your employee or former employees. This reporting requirement does not apply to the exercise of a statutory stock option, or the sale or disposition of stock acquired pursuant to the exercise of a statutory stock option. Include in boxes 1, 3 (up to $142,800 for 2021) and 5 of Form W-2.

W Show any employer contributions and employee's pretax contributions to a Health Savings Account (HSA). An employer's contribution to an HSA is not subject to federal income tax withholding, Social Security, Medicare, federal unemployment, or railroad retirement taxes if it is reasonable to believe at the time of payment that the contribution will be excluded from employee's income. However, if it is not reasonable to believe at the time of payment that the contribution will be excludable from the employee's income, employer contributions are subject to income tax withholding, Social Security, Medicare, and federal unemployment taxes (or railroad retirement taxes, if applicable) and must be reported in boxes 1, 3, and 5 (and on Form 940).

Employers must report all employer and employee pretax contributions to an HSA in box 12 of Form W-2 with code W even if the contribution is not reported as wages in boxes 1, 3, or 5.

Y   Used to report all deferrals to (contributions to) a IRC 409A nonqualified deferred compensation plan in the calendar year. Note that reporting pursuant to this code is indefinitely suspended by the IRS.

Z   Used to report income from a nonqualified deferred compensation plan that fails to meet IRC §409A requirements. This amount is also included in Box 1.

Code AA   Show designated Roth contributions to an IRC §401(k) plan.

Code BB   Show designated Roth contributions to an IRC §403(b) salary reduction agreement.

Code CC: Applied only for tax year 2010.

Code DD: Used to report the cost of employer-sponsored health coverage required by the Affordable Care Act. This amount is not subject to employment tax or withholding and is not reported on the Form W-2 in boxes 1, 3, or 5. Businesses filing fewer than 250 Forms W-2 in 2020 are not required to use Code DD in 2021.

Code EE: Used to report designated Roth contributions under a governmental IRC §457(b) plan. IRC §402A requires separate reporting of the yearly designated Roth contributions. Designated Roth contributions to 401(k) plans are reported using code AA in box 12; designated Roth contributions under 403(b) salary reduction agreements are reported using code BB in box 12; and designated Roth contributions under a governmental IRC §457(b) plan are reported using Code EE in box 12. Do not use Code EE to report elective deferrals under Code G.

Code FF: Permitted benefits under a qualified small employer health reimbursement arrangement (QSEHRA). Use this code to report the total amount of permitted benefits under a QSEHRA.

Code GG: Under the TCJA and effective January 1, 2018, employees have the option to defer federal income tax and federal income tax withholding on certain stock transactions under new IRC §83(i). Code GG is used to report the amount includible in gross income from qualified equity grants under IRC §83(i)(1)(A) for the calendar year.

Code HH: Under the TCJA and effective January 1, 2018, employees have the option to defer federal income tax and federal income tax withholding on certain stock transactions under new IRC §83(i). Code HH is used to report the aggregrate amount of income deferred under IRC §83(i) elections as of the close of the calender year.

Box 10: Report in this box the total dependent care (child care) benefits provided by the employer or pretax contributions made by employees during the year through an employer's flexible benefits plan (sometimes called a "Section 125" or "cafeteria" plan). Any amount over $5,000 ($10,500 for 2021 only) is taxable and is reported in:

- Box 1 (wages, tips and other compensation)

- Box 3 (Social Security wages up to $142,800 for 2021)

- Box 5 (Medicare wages)

Box 13: Following are the boxes that must be checked if they apply.

Statutory employee. There are two types of employees, common law (which defines most employees) and statutory. The wages of a common-law employee are subject to all the applicable federal employment and withholding taxes (i.e., federal income tax withholding, Social Security and Medicare, and federal unemployment tax). However, the wages of a statutory employee are not subject to federal income tax withholding but are subject to FICA and FUTA. Workers meeting the definition of a statutory employee are:

1. drivers who distribute beverages (other than milk), meats, vegetables, fruits, or bakery products, or who pick up and deliver laundry or dry cleaning, if the driver is an agent of the employer or is paid by commission;

2. full-time life insurance sales agents whose principal business activity is selling life insurance or annuity contracts, or both, primarily for one life insurance company;

3. individuals who work at home on materials or goods that the employer supplies and that must be returned to the employer or to a person the employer names, if the employer also furnishes specifications for the work to be done; and

4. full-time traveling or city salespeople who work on the employer's behalf and turn in orders to the employer from wholesalers, retailers, contractors, or operators of hotels, restaurants, or other similar establishments. The goods sold must be merchandise for resale or supplies for use in the buyer's business operation. The work performed for the employer must be the salesperson's principal business activity.

Third-party sick pay. Check this box only if you are a third-party sick pay payer filing Forms W-2 for an insured's employee or are an employer reporting sick payments made by a third party. If more than one box applies (e.g., this box and the "941" box), check both this box and the "941" box and file a single Form W-3 for the regular and "third-party sick pay" Forms W-2. The third-party payer also should check box 13 of Form W-3.

Retirement plan. Check the retirement plan box if the employee was an active participant (for any part of the year) in any of the following:

1. A qualified pension, profit-sharing, or stock-bonus plan described in IRC §401(a) (including a §401(k) plan).

2. An annuity plan described in IRC §403(a).

3. An annuity contract or custodial account described in IRC §403(b).

4. A simplified employee pension (SEP) plan described in IRC §408(k).

5. A SIMPLE retirement account described in IRC §408(p).

6. A trust described in IRC § 501(c)(18).

7. A plan for federal, state, or local government employees or by an agency or instrumentality thereof (other than a IRC §457(b) plan).

DO NOT check the retirement plan box for any individual who made contributions to a nonqualified §457 plan or a nonqualified deferred compensation plan.

Box 14: Optionally, report in this box the value of certain taxable fringe benefits included in Box 1. Also at the employer's option, such items as union dues withheld, health insurance contributions under a flex plan, taxable moving expenses, withheld state disability insurance contributions, and charitable contributions made during the year may be reported in this box. If an employer reports 100% of a vehicle's use in Box 1, this amount must be indicated separately in Box 14 or provided to the employee in a separate, written notice. Do not report in Box 14 amounts reported in Boxes 10 or 13.

Quarterly and Year-End Reporting for Fringe Benefits

The table in Figure 3-1, page 55, summarizes where employers are required to report fringe benefits on the W-2 and other federal employment forms and information statements.

Figure 3-1

BENEFIT TYPE	W-2 Box 1	W-2 Box 3/5	W-2 Box 10	W-2 Box 12[10]	W-2 Box 13[6]	W-2 Box 14	941 Line 2	941 Lines 5a and 5c	940 Part 2 Line 3	940 Part 2 Line 4[9]
Adoption Assistance not Exceeding $14,440 for 2021	out	in	out	In ("T")[14]	out	out	out	in	in	out
Business Expenses: Unsubstantiated or Excess Payments[1]	in	in	out	in ("L")	out	out	in	in	in	out
Dependent Care Assistance Under $10,500[2]	out	out	In[2]	out	out	out	out	out	in	in
Group-Term Life Over $50,000	in	in	out	in ("C")	out	out	in	in	in	in
Group-Term Life: Former Employees	in	in	out	in[8]	out	out	in	in[12]	in	in
Health plan, aggregate employer cost (16)	out	out	out	In ("DD")	out	out	out	out	out	out
Third-Party Sick Pay: Taxable Portion[11]	in	in	out	out	out	out	In[7]	in	in	out
Health insurance-employer provided	out	out	out	In ("DD")[16]	out	out	out	out	out	out
Health Savings Account – employer and employee pretax	out	out	out	In ("W")	out	out	out	out	out	out
Third-Party Sick Pay: Nontaxable Portion[11]	out	out	out	in ("J")	out	out	out	out	in	in
Tips: FICA Not Withheld[3]	in	in	out	in ("A/B")	out	out	in	in[12]	in	out
Tips: Allocated[4]	out	out	out	out	out	out	out	out	out	out
Reimbursed Moving Expenses: Taxable	in	in	out	out	out	in[13]	in	in	in	out
Reimbursed Moving Expenses: Nontaxable	out[13]	out	out	Out[13] ("P")	out	in[13]	out[13]	out	in	in
§401(k) Pretax Contributions	out	in	out	in ("D")	in[6]	out	out	in	in	out
Roth §401(k) Post tax Contributions	in	in	out	In ("AA")	In[6]	out	in	in	in	out
Roth §457(b) Post tax Contributions	in	in	out	In ("EE")	out	out	in	in	in	out
SEP: Employer Contributions	out	out	out	out	In[6]	out	out	out	out	out
SEP: Employee Contributions	out	in	out	in ("F")	in[6]	out	out	in	in	out
§125 Pretax Contributions	out	out	out	out	out	out	out	out	in	in
§501(c)(18)(D) Plans	in	in	out	in ("H")	in[6]	out	in	in	in	out
Personal Use Company Car	in	in	out	out	out	In[15]	in	in	in	out
Wages Paid After Death: Year of Death[5]	out	in	out	out	out	out	out	out	in	out
Wages Paid After Death: Year After Death[5]	out	out	out	out	out	out	out	out	out	out

* This chart was reprinted from Principles of Payroll Administration, Debera J. Salam © Copyright 2021. All rights reserved.

Using the Fringe Benefits Reporting Chart

"In" indicates that the benefit is reported in this area of the form. "Out" indicates that the benefit is not reported in this area of the form.

(1) The amount equal to the government-specified rate is reported in the W-2 in box 12; the excess or unsubstantiated reimbursement is reported in boxes 1,3, and 5.

(2) Report 100% of employer-provided dependent care assistance in Box 10, even if the value exceeds $5,000 ($10,500 for 2021 only). Also report the excess over $5,000 per year in boxes 1, 3, and 5 of the W-2. Remind dependent care assistance plan participants to include Form 2441 with their federal tax return or the taxpayer may be disallowed the $5,000 exclusion.

(3) Report wages even though FICA tax not withheld. Report in box 12 of the W-2 an "A" for Social Security tax not collected from tips and a "B" for Medicare tax not collected and do not report in boxes 4 and 6 of the W-2.

(4) This amount is reported in box 8 only.

(5) The federal taxable amount of the payment should be reported on the 1099-MISC (rather than box 1 of the W-2) and issued to the beneficiary or recipient of the wages. Wages paid after death but in the same year as death are FICA and FUTA taxable and reported as such on the W-2, 941, and 940. Wages paid in the year after death are not taxable for FICA or FUTA, and are not reported on the W-2, 941, or 940 but only on the 1099-MISC. Federal taxable income in connection with nonqualified deferred compensation that is paid to the beneficiary of a deceased employee is reported on Form 1099-R.

(6) Box 13 "retirement plan," is checked for all participants in a retirement plan. This may include those employees who are eligible but elected not to participate. Discuss with your organization's benefits consultant.

(7) See the 941 instructions for line 2.

(8) Report taxable group-term life insurance over $50,000 in box 12 with the amount preceded by a "C." Report uncollected social security tax from former employees' taxable group-term life insurance in box 12 preceded by an "M." Report uncollected Medicare tax in box 12 preceded by an "N." You must show the taxable group-term life in box 12 preceded by Code C to avoid being assessed the amounts reported in box 12, Codes M and N.

(9) Check one of the boxes as appropriate for the wage type that is exempt from FUTA. For instance, check box 4(a), "fringe benefits" for pretax health contributions under a cafeteria plan arrangement and 4(b), "group-term life" for taxable group-term life over $50,000.

(10) Letters shown in this column must precede the dollar amount in box 12. There must be at least one space between the code and the dollar amount.

(11) Sick pay received in the first six months from the last day of the month that the employee last worked is reported in boxes 1, 3, and 5 of the Form W-2. Sick pay received after this six-month coverage period is reported in box 1 of the W-2 only. Report nontaxable sick pay in box 12 with the code J. Form 8922 is required if Forms 941 and W-2 will not agree (usually applies to the third-party payer).

(12) Show a credit for the amount of Social Security and/or Medicare tax not withheld from tips and/or group-term life insurance over $50,000 on line 9 of the 941.

(13) *For expenses incurred through December 31, 2017:* Exclude nontaxable amounts from box 1 of the W-2 and Line 2 of the 941. Taxable relocation expenses are also reported as Social Security and Medicare wages on the Forms W-2 and 941. Report nontaxable relocation reimbursements made directly to employees in box 12 of the W-2 preceded by a "P." Do not report nontaxable payments made directly to third parties in box 12; however, include these amounts on Form 940, Part 2, Line 3 and Part 2, Line 4 (check box 4e). Box 14 reporting is optional.
For expenses incurred on and after January 1, 2018: Reimbursements or payments made to third parties for moving expenses are no longer excluded from taxable wages. An exception applies to moving expenses incurred by members of the Armed Forces. Use box 12, Code P only for reimbursements made to the Armed Forces.

(14) When reporting adoption assistance in box 12, exclude amounts forfeited under an adoption assistance flexible spending account.

(15) If 100% of a vehicle's use is reported in box 1 of the W-2, show the amount included in box 1 in box 14 of the W-2, or provide a separate statement to employee with this information.

(16) Under the Affordable Care Act of 2010, and effective in 2012, employers are required to report in Form W-2, box 12, code DD the aggregate cost of employer-provided group health care if they filed 250 or more Forms W-2 in the previous tax year. This amount is informational only and has no effect on taxable wages.

---

[1]Effective in 2018 and through 2025, applies only to the U.S. Armed Forces.

QUIZ 1   REPORTING FOR FRINGE BENEFITS

Problem I.

Answer each statement True or False assuming it is tax year 2021.

1. Under the special accounting rule, certain noncash fringe benefits provided to employees between November and December 2021 may be reported in 2022.

    a. True   b. False

2. The value of taxable fringe benefits received by employees may be treated as paid and taxed at any frequency provided they are taxed by the end of the year.

    a. True   b. False

3. If an employer elects to use the special accounting rule, it must notify employees by January 31 of the year in which the election is made.

    a. True   b. False

4. Box 12 of the W-2 is where employers report total employee pretax contributions to a health care plan.

    a. True   b. False

5. Only nontaxable third-party sick pay is reported in Box 12.

    a. True   b. False

Problem II.

Fill in the blanks assuming it is tax year 2021.

1. Under the special accounting rule, certain noncash fringe benefits received during the months of _____ and _____ 2021 may be treated as having been received in _____.

2. Noncash fringe benefits must be reported and taxed at least

    _____.

3. The dollar amounts reported in Box 12 of the W-2 should include decimal points but not _____ _____ or _____.

4. If an employee made contributions to a §401(k) plan, the employer should, in addition to Boxes 3 and 5, complete Boxes _____ and _____ of the W-2.

5. Taxable group-term life insurance is reported on the W-2 in Boxes _____, _____, _____, and _____.

Problem III.

Multiple choice. Circle the correct answer assuming it is tax year 2021. (Answers may be found in the text or in the table in Figure 3-1.)

1. Dependent care benefits must be reported on the W-2 in Box:

    a. 14   b. 10   c. 12   d. 13

2. Nontaxable third-party sick pay is reported on the W-2 in Box:

    a. 1   b. 14   c. 12   d. 13

3. Wages paid after an employee's death, but in the same year in which the death occurred must *not* appear on the W-2 in Box:

    a. 14   b. 3   c. 5   d. 1

4. An example of a benefit reported in Box 14 of the W-2 is:

    a. dependent care assistance
    b. charitable contributions
    c. group-term life over $50,000
    d. SEP contributions

5. An example of a benefit not reported on Line 2 of the 941 is:

    a. group-term life over $50,000
    b. allocated tips
    c. taxable moving expense reimbursements
    d. unsubstantiated business expense reimbursements

6. An employer that wants to show §401(k) contributions of $2,500.75 in Box 12 of the W-2 would write it as:

    a. $2,500.75
    b. D 2,500.75
    c. D 2500.75
    d. D $2500.75

7. For 2021, relocation reimbursements made directly to employees of a for-profit business must be reported in which box or boxes of Form W-2?

    a. Boxes 10 and 12
    b. Box 14
    c. Box 12
    d. Boxes 1, 3 and 5

QUIZ 1   *Solutions and Explanations*

Problem I.

1. True
   Only noncash fringe benefits received by the employee in November and December 2021 may be reported in 2022.

2. False
   Only *noncash* fringe benefits may be taxed once a year. All other benefits are taxable when received.

3. False
   Employers are required to give notice between the date that employees receive their final paycheck of the year and January 31 of the following year.

4. False
   Box 12 is used for reporting certain taxable and non-taxable benefits. Box 14 is used, at the employer's option, to report information not reported in Box 12 such as payments of union dues withheld, employee pretax health insurance contributions, taxable moving expense reimbursements, educational assistance payments made during the year, or any other notice that the employer wishes to include.

5. True

Problem II.

1. November, December, 2022

2. annually

3. dollar signs, commas

4. 12, 13

5. 1, 3, 5, 12

Problem III.

1. b

2. c

3. d

4. b

5. b

6. c

7. d

QUIZ 2   REPORTING FOR FRINGE BENEFITS

Problem I.

Answer the following statements True or False assuming it is tax year 2021.

1. The value of employer-provided health coverage is reported on Form W-2 using Code DD.

    a. True   b. False

2. All moving expense reimbursements paid to non-military employees are reported in Box 12 of the W-2.

    a. True   b. False

3. Employees must be notified of the frequency with which an employer recognizes and withholds taxes on the value of noncash fringe benefits.

    a. True   b. False

4. Box 14 of the W-2 may be used to report information such as total union dues withheld for the year.

    a. True   b. False

5. Under the special accounting rule, if an employer does not expect to have enough time to compute taxable income for certain noncash fringe benefits received by employees during December, it may defer withholding and reporting on the benefits until the following year.

    a. True   b. False

Problem II.

Fill in the blanks assuming it is tax year 2021.

1. If Joe made contributions to a SEP, the employer should complete Boxes _____, _____, _____, and _____ of the W-2.

2. The letter code used in Box 12 of the W-2 to report the aggregate cost of employer-provided health insurance _____.

3. An employer's option to postpone taxation and reporting of certain noncash fringe benefits received by employees during the last 2 months of one year to the following year is called the _____ _____ _____.

4. In tax year 2021, the four boxes on the W-2 for reporting fringe benefits are _____, _____, _____, and _____.

5. Wages paid after an employee's death, but in the same year that the death occurred, are reported on two information returns, the W-2 and the _____ (see the table in Figure 3-1).

Problem III.

Multiple choice. Circle the correct answer assuming it is tax year 2021. (Answers may be found in the text or in the table in Figure 3-1.)

1. An example of a benefit not reported on Line 2 of the 941 is:

    a. substantiated expense advance
    b. personal use of a company-owned vehicle
    c. cash gift of $25
    d. group-term life over $50,000

2. An example of a benefit reported in Box 12 of the W-2 is:

    a. personal use of company-owned vehicle
    b. cafeteria plan contributions
    c. dependent care assistance
    d. group-term life over $50,000

3. Wages paid the year after an employee's death are reported on which of the following federal forms?

    a. 1099-MISC   b. W-2   c. 940   d. 941

4. Taxable group-term life is reported on the W-2 in Boxes 1, 3, 5, and . . .

    a. 10   b. 14   c. 12   d. 13

5. Taxable third-party sick pay received in the first 6 months of disability is reported on the W-2 in Boxes 1, 3, and . . .

    a. 12   b. 5   c. 14   d. 13

QUIZ 2 *Solutions and Explanations*

Problem I.

1. True

2. False

3. False

4. True

5. True

Problem II.

1. 3, 5, 12, 13

2. DD

3. special accounting rule

4. 10, 12, 13 and 14

5. 1099-MISC

Problem III.

1. a

2. d

3. a

4. c

5. b

EMPLOYEE BUSINESS EXPENSES

Introduction

Most employers provide employees with allowances, advances or reimbursements to cover business expenses. The IRS has rules to ensure that these payments to employees can be verified as covering *business-related* expenses—expenses incurred by the employee on behalf of the employer. Employers have a number of options for verifying that employees meet the substantiation requirements, each of which should be carefully considered.

Tax-Free Allowances, Advances and Reimbursements

A business-expense *allowance* is usually a lump sum given by the employer to the employee on a regular basis to cover the employee's estimated recurring business expenses.

A business-expense *advance* is usually money given to the employee prior to a particular trip or purchase to cover costs.

A business-expense *reimbursement* is an employer's repayment of business-related expenses incurred by the employee.

Employer allowances, advances and reimbursements for business-related expenses are tax-free only if provided under an *accountable plan*. An accountable plan is one that includes the following requirements:

1. The expense is ordinary, necessary and related to the employer's trade or business.

2. The expense is not related to the employee's personal, living or family expenses.

3. The employee is required to substantiate that the expense is business-related with receipts and documents that show the amount, time, place, and business purpose.

4. The employee is required to return all monies not used for business-related expenses and all monies for expenses that are not substantiated within a reasonable *and specified period of time.*

The IRS has no specific rules for when an employee must substantiate business expenses. However, it offers these guidelines:

1. An advance or allowance should not be given more than 30 days before the employee will incur the expense. (Some employers offer a "permanent advance"—a one-time payment that the employee need not substantiate as business-related and which generally is returned to the employer when the employee terminates. Under IRS guidelines, a "permanent advance" is not tax-free.)

2. An allowance, advance or reimbursement should be substantiated within 60 days after the employee receives the money or incurs the expense.

3. Any portion of an advance, allowance or reimbursement that cannot be substantiated should be returned to the employer within 120 days of the day that the employee receives the money or incurs the expense.

4. In lieu of these three guidelines the employer may submit to employees a statement of unsubstantiated allowances, advances and reimbursements no less than quarterly. The employee should substantiate expenses and/or return any excess within 120 days of receiving this statement.

> **PROBLEM 1:** On October 1, Joan drives out of state on a 3-day business trip. What is the earliest date the IRS recommends that Joan's employer give her a travel advance?
>
> **SOLUTION 1:** September 1—30 days before she is expected to incur travel expenses.
>
> **PROBLEM 2:** Philip returns from a business trip on October 15. If his employer does not issue statements of unsubstantiated allowances, advances and reimbursements, what is the latest date Philip should substantiate his expenses according to IRS recommendations?
>
> **SOLUTION 2:** December 14—within 60 days of incurring the expenses (the date he returns from the trip).

Unsubstantiated Expenses

If an employee fails to substantiate a business expense or return excess amounts within a reasonable period of time, the unsubstantiated or unreturned portion becomes taxable for FIT, FITW, FICA and FUTA and is reported as taxable wages on the W-2, 940 and 941.

Amounts neither substantiated nor returned are costly. Employers incur FUTA and FICA tax expenses and employees incur FICA and FITW on these amounts. To avoid these costs, employers are advised to consider the advantages and disadvantages of expense allowances, advances or reimbursements and determine which approach is most suitable for their business.

> **PROBLEM 3:** On August 19, 2021, Tania receives a travel advance of $500. She submits receipts and indicates the time, place and business purpose of $300 in expenses. She neither substantiates nor returns the remaining $200. Is any portion of the advance taxable? If so, which taxes apply?
>
> **SOLUTION 3:** $200 of the advance is taxable because it was neither substantiated nor returned. The $200 is subject to FIT, FITW, FICA, and FUTA.

Employer Payment Options for Business Expenses

Employers have several options for paying employee business expenses, including dollar-for-dollar reimbursement of all expenses, specified rates for employees' use of a personal car, and specified rates for lodging and meal expenses incurred during overnight travel.

1. **Dollar-for-dollar reimbursement.** Under this method, the employee must submit receipts for all but "de minimis" expenses (de minimis expenses are generally expenses of less than $75 or occasional parking fees or tolls). This method is most practical for travel expenses such as lodging, business entertainment, meals, and cab fare, but not for an employee's use of his or her personal car for company business.

> **Advantage:** The employer does not incur the risk of payroll taxes associated with allowances or advances that are not substantiated or repaid.
>
> **Disadvantage:** Collecting, verifying and storing receipts can be an administrative burden.

2. Business standard mileage rate for employee use of a personal car. This is the simplest, most tax-favored way to reimburse an employee for business use of a personal car. Effective January 1, 2021 the maximum tax-free reimbursement for business use of a personal car is $0.56 for each business mile driven. This rate includes depreciation, maintenance, insurance, and gasoline. The employee submits only a statement indicating the time, place and business purpose of the travel, but no receipts. Expenses incurred for occasional parking and tolls may be reimbursed separately provided employees indicate the time, place, and business purpose of the expense.

To qualify as tax-free, allowances, advances and reimbursements for personal-auto use must meet the following criteria:

1. The employee must substantiate the reimbursement by indicating the time, place and business purpose of the travel.

2. Amounts in excess of the government-specified mileage rate of $0.56 per mile effective January 1, 2021 must be treated as wages subject to FIT, FITW, FICA, and FUTA.

> **PROBLEM 4:** On March 25, 2021, BusCo reimburses Jose at the rate of $0.57 per mile for a 100-mile business trip made in his car on March 12. He substantiates the time, place and business purpose of the travel. How much, if any, of this reimbursement is taxable, and which taxes apply?

> **SOLUTION 4:** $1 of Jose's reimbursement is taxable. To calculate:

> $0.57 per mile (employer rate) − $0.56 per mile (government-specified rate) = $.01 × 100 miles driven for business, or $1.

This excess over the government-specified rate is subject to FIT, FITW, FICA, and FUTA. The first $0.56 reimbursed for each mile driven is tax-free effective January 1, 2021 (and the first $0.575 per mile was tax free effective January 1, 2020 through December 31, 2020).

> **PROBLEM 5:** If the employee in Problem 4 had not indicated the time, place and business purpose of his trip, what portion of the reimbursement would be taxable, and what taxes would apply?

> **SOLUTION 5:** The entire $57.00 of the reimbursement (100 miles × $0.57 per mile) would be taxable, subject to FIT, FITW, FICA, and FUTA.

3. **Federal per diem rate and the high-low substantiation method.**
Government-specified per diem (daily) rates cover employees' business-related travel expenses (such as lodging and meals) and certain incidental expenses (such as laundry, cleaning, pressing, and tips). However, the per diem rate does not include certain expenses such as cab fare, phone calls, faxes, or wires. These expenses may be reimbursed separately from the per diem rate, but receipts generally are required for substantiation of expenses. Federal per diem rates vary depending on the employee's destination.

NOTE: Receipts generally are not required for amounts of $75 or less.

To qualify as tax-free, advances, reimbursements and allowances for lodging, meals and incidental expenses must meet the following requirements:

1. The employee must substantiate the reimbursement by indicating time, place and business purpose of the travel.

2. Amounts in excess of the government-specified per diem must be treated as wages subject to FIT, FITW, FICA, and FUTA.

Because the list of federal per diem rates is very long, employers may use the simpler high-low substantiation method. This method provides one set of rates for "high-cost" areas and another set of rates for all other areas (or "low-cost" areas).

The federal per diem rates in effect as of January 1, 2021 (or alternatively, October 1, 2020) and through December 31, 2021 (or alternatively September 30, 2021) for the continental United States (CONUS) under the high-low substantiation method are as follows:

*Lodging, Meals and Incidental Expenses**

High-cost areas: $292 (was $297) per day
Low-cost (all other) areas: $198 per your alert and IRS Notice 2020-71 (was $200) per day

*Lodging Only**

High-cost areas: $221 (was $226) per day
Low-cost (all other) areas: $138 (was $135) per day

Note: Room tax may be reimbursed separately provided proper substantiation is provided.

---

* For travel in continental U.S. only.

Meals and Incidental Expenses Only*

High-cost areas: $71 per day
Low-cost (all other) areas: $60 per day

Incidental Expenses Only*

High-cost areas: $5 per day
Low-cost areas: $5 per day

High cost areas are shown in Figure 4-1 (page 71)—all areas not shown are in the low-cost category.

Note: Some localities are classified as high cost for a limited period each year, making use of the high-low substantiation method more complex.

Advantages: Reduces administrative burden of collecting and retaining receipts and helps control the employer's travel expenses.

Disadvantages: If the employer pays in excess of the government-specified rates, both the employer and the employee pay tax on the excess. To avoid these taxes, the employer must reimburse at rates that may be too low to cover actual expenses, and employees may resist accepting travel assignments.

NOTE: The per diem rates for travel in the continenetal United States (CONUS) are available on the General Services Administration (GSA) website at at *https://www.gsa.gov/travel/plan-book/per-diem-rates*. Per diem rates for travel outisde the continental United States (OCONUS) are available on the U.S. Department of Defense website at *https://www.defensetravel.dod.mil/site/perdiemCalc.cfm*. Foreign per diem rates are found on the U.S. Department of State website at *https://aoprals.state.gov/content.asp?content_id=184&menu_id=78*.

PROBLEM 6: Sales representative Joan is sent to New York City for 2 days in October 2021 to close a sales contract. Her employer uses the per diem method to reimburse employees for travel expenses. She is given an advance of $632 ($316 per day) for lodging, meals and incidentals for a 2-night stay. She substantiates the time, place and business purpose of her trip. What portion of this advance, if any, is taxable under the high-low substantiation method?

---

* For travel in continental U.S. only.

Figure 4-1

High-Cost Localities of Under the High-Low Substantiation Method
(Effective October 1, 2020 through September 30, 2021)

Key City	County/Other Defined Location	Key City	County/Other Defined Location
Arizona		**Maine**	
Sedona (Oct 1–Dec 1, Mar 1–Apr 30, and Sept 1–Sept 30	City Limits of Sedona	Bar Harbor/Rockport (July 1–Aug 31)	Hancock and Knox
California		Kennebunk/Kittery/Sanford (July 1–Aug 31)	York
Los Angeles (Oct 1–Oct 31 and Jan 1–Sept 30)	Los Angeles, Orange, Ventura, Edwards AFB less the city of Santa Monica	**Maryland**	
		Ocean City (July 1–Aug 31)	Worcester
Mill Valley/San Rafael/Novato (Oct 1–Oct 31 and June 1–Sept 30)	Marin	Washington DC Metro Area	Montgomery and Prince George's
Monterey (June 1–Aug 31)	Monterey	**Massachusetts**	
Napa (Oct 1–Nov 30 and Apr 1–Sept 30)	Napa	Boston/Cambridge (Oct 1–Nov 30 and Mar 1–Sept 30)	Suffolk, City of Cambridge
Oakland	Alameda	Falmouth (July 1–Aug 31)	City Limits of Falmouth
San Diego (Feb 1–July 31)	San Diego	Hyannis (July 1–Aug 31)	Barnstable less the city of Faimouth
San Francisco	San Francisco	Martha's Vineyard (June 1–Sep 30)	Dukes
Santa Barbara	Santa Barbara	Nantucket (June 1–Sept 30)	Nantucket
San Mateo/Foster City/Belmont	San Mateo	**Michigan**	
Santa Monica	City Limits of Santa Monica	Petoskey (July 1–Aug 31)	Emmet
Sunnyvale/Palo Alto/San Jose	Santa Clara	Traverse City (July 1–Aug 31)	Grand Traverse
Colorado		**Montana**	
Aspen (Oct 1–Mar 31 and June 1–Sept 30)	Pitkin	Big Sky/West Yellowstone/Gardiner June 1–Sept 30)	Gallatin and Park
Crested Butte/Gunnison (Dec 1–Mar 31)	Gunnnison	**New Mexico**	
		Carlsbad	Eddy
Denver/Aurora (Oct 1–Oct 31 and Apr 1–Sept 30)	Denver, Adams, Arapahoe, Jefferson	**New York**	
		Lake Placid (July 1–Aug 31)	Essex
Grand Lake (Dec 1–Mar 31)	Grand	New York City (Oct 1–Dec 31 and Mar 1–Sept 30)	Bronx, Kings, New York, Queens, and Richmond
Silverthorne/Breckenridge (Dec 1–Mar 31)	Summit	**Oregon**	
Telluride	San Miguel	Portland (Oct 1–Oct 31 and June 1–Sept 30)	Multnomah
Vail	Eagle	Seaside (July 1–Aug 31)	Clatsop
Delaware		**Pennsylvania**	
Lewes (July 1–Aug 31)	Sussex	Hershey (June 1–Aug 31)	Hershey
District of Columbia		Philadelphia (Oct 1–Nov 30, Mar 1–June 30, and Sept 1–Sept 30)	Philadelphia
Washington DC	Also the cities of Alexandra, Falls Church, Fairfax; and the counties of Arlington and Fairfax in Virginia; and the counties of Montgomery and Prince George's in Maryland.) (See also Maryland and Virginia.)	**Rhode Island**	
		Jamestown/Middletown/Newport (Oct 1–Oct 31 and June 1–Sept 30)	Newport
		South Carolina	
		Charleston (Oct 1–Nov 30 and Mar 1–Sept 30)	Charleston, Berkley, and Dorchester
Florida		**Tennessee**	
Boca Raton/Delray Beach/Jupiter (Dec 1–Apr 30)	Palm Beach and Hendry	Nashville	Davidson
Fort Lauderdale (Jan 1–Apr 30)	Broward	**Utah**	
Fort Meyers (Feb 1–Mar 31)	Lee	Park City (Dec 1–Mar 31)	Summit
Fort Walton Beach/De Funiak Springs (June 1–July 31)	Okaloosa and Walton	**Virginia**	
		Virginia Beach (June 1–Aug 31)	City of Virginia Beach
Gulf Breeze (Oct 1–July 31)	Santa Rosa	Wallops Island (July 1–Aug 31)	Accomack
Key West (Oct 1–July 31)	Monroe	Washington, DC Metro Area	Cities of Alexandria, Fairfax, and Falls Church; Counties of Arlington and Fairfax
Miami (Dec 1–Mar 31)	Miami-Dade		
Naples (Dec 1–Apr 30)	Collier		
Vero Beach (Dec 1–April 30)	Indian River		
Georgia		**Washington**	
Jekyll Island/Brunswick (Mar 1–July 31)	Glynn	Seattle	King
Illinois		Vancouver (Oct 1–Oct 31 and June 1–Sept 30)	Clark, Cowlitz and Skamania
Chicago (Oct 1–Nov 30 and Apr 1–Sept 30)	Cook and Lake	**Wyoming**	
		Cody (June 1–Sept 30)	Park
		Jackson/Pinedale (June 1–Sept 30)	Teton and Sublette

SOLUTION 6: $48 of the advance is taxable under the high-low substantiation method. To calculate:

$316 employer per diem – $292 per day government-specified rate for New York City under the high-low substantiation method = $24 × 2 days = $48 over the government-specified rate that is taxable as income.

PROBLEM 7: If the employee in Problem 6 did not substantiate the time, place and business purpose of her trip, how much of her $632 advance would be taxable?

SOLUTION 7: The entire advance of $632 would be taxable.

Reporting of Taxable Employer Payments

Employers report 100% of the amount of unsubstantiated or unreturned business-expense allowances, advances and reimbursements in Box 1 of the W-2. Any unsubstantiated or unreturned excess is also reported in Box 3 (up to the 2021 Social Security wage limit of $142,800) and 5 (there is no Medicare wage limit).

When an employer's mileage or per diem rate is higher than the federal rate and employees meet substantiation requirements, the total allowances, advances or reimbursements ***equal to the government-specified rate*** are reported in Box 12 using Code L. The excess over the government-specified rate is reported in Boxes 1, 3 and 5. If the employer's mileage or per diem rate is less than or equal to the federal rate, nothing is reported on the W-2. Check the table "Figure 3-1: Fringe Benefits Reporting for Federal Forms for 2021" on page 55.

PROBLEM 8: On May 6, 2021, ACME reimburses Ramon $0.590 per mile for business use of his personal car for a 150-mile trip. How is the excess reimbursement of $4.50 (150 miles × $0.03) reported on Ramon's W-2 for 2021?

SOLUTION 8: The excess $4.50 is reported in Boxes 1, 3 and 5 of the Form W-2, and $84.00, the amount equal to the government-specified rate ($0.56 × 150 miles), is reported in Box 12 (Code L) of Ramon's W-2. Remember that dollar signs and commas are not used in Box 12 or anywhere on the W-2.

QUIZ 1 EMPLOYEE BUSINESS EXPENSES

Problem I.

Fill in the blanks.

1. A business-expense reimbursement is tax-free if the employee substantiates the _____, _____, _____, and _____ of the expense.

2. The IRS recommends that an allowance, advance or reimbursement be provided to the employee no more than _____ days before the employee will incur the expense.

3. Under IRS guidelines, an employee should be given no more than _____ days to return the portion of an expense advance or allowance that is not used for business.

4. Unsubstantiated expense reimbursements can be costly to the _____ and _____.

5. The government-specified business standard mileage rate is _____ per mile effective January 1, 2021.

Problem II.

Answer each question True or False.

1. The government-specified business standard mileage rate effective January 1, 2021, is $0.56 per mile.

    a. True   b. False

2. The government-specified business standard mileage rate includes the cost of depreciation, maintenance, gasoline, parking fees, and tolls.

    a. True   b. False

3. Under the government-specified business per diem rate option, employees need not substantiate the amount of the expense.

    a. True   b. False

4. Generally, expenses such as occasional parking and tolls do not need to be substantiated with documents/receipts.

   a. True   b. False

5. The IRS recommends that employees substantiate an expense for which they have received an allowance, advance or reimbursement within 365 days from the date incurred.

   a. True   b. False

Problem III.

Multiple choice. Circle the correct answer.

1. The government-specified business standard mileage rate effective January 1, 2021, is:

   a. $0.140   b. $0.56   c. $0.575   d. $0.200

2. If XYZ Co reimburses employees $292 per day in May 2021 for lodging, meals and incidental expenses incurred in St. Louis, Missouri, the daily taxable amount under the high-low substantiation method would be . . .

   a. $0   b. $292   c. $200   d. $94

3. Under IRS guidelines, an expense advance or allowance should be given to an employee no more than how many days before the business expense will be incurred?

   a. 120   b. 90   c. 30   d. 60

4. WidgeCo reimburses Mai-Lee $295 for substantiated lodging, meals and incidentals for 1 night's travel in October 2021 to New York City. What amount would be reported on her 2021 W-2 in Boxes 1 and 12?

   a. Box 1: 3.00, Box 12: 292
   b. Box 1: 295, Box 12: 292
   c. Box 1: 295, Box 12: 3.00
   d. Box 1: 295, Box 12: 300

5. ACME reimburses Fran $0.57 per mile for 100 business miles that she drove in her own car in February 2021. Assuming that Fran substantiates this reimbursement, how much of it is taxable to her?

    a. $0   b. $57.50   c. $56.00   d. $1.00

QUIZ 1 Solutions and Explanations

Problem I.

1. amount, time, place, business purpose

2. 30

3. 120

4. employer, employee (in any order)

5. $0.56

Problem II.

1. True

2. False
   The government-specified business standard mileage rate does not include parking fees and tolls.

3. True
   (employee must substantiate the time, place, and business purpose, but not the amount)

4. True
   (employee must substantiate the time, place, and business purpose)

5. False
   The period suggested by the IRS is 60 days.

Problem III.

    1. b

    2. d

    $292 − $198 (2021 government-specified per diem rate for low-cost areas) = $94 excess per day that is taxable

    3. c

    4. a

    ($295 − $292 = $3 taxable, $292 nontaxable)

    5. d

    $.01 ($0.57 − $0.56) per mile excess × 100 mi. = $1.00 excess that is taxable.

Mastering Payroll II

QUIZ 2   EMPLOYEE BUSINESS EXPENSES

Problem I.

Fill in the blanks.

1. Under IRS guidelines, employees should substantiate reimbursements or return unused portions of expense allowances, advances and reimbursements within _____ days of their employer's issuing its statement of unsubstantiated expenses, advances and allowances.

2. The IRS offers simplified per diem rates under a safe harbor rule called the _____ – _____ _____ _____.

3. To which three payroll taxes is an unsubstantiated expense reimbursement potentially subject?   1. _____ 2. _____ 3. _____.

4. The advantage of using the government-specified per diem rate is that even though the employees must indicate time, place and business purpose of travel, no _____ are required for substantiation of the amount of the expense.

Problem II.

Answer each question True or False.

1. The government-specified per diem for incidental expenses does not include the cost of phone calls or telegrams.

    a. True   b. False

2. The government-specified business standard mileage rate on January 1, 2021, is $0.56 for all business miles driven by employees in their personal cars during the year.

    a. True   b. False

3. If an employee is reimbursed at a per diem rate that is higher than the government-specified rate, 100% of the reimbursement is taxable.

    a. True   b. False

4. IRS guidelines recommend that unused portions of an allowance or advance be returned to the employer within 30 days.

    a. True   b. False

5. The highest tax-free per diem rate allowed for lodging, meals and incidental expenses in a high cost area under the high-low substantiation method effective January 1, 2021, is $198.

    a. True   b. False

Problem III.

Multiple choice. Circle the correct answer.

1. Unsubstantiated allowances, advances and reimbursements are . . .

    a. subject to FICA only
    b. subject to FICA and FUTA only
    c. reported as taxable wages only
    d. subject to FICA, FUTA and FITW

2. If Pete is reimbursed at a rate of $0.57 per mile for 200 substantiated business miles driven in his personal car during July 2021, the reimbursement would be reported on his 2021 W-2 as follows:

    a. Box 1: 112.00, Box 12: 2.00
    b. Box 1: 2.00, Box 12: 112.00
    c. Box 1: 2.00, Box 12: 116.00
    d. Box 1: 2.00, Box 12: 2.00

3. Under the high-low substantiation method and effective January 1, 2021, if an employer reimburses an employee for substantiated lodging, meals and incidental expenses for travel to San Francisco at a per diem rate of $300, how much of the daily amount is taxable?

    a. $300   b. $100   c. $8   d. $292

4. Under the high-low substantiation method and effective January 1, 2021, the per diem reimbursement rate for lodging only in a high-cost area is:

    a. $292   b. $221   c. $200   d. $140

QUIZ 2   *Solutions and Explanations*

Problem I.

1. 120

2. high-low substantiation method

3. FICA, FUTA and FITW

4. receipts

Problem II.

1. True

2. True

3. False
Only the excess is taxable, unless the employee fails to substantiate the advance, allowance or reimbursement, in which case it is all taxable.

4. False
The IRS recommends 120 days.

5. False
The highest government-specified per diem under the high-low effective January 1, 2021, is $292.

Problem III.

1. d

2. b
$0.56 × 200 = $112 nontaxable (box 12)
$0.57 − $0.56 = 0.01 × 200 = $2.00 taxable (box 1)

3. c
$300 company per diem − $292 government-specified rate = $8 per day taxable excess

4. b
(Lodging, meals, and incidentals of $292 − meals and incidentals only of $71)

Section 5
PERSONAL USE OF COMPANY-PROVIDED VEHICLES

Introduction

Many employers own or lease cars that employees drive for business and/or personal use. The IRS has rules for determining the value of employees' personal use of company-provided vehicles for wage and tax purposes. The value of the personal use of a company-provided vehicle is subject to FIT, FICA and FUTA, but employers may elect not to withhold federal income tax.

Taxable Vehicle Use

Employee use of a company-provided vehicle in connection with the employer's trade or business is tax-free as a working condition fringe. However, personal (nonbusiness-related) use, such as commuting,* household errands and vacation travel is subject to FIT, FICA and FUTA. An employer may elect to waive FITW on the value of personal vehicle use provided that: (a) the election is made at the beginning of the year in which the election applies; and (b) the employer notifies all employees affected by the election no later than January 31 of the year in which the election will apply, or 30 days from the day the vehicle is first made available.

> **PROBLEM 1:** Since 2008, Ernie's has allowed repair personnel to commute in company trucks. It has withheld FICA and FIT on the value of employees' personal use of its trucks. On January 1, 2021, Ernie's elects to stop withholding federal income tax on the value of employees' personal use of its trucks. By when must Ernie's notify employees affected by this election?
>
> **SOLUTION 1:** By January 31, 2021.

Three Special Valuation Methods

The IRS offers employers several safe-harbor methods (exceptions allowing for simpler or more lenient treatment) for determining the value of an employee's vehicle use. Generally, once an employer elects to use a particular method, it must use that method every year for as long as the vehicle qualifies for it.

---

* *Commuting* is defined as travel to and from work.

1. **Annual lease value method.** Employers wishing to use a special valuation method must use the annual lease value for any "luxury" vehicle. A luxury vehicle is defined by its annual adjusted value. Below is a table showing the annual adjusted value for each year since 1990.

Luxury Vehicle Annual Adjusted Value	
Before January 1, 1990	12,800
After January 1, 1990	13,200
1991	13,400
1992	13,900
1993	14,200
1994	14,700
1995	15,200
1996	15,400
1997	15,700
1998	15,600
1999	15,500
2000–2001	15,400
2002	15,300
2003	15,200
2004–2005	14,800
2006	15,000
2007	15,100
2008–2009	15,000
2010–2011	15,300
2012	15,900
2013–2015	16,000
2016–2017	15,900
2018	50,000
2019	50,400
2020	50,400
2021	51,100*
*See IRS Notice 2021-02	

To determine the value of an employee's use of a company-provided vehicle under this method, an employer may use the actual price a buyer would pay to lease a comparable vehicle in an arm's-length transaction (that is, a transaction between two parties that are independent of one another and not related in any way that would impair their objectivity). This requires consulting the blue book to ascertain the vehicle's value. All car dealers have a blue book that lists the value of current and prior-year car makes and models. The employer finds the current value of the company vehicle as of the day it was first made available to the employee and compares this value to the "IRS Annual Lease Value Table" (Figure 5-1, page 83).

A vehicle's value may be reevaluated every four years. If the car is used by the employee for less than a year, the annual lease value is prorated by dividing the annual lease value by 365 days and multiplying the daily rate by the number of days the employee uses the vehicle. The annual lease value

Section 5–Personal Use of Company-Provided Vehicles

Figure 5-1
IRS Annual Lease Value Table*

Automobile Fair Market Value (FMV) (1)	Annual Lease Value (2)	Automobile Fair Market Value (FMV) (1)	Annual Lease Value (2)
$ 0 to $ 999	$ 600	$21,000 to $21,999	$ 5,850
1,000 to 1,999	850	22,000 to 22,999	6,100
2,000 to 2,999	1,100	23,000 to 23,999	6,350
3,000 to 3,999	1,350	24,000 to 24,999	6,600
4,000 to 4,999	1,600	25,000 to 25,999	6,850
5,000 to 5,999	1,850	26,000 to 27,999	7,250
6,000 to 6,999	2,100	28,000 to 29,999	7,750
7,000 to 7,999	2,350	30,000 to 31,999	8,250
8,000 to 8,999	2,600	32,000 to 33,999	8,750
9,000 to 9,999	2,850	34,000 to 35,999	9,250
10,000 to 10,999	3,100	36,000 to 37,999	9,750
11,000 to 11,999	3,350	38,000 to 39,999	10,250
12,000 to 12,999	3,600	40,000 to 41,999	10,750
13,000 to 13,999	3,850	42,000 to 43,999	11,250
14,000 to 14,999	4,100	44,000 to 45,999	11,750
15,000 to 15,999	4,350	46,000 to 47,999	12,250
16,000 to 16,999	4,600	48,000 to 49,999	12,750
17,000 to 17,999	4,850	50,000 to 51,999	13,250
18,000 to 18,999	5,100	52,000 to 53,999	13,750
19,000 to 19,999	5,350	54,000 to 55,999	14,250
20,000 to 20,999	5,600	56,000 to 57,999	14,750
		58,000 to 59,999	15,250

*For automobiles with a FMV of more than $59,999, the annual lease value equals (.25 × the FMV of the car) + $500.

rate does not include the value of employer-provided fuel. Employer-provided fuel may be valued at actual cost, or at 5.5 cents for each mile driven.

PROBLEM 2: During the year, Mary drives a company-owned vehicle valued at $17,000 for 60 days and buys her own fuel. Assuming no business use, how much taxable income must be recognized for Mary's personal use of the company vehicle?

SOLUTION 2: $797.40 taxable income must be recognized for Mary's personal use of the company vehicle. To calculate:

$17,000 market value of car = $4,850 annual lease value
   (See the table in Figure 5-1, page 83)

$4,850 annual lease value ÷ 365 days = $13.29 per day

$13.29 × 60 days = $797.40 taxable income

83

Allocation versus 100% use under the lease value method: Employers have two reporting options.

A. **Report 100% of annual lease value.** Employers may report 100% of the annual lease value plus the value of employer-provided fuel. This option offers the advantage of reduced recordkeeping but may result in increased FICA and FUTA tax expenses for the employer because taxes are paid on business use that is otherwise tax-free.

B. **Report only the annual lease value of personal use.** To use this option, the employer must obtain from the employee a record of total business and personal miles. To determine the value of personal use, the percentage of personal use is multiplied by the annual lease value. The value of any employer-provided fuel is added to this amount.

> **PROBLEM 3:** George uses a company-owned vehicle valued at $15,000 for the full year. He drives 10,000 miles, of which 3,000 were personal. His employer provides all fuel. If his employer chooses to report only the value of George's personal use of the car, how much income would it report for him?
>
> **SOLUTION 3:** $1,470 taxable income for George for his personal use of the company car. To calculate:
>
> The annual lease value of a $15,000 car is $4,350 per year (see the table in Figure 5-1, page 83)
>
> 3,000 miles personal use ÷ 10,000 total miles driven = 30% personal use
>
> $4,350 annual lease value × 30% personal use = $1,305 annual lease value for personal use
>
> 3,000 miles × $0.055 per mile = $165 for personal fuel
>
> $1,305 taxable income for personal mileage + $165 taxable income for employer-provided fuel = $1,470 total taxable income

2. **Apply the vehicle cents-per-mile method.** This method may be used only when two requirements are met:

a. At least 50% of the vehicle's total annual mileage is related to the employer's trade or business, or the vehicle is used each day to transport at least 3 employees to or from work (for example, as part of a company-sponsored van pool);

b. The value of the vehicle does not exceed $51,100 for 2021 ($50,400 for 2020). See page 82. **Note:** Effective 1-1-98, this method may be used for leased vehicles.

Under this method, each personal mile driven by the employee is multiplied by the government-specified business standard mileage rate, effective January 1, 2021, $0.56 per mile, regardless of how many miles the employee drives. If the employer does not provide fuel to the employee, the rate may be reduced by $0.055.

Allocation versus 100% use under the vehicle cents-per-mile method. An employer that uses the vehicle cents-per-mile method has no choice. It must report as taxable income *only* the personal miles driven by the employee. The employee is required to submit a record of personal miles driven during the period and to substantiate business miles driven with a statement indicating time, place and business purpose.

> **PROBLEM 4:** Randolph drives 7,000 miles during August 2021 in a new car valued at $30,000. Total mileage includes 1,000 personal miles. His employer furnishes fuel. Can his employer use the vehicle cents-per-mile method? If so, how much taxable income should the employer report?

> **SOLUTION 4:** Yes, his employer may use the vehicle cents-per-mile method—and it will report $560 (1,000 miles × $.56) taxable income for Randolph. The vehicle cents-per-mile method can be used because the car was valued at less than $51,100 for 2021, and more than 50% of its use is for the employer's business.

3. **Commuting valuation method.** This method may be used when three requirements are met:

a. The employer, for its own benefit, requires employees to commute in a company-provided vehicle for valid noncompensatory business purposes. For example, a service truck containing valuable equipment must be taken to the employee's home overnight because it is unsafe to leave the vehicle in the employer's parking lot.

b. There is a written employer plan or policy stating that the vehicle may not be used for any personal use other than commuting.

c. The vehicle is owned or leased by the employer and provided to one or more employees for use in connection with the employer's trade or business or to transport employees in a company-sponsored van pool.

Under this method, the value of an employer-provided van pool is $1.50 for each one-way commute, or $3 per round trip. This flat rate applies regardless of the number of miles the employee commutes. (**Note:** Effective January 1, 2021, up to $270 per month of van pool benefits may be tax free. See page 32 for more details.) The commuting valuation method also may be used when the employee, for business reasons, is *required* to commute in a company-provided vehicle. However, the commuting valuation method may *never* be used for employees of the *control group* (e.g., company officers who own 1% or more of its stock).

Requirements for Using the Special Valuation Methods

Employers are required to notify employees of the special valuation rule (cents-per-mile, commuting valuation or annual lease value method) they will use to determine the fair market value of personal use of a company-provided vehicle. The IRS clarifies that an employer or employee may use the special valuation rules only when:

1. the employer treats the value of the personal vehicle use as income in the prescribed time;

2. the employee includes the value of the personal vehicle use as income in the prescribed time;

3. the employee is not a control employee of the employer as defined in §1.61-21(f)(5) and (f)(6); or

4. the employer demonstrates a good faith effort to treat the value of this noncash fringe benefit correctly for reporting purposes (e.g., includes the noncash fringe benefit in taxable income no later than December 31 of the tax year in which the benefit is received).

If none of these conditions is met, the employer or employee cannot use the special valuation rules.

Reporting Personal Use of Company Vehicles

The value of the personal use of a company-provided vehicle must be reported on the employee's W-2, in Boxes 1, 3 and 5. If the employer reports 100% of the vehicle's use in Box 1 of the W-2, this amount must be identified separately on the W-2 in Box 14, or in lieu of reporting in Box 14 the employee must be provided with a special statement to this effect at the end of the calendar year.

QUIZ 1   PERSONAL USE OF COMPANY-PROVIDED VEHICLES

Problem I.

Fill in the blanks. Answers may be more than one word.

1. Personal use of a company-provided vehicle is considered wages subject to _____, _____ and _____.

2. _____ is the only withholding tax that may be waived on the value of an employee's personal use of a company-provided vehicle.

3. Employers must use the _____ method for vehicles placed in service after January 1, 2021, with a value exceeding $51,100.

4. When prorating the employee's personal use of a company-provided vehicle under the annual lease value method, divide the annual lease value rate by _____, then multiply the result by the number of _____ the vehicle was in use.

5. The commuting valuation method may not be used for employees who are part of the _____.

Problem II.

Calculate the taxable income for the benefits provided in each problem.

1. Chen drives 3,000 business miles and 2,000 personal miles during February 2021 in a company-provided vehicle. The employer uses the vehicle cents-per-mile method and does not provide fuel. $_____

2. In April 2021, Ruth is allowed to commute in a free company van pool. She makes 90 round trips in the pool during the month. Her employer uses the commuting valuation method. $_____

3. During 2021, Hans drives 3,000 business miles and 500 personal miles in a company-provided car valued at $14,000, and his employer provides fuel. The company uses the annual lease value method and reports only his personal use of the car. $_____

4. During August 2021, Regina drives 300 personal miles in a company-provided car for which her employer provides fuel. The company uses the cents-per-mile method. $_____

5. In 2021, Greg uses a company-provided car valued at $13,000 for 90 days. He drives 2,500 miles that include 300 miles for personal use. His employer uses the annual lease value method and will report 100% of Greg's vehicle use as personal income. It does not provide fuel. $_____

Problem III.

Multiple choice. Circle the correct answer.

1. Under the annual lease value method, after how many years may a vehicle's annual lease value be reevaluated?

    a. 1   b. 3   c. 4   d. 7

2. The cents-per-mile method may not be used for vehicles placed in service in 2021 with a value exceeding . . .

    a. $50,400   b. $15,900   c. $16,000   d. $51,100

3. Which of the following methods would be used to determine the value of an employer-provided van pool?

    a. cents-per-mile method
    b. annual lease value method
    c. commuting valuation method
    d. general valuation standard method

4. The annual lease value of a vehicle valued at $18,000 is:

    a. $5,100   b. $4,850   c. $5,350   d. $4,600

5. What is the fair market value of each round-trip commute an employee makes under the commuting valuation method?

    a. $3.00   b. $3.50   c. $1.00   d. $1.50

QUIZ 1   *Solutions and Explanations*

Problem I.

1. FIT, FICA, FUTA
   (Federal income tax withholding may be waived at the employer's option.)

2. FITW

3. annual lease value

4. 365, days

5. control group

Problem II.

1. $1,010
   To calculate:

   $0.56 per mile − $0.055 value of fuel not provided = $0.505 adjusted per-mile rate

   2,000 miles personal use × $0.505 per mile = $1,010 taxable income.

2. $0
   To calculate:

   90 trips × $3 = $270 fair market value

   $270 − $270 (January 1, 2021 tax-free limit) = $0

3. $613.80
   To calculate:

   $14,000 car = $4,100 annual lease value

   500 miles for personal use ÷ 3,500 total miles = 14.3% personal use

   $4,100 annual lease value × 0.143 (14.3%) = $586.30 taxable annual lease value

   500 miles × $0.055 per gallon for employer-provided fuel = $27.50 taxable fuel

   $586.30 taxable income for personal use of car + $27.50 taxable income for employer-provided fuel = $613.80 total taxable income

4. $168.00
To calculate:

300 miles personal use × $0.56 = $168.00 taxable income

5. $949.50
To calculate:

$13,000 car = $3,850 annual lease value

$3,850 taxable use of car ÷ 365 days × 90 days = $949.50
  taxable income

Problem III.

1. c

2. d

3. c

4. a

5. a
($1.50 × 2)

QUIZ 2   PERSONAL USE OF COMPANY-PROVIDED VEHICLES

Problem I.

Fill in the blanks. Answers may be more than one word.

1. When an employer elects not to withhold federal income tax on the value of an employee's personal use of a company-owned vehicle, it must notify employees of its decision no later than _____ of the year in which the election is made.

2. If a vehicle is first made available to an employee in May and the employer has elected not to withhold federal income tax from the fair market value of his personal use, this employee must be notified of the employer's election within _____ days of when the vehicle was first made available to the employee.

3. If an employer elects to report _____% of the vehicle use under the annual lease value method, it eliminates the need for recordkeeping and lengthy calculations.

4. The employee's use of a company-provided vehicle is tax-free if the use is connected to the employer's _____ or _____.

5. The safe harbor options that the IRS allows for determining the value of an employee's personal use of a company-provided vehicle are the _____, _____ and _____ methods.

Problem II.

Compute taxable income for the benefits provided in each problem.

1. The value of an employee's company-provided car is $19,000. The employee drove a total of 4,500 miles in 2021 that included 900 miles for personal use. The employer provided fuel. The employer uses the annual lease value method and reports only personal use. $_____

2. An employee drives 5,500 business miles and 1,500 personal miles during March 2021. The employer does not provide fuel. The vehicle cents-per-mile method is used. $_____

3. An employee drives 500 personal miles in a company-provided car during August 2021. The employer provides fuel. The vehicle cents-per-mile method is used. $_____

4. During 2021, an employee drives a company-provided car valued at $15,500 for 120 days. The employee drives 2,400 business miles and 600 personal miles. The employer does not provide fuel. The annual lease value method is used, and the employer reports 100% of usage as wages. $_____

5. It is 2021 and an employee participating in a free company van pool takes 32 round trips during the month. The employer uses the commuting valuation method. $_____

Problem III.

Multiple choice. Circle the correct answer.

1. Which of the following IRS valuation methods is most appropriate for a company officer using a company-provided car that was placed in service in 2021 and valued at $60,000?

    a. annual lease value
    b. cents-per-mile
    c. commuting valuation
    d. general valuation standard

2. To prorate partial-year use of a vehicle under the annual lease value method, the annual lease value rate is divided by:

    a. 52 weeks
    b. 12 months
    c. 365 days
    d. 24 semimonthly periods

3. When withholding taxes on the value of an employee's personal use of a company car, which of the following taxes is withheld at the employer's option?

    a. FICA tax
    b. federal income tax
    c. FUTA tax
    d. FICA and FUTA

4. To determine the value of employer-provided fuel, the number of miles driven is multiplied by:

    a. $0.575   b. $0.055   c. $0.170   d. $0.56

5. The annual lease value of a car worth $23,000 is:

    a. $6,100   b. $6,350   c. $6,600   d. $5,850

QUIZ 2   *Solutions and Explanations*

Problem I.

1. January 31

2. 30

3. 100%

4. trade, business

5. annual lease value, vehicle cents-per-mile, commuting valuation

Problem II.

1. $1,119.50
To calculate:

$19,000 car = $5,350 annual lease value

900 miles for personal use ÷ 4,500 miles total use = 20% personal use

$5,350 annual lease value × 20% personal miles driven = $1,070 taxable income

900 personal miles × $0.055 per mile for fuel = $49.50 taxable income for fuel

$1,070 + $49.50 = $1,119.50 total taxable income

2. $757.50
To calculate:

$0.56 per mile – $0.055 employer-provided fuel = $0.505 adjusted per mile rate

1,500 personal miles × $0.505 per mile adjusted rate = $757.50 taxable income

3. $280.00
To calculate:

500 personal miles × $0.56 per mile = $280.00 taxable income

4. $1,430.40
To calculate:

$15,500 car = $4,350 annual lease value

$4,350 ÷ 365 days = $11.92 per day

$11.92 per day × 120 days = $1,430.40 taxable income

5. $0
To calculate:

32 round trips × $3 = $96 fair market value

$96 − $270 (January 1, 2021 tax-free limit) = $0 taxable income

Problem III.

1. a

2. c

3. b

4. b

5. b

SALARY REDUCTION AND FLEXIBLE BENEFIT PLANS

Introduction

Employees may defer or reduce taxable income by making contributions to their employer's deferred compensation plan or flexible benefit plan.

Salary Reduction Plans

The two most common deferred compensation plans (called "cash or deferred-salary arrangements") offered by employers are Section* 401(k) and simplified employee pension plans (SEP) under Section 408(k)(6). A salary reduction plan encourages employees to set aside income for retirement by permitting them to make *elective deferrals*—pretax contributions of a portion of their salary. Federal income tax is deferred from pretax contributions until the employee withdraws money from the fund, generally at retirement age. However, a pretax contribution is not exempt from FICA or FUTA.

> **EXAMPLE:** Susan makes a pretax contribution of 4% of her weekly salary of $500 to her employer's SEP. FIT is withheld on only $480. To calculate:
>
> $500 gross − $20 elective deferral [$500 × 4%] = $480 FIT taxable
> $500 gross less $0 = $500 FICA taxable

Other taxes: Although employees' pretax contributions to a Section 401(k) or 408(k)(6) plan are exempt from FIT, they are not exempt from FICA or FUTA.

PROBLEM 1: During 2021, Sam contributes 2% of his $400 weekly gross to his employer's SEP. Using a 2021 FICA rate of 7.65% and an FITW rate of 15%, what is Sam's weekly net pay?

---

* "Section" refers to the section of the tax code that covers the benefit. It is provided here for reference. Some benefits are nicknamed after their section in the tax code, such as a "401(k)."

SOLUTION 1: $302.60. To calculate:

Weekly gross		$400.00
Less: SEP contribution (400 × 2%)		− 8.00
Taxable portion of salary		392.00
FITW at 15% ($392 × 0.15)	−58.80	
FICA at 7.65% ($400 × 0.0765)*	−30.60	
Total taxes withheld		− 89.40
Net pay		$302.60

* Pretax contributions are not exempt from FICA. Therefore, Sam's FICA taxable wages aren't decreased by his contribution.

Limitations on salary reduction plans: For 2021, an employee's elective deferral may not exceed $19,500 [under 401(k) and SEP] and $13,500 under a SIMPLE plan. This limitation, which typically changes each year, is announced by the IRS in the months of October, November or December of the year preceding the year the limit applies.

Reporting for salary reduction plans: Total pretax contributions (elective deferrals) for the year are reported as FICA wages in Boxes 3 and 5 of the W-2 and Lines 5a and 5c (and 5d if applicable) of the 941, and as total payments on Line 3, Part 2 of the 940. They are also reported in Box 12 of the W-2, using Code F for SEP contributions, Code S for SIMPLE contributions, and Code D for 401(k) contributions. Box 13 ("Retirement Plan") must be checked. Elective deferrals are not reported in Box 1 of the W-2 or on Line 2 of the 941. For details on reporting requirements see the table "3.1: Fringe Benefits Reporting for Federal Forms for 2021" on page 55. Employers filing Form 944 should see the forms instructions for reporting FICA wages.

Flexible Benefit Plans

A flexible benefit or cafeteria plan (Section 125) is an employer-sponsored program that allows employees to elect benefits from a "menu" of options—thus, the term "cafeteria" plan. The cafeteria plan is attractive to a diverse workforce with varying benefits needs. Some benefits may be purchased with pretax dollars, an added financial bonus. This course covers only pretax contributions.

Under a qualified* flexible benefit plan, employees can pay for benefits such as medical and dental insurance with pretax dollars. (Normally, employees pay for medical or dental insurance and other benefits with after tax dollars.) In other words, payments for health insurance premiums can actually decrease the employee's taxable income. And most contributions are completely tax-free—rather than tax-deferred as with a SEP or a 401(k).

> **EXAMPLE:** Stephen's employer has a flexible benefit plan. From his $350 weekly gross, the employer deducts $50 for his medical insurance premium. Total taxes come to 30% of $300, or $90, giving him net pay of $210:
>
> $350 gross – $50 medical insurance premium – $90 for taxes = $210 net pay
>
> **EXAMPLE:** Stewart's employer has no flexible benefit plan. It deducts taxes of 30% from his $350 weekly gross, reducing it to $245, then deducts $50 for his medical insurance premium, giving him net pay of $195.
>
> $350 gross – $105 for taxes = $245 – $50 medical insurance premium = $195 net pay
>
> **Note that** he pays more tax than Stephen and therefore has a lower take-home pay amount.

Restrictions: Pretax contributions are permitted only when the benefit purchased is tax-free. For instance, employees can make pretax contributions for medical insurance, but not as reimbursement for the personal use of an employer-provided vehicle, which is a taxable benefit.

Effect on other taxes: Pretax contributions to a flexible benefit plan are exempt from FITW, FICA and FUTA (except with respect to adoption assistance which is only exempt from FIT) and generally from state income tax. State laws vary concerning the exclusion of pretax contributions to a flexible benefit plan for unemployment tax purposes. Employers are advised to check their state's laws.

> **PROBLEM 2:** In 2021, Darlene is paid $600 each weekly period and makes a pretax contribution of $100 for dependent-care assistance to her employer's flexible benefit plan. The FITW rate is 15%, FICA is 7.65%, and state income tax is 10%. (Dependent-care assistance is taxable under state law.) What is her net pay?

---

* For details on "qualified" plans, consult your tax advisor or benefits consultant.

SOLUTION 2. $326.75. To calculate:

Weekly gross		$600.00
Less: Dependent care/flex. benefit plan*		−100.00
Taxable portion of salary		500.00
FITW at 15% ($500 × 0.15)	−75.00	
FICA at 7.65% ($500 × 0.0765)	−38.25	
State inc. tax at 10% ($600 × 0.10)	−60.00	
Total taxes withheld		−173.25
Net pay		$326.75

Reporting for flexible benefit plans: Total employee pretax contributions are included in Line 3, Part 2 of the 940 and also in Line 4, Part 2 because they are exempt from FUTA. Note: Check 4a "Fringe Benefits." *They are not reported as FIT or FICA wages on the W-2 or 941 (or 944).* State reporting rules vary.

The election to pay for benefits such as health insurance with pretax contributions is not arbitrary. The employer must adopt a formal written plan and apply certain tests to the plan to ensure that it does not disproportionately favor highly paid employees. In addition, Form 5500, "Annual Return/Report of Employee Benefit Plan," must be electronically filed with the Department of Labor, Employee Benefits Security Administration by the last day of the seventh month following the end of the plan year.

Authorization for Employee Deductions

In general, there are no restrictions on the kinds of voluntary contributions or payments that an employee may make through payroll deduction (all the contributions mentioned in this section are voluntary). *However, it is important for an employer to be able to prove that a particular deduction was voluntary.* For this reason, employees should be asked to sign a payroll deduction authorization form for *each voluntary deduction that will be taken from their pay during the year.* See Section 10 for more on deductions from pay.

---

* Dependent care assistance benefits are reported only in Box 10 of Form W-2.

QUIZ 1   SALARY REDUCTION AND FLEXIBLE BENEFIT PLANS

Problem I.

Fill in the blanks. Answers may be more than one word.

1. The two most common qualified deferred compensation plans employers offer are _____ and _____.

2. A flexible benefit plan is also known as a _____ because it may give the employee a menu of benefits from which to choose.

3. Employee contributions to retirement or flexible benefit plans that reduce taxable income are _____ contributions.

4. Pretax contributions to a flexible benefit plan are _____, but pretax contributions to salary reduction plans are _____.

5. Total employee pretax contributions to a salary reduction plan are reported in Boxes _____, _____, _____, and _____ of the W-2 and on Lines _____ and _____ of the 941.

Problem II.

Calculate net pay for each problem. Assume that the FICA rate is 7.65%, FITW is 15% and no employee earned more than $50,000.

1. Keith is paid $700 per week and contributes 3% to his employer's SEP.
    $_____

2. Miguel is paid $850 each semimonthly period and makes a $75 pretax contribution for medical insurance to his employer's flexible benefit plan.
    $_____

3. Regina is paid $400 per week. She makes a 2% pretax contribution to her employer's SEP and a $50 pretax contribution for medical insurance to her employer's flexible benefit plan. $_____

Problem III.

Multiple choice. Circle the correct answer.

1. For 2021, an employee's annual pretax contribution to a Section 401(k) is limited to:

   a. $19,000   b. $13,500   c. $13,000   d. $19,500

2. A pretax contribution to a 401(k) is not reported on the . . .

   a. W-2, Box 3
   b. W-2, Box 5
   c. W-2, Box 1
   d. W-2, Box 12

3. Pretax contributions for benefits other than adoption assistance to a flexible benefit plan are exempt from:

   a. FICA
   b. FITW
   c. FUTA
   d. all of the above

QUIZ 1   Solutions and Explanations

Problem I.

1. Section 401(k) and SEP

2. cafeteria plan

3. pretax

4. tax-free, tax-deferred

5. (Boxes) 3, 5, 12, 13, (Lines) 5a and 5c (and possibly 5d)

Problem II.

1. $523.60
   To calculate:

Weekly gross	$700.00
Less: SEP contribution ($700 × 0.03 [3%] = $21)	– 21.00
Taxable portion of salary	679.00
FITW at 15% ($679 × 0.15) –101.85	
FICA at 7.65% ($700 × 0.0765) – 53.55*	
Total taxes	–155.40
Net pay	$523.60

* Pretax SEP contributions are not exempt from FICA. Therefore, FICA taxable wages are not decreased by this contribution.

2. $599.46
To calculate:

Semimonthly gross	$850.00
Less: Medical ins. contribution	− 75.00
Taxable portion of salary	775.00
FITW at 15% ($775 × 0.15) −116.25	
FICA at 7.65% ($775 × 0.0765) − 59.29	
Total taxes	−175.54
Net pay	$599.46

3. $263.92
To calculate:

Weekly gross	$400.00
Less: SEP contribution ($400 × 0.02 [2%] = $8) − 8.00	
Less: Medical ins. contribution −50.00	
Total contributions	− 58.00
Taxable portion of salary	342.00
FITW at 15% ($342 × 0.15) −51.30	
FICA at 7.65% ($350 × 0.0765) −26.78[*]	
Total taxes	− 78.08
Net pay	$263.92

[*] Pretax SEP contributions are not exempt from FICA. Therefore, FICA taxable wages are not decreased by this contribution; however, pretax contributions under a cafeteria plan are exempt from FICA.

Problem III.

1. d

2. c

3. d

QUIZ 2   SALARY REDUCTION AND FLEXIBLE BENEFIT PLANS

Problem I.

Fill in the blanks. Answers may be more than one word.

1. In general, a discriminatory plan is one that disproportionately favors _____ or key employees.

2. An employee's elective deferral to a 401(k) may not exceed $_____ for 2021.

3. When an employee makes a contribution that does not reduce taxable income, this is referred to as a (an) _____ deduction.

4. Pretax contributions to a SEP are _____, while pretax contributions to a cafeteria plan are _____.

5. An employee's pretax contributions to a 401(k) are exempt from _____ and _____.

Problem II.

Calculate net pay in the following examples. Assume that the FICA rate is 7.65%, FITW is 15% and no employee earned more than $50,000.

1. Robert is paid $475 per week and makes a pretax contribution of $75 for medical insurance to his employer's flexible benefit plan. $_____

2. Laura is paid $350 per week and makes a 4% pretax contribution to her employer's 401(k) plan. $_____

3. Gunther is paid $400 per week and makes a 3% pretax contribution to his employer's SEP and a pretax contribution of $70 for medical insurance through his employer's flexible benefit plan. $_____

Problem III.

Multiple choice. Circle the correct answer.

1. Pretax contributions made to a SEP or 401(k) are exempt from:

   a. FICA
   b. FUTA
   c. FITW
   d. all of the above

2. Total annual pretax contributions to a SEP are included on the W-2 in Boxes 3, 12, and . . .

   a. 1   b. 5   c. 11   d. 10

3. Pretax contributions to a flexible benefit plan are reported as income on the . . .

   a. W-2, Box 1
   b. 941, Line 2
   c. W-2, Box 12
   d. none of the above

QUIZ 2   *Solutions and Explanations*

Problem I.

   1. highly compensated employees

   2. $19,500

   3. after tax

   4. tax-deferred, tax-free

   5. FIT and FITW

Problem II.

   1. $309.40
   To calculate:

Weekly gross	$475.00
Less: Medical ins. contribution	– 75.00
Taxable portion of salary	400.00
FITW at 15% ($400 × 0.15)	60.00
FICA at 7.65% ($400 × 0.0765)	–30.60
Total taxes	– 90.60
Net pay	$309.40

2. $258.82

To calculate:

Weekly gross		$350.00
Less: 401(k) contribution ($350 × 0.04 [4%] = $14)		− 14.00
Taxable portion of salary		336.00
FITW at 15% ($336 × 0.15)	−50.40	
FICA at 7.65% ($350 × 0.0765)	−26.78*	
Total taxes		− 77.18
Net pay		$258.82

* Pretax Section 401(k) contributions are not exempt from FICA. Therefore, FICA taxable wages are not decreased by this contribution.

3. $245.05

To calculate:

Weekly gross		$400.00
Less: SEP contribution ($400 × 0.03 [3%] = $12)	−12.00	
Less: Medical ins. contribution	−70.00	
Total contributions		− 82.00
Taxable portion of salary		318.00
FITW at 15% ($318 × 0.15)	−47.70	
FICA at 7.65% ($330 × 0.0765)	−25.25*	
Total taxes		− 72.95
Net pay		$245.05

* Pretax SEP contributions are not exempt from FICA. Therefore, FICA taxable wages are not decreased by this contribution.

Problem III.

1. c

2. b

3. d

Section 7
DISABILITY AND THIRD-PARTY SICK PAY

Introduction

Understanding basic terminology is important.

Disability pay. General term that describes payment for an illness or accident that *may or may not be job-related.*

Sick pay. Employer-paid time off for illness or injury provided under a plan or system of the employer or a third party.

Third-party sick pay. Payment for a *nonjob-related* illness, accident or disability that is paid by an insurance company or state fund. Premiums may be paid by the employer, employee or both.

Workers' compensation. Payment for a *job-related* illness, accident or disability that is paid by an insurance company or state fund. (See Section 12 for more on workers' compensation insurance.)

It should be noted that these terms are often used interchangeably (and sometimes incorrectly).

State Disability Insurance

Some states require employees and/or employers to pay state disability insurance (SDI) tax to fund a state disability plan. If the employee qualifies, payments are made by the state to cover certain periods when the employee is disabled due to a nonjob-related accident or illness. States that have this kind of disability plan include California,* Hawaii, New Jersey, New York, Puerto Rico, and Rhode Island*.

Note also that some states also require that employees and/or employers pay contributions for state paid family and medical leave insurance.

---

* California and Rhode Island do not require that employers pay SDI. Therefore, disability pay provided under the state plans of California and Rhode Island is not taxable to the employee.

107

Taxable and Nontaxable
Third-Party Sick Pay

1. **Federal income taxable.** Although third-party sick pay is subject to federal income tax (FIT), it is *not* subject to federal income tax withholding (FITW). If the employee prefers that federal income tax be withheld, such a request is made on Form W-4S.

Exception: Federal income tax must be withheld from third-party sick payments that are paid to employees who are permanently disabled and separated from employment. Form W-4 is used to determine the amount to withhold at the employee's option.

The percentage of disability pay subject to FIT is based on the percentage of SDI tax or insurance premium that the employee pays. For instance, if the employee pays 100% of the SDI tax or insurance premium cost, then 100% of the payment to the employee is tax-free. If the employee pays only 25% of the SDI tax or premium, then 25% of the disability pay is tax-free. If the employee pays no part of the premium or tax (because the employer pays 100%), then 100% of disability pay is FIT taxable. (See number 2 below for FICA and FUTA tax treatment.)

Note that employee pretax contributions for third-party sick pay are treated as employer contributions.

EXAMPLE: George's employer pays 80% of his disability insurance premiums. Later, he receives $1,000 in third-party sick pay. Because his employer pays 80% of the insurance premium, $800 of the $1,000 payment is federal income taxable ($1,000 × 80% = $800).

PROBLEM 1: DelCo provides disability insurance to its employees and pays 35% of the premium. Becky is out sick and receives $1,800 in third-party sick pay. How much of the payment is FIT taxable?

SOLUTION 1: $630 of the third-party sick pay is FIT taxable. To calculate:

$1,800 third-party payment × 35% (the percentage of the premium paid by her employer) = $630

2. **FICA and FUTA taxable.** The percentage of disability pay subject to FICA and FUTA follows the rules for federal income tax, except that disability pay is taxable only in the first six months following the last day

of the month in which the employee last worked. Thus, if an employee does not receive disability pay until after the end of the six-month coverage period, the disability pay is not FICA or FUTA taxable.

Exception: Third-party sick payments that are paid to employees who are permanently disabled and, as a result, are separated from employment, are exempt from FICA and FUTA.

> **PROBLEM 2:** Tina is out on disability for 7 months. She receives $3,500 in disability pay from the insurance company in the 6-month coverage period and $650 during the 7th month. If her employer paid 35% of the premium, how much of the disability pay is subject to FIT and how much to FICA and FUTA?
>
> **SOLUTION 2:** $1,452.50 is FIT taxable and $1,225 is subject to FICA and FUTA. Because her employer pays 35% of the premium, 35% of her total disability pay is FIT taxable ($3,500 + $650 = $4,150 × 35% = $1,452.50); and 35% of payments made during the 6-month coverage period is subject to FICA and FUTA taxes ($3,500 × 35% = $1,225).
>
> **PROBLEM 3:** George became disabled on December 28, 2020. His disability payments begin on July 5, 2021, and he receives a total of $2,700 for the year. His employer has been paying 60% of the insurance premium. How much of the $2,700 is FIT taxable and subject to FICA and FUTA?
>
> **SOLUTION 3:** $1,620 is FIT taxable ($2,700 × 60% = $1,620). However, the $2,700 is not subject to FICA or FUTA because payments did not begin until after the first 6 months that George was disabled.

Withholding and Employment Taxes on Third-Party Sick Pay

1. **Sick pay provided by the employer.** Paid time off is subject to FITW, FICA and FUTA.

2. **Employer's self-insured plan.** Disability pay provided through an employer's self-insured plan is not subject to FICA or FUTA after the six-month coverage period. FITW applies for the entire period.

3. **Third-party sick payments.** The third-party payer, such as an insurance company or state fund, is required to withhold FICA on the taxable portion of disability pay during the six-month coverage period. FITW is withheld at the employee's option. An employee may request that federal income tax be withheld by completing Form W-4S and submitting it to the third-party payer. The employer is responsible for paying FUTA and for paying the employer's share of FICA on the taxable portion of third-party disability payments. The third-party payer must provide the employer with statements of disability payments made to employees so that the employer can make timely payments of its taxes. If these statements are not sent to the employer by January 15 following the year the disability is paid, the third-party payer becomes responsible for paying FICA and FUTA and for filing the necessary returns.

Exception: If an employee is permanently disabled and separated from employment, federal income tax withholding is mandatory and is based on Form W-4. However, the payments are exempt from FICA and FUTA for all months the payments are received. In this case, the third-party payer cannot transfer liability for reporting (Form 941 and Form W-2) to the employer. It is the third-party payer's responsibility to report all payments made to permanently disabled individuals who are separated from employment.

CAUTION: When employers fail to notify third-party payers of employee contributions to insurance premiums, the insurer is required to assume that 100% of the disability payments are taxable. This may result in tax over-payments by both employer and employee. To avoid this, employers must tell the insurance company what percentage of the premium is paid by the employee and the employer.

Reporting for Third-Party Sick Pay

Form W-2. Employers are responsible for reporting disability payments on the employee's W-2 (and the W-3), *even though the payments were made by a third party*. Federal income tax withheld by the third-party payer is reported in Box 14 of the W-3 by the employer.

Exception: If an employee is permanently disabled and separated from employment, the responsibility for reporting payments on Form 941 and Form W-2 (payments are exempt from FICA and FUTA) cannot be transferred to the employer. Reporting for these individuals is the sole responsibility of the third-party payer.

The taxable portion of disability pay is reported in Boxes 1, 3 and 5; the non-taxable portion in Box 12, using Code J. Third-party payers are required to furnish employers with an annual statement of disability payments no later than January 15 of the year following the year in which payments were made. If a third-party payer fails to provide this statement, it becomes the third-party payer's responsibility to prepare and file all required returns.

Form 941 (and 944). Employers report taxable third-party sick pay on Line 2 and the amount subject to FICA tax on Lines 5a and 5c (and 5d if applicable) of the 941. An adjustment is made for the amount of FICA withheld by the third-party payer by deducting it on Line 8. When Line 8 is completed in this way, the 941 agrees with taxes actually deposited by the employer.

Form 940. Third-party payments for sick pay are reported on Line 3, Part 2. Nontaxable payments are reported in Line 4, Part 2 as "exempt." Check 4a "Fringe Benefits" on Line 4.

Avoiding Employer Tax Overpayments

Because third parties make taxable disability payments to employees, employers should keep payroll records fully up to date. FICA and FUTA taxes both have wage ceilings. Failure to record sick payments by third-party payers may result in an overpayment of these taxes.

> **EXAMPLE:** Margaret received $5,000 in third-party payments from January to June 2021. Her employer paid FUTA on the payments. After returning to work in July, she received another $5,000 in wages through the end of the year. Her employer is required to pay FUTA tax on the first $2,000 of these wages ($7,000 FUTA ceiling − $5,000 in third-party payments = $2,000 FUTA taxable wages). If Margaret's employer had failed to consider the $5,000 in third-party sick payments, it would have overpaid its FUTA tax.

QUIZ 1   DISABILITY AND THIRD-PARTY SICK PAY

Problem I.

Fill in the blanks. Answers may be more than one word.

1. Sick pay from a party other than the employer is called _____.

2. Six states have their own disability insurance plans. Name two:
_____ and _____.

3. Third-party sick pay refers to payments that are made for illness or injury that (is/is not) _____ related to the employee's job.

4. For FICA and FUTA purposes, taxable third-party sick pay is generally subject to FICA and FUTA taxes during the first _____ months of disability.

5. If an employer pays 75% of the cost of the disability insurance, then _____ of the employee's disability pay is federal taxable.

Problem II.

For each problem, determine the amount of third-party sick pay that is FIT, FICA and FUTA taxable. Assume that the employee has received no wages prior to disability.

1. Louis becomes disabled on May 29 and returns to work on November 15. He received $4,500 in disability pay. His employer pays 100% of the premium.
FIT taxable $_____
FICA taxable $_____
FUTA taxable $_____

2. Maria is disabled on December 31 and returns to work on July 31. She receives $750 in disability for each month she is out. Her employer pays 45% of the premium.
FIT taxable $_____
FICA taxable $_____
FUTA taxable $_____

3. Matthew is disabled on January 20 and returns to work on July 10. He receives $5,500 in disability pay. His employer pays 70% of the premium.
   FIT taxable $_____
   FICA taxable $_____
   FUTA taxable $_____

4. Berta is disabled on February 28 but does not receive disability pay until September 1. She then receives $550 for each month she was off from work. She returns to work on September 1. Her employer pays 100% of the premium.
   FIT taxable $_____
   FICA taxable $_____
   FUTA taxable $_____

5. Steven becomes disabled on April 30. He receives $700 for each month that he is off work. He returns to work on October 31. The employer pays 60% of the insurance premium.
   FIT taxable $_____
   FICA taxable $_____
   FUTA taxable $_____

Problem III.

Multiple choice. Circle the correct answer.

1. Third-party payers are required to furnish an employer with an annual statement of disability payments made to its employees no later than _____ of the year following the year in which the payments were made.

   a. January 31
   b. February 28
   c. January 15
   d. January 1

2. Taxable third-party sick payments made during the first 6 months of disability are _____ taxable.

   a. FIT
   b. FICA
   c. FUTA
   d. all of the above

3. An employee may request that federal income tax be withheld from third-party sick pay by completing Form . . .

a. W-4S   b. W-2P   c. W-4   d. W-2

QUIZ 1 *Solutions and Explanations*

Problem I.

1. third-party sick pay

2. Any two of the following: California, Hawaii, New Jersey, New York, Rhode Island, Puerto Rico

3. is not

4. 6

5. 75%

Problem II.

1. FIT taxable, $4,500; FICA taxable, $4,500; FUTA taxable, $4,500. Because the employee was disabled for less than 6 months, all payments for the period are FIT, FICA and FUTA taxable. The employer pays 100% of insurance premiums, making 100% of payments taxable.

2. FIT taxable, $2,362.50; FICA taxable, $2,025; FUTA taxable, $2,025. Only the first 6 months are taxable for FICA and FUTA (not the 7th month). The employer pays 45% of the insurance premium, making 45% of disability pay taxable. To calculate:

   $750 × 7 months = $5,250 × 45% = $2,362.50 FIT taxable

   $750 × 6 months = $4,500 × 45% = $2,025 FICA/FUTA taxable

3. FIT taxable, $3,850; FICA taxable, $3,850; FUTA taxable, $3,850. The employee was disabled for less than 6 months, making the entire period of disability subject to FICA and FUTA. Because the employer pays 70% of the insurance premium, 70% of disability pay is taxable. To calculate:

   $5,500 × 70% = $3,850 FIT, FICA and FUTA taxable

4. FIT taxable, $3,300; FICA taxable, $0; FUTA taxable, $0. Although the employee was disabled for 6 months, payments were not made until the 7th month. Thus, none of the disability pay is subject to FICA or FUTA. Because the employer pays 100% of the insurance premium, 100% of the disability pay is FIT taxable. To calculate:

$550 × 6 months = $3,300 FIT taxable

5. FIT taxable, $2,520; FICA taxable, $2,520; FUTA taxable, $2,520. Because the employee was disabled for 6 months, the entire period of disability is potentially subject to FICA and FUTA tax. The employer pays 60% of the insurance premium, making 60% of disability payments taxable. To calculate:

$700 × 6 months = $4,200 × 60% = $2,520 FICA, FUTA
   and FIT taxable

Problem III.

1. c

2. d

3. a

QUIZ 2   DISABILITY AND THIRD-PARTY SICK PAY

Problem I.

Fill in the blanks. Answers may be more than one word.

1. FITW is mandatory under a (an) _____ self-insured plan, but optional for disability payments made by a (an) _____ .

2. In states that operate a disability plan, employers and/or employees may be required to pay _____ .

3. When an employer makes an entry on a 941 for FICA tax withheld by a third-party payer, the amount of FICA withheld by the third-party payer is reported on Line _____ .

4. Pay for work-related disability is covered by _____ .

5. Employers report third-party sick pay on Lines _____ , _____ and _____ of the 941.

Problem II.

For each problem, determine the amount of disability pay that is FIT, FICA and FUTA taxable. Assume that the employee has received no wages prior to disability.

1. Marcy is disabled on October 15 and does not return to work until Dec. 15. She receives total disability pay of $850. Her employer pays 80% of the insurance premium.
   FIT taxable $_____
   FICA taxable $_____
   FUTA taxable $_____

2. Robert is disabled on December 31 and does not return to work until October 1 of the following year. He receives $450 for each month that he is out. His employer pays 65% of the insurance premium.
   FIT taxable $_____
   FICA taxable $_____
   FUTA taxable $_____

3. Nancy is disabled on July 31 and does not return to work until December 15. She receives a total of $1,500 in disability pay. Her employer pays 100% of the insurance premium.
   FIT taxable $_____
   FICA taxable $_____
   FUTA taxable $_____

4. Juan is disabled on May 30. He returns to work on December 1. He then receives $350 for each month that he was out. His employer pays 100% of the insurance premium.
   FIT taxable $_____
   FICA taxable $_____
   FUTA taxable $_____

5. Andrea is disabled on February 25 and does not return to work until July 1. She receives $4,300 in disability pay. Her employer pays 35% of the insurance premium.
   FIT taxable $_____
   FICA taxable $_____
   FUTA taxable $_____

Problem III.

Multiple choice. Circle the correct answer.

1. Employers show an adjustment for FICA tax withheld by third-party payers on the 941, Line . . .

   a. 3   b. 8   c. 5a   d. 7

2. Third-party sick pay received after the first 6 months of disability is subject to . . .

   a. FUTA
   b. FICA
   c. FICA and FUTA
   d. none of the above

3. Employers report taxable disability payments made by third-party payers on Form:

   a. 940
   b. 941
   c. W-2
   d. all of the above

QUIZ 2   *Solutions and Explanations*

Problem I.

1. employer-funded, third-party payer

2. SDI tax

3. 8

4. workers' compensation insurance

5. 2, 5a and 5c (and possibly 5d)

Problem II.

1. FIT taxable, $680; FICA taxable, $680; FUTA taxable, $680. Because the employee was disabled for 2 months, payments for the entire period are subject to FICA and FUTA. The employer pays 80% of the insurance premium, making 80% of the employee's disability pay taxable. To calculate:

$850 × 80% = $680 FIT, FICA and FUTA taxable

2. FIT taxable, $2,632.50; FICA taxable, $1,755; FUTA taxable, $1,755. Although the employee was disabled for 9 months, only the first 6 months are FICA and FUTA taxable. Because the employer pays 65% of the insurance premium, 65% of the disability pay is taxable.

$450 × 9 months = $4,050 × 65% = $2,632.50 FIT taxable

$450 × 6 months = $2,700 × 65% = $1,755 FICA
    and FUTA taxable

3. FIT taxable, $1,500; FICA taxable, $1,500; FUTA taxable, $1,500. The employee was disabled for 4 months, making the entire period of disability FIT taxable and subject to FICA and FUTA. Because the employer pays 100% of the insurance premium, 100% of disability pay is taxable.

4. FIT taxable, $2,100; FICA taxable, $0; FUTA taxable, $0. Although the employee was disabled for 6 months, he did not receive any disability pay until the 7th month. As a result, his disability pay is not subject to FICA or FUTA. However, because the employer pays 100% of the insurance, 100% of the disability payments are FIT taxable. To calculate:

$350 × 6 months = $2,100 FIT taxable

5. FIT taxable, $1,505; FICA taxable, $1,505; FUTA taxable, $1,505. Because the employee was disabled for 4 months, disability pay for the entire period is subject to FICA and FUTA. The employer pays 35% of the insurance premium, making 35% of the disability payments FIT taxable. To calculate:

$4,300 × 35% = $1,505 FIT, FICA and FUTA taxable

Problem III.

1. b

2. d

3. d

GROUP-TERM LIFE INSURANCE

Introduction

Life insurance is a popular employee benefit offered in a variety of types. However, only one type—group-term life insurance—qualifies for tax-favored treatment. Among the plans that employers may provide are:

Employer-sponsored group-term life insurance. The death benefit or "insurance coverage" is paid to the beneficiaries named by the employee. The value of coverage is tax-free under federal and most state laws up to $50,000.

The premium cost paid by the employer on the first $50,000 of coverage is tax-free to the employee provided the plan does not disproportionately favor highly compensated employees.

Employer-sponsored dependent-term life insurance. This insurance is like group-term life insurance except that it covers an employee's dependent (rather than the employee), and the death benefit is paid to the employee or designated beneficiary. If the coverage amount is $2,000 or less, it is tax-free as a de minimis fringe benefit under federal and most state laws.

Individual life insurance. This insurance may be purchased by the employer or employee individually or for classes of employees—(e.g., officers, managers and clerical staff). Employer-paid premiums are considered wages subject to FIT, FITW, FICA, and FUTA. However, if the employer is the designated beneficiary, the insurance is tax-free to the employee (but is not a deductible business expense to the company).

Taxable Income on Group-Term
Life Insurance

Taxable income is based on coverage rather than premium cost, and the first $50,000 per month of coverage generally is tax-free. Typically, coverage is equal to a multiple of an employee's salary, such as three times annual salary. It also may be determined by job category—such as $10,000 coverage for clerical employees and $30,000 coverage for sales personnel. Many policies place a cap on the death benefit, such as twice an employee's annual salary up to a limit of $100,000.

PROBLEM 1: Raul's employer provides life insurance coverage equal to twice his annual salary of $35,000. What portion of his coverage, if any, is taxable?

SOLUTION 1: $20,000 of his coverage is taxable. To calculate:

$35,000 annual salary $\times$ 2 = $70,000 coverage

$70,000 coverage $-$ $50,000 tax-free maximum = $20,000 taxable

Calculating the Taxable Value

To determine the taxable value of an employee's coverage, employers use the IRS Uniform Premium Table I (Figure 8-1), which lists a dollar value for each $1,000 of group-term life insurance coverage over $50,000 per month. The value must be determined on a monthly basis. Therefore, a policy that provides $80,000 of coverage provides $80,000 per month.

Figure 8-1
IRS Uniform Premium Table I
Effective July 1, 1999

Cost per $1,000 5-year age bracket	protection for one month
Under age 25	$ .05
Age 25–29	$ .06
Age 30–34	$ .08
Age 35–39	$ .09
Age 40–44	$ .10
Age 45–49	$ .15
Age 50–54	$ .23
Age 55–59	$ .43
Age 60–64	$ .66
Age 65–69	$1.27
Age 70 and over	$2.06

EXAMPLE: Thomas's coverage under his employer's group-term life insurance plan is $60,000. Thomas will be 30 years old on November 15, 2021. To calculate the taxable income on this coverage:

A. $60,000 total coverage − $50,000 tax-free limit = $10,000 taxable coverage

B. $10,000 taxable coverage ÷ $1,000 (from IRS table, Figure 8-2) = 10

C. 10 × $0.08 (rate for age 30) = $.80 *monthly* IRS value

D. $.80 × 12 months = $9.60 taxable income for the year

Under IRS rules, employers must use the employee's age as of December 31 for the entire year. Thus, in the example above, although Thomas is 29 years old for most of the year (January through October), his employer must use the rate for a 30-year-old employee.

PROBLEM 2: Karen's coverage under her employer's group-term life insurance plan is $85,000. She will be 50 years old on April 3, 2021. What is her taxable income on this coverage for the year?

SOLUTION 2: $96.60 taxable income for the year. To calculate:

A. $85,000 total coverage − $50,000 tax-free limit = $35,000 taxable coverage

B. $35,000 taxable coverage ÷ $1,000 (from IRS table, Figure 8-2) = 35

C. 35 × $0.23 (rate for age 50) = $8.05 monthly IRS value

D. $8.05 × 12 months = $96.60 taxable income for the year

Adjustments for Employee Contributions

If an employee pays the premium cost, or a portion of it with after-tax dollars, the contribution is subtracted from the value of the insurance (per IRS Table I) to determine the net taxable amount. *Pretax contributions to the premium cost do not reduce the taxable amount.*

PROBLEM 3: Mike's coverage under his employer's group-term life plan is $87,000. Mike will be 27 years old on March 21. For the year, he contributes $20 on an after-tax basis toward the insurance premium. What is the taxable income on his coverage for the year?

SOLUTION 3: $6.64 taxable income per year. To calculate:

A. $87,000 total coverage − $50,000 tax-free limit = $37,000 taxable coverage

B. $37,000 taxable coverage ÷ $1,000 (from IRS table) = 37

C. 37 × $0.06 (rate for age 27) = $2.22 monthly IRS value

D. $2.22 × 12 months = $26.64 taxable income for the year

E. $26.64 − $20.00 (Mike's annual contribution) = $6.64 net taxable income for the year

PROBLEM 4: Suppose that in problem 3, Mike's $20 contribution toward the insurance premium was paid with pretax dollars. What would his taxable income be for the year?

SOLUTION 4: $26.64 taxable income for the year. The annual contribution of $20 toward the premium cost would not be deducted from taxable income because it was a pretax contribution.

Discriminatory Group-Term Life Plans

A group-term life insurance plan is considered discriminatory unless it passes an eligibility test showing that at least 70% of all employees are eligible to participate in the plan and at least 85% of eligible employees who participate are not key employees.

For the eligibility test, employers may exclude:

1. Employees who have not completed three years of service, or are part-time or seasonal.

2. Employees who are nonresident aliens and have not earned U.S.-source income.

3. Employees covered by a collective bargaining agreement in which the benefit is provided.

If an employer's group-term life plan is discriminatory (disproportionately favors key employees and/or shareholders), these individuals are not entitled to tax-favored treatment on the first $50,000 of coverage. Taxable income is based on the actual cost of the insurance or value of the coverage using IRS Uniform Premium Table I, *whichever is greater.*

For details on discriminatory group-term life insurance plans, employers are advised to consult a benefits consultant, tax advisor or legal counsel.

Former Employees

Employers need not withhold FICA on the value of group-term life insurance given to *former* employees (unlike group-term life provided to *current* employees, on which employers must withhold FICA). But even the FICA not withheld is reported on the W-2. The uncollected Social Security tax is reported on the W-2 in Box 12 preceded by Code M; the uncollected Medicare tax is reported in Box 12 preceded by Code N.

CAUTION: Be sure to also report the value of the taxable group-term life insurance in Form W-2, Box 12, Code C, otherwise the IRS may try to collect the tax reported in Box 12, Codes M and N.

Note: Codes M and N are not used to reflect the Additional Medicare Tax of 0.9% (on wages over $200,000) that is not withheld on former employees' group-term life insurance.

Taxation and Reporting

FITW. Not mandatory, even though this benefit is reported as federal taxable wages subject to FIT.

FICA and FUTA. Subject to FICA, but exempt from FUTA.

Required reporting includes:

Form W-2. Taxable portion is reported in Boxes 1, 3, 5, and 12 (Code C).

Form 941 (and 944). Taxable portion is reported on Lines 2, 5a and 5c (and 5d if applicable).

Form 940. Taxable portion is included in Part 2, Line 3 as total payments and in Part 2, Line 4 as an exempt payment. Check 4b, "Group term life insurance" on Line 4.

As long as an employer withholds FICA tax from taxable group-term life and reports the payments and taxes by the end of the year, it may collect taxes and report them at whatever frequency it chooses. However, frequent collection and reporting of taxes can prevent tax underpayments, because any FICA not paid by an employee prior to termination becomes the employer's obligation.

Note: The IRS has clarified that the special accounting rule may not be used for taxable group-term life insurance.

QUIZ 1 GROUP-TERM LIFE INSURANCE

Problem I.

Fill in the blanks. Answers may be more than one word.

1. The value of the first $_____ of group-term life insurance is tax-free.

2. To determine the value of group-term life insurance over $50,000, employers use the IRS _____.

3. A group-term life plan passes the eligibility test when at least _____% of the employees are eligible to participate in the plan and at least _____% of all employees who participate are not key employees.

4. For taxation of group-term life insurance coverage over $50,000, FITW is (mandatory/optional) _____ and FICA withholding is (mandatory/optional) _____.

5. If a group-term life insurance plan is discriminatory, taxable income is equal to the value of the insurance as determined under IRS Table I, or the insurance _____, whichever is _____.

Problem II.

Compute the annual taxable income under the employer's group-term life insurance plan for each of the following:

1. Marsha's group-term life insurance coverage is $110,000. She will be 48 years old on February 10, 2021. $_____

2. Mark's group-term life insurance coverage is $45,000. He will be 45 years old on December 10, 2021. $_____

3. Ann's group-term life insurance coverage is $89,000. She will be 45 years old on September 30, 2021. She contributes $40 on an after-tax basis toward the premium for the year. $_____

4. Todd's group-term life insurance coverage is $75,000. He will be 36 years old on April 1, 2021. He contributes $35 in pretax contributions toward the premium for the year. $_____

5. Ed's group-term life insurance coverage is $85,000. He will be 64 years old on August 10, 2021. $_____

Problem III.

Multiple choice. Circle the correct answer.

1. Which of the following group-term life plans would be considered discriminatory?

   a. 65% of employees are eligible to participate
   b. at least 85% of those participating are not key employees
   c. 75% of employees are eligible to participate
   d. at least 90% of those participating are not key employees

2. If an employer pays the premium for employees' group-term life insurance, the benefit is subject to:

   a. FICA and FIT
   b. FICA and FUTA
   c. FITW
   d. FICA, FIT and FUTA

3. Dependent group-term life insurance is tax-free when coverage is equal to or less than . . .

   a. $5,000   b. $10,500   c. $50,000   d. $2,000

4. Uncollected Social Security tax from former employees' wages is reported on the W-2 in Box 12 preceded by what Code?

   a. G   b. F   c. M   d. N

QUIZ 1   *Solutions and Explanations*

Problem I.

1. $50,000

2. Uniform Premium Table I

3. 70, 85

4. optional, mandatory

5. premium cost, greater

Problem II.

1. $108.00
   To calculate:

   A. $110,000 total coverage − $50,000 tax-free limit = $60,000 taxable coverage

   B. $60,000 taxable coverage ÷ $1,000 (from IRS table, Figure 8-2) = 60

   C. 60 × $0.15 (rate for age 48) = $9.00 monthly IRS value

   D. $9.00 × 12 months = $108.00 taxable income

2. $0
   To calculate:
   A. $45,000 − $50,000 = $0 taxable

3. $30.20
   To calculate:

   A. $89,000 total coverage − $50,000 tax-free limit = $39,000 taxable coverage

   B. $39,000 taxable coverage ÷ $1,000 (from IRS table, Figure 8-2) = 39

   C. 39 × $0.15 (rate for age 45) = $5.85 monthly IRS value

   D. $5.85 × 12 months = $70.20 taxable

   E. $70.20 taxable income − $40 contribution = $30.20 net taxable income

4. $27
To calculate:

A. $75,000 total coverage − $50,000 tax-free limit = $25,000 taxable coverage

B. $25,000 taxable coverage ÷ $1,000 (from IRS table, Figure 8-2) = 25

C. 25 × $0.09 (rate for age 36) = $2.25 monthly IRS value

D. $2.25 × 12 months = $27 taxable income

E. Tod's contributions are not used to reduce taxable income because they were pretax contributions.

5. $277.20
To calculate:

A. $85,000 total coverage − $50,000 tax-free limit = $35,000 taxable coverage

B. $35,000 taxable coverage ÷ $1,000 (from IRS table, Figure 8-2) = 35

C. 35 × $0.66 (rate for age 64) = $23.10 monthly IRS value

D. $23.10 × 12 months = $277.20 taxable

Problem III.

1. a

2. a

3. d

4. c

QUIZ 2   GROUP-TERM LIFE INSURANCE

Problem I.

Fill in the blanks.

1. Under the eligibility test, employees with less than _____ years of service may be excluded.

2. Taxable group-term life insurance is not subject to _____ or _____ but is subject to _____.

3. A group-term life insurance plan is discriminatory if it disproportionately favors _____ employees.

4. Dependent group-term life is tax-free if coverage is equal to or less than $_____.

5. If an employee designates his or her spouse as the beneficiary under an individual life insurance policy, the insurance is _____ to the employee.

Problem II.

Compute the annual taxable income under the employer's group-term life plan for the following:

1. Margaret's group-term life insurance coverage is $91,000. She will be 38 years old on August 12, 2021. She contributes $32 on an after-tax basis toward the annual premium. $_____

2. Randy's group-term life insurance coverage is $65,000. He will be 43 years old on December 3, 2021. His pretax contribution to the premium is $10. $_____

3. Ralph's group-term life insurance coverage is $35,000. He will be 38 years old on July 15, 2021. $_____

4. Albert's group-term life insurance coverage is $150,000. He will be 42 years old on September 3, 2021. $_____

5. Donna's group-term life insurance coverage is $73,000. She will be 54 years old on August 28, 2021. She contributes $50 on an after-tax basis toward the annual premium. $_____

Problem III.

Multiple choice. Circle the correct answer.

1. Group-term life insurance over $50,000 is exempt from . . .

    a. FICA only
    b. FICA and FITW
    c. FUTA and FITW
    d. FUTA, FICA and FITW

2. Group-term life insurance over $50,000 must be taxed and reported at least . . .

    a. quarterly
    b. biweekly
    c. monthly
    d. annually

3. Taxable group-term life insurance is reported on the W-2, Box 12 using Code _____.

    a. B   b. C   c. L   d. D

4. Uncollected Medicare tax from former employees' group-term life is reported on the W-2 in Box 12 preceded by what Code?

    a. G   b. F   c. M   d. N

QUIZ 2   *Solutions and Explanations*

Problem I.

1. three

2. FUTA, FITW, FICA

3. key

4. $2,000

5. taxable

Problem II.

1. $12.28
   To calculate:

   A. $91,000 total coverage − $50,000 tax-free limit = $41,000 taxable coverage

   B. $41,000 taxable coverage ÷ $1,000 (from IRS table, Figure 8-2) = 41

   C. 41 × $0.09 (rate for age 38) = $3.69 monthly IRS value

   D. $3.69 × 12 months = $44.28 taxable income

   E. $44.28 − $32.00 contribution = $12.28 net taxable income

2. $18.00
   To calculate:

   A. $65,000 total coverage − $50,000 tax-free = $15,000 taxable coverage

   B. $15,000 taxable coverage ÷ $1,000 (from IRS table, Figure 8-2) = 15

   C. 15 × $0.10 (rate for age 43) = $1.50 monthly IRS value

   D. $1.50 × 12 months = $18.00 taxable income

   Pretax contributions may not be used to reduce taxable income.

3. $0

To calculate:

A. $35,000 total coverage − $50,000 tax-free limit = $0 taxable

4. $120

To calculate:

A. $150,000 total coverage − $50,000 tax-free limit = $100,000 taxable coverage

B. $100,000 taxable coverage ÷ $1,000 (from IRS table, Figure 8-2) = 100

C. 100 × $0.10 (rate for age 42) = $10 monthly IRS value

D. $10 × 12 months = $120 taxable income

5. $13.48

To calculate:

A. $73,000 total coverage − $50,000 tax-free limit = $23,000 taxable coverage

B. $23,000 taxable coverage ÷ $1,000 (from IRS table, Figure 8-2) = 23

C. 23 × $0.23 (rate for age 54) = $5.29 monthly IRS value

D. $5.29 × 12 months = $63.48 taxable

E. $63.48 − $50 (Donna's contributions) = $13.48 net taxable income.

Problem III.

1. c

2. d

3. b

4. d

Section 9
IMPUTED INCOME AND GROSS-UP

Introduction

Normally, taxes are withheld from wages before employees are paid. But sometimes employees are given bonuses or other cash payments from which no taxes have been withheld. When this occurs, taxes must be withheld after the compensation is received by the employee. The employer must *impute income* to the employee's next paycheck. In other instances, an employer may decide to pay the employee's share of taxes as part of the bonus. But by paying the employee's taxes, the employer increases the employee's taxable earnings and taxes. To account for these added taxes, the employer generally must *gross up* the bonus.

Imputed Income

An employee is given a cash bonus from which no tax is withheld. Assuming that this bonus is subject to FITW and FICA, how can taxes be withheld from the employee after the fact?

One correct method is to impute (add) the bonus to a future paycheck and withhold tax on the total.

EXAMPLE: AlCorp discovers that Gerhardt's supervisor gave him a cash bonus of $50 from the petty cash fund and withheld no taxes. AlCorp must collect the taxes from Gerhardt's next paycheck by imputing the $50 in income to it. Gerhardt's next payroll check would normally be $425 gross. Assuming it is 2021 and for hypothetical purposes only, Gerhardt is in the 15% tax bracket, here is the calculation:

Worksheet for Imputed Income			
1. Regular wages (Salary Expense)			$425.00
2. Federal income taxable (Form W-2, Box 1)			
a. regular wages	$425.00		
b. imputed income	50.00		
c. tax on $475 × 15%		−71.25	
3. FICA taxable (Form W-2, Boxes 3 and 5)			
a. regular wages	$425.00		
b. imputed income	50.00		
c. tax on $475 × 7.65%		−36.34	
4. Total taxes (Line 2 + Line 3)			−107.59
5. Net pay (Line 1 − Line 4)			$317.41

As this example illustrates, Gerhardt paid taxes on the $50 cash bonus from his next paycheck, reducing his net pay for the period by the taxes owed on the bonus.

> **PROBLEM 1:** Francesca receives a cash bonus of $75. No taxes were withheld. She is scheduled to receive her next regular paycheck of $500 on September 23, 2021. Assuming a federal income tax withholding rate of 15%, what should her employer do?
>
> **SOLUTION 1:** On the September 23, 2021 paycheck, the employer should impute (add) the $75 bonus to her paycheck as follows:

Worksheet for Francesca

---

1. Regular wages (Salary Expense)			$500.00
2. Federal income taxable (Form W-2, Box 1)			
a. regular wages	$500.00		
b. imputed income	75.00		
c. tax on $575 × 15%		−86.25	
3. FICA taxable (Form W-2, Boxes 3 and 5)			
a. regular wages	$500.00		
b. imputed income	75.00		
c. tax on $575 at 7.65%		−43.99	
4. Total taxes (Line 2 + Line 3)			−130.24
5. Net pay (Line 1 − Line 4)			$369.76

Gross-up

In some instances, an employer may decide to pay the employee's share of taxes. This payment of taxes is additional taxable income to the employee, so the employer will pay taxes on the tax payment—adding still more taxable income, and so on. This is known as the *pyramiding effect*.

> **EXAMPLE:** Andrea's FICA and FITW tax obligation on a $600 bonus is $160. As part of her bonus, Andrea's employer decides to pay these taxes for her. But when her employer does this, the $160 becomes income on which she owes $43 in taxes. When her employer pays the $43, it becomes taxable income to her on which she owes $12 in taxes and so on, *pyramiding* upward. To simplify this endless chain of calculations, an algebraic formula known as "gross-up" is used. Here is how it works:

Gross-up Worksheet

A. Wage payment before tax.

    1. Determine the percentage of federal income tax to withhold.

    2. Determine the percentage of FICA tax to withhold (for 2021, this is 6.2% of the first $142,800 in covered wages for Social Security and 1.45% of all covered wages for Medicare).

    3. Determine the percentage of state income tax to withhold (this can be done by finding the tax percentage that would apply to the employee's estimated annual earnings).

    4. Add the percentages from Lines 1, 2 and 3 to get the total tax percentage.

    5. Subtract the total in Line 4 from 100%.

    6. Divide the wage payment by the result in Line 5. This is the new gross wage amount.

B. Check the result in Line 6 by subtracting the taxes to be withheld. The result should agree with A.

> **EXAMPLE:** Rosie's employer has decided to pay the employees' taxes on their annual bonus checks. Rosie is due a bonus of $1,000, which is subject to FITW (27%), FICA (7.65%) and state income tax (13%).

Gross-up Worksheet for Rosie

A.		$1,000.00
1. Federal tax percentage	27.00%	
2. FICA percentage	7.65%	
3. State tax percentage	13.00%	
4. Total tax percentage =	47.65%	
5. 100% – Line 4 =		52.35%
6. Line A divided by Line 5		1,910.22
($1,000 ÷ 0.5235)		

B. To verify:
$1,910.22 gross – $910.22 in taxes [$1,910.22 × 47.65%] = $1,000.00, the amount in Line A. The calculation is verified because the result is equal to the amount in A.

Other Uses for the Gross-up Formula

The gross-up formula also can be used when you know what net pay is and want to determine gross.

PROBLEM 3: ACME wants to give each employee a net (after-tax) bonus check of $500. What is gross pay, assuming a net of $500 and that FITW is 27%, FICA is 7.65% and state tax is 13%?

SOLUTION 3:

Gross-up Worksheet for ACME

A.		$500.00
1. Federal tax percentage	27.00%	
2. FICA percentage	7.65%	
3. State tax percentage	13.00%	
4. Total tax percentage	47.65%	
5. 100% − Line 4 =		52.35%
6. Line A divided by Line 5		955.11

($500 ÷ 0.5235) in gross wages will be required to yield a net of $500

B. To verify:

$955.11 gross − $455.11 in taxes [$955.11 × 47.65%] = $500.00, the amount in Line A. The calculation is verified.

Domestic and Agricultural Employees

The IRS does not require that the gross-up computation be used when FICA tax is paid on behalf of domestic or agricultural employees [IRC §3121(a)(6)]. Instead, employers are instructed to report only the amount of FICA paid on behalf of an employee in Form W-2, Box 1 (wages, tips and other compensation).

EXAMPLE: Assume the same facts as in Problem 3 except that the employee is a domestic worker. FICA and FIT taxable wages are computed as follows:

1. $500.00 × 7.65% = $38.25

2. $500.00 + $38.25 = $538.25 (FIT taxable wages, report in Box 1 of Form W-2)

3. Report only $500.00 as FICA wages (report in Boxes 3 and 5 of Form W-2)

For more information, refer to IRS Publication 926, "Household Employer's Tax Guide" on the IRS Website at *www.irs.gov*.

QUIZ 1   IMPUTED INCOME AND GROSS-UP

Problem I.

Compute gross or net pay for each question. Assume that FITW is 15%, FICA is 7.65%, but that there is no state income tax unless specified.

1. PlumbCo pays Mary a cash bonus of $15. Federal income tax is withheld at the time of payment, but not FICA tax. If her gross wages for each pay period are $550, what is her net pay on November 13th? $_____

2. The shop supervisor at WidgeCo gives Tony a cash bonus of $100 and withholds no taxes. Tony's next paycheck will be $1,000 in gross wages. If the FITW and FICA applicable to the bonus are withheld from this paycheck, what will his net pay be? $_____

3. AlCo wants to give each employee a net cash bonus of $300. Jose has 11% of his gross wages withheld for state income tax as well as FITW and FICA. What will be the gross amount of Jose's bonus check? $_____

4. As the result of an error, FITW and FICA on $65 of Jane's gross wages were not withheld. Her regular gross wages for each period are $1,000. If the $65 is imputed against her next paycheck, what will her net pay be? $_____

5. As an added inducement for employees to relocate, DelCo offers to pay the employee portion of FITW and FICA on bonus payments. Fred receives a relocation bonus of $1,500. How much taxable income is reported on his bonus? $_____

Problem II.

Fill in the blanks. Answers may be more than one word.

1. When taxes must be withheld after wages are paid, the untaxed wages are treated as _____ on the employee's next paycheck.

2. When an employer pays an employee's tax, it must use a calculation known as _____ to determine total taxable gross wages.

3. When an employer decides to give employees a net bonus or other payment, it can calculate how much gross wages must be paid to arrive at that net amount by using an algebraic method known as _____.

4. When using gross-up, an employer must include FITW, FICA and _____ and _____ income tax.

QUIZ 1   *Solutions and Explanations*

Problem I.

1. $424.28
To calculate:

1. Regular wages		$550.00
2. Federal income taxable		
a. regular wages	$550.00	
b. imputed income	N/A	
c. tax on $550 × 15%		−82.50
3. FICA taxable		
a. regular wages	$550.00	
b. imputed income	15.00	
c. tax on $565 × 7.65%		−43.22
4. Total taxes (Line 2 + Line 3)		−125.72
5. Net pay (Line 1 − Line 4)		$424.28

2. $750.85
To calculate:

1. Regular wages		$1,000.00
2. Federal income taxable		
a. regular wages	$1,000.00	
b. imputed income	100.00	
c. tax on $1,100.00 × 15%		−165.00
3. FICA taxable		
a. regular wages	$1,000.00	
b. imputed income	100.00	
c. tax on $1,100.00 × 7.65%		− 84.15
4. Total taxes (Line 2 + Line 3)		− 249.15
5. Net pay (Line 1 − Line 4)		$ 750.85

3. $452.15

To calculate:

A. $300.00

   1. Federal tax percentage   15.00%

   2. FICA percentage   7.65%

   3. State tax percentage   <u>11.00%</u>

   4. Total tax percentage   33.65%

   5. 100% − 33.65% (Line 4) =   66.35%

   6. Line A ÷ Line 5

       $300 ÷ 0.6635 (66.35%)   = <u>$452.15</u>

                                        new amount of gross wages

B. To verify:

    $452.15 − $152.15 ($452.15 × .3365 [33.65%]) = $300,
the amount in Line A

The calculation is verified because the result is equal to the amount in A.

4. $758.78

To calculate:

   1. Regular wages $1,000.00

   2. Federal income taxable

       a. regular wages $1,000.00

       b. imputed income   65.00

       c. tax on $1,065.00 × 15%   −159.75

   3. FICA taxable

       a. regular wages $1,000.00

       b. imputed income   65.00

       c. tax on $1,065.00 × 7.65%   <u>− 81.47</u>

   4. Total taxes (Line 2 + Line 3)   − 241.22

   5. Net pay (Line 1 − Line 4)   <u>$ 758.78</u>

5. $1,939.24

To calculate:

A. $1,500.00

  1. Federal tax percentage   15.00%

  2. FICA percentage   7.65%

  3. Total tax percentage   22.65%

  4. 100% − 22.65% (Line 3) =   77.35%

  5. Line A ÷ Line 4

     $1,500 ÷ 0.7735 (77.35%) = $1,939.24

                                   new amount of gross wages

B. To verify:

    $1,939.24 − $439.24 ($1,939.24 × .2265 [22.65%]) =

      $1,500.00, the amount in Line A

The calculation is verified.

Problem II.

  1. imputed income

  2. gross-up

  3. gross-up

  4. state, local

QUIZ 2   IMPUTED INCOME AND GROSS-UP

Problem I.

Compute gross or net pay for each question. Assume that FITW is 15%, FICA is 7.65%, but that there is no state income tax unless specified.

1. When PlumbCo gives Susan a cash bonus of $20 on October 12, it withholds federal income tax but not FICA. Her gross wages for each pay period are normally $600. What is Susan's net pay on October 15th?
$_____

2. Matthew receives a cash bonus of $200 from which no taxes are withheld. Taxes due on the bonus will be withheld from Matthew's next weekly paycheck. Assuming he is paid $1,000 each weekly period, what will his net pay be? $_____

3. AlCo gives each employee a net cash bonus of $350. What will each employee's gross wages have to be to arrive at the $350 net after deducting FITW, FICA and state income tax of 11%? $_____

4. On her next paycheck, Ronnie must have tax withheld on an additional $50 that went untaxed on her last paycheck. Normally, her gross wages are $1,500. What will be her net pay after the $50 is imputed against these wages? $_____

5. To speed automation of its offices, ZapCo offers all office workers who agree to be trained a special bonus that includes payment of their federal taxes on the bonus. Harry receives a training bonus of $2,000. How much taxable income is reported on his bonus? $_____

Problem II.

Fill in the blanks. Answers may be more than one word.

1. When income is imputed, it is _____ to the employee's taxable wages so that taxes can be withheld from the imputed amount.

2. If an employer discovers that an employee received payment on which no taxes were withheld, it should treat that payment as _____ on the employee's next paycheck.

3. When an employer decides to pay an employee's taxes as part of a bonus, it uses the gross-up formula to avoid the long string of calculations created by the _____.

4. The gross-up formula is useful when the net (after tax) payment is known, but the employer does not know what the _____ wage amount is.

5. The gross-up computation is not used for wages paid to _____ and _____ employees.

QUIZ 2   Solutions and Explanations

Problem I.

1. $462.57

To calculate:

1. Regular wages			$600.00
2. Federal income taxable			
a. regular wages	$600.00		
b. imputed income	N/A		
c. tax on $600 × 15%		−90.00	
3. FICA taxable			
a. regular wages	$600.00		
b. imputed income	$20.00		
c. tax on $620 × 7.65%		−47.43	
4. Total taxes (Line 2 + 3)			−137.43
5. Net pay (Line 1 − Line 4)			$462.57

2. $728.20

To calculate:

1. Regular wages			$1,000.00
2. Federal income taxable			
a. regular wages	$1,000.00		
b. imputed income	200.00		
c. tax on $1,200.00 × 15%		−180.00	
3. FICA taxable			
a. regular wages	$1,000.00		
b. imputed income	200.00		
c. tax on $1,200.00 × 7.65%		− 91.80	
4. Total taxes (Line 2 + Line 3)			− 271.80
5. Net pay (Line 1 − Line 4)			$ 728.20

3. $527.51
To calculate:

A. $350.00
1. Federal tax percentage   15.00%
2. FICA percentage   7.65%
3. State tax percentage   <u>11.00%</u>
4. Total tax percentage   33.65%
5. 100% − 33.65% (Line 4) =   66.35%
6. Line A ÷ Line 5
    $350 ÷ 0.6635 (66.35%)   = <u>$527.51</u>
           new amount of gross wages

B. To verify:
   $527.51 − $177.51 ($527.51 × .3365 [33.65%]) =
   $350.00, the amount in Line A
The calculation is verified because the result is equal to the amount in Line A.

4. $1,148.93
To calculate:

1. Regular wages $1,500.00
2. Federal income taxable
   a. regular wages $1,500.00
   b. imputed income   50.00
   c. tax on $1,550.00 × 15%   −232.50
3. FICA taxable
   a. regular wages $1,500.00
   b. imputed income   50.00
   c. tax on $1,550.00 × 7.65%   <u>− 118.57</u>
4. Total taxes (Line 2 + Line 3)   <u>−351.07</u>
5. Net pay (Line 1 − Line 4)   <u>$1,148.93</u>

5. $2,585.65
To calculate:

A. $2,000.00

1. Federal tax percentage   15.00%
2. FICA percentage   7.65%
3. Total tax percentage   22.65%
4. 100% − 22.65% (Line 3) =   77.35%
5. Line A ÷ Line 4
    $2,000 ÷ 0.7735 (77.35%)   = $2,585.65
                                          new amount of gross wages

B. To verify:
    $2,585.65 − $585.65 ($2,585.65 × .2265 [22.65%]) =
    $2,000.00, the amount in Line A

The calculation is verified.

Problem II.

1. added

2. imputed income

3. pyramiding effect

4. gross

5. domestic, agricultural

Section 10
IMPUTED INCOME FOR FRINGE BENEFITS

Introduction

Because most fringe benefits are not paid in cash, taxes cannot be withheld at the time that they are provided to employees. Instead, taxes are collected from regular wages by *imputing* (adding) the value of the benefit to the appropriate taxable amounts.

Calculating Imputed Income

Income is imputed as shown below:

EXAMPLE: CarCo buys auto mechanic George a $50 book on plumbing. Because a book on plumbing is unrelated to George's present job, it is a taxable benefit subject to FITW, FICA and FUTA. Assuming FITW of 15% and FICA of 7.65% on regular wages of $425, here's how CarCo would impute this $50 to George's next paycheck and collect taxes on it:

Worksheet for Imputed Income		
1. Regular wages (Salary Expense)		$ 425.00
2. Federal income taxable		
a. regular wages	425.00	
b. imputed income	50.00	
c. FITW on $475 × 15%		−71.25
3. FICA taxable		
a. regular wages	425.00	
b. imputed income	50.00	
c. FICA on $475 × 7.65%		−36.34
4. Total taxes (Line 2 + Line 3)		−107.59
5. Net pay (Line 1 − Line 4)		$317.41

PROBLEM 1: Charlie uses a company-owned vehicle for personal use. His employer will collect FITW and FICA for this benefit from each semimonthly paycheck due on the 15th. If Charlie is paid $500 gross on March 15 and the value of his personal use of the vehicle is $75 for the month, what is Charlie's net pay for March 15? (Assume a FITW rate of 15% and a FICA rate of 7.65%.)

SOLUTION 1: $369.76 net pay.

Worksheet for Charlie's March 1 Paycheck		
1. Regular wages (Salary Expense)		$500.00
2. Federal income taxable		
a. regular wages	500.00	
b. imputed income	75.00	
c. FITW on $575 × 15%		−86.25
3. FICA taxable		
a. regular wages	500.00	
b. imputed income	75.00	
c. FICA on $575 at 7.65%		−43.99
4. Total taxes (Line 2 + Line 3)		−130.24
5. Net pay (Line 1 − Line 4)		$369.76

The imputed income calculation is more complicated when a benefit or payment is subject to some federal and state taxes but not to others. For instance, the value of group-term life insurance over $50,000 is subject to FICA but not to FITW. Although most newer computer programs perform this calculation automatically, a worksheet can be helpful for manually prepared payroll checks.

EXAMPLE: Keith receives group-term life insurance over $50,000 and must recognize $5 taxable income each month on the excess. His employer withholds FICA from this benefit from wages paid on the last day of the month. Keith is due $425 in gross wages on his paycheck of June 30. What is his net pay?

Worksheet for Imputed Income with Varying Tax Liability		
1. Regular wages		$425.00
2. Federal income taxable		
a. regular wages	425.00	
b. imputed income	N/A	
c. FITW on $425 × 15%		−63.75
3. FICA taxable		
a. regular wages	425.00	
b. imputed income	5.00	
c. FICA on $430 ($425 + $5) × 7.65%		−32.90
4. Total taxes (Line 2 + Line 3)		− 96.65
5. Net pay (Line 1 − Line 4)		$328.35

As this example illustrates, the $5 imputed monthly income for group-term life insurance over $50,000 increases Keith's taxable wages for gross income and FICA (Line 3), but not for FITW (Line 2c). The $5.00 of imputed income is included in Box 1 of the W-2, but the amount is not subject to federal income tax withholding.

PROBLEM 2: Sally receives group-term life insurance over $50,000 and must recognize $10 in taxable income per month. Her employer collects FICA tax related to the benefit from wages paid on the 15th of the month. Sally is due $525 gross wages on her paycheck of October 15. Using a FITW rate of 15% and a FICA rate of 7.65%, what will her net pay be?

SOLUTION 2: $405.32. To calculate:

Worksheet for Sally's October 15 Paycheck		
1. Regular wages		$525.00
2. Federal income taxable		
a. regular wages	525.00	
b. imputed income	N/A	
c. FITW on $525 × 15%		−78.75
3. FICA taxable		
a. regular wages	525.00	
b. imputed income	10.00	
c. FICA on $535 ($525 + $10) × 7.65%		−40.93
4. Total taxes (Line 2 + Line 3)		−119.68
5. Net pay (Line 1 − Line 4)		$405.32

QUIZ 1   IMPUTED INCOME FOR FRINGE BENEFITS

Problem I.

Compute net pay for each question. Assume that FITW is 15%, FICA is 7.65%, but no state income tax applies unless specified. Assume no employee earned more than $50,000 for the year.

1. ACME purchases group-term life insurance for employees. Life insurance coverage is two times the annual salary. ACME imputes the taxable portion of this benefit to paychecks delivered on the 15th of each month. Mary must recognize $15 per month in federal taxable income for this benefit. Her employer has elected not to withhold federal income tax on the value of this benefit. If her gross wages are normally $550, what is her net pay on November 15th? $_____

2. Jane's personal use of a company-owned vehicle is valued at $65, which will be imputed for employment tax and withholding purposes to her February 15 paycheck. If her gross wages are normally $1,000, what is her net pay on February 15? $_____

3. Mark's personal use of a company-owned vehicle is valued at $25, which will be imputed to his April 15 paycheck. His employer has elected not to withhold federal income tax on the value of this benefit. If his gross wages are normally $1,500, what is his net pay? $_____

QUIZ 1 Solutions and Explanations

Problem I.

1. $424.28
To calculate:

1. Regular wages		$550.00
2. Federal income taxable		
a. regular wages	550.00	
b. imputed income subject to FITW	N/A	
c. FITW on $550 × 15%		−82.50
3. FICA taxable		
a. regular wages	550.00	
b. imputed income subject to FICA	15.00	
c. FICA on $565 ($550 + $15) × 7.65%		−43.22
4. Total taxes (Line 2 + Line 3)		−125.72
5. Net pay (Line 1 − Line 4)		$424.28

2. $758.78
To calculate:

1. Regular wages		$1,000.00
2. Federal income taxable		
a. regular wages	1,000.00	
b. imputed income	65.00	
c. FITW on $1,065 ($1,000 + $65) × 15%		−159.75
3. FICA taxable		
a. regular wages	1,000.00	
b. imputed income	65.00	
c. FICA on $1,065 ($1,000 + $65) × 7.65%		− 81.47
4. Total taxes (Line 2 + Line 3)		−241.22
5. Net pay (Line 1 − Line 4)		$758.78

3. $1,158.34
To calculate:

1. Regular wages		$1,500.00
2. Federal income taxable		
a. regular wages	1,500.00	
b. imputed income (employer elected not to withhold)	N/A	
c. FITW on $1,500 × 15%		− 225.00
3. FICA taxable		
a. regular wages	1,500.00	
b. imputed income	25.00	
c. FICA on $1,525 ($1,500 + $25) × 7.65%		− 116.66
4. Total taxes (Line 2 + Line 3)		− 341.66
5. Net pay (Line 1 − Line 4)		$1,158.34

QUIZ 2   IMPUTED INCOME FOR FRINGE BENEFITS

Problem I.

Compute net pay for each question. Assume that FITW is 15%, FICA is 7.65%, but no state income tax applies unless specified. Assume no employee earned more than $50,000 for the year.

1. ACME purchases group-term life insurance for its employees. Life insurance coverage is two times the annual salary. ACME imputes the value of this benefit to paychecks dated the 15th of each month. Susan must recognize $20 per month in taxable income for the benefit. Her employer does not withhold federal income tax from taxable group term life. Assuming that Susan's gross pay is normally $600, what is her net pay on October 15th?
   $_____

2. Brigit is reimbursed for travel expenses of $250. The reimbursement is tax-free for FITW and FICA purposes, but is subject to state income tax withholding at 3%. The benefit will be imputed to Brigit's May 15 paycheck. If her gross wages on May 15 are $950, what is her net pay?
   $_____

3. Fran drives a company-owned vehicle for personal business. Her personal use is valued at $50. This taxable income will be imputed for employment tax and withholding purposes to her August 28 paycheck, which is $1,500. What is her net pay? $_____

QUIZ 2   Solutions and Explanations

Problem I.

1. $462.57

To calculate:

1. Regular wages		$600.00
2. Federal income taxable		
a. regular wages	600.00	
b. imputed income subject to FITW	N/A	
c. FITW on $600 × 15%		−90.00
3. FICA taxable		
a. regular wages	600.00	
b. imputed income subject to FICA	20.00	
c. FICA on $620 ($600 + $20)		
× 7.65%		<u>−47.43</u>
4. Total taxes (Line 2 + Line 3)		<u>−137.43</u>
5. Net pay (Line 1 − Line 4)		<u>$462.57</u>

2. $698.82

To calculate:

1. Regular wages		$950.00
2. Federal income taxable		
a. regular wages	950.00	
b. imputed income	N/A	
c. FITW on $950 × 15%		−142.50
3. State taxable		
a. regular wages	950.00	
b. imputed income	250.00	
c. state tax on $1,200		
($950 + $250) × 3%		− 36.00
4. FICA taxable		
a. regular wages	950.00	
b. imputed income	N/A	
c. FICA on $950 × 7.65%		<u>− 72.68</u>
5. Total taxes (Line 2 + Line 2a + Line 3)		<u>−251.18</u>
6. Net pay (Line 1 − Line 4)		<u>$698.82</u>

3. $1,148.92
To calculate:

1. Regular wages		$1,500.00
2. Federal income taxable		
a. regular wages	1,500.00	
b. imputed income	50.00	
c. FITW on $1,550		
($1,500 + $50) × 15%		−232.50
3. FICA taxable		
a. regular wages	1,500.00	
b. imputed income	50.00	
c. FICA on $1,550		
($1,500 + $50) × 7.65%		− 118.58
4. Total taxes (Line 2 + Line 3)		− 351.08
5. Net pay (Line 1 − Line 4)		$1,148.92

INVOLUNTARY DEDUCTIONS FROM PAY

Introduction

In addition to making voluntary deductions from employees' pay for items such as contributions to medical insurance plans and retirement plans, employers may be required to make involuntary deductions. These deductions, also called attachments or garnishments, may be required for child support and alimony, federal and state tax levies (for tax debts), creditor garnishments, delinquent student loans and other federal debts, and certain involuntary employer deductions.

Child Support and Alimony

Under federal and state laws, some employees are required to make child support and/or alimony payments through payroll deduction. The employer is notified through a state agency or court if deductions must be made from an employee's wages. The notice will include the amount of the deduction, and the remittance address. Because state agency notices and court orders are legal documents, they must be read carefully and observed to the letter. Employers are advised to consult the withholding agency to interpret the requirements of an order or notice and to instruct those responsible for preparing paychecks. Failure to observe a wage withholding order can result in severe penalties. An employer can be held responsible for making all payments not withheld from the employee's wages and may be assessed punitive damages.

Federal and State Tax Levies

The IRS and many state taxing authorities have the right to attach the wages of an employee who fails to pay income or other taxes. The employer must honor this attachment, or "levy," until the taxing authority (e.g., IRS) has issued a written "Release of Levy" to the employer. Employers should *never* accept *oral* instructions to stop a levy—even from the IRS.

There are restrictions on the percentage of wages the IRS can attach.

For levies received by an employer prior to July 1, 1989: $75 per week of take-home (net) pay is exempt from levy, plus an additional $25 per week for each allowance the employee is allowed to take. The employee notifies the employer of these allowances by completing IRS Form 668-W(c)(DO), Parts 2–5 (see Form 668-W(c)(DO) in the "Forms Appendix").

> **EXAMPLE:** WidgeCo is notified by the IRS that Fran owes back taxes of $400. She is paid $500 per week and claims 1 allowance on the 668-W(c)(DO). To calculate her net pay under the levy:

Gross wages		$500.00
FITW at 15%	−75.00	
FICA at 7.65%	−38.25	
Medical insurance	−50.00	
Total deductions		−163.25
A. Net pay before levy		336.75
B. Exempt from levy ($75 + $25)		−100.00
C. IRS levy (Line A − Line B)		−236.75
Net pay (should be equal to Line B)		$100.00

For levies received by an employer after July 1, 1989: The amount exempt from levy is equal to the sum of the standard deduction and total allowances permitted, divided by the number of pay periods per year that the employee is paid (i.e., weekly, biweekly, etc.). The employee claims personal allowances by completing the 668-W(c)(DO), Parts 2–5. The IRS levy notice contains a table that provides the computed value of the wages exempt from levy.

For purposes of illustration, the table on the following page shows some of the exempt amounts on a weekly levy table.

Refer to IRS Publication 1494 for the amounts exempt from levy for each tax year. You can download Publication 1494 on the IRS website at *www.irs.gov*.

See IRS Notice 1439 for instructions on figuring the amount from levy starting in tax year 2018, available on the IRS website at *https://www.irs.gov/pub/irs-pdf/n1439.pdf*.

Exempt Amounts on a Weekly Levy
Single Employee, 1 Dependent

2010:	$179.81
2011:	$182.69
2012	$187.50
2013	$192.31
2014	$195.19
2015	$198.08
2016	$199.04
2017	$200.00
2018	$310.58
2019	$315.39
2020	$321.15
2021	$324.04

If an employee submits Form 668-W(c)(DO) requesting a change in marital status or number of dependent, the employer is to use the wage-exempt table in effect in the year that the employee requests the change. However, employers are not allowed to change automatically the amount exempt from levy each year based on the new year's tables.

EXAMPLE: On September 15, 2020, WidgeCo receives an IRS levy of $50,000 for Matthew, who claims single with 1 dependent on the 668-W(c)(DO). He does not change his 668-W(c)(DO) for 2021. According to the weekly levy table above, $321.15 of weekly take-home (net) pay is exempt from federal levy and not the 2021 amount of $324.04. (*Note:* The form used to determine an employee's marital status and number of allowances for tax levy purposes is Parts 2–5 of the 668-W(c)(DO) and not the Form W-4).

PROBLEM 1: On June 15, 2020, ACME, Inc. receives an IRS levy of $400 for employee Matthew. He is single and is entitled to 1 allowance. How much of his weekly take-home pay is exempt from levy?

SOLUTION 1: $321.15 of weekly take-home pay is exempt from levy. See the weekly levy table above.

PROBLEM 2: On July 12, 2019, ACME receives an IRS levy of $700 for Francesca who is single and entitled to 1 personal allowance. How much of her weekly take-home pay is exempt from levy?

SOLUTION 2: $315.39 of weekly take-home pay is exempt from levy. See the weekly levy table above.

Creditor Garnishments

A garnishment order may be issued to the employer of an employee who owes a creditor money. The employer is required to make deductions from the employee's paycheck and send the amounts withheld to the creditor. Creditor garnishments are regulated by both federal and state laws. Some states, such as Texas, do not allow creditor garnishments at all. If state law allows for a greater restriction on the amount that can be deducted from an employee's wages, then the employer must comply with state law. If federal law allows for a greater restriction on the deduction amount, then the employer complies with federal law rather than state law.

Student Loans and Administrative Wage Garnishments

Wage attachment orders for student loans and other federal debts, such as HUD or VHA loans, are issued by various agencies of the federal government either directly or through private collection firms. The deduction limits on these federal debts are as follows:

- Student Loans Issued Through State Guaranty Agencies: The deduction limit on a wage withholding order for a defaulted student loan is 15% of disposable pay.

- Administrative Wage Garnishment (AWG): The limit on deductions from wages for an AWG (that is, garnishments for unpaid student loans made directly by the U.S. Department of Education and for other federal loans) is 15% of disposable pay.

If an employee has more than one garnishment, and one is a student loan or AWG, the maximum deduction on all AWG garnishments for this employee is 25%. For example, if 20% of an employee's disposable pay is being deducted for a federal tax levy and the employer receives an AWG, the employer may deduct only 5% for the AWG. At this point the employer will have reached the 25% maximum deduction for multiple federal garnishments.

Note: Although some states impose deduction limits at 15%, these limits cannot supercede the federal limits. In other words, for more than one AWG federal garnishment you must deduct a maximum of 25% even if the state limit is lower.

Disposable Pay

Wage withholding orders, such as those for child support, and creditor garnishments may instruct an employer to deduct a percentage of the employee's *disposable pay,* defined as gross wages less deductions required by law such as federal, state and local taxes. However, disposable pay does not include voluntary deductions for health insurance, savings bonds, uniforms, etc. ***Note:*** For an administrative wage order, health insurance is deducted from gross pay to compute disposable pay.

PROBLEM 3: Craig is paid $500 gross, has $75 deducted for FITW, $38 for FICA, and $50 for medical insurance. What is his *disposable pay*?

SOLUTION 3: His disposable pay is $387. To calculate:

$500 gross − $75 FITW − $38 FICA = $387

The $50 deduction for medical insurance is not included in the calculation for disposable pay.

Employer Deductions

An employer covered by federal wage and hour law is restricted from making involuntary deductions from employees' pay. Generally, an employer may not make an involuntary deduction if it brings an employee's gross wages for the workweek below the federal minimum hourly wage of $7.25. No deduction is allowed in a workweek in which overtime is worked. There is no limit on the amount that can be deducted for voluntary contributions.

PROBLEM 4: ACME's policy requires employees to pay for damaged tools. Drew owes $100 and his payments will begin with the paycheck of November 11, 2021, for a chain saw that he damaged. If his gross pay is $320 for 40 hours in the workweek, how much can ACME deduct?

SOLUTION 4: It can deduct a maximum of $30.00 from Drew's pay. To calculate:

$320 ÷ 40 hours = $8.00 per hour.

$8.00 per hour − $7.25 federal minimum wage =
    $.75 × 40 hours = $30.00

QUIZ 1   INVOLUNTARY DEDUCTIONS FROM PAY

Problem I.

Mark each statement True or False.

1. Disposable pay is net pay.

    a. True   b. False

2. Federal income tax is one example of a voluntary deduction.

    a. True   b. False

3. For levies issued prior to July 1, 1989, the amount exempt from levy is $75 per week plus $25 for each additional allowance.

    a. True   b. False

4. Employees should authorize all voluntary deductions.

    a. True   b. False

5. Employees must authorize all involuntary deductions.

    a. True   b. False

Problem II.

Calculate the involuntary deduction permitted in each case.

1. On June 30, 2021, WidgeCo receives an IRS Notice of Levy for Fran whose weekly take-home pay is $450. She is single and entitled to 1 dependent. How much of her paycheck is the IRS entitled to?
$_____

2. Matthew must pay his employer for damaged tools. For the week ending October 1, 2021, he earns $330 for 40 hours straight time ($8.25 per hour) and $12.38 for 1 hour overtime. If his employer is covered by federal wage and hour law, what is the maximum it may deduct for the damages?
$_____

3. On July 14, 2020, Gunther's employer receives an IRS Notice of Levy for taxes that he owes. His weekly take-home pay before the levy is $435. He is single and entitled to 1 dependent. How much of this wage payment is the IRS entitled to? $_____

4. Mary's employer receives a child support order stating that 55% of her disposable pay, or $200, whichever is less, should be deducted for child support. Her gross wages are $500. Her withholding includes federal tax of $75, FICA tax of $38 and a credit union deduction of $30. How much should be deducted for child support?
$_____

5. On October 7, 2021, Bob's employer receives a student loan garnishment from a State Guaranty Agency. His disposable pay is $350. How much can be deducted from his wages for this attachment? $_____

Problem III.

Multiple choice. Circle the correct answer.

1. For levies first issued in 2021, the amount per week exempt from levy is . . .

    a. $324.04   b. $75.00   c. $199.04   d. $321.15

2. Which of the following is a voluntary deduction?

    a. state tax
    b. federal tax
    c. U.S. Savings Bonds
    d. FICA tax

3. Which of the following is an involuntary deduction?

    a. credit union dues
    b. health insurance
    c. United Way contribution
    d. child support

4. Which of the following is included in the calculation for disposable pay?

    a. U.S. Savings Bonds
    b. credit union dues
    c. United Way contribution
    d. FICA tax

5. Which of the following is not an attachment?

    a. child support
    b. federal income tax
    c. creditor garnishment
    d. IRS levy

QUIZ 1   *Solutions and Explanations*

Problem I.

1. False

2. False

3. True

4. True

5. False

Problem II.

1. $125.96
To calculate:

A. Net pay before levy	$450.00
B. Exempt from levy (2021)	324.04
	$125.96

2. $0
Nothing can be deducted because the employee worked in excess of 40 hours in the workweek.

3. $113.85
To calculate:

A. Net pay before levy	$435.00
B. Exempt from levy (2020)	–321.15
	$113.85

4. $200
To calculate:

$500 gross − $75 FITW − $38 FICA = $387
$387 × 55% = $212.85

Because $200 is less than $212.85, the $200 should be deducted under the child support order. The $30 credit union deduction is not included in the disposable pay calculation.

5. $52.50
To calculate:

A. Disposable pay	$350.00
B. Less 85% exempt	− 297.50
C. Student Loan Garnishment (15% of A)	$ 52.50

Problem III.

1. a

2. c

3. d

4. d

5. b

QUIZ 2   INVOLUNTARY DEDUCTIONS FROM PAY

Problem I.

Mark each statement True or False.

1. A United Way contribution is an after tax deduction.

   a. True   b. False

2. An employer is served with garnishment for a student loan provided directly through the U.S. Department of Education on July 2, 2021. The maximum deduction allowed is 10% of disposable pay.

   a. True   b. False

3. Employers may attach employees' overtime pay for involuntary deductions.

   a. True   b. False

4. Federal income tax is one example of an attachment.

   a. True   b. False

5. Disposable pay is not necessarily the same as take-home pay.

   a. True   b. False

Problem II.

Calculate the involuntary deduction in each case.

1. On June 25, 2020, ACME received an IRS Notice of Levy for Carson whose weekly take-home pay is normally $450. He is single and entitled to 1 dependent. How much of the weekly wage payment is the IRS entitled to in 2021 if he has not requested a change since 2020?
   $_____

2. Mike must pay his employer for damaged tools. For the week ending September 3, 2021, his gross pay is $324 straight time ($8.10 per hour), and no overtime hours were worked in the workweek. What is the maximum his employer may deduct for the damaged tools (assuming that the employer is covered by federal wage and hour law)? $_____

3. On July 10, 2020, PlumbCo receives an IRS Notice of Levy for Simon whose weekly take-home pay is $350. He is single and entitled to 1 dependent. How much of his weekly paycheck is the IRS entitled to? $_____

4. WidgeCo receives a child support order for Martha stating that 55% of her disposable pay, or $275, whichever is less, must be deducted for child support. Her gross wages are $600, FITW is $75, FICA tax is $45, and her U.S. Savings Bond deduction is $50. How much should be deducted for child support? $_____

5. On October 8, 2020, ACME received an IRS Notice of Levy for Ellis whose weekly take-home pay on October 15, 2021, is $390. He is single and entitled to 1 dependent. How much of his paycheck is the IRS entitled to, assuming he did not request that the exempt amount be recomputed since 2020? $_____

Problem III.

Multiple choice. Circle the correct answer.

1. For 2020, the amount per week exempt from IRS levy for a single employee with 1 allowance is:

    a. $324.04   b. $75.00   c. $315.39   d. $321.15

2. Which of the following is not included in the calculation of disposable pay?

    a. state tax
    b. county tax
    c. FICA
    d. uniform deductions

3. Which of the following is an attachment?

    a. state tax
    b. county tax
    c. child support
    d. FICA

4. Assuming it is July 1, 2021, what is the maximum deduction allowed for a student loan garnishment is:

    a. 10%   b. 15%   c. 20%   d. 5%

5. Which of the following is not a voluntary deduction?

    a. FICA
    b. credit union dues
    c. United Way contribution
    d. uniform deduction

QUIZ 2   Solutions and Explanations

Problem I.

1. True

2. False
The deduction limit is 15%.

3. False

4. False

5. True

Problem II.

1. $128.85
To calculate:

A. Net pay before levy	$450.00
B. Exempt from levy (2020)	−321.15
C. IRS levy (Line A − Line B)	$128.85

2. $34
To calculate:

$324 ÷ 40 hours = $8.10 per hour

$8.10 − $7.25 (federal minimum wage) = $.85

$.85 × 40 hours = $34.00

3. $28.85
To calculate:

A. Net pay before levy	$350.00
B. Exempt from levy (2020)	–321.15
C. IRS levy (Line A – Line B)	$28.85

4. $264.00
To calculate:

$600 gross – $75 FITW – $45 FICA = $480
$480 × 55% = $264.00

Because $264.00 is less than $275, the $264.00 should be deducted for child support. The $50 savings bond deduction is not included in the calculation for disposable pay.

5. $68.85
To calculate:

A. Net pay before levy	$390.00
B. Exempt from levy (2020)	–321.15*
C. IRS Levy (Line A – Line B)	$ 68.85

* The employee did not request that the exempt amount be changed; therefore, the 2020 exempt amount remains in effect.

Problem III.

1. d

2. d

3. c

4. b

5. a

Section 12
WORKERS' COMPENSATION INSURANCE

Introduction

Most all states (exceptions apply in certain states, such as Texas) require that employers insure their employees from work-related accident or illness. This kind of insurance is called "workers' compensation." It guarantees that employees who become injured or ill as a result of their jobs will receive reimbursement for medical expenses and disability pay for the time they cannot work.

State Variations

Depending on the laws of the individual state, workers' compensation insurance may be provided by a private insurance company, employer-funded plan or a state fund. In the majority of states, however, private carriers, rather than the state, are the primary or sole providers of workers' compensation insurance.

Monopolistic Versus Competitive States

In a *monopolistic state*, the employer is not allowed to be self-insured or to carry workers' compensation insurance with a private insurance company. The state is the sole provider of workers' compensation insurance. All premiums are paid directly to the state. Monopolistic states include North Dakota, Ohio, Puerto Rico, the Virgin Islands, Washington, and Wyoming.

In the *competitive rating states*, the individual insurance company files their own rates and rules with the state. The competitive rating states are listed on the following page.

Note that Texas does not require that employers carry worker's compensation insurance; however, employers are liable for the medical and related costs of their workers' injuries.

This section covers the general principles for workers' compensation insurance provided by private carriers. Certain general principles apply to workers' compensation insurance in those states that are not monopolistic.

Alabama	Missouri
Alaska	Montana
Arkansas	Nebraska
Colorado	New Hampshire
Connecticut	New Mexico
District of Columbia	Oklahoma
Georgia	Oregon
Hawaii	Rhode Island
Illinois	South Dakota
Kansas	Tennessee
Kentucky	Vermont
Louisiana	Virginia
Maine	Utah
Maryland	West Virginia
Mississippi	

Workers' Compensation Classification Codes

The rate that an employer pays for workers' compensation insurance is based on the nature of the work the company does and, in some instances, on each employee's job. The more hazardous the work, the higher the rate. For instance, a machine shop pays a higher workers' compensation rate than an appliance store does.

Governing Class Code

The insurer identifies the nature of the employer's work and assigns it a "governing class code." The premium is calculated by multiplying the employee's wages by the rate for the employer's governing class code.

Standard Exception Codes

Certain jobs are so common to all companies that they can be rated separately from the assigned governing class codes. Examples of standard exception codes include:

- **8810-office/administrative.** Employees who can fulfill assigned clerical or administrative duties without leaving the office environment.

- **8742-sales person/traveling manager/messenger.** Office employees who must leave the office or travel to carry out sales management responsibilities.

- **7380-delivery driver/route salesperson/ chauffeur.** Employees who deliver or pick up inventory for their company.

Assigning standard exception codes wherever possible can lower an employer's insurance premium.

> **EXAMPLE:** California-based WeldCo is a machine shop with a governing class code of 3632. Assume that the rate in California for this governing class code is $6.81 per $100 of wages. However, WeldCo's bookkeeper works only in the office and can be assigned a standard exception code (8810) at a rate of just $0.72 per $100—89% less than the rate of the machine shop employees.*
>
> * These are not the actual California rates.

Wages to Include or Exclude

In calculating the workers' compensation premium (employee wages × applicable rate), the following are examples of payments to employees that generally are excluded from the premium calculation under state law:

- travel expenses

- severance pay or pay in lieu of vacation

- rewards for invention/discovery

- supper money

- stock options (some stock options may be included)

- club memberships

- insurance payments (third-party sick pay or workers' compensation)

- employee discounts

- premium pay (overtime pay rate less regular hourly pay rate— e.g., if overtime is $13.50 per hour and the regular rate is $9 per hour, $4.50 per hour is excludable)

- reinstatement wages

- tips

- educational assistance plan reimbursements

- personal use of a company-owned vehicle

- uniform allowances

Paying the Workers' Compensation Premium

Generally, employers are provided with an annual estimated premium at the end of the policy year. An audit is conducted each year to determine the actual premium cost. If necessary, an adjustment is made to the premium at this time.

Taxation and Reporting

Workers' compensation payments to employees for illness or injury are exempt from FITW, FICA and FUTA and therefore are not reported by the employer.

QUIZ 1 WORKERS' COMPENSATION INSURANCE

Problem I.

Fill in the blanks.

1. In _____ states, employers may use either the state fund or a private insurance company for workers' compensation insurance.

2. The code used to rate the nature of the employer's work is called the

   _____ _____ _____.

3. Workers' compensation insurance provides medical and disability benefits to employees for _____-_____ accidents or illnesses.

4. Washington and Wyoming are examples of _____ states.

5. Generally, premium overtime is/is not _____ included in wages to calculate a workers' compensation insurance premium.

6. Name one state in which workers' compensation insurance is not mandatory. _____

Problem II.

Answer each statement True or False.

1. Code 8810 for office and administrative employees is an example of a governing class code.

   a. True   b. False

2. A standard exception code may be used for machine shop supervisors.

   a. True   b. False

3. Generally, holiday pay is included in wages for calculating a workers' compensation insurance premium.

   a. True   b. False

4. The workers' compensation rate under a standard exception code is often lower than the rate that applies to the governing class code.

 a. True   b. False

5. New York is an example of a monopolistic state.

 a. True   b. False

Problem III.

Multiple choice. Circle the correct answer.

1. Which of the following is a competitive rating state?

 a. Arizona
 b. North Dakota
 c. Colorado
 d. Florida

2. A traveling salesperson of a machine shop could be classified under which of the following standard exception codes?

 a. 8810   b. 8742   c. 7380   d. 3632

3. Which of the following payments would generally be included in wages when determining the workers' compensation premium?

 a. holiday pay
 b. third-party sick pay
 c. severance pay
 d. personal use of company-owned vehicle

QUIZ 1   Solutions and Explanations

Problem I.

    1. competitive rating

    2. governing class code

    3. job-related

    4. monopolistic

    5. is not

    6. Texas

Problem II.

    1. False

    2. False

    3. True

    4. True

    5. False

Problem III.

    1. c

    2. b

    3. a

QUIZ 2   WORKERS' COMPENSATION INSURANCE

Problem I.

Fill in the blanks.

1. In a _____ state, the employer may not purchase workers' compensation insurance from a private carrier.

2. Workers' compensation insurance provides _____ and _____ benefits for employees injured on the job.

3. For certain jobs common to most companies, special codes called _____ _____ _____ may be used.

4. Tennessee and Vermont are examples of _____ states.

5. Workers' comp payments to employees for job-related sickness or injury (are/are not) _____ subject to FITW, FICA, and FUTA.

Problem II.

Mark each statement True or False.

1. Workers' compensation rules vary by state.

   a. True   b. False

2. Bob delivers parts for WeldCo, a machine shop. He may be assigned the standard exception code of 8810.

   a. True   b. False

3. Generally, severance pay is included in wages when determining a workers' compensation premium.

   a. True   b. False

4. Maine is an example of a competitive rating state.

   a. True   b. False

5. An office secretary of a printing shop who spends all of her time in the office should be assigned the governing class code.

a. True   b. False

Problem III.

Multiple choice. Circle the correct answer.

1. Which of the following is a monopolistic state?

a. Texas
b. Colorado
c. Washington
d. Wisconsin

2. Workers' compensation benefits paid to employees for job-related accidents or illnesses are subject to . . .

a. FITW
b. FICA
c. FUTA
d. none of the above

3. Which of the following payments generally would be excluded from wages in determining the workers' compensation premium?

a. tips
b. regular wages
c. jury duty
d. commissions

QUIZ 2   Solutions and Explanations

Problem I.

    1. monopolistic

    2. disability, medical

    3. standard exception codes

    4. competitive rating

    5. are not

Problem II.

    1. True

    2. False

    3. False

    4. True

    5. False

Problem III.

    1. c

    2. d

    3. a

GLOSSARY OF KEY TERMS

Accountable plan: See page 65.

Alternative flat tax: For 2018 through 2025, a 22% tax rate that may be used to compute withholding on *supplemental wages* (see page 191) of $1 million or less. For 2018 through 2025, supplemental wages in excess of $1 million in the year are subject to a mandatory 37% rate without regard to the employee's Form W-4.

Annual lease value method: Method for valuing employee use of a company-provided vehicle based on the actual price a buyer would pay to lease a comparable vehicle in an arm's-length transaction. Required method for any vehicle placed in service in 2021 with a value exceeding $51,100 (indexed each year for inflation).

Business-expense allowance: Generally, a lump sum given by the employer to an employee annually or on a regular basis to cover the employee's estimated business expenses.

Business-expense advance: Generally, monies given to an employee prior to a particular trip or purchase to cover the business costs incurred.

Business-expense reimbursement: Employer repayment of business-related expenses incurred by an employee on its behalf.

Business-related expenses: Expenses incurred by an employee on behalf of his or her employer.

Business standard mileage rate: Rate allowed for business use of a personal car. Effective January 1, 2021, the rate is $0.56 per mile ($.575 per mile effective January 1, 2020 through December 31, 2020).

"Cafeteria" plan: A *flexible benefit plan* (see page 187).

Circular E: IRS Publication 15 issued each December containing information about the federal payroll taxes and reporting requirements that apply. The federal income tax withholding tables for the year are contained in Publication 15-T.

Commuting: Employee travel to or from the employer's principal place of business.

Commuting valuation method: Method under which the IRS allows employers to compute a flat taxable amount of $1.50 for each one-way commute, or $3 per round trip, regardless of the number of miles the employee commutes in a free employer-provided van pool or when the employer requires employees to use a company-provided vehicle for commuting.

Competitive rating state: A state in which the individual workers' compensation insurance company files its own rates and rules with the state.

Creditor garnishment: An order issued to an employer requiring it to withhold a portion of an employee's salary and send it to a creditor to which the employee owes money.

De minimis expenses: Occasional expenses of generally $75 or less (such as occasional parking or tolls) for which the IRS doesn't require receipts as part of the substantiation requirements under an accountable plan.

De minimis fringe benefit: A benefit that is tax-free because its value is so small ("de minimis") that accounting for it would be unreasonable or impractical.

Disability pay: A general term that describes payment for an illness or accident that *may or may not be job-related*.

Discriminatory group-term life plans: A group-term life insurance plan is considered discriminatory unless it passes an eligibility test showing that at least 70% of all employees are eligible to participate in the plan and at least 85% of all employees who participate are not key employees.

Disposable pay: Gross wages less deductions required by law such as federal, state and local taxes, but generally not voluntary deductions such as health insurance or U.S. Savings Bonds contributions unless specified in the law or the withholding order.

Dollar-for-dollar reimbursement: A method of reimbursing employees for business-related expenses under which the employee must submit verification (such as receipts) for all but *de minimis* (see above) expenses.

Educational assistance plan: A fringe benefit that provides reimbursement to an employee for nonjob-related undergraduate or graduate education.

EFTPS: Electronic Federal Tax Payment System—the federal system used for employers' electronic remittance of federal taxes.

EIN: Employer Identification Number.

Elective deferrals: An employee's pretax contribution of a portion of his or her salary to an employer-sponsored retirement plan.

Employee: Under IRS guidelines, an individual is considered an employee when the employer exercises control over who will do the work, what the person will do, how it will be done, and when it will be done and if the *safe harbor rules* (see page 190) do not apply (e.g., a past IRS audit, common industry practice).

Employer-sponsored group-term life insurance: Death benefit is paid under an insurance policy to beneficiaries named by the employee.

Employer-sponsored dependent-term life insurance: Like group-term life insurance except that coverage is for a dependent named by the employee and the death benefit is paid to the employee or designated beneficiary.

Federal (or state) tax levy: Attachment of an employee's wages by the IRS (or state taxing authority) for failure to pay tax owed.

Federal per diem rate: The government-specified daily rate an employer may use to cover employee business-related travel expenses such as lodging, meals and certain incidental expenses (e.g., laundry, cleaning and pressing, fees, tips).

FICA: Federal Insurance Contributions Act. See *Social Security tax* and *Medicare tax*.

FIT: Federal income tax.

FITW: Federal income tax withholding.

Flexible benefit plan: An employer-sponsored program that allows employees to elect benefits from a "menu" of options. Also known as a "cafeteria" plan.

Form 8109: No longer used as of January 1, 2011. Formerly, employees used this Form 8109, *Federal Tax Deposit Coupon* to deposit FICA, FITW, FUTA, and other nonpayroll taxes at authorized financial institutions.

Form 940: Employer's Annual Federal Unemployment Tax Return—used to compute the employer's annual federal unemployment tax (*FUTA*; see below) liability and to report quarterly payments.

Form 941: Employer's Quarterly Federal Tax Return—used to report quarterly wage and tax information and any tax liability due. (Note that IRS authorized employers with annual liability of $1,000 or less may file an annual Form 944.)

Form 1099: Various forms (1099-MISC, 1099-NEC, 1099-DIV, etc.)—used to report nonwage income such as commissions, fees, royalties, and dividends.

Form W-4: Federal Employees' Withholding Certificate—informs the employer which tax tables or rate schedules to use to determine the amount of federal income tax to withhold from an employee's wages.

Form W-2: Wage and Tax Statement—the employee's annual summary of total taxable wages paid and taxes withheld.

Form W-3: Transmittal of Wage and Tax Statements—a form that serves both to submit paper Forms W-2 to the Social Security Administration and as an employer's annual reconciliation of wage and tax information.

FUTA: Federal Unemployment Tax Act—tax paid by most private employers to the federal unemployment fund.

Gross-up: Process of calculating an employee's gross pay based on net pay and a formula for calculating taxable income when the employer pays the employee's share of taxes on a bonus or other payment.

HI tax: Hospital insurance (also referred to as *Medicare tax*; see page 189)—one of three kinds of insurance that make up FICA tax. The others are *OASDI* and the Additional Medicare tax of 0.9% withholding on wages in excess of $200,000 (see page 189).

High-low substantiation method: Method for reimbursing employee expenses for business-related travel that uses one set of rates for "high-cost" areas and another set of rates for all other areas.

HSA (Health Savings Account): A tax-exempt fund that is allowed for employees with high-deductible health insurance plans.

Imputed income: Income from which no taxes have been withheld (such as a cash bonus, commission or other payment) that is added to an employee's next paycheck so that taxes may be collected on it.

Individual life insurance: May be purchased by the employer or employee individually or for classes of employees (for example, officers, managers and clerical staff). Premiums paid by the employer are considered wages subject to FITW, FICA and FUTA. However, if the company, rather than the employee, designates the beneficiary, the insurance is tax-free to the employee.

IRS: Internal Revenue Service.

Medicare tax: Federal insurance program (also called Medicare hospital insurance, or *HI tax*; see page 188). Employers and employees pay 1.45% on all covered wages. For 2021, employers withhold an Additional Medicare tax of 0.9% on wages in excess of $200,000; however, there is no employer matching contribution.

Monopolistic state: A state in which the employer is not allowed to be self-insured or to carry workers' compensation insurance with a private insurance company.

No-additional-cost services fringe benefit: Free services offered to employees by their employer that are tax-free.

OASDI tax: Old Age, Survivors, and Disability Insurance—one of three kinds of federal insurance that make up FICA tax; the others are *HI tax* and the additional Medicare tax (see page 188). Also see *Social Security tax*.

Overtime pay: Defined under federal law as 1½ times an employee's regular rate of pay, but may be higher based on company policy or union contract.

Percentage method: A more accurate, but more complicated method of determining the amount of federal income tax to withhold from an employee's paycheck. Generally used by firms that use computerized payroll systems.

Premium pay: Under federal law, the additional ½-times-regular-pay added to base pay to yield the hourly overtime rate.

Qualified employee discounts: Tax-free discounts for employees on goods or services sold by the employer.

Release of Levy: Written notice from the IRS that relieves an employer of the responsibility for deducting portions of an employee's pay for back taxes.

Safe harbor rules: IRS-approved shortcuts or exceptions that provide simpler or more lenient methods for complying with regulations.

Section 401(k): An employer's retirement arrangement that may be funded wholly or in part by employees as part of a cash or deferred-salary reduction arrangement.

Section 408(k)(6): A simplified employee pension plan (SEP).

Section 125: An employee sponsored *flexible benefit plan* (see page 187).

SEP: Simplified employee pension plan.

Sick pay: Disability pay provided under a definite plan or system of the employer or a third-party payer (i.e., insurance carrier or state fund).

SIMPLE: Savings Incentive Match Plan for Employees, or the SIMPLE retirement plan, is a less complicated retirement plan for employers with 100 or fewer employees.

Social Security tax: Tax on almost all U.S. employees regardless of age (exceptions apply to federal and certain state and local employees) as required under the Federal Insurance Contributions Act (FICA). Employers and employees pay this tax based on a percentage rate and taxable wage base. For 2021, the employer and the employee pay 6.2% on taxable wages up to $142,800.

Special accounting rule: An option that permits employers to treat noncash fringe benefits provided to employees in the last two months of the year as having been received by employees in the following year. Does not apply to group-term life insurance over $50,000.

SSA: Social Security Administration.

SIT: State income tax—used in entries that record payroll distribution on check stubs.

SSN: Social Security Number.

Supplemental wages: Payments in addition to regular wages such as commissions, bonuses, vacation pay in lieu of vacation, vacation pay given at termination, severance pay, retroactive increases, and overtime pay.

Taxpayer Identification Number (TIN): A Social Security Number (SSN) or Employer Identification Number (EIN).

Third-party sick pay: Payment for a nonjob-related illness, accident or disability from an insurance company or state fund.

TIN: *Taxpayer Identification Number* (see above).

Vehicle cents-per-mile method: Under this method, each personal mile driven by the employee is multiplied by the government-specified business standard mileage rate ($0.56 effective January 1, 2021).

Wage-bracket method: Easier and faster method of determining the amount of federal income tax to withhold from an employee's paycheck. Generally used when paychecks are prepared manually.

Worker's compensation: Payment for a job-related illness, accident or disability that is paid by an insurance company or state fund.

Working condition fringe benefit: A tax-free reimbursement of work-related expenses incurred by employees on behalf of their employer.

BIBLIOGRAPHY

Internal Revenue Service. "Circular E Employer's Tax Guide," Publication 15 (January 2021).

Internal Revenue Service. "Publication 15-A, Employer's Supplemental Tax Guide (Supplement to Circular E, Employer's Tax Guide, Publication 15)."

Internal Revenue Service. "Publication 15-B, Employer's Tax Guide to Fringe Benefits."

Internal Revenue Service, "Publication 15-T, Federal Income Tax Withholding Methods."

APPENDIX

Forms for
Mastering Payroll II

CONTENTS

*2020 form; 2021 form will not be released by IRS until late in 2021.

Form W-4 (Page 1)

Form W-4
(Rev. December 2020)
Department of the Treasury
Internal Revenue Service

Employee's Withholding Certificate

▶ Complete Form W-4 so that your employer can withhold the correct federal income tax from your pay.
▶ Give Form W-4 to your employer.
▶ Your withholding is subject to review by the IRS.

OMB No. 1545-0074

2021

Step 1:
Enter Personal Information

(a) First name and middle initial	Last name	(b) Social security number

Address

City or town, state, and ZIP code

▶ **Does your name match the name on your social security card?** If not, to ensure you get credit for your earnings, contact SSA at 800-772-1213 or go to *www.ssa.gov*.

(c) ☐ Single or **Married filing separately**
☐ **Married filing jointly** or **Qualifying widow(er)**
☐ **Head of household** (Check only if you're unmarried and pay more than half the costs of keeping up a home for yourself and a qualifying individual.)

Complete Steps 2–4 ONLY if they apply to you; otherwise, skip to Step 5. See page 2 for more information on each step, who can claim exemption from withholding, when to use the estimator at *www.irs.gov/W4App*, and privacy.

Step 2:
Multiple Jobs or Spouse Works

Complete this step if you (1) hold more than one job at a time, or (2) are married filing jointly and your spouse also works. The correct amount of withholding depends on income earned from all of these jobs.

Do **only one** of the following.

(a) Use the estimator at *www.irs.gov/W4App* for most accurate withholding for this step (and Steps 3–4); **or**

(b) Use the Multiple Jobs Worksheet on page 3 and enter the result in Step 4(c) below for roughly accurate withholding; **or**

(c) If there are only two jobs total, you may check this box. Do the same on Form W-4 for the other job. This option is accurate for jobs with similar pay; otherwise, more tax than necessary may be withheld . . . . . ▶ ☐

TIP: To be accurate, submit a 2021 Form W-4 for all other jobs. If you (or your spouse) have self-employment income, including as an independent contractor, use the estimator.

Complete Steps 3–4(b) on Form W-4 for only ONE of these jobs. Leave those steps blank for the other jobs. (Your withholding will be most accurate if you complete Steps 3–4(b) on the Form W-4 for the highest paying job.)

Step 3:
Claim Dependents

If your total income will be $200,000 or less ($400,000 or less if married filing jointly):

Multiply the number of qualifying children under age 17 by $2,000 ▶ $ _____

Multiply the number of other dependents by $500 . . . . ▶ $ _____

Add the amounts above and enter the total here . . . . | 3 | $

Step 4 (optional):
Other Adjustments

(a) **Other income (not from jobs).** If you want tax withheld for other income you expect this year that won't have withholding, enter the amount of other income here. This may include interest, dividends, and retirement income . . . . | 4(a) | $

(b) **Deductions.** If you expect to claim deductions other than the standard deduction and want to reduce your withholding, use the Deductions Worksheet on page 3 and enter the result here . . . . | 4(b) | $

(c) **Extra withholding.** Enter any additional tax you want withheld each **pay period** . | 4(c) | $

Step 5:
Sign Here

Under penalties of perjury, I declare that this certificate, to the best of my knowledge and belief, is true, correct, and complete.

▶ _____
Employee's signature (This form is not valid unless you sign it.)

▶ **Date**

Employers Only

Employer's name and address	First date of employment	Employer identification number (EIN)

For Privacy Act and Paperwork Reduction Act Notice, see page 3.

Cat. No. 10220Q

Form **W-4** (2021)

Form W-4 (Page 2)

General Instructions

Future Developments

For the latest information about developments related to Form W-4, such as legislation enacted after it was published, go to *www.irs.gov/FormW4*.

Purpose of Form

Complete Form W-4 so that your employer can withhold the correct federal income tax from your pay. If too little is withheld, you will generally owe tax when you file your tax return and may owe a penalty. If too much is withheld, you will generally be due a refund. Complete a new Form W-4 when changes to your personal or financial situation would change the entries on the form. For more information on withholding and when you must furnish a new Form W-4, see Pub. 505, Tax Withholding and Estimated Tax.

Exemption from withholding. You may claim exemption from withholding for 2021 if you meet both of the following conditions: you had no federal income tax liability in 2020 **and** you expect to have no federal income tax liability in 2021. You had no federal income tax liability in 2020 if (1) your total tax on line 24 on your 2020 Form 1040 or 1040-SR is zero (or less than the sum of lines 27, 28, 29, and 30), or (2) you were not required to file a return because your income was below the filing threshold for your correct filing status. If you claim exemption, you will have no income tax withheld from your paycheck and may owe taxes and penalties when you file your 2021 tax return. To claim exemption from withholding, certify that you meet both of the conditions above by writing "Exempt" on Form W-4 in the space below Step 4(c). Then, complete Steps 1(a), 1(b), and 5. Do not complete any other steps. You will need to submit a new Form W-4 by February 15, 2022.

Your privacy. If you prefer to limit information provided in Steps 2 through 4, use the online estimator, which will also increase accuracy.

As an alternative to the estimator: if you have concerns with Step 2(c), you may choose Step 2(b); if you have concerns with Step 4(a), you may enter an additional amount you want withheld per pay period in Step 4(c). If this is the only job in your household, you may instead check the box in Step 2(c), which will increase your withholding and significantly reduce your paycheck (often by thousands of dollars over the year).

When to use the estimator. Consider using the estimator at *www.irs.gov/W4App* if you:

1. Expect to work only part of the year;

2. Have dividend or capital gain income, or are subject to additional taxes, such as Additional Medicare Tax;

3. Have self-employment income (see below); or

4. Prefer the most accurate withholding for multiple job situations.

Self-employment. Generally, you will owe both income and self-employment taxes on any self-employment income you receive separate from the wages you receive as an employee. If you want to pay these taxes through withholding from your wages, use the estimator at *www.irs.gov/W4App* to figure the amount to have withheld.

Nonresident alien. If you're a nonresident alien, see Notice 1392, Supplemental Form W-4 Instructions for Nonresident Aliens, before completing this form.

Specific Instructions

Step 1(c). Check your anticipated filing status. This will determine the standard deduction and tax rates used to compute your withholding.

Step 2. Use this step if you (1) have more than one job at the same time, or (2) are married filing jointly and you and your spouse both work.

Option **(a)** most accurately calculates the additional tax you need to have withheld, while option **(b)** does so with a little less accuracy.

If you (and your spouse) have a total of only two jobs, you may instead check the box in option **(c)**. The box must also be checked on the Form W-4 for the other job. If the box is checked, the standard deduction and tax brackets will be cut in half for each job to calculate withholding. This option is roughly accurate for jobs with similar pay; otherwise, more tax than necessary may be withheld, and this extra amount will be larger the greater the difference in pay is between the two jobs.

 Multiple jobs. *Complete Steps 3 through 4(b) on only one Form W-4. Withholding will be most accurate if you do this on the Form W-4 for the highest paying job.*

Step 3. This step provides instructions for determining the amount of the child tax credit and the credit for other dependents that you may be able to claim when you file your tax return. To qualify for the child tax credit, the child must be under age 17 as of December 31, must be your dependent who generally lives with you for more than half the year, and must have the required social security number. You may be able to claim a credit for other dependents for whom a child tax credit can't be claimed, such as an older child or a qualifying relative. For additional eligibility requirements for these credits, see Pub. 972, Child Tax Credit and Credit for Other Dependents. You can also include **other tax credits** in this step, such as education tax credits and the foreign tax credit. To do so, add an estimate of the amount for the year to your credits for dependents and enter the total amount in Step 3. Including these credits will increase your paycheck and reduce the amount of any refund you may receive when you file your tax return.

Step 4 (optional).

Step 4(a). Enter in this step the total of your other estimated income for the year, if any. You shouldn't include income from any jobs or self-employment. If you complete Step 4(a), you likely won't have to make estimated tax payments for that income. If you prefer to pay estimated tax rather than having tax on other income withheld from your paycheck, see Form 1040-ES, Estimated Tax for Individuals.

Step 4(b). Enter in this step the amount from the Deductions Worksheet, line 5, if you expect to claim deductions other than the basic standard deduction on your 2021 tax return and want to reduce your withholding to account for these deductions. This includes both itemized deductions and other deductions such as for student loan interest and IRAs.

Step 4(c). Enter in this step any additional tax you want withheld from your pay **each pay period**, including any amounts from the Multiple Jobs Worksheet, line 4. Entering an amount here will reduce your paycheck and will either increase your refund or reduce any amount of tax that you owe.

Appendix

Form W-4 (Page 3)

Form W-4 (2021)   Page **3**

Step 2(b)—Multiple Jobs Worksheet *(Keep for your records.)*

If you choose the option in Step 2(b) on Form W-4, complete this worksheet (which calculates the total extra tax for all jobs) on **only ONE** Form W-4. Withholding will be most accurate if you complete the worksheet and enter the result on the Form W-4 for the highest paying job.

Note: If more than one job has annual wages of more than $120,000 or there are more than three jobs, see Pub. 505 for additional tables; or, you can use the online withholding estimator at *www.irs.gov/W4App.*

1   **Two jobs.** If you have two jobs or you're married filing jointly and you and your spouse each have one job, find the amount from the appropriate table on page 4. Using the "Higher Paying Job" row and the "Lower Paying Job" column, find the value at the intersection of the two household salaries and enter that value on line 1. Then, **skip** to line 3 . . . .   **1** $ _____

2   **Three jobs.** If you and/or your spouse have three jobs at the same time, complete lines 2a, 2b, and 2c below. Otherwise, skip to line 3.

   a   Find the amount from the appropriate table on page 4 using the annual wages from the highest paying job in the "Higher Paying Job" row and the annual wages for your next highest paying job in the "Lower Paying Job" column. Find the value at the intersection of the two household salaries and enter that value on line 2a . . . .   **2a** $ _____

   b   Add the annual wages of the two highest paying jobs from line 2a together and use the total as the wages in the "Higher Paying Job" row and use the annual wages for your third job in the "Lower Paying Job" column to find the amount from the appropriate table on page 4 and enter this amount on line 2b . . . .   **2b** $ _____

   c   Add the amounts from lines 2a and 2b and enter the result on line 2c . . . .   **2c** $ _____

3   Enter the number of pay periods per year for the highest paying job. For example, if that job pays weekly, enter 52; if it pays every other week, enter 26; if it pays monthly, enter 12, etc. . . . . .   **3** _____

4   **Divide** the annual amount on line 1 or line 2c by the number of pay periods on line 3. Enter this amount here and in **Step 4(c)** of Form W-4 for the highest paying job (along with any other additional amount you want withheld) . . . .   **4** $ _____

Step 4(b)—Deductions Worksheet *(Keep for your records.)*

1   Enter an estimate of your 2021 itemized deductions (from Schedule A (Form 1040)). Such deductions may include qualifying home mortgage interest, charitable contributions, state and local taxes (up to $10,000), and medical expenses in excess of 7.5% of your income . . . .   **1** $ _____

2   Enter: { • $25,100 if you're married filing jointly or qualifying widow(er)
              • $18,800 if you're head of household
              • $12,550 if you're single or married filing separately }   . . . .   **2** $ _____

3   If line 1 is greater than line 2, subtract line 2 from line 1 and enter the result here. If line 2 is greater than line 1, enter "-0-" . . . .   **3** $ _____

4   Enter an estimate of your student loan interest, deductible IRA contributions, and certain other adjustments (from Part II of Schedule 1 (Form 1040)). See Pub. 505 for more information . . . .   **4** $ _____

5   **Add** lines 3 and 4. Enter the result here and in **Step 4(b)** of Form W-4 . . . .   **5** $ _____

Privacy Act and Paperwork Reduction Act Notice. We ask for the information on this form to carry out the Internal Revenue laws of the United States. Internal Revenue Code sections 3402(f)(2) and 6109 and their regulations require you to provide this information; your employer uses it to determine your federal income tax withholding. Failure to provide a properly completed form will result in your being treated as a single person with no other entries on the form; providing fraudulent information may subject you to penalties. Routine uses of this information include giving it to the Department of Justice for civil and criminal litigation; to cities, states, the District of Columbia, and U.S. commonwealths and possessions for use in administering their tax laws; and to the Department of Health and Human Services for use in the National Directory of New Hires. We may also disclose this information to other countries under a tax treaty, to federal and state agencies to enforce federal nontax criminal laws, or to federal law enforcement and intelligence agencies to combat terrorism.

You are not required to provide the information requested on a form that is subject to the Paperwork Reduction Act unless the form displays a valid OMB control number. Books or records relating to a form or its instructions must be retained as long as their contents may become material in the administration of any Internal Revenue law. Generally, tax returns and return information are confidential, as required by Code section 6103.

The average time and expenses required to complete and file this form will vary depending on individual circumstances. For estimated averages, see the instructions for your income tax return.

If you have suggestions for making this form simpler, we would be happy to hear from you. See the instructions for your income tax return.

Form W-4 (Page 4)

Form W-4 (2021)   Page **4**

Married Filing Jointly or Qualifying Widow(er)

Higher Paying Job Annual Taxable Wage & Salary	Lower Paying Job Annual Taxable Wage & Salary											
	$0 - 9,999	$10,000 - 19,999	$20,000 - 29,999	$30,000 - 39,999	$40,000 - 49,999	$50,000 - 59,999	$60,000 - 69,999	$70,000 - 79,999	$80,000 - 89,999	$90,000 - 99,999	$100,000 - 109,999	$110,000 - 120,000
$0 - 9,999	$0	$190	$850	$890	$1,020	$1,020	$1,020	$1,020	$1,020	$1,100	$1,870	$1,870
$10,000 - 19,999	190	1,190	1,890	2,090	2,220	2,220	2,220	2,220	2,300	3,300	4,070	4,070
$20,000 - 29,999	850	1,890	2,750	2,950	3,080	3,080	3,080	3,160	4,160	5,160	5,930	5,930
$30,000 - 39,999	890	2,090	2,950	3,150	3,280	3,280	3,360	4,360	5,360	6,360	7,130	7,130
$40,000 - 49,999	1,020	2,220	3,080	3,280	3,410	3,490	4,490	5,490	6,490	7,490	8,260	8,260
$50,000 - 59,999	1,020	2,220	3,080	3,280	3,490	4,490	5,490	6,490	7,490	8,490	9,260	9,260
$60,000 - 69,999	1,020	2,220	3,080	3,360	4,490	5,490	6,490	7,490	8,490	9,490	10,260	10,260
$70,000 - 79,999	1,020	2,220	3,160	4,360	5,490	6,490	7,490	8,490	9,490	10,490	11,260	11,260
$80,000 - 99,999	1,020	3,150	5,010	6,210	7,340	8,340	9,340	10,340	11,340	12,340	13,260	13,460
$100,000 - 149,999	1,870	4,070	5,930	7,130	8,260	9,320	10,520	11,720	12,920	14,120	15,090	15,290
$150,000 - 239,999	2,040	4,440	6,500	7,900	9,230	10,430	11,630	12,830	14,030	15,230	16,190	16,400
$240,000 - 259,999	2,040	4,440	6,500	7,900	9,230	10,430	11,630	12,830	14,030	15,270	17,040	18,040
$260,000 - 279,999	2,040	4,440	6,500	7,900	9,230	10,430	11,630	12,870	14,870	16,870	18,640	19,640
$280,000 - 299,999	2,040	4,440	6,500	7,900	9,230	10,470	12,470	14,470	16,470	18,470	20,240	21,240
$300,000 - 319,999	2,040	4,440	6,500	7,940	10,070	12,070	14,070	16,070	18,070	20,070	21,840	22,840
$320,000 - 364,999	2,720	5,920	8,780	10,980	13,110	15,110	17,110	19,110	21,190	23,490	25,560	26,860
$365,000 - 524,999	2,970	6,470	9,630	12,130	14,560	16,860	19,160	21,460	23,760	26,060	28,130	29,430
$525,000 and over	3,140	6,840	10,200	12,900	15,530	18,030	20,530	23,030	25,530	28,030	30,300	31,800

Single or Married Filing Separately

Higher Paying Job Annual Taxable Wage & Salary	Lower Paying Job Annual Taxable Wage & Salary											
	$0 - 9,999	$10,000 - 19,999	$20,000 - 29,999	$30,000 - 39,999	$40,000 - 49,999	$50,000 - 59,999	$60,000 - 69,999	$70,000 - 79,999	$80,000 - 89,999	$90,000 - 99,999	$100,000 - 109,999	$110,000 - 120,000
$0 - 9,999	$440	$940	$1,020	$1,020	$1,410	$1,870	$1,870	$1,870	$1,870	$2,030	$2,040	$2,040
$10,000 - 19,999	940	1,540	1,620	2,020	3,020	3,470	3,470	3,470	3,640	3,840	3,840	3,840
$20,000 - 29,999	1,020	1,620	2,100	3,100	4,100	4,550	4,550	4,720	4,920	5,120	5,120	5,120
$30,000 - 39,999	1,020	2,020	3,100	4,100	5,100	5,550	5,720	5,920	6,120	6,320	6,320	6,320
$40,000 - 59,999	1,870	3,470	4,550	5,550	6,690	7,340	7,540	7,740	7,940	8,140	8,150	8,150
$60,000 - 79,999	1,870	3,470	4,690	5,890	7,090	7,740	7,940	8,140	8,340	8,540	9,190	9,990
$80,000 - 99,999	2,000	3,810	5,090	6,290	7,490	8,140	8,340	8,540	9,390	10,390	11,190	11,990
$100,000 - 124,999	2,040	3,840	5,120	6,320	7,520	8,360	9,360	10,360	11,360	12,360	13,410	14,510
$125,000 - 149,999	2,040	3,840	5,120	6,910	8,910	10,360	11,360	12,450	13,750	15,050	16,160	17,260
$150,000 - 174,999	2,220	4,830	6,910	8,910	10,910	12,600	13,900	15,200	16,500	17,800	18,910	20,010
$175,000 - 199,999	2,720	5,320	7,490	9,790	12,090	13,850	15,150	16,450	17,750	19,050	20,150	21,250
$200,000 - 249,999	2,970	5,880	8,260	10,560	12,860	14,620	15,920	17,220	18,520	19,820	20,930	22,030
$250,000 - 399,999	2,970	5,880	8,260	10,560	12,860	14,620	15,920	17,220	18,520	19,820	20,930	22,030
$400,000 - 449,999	2,970	5,880	8,260	10,560	12,860	14,620	15,920	17,220	18,520	19,910	21,220	22,520
$450,000 and over	3,140	6,250	8,830	11,330	13,830	15,790	17,290	18,790	20,290	21,790	23,100	24,400

Head of Household

Higher Paying Job Annual Taxable Wage & Salary	Lower Paying Job Annual Taxable Wage & Salary											
	$0 - 9,999	$10,000 - 19,999	$20,000 - 29,999	$30,000 - 39,999	$40,000 - 49,999	$50,000 - 59,999	$60,000 - 69,999	$70,000 - 79,999	$80,000 - 89,999	$90,000 - 99,999	$100,000 - 109,999	$110,000 - 120,000
$0 - 9,999	$0	$820	$930	$1,020	$1,020	$1,020	$1,420	$1,870	$1,870	$1,910	$2,040	$2,040
$10,000 - 19,999	820	1,900	2,130	2,220	2,220	2,620	3,620	4,070	4,110	4,310	4,440	4,440
$20,000 - 29,999	930	2,130	2,360	2,450	2,850	3,850	4,850	5,340	5,540	5,740	5,870	5,870
$30,000 - 39,999	1,020	2,220	2,450	2,940	3,940	4,940	5,980	6,630	6,830	7,030	7,160	7,160
$40,000 - 59,999	1,020	2,470	3,700	4,790	5,800	7,000	8,200	8,850	9,050	9,250	9,380	9,380
$60,000 - 79,999	1,870	4,070	5,310	6,600	7,800	9,000	10,200	10,850	11,050	11,250	11,520	12,320
$80,000 - 99,999	1,880	4,280	5,710	7,000	8,200	9,400	10,600	11,250	11,590	12,590	13,520	14,320
$100,000 - 124,999	2,040	4,440	5,870	7,160	8,360	9,560	11,240	12,690	13,690	14,690	15,670	16,770
$125,000 - 149,999	2,040	4,440	5,870	7,240	9,240	11,240	13,240	14,690	15,890	17,190	18,420	19,520
$150,000 - 174,999	2,040	4,920	7,150	9,240	11,240	13,290	15,590	17,340	18,640	19,940	21,170	22,270
$175,000 - 199,999	2,720	5,920	8,150	10,440	12,740	15,040	17,340	19,090	20,390	21,690	22,920	24,020
$200,000 - 249,999	2,970	6,470	9,000	11,390	13,690	15,990	18,290	20,040	21,340	22,640	23,880	24,980
$250,000 - 349,999	2,970	6,470	9,000	11,390	13,690	15,990	18,290	20,040	21,340	22,640	23,880	24,980
$350,000 - 449,999	2,970	6,470	9,000	11,390	13,690	15,990	18,290	20,040	21,340	22,640	23,900	25,200
$450,000 and over	3,140	6,840	9,570	12,160	14,660	17,160	19,660	21,610	23,110	24,610	26,050	27,350

Form 940 (Page 1)

Form 940 for 2020: **Employer's Annual Federal Unemployment (FUTA) Tax Return**

Department of the Treasury — Internal Revenue Service

850113

OMB No. 1545-0028

Employer identification number (EIN) ☐☐ – ☐☐☐☐☐☐☐

Name *(not your trade name)*

Trade name *(if any)*

Address

Number   Street   Suite or room number

City   State   ZIP code

Foreign country name   Foreign province/county   Foreign postal code

Type of Return
(Check all that apply.)

☐ **a.** Amended

☐ **b.** Successor employer

☐ **c.** No payments to employees in 2020

☐ **d.** Final: Business closed or stopped paying wages

Go to *www.irs.gov/Form940* for instructions and the latest information.

Read the separate instructions before you complete this form. Please type or print within the boxes.

Part 1:   Tell us about your return. If any line does NOT apply, leave it blank. See instructions before completing Part 1.

1a If you had to pay state unemployment tax in one state only, enter the state abbreviation . **1a** ☐☐

1b If you had to pay state unemployment tax in more than one state, you are a multi-state employer . . . . **1b** ☐ Check here. Complete Schedule A (Form 940).

2 If you paid wages in a state that is subject to CREDIT REDUCTION . . . . **2** ☐ Check here. Complete Schedule A (Form 940).

Part 2:   Determine your FUTA tax before adjustments. If any line does NOT apply, leave it blank.

3 Total payments to all employees . . . . **3** ☐ .

4 Payments exempt from FUTA tax . . . . . **4** ☐ .

Check all that apply: **4a** ☐ Fringe benefits   **4c** ☐ Retirement/Pension   **4e** ☐ Other
                                4b ☐ Group-term life insurance   **4d** ☐ Dependent care

5 Total of payments made to each employee in excess of $7,000 . . . . **5** ☐ .

6 Subtotal (line 4 + line 5 = line 6) . . . . **6** ☐ .

7 Total taxable FUTA wages (line 3 – line 6 = line 7). See instructions . . . . **7** ☐ .

8 FUTA tax before adjustments (line 7 x 0.006 = line 8) . . . . **8** ☐ .

Part 3:   Determine your adjustments. If any line does NOT apply, leave it blank.

9 If ALL of the taxable FUTA wages you paid were excluded from state unemployment tax, multiply line 7 by 0.054 (line 7 × 0.054 = line 9). Go to line 12 . . . . **9** ☐ .

10 If SOME of the taxable FUTA wages you paid were excluded from state unemployment tax, OR you paid ANY state unemployment tax late (after the due date for filing Form 940), complete the worksheet in the instructions. Enter the amount from line 7 of the worksheet . . **10** ☐ .

11 If credit reduction applies, enter the total from Schedule A (Form 940) . . . . . . **11** ☐ .

Part 4:   Determine your FUTA tax and balance due or overpayment. If any line does NOT apply, leave it blank.

12 Total FUTA tax after adjustments (lines 8 + 9 + 10 + 11 = line 12) . . . . **12** ☐ .

13 FUTA tax deposited for the year, including any overpayment applied from a prior year **13** ☐ .

14 Balance due. If line 12 is more than line 13, enter the excess on line 14.
 • If line 14 is more than $500, you must deposit your tax.
 • If line 14 is $500 or less, you may pay with this return. See instructions . . . . . **14** ☐ .

15 Overpayment. If line 13 is more than line 12, enter the excess on line 15 and check a box below **15** ☐ .

▶ You **MUST** complete both pages of this form and **SIGN** it.   Check one: ☐ Apply to next return. ☐ Send a refund.

Next ▶

For Privacy Act and Paperwork Reduction Act Notice, see the back of the Payment Voucher.   Cat. No. 11234O   Form **940** (2020)

Form 940 (Page 2)

850212

Name *(not your trade name)*	Employer identification number (EIN)

Part 5: Report your FUTA tax liability by quarter only if line 12 is more than $500. If not, go to Part 6.

16   Report the amount of your FUTA tax liability for each quarter; do NOT enter the amount you deposited. If you had no liability for a quarter, leave the line blank.

16a   **1st quarter** (January 1 – March 31) . . . .   **16a**   [.   ]

16b   **2nd quarter** (April 1 – June 30) . . . .   **16b**   [.   ]

16c   **3rd quarter** (July 1 – September 30) . . . .   **16c**   [.   ]

16d   **4th quarter** (October 1 – December 31) . . . . . .   **16d**   [.   ]

17   **Total tax liability for the year** (lines 16a + 16b + 16c + 16d = line 17)   **17**   [.   ]   **Total must equal line 12.**

Part 6:   May we speak with your third-party designee?

Do you want to allow an employee, a paid tax preparer, or another person to discuss this return with the IRS? See the instructions for details.

☐ **Yes.**   Designee's name and phone number   [   ]   [   ]

       Select a 5-digit personal identification number (PIN) to use when talking to the IRS.   [ ] [ ] [ ] [ ] [ ]

☐ **No.**

Part 7:   Sign here. You MUST complete both pages of this form and SIGN it.

Under penalties of perjury, I declare that I have examined this return, including accompanying schedules and statements, and to the best of my knowledge and belief, it is true, correct, and complete, and that no part of any payment made to a state unemployment fund claimed as a credit was, or is to be, deducted from the payments made to employees. Declaration of preparer (other than taxpayer) is based on all information of which preparer has any knowledge.

✗ **Sign your name here**   [   ]   Print your name here   [   ]

                                Print your title here   [   ]

Date   [/   /   ]   Best daytime phone   [   ]

Paid Preparer Use Only   Check if you are self-employed ☐

Preparer's name	[ ]	PTIN [ ]
Preparer's signature	[ ]	Date [/ /]
Firm's name (or yours if self-employed)	[ ]	EIN [ ]
Address	[ ]	Phone [ ]
City	[ ] State [ ]	ZIP code [ ]

Form **940** (2020)

Form 940 Instructions (Page 1)

20**20**

Department of the Treasury
Internal Revenue Service

Instructions for Form 940

Employer's Annual Federal Unemployment (FUTA) Tax Return

Section references are to the Internal Revenue Code unless otherwise noted.

Future Developments

For the latest information about developments related to Form 940 and its instructions, such as legislation enacted after they were published, go to *IRS.gov/Form940*.

What's New

Credit reduction state. A state that hasn't repaid money it borrowed from the federal government to pay unemployment benefits is a "credit reduction state." The Department of Labor determines these states. If an employer pays wages that are subject to the unemployment tax laws of a credit reduction state, that employer must pay additional federal unemployment tax when filing its Form 940.

For 2020, the U.S. Virgin Islands (USVI) is the only credit reduction state. If you paid any wages that are subject to the unemployment compensation laws of the USVI, your credit against federal unemployment tax will be reduced based on the credit reduction rate for the USVI. Use Schedule A (Form 940) to figure the credit reduction. For more information, see the Schedule A (Form 940) instructions or visit IRS.gov.

Reminders

Moving expense and bicycle commuting reimbursements are subject to FUTA tax. The Tax Cuts and Jobs Act (P.L. 115-97) suspends the exclusion for qualified moving expense reimbursements from your employee's income under section 132 and the deduction from the employee's income under section 217, as well as the exclusion for qualified bicycle commuting reimbursements from your employee's income under section 132, beginning after 2017 and before 2026. Therefore, moving expense and bicycle commuting reimbursements aren't exempt from FUTA tax during this period. Don't include moving expense or bicycle commuting reimbursements on Form 940, line 4. For more information about fringe benefits, see Pub. 15-B.

Certification program for professional employer organizations (PEOs). The Stephen Beck, Jr., Achieving a Better Life Experience Act of 2014 required the IRS to establish a voluntary certification program for PEOs. PEOs handle various payroll administration and tax reporting responsibilities for their business clients and are typically paid a fee based on payroll costs. To become and remain certified under the certification program, certified professional employer organizations (CPEOs) must meet various requirements described in sections 3511 and 7705 and related published guidance. Certification as a CPEO may affect the employment tax liabilities of both the CPEO and its customers. A CPEO is generally treated for employment tax purposes as the employer of any individual who performs services for a customer of the CPEO and is covered by a contract described in section 7705(e)(2) between the CPEO and the customer (CPEO contract), but only for wages and other compensation paid to the individual by the CPEO. To become a CPEO, the organization must apply through the IRS Online Registration System. For more information or to apply to become a CPEO, visit the IRS website at *IRS.gov/CPEO*.

For wages paid to a work site employee, a CPEO is eligible for the credit for state unemployment tax paid to a state unemployment fund, whether the CPEO or a customer of the CPEO made the contribution. In addition, a CPEO is allowed the additional credit if the CPEO is permitted, under state law, to collect and remit contributions to the state unemployment fund with respect to a work site employee. For more information on the credit, see *Credit for State Unemployment Tax Paid to a State Unemployment Fund*, later.

CPEOs must generally file Form 940 and Schedule R (Form 940), Allocation Schedule for Aggregate Form 940 Filers, electronically. For more information about a CPEO's requirement to file electronically, see Rev. Proc. 2017-14, 2017-3 I.R.B. 426, available at *IRS.gov/irb/ 2017-03_IRB#RP-2017-14*.

Outsourcing payroll duties. Generally, as an employer, you're responsible to ensure that tax returns are filed and deposits and payments are made, even if you contract with a third party to perform these acts. You remain responsible if the third party fails to perform any required action. Before you choose to outsource any of your payroll and related tax duties (that is, withholding, reporting, and paying over social security, Medicare, FUTA, and income taxes) to a third-party payer, such as a payroll service provider or reporting agent, go to *IRS.gov/ OutsourcingPayrollDuties* for helpful information on this topic. If a CPEO pays wages and other compensation to an individual performing services for you, and the services are covered by a contract described in section 7705(e)(2) between you and the CPEO (CPEO contract), then the CPEO is generally treated for employment tax purposes as the employer, but only for wages and other compensation paid to the individual by the CPEO. However, with respect to certain employees covered by a CPEO contract, you may also be treated as an employer of the employees and, consequently, may also be liable for federal employment taxes imposed on wages and other compensation paid by the CPEO to such employees. For more information on the different types of third-party payer arrangements, see section 16 in Pub. 15.

Aggregate Form 940 filers. Approved section 3504 agents and CPEOs must complete Schedule R (Form

Sep 23, 2020

Cat. No. 13660I

Form 940 Instructions (Page 2)

940) when filing an aggregate Form 940. Aggregate Forms 940 are filed by agents of home care service recipients approved by the IRS under section 3504. To request approval to act as an agent for an employer, the agent files Form 2678 with the IRS unless you're a state or local government agency acting as an agent under the special procedures provided in Rev. Proc. 2013-39, 2013-52 I.R.B. 830, available at *IRS.gov/irb/ 2013-52_IRB#RP-2013-39*.

Aggregate Forms 940 are also filed by CPEOs approved by the IRS under section 7705. CPEOs file Form 8973, Certified Professional Employer Organization/ Customer Reporting Agreement, to notify the IRS that they started or ended a service contract with a customer. CPEOs must generally file Form 940 and Schedule R electronically. For more information about a CPEO's requirement to file electronically, see Rev. Proc. 2017-14, 2017-3 I.R.B. 426, available at *IRS.gov/irb/ 2017-03_IRB#RP-2017-14*.

If you change your business name, business address, or responsible party. Notify the IRS immediately if you change your business name, business address, or responsible party.
• Write to the IRS office where you file your returns (using the *Without a payment* address under *Where Do You File*, later) to notify the IRS of any business name change. See Pub. 1635 to see if you need to apply for a new employer identification number (EIN).
• Complete and mail Form 8822-B to notify the IRS of a business address or responsible party change. Don't mail Form 8822-B with your Form 940. For a definition of "responsible party," see the Instructions for Form SS-4.

Federal tax deposits must be made by electronic funds transfer (EFT). You must use EFT to make all federal tax deposits. Generally, an EFT is made using the Electronic Federal Tax Payment System (EFTPS). If you don't want to use EFTPS, you can arrange for your tax professional, financial institution, payroll service, or other trusted third party to make electronic deposits on your behalf. Also, you may arrange for your financial institution to initiate a same-day wire payment on your behalf. EFTPS is a free service provided by the Department of the Treasury. Services provided by your tax professional, financial institution, payroll service, or other third party may have a fee.

For more information on making federal tax deposits, see section 11 of Pub. 15. To get more information about EFTPS or to enroll in EFTPS, go to *EFTPS.gov*, or call 800-555-4477, 800-733-4829 (TDD), or 800-244-4829 (Spanish). Additional information about EFTPS is also available in Pub. 966.

Electronic filing and payment. Businesses can enjoy the benefits of filing and paying their federal taxes electronically. Whether you rely on a tax professional or handle your own taxes, the IRS offers you convenient programs to make filing and paying easier. Spend less time worrying about taxes and more time running your business. Use *e-file* and EFTPS to your benefit.
• For *e-file*, go to *IRS.gov/EmploymentEfile* for additional information. A fee may be charged to file electronically.

• For EFTPS, go to *EFTPS.gov*, or call one of the numbers provided under *Federal tax deposits must be made by electronic funds transfer (EFT)*, earlier.

Electronic funds withdrawal (EFW). If you file Form 940 electronically, you can e-file and use EFW to pay the balance due in a single step using tax preparation software or through a tax professional. However, don't use EFW to make federal tax deposits. For more information on paying your taxes using EFW, go to *IRS.gov/EFW*.

Credit or debit card payments. You may pay your FUTA tax shown on line 14 using a credit or debit card. Your payment will be processed by a payment processor who will charge a processing fee. Don't use a credit or debit card to pay taxes that are required to be deposited (see *When Must You Deposit Your FUTA Tax*, later). For more information on paying your taxes with a credit or debit card, go to *IRS.gov/PayByCard*.

Online payment agreement. You may be eligible to apply for an installment agreement online if you can't pay the full amount of tax you owe when you file your return. For more information, see *What if you can't pay in full*, later.

Disregarded entities and qualified subchapter S subsidiaries (QSubs). Business entities that are disregarded as separate from their owner, including QSubs, are required to withhold and pay employment taxes and file employment tax returns using the name and EIN of the disregarded entity. For more information, see *Disregarded entities*, later.

State unemployment information. When you registered as an employer with your state, the state assigned you a state reporting number. If you don't have a state unemployment account and state experience tax rate, or if you have questions about your state account, you must contact your state unemployment agency. For a list of state unemployment agencies, visit the U.S. Department of Labor's website at *oui.doleta.gov/ unemploy/agencies.asp*.

Photographs of missing children. The IRS is a proud partner with the *National Center for Missing & Exploited Children® (NCMEC)*. Photographs of missing children selected by the Center may appear in instructions on pages that would otherwise be blank. You can help bring these children home by looking at the photographs and calling 1-800-THE-LOST (1-800-843-5678) if you recognize a child.

How Can You Get More Help?

If you want more information about this form, see Pub. 15, visit our website at IRS.gov, or call the Business and Specialty Tax Line toll free at 800-829-4933 or 800-829-4059 (TDD/TTY for persons who are deaf, hard of hearing, or have a speech disability), Monday–Friday from 7:00 a.m. to 7:00 p.m. local time (Alaska and Hawaii follow Pacific time).

For a list of related employment tax topics, go to *IRS.gov/EmploymentTaxes*. You can order forms, instructions, and publications at *IRS.gov/OrderForms*.

Form 940 Instructions (Page 3)

General Instructions

What's the Purpose of Form 940?

These instructions give you some background information about Form 940. They tell you who must file the form, how to fill it out line by line, and when and where to file it.

Use Form 940 to report your annual Federal Unemployment Tax Act (FUTA) tax. Together with state unemployment tax systems, the FUTA tax provides funds for paying unemployment compensation to workers who have lost their jobs. Most employers pay both a federal and a state unemployment tax. Only employers pay FUTA tax. Don't collect or deduct FUTA tax from your employees' wages.

The FUTA tax applies to the first $7,000 you pay to each employee during a calendar year after subtracting any payments exempt from FUTA tax.

Who Must File Form 940?

Except as noted below, if you answer "Yes" to either one of these questions, you must file Form 940.
• Did you pay wages of $1,500 or more to employees in any calendar quarter during 2019 or 2020?
• Did you have one or more employees for at least some part of a day in any 20 or more different weeks in 2019 or 20 or more different weeks in 2020? Count all full-time, part-time, and temporary employees. However, if your business is a partnership, don't count its partners.

If your business was sold or transferred during the year, each employer who answered "Yes" to at least one question above must file Form 940. However, don't include any wages paid by the predecessor employer on your Form 940 unless you're a successor employer. For details, see *Successor employer* under *Type of Return*, later.

If you're not liable for FUTA tax for 2020 because you made no payments to employees in 2020, check box c in the top right corner of the form. Then go to Part 7, sign the form, and file it with the IRS.

If you won't be liable for filing Form 940 in the future because your business has closed or because you stopped paying wages, check box d in the top right corner of the form. For more information, see *Final: Business closed or stopped paying wages* under *Type of Return*, later.

For Employers of Household Employees . . .

If you're a household employer, you must pay FUTA tax on wages that you paid to your household employees only if you paid cash wages of $1,000 or more in any calendar quarter in 2019 or 2020.

A household employee performs household work in a:
• Private home,
• Local college club, or
• Local chapter of a college fraternity or sorority.

Generally, employers of household employees must file Schedule H (Form 1040) instead of Form 940.

However, if you have other employees in addition to household employees, you can choose to include the FUTA taxes for your household employees on Form 940 instead of filing Schedule H (Form 1040). If you choose to include household employees on your Form 940, you must also file Form 941, Employer's QUARTERLY Federal Tax Return; Form 943, Employer's Annual Federal Tax Return for Agricultural Employees; or Form 944, Employer's ANNUAL Federal Tax Return, to report social security, Medicare, and any withheld federal income taxes for your household employees. See Pub. 926 for more information.

For Agricultural Employers . . .

File Form 940 if you answer "Yes" to either of these questions.
• Did you pay cash wages of $20,000 or more to farmworkers during any calendar quarter in 2019 or 2020?
• Did you employ 10 or more farmworkers during some part of the day (whether or not at the same time) during any 20 or more different weeks in 2019 or 20 or more different weeks in 2020?

Count wages you paid to aliens who were admitted to the United States on a temporary basis to perform farmwork (workers with H-2A visas). However, wages paid to "H-2A visa workers" aren't subject to FUTA tax. See Pub. 51 for more information.

For Indian Tribal Governments . . .

Services rendered by employees of a federally recognized Indian tribal government employer (including any subdivision, subsidiary, or business enterprise wholly owned by the tribe) are exempt from FUTA tax and no Form 940 is required. However, the tribe must have participated in the state unemployment system for the full year and be in compliance with applicable state unemployment law. For more information, see section 3309(d).

For Tax-Exempt Organizations . . .

Religious, educational, scientific, charitable, and other organizations described in section 501(c)(3) and exempt from tax under section 501(a) aren't subject to FUTA tax and don't have to file Form 940.

For State or Local Government Employers . . .

Services rendered by employees of a state, or a political subdivision or instrumentality of the state, are exempt from FUTA tax and no Form 940 is required.

When Must You File Form 940?

The due date for filing Form 940 for 2020 is February 1, 2021. However, if you deposited all your FUTA tax when it was due, you may file Form 940 by February 10, 2021.

If we receive Form 940 after the due date, we will treat Form 940 as filed on time if the envelope containing Form 940 is properly addressed, contains sufficient postage, and is postmarked by the U.S. Postal Service on or before the due date, or sent by an IRS-designated private delivery service (PDS) on or before the due date. However, if you don't follow these guidelines, we will generally consider Form 940 filed when it is actually received. For more information about PDSs, see *Where Do You File*, later.

Instructions for Form 940 (2020) -3-

Form 940 Instructions (Page 4)

If any due date for filing falls on a Saturday, Sunday, or legal holiday, you may file your return on the next business day.

Where Do You File?

You're encouraged to file Form 940 electronically. Go to *IRS.gov/EmploymentEfile* for more information on electronic filing. If you file a paper return, where you file depends on whether you include a payment with Form 940. Mail your return to the address listed for your location in the table that follows.

PDSs can't deliver to P.O. boxes. You must use the U.S. Postal Service to mail an item to a P.O. box address. Go to *IRS.gov/PDS* for the current list of PDSs. For the IRS mailing address to use if you're using a PDS, go to *IRS.gov/PDSstreetAddresses*. Select the mailing address listed on the webpage that is in the same state as the address to which you would mail returns filed without a payment, as shown in the table that follows.

Mailing Addresses for Form 940

If you're in . . .	Without a payment . . .	With a payment . . .
Connecticut, Delaware, District of Columbia, Georgia, Illinois, Indiana, Kentucky, Maine, Maryland, Massachusetts, Michigan, New Hampshire, New Jersey, New York, North Carolina, Ohio, Pennsylvania, Rhode Island, South Carolina, Tennessee, Vermont, Virginia, West Virginia, Wisconsin	Department of the Treasury Internal Revenue Service Kansas City, MO 64999-0046	Internal Revenue Service P.O. Box 806531 Cincinnati, OH 45280-6531
Alabama, Alaska, Arizona, Arkansas, California, Colorado, Florida, Hawaii, Idaho, Iowa, Kansas, Louisiana, Minnesota, Mississippi, Missouri, Montana, Nebraska, Nevada, New Mexico, North Dakota, Oklahoma, Oregon, South Dakota, Texas, Utah, Washington, Wyoming	Department of the Treasury Internal Revenue Service Ogden, UT 84201-0046	Internal Revenue Service P.O. Box 932000 Louisville, KY 40293-2000
Puerto Rico, U.S. Virgin Islands	Internal Revenue Service P.O. Box 409101 Ogden, UT 84409	Internal Revenue Service P.O. Box 932000 Louisville, KY 40293-2000
If the location of your legal residence, principal place of business, office, or agency is not listed	Internal Revenue Service P.O. Box 409101 Ogden, UT 84409	Internal Revenue Service P.O. Box 932000 Louisville, KY 40293-2000
EXCEPTION for tax-exempt organizations; federal, state, and local governments; and Indian tribal governments, regardless of your location	Department of the Treasury Internal Revenue Service Ogden, UT 84201-0046	Internal Revenue Service P.O. Box 932000 Louisville, KY 40293-2000

⚠️ **CAUTION** *Your filing address may have changed from that used to file your employment tax return in prior years.*

Credit for State Unemployment Tax Paid to a State Unemployment Fund

Generally, you get a credit for amounts you pay to a state (including the District of Columbia, Puerto Rico, and the USVI) unemployment fund by February 1, 2021 (or February 10, 2021, if that is your Form 940 due date). Your FUTA tax will be higher if you don't pay the state unemployment tax timely. If you didn't pay all state unemployment tax by the due date of Form 940, see the line 10 instructions. For wages paid to a work site employee, a CPEO is eligible for the credit whether the CPEO or a customer of the CPEO made the contribution with respect to a work site employee.

State unemployment taxes are sometimes called "contributions." These contributions are payments that a state requires an employer to make to its unemployment fund for the payment of unemployment benefits. They don't include:
- Any payments deducted or deductible from your employees' pay;
- Penalties, interest, or special administrative taxes; and
- Voluntary amounts you paid to get a lower assigned state experience rate.

Additional credit. You may receive an additional credit if you have a state experience rate lower than 5.4% (0.054). This applies even if your rate varies during the year. This additional credit is the difference between your actual state unemployment tax payments and the amount you would have been required to pay at 5.4%. For wages paid to a work site employee, the CPEO is allowed the additional credit if the CPEO is allowed, under state law, to collect and remit contributions to the state unemployment fund with respect to a work site employee.

-4-

Instructions for Form 940 (2020)

Form 940 Instructions (Page 5)

Special credit for successor employers. You may be eligible for a credit based on the state unemployment taxes paid by a predecessor. You may claim this credit if you're a successor employer who acquired a business in 2020 from a predecessor who wasn't an employer for FUTA purposes and, therefore, wasn't required to file Form 940 for 2020. See section 3302(e). You can include amounts paid by the predecessor on the Worksheet—Line 10 as if you paid them. For details on successor employers, see *Successor employer* under *Type of Return*, later. If the predecessor was required to file Form 940, see the line 5 instructions.

When Must You Deposit Your FUTA Tax?

Although Form 940 covers a calendar year, you may have to deposit your FUTA tax before you file your return. If your FUTA tax is more than $500 for the calendar year, you must deposit at least one quarterly payment.

You must determine when to deposit your tax based on the amount of your quarterly tax liability. If your FUTA tax is $500 or less in a quarter, carry it over to the next quarter. Continue carrying your tax liability over until your cumulative tax is more than $500. At that point, you must deposit your tax for the quarter. Deposit your FUTA tax by the last day of the month after the end of the quarter. If your tax for the next quarter is $500 or less, you're not required to deposit your tax again until the cumulative amount is more than $500.

Fourth quarter liabilities. If your FUTA tax for the fourth quarter (plus any undeposited amounts from earlier quarters) is more than $500, deposit the entire amount by February 1, 2021. If it is $500 or less, you can either deposit the amount or pay it with your Form 940 by February 1, 2021.

In years when there are credit reduction states, you must include liabilities owed for credit reduction with your fourth quarter deposit.

When To Deposit Your FUTA Tax

If your undeposited FUTA tax is more than $500 on . . .*	Deposit your tax by . . .
March 31	April 30
June 30	July 31
September 30	October 31
December 31	January 31

*Also, see the instructions for line 16.

TIP *If any deposit due date falls on a Saturday, Sunday, or legal holiday, you may deposit on the next business day. See* Timeliness of federal tax deposits*, later.*

How Do You Figure Your FUTA Tax Liability for Each Quarter?

You owe FUTA tax on the first $7,000 you pay to each employee during the calendar year after subtracting any payments exempt from FUTA tax. The FUTA tax is 6.0% (0.060) for 2020. Most employers receive a maximum credit of up to 5.4% (0.054) against this FUTA tax. Every quarter, you must figure how much of the first $7,000 of each employee's annual wages you paid during that quarter.

Figure Your Tax Liability

Before you can figure the amount to deposit, figure your FUTA tax liability for the quarter. To figure your tax liability, add the first $7,000 of each employee's annual wages you paid during the quarter for FUTA wages paid and multiply that amount by 0.006.

The tax rates are based on your receiving the maximum credit against FUTA taxes. You're entitled to the maximum credit if you paid all state unemployment tax by the due date of your Form 940 or if you weren't required to pay state unemployment tax during the calendar year due to your state experience rate.

Example. During the first quarter, you had three employees: Mary Smith, George Jones, and Jane Moore. You paid $11,000 to Mary, $2,000 to George, and $4,000 to Jane. None of the payments made were exempt from FUTA tax.

To figure your liability for the first quarter, add the first $7,000 of each employee's wages subject to FUTA tax:

$7,000	Mary's wages subject to FUTA tax
2,000	George's wages subject to FUTA tax
+ 4,000	Jane's wages subject to FUTA tax
$13,000	Total wages subject to FUTA tax for the first quarter

$13,000	Total wages subject to FUTA tax for the first quarter
x 0.006	Tax rate (based on maximum credit of 5.4%)
$78	Your liability for the first quarter

In this example, you don't have to make a deposit because your liability is $500 or less for the first quarter. However, you must carry this liability over to the second quarter.

If any wages subject to FUTA tax aren't subject to state unemployment tax, you may be liable for FUTA tax at the maximum rate of 6.0%. For instance, in certain states, wages paid to corporate officers, certain payments of sick pay by unions, and certain fringe benefits are excluded from state unemployment tax.

Example. Mary Smith and George Jones are corporate officers whose wages are excluded from state unemployment tax in your state. Jane Moore's wages aren't excluded from state unemployment tax. During the first quarter, you paid $11,000 to Mary, $2,000 to George, and $4,000 to Jane.

$ 9,000	Total FUTA wages for Mary and George in first quarter
x 0.060	Tax rate
$540	Your liability for the first quarter for Mary and George

$4,000	Total FUTA wages subject to state unemployment tax
x 0.006	Tax rate (based on maximum credit of 5.4%)
$24	Your liability for the first quarter for Jane

$540	Your liability for the first quarter for Mary and George
+ 24	Your liability for first quarter for Jane
$564	Your liability for the first quarter for Mary, George, and Jane

In this example, you must deposit $564 by April 30 because your liability for the first quarter is more than $500.

How Must You Deposit Your FUTA Tax?

You Must Deposit Your FUTA Tax Using EFT

You must use EFT to make all federal tax deposits. Generally, an EFT is made using EFTPS. If you don't want to use EFTPS, you can arrange for your tax professional, financial institution, payroll service, or other trusted third party to make electronic deposits on your behalf. Also, you may arrange for your financial institution to initiate a same-day wire payment on your behalf. EFTPS is a free service provided by the Department of the Treasury. Services provided by your tax professional, financial institution, payroll service, or other third party may have a fee.

For more information on making federal tax deposits, see Pub. 966. To get more information about EFTPS or to enroll in EFTPS, go to *EFTPS.gov*, or call one of the following numbers.
• 800-555-4477 (toll free)
• 800-244-4829 (Spanish)
• 800-733-4829 (TDD)

If your business is new, the IRS will automatically pre-enroll you in EFTPS when you apply for an EIN. Follow the instructions on your EIN package to activate your enrollment.

 For an EFTPS deposit to be on time, you must submit the deposit by 8 p.m. Eastern time the day before the date the deposit is due.

Same-day wire payment option. If you fail to submit a deposit transaction on EFTPS by 8 p.m. Eastern time the day before the date a deposit is due, you can still make your deposit on time by using the Federal Tax Collection Service (FTCS) to make a same-day wire payment. To use the same-day wire payment method, you will need to make arrangements with your financial institution ahead of time. Please check with your financial institution regarding availability, deadlines, and costs. Your financial institution may charge you a fee for payments made this way. To learn more about the information you will need to give your financial institution to make a same-day wire payment, go to *IRS.gov/SameDayWire*.

Timeliness of federal tax deposits. If a deposit is required to be made on a day that isn't a business day, the deposit is considered timely if it is made by the close of the next business day. A business day is any day other than a Saturday, Sunday, or legal holiday. The term "legal holiday" for deposit purposes includes only those legal holidays in the District of Columbia. Legal holidays in the District of Columbia are provided in section 11 of Pub. 15.

How Can You Avoid Penalties and Interest?

You can avoid paying penalties and interest if you do all of the following.
• Deposit and pay your tax when it is due.
• File your fully completed Form 940 accurately and on time.
• Attach Schedule R (Form 940) if required.
• Ensure your tax payments are honored by your financial institution.

Penalties and interest are charged on taxes paid late and returns filed late at a rate set by law. See sections 11 and 12 of Pub. 15 for details.

Use Form 843 to request abatement of assessed penalties or interest. Don't request abatement of assessed penalties or interest on Form 940.

If you receive a notice about a penalty after you file this return, reply to the notice with an explanation and we will determine if you meet reasonable-cause criteria. Don't attach an explanation when you file your return.

Can You Amend a Return?

You use the 2020 Form 940 to amend a return that you previously filed for 2020. If you're amending a return for a previous year, use that previous year's Form 940.

Follow the steps below to amend your return.
• Use a paper return to amend a Form 940 filed under an electronic filing program.
• Check the amended return box in the top right corner of Form 940, page 1, box a.
• Fill in all the amounts that should have been on the original form.
• Sign the form.
• Attach an explanation of why you're amending your return. For example, tell us if you're filing to claim credit for tax paid to your state unemployment fund after the due date of Form 940.
• File the amended return using the *Without a payment* address (even if a payment is included) under *Where Do You File*, earlier.
• If you file an amended return for an aggregate Form 940, be sure to attach Schedule R (Form 940). Complete Schedule R (Form 940) only for employers who have adjustments on the amended Form 940.

Completing Your Form 940

Follow These Guidelines To Correctly Fill Out the Form

Make entries on Form 940 as follows to enable accurate scanning and processing.
• Make sure your business name and EIN are on every page of the form and any attachments.
• If you type or use a computer to fill out your form, use a 12-point Courier font, if possible. Portable Document

-6-

Instructions for Form 940 (2020)

Form 940 Instructions (Page 7)

Format (PDF) forms on IRS.gov have fillable fields with acceptable font specifications.

• Don't enter dollar signs and decimal points. Commas are optional. Enter dollars to the left of the preprinted decimal point and cents to the right of it.

• You may choose to round your amounts to the nearest dollar, instead of reporting cents on this form. If you choose to round, you must round all entries. To round, drop the amounts under 50 cents and increase the amounts from 50 to 99 cents to the next dollar. For example, $1.49 becomes $1.00 and $2.50 becomes $3.00. If you use two or more amounts to figure an entry on the form, use cents to figure the answer and round the answer only.

• If you have a line with the value of zero, leave it blank.

Employer Identification Number (EIN), Name, Trade Name, and Address

Enter Your Business Information at the Top of the Form

Enter your EIN, name, and address in the spaces provided. You must enter your name and EIN here and on page 2. Enter the business (legal) name that you used when you applied for your EIN on Form SS-4. For example, if you're a sole proprietor, enter "Ronald Smith" on the *Name* line and "Ron's Cycles" on the *Trade Name* line. Leave the *Trade Name* line blank if it is the same as your *Name*.

If you pay a tax preparer to fill out Form 940, make sure the preparer shows your business name exactly as it appeared when you applied for your EIN.

Employer identification number (EIN). To make sure that businesses comply with federal tax laws, the IRS monitors tax filings and payments by using a numerical system to identify taxpayers. A unique nine-digit EIN is assigned to all corporations, partnerships, and some sole proprietors. Businesses needing an EIN must apply for a number and use it throughout the life of the business on all tax returns, payments, and reports.

Your business should have only one EIN. If you have more than one and aren't sure which one to use, write to the IRS office where you file your returns (using the *Without a payment* address under <u>Where Do You File</u>, earlier) or call the IRS at 800-829-4933 (toll free). If you're outside the United States, call 267-941-1000 (toll call).

If you don't have an EIN, you may apply for one by visiting <u>*IRS.gov/EIN*</u>. You may also apply for an EIN by faxing or mailing Form SS-4 or SS-4PR to the IRS. If the principal business was created or organized outside of the United States or U.S. territories, you may also apply for an EIN by calling 267-941-1099 (toll call). If you haven't received your EIN by the due date of Form 940, write "Applied For" and the date you applied in the space shown for the number.

 If you're filing your tax return electronically, a valid EIN is required at the time the return is filed. If a valid EIN isn't provided, the return won't be accepted. This may result in penalties.

TIP *Always be sure the EIN on the form you file exactly matches the EIN that the IRS assigned to your business. Don't use a social security number (SSN) or individual taxpayer identification number (ITIN) on forms that ask for an EIN. Filing a Form 940 with an incorrect EIN or using the EIN of another's business may result in penalties and delays in processing your return.*

Tell Us if You Change Your Business Name, Business Address, or Responsible Party

Notify the IRS immediately if you change your business name, business address, or responsible party.

Name change. Write to the IRS office where you filed your return (using the *Without a payment* address under <u>Where Do You File</u>, earlier) to notify the IRS of any name change. See Pub. 1635 to see if you also need to apply for a new EIN.

Address or responsible party change. Complete and mail Form 8822-B to notify the IRS of an address or responsible party change. Don't mail Form 8822-B with your Form 940. For a definition of "responsible party," see the Instructions for Form SS-4.

Type of Return

Review the box at the top of the form. If any line applies to you, check the appropriate box to tell us which type of return you're filing. You may check more than one box.

Amended. If this is an amended return that you're filing to correct a return that you previously filed, check box a.

Successor employer. Check box b if you're a successor employer and:

• You're reporting wages paid before you acquired the business by a predecessor who was required to file a Form 940 because the predecessor was an employer for FUTA tax purposes, or

• You're claiming a special credit for state unemployment tax paid before you acquired the business by a predecessor who wasn't required to file a Form 940 because the predecessor wasn't an employer for FUTA tax purposes.

A successor employer is an employer who:

• Acquires substantially all the property used in a trade or business of another person (predecessor) or used in a separate unit of a trade or business of a predecessor; and

• Immediately after the acquisition, employs one or more people who were employed by the predecessor.

No payments to employees in 2020. If you're not liable for FUTA tax for 2020 because you made no payments to employees in 2020, check box c. Then go to Part 7, sign the form, and file it with the IRS.

Final: Business closed or stopped paying wages. If this is a final return because you went out of business or stopped paying wages and you won't be liable for filing Form 940 in the future, check box d. Complete all applicable lines on the form, sign it in Part 7, and file it with the IRS. Also attach a statement to your return showing the name of the person keeping the payroll records and the address where those records will be kept.

Form 940 Instructions (Page 8)

Disregarded entities. A disregarded entity is required to file Form 940 using its name and EIN, not the name and EIN of its owner. An entity that has a single owner and is disregarded as separate from its owner for federal income tax purposes is treated as a separate entity for purposes of payment and reporting federal employment taxes. If the entity doesn't currently have an EIN, it must apply for one using one of the methods under *Employer identification number (EIN)*, earlier. Disregarded entities include single-owner limited liability companies (LLCs) that haven't elected to be taxed as a corporation for federal income tax purposes, QSubs, and certain foreign entities treated as disregarded entities for U.S. income tax purposes. Although a disregarded entity is treated as a separate entity for employment tax purposes, it isn't subject to FUTA tax if it is owned by a tax-exempt organization under section 501(c)(3) and isn't required to file Form 940. For more information, see *Disregarded entities and qualified subchapter S subsidiaries* in the *Introduction* section of Pub. 15.

Specific Instructions
Part 1: Tell Us About Your Return

1. If You Were Required To Pay Your State Unemployment Tax In . . .

You must complete line 1a or line 1b even if you weren't required to pay any state unemployment tax because your state unemployment tax rate(s) was zero. You may leave lines 1a and 1b blank only if all of the wages you paid to all employees in all states were excluded from state unemployment tax. If you leave lines 1a and 1b blank, and line 7 is more than zero, you must complete line 9 because all of the taxable FUTA wages you paid were excluded from state unemployment tax.

Identify the state(s) where you were required to pay state unemployment taxes.

1a. One state only. Enter the two-letter U.S. Postal Service abbreviation for the state where you were required to pay your state unemployment tax on line 1a. For a list of state abbreviations, see the Schedule A (Form 940) instructions or visit the website for the U.S. Postal Service at *USPS.com*.

1b. More than one state (you're a multi-state employer). Check the box on line 1b. Then fill out Schedule A (Form 940) and attach it to your Form 940.

2. If You Paid Wages in a State That Is Subject to Credit Reduction

A state that hasn't repaid money it borrowed from the federal government to pay unemployment benefits is called a "credit reduction state." The U.S. Department of Labor determines which states are credit reduction states.

If you paid wages that are subject to the unemployment tax laws of a credit reduction state, you may have to pay more FUTA tax when filing your Form 940.

For tax year 2020, the USVI is the only credit reduction state. If you paid wages subject to the unemployment tax laws of the USVI, check the box on line 2 and fill out

Schedule A (Form 940). See the instructions for line 9 before completing the Schedule A (Form 940).

Part 2: Determine Your FUTA Tax Before Adjustments

If any line in Part 2 doesn't apply, leave it blank.

3. Total Payments to All Employees

Report the total payments you made during the calendar year on line 3. Include payments for the services of all employees, even if the payments aren't taxable for FUTA. Your method of payment doesn't determine whether payments are wages. You may have paid wages hourly, daily, weekly, monthly, or yearly. You may have paid wages for piecework or as a percentage of profits. Include the following.

- **Compensation,** such as the following.
  - —Salaries, wages, commissions, fees, bonuses, vacation allowances, and amounts you paid to full-time, part-time, or temporary employees.
- **Fringe benefits**, such as the following.
  - —Sick pay (including third-party sick pay if liability is transferred to the employer). For details on sick pay, see Pub. 15-A, Employer's Supplemental Tax Guide.
  - —The value of goods, lodging, food, clothing, and non-cash fringe benefits.
  - —Section 125 (cafeteria) plan benefits.
- **Retirement/Pension**, such as the following.
  - —Employer contributions to a 401(k) plan, payments to an Archer MSA, payments under adoption assistance programs, and contributions to SIMPLE retirement accounts (including elective salary reduction contributions).
  - —Amounts deferred under a non-qualified deferred compensation plan.
- **Other payments**, such as the following.
  - —Tips of $20 or more in a month that your employees reported to you.
  - —Payments made by a predecessor employer to the employees of a business you acquired.
  - —Payments to nonemployees who are treated as your employees by the state unemployment tax agency.

 Wages may be subject to FUTA tax even if they are excluded from your state's unemployment tax.

For details on wages and other compensation, see section 5 of Pub. 15-A.

Example

You had three employees. You paid $44,000 to Joan Rose, $8,000 to Sara Blue, and $16,000 to John Green.

$44,000	Amount paid to Joan
8,000	Amount paid to Sara
+ 16,000	Amount paid to John
$68,000	Total payments to employees. You would enter this amount on line 3.

-8-

Form 940 Instructions (Page 9)

4. Payments Exempt From FUTA Tax

If you enter an amount on line 4, check the appropriate box or boxes on lines 4a through 4e to show the types of payments exempt from FUTA tax. **You only report a payment as exempt from FUTA tax on line 4 if you included the payment on line 3.**

Some payments are exempt from FUTA tax because the payments aren't included in the definition of wages or the services aren't included in the definition of employment. Payments exempt from FUTA tax may include the following.

- **Fringe benefits**, such as the following.

    —The value of certain meals and lodging.
    —Contributions to accident or health plans for employees, including certain employer payments to a health savings account or an Archer MSA.
    —Payments for benefits excluded under section 125 (cafeteria) plans.

- **Group-term life insurance.** For information about group-term life insurance and other payments for fringe benefits that may be exempt from FUTA tax, see Pub. 15-B.

- **Retirement/Pension**, such as employer contributions to a qualified plan, including a SIMPLE retirement account (other than elective salary reduction contributions) and a 401(k) plan.

- **Dependent care**, such as payments (up to $5,000 per employee, $2,500 if married filing separately) for a qualifying person's care that allows your employees to work and that would be excludable by the employee under section 129.

- **Other payments**, such as the following.

    —All non-cash payments and certain cash payments for agricultural labor, and all payments to "H-2A" visa workers. See *For Agricultural Employers*, earlier, or see Pub. 51.
    —Payments made under a workers' compensation law because of a work-related injury or sickness. See section 6 of Pub. 15-A.
    —Payments for domestic services if you didn't pay cash wages of $1,000 or more (for all domestic employees) in any calendar quarter in 2019 or 2020, or if you file Schedule H (Form 1040). See *For Employers of Household Employees*, earlier, or Pub. 926.
    —Payments for services provided to you by your parent, spouse, or child under the age of 21. See section 3 of Pub. 15.
    —Payments for certain fishing activities. See Pub. 334, Tax Guide for Small Business.
    —Payments to certain statutory employees. See section 1 of Pub. 15-A.
    —Payments to nonemployees who are treated as your employees by the state unemployment tax agency.

See section 3306 and its related regulations for more information about FUTA taxation of retirement plan contributions, dependent care payments, and other payments.

For more information on payments exempt from FUTA tax, see section 15 in Pub. 15.

Example

You had three employees. You paid $44,000 to Joan Rose, including $2,000 in health insurance benefits. You paid $8,000 to Sara Blue, including $500 in retirement benefits. You paid $16,000 to John Green, including $2,000 in health and retirement benefits.

$ 2,000	Health insurance benefits for Joan
500	Retirement benefits for Sara
+ 2,000	Health and retirement benefits for John
$4,500	Total payments exempt from FUTA tax. You would enter this amount on line 4 and check boxes 4a and 4c.

5. Total of Payments Made to Each Employee in Excess of $7,000

Only the first $7,000 you paid to each employee in a calendar year, after subtracting any payments exempt from FUTA tax, is subject to FUTA tax. This $7,000 is called the *FUTA wage base.*

Enter on line 5 the total of the payments over the FUTA wage base you paid to each employee during 2020 **after subtracting any payments exempt from FUTA tax shown on line 4.**

Following Our Example

You had three employees. You paid $44,000 to Joan Rose, $8,000 to Sara Blue, and $16,000 to John Green, including a total of $4,500 in payments exempt from FUTA tax for all three employees. To determine the total payments made to each employee in excess of the FUTA wage base, the payments exempt from FUTA tax and the FUTA wage base must be subtracted from total payments. These amounts are shown in parentheses.

Employees	Joan	Sara	John
Total payments to employees	$44,000	$8,000	$16,000
Payments exempt from FUTA tax	(2,000)	(500)	(2,000)
FUTA wage base	(7,000)	(7,000)	(7,000)
	$35,000	$ 500	$ 7,000

Total of payments made to each employee in excess of the FUTA wage base. You would enter this amount on line 5. $42,500

If you're a successor employer . . . When you figure the payments made to each employee in excess of the FUTA wage base, you may include the payments that the predecessor made to the employees who continue to work for you **only** if the predecessor was an employer for FUTA tax purposes resulting in the predecessor being required to file Form 940.

Instructions for Form 940 (2020)   -9-

Form 940 Instructions (Page 10)

Example for Successor Employers

During the calendar year, the predecessor employer paid $5,000 to Susan Jones. You acquired the predecessor's business. After the acquisition, you employed Susan and paid Susan an additional $3,000 in wages. None of the amounts paid to Susan were payments exempt from FUTA tax.

$5,000	Wages paid by predecessor employer
+ 3,000	Wages paid by you
$8,000	Total payments to Susan. You would include this amount on line 3.

$8,000	Total payments to Susan
− 7,000	FUTA wage base
$1,000	Payments made to Susan in excess of the FUTA wage base

$1,000	Payments made to Susan in excess of the FUTA wage base
+ 5,000	Taxable FUTA wages paid by predecessor employer
$6,000	You would include this amount on line 5.

6. Subtotal

To figure your subtotal, add the amounts on lines 4 and 5 and enter the result on line 6.

```
  line 4
+ line 5
  line 6
```

7. Total Taxable FUTA Wages

To figure your total taxable FUTA wages, subtract line 6 from line 3 and enter the result on line 7.

```
  line 3
− line 6
  line 7
```

8. FUTA Tax Before Adjustments

To figure your total FUTA tax before adjustments, multiply line 7 by 0.006 and then enter the result on line 8.

```
   line 7
x 0.006
   line 8
```

Part 3: Determine Your Adjustments

If any line in Part 3 doesn't apply, leave it blank.

9. If ALL of the Taxable FUTA Wages You Paid Were Excluded From State Unemployment Tax . . .

 Line 9 doesn't apply to FUTA wages on which you paid no state unemployment tax only because the state assigned you a tax rate of 0%.

If all of the taxable FUTA wages you paid were excluded from state unemployment tax, multiply line 7 by 0.054 and enter the result on line 9.

```
   line 7
x 0.054
   line 9
```

If you weren't required to pay state unemployment tax because all of the wages you paid were excluded from state unemployment tax, you must pay FUTA tax at the 6.0% (0.060) rate. For example, if your state unemployment tax law excludes wages paid to corporate officers or employees in specific occupations, and the only wages you paid were to corporate officers or employees in those specific occupations, you must pay FUTA tax on those wages at the full FUTA rate of 6.0% (0.060). When you figured the FUTA tax before adjustments on line 8, it was based on the maximum allowable credit (5.4%) for state unemployment tax payments. Because you didn't pay state unemployment tax, you don't have a credit and must figure this adjustment.

If line 9 applies to you, lines 10 and 11 don't apply to you. Therefore, leave lines 10 and 11 blank. Don't fill out the worksheet in these instructions. Complete Schedule A (Form 940) only if you're a multi-state employer.

10. If SOME of the Taxable FUTA Wages You Paid Were Excluded From State Unemployment Tax, or You Paid Any State Unemployment Tax Late . . .

You must fill out the worksheet on the next page if:
• Some of the taxable FUTA wages you paid were excluded from state unemployment tax, or
• Any of your payments of state unemployment tax were late.
The worksheet takes you step by step through the process of figuring your credit. At the end of the worksheet you'll find an example of how to use it. Don't complete the worksheet if line 9 applied to you (see the instructions for line 9, earlier).

Before you can properly fill out the worksheet, you will need to gather the following information.
• Taxable FUTA wages (Form 940, line 7).
• Taxable state unemployment wages (state and federal wage bases may differ).
• The experience rates assigned to you by the states where you paid wages.
• The amount of state unemployment taxes you paid on time. (*On time* means that you paid the state unemployment taxes by the due date for filing Form 940.)
• The amount of state unemployment taxes you paid late. (*Late* means after the due date for filing Form 940.)

 Don't include any penalties, interest, or unemployment taxes deducted from your employees' pay in the amount of state unemployment taxes. Also, don't include as state unemployment taxes any special administrative taxes or voluntary contributions you paid to get a lower assigned experience rate or any surcharges, excise taxes, or employment and training taxes. (These items are generally listed as separate items on the state's quarterly wage report.)

-10-

Instructions for Form 940 (2020)

Form 940 Instructions (Page 11)

For line 3 of the worksheet:
• If any of the experience rates assigned to you were less than 5.4% for any part of the calendar year, you must list each assigned experience rate separately on the worksheet.
• If you were assigned six or more experience rates that were less than 5.4% for any part of the calendar year, you must use another sheet to figure the additional credits and then include those additional credits in your line 3 total.

After you complete the worksheet, enter the amount from line 7 of the worksheet on Form 940, line 10. **Don't attach the worksheet to your Form 940.** Keep it with your records.

Instructions for Form 940 (2020)   -11-

Form 940 Instructions (Page 12)

Worksheet—Line 10

Keep for Your Records

Before you begin: Read the *Example* on the next page before completing this worksheet.

Use this worksheet to figure your credit if:

√ Some of the wages you paid were excluded from state unemployment tax, OR
√ You paid any state unemployment tax late.

For this worksheet, **don't round your figures.**

Before you can properly fill out this worksheet, you must gather this information:

- Taxable FUTA wages (Form 940, line 7).

- Taxable state unemployment wages.

- The experience rates assigned to you by the states where you paid wages.

- The amount of state unemployment taxes you paid on time. (*On time* means that you paid the state unemployment taxes by the due date for filing Form 940.) Include any state unemployment taxes you paid on nonemployees who were treated as employees by your state unemployment agency.

- The amount of state unemployment taxes you paid late. (*Late* means after the due date for filing Form 940.)

1. **Maximum allowable credit** — Enter Form 940, line 7 (Form 940, line 7 x 0.054 = line 1).   _____ . x 0.054 on line 1   1. _____ .

2. **Credit for timely state unemployment tax payments** — How much did you pay on time?   2. _____ .

   • If line 2 is **equal to** or **more than** line 1, **STOP here.** (STOP) You've completed the worksheet. Leave Form 940, line 10, blank.

   • If line 2 is **less than** line 1, continue this worksheet.

3. **Additional credit** — Were ALL of your assigned experience rates 5.4% or more?

   • **If yes,** enter zero on line 3. Then go to line 4 of this worksheet.

   • **If no,** fill out the computations below. List ONLY THOSE STATES for which your assigned experience rate for any part of the calendar year was less than 5.4%.

State	Computation rate The difference between 5.4% (0.054) and your assigned experience rate (0.054 – .XXX (assigned experience rate) = computation rate)		Taxable state unemployment wages at assigned experience rate		Additional Credit
1. _____	_____ .	x	_____ .	=	_____ .
2. _____	_____ .	x	_____ .	=	_____ .
3. _____	_____ .	x	_____ .	=	_____ .
4. _____	_____ .	x	_____ .	=	_____ .
5. _____	_____ .	x	_____ .	=	_____ .

If you need more lines, use another sheet and include those additional credits in the total.   **Total** _____ .

Enter the total on line 3.

3. _____ .

4. **Subtotal** (line 2 + line 3 = line 4)   4. _____ .

   • If line 4 is equal to or more than line 1, **STOP here.** (STOP) You've completed the worksheet. Leave Form 940, line 10, blank.

   • If line 4 is less than line 1, continue this worksheet.

5. **Credit for paying state unemployment taxes late:**

   5a. **What is your remaining allowable credit?** (line 1 – line 4 = line 5a)   5a. _____ .

   5b. **How much state unemployment tax did you pay late?**   5b. _____ .

   5c. **Which is smaller, line 5a or line 5b?** Enter the smaller number here.   5c. _____ .

   5d. **Your allowable credit for paying state unemployment taxes late** (line 5c x 0.900 = line 5d)   5d. _____ .

6. **Your FUTA credit** (line 4 + line 5d = line 6)   6. _____ .

   • If line 6 is equal to or more than line 1, **STOP here.** (STOP) You've completed the worksheet. Leave Form 940, line 10, blank.

   • If line 6 is less than line 1, continue this worksheet.

7. **Your adjustment** (line 1 – line 6 = line 7)   Enter line 7 from this worksheet on Form 940, line 10.   7. _____ .

Don't attach this worksheet to your Form 940. Keep it for your records.

Form 940 Instructions (Page 13)

Example for Using the Worksheet

Jill Brown and Tom White are corporate officers whose wages are excluded from state unemployment tax in your state. Jack Davis's wages aren't excluded from state unemployment tax. During 2020, you paid $44,000 to Jill, $22,000 to Tom, and $16,000 to Jack. Your state's wage base is $8,000. You paid some state unemployment tax on time, some late, and some remains unpaid.

Here are the records:

Total taxable FUTA wages (Form 940, line 7)	$21,000.00
Taxable state unemployment wages	$ 8,000.00
Experience rate for 2020	0.041 (4.1%)
State unemployment tax paid on time	$100.00
State unemployment tax paid late	$78.00
State unemployment tax not paid	$150.00

1. Maximum allowable credit

$21,000.00 (Form 940, line 7)
x 0.054 (maximum credit rate)
$1,134.00   **1.** $1,134.00

2. Credit for timely state unemployment tax payments   **2.** $100.00

3. Additional credit

0.054 (maximum credit rate) $8,000
− 0.041 (your experience rate)   x 0.013
0.013 (your computation rate) $104.00   **3.** $104.00

4. Subtotal (line 2 + line 3)

$100.00
+ 104.00
$204.00   **4.** $204.00

5. Credit for paying state unemployment taxes late

5a. **Remaining allowable credit: (line 1 − line 4)**

$1,134.00
− 204.00
$930.00   **5a.** $930.00

5b. **State unemployment tax paid late**   **5b.** $78.00

5c. **Which is smaller?** Line 5a or line 5b?   **5c.** $78.00

5d. **Allowable credit (for paying late)**

$78.00
x 0.900
$70.20   **5d.** $70.20

6. Your FUTA credit (line 4 + line 5d)

$204.00
+ 70.20
$274.20   **6.** $274.20

7. Your adjustment (line 1 − line 6)

$1,134.00
− 274.20
$859.80   **7.** $859.80

* You would enter line 7 from this worksheet on Form 940, line 10.

11. If Credit Reduction Applies . . .

If you paid FUTA taxable wages that were also subject to state unemployment taxes in any states that are subject to credit reduction, enter the total amount from Schedule A (Form 940) on Form 940, line 11. However, if you entered an amount on line 9 because all the FUTA taxable wages you paid were excluded from state unemployment tax, skip line 11 and go to line 12.

Part 4: Determine Your FUTA Tax and Balance Due or Overpayment

If any line in Part 4 doesn't apply, leave it blank.

12. Total FUTA Tax After Adjustments

Add the amounts shown on lines 8, 9, 10, and 11, and enter the result on line 12.

line 8
line 9
line 10
+ line 11
line 12

 If line 9 is greater than zero, lines 10 and 11 must be zero because they don't apply.

13. FUTA Tax Deposited for the Year

Enter the amount of FUTA tax that you deposited for the year, including any overpayment that you applied from a prior year.

14. Balance Due

If line 13 is less than line 12, enter the difference on line 14.

line 12
− line 13
line 14

If line 14 is:
• More than $500, you must deposit your tax. See *When Must You Deposit Your FUTA Tax*, earlier.
• $500 or less, you can deposit your tax, pay your tax with a credit card or debit card, pay your tax by EFW if filing electronically, or pay your tax by check or money order with your return. For more information on electronic payment options, go to *IRS.gov/Payments*.
• Less than $1, you don't have to pay it.

If you don't deposit as required and pay any balance due with Form 940, you may be subject to a penalty.

If you pay by EFT, credit card, or debit card, file your return using the *Without a payment* address under *Where Do You File*, earlier. Don't file Form 940-V, Payment Voucher.

Form 940 Instructions (Page 14)

What if you can't pay in full? If you can't pay the full amount of tax you owe, you can apply for an installment agreement online. You can apply for an installment agreement online if:
- You can't pay the full amount shown on line 14,
- The total amount you owe is $25,000 or less, and
- You can pay the liability in full in 24 months.

To apply using the Online Payment Agreement Application, go to *IRS.gov/OPA*.

Under an installment agreement, you can pay what you owe in monthly installments. There are certain conditions you must meet to enter into and maintain an installment agreement, such as paying the liability within 24 months, and making all required deposits and timely filing tax returns during the length of the agreement.

If your installment agreement is accepted, you will be charged a fee and you will be subject to penalties and interest on the amount of tax not paid by the due date of the return.

15. Overpayment

If line 13 is more than line 12, enter the difference on line 15.

$$
\begin{array}{r}
\text{line 13} \\
- \text{line 12} \\
\hline
\text{line 15}
\end{array}
$$

If you deposited more than the FUTA tax due for the year, you may choose to have us either:
- Apply the refund to your next return, or
- Send you a refund.

Check the appropriate box on line 15 to tell us which option you select. Check only one box on line 15. If you don't check either box or if you check both boxes, we will generally apply the overpayment to your next return. Regardless of any box you check or don't check, we may apply your overpayment to any past due tax account that is shown in our records under your EIN.

If line 15 is less than $1, we will send you a refund or apply it to your next return only if you ask for it in writing.

Part 5: Report Your FUTA Tax Liability by Quarter Only if Line 12 Is More Than $500

Fill out Part 5 only if line 12 is more than $500. If line 12 is $500 or less, leave Part 5 blank and go to Part 6.

16. Report the Amount of Your FUTA Tax Liability for Each Quarter

Enter the amount of your FUTA tax liability for each quarter on lines 16a–d. Don't enter the amount you deposited. If you had no liability for a quarter, leave the line blank.

16a. 1st quarter (January 1 to March 31)
16b. 2nd quarter (April 1 to June 30)
16c. 3rd quarter (July 1 to September 30)
16d. 4th quarter (October 1 to December 31)

To figure your FUTA tax liability for the fourth quarter, complete Form 940 through line 12. Then copy the amount from line 12 onto line 17. Lastly, subtract the sum of lines 16a through 16c from line 17 and enter the result on line 16d.

Example

You paid wages on March 28 and your FUTA tax on those wages was $200. You weren't required to make a deposit for the 1st quarter because your accumulated FUTA tax was $500 or less. You paid additional wages on June 28 and your FUTA tax on those wages was $400. Because your accumulated FUTA tax for the 1st and 2nd quarters exceeded $500, you were required to make a deposit of $600 by July 31.

You would enter $200 on line 16a because your liability for the 1st quarter is $200. You would also enter $400 on line 16b to show your 2nd quarter liability.

 In years when there are credit reduction states, you must include liabilities owed for credit reduction with your fourth quarter deposit. You may deposit the anticipated extra liability throughout the year, but it isn't due until the due date for the deposit for the fourth quarter, and the associated liability should be recorded as being incurred in the fourth quarter.

17. Total Tax Liability for the Year

Your total tax liability for the year must equal line 12. Copy the amount from line 12 onto line 17.

Part 6: May We Speak With Your Third-Party Designee?

If you want to allow an employee, your paid tax preparer, or another person to discuss your Form 940 with the IRS, check the "Yes" box. Then enter the name and phone number of the person you choose as your designee. Be sure to give us the specific name of a person—not the name of the firm that prepared your tax return.

Have your designee select a five-digit personal identification number (PIN) that he or she must use as identification when talking to the IRS about your form.

By checking "Yes," you authorize us to talk to your designee about any questions that we may have while we process your return. Your authorization applies only to this form, for this year; it doesn't apply to other forms or other tax years.

You're authorizing your designee to:
- Give us any information that is missing from your return,
- Ask us for information about processing your return, and
- Respond to certain IRS notices that you have shared with your designee about math errors and in preparing your return. We won't send notices to your designee.

You're not authorizing your designee to:
- Receive any refund check,
- Bind you to anything (including additional tax liability), or
- Otherwise represent you before the IRS.

Form 940 Instructions (Page 15)

The authorization will automatically expire 1 year after the due date for filing your Form 940 (regardless of extensions). If you or your designee want to end the authorization before it expires, write to the IRS office for your location using the *Without a payment* address under *Where Do You File*, earlier.

If you want to expand your designee's authorization or if you want us to send your designee copies of your notices, see Pub. 947.

Part 7: Sign Here (Approved Roles)

You MUST Fill Out Both Pages of This Form and SIGN It

Failure to sign will delay the processing of your return.

On page 2 in Part 7, sign and print your name and title. Then enter the date and the best daytime telephone number, including area code, where we can reach you if we have any questions.

Who Must Sign Form 940?

The following persons are authorized to sign the return for each type of business entity.
- **Sole proprietorship**—The individual who owns the business.
- **Partnership (including a limited liability company (LLC) treated as a partnership) or unincorporated organization**—A responsible and duly authorized partner, member, or officer having knowledge of its affairs.
- **Corporation (including an LLC treated as a corporation)**—The president, vice president, or other principal officer duly authorized to sign.
- **Single-member LLC treated as a disregarded entity for federal income tax purposes**—The owner of the LLC or a principal officer duly authorized to sign.
- **Trust or estate**—The fiduciary.

Form 940 may also be signed by a duly authorized agent of the taxpayer if a valid power of attorney or reporting agent authorization (Form 8655) has been filed.

Alternative signature method. Corporate officers or duly authorized agents may sign Form 940 by rubber stamp, mechanical device, or computer software program. For details and required documentation, see Rev. Proc. 2005-39, 2005-28 I.R.B. 82, available at *IRS.gov/irb/2005-28_IRB#RP-2005-39*.

Paid preparers. A paid preparer must sign Form 940 and provide the information in the *Paid Preparer Use Only* section of Part 7 if the preparer was paid to prepare Form 940 and isn't an employee of the filing entity. Paid preparers must sign paper returns with a manual signature. The preparer must give you a copy of the return in addition to the copy to be filed with the IRS.

If you're a paid preparer, enter your Preparer Tax Identification Number (PTIN) in the space provided. Include your complete address. If you work for a firm, write the firm's name and the EIN of the firm. You can apply for a PTIN online or by filing Form W-12. For more information about applying for a PTIN online, go to *IRS.gov/PTIN*. You can't use your PTIN in place of the EIN of the tax preparation firm.

Generally, don't complete the *Paid Preparer Use Only* section if you're filing the return as a reporting agent and have a valid Form 8655 on file with the IRS. However, a reporting agent must complete this section if the reporting agent offered legal advice, for example, by advising the client on determining whether its workers are employees or independent contractors for federal tax purposes.

Privacy Act and Paperwork Reduction Act Notice. We ask for the information on Form 940 to carry out the Internal Revenue laws of the United States. We need it to figure and collect the right amount of tax. Subtitle C, Employment Taxes, of the Internal Revenue Code imposes unemployment tax under the Federal Unemployment Tax Act. Form 940 is used to determine the amount of the taxes that you owe. Section 6011 requires you to provide the requested information if the tax is applicable to you. Section 6109 requires you to provide your identification number. If you fail to provide this information in a timely manner, or provide false or fraudulent information, you may be subject to penalties.

You're not required to provide the information requested on a form that is subject to the Paperwork Reduction Act unless the form displays a valid OMB control number. Books or records relating to a form or its instructions must be retained as long as their contents may become material in the administration of any Internal Revenue law.

Generally, tax returns and return information are confidential, as required by section 6103. However, section 6103 allows or requires the IRS to disclose or give the information shown on your tax return to others as described in the Code. For example, we may disclose your tax information to the Department of Justice for civil and criminal litigation, and to cities, states, the District of Columbia, and U.S. commonwealths and possessions to administer their tax laws. We may also disclose this information to other countries under a tax treaty, to federal and state agencies to enforce federal nontax criminal laws, or to federal law enforcement and intelligence agencies to combat terrorism.

If you have comments concerning the accuracy of these time estimates or suggestions for making these forms simpler, we would be happy to hear from you. You can send us comments from *IRS.gov/FormComments*. Or you can send your comments to Internal Revenue Service, Tax Forms and Publications Division, 1111 Constitution Ave. NW, IR-6526, Washington, DC 20224. Don't send Form 940 to this address. Instead, see *Where Do You File*, earlier.

Instructions for Form 940 (2020) -15-

Form 940 Instructions (Page 16)

Estimated Average Times

The time needed to complete and file this form will vary depending on individual circumstances. The estimated average time is:		
Form	**Recordkeeping**	**Preparing, copying, assembling, and sending the form to the IRS**
Schedule A (Form 940)	16 hr., 1 min.	15 min.
Worksheet (Form 940)	1 hr., 41 min.	21 min.

Form 940 Schedule A (Page 1)

Schedule A (Form 940) for 2020:

Multi-State Employer and Credit Reduction Information
Department of the Treasury — Internal Revenue Service

860312

OMB No. 1545-0028

See the instructions on page 2. File this schedule with Form 940.

Employer identification number (EIN) ☐☐ – ☐☐☐☐☐☐☐

Name *(not your trade name)*

Place an "X" in the box of EVERY state in which you had to pay state unemployment tax this year. For the U.S. Virgin Islands, enter the FUTA taxable wages and the reduction rate (see page 2). Multiply the FUTA taxable wages by the reduction rate and enter the credit reduction amount. Don't include in the *FUTA Taxable Wages* box wages that were excluded from state unemployment tax (see the instructions for Step 2). If any states don't apply to you, leave them blank.

Postal Abbreviation	FUTA Taxable Wages	Reduction Rate	Credit Reduction	Postal Abbreviation	FUTA Taxable Wages	Reduction Rate	Credit Reduction
☐ AK	.		.	☐ NC	.		.
☐ AL	.		.	☐ ND	.		.
☐ AR	.		.	☐ NE	.		.
☐ AZ	.		.	☐ NH	.		.
☐ CA	.		.	☐ NJ	.		.
☐ CO	.		.	☐ NM	.		.
☐ CT	.		.	☐ NV	.		.
☐ DC	.		.	☐ NY	.		.
☐ DE	.		.	☐ OH	.		.
☐ FL	.		.	☐ OK	.		.
☐ GA	.		.	☐ OR	.		.
☐ HI	.		.	☐ PA	.		.
☐ IA	.		.	☐ RI	.		.
☐ ID	.		.	☐ SC	.		.
☐ IL	.		.	☐ SD	.		.
☐ IN	.		.	☐ TN	.		.
☐ KS	.		.	☐ TX	.		.
☐ KY	.		.	☐ UT	.		.
☐ LA	.		.	☐ VA	.		.
☐ MA	.		.	☐ VT	.		.
☐ MD	.		.	☐ WA	.		.
☐ ME	.		.	☐ WI	.		.
☐ MI	.		.	☐ WV	.		.
☐ MN	.		.	☐ WY	.		.
☐ MO	.		.	☐ PR	.		.
☐ MS	.		.	☐ VI	.	.	.
☐ MT	.						

Total Credit Reduction. Add all amounts shown in the *Credit Reduction* boxes. Enter the total here and on Form 940, line 11 . . . . ☐ .

For Privacy Act and Paperwork Reduction Act Notice, see the Instructions for Form 940.   Cat. No. 16997C   **Schedule A (Form 940) 2020**

Form 940 Schedule A (Page 2)

Instructions for Schedule A (Form 940) for 2020:

860412

Multi-State Employer and Credit Reduction Information

Specific Instructions: Completing Schedule A

Step 1. Place an "X" in the box of every state (including the District of Columbia, Puerto Rico, and the U.S. Virgin Islands) in which you had to pay state unemployment taxes this year, even if the state's credit reduction rate is zero.

Note: Make sure that you have applied for a state reporting number for your business. If you don't have an unemployment account in a state in which you paid wages, contact the state unemployment agency to receive one. For a list of state unemployment agencies, visit the U.S. Department of Labor's website at *https://oui.doleta.gov/unemploy/agencies.asp.*

The table below provides the two-letter postal abbreviations used on Schedule A.

State	Postal Abbreviation	State	Postal Abbreviation
Alabama	AL	Montana	MT
Alaska	AK	Nebraska	NE
Arizona	AZ	Nevada	NV
Arkansas	AR	New Hampshire	NH
California	CA	New Jersey	NJ
Colorado	CO	New Mexico	NM
Connecticut	CT	New York	NY
Delaware	DE	North Carolina	NC
District of Columbia	DC	North Dakota	ND
Florida	FL	Ohio	OH
Georgia	GA	Oklahoma	OK
Hawaii	HI	Oregon	OR
Idaho	ID	Pennsylvania	PA
Illinois	IL	Rhode Island	RI
Indiana	IN	South Carolina	SC
Iowa	IA	South Dakota	SD
Kansas	KS	Tennessee	TN
Kentucky	KY	Texas	TX
Louisiana	LA	Utah	UT
Maine	ME	Vermont	VT
Maryland	MD	Virginia	VA
Massachusetts	MA	Washington	WA
Michigan	MI	West Virginia	WV
Minnesota	MN	Wisconsin	WI
Mississippi	MS	Wyoming	WY
Missouri	MO	Puerto Rico	PR
		U.S. Virgin Islands	VI

Credit reduction state. For 2020, the U.S. Virgin Islands (USVI) is the only credit reduction state. The credit reduction rate is 0.03 (3.0%).

Step 2. You're subject to credit reduction if you paid FUTA taxable wages that were also subject to state unemployment taxes in the USVI.

In the *FUTA Taxable Wages* box, enter the total FUTA taxable wages that you paid in the USVI. (The FUTA wage base for all states is $7,000.) However, don't include in the *FUTA Taxable Wages* box wages that were excluded from state unemployment tax. For example, if you paid $5,000 in FUTA taxable wages in the USVI but $1,000 of those wages were excluded from state unemployment tax, report $4,000 in the *FUTA Taxable Wages* box.

Note: Don't enter your state unemployment wages in the *FUTA Taxable Wages* box.

Enter the reduction rate and then multiply the total FUTA taxable wages by the reduction rate.

Enter your total in the *Credit Reduction* box at the end of the line.

Step 3. Total credit reduction

To calculate the total credit reduction, add up all of the *Credit Reduction* boxes and enter the amount in the *Total Credit Reduction* box.

Then enter the total credit reduction on Form 940, line 11.

Example 1

You paid $20,000 in wages to each of three employees in State A. State A is subject to credit reduction at a rate of 0.03 (3.0%). Because you paid wages in a state that is subject to credit reduction, you must complete Schedule A and file it with Form 940.

Total payments to all employees in State A $60,000

Payments exempt from FUTA tax
(see the Instructions for Form 940) $0

Total payments made to each employee in excess of $7,000 (3 x ($20,000 - $7,000)) $39,000

Total FUTA taxable wages you paid in State A entered in the *FUTA Taxable Wages* box ($60,000 - $0 - $39,000) . . . $21,000

Credit reduction rate for State A 0.03

Total credit reduction for State A ($21,000 x 0.03) $630.00

 Don't include in the FUTA Taxable Wages *box wages in excess of the $7,000 wage base for each employee subject to state unemployment insurance in the credit reduction state. The credit reduction applies only to FUTA taxable wages that were also subject to state unemployment tax.*

In this case, you would write $630.00 in the *Total Credit Reduction* box and then enter that amount on Form 940, line 11.

Example 2

You paid $48,000 ($4,000 a month) in wages to Mary Smith and no payments were exempt from FUTA tax. Mary worked in State B (not subject to credit reduction) in January and then transferred to State C (subject to credit reduction) on February 1. Because you paid wages in more than one state, you must complete Schedule A and file it with Form 940.

The total payments in State B that aren't exempt from FUTA tax are $4,000. Since this payment to Mary doesn't exceed the $7,000 FUTA wage base, the total FUTA taxable wages paid in State B are $4,000.

The total payments in State C that aren't exempt from FUTA tax are $44,000. However, $4,000 of FUTA taxable wages was paid in State B with respect to Mary. Therefore, the total FUTA taxable wages with respect to Mary in State C are $3,000 ($7,000 (FUTA wage base) - $4,000 (total FUTA taxable wages paid in State B)). Enter $3,000 in the *FUTA Taxable Wages* box, multiply it by the *Reduction Rate*, and then enter the result in the *Credit Reduction* box.

Attach Schedule A to Form 940 when you file your return.

Form 940 Schedule R (Page 1)

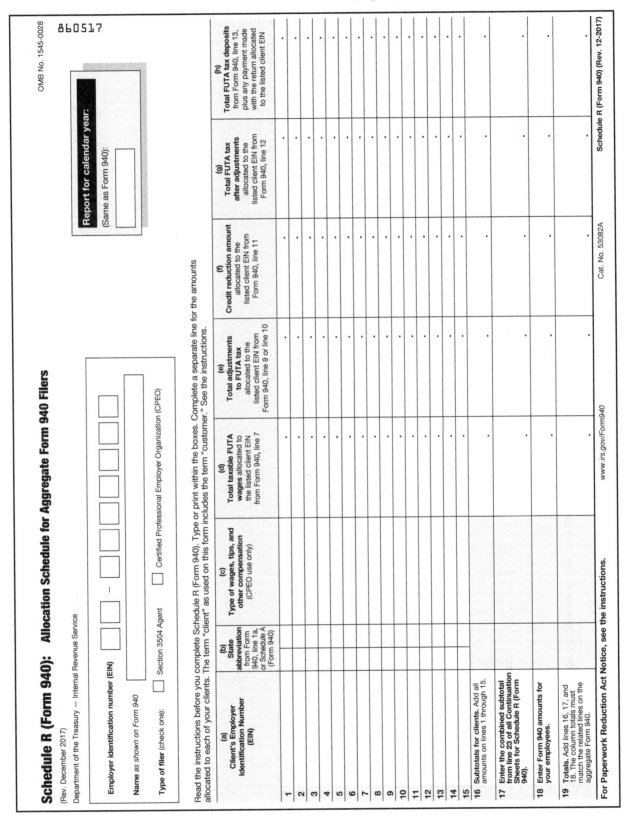

Form 940 Schedule R (Page 2)

860617

Continuation Sheet for Schedule R (Form 940)
Page ___ of ___
(Rev. December 2017)

Employer identification number (EIN) ☐☐ – ☐☐☐☐☐☐☐

Name *as shown on Form 940*

Report for calendar year:
(Same as Form 940):

Type of filer (check one): ☐ Section 3504 Agent ☐ Certified Professional Employer Organization (CPEO)

	(a) Client's Employer Identification Number (EIN)	(b) State abbreviation from Form 940, line 1a, or Schedule A (Form 940)	(c) Type of wages, tips, and other compensation (CPEO use only)	(d) Total taxable FUTA wages allocated to the listed client EIN from Form 940, line 7	(e) Total adjustments to FUTA tax allocated to the listed client EIN from Form 940, line 9 or line 10	(f) Credit reduction amount allocated to the listed client EIN from Form 940, line 11	(g) Total FUTA tax after adjustments allocated to the listed client EIN from Form 940, line 12	(h) Total FUTA tax deposits from Form 940, line 13, plus any payment made with the return allocated to the listed client EIN
1								
2								
3								
4								
5								
6								
7								
8								
9								
10								
11								
12								
13								
14								
15								
16								
17								
18								
19								
20								
21								
22								
23	**Subtotals for clients.** Add lines 1 through 22. Include the subtotals from line 23 on Schedule R (Form 940), line 17.							

Schedule R (Form 940) (Rev. 12-2017)

Form 940 Schedule R (Page 3)

Schedule R (Form 940) (Rev. 12-2017)

Section references are to the Internal Revenue Code unless otherwise noted.

Future Developments

For the latest information about developments related to Schedule R and its instructions, such as legislation enacted after they were published, go to *www.irs.gov/Form940.*

What's New

A certified professional employer organization (CPEO) must attach Schedule R to its aggregate Form 940, Employer's Annual Federal Unemployment (FUTA) Tax Return.

General Instructions

Purpose of Schedule R

Use Schedule R to allocate the aggregate information reported on Form 940 to each client. For purposes of Schedule R, the term "client" means (a) a home care service recipient identified on the Form 2678, Employer/Payer Appointment of Agent; (b) a customer who enters into a contract that meets the requirements under section 7705(e)(2); or (c) a client who enters into a service agreement described under Regulations section 31.3504-2(b)(2) with a CPEO. If you have more than 15 clients, complete as many continuation sheets as necessary. Attach Schedule R, including any continuation sheets, to your aggregate Form 940.

Who Must File?

You must complete Schedule R if you file an aggregate Form 940. Aggregate Forms 940 are filed by agents of home care service recipients approved by the IRS under section 3504 and by CPEOs. To request approval to act as an agent for a home care service recipient, you must file Form 2678 with the IRS, unless you are a state or local government agency acting as agent under the special procedures provided in Rev. Proc. 2013-39. Form 2678 must be previously filed and approved by the IRS before filing Schedule R. To become a CPEO, you must apply through the IRS Online Registration System. Visit *www.irs.gov/CPEO* for more information.

When Must You File?

If you're an aggregate Form 940 filer, file Schedule R with your aggregate Form 940 every year when your Form 940 is due. Agents may file Form 940 and Schedule R electronically or by paper submission. CPEOs generally must file Form 940 and Schedule R electronically. For more information about a CPEO's requirement to file electronically, see Rev. Proc. 2017-14, 2017-3 I.R.B. 426, available at *www.irs.gov/irb/2017-03_IRB/ar14.html.*

Specific Instructions

Completing Schedule R

Enter Your Business Information

Carefully enter your employer identification number (EIN) and the name of your business at the top of the schedule. Make sure they exactly match the EIN and name shown on the attached Form 940. Check one of the "Type of filer" boxes to tell us if you're a section 3504 agent or a CPEO.

Calendar Year

Enter the calendar year for which you are filing your Form 940. Make sure that the year entered on the top of Schedule R matches the year on the attached Form 940.

Client and Employee Information

On Schedule R, including any continuation sheets, you must report the following for each client.

Note: When entering amounts over 999.99 on Schedule R, don't enter commas.

Column a. Your client's EIN.

Column b. The state abbreviation of the client's location.

Column c (CPEO Use Only). Type of wages, tips, and other compensation. Enter a code to report the type of wages, tips, and other compensation paid to the individual(s) performing services for the client. If you paid more than one type of wages, tips, or other compensation, you must use more than one line to report for that client and enter the applicable code for each line. The following four codes are the only entries that can be made in column c.

- A: Wages, tips, and other compensation paid under section 3511(a).
- B: Wages, tips, and other compensation paid under section 3511(c).
- C: Wages, tips, and other compensation not reported under Code A or Code B paid as a payor under a service agreement described in Regulations section 31.3504-2(b)(2).
- D: Wages, tips, and other compensation paid as an agent under Regulations section 31.3504-1.

Column d. Total taxable FUTA wages allocated to the listed client EIN from Form 940, line 7.

Column e. Total adjustments to FUTA tax allocated to the listed client EIN from Form 940, line 9 or 10.

Column f. Credit reduction amount allocated to the listed client EIN from Form 940, line 11.

Column g. Total FUTA tax after adjustments allocated to the listed client EIN from Form 940, line 12.

Column h. Total FUTA tax deposits from Form 940, line 13, plus any other payments allocated to the listed client EIN.

You must also report the same information for your employees on Schedule R, line 18.

Compare the total of each column on Schedule R, line 19 (including your information from Schedule R, line 18) to the amounts reported on the aggregate Form 940. For each column total, the relevant line from Form 940 is noted in the column heading.

If the totals on Schedule R, line 19, don't match the totals on Form 940, there is an error that must be corrected before submitting Form 940 and Schedule R.

Paperwork Reduction Act Notice. We ask for the information on Schedule R to carry out the Internal Revenue laws of the United States. You are required to give us this information. We need it to ensure that you are complying with these laws and to allow us to figure and collect the right amount of tax.

You're not required to provide the information requested on a form that is subject to the Paperwork Reduction Act unless the form displays a valid OMB control number. Books or records relating to a form or its instructions must be retained as long as their contents may become material in the administration of any Internal Revenue law. Generally, tax returns and return information are confidential, as required by section 6103.

The time needed to complete and file Schedule R will vary depending on individual circumstances. The estimated average time is:

Recordkeeping	. 11 hr.
Learning about the law or the form	. 18 min.
Preparing, copying, and assembling the form	. 29 min.

If you have comments concerning the accuracy of these time estimates or suggestions for making Schedule R simpler, we would be happy to hear from you. You can send us comments from *www.irs.gov/FormComments.* Or you can send your comments to Internal Revenue Service, Tax Forms and Publications Division, 1111 Constitution Ave., NW, IR-6526, Washington, DC 20224. Don't send Schedule R to this address. Instead, see *Where Do You File?* in the Instructions for Form 940.

Form 941 (Page 1)

Form **941 for 2021:** **Employer's QUARTERLY Federal Tax Return**
(Rev. March 2021)
Department of the Treasury — Internal Revenue Service

950121

OMB No. 1545-0029

Employer identification number (EIN) ☐☐ – ☐☐☐☐☐☐☐

Name *(not your trade name)* _____

Trade name *(if any)* _____

Address _____
Number   Street   Suite or room number

_____
City   State   ZIP code

_____
Foreign country name   Foreign province/county   Foreign postal code

Report for this Quarter of 2021
(Check one.)

☐ **1:** January, February, March

☐ **2:** April, May, June

☐ **3:** July, August, September

☐ **4:** October, November, December

Go to *www.irs.gov/Form941* for instructions and the latest information.

Read the separate instructions before you complete Form 941. Type or print within the boxes.

Part 1: **Answer these questions for this quarter.**

1. Number of employees who received wages, tips, or other compensation for the pay period including: *Mar. 12* (Quarter 1), *June 12* (Quarter 2), *Sept. 12* (Quarter 3), or *Dec. 12* (Quarter 4)   **1** _____

2. Wages, tips, and other compensation . . . .   **2** _____

3. Federal income tax withheld from wages, tips, and other compensation . . . . . .   **3** _____

4. If no wages, tips, and other compensation are subject to social security or Medicare tax   ☐ Check and go to line 6.

	Column 1		Column 2
5a Taxable social security wages . .	_____	× 0.124 =	_____
5a (i) Qualified sick leave wages . .	_____	× 0.062 =	_____
5a (ii) Qualified family leave wages .	_____	× 0.062 =	_____
5b Taxable social security tips . . .	_____	× 0.124 =	_____
5c Taxable Medicare wages & tips . .	_____	× 0.029 =	_____
5d Taxable wages & tips subject to Additional Medicare Tax withholding	_____	× 0.009 =	_____

5e. Total social security and Medicare taxes. Add Column 2 from lines 5a, 5a(i), 5a(ii), 5b, 5c, and 5d   **5e** _____

5f. Section 3121(q) Notice and Demand—Tax due on unreported tips (see instructions) . .   **5f** _____

6. Total taxes before adjustments. Add lines 3, 5e, and 5f . . . .   **6** _____

7. Current quarter's adjustment for fractions of cents . . . .   **7** _____

8. Current quarter's adjustment for sick pay . . . .   **8** _____

9. Current quarter's adjustments for tips and group-term life insurance . . . . .   **9** _____

10. Total taxes after adjustments. Combine lines 6 through 9 . . . . . .   **10** _____

11a. Qualified small business payroll tax credit for increasing research activities. Attach Form 8974   **11a** _____

11b. Nonrefundable portion of credit for qualified sick and family leave wages from Worksheet 1   **11b** _____

11c. Nonrefundable portion of employee retention credit from Worksheet 1 . . . . . .   **11c** _____

▶ **You MUST complete all three pages of Form 941 and SIGN it.**   Next ▶

For Privacy Act and Paperwork Reduction Act Notice, see the back of the Payment Voucher.   Cat. No. 17001Z   Form **941** (Rev. 3-2021)

Form 941 (Page 2)

950221

Name *(not your trade name)*	Employer identification number (EIN)

Part 1:   **Answer these questions for this quarter.** *(continued)*

11d   **Total nonrefundable credits.** Add lines 11a, 11b, and 11c . . . . **11d** [.   ]

12   **Total taxes after adjustments and nonrefundable credits.** Subtract line 11d from line 10 . **12** [.   ]

13a   Total deposits for this quarter, including overpayment applied from a prior quarter and overpayments applied from Form 941-X, 941-X (PR), 944-X, or 944-X (SP) filed in the current quarter **13a** [.   ]

13b   Reserved for future use . . . . **13b** [.   ]

13c   Refundable portion of credit for qualified sick and family leave wages from Worksheet 1 **13c** [.   ]

13d   Refundable portion of employee retention credit from Worksheet 1 . . . . **13d** [.   ]

13e   **Total deposits and refundable credits.** Add lines 13a, 13c, and 13d . . . . **13e** [.   ]

13f   Total advances received from filing Form(s) 7200 for the quarter . . . . **13f** [.   ]

13g   **Total deposits and refundable credits less advances.** Subtract line 13f from line 13e . . . . **13g** [.   ]

14   **Balance due.** If line 12 is more than line 13g, enter the difference and see instructions . . . **14** [.   ]

15   **Overpayment.** If line 13g is more than line 12, enter the difference [.   ] Check one: ☐ Apply to next return.   ☐ Send a refund.

Part 2:   **Tell us about your deposit schedule and tax liability for this quarter.**

If you're unsure about whether you're a monthly schedule depositor or a semiweekly schedule depositor, see section 11 of Pub. 15.

16   Check one: ☐   **Line 12 on this return is less than $2,500 or line 12 on the return for the prior quarter was less than $2,500, and you didn't incur a $100,000 next-day deposit obligation during the current quarter.** If line 12 for the prior quarter was less than $2,500 but line 12 on this return is $100,000 or more, you must provide a record of your federal tax liability. If you're a monthly schedule depositor, complete the deposit schedule below; if you're a semiweekly schedule depositor, attach Schedule B (Form 941). Go to Part 3.

     ☐   **You were a monthly schedule depositor for the entire quarter.** Enter your tax liability for each month and total liability for the quarter, then go to Part 3.

         Tax liability: **Month 1**   [.   ]

                 Month 2   [.   ]

                 Month 3   [.   ]

         Total liability for quarter   [.   ]   **Total must equal line 12.**

     ☐   **You were a semiweekly schedule depositor for any part of this quarter.** Complete Schedule B (Form 941), Report of Tax Liability for Semiweekly Schedule Depositors, and attach it to Form 941. Go to Part 3.

▶ **You MUST complete all three pages of Form 941 and SIGN it.**   Next ▶

Page **2**   Form **941** (Rev. 3-2021)

Form 941 (Page 3)

950921

Name *(not your trade name)*   **Employer identification number (EIN)**

Part 3:   Tell us about your business. If a question does NOT apply to your business, leave it blank.

17 If your business has closed or you stopped paying wages . . . . ☐ Check here, and

enter the final date you paid wages [/ /] ; also attach a statement to your return. See instructions.

18 If you're a seasonal employer and you don't have to file a return for every quarter of the year . . . ☐ Check here.

19 Qualified health plan expenses allocable to qualified sick leave wages . . . . 19 [.]

20 Qualified health plan expenses allocable to qualified family leave wages . . . . 20 [.]

21 Qualified wages for the employee retention credit . . . . 21 [.]

22 Qualified health plan expenses allocable to wages reported on line 21 . . . . 22 [.]

23 Credit from Form 5884-C, line 11, for this quarter . . . . 23 [.]

24 Reserved for future use . . . . 24 [.]

25 Reserved for future use . . . . 25 [.]

Part 4:   May we speak with your third-party designee?

Do you want to allow an employee, a paid tax preparer, or another person to discuss this return with the IRS? See the instructions for details.

☐ Yes. Designee's name and phone number [   ] [   ]

Select a 5-digit personal identification number (PIN) to use when talking to the IRS. [ ][ ][ ][ ][ ]

☐ No.

Part 5:   Sign here. You MUST complete all three pages of Form 941 and SIGN it.

Under penalties of perjury, I declare that I have examined this return, including accompanying schedules and statements, and to the best of my knowledge and belief, it is true, correct, and complete. Declaration of preparer (other than taxpayer) is based on all information of which preparer has any knowledge.

X **Sign your name here** [   ]   Print your name here [   ]

Print your title here [   ]

Date [/ /]   Best daytime phone [   ]

Paid Preparer Use Only   Check if you're self-employed . . . ☐

Preparer's name [   ]   PTIN [   ]

Preparer's signature [   ]   Date [/ /]

Firm's name (or yours if self-employed) [   ]   EIN [   ]

Address [   ]   Phone [   ]

City [   ] State [   ]   ZIP code [   ]

Page **3**   Form **941** (Rev. 3-2021)

Instructions for Form 941

**Department of the Treasury
Internal Revenue Service**

(Rev. March 2021)

Employer's QUARTERLY Federal Tax Return

Section references are to the Internal Revenue Code unless otherwise noted.

Future Developments

For the latest information about developments related to Form 941 and its instructions, such as legislation enacted after they were published, go to *IRS.gov/Form941*.

At the time these instructions went to print, Congress was considering changes to coronavirus (COVID-19) tax relief. If new legislation impacts these instructions, updates will be posted to *IRS.gov/Form941*. You may also go to *IRS.gov/Coronavirus* for the latest information about COVID-19 tax relief.

What's New

Social security and Medicare tax for 2021. The rate of social security tax on taxable wages, except for qualified sick leave wages and qualified family leave wages, is 6.2% each for the employer and employee or 12.4% for both. Qualified sick leave wages and qualified family leave wages aren't subject to the employer share of social security tax; therefore, the tax rate on these wages is 6.2%. The social security wage base limit is $142,800.

The Medicare tax rate is 1.45% each for the employee and employer, unchanged from 2020. There is no wage base limit for Medicare tax.

Social security and Medicare taxes apply to the wages of household workers you pay $2,300 or more in cash wages in 2021. Social security and Medicare taxes apply to election workers who are paid $2,000 or more in cash or an equivalent form of compensation in 2021.

The COVID-19 related employee retention credit and the credit for qualified sick and family leave wages have been extended. The Families First Coronavirus Response Act (FFCRA) and the Coronavirus Aid, Relief, and Economic Security (CARES) Act were both amended by recent legislation. The FFCRA requirement that employers provide paid sick and family leave for reasons related to COVID-19 (the employer mandate) expired on December 31, 2020; however, the COVID-related Tax Relief Act of 2020 extends the periods for which employers providing leave that otherwise meets the requirements of the FFCRA may continue to claim tax credits for wages paid for leave taken before April 1, 2021. For more information about the credit for qualified sick and family leave wages, and to see if future legislation extends the dates through which the credit may be claimed, go to *IRS.gov/PLC*.

The Taxpayer Certainty and Disaster Tax Relief Act of 2020 modifies the calculation of the employee retention credit and extends the date through which the credit may be claimed to qualified wages paid through June 30, 2021. For more information about the employee retention credit, and to see if future legislation extends the dates through which credit may be claimed, go to *IRS.gov/ERC*.

Advance payment of COVID-19 credits extended. Form 7200, Advance Payment of Employer Credits Due to COVID-19, may be filed to request an advance payment for the credit for qualified sick and family leave wages through April 30, 2021. Form 7200 may be filed to request an advance payment for the employee retention credit through August 2, 2021. Form(s) 7200 can't be filed for quarters beginning after March 31, 2021, unless the credit for qualified sick and family leave wages is extended to leave taken after March 31, 2021; or for quarters beginning after June 30, 2021, unless the employee retention credit is extended to wages paid after June 30, 2021. For more information, including information on which employers are eligible to request an advance payment and the amount that can be advanced, see the Instructions for Form 7200. To see if future legislation extends these credits, see *IRS.gov/PLC*, *IRS.gov/ERC*, *IRS.gov/Form941*, and *IRS.gov/Form7200*.

Deferral of the employer share of social security tax expired. The CARES Act allowed employers to defer the deposit and payment of the employer share of social security tax. The deferred amount of the employer share of social security tax was only available for deposits due on or after March 27, 2020, and before January 1, 2021, as well as deposits and payments due after January 1, 2021, that are required for wages paid on or after March 27, 2020, and before January 1, 2021. Therefore, the line previously used for the employer deferral has been "Reserved for future use." One-half of the employer share of social security tax is due by December 31, 2021, and the remainder is due by December 31, 2022. Because both December 31, 2021, and December 31, 2022, are nonbusiness days, payments made on the next business day will be considered timely. Any payments or deposits you make before December 31, 2021, are first applied against your payment due on December 31, 2021, and then applied against your payment due on December 31, 2022. For more information about the deferral of employment tax deposits, go to *IRS.gov/ETD*. See *Paying the deferred amount of the employer share of social security tax* and *How to pay the deferred amount of the employer and employee share of social security tax*, later, for information about paying the deferred amount of the employer share of social security tax.

Deferral of the employee share of social security tax expired. The Presidential Memorandum on Deferring Payroll Tax Obligations in Light of the Ongoing COVID-19 Disaster, issued on August 8, 2020, directed the Secretary of the Treasury to defer the withholding, deposit, and payment of the employee share of social security tax on wages paid during the period from September 1, 2020, through December 31, 2020. The deferral of the withholding and payment of the employee share of social security tax was available for employees whose social security wages paid for a biweekly pay period were less than $4,000, or the equivalent threshold amount for other pay periods. The line previously used for the employee deferral has been "Reserved for future use." The COVID-related Tax Relief Act of 2020 defers the due date for the withholding and payment of the employee share of social security tax until the period beginning on January 1, 2021, and ending on December 31, 2021. For more information about the deferral of employee

Mar 09, 2021   Cat. No. 14625L

Form 941 Instructions (Page 2)

social security tax, see Notice 2020-65, 2020-38 I.R.B. 567, available at *IRS.gov/irb/2020-38_IRB#NOT-2020-65*, and Notice 2021-11, 2021-06 I.R.B. 827, available at *IRS.gov/irb/2021-06_IRB#NOT-2021-11*. Also see *Paying the deferred amount of the employee share of social security tax* and *How to pay the deferred amount of the employer and employee share of social security tax*, later, for information about paying the deferred amount of the employee share of social security tax. For information about how to report the deferred amount of the employee share of social security tax on Form W-2 and Form W-2c for 2020, see *IRS.gov/FormW2* and the 2021 General Instructions for Forms W-2 and W-3.

New payroll tax credit for certain tax-exempt organizations affected by qualified disasters. Section 303(d) of the Taxpayer Certainty and Disaster Tax Relief Act of 2020 allows for a new payroll tax credit for certain tax-exempt organizations affected by certain qualified disasters **not** related to COVID-19. This credit may still be available to certain tax-exempt organizations during the first and second quarters of 2021. This new credit will be claimed on new Form 5884-D (not on Form 941). Form 5884-D is filed after the Form 941 for the quarter for which the credit is being claimed has been filed. If you will claim this credit on Form 5884-D for a calendar quarter of 2021 and you're also claiming a credit for qualified sick and family leave wages and/or the employee retention credit in that quarter, you must include any credit that will be claimed on Form 5884-D on Worksheet 1 for the Form 941 for that quarter. For more information about this credit, go to *IRS.gov/Form5884D*.

⚠️ **CAUTION** *Don't use an earlier revision of Form 941 to report taxes for 2021. Don't use the March 2021 revision of Form 941 to report taxes for any quarter ending before January 1, 2021. Prior revisions of Form 941 are available at IRS.gov/Form941 (select the link for "All Form 941 Revisions" under "Other Items You May Find Useful").*

Reminders

Paying the deferred amount of the employer share of social security tax. One-half of the employer share of social security tax is due by December 31, 2021, and the remainder is due by December 31, 2022. Because both December 31, 2021, and December 31, 2022, are nonbusiness days, payments made on the next business day will be considered timely. Any payments or deposits you make before December 31, 2021, are first applied against your payment due on December 31, 2021, and then applied against your payment due on December 31, 2022. For example, if your employer share of social security tax for the third quarter of 2020 was $20,000 and you deposited $5,000 of the $20,000 during the third quarter of 2020 and you deferred $15,000 on Form 941, line 13b, then you must pay $5,000 by December 31, 2021, and $10,000 by December 31, 2022. However, if your employer share of social security tax for the third quarter of 2020 was $20,000 and you deposited $15,000 of the $20,000 during the third quarter of 2020 and you deferred $5,000 on Form 941, line 13b, then you don't need to pay any deferred amount by December 31, 2021, because 50% of the amount that could have been deferred ($10,000) has already been paid and is first applied against your payment that would be due on December 31, 2021. Accordingly, you must pay the $5,000 deferral by December 31, 2022. For additional information, go to *IRS.gov/ETD*.

Paying the deferred amount of the employee share of social security tax. The due date for the withholding and payment of the employee share of social security tax is postponed until the period beginning on January 1, 2021, and ending on December 31, 2021. The employer must withhold and pay the total deferred employee share of social security tax ratably from wages paid to the employee between January 1, 2021, and December 31, 2021. If necessary, the employer may make arrangements to otherwise collect the total deferred taxes from the employee. The employer is liable to pay the deferred taxes to the IRS and must do so before January 1, 2022, to avoid interest, penalties, and additions to tax on those amounts. Because January 1, 2022, is a nonbusiness day, payments made on January 3, 2022, will be considered timely. For more information about the deferral of the employee share of social security tax, see *Notice 2020-65* and *Notice 2021-11*.

How to pay the deferred amount of the employer and employee share of social security tax. You may pay the amount you owe electronically using the Electronic Federal Tax Payment System (EFTPS), by credit or debit card, or by a check or money order. The preferred method of payment is EFTPS. For more information, go to *EFTPS.gov*, or call 800-555-4477 or 800-733-4829 (TDD). To pay the deferred amount using EFTPS, select Form 941, the calendar quarter in 2020 to which the payment relates, and the option for payment due on an IRS notice. The IRS expects EFTPS to be updated on or around March 19, 2021, to provide a specific option to pay the deferred amount in lieu of selecting the option of making a payment due on an IRS notice.

To pay by credit or debit card, go to *IRS.gov/PayByCard*. If you pay by check or money order, include a 2020 Form 941-V, Payment Voucher, for the quarter in which you originally deferred the deposit and payment. Darken the circle identifying the quarter for which the payment is being made. The 2020 Form 941-V is on page 5 of Form 941 and is available at *IRS.gov/Form941* (select the link for "All Form 941 Revisions" under "Other Items You May Find Useful"). Make the check or money order payable to "United States Treasury." Enter your EIN, "Form 941," and the calendar quarter in which you originally deferred the deposit and payment (for example, "2nd Quarter 2020").

Payments should be sent to:

Department of the Treasury Internal Revenue Service Ogden, UT 84201-0030	or	Department of the Treasury Internal Revenue Service Kansas City, MO 64999-0030

Send your payment to the address above that is in the same state as the address to which you would mail returns filed without a payment, as shown under *Where Should You File*, later. For more information about the deferral of social security tax, go to *IRS.gov/ETD* and see *Notice 2020-65* and *Notice 2021-11*.

2021 withholding tables. The federal income tax withholding tables are included in Pub. 15-T, Federal Income Tax Withholding Methods.

Qualified small business payroll tax credit for increasing research activities. For tax years beginning after 2015, a qualified small business may elect to claim up to $250,000 of its credit for increasing research activities as a payroll tax credit against the employer share of social security tax. The

-2-

Instructions for Form 941 (Rev. 3-2021)

Form 941 Instructions (Page 3)

payroll tax credit election must be made on or before the due date of the originally filed income tax return (including extensions). The portion of the credit used against the employer share of social security tax is allowed in the first calendar quarter beginning after the date that the qualified small business filed its income tax return. The election and determination of the credit amount that will be used against the employer share of social security tax are made on Form 6765, Credit for Increasing Research Activities. The amount from Form 6765, line 44, must then be reported on Form 8974, Qualified Small Business Payroll Tax Credit for Increasing Research Activities. Form 8974 is used to determine the amount of the credit that can be used in the current quarter. The amount from Form 8974, line 12, is reported on Form 941, line 11a. If you're claiming the research payroll tax credit on your Form 941, you must attach Form 8974 to that Form 941. For more information about the payroll tax credit, see Notice 2017-23, 2017-16 I.R.B. 1100, available at *IRS.gov/irb/2017-16_IRB#NOT-2017-23*, and *IRS.gov/ResearchPayrollTC*. Also see *Adjusting tax liability for nonrefundable credits claimed on lines 11a, 11b, and 11c*, later.

Certification program for professional employer organizations (PEOs). The Stephen Beck, Jr., ABLE Act of 2014 required the IRS to establish a voluntary certification program for PEOs. PEOs handle various payroll administration and tax reporting responsibilities for their business clients and are typically paid a fee based on payroll costs. To become and remain certified under the certification program, certified professional employer organizations (CPEOs) must meet various requirements described in sections 3511 and 7705 and related published guidance. Certification as a CPEO may affect the employment tax liabilities of both the CPEO and its customers. A CPEO is generally treated for employment tax purposes as the employer of any individual who performs services for a customer of the CPEO and is covered by a contract described in section 7705(e)(2) between the CPEO and the customer (CPEO contract), but only for wages and other compensation paid to the individual by the CPEO. To become a CPEO, the organization must apply through the IRS Online Registration System. For more information or to apply to become a CPEO, go to *IRS.gov/CPEO*.

CPEOs must generally file Form 941 and Schedule R (Form 941), Allocation Schedule for Aggregate Form 941 Filers, electronically. For more information about a CPEO's requirement to file electronically, see Rev. Proc. 2017-14, 2017-3 I.R.B. 426, available at *IRS.gov/irb/2017-03_IRB#RP-2017-14*.

Outsourcing payroll duties. Generally, as an employer, you're responsible to ensure that tax returns are filed and deposits and payments are made, even if you contract with a third party to perform these acts. You remain responsible if the third party fails to perform any required action. Before you choose to outsource any of your payroll and related tax duties (that is, withholding, reporting, and paying over social security, Medicare, FUTA, and income taxes) to a third-party payer, such as a payroll service provider or reporting agent, go to *IRS.gov/OutsourcingPayrollDuties* for helpful information on this topic. If a CPEO pays wages and other compensation to an individual performing services for you, and the services are covered by a contract described in section 7705(e)(2) between you and the CPEO (CPEO contract), then the CPEO is generally treated for employment tax purposes as the employer, but only for wages and other

compensation paid to the individual by the CPEO. However, with respect to certain employees covered by a CPEO contract, you may also be treated as an employer of the employees and, consequently, may also be liable for federal employment taxes imposed on wages and other compensation paid by the CPEO to such employees. For more information on the different types of third-party payer arrangements, see section 16 of Pub. 15.

Aggregate Form 941 filers. Approved section 3504 agents and CPEOs must complete and file Schedule R (Form 941) when filing an aggregate Form 941. Aggregate Forms 941 are filed by agents approved by the IRS under section 3504. To request approval to act as an agent for an employer, the agent files Form 2678 with the IRS unless you're a state or local government agency acting as an agent under the special procedures provided in Rev. Proc. 2013-39, 2013-52 I.R.B. 830, available at *IRS.gov/irb/2013-52_IRB#RP-2013-39*. Aggregate Forms 941 are also filed by CPEOs approved by the IRS under section 7705. To become a CPEO, the organization must apply through the IRS Online Registration System at *IRS.gov/CPEO*. CPEOs file Form 8973, Certified Professional Employer Organization/Customer Reporting Agreement, to notify the IRS that they started or ended a service contract with a customer. CPEOs must generally file Form 941 and Schedule R (Form 941) electronically. For more information about a CPEO's requirement to file electronically, see Rev. Proc. 2017-14, 2017-3 I.R.B. 426, available at *IRS.gov/irb/2017-03_IRB#RP-2017-14*. The June 2020 revision of Schedule R won't be revised for 2021. If a line on Form 941 is "Reserved for future use," don't enter any amounts in the corresponding columns on Schedule R.

Other third-party payers that file aggregate Forms 941, such as non-certified PEOs, must complete and file Schedule R (Form 941) if they have clients that are claiming the qualified small business payroll tax credit for increasing research activities, the credit for qualified sick and family leave wages, or the employee retention credit.

TIP *If both an employer and a section 3504 authorized agent (or CPEO or other third-party payer) paid wages to an employee during a quarter, both the employer and the section 3504 authorized agent (or CPEO or other third-party payer, if applicable) should file Form 941 reporting the wages each entity paid to the employee during the applicable quarter and issue Forms W-2 reporting the wages each entity paid to the employee during the year.*

If a third-party payer of sick pay is also paying qualified sick leave wages on behalf of an employer, the third party would be making the payments as an agent of the employer. The employer is required to do the reporting and payment of employment taxes with respect to the qualified sick leave wages and claim the credit for the qualified sick leave wages, unless the employer has an agency agreement with the third-party payer that requires the third-party payer to do the collecting, reporting, and/or paying or depositing employment taxes on the qualified sick leave wages. If the employer has an agency agreement with the third-party payer, the third-party payer includes the qualified sick leave wages on the third party's aggregate Form 941, claims the sick leave credit on behalf of the employer on the aggregate Form 941, and separately reports the credit allocable to the employers on Schedule R (Form 941). See section 6 of Pub. 15-A, Employer's Supplemental Tax Guide, for more information about sick pay reporting.

Form 941 Instructions (Page 4)

Work opportunity tax credit for qualified tax-exempt organizations hiring qualified veterans. Qualified tax-exempt organizations that hire eligible unemployed veterans may be able to claim the work opportunity tax credit against their payroll tax liability using Form 5884-C. For more information, go to *IRS.gov/WOTC*.

Correcting a previously filed Form 941. If you discover an error on a previously filed Form 941, make the correction using Form 941-X. Form 941-X is filed separately from Form 941. For more information, see the Instructions for Form 941-X, section 13 of Pub. 15, or go to *IRS.gov/CorrectingEmploymentTaxes*.

Federal tax deposits must be made by electronic funds transfer (EFT). You must use EFT to make all federal tax deposits. Generally, an EFT is made using EFTPS. If you don't want to use EFTPS, you can arrange for your tax professional, financial institution, payroll service, or other trusted third party to make electronic deposits on your behalf. Also, you may arrange for your financial institution to initiate a same-day wire payment on your behalf. EFTPS is a free service provided by the Department of the Treasury. Services provided by your tax professional, financial institution, payroll service, or other third party may have a fee.

For more information on making federal tax deposits, see section 11 of Pub. 15. To get more information about EFTPS or to enroll in EFTPS, go to *EFTPS.gov*, or call 800-555-4477 or 800-733-4829 (TDD). Additional information about EFTPS is also available in Pub. 966.

> ⚠ **CAUTION** *For an EFTPS deposit to be on time, you must submit the deposit by 8 p.m. Eastern time the day before the date the deposit is due.*

Same-day wire payment option. If you fail to submit a deposit transaction on EFTPS by 8 p.m. Eastern time the day before the date a deposit is due, you can still make your deposit on time by using the Federal Tax Collection Service (FTCS) to make a same-day wire payment. To use the same-day wire payment method, you will need to make arrangements with your financial institution ahead of time. Please check with your financial institution regarding availability, deadlines, and costs. Your financial institution may charge you a fee for payments made this way. To learn more about the information you will need to give your financial institution to make a same-day wire payment, go to *IRS.gov/SameDayWire*.

Timeliness of federal tax deposits. If a deposit is required to be made on a day that isn't a business day, the deposit is considered timely if it is made by the close of the next business day. A business day is any day other than a Saturday, Sunday, or legal holiday. The term "legal holiday" for deposit purposes includes only those legal holidays in the District of Columbia. Legal holidays in the District of Columbia are provided in section 11 of Pub. 15.

Electronic filing and payment. Businesses can enjoy the benefits of filing tax returns and paying their federal taxes electronically. Whether you rely on a tax professional or handle your own taxes, the IRS offers you convenient programs to make filing and paying easier. Spend less time worrying about taxes and more time running your business. Use e-file and EFTPS to your benefit.

• For e-file, go to *IRS.gov/EmploymentEfile* for additional information. A fee may be charged to file electronically.

• For EFTPS, go to *EFTPS.gov*, or call EFTPS Customer Service at 800-555-4477 or 800-733-4829 (TDD) for additional information.

• For electronic filing of Forms W-2, Wage and Tax Statement, go to *SSA.gov/employer*. You may be required to file Forms W-2 electronically. For details, see the General Instructions for Forms W-2 and W-3.

> ⚠ **CAUTION** *If you're filing your tax return or paying your federal taxes electronically, a valid employer identification number (EIN) is required at the time the return is filed or the payment is made. If a valid EIN isn't provided, the return or payment won't be processed. This may result in penalties. See* Employer identification number (EIN), *later, for information about applying for an EIN.*

Electronic funds withdrawal (EFW). If you file Form 941 electronically, you can e-file and use EFW to pay the balance due in a single step using tax preparation software or through a tax professional. However, don't use EFW to make federal tax deposits. For more information on paying your taxes using EFW, go to *IRS.gov/EFW*.

Credit or debit card payments. You can pay the balance due shown on Form 941 by credit or debit card. Your payment will be processed by a payment processor who will charge a processing fee. Don't use a credit or debit card to make federal tax deposits. For more information on paying your taxes with a credit or debit card, go to *IRS.gov/PayByCard*.

Online payment agreement. You may be eligible to apply for an installment agreement online if you can't pay the full amount of tax you owe when you file your return. For more information, see *What if you can't pay in full*, later.

Paid preparers. If you use a paid preparer to complete Form 941, the paid preparer must complete and sign the paid preparer's section of the form.

Where can you get telephone help? For answers to your questions about completing Form 941 or tax deposit rules, you can call the IRS at 800-829-4933 or 800-829-4059 (TDD/TTY for persons who are deaf, hard of hearing, or have a speech disability), Monday–Friday from 7:00 a.m. to 7:00 p.m. local time (Alaska and Hawaii follow Pacific time).

Photographs of missing children. The IRS is a proud partner with the *National Center for Missing & Exploited Children® (NCMEC)*. Photographs of missing children selected by the Center may appear in instructions on pages that would otherwise be blank. You can help bring these children home by looking at the photographs and calling 1-800-THE-LOST (1-800-843-5678) if you recognize a child.

General Instructions:
Purpose of Form 941

These instructions give you some background information about Form 941. They tell you who must file Form 941, how to complete it line by line, and when and where to file it.

If you want more in-depth information about payroll tax topics relating to Form 941, see Pub. 15 or go to *IRS.gov/EmploymentTaxes*.

Federal law requires you, as an employer, to withhold certain taxes from your employees' pay. Each time you pay wages, you must withhold—or take out of your employees' pay—certain amounts for federal income tax, social security

-4-   **Instructions for Form 941 (Rev. 3-2021)**

Form 941 Instructions (Page 5)

tax, and Medicare tax. You must also withhold Additional Medicare Tax from wages you pay to an employee in excess of $200,000 in a calendar year. Under the withholding system, taxes withheld from your employees are credited to your employees in payment of their tax liabilities.

Federal law also requires you to pay any liability for the employer share of social security and Medicare taxes. This share of social security and Medicare taxes isn't withheld from employees.

Who Must File Form 941?

If you pay wages subject to federal income tax withholding or social security and Medicare taxes, you must file Form 941 quarterly to report the following amounts.
• Wages you've paid.
• Tips your employees reported to you.
• Federal income tax you withheld.
• Both the employer and the employee share of social security and Medicare taxes.
• Additional Medicare Tax withheld from employees.
• Current quarter's adjustments to social security and Medicare taxes for fractions of cents, sick pay, tips, and group-term life insurance.
• Qualified small business payroll tax credit for increasing research activities.
• Credit for qualified sick and family leave wages.
• Employee retention credit.
• Total advances received from filing Form(s) 7200 for the quarter.

Don't use Form 941 to report backup withholding or income tax withholding on nonpayroll payments such as pensions, annuities, and gambling winnings. Report these types of withholding on Form 945, Annual Return of Withheld Federal Income Tax. Also, don't use Form 941 to report unemployment taxes. Report unemployment taxes on Form 940, Employer's Annual Federal Unemployment (FUTA) Tax Return.

After you file your first Form 941, you must file a return for each quarter, even if you have no taxes to report, unless you filed a final return or one of the exceptions listed next applies.

Exceptions

Special rules apply to some employers.
• If you received notification to file **Form 944,** you must file Form 944 annually; don't file Form 941 quarterly.
• **Seasonal employers** don't have to file a Form 941 for quarters in which they have no tax liability because they have paid no wages. To tell the IRS that you won't file a return for one or more quarters during the year, check the box on line 18 every quarter you file Form 941. See section 12 of Pub. 15 for more information.
• Employers of **household employees** don't usually file Form 941. See Pub. 926 and Schedule H (Form 1040) for more information.
• Employers of **farm employees** don't file Form 941 for wages paid for agricultural labor. See Form 943 and Pub. 51 for more information.

 If none of the these exceptions apply and you haven't filed a final return, you must file Form 941 each quarter even if you didn't pay wages during the quarter. Use IRS e-file, if possible.

Requesting To File Forms 941 Instead of Form 944, or Requesting To File Form 944 Instead of Forms 941

Requesting to file Forms 941 instead of Form 944. Employers that would otherwise be required to file Form 944, Employer's ANNUAL Federal Tax Return, may contact the IRS to request to file quarterly Forms 941 instead of annual Form 944. To request to file quarterly Forms 941 to report your social security and Medicare taxes for the 2021 calendar year, you must either call the IRS at 800-829-4933 between January 1, 2021, and April 1, 2021, or send a written request postmarked between January 1, 2021, and March 15, 2021. After you contact the IRS, the IRS will send you a written notice that your filing requirement has been changed to Forms 941. You must receive written notice from the IRS to file Forms 941 instead of Form 944 before you may file these forms. If you don't receive this notice, you must file Form 944 for calendar year 2021.

Requesting to file Form 944 instead of Forms 941. If you're required to file Forms 941 but believe your employment taxes for calendar year 2021 will be $1,000 or less, you may request to file Form 944 instead of Forms 941 by calling the IRS at 800-829-4933 between January 1, 2021, and April 1, 2021, or sending a written request postmarked between January 1, 2021, and March 15, 2021. After you contact the IRS, the IRS will send you a written notice that your filing requirement has been changed to Form 944. You must receive written notice from the IRS to file Form 944 instead of Forms 941 before you may file this form. If you don't receive this notice, you must file Forms 941 for calendar year 2021.

Where to send written requests. Written requests should be sent to:

Department of the Treasury
Internal Revenue Service
Ogden, UT 84201-0038

or

Department of the Treasury
Internal Revenue Service
Cincinnati, OH 45999-0038

If you would mail your return filed without a payment to Ogden, as shown under *Where Should You File*, later, send your request to the Ogden address shown above. If you would mail your return filed without a payment to Kansas City, send your request to the address for Cincinnati shown above. For more information about these procedures, see Rev. Proc. 2009-51, 2009-45 I.R.B. 625, available at *IRS.gov/irb/2009-45_IRB#RP-2009-51.*

What if You Reorganize or Close Your Business?

If You Sell or Transfer Your Business . . .

If you sell or transfer your business during the quarter, you and the new owner must each file a Form 941 for the quarter in which the transfer occurred. Report only the wages you paid.

When two businesses merge, the continuing firm must file a return for the quarter in which the change took place and the other firm should file a final return.

Changing from one form of business to another—such as from a sole proprietorship to a partnership or corporation—is considered a transfer. If a transfer occurs, you may need a

Form 941 Instructions (Page 6)

new EIN. See Pub. 1635 and section 1 of Pub. 15 for more information.

Attach a statement to your return with:
• The new owner's name (or the new name of the business);
• Whether the business is now a sole proprietorship, partnership, or corporation;
• The kind of change that occurred (a sale or transfer);
• The date of the change; and
• The name of the person keeping the payroll records and the address where those records will be kept.

If Your Business Has Closed . . .

If you permanently go out of business or stop paying wages to your employees, you must file a final return. To tell the IRS that Form 941 for a particular quarter is your final return, check the box on line 17 and enter the final date you paid wages. Also attach a statement to your return showing the name of the person keeping the payroll records and the address where those records will be kept.

See *Terminating a business* in the General Instructions for Forms W-2 and W-3 for information about earlier dates for the expedited furnishing and filing of Forms W-2 when a final Form 941 is filed.

If you participated in a statutory merger or consolidation, or qualify for predecessor-successor status due to an acquisition, you should generally file Schedule D (Form 941), Report of Discrepancies Caused by Acquisitions, Statutory Mergers, or Consolidations. See the Instructions for Schedule D (Form 941) to determine whether you should file Schedule D (Form 941) and when you should file it.

When Must You File?

File your initial Form 941 for the quarter in which you first paid wages that are subject to social security and Medicare taxes or subject to federal income tax withholding. See the table titled *When To File Form 941*, later.

Then you must file for every quarter after that—every 3 months—even if you have no taxes to report, unless you're a seasonal employer or are filing your final return. See *Seasonal employers* and *If Your Business Has Closed*, earlier.

File Form 941 only once for each quarter. If you filed electronically, don't file a paper Form 941. For more information about filing Form 941 electronically, see *Electronic filing and payment*, earlier.

When To File Form 941

Your Form 941 is due by the last day of the month that follows the end of the quarter.

The Quarter Includes . . .	Quarter Ends	Form 941 Is Due
1. January, February, March	March 31	April 30
2. April, May, June	June 30	July 31
3. July, August, September	September 30	October 31
4. October, November, December	December 31	January 31

For example, you must generally report wages you pay during the first quarter—which is January through March—by April 30. If you made timely deposits in full payment of your taxes for the quarter, you may file by the 10th day of the 2nd

month that follows the end of the quarter. For example, you may file Form 941 by May 10 if you made timely deposits in full payment of your taxes for the 1st quarter.

If we receive Form 941 after the due date, we will treat Form 941 as filed on time if the envelope containing Form 941 is properly addressed, contains sufficient postage, and is postmarked by the U.S. Postal Service on or before the due date, or sent by an IRS-designated private delivery service (PDS) on or before the due date. If you don't follow these guidelines, we will generally consider Form 941 filed when it is actually received. For more information about PDSs, see *Where Should You File*, later.

If any due date for filing falls on a Saturday, Sunday, or legal holiday, you may file your return on the next business day.

How Should You Complete Form 941?

Type or print your EIN, name, and address in the spaces provided. Also enter your name and EIN on the top of pages 2 and 3. Don't use your social security number (SSN) or individual taxpayer identification number (ITIN). Generally, enter the business (legal) name you used when you applied for your EIN. For example, if you're a sole proprietor, enter "Haleigh Smith" on the "Name" line and "Haleigh's Cycles" on the "Trade name" line. Leave the "Trade name" line blank if it is the same as your "Name."

If you use a tax preparer to fill out Form 941, make sure the preparer shows your business name exactly as it appeared when you applied for your EIN.

Employer identification number (EIN). To make sure businesses comply with federal tax laws, the IRS monitors tax filings and payments by using a numerical system to identify taxpayers. A unique nine-digit EIN is assigned to all corporations, partnerships, and some sole proprietors. Businesses needing an EIN must apply for a number and use it throughout the life of the business on all tax returns, payments, and reports.

Your business should have only one EIN. If you have more than one and aren't sure which one to use, write to the IRS office where you file your returns (using the *Without a payment* address under *Where Should You File*, later) or call the IRS at 800-829-4933.

If you don't have an EIN, you may apply for one online by visiting *IRS.gov/EIN*. You may also apply for an EIN by faxing or mailing Form SS-4 to the IRS. If the principal business was created or organized outside of the United States or U.S. territories, you may also apply for an EIN by calling 267-941-1099 (toll call). If you haven't received your EIN by the due date of Form 941, file a paper return and write "Applied For" and the date you applied in this entry space.

 If you're filing your tax return electronically, a valid EIN is required at the time the return is filed. If a valid EIN isn't provided, the return won't be accepted. This may result in penalties.

 Always be sure the EIN on the form you file exactly matches the EIN the IRS assigned to your business. Don't use your SSN or ITIN on forms that ask for an EIN. If you used an EIN (including a prior owner's EIN) on Form 941 that is different from the EIN reported on Form W-3, see Box h—Other EIN used this year *in the General Instructions for Forms W-2 and W-3. Filing a Form 941 with*

-6-

Form 941 Instructions (Page 7)

an incorrect EIN or using another business's EIN may result in penalties and delays in processing your return.

If you change your business name, business address, or responsible party... Notify the IRS immediately if you change your business name, business address, or responsible party.
• Write to the IRS office where you file your returns (using the *Without a payment* address under *Where Should You File*, later) to notify the IRS of any business name change. See Pub.1635 to see if you need to apply for a new EIN.
• Complete and mail Form 8822-B to notify the IRS of a business address or responsible party change. Don't mail Form 8822-B with your Form 941. For a definition of "responsible party," see the Instructions for Form SS-4.

Check the Box for the Quarter

Under "Report for this Quarter of 2021" at the top of Form 941, check the appropriate box of the quarter for which you're filing. Make sure the quarter checked is the same as shown on any attached Schedule B (Form 941), Report of Tax Liability for Semiweekly Schedule Depositors, and, if applicable, Schedule R (Form 941).

Completing and Filing Form 941

Make entries on Form 941 as follows to enable accurate scanning and processing.
• Use 10-point Courier font (if possible) for all entries if you're typing or using a computer to complete your form. Portable Document Format (PDF) forms on IRS.gov have fillable fields with acceptable font specifications.
• Don't enter dollar signs and decimal points. Commas are optional. Enter dollars to the left of the preprinted decimal point and cents to the right of it. Don't round entries to whole dollars. Always show an amount for cents, even if it is zero.
• Leave blank any data field (except lines 1, 2, and 12) with a value of zero.
• Enter negative amounts using a minus sign (if possible). Otherwise, use parentheses.
• Enter your name and EIN on all pages.
• Enter your name, EIN, "Form 941," and the tax year and quarter on all attachments.
• Staple multiple sheets in the upper left corner when filing.

Complete all three pages. You must complete all three pages of Form 941 and sign on page 3. Failure to do so may delay processing of your return.

Required Notice to Employees About the Earned Income Credit (EIC)

To notify employees about the EIC, you must give the employees one of the following items.

• Form W-2 which has the required information about the EIC on the back of Copy B.
• A substitute Form W-2 with the same EIC information on the back of the employee's copy that is on Copy B of the IRS Form W-2.
• Notice 797, Possible Federal Tax Refund Due to the Earned Income Credit (EIC).
• Your written statement with the same wording as Notice 797.

For more information, see section 10 of Pub. 15, Pub. 596, and *IRS.gov/EIC*.

Reconciling Forms 941 and Form W-3

The IRS matches amounts reported on your four quarterly Forms 941 with Form W-2 amounts totaled on your yearly Form W-3, Transmittal of Wage and Tax Statements. If the amounts don't agree, you may be contacted by the IRS or the Social Security Administration (SSA). The following amounts are reconciled.
• Federal income tax withholding.
• Social security wages.
• Social security tips.
• Medicare wages and tips.

For more information, see section 12 of Pub. 15 and the Instructions for Schedule D (Form 941).

Where Should You File?

You're encouraged to file Form 941 electronically. Go to *IRS.gov/EmploymentEfile* for more information on electronic filing. If you file a paper return, where you file depends on whether you include a payment with Form 941. Mail your return to the address listed for your location in the table that follows.

PDSs can't deliver to P.O. boxes. You must use the U.S. Postal Service to mail an item to a P.O. box address. Go to *IRS.gov/PDS* for the current list of PDSs. For the IRS mailing address to use if you're using a PDS, go to *IRS.gov/PDSstreetAddresses*. Select the mailing address listed on the webpage that is in the same state as the address to which you would mail returns filed without a payment, as shown next.

Form 941 Instructions (Page 8)

Mailing Addresses for Form 941

If you're in . . .	Without a payment . . .	With a payment . . .
Connecticut, Delaware, District of Columbia, Georgia, Illinois, Indiana, Kentucky, Maine, Maryland, Massachusetts, Michigan, New Hampshire, New Jersey, New York, North Carolina, Ohio, Pennsylvania, Rhode Island, South Carolina, Tennessee, Vermont, Virginia, West Virginia, Wisconsin	Department of the Treasury Internal Revenue Service Kansas City, MO 64999-0005	Internal Revenue Service P.O. Box 806532 Cincinnati, OH 45280-6532
Alabama, Alaska, Arizona, Arkansas, California, Colorado, Florida, Hawaii, Idaho, Iowa, Kansas, Louisiana, Minnesota, Mississippi, Missouri, Montana, Nebraska, Nevada, New Mexico, North Dakota, Oklahoma, Oregon, South Dakota, Texas, Utah, Washington, Wyoming	Department of the Treasury Internal Revenue Service Ogden, UT 84201-0005	Internal Revenue Service P.O. Box 932100 Louisville, KY 40293-2100
No legal residence or principal place of business in any state	Internal Revenue Service P.O. Box 409101 Ogden, UT 84409	Internal Revenue Service P.O. Box 932100 Louisville, KY 40293-2100
Special filing address for exempt organizations; federal, state, and local governmental entities; and Indian tribal governmental entities, regardless of location	Department of the Treasury Internal Revenue Service Ogden, UT 84201-0005	Internal Revenue Service P.O. Box 932100 Louisville, KY 40293-2100

 Your filing address may have changed from that used to file your employment tax return in prior years. Don't send Form 941 or any payments to the SSA.

Depositing Your Taxes

 You must deposit all depository taxes electronically by EFT. For more information, see Federal tax deposits must be made by electronic funds transfer (EFT) *under* Reminders, *earlier.*

Must You Deposit Your Taxes?

You may have to deposit the federal income taxes you withheld and both the employer and employee social security taxes and Medicare taxes.

- **If your total taxes after adjustments and nonrefundable credits (line 12) are less than $2,500 for the current quarter or the prior quarter, and you didn't incur a $100,000 next-day deposit obligation during the current quarter.** You don't have to make a deposit. To avoid a penalty, you must pay any amount due in full with a timely filed return or you must deposit any amount you owe by the due date of the return. For more information on paying with a timely filed return, see the instructions for line 14, later. If you're not sure your total tax liability for the current quarter will be less than $2,500 (and your liability for the prior quarter wasn't less than $2,500), make deposits using the semiweekly or monthly rules so you won't be subject to failure-to-deposit (FTD) penalties.
- **If your total taxes after adjustments and nonrefundable credits (line 12) are $2,500 or more for the current quarter and the prior quarter.** You must make deposits according to your deposit schedule. See section 11 of Pub. 15 for information about payments made under the accuracy of deposits rule and for rules about federal tax deposits.

Reducing your deposits for COVID-19 credits. Employers eligible to claim the credit for qualified sick and family leave wages and/or the employee retention credit can reduce their deposits by the amount of their anticipated credits. Employers won't be subject to an FTD penalty for reducing their deposits if certain conditions are met. See the instructions for line 11b and line 11c for more information on these credits. For more information on reducing deposits, see Notice 2020-22, 2020-17 I.R.B. 664, available at IRS.gov/irb/2020-17_IRB#NOT-2020-22. Also see

IRS.gov/ERC and IRS.gov/PLC for more information, including examples, about reducing deposits. See the instructions for line 16, later, for information on adjusting tax liabilities reported on line 16 or Schedule B (Form 941) for nonrefundable credits.

When Must You Deposit Your Taxes?

Determine if You're a Monthly or Semiweekly Schedule Depositor for the Quarter

The IRS uses two different sets of deposit rules to determine when businesses must deposit their social security, Medicare, and withheld federal income taxes. These schedules tell you when a deposit is due after you have a payday.

Your deposit schedule isn't determined by how often you pay your employees. Your deposit schedule depends on the total tax liability you reported on Form 941 during the previous 4-quarter lookback period (July 1 of the second preceding calendar year through June 30 of the preceding calendar year). See section 11 of Pub. 15 for details. If you filed Form 944 in either 2019 or 2020, your lookback period is the 2019 calendar year.

Before the beginning of each calendar year, determine which type of deposit schedule you must use.
- If you reported $50,000 or less in taxes during the lookback period, you're a **monthly schedule depositor**.
- If you reported more than $50,000 of taxes during the lookback period, you're a **semiweekly schedule depositor**.

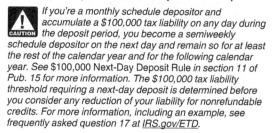 *If you're a monthly schedule depositor and accumulate a $100,000 tax liability on any day during the deposit period, you become a semiweekly schedule depositor on the next day and remain so for at least the rest of the calendar year and for the following calendar year. See* $100,000 Next-Day Deposit Rule *in section 11 of Pub. 15 for more information. The $100,000 tax liability threshold requiring a next-day deposit is determined before you consider any reduction of your liability for nonrefundable credits. For more information, including an example, see frequently asked question 17 at IRS.gov/ETD.*

Instructions for Form 941 (Rev. 3-2021)

Form 941 Instructions (Page 9)

What About Penalties and Interest?

Avoiding Penalties and Interest

You can avoid paying penalties and interest if you do all of the following.
- Deposit or pay your taxes when they are due, unless you meet the requirements discussed in *Notice 2020-22* or *IRS.gov/ETD*, or you have chosen to use the relief provided in *Notice 2020-65* and *Notice 2021-11*.
- File your fully completed Form 941 on time.
- Report your tax liability accurately.
- Submit valid checks for tax payments.
- Furnish accurate Forms W-2 to employees.
- File Form W-3 and Copy A of Forms W-2 with the SSA on time and accurately.

Penalties and interest are charged on taxes paid late and returns filed late at a rate set by law. See sections 11 and 12 of Pub. 15 for details.

Use Form 843 to request abatement of assessed penalties or interest. Don't request abatement of assessed penalties or interest on Form 941 or Form 941-X.

If you receive a notice about a penalty after you file this return, reply to the notice with an explanation and we will determine if you meet reasonable-cause criteria. Don't attach an explanation when you file your return.

⚠️ **CAUTION** *If federal income, social security, and Medicare taxes that must be withheld (that is, trust fund taxes) aren't withheld or aren't deposited or paid to the United States Treasury, the trust fund recovery penalty may apply. The penalty is 100% of the unpaid trust fund tax. If these unpaid taxes can't be immediately collected from the employer or business, the trust fund recovery penalty may be imposed on all persons who are determined by the IRS to be responsible for collecting, accounting for, or paying over these taxes, and who acted willfully in not doing so. For more information, see section 11 of Pub. 15. The trust fund recovery penalty won't apply to any amount of trust fund taxes an employer holds back in anticipation of any credits they are entitled to. It also won't apply to applicable taxes deferred under Notice 2020-65 and Notice 2021-11 before January 1, 2022.*

Adjustment of Tax on Tips

If, by the 10th of the month after the month you received an employee's report on tips, you don't have enough employee funds available to withhold the employee share of social security and Medicare taxes, you no longer have to collect it. Report the entire amount of these tips on line 5b (Taxable social security tips), line 5c (Taxable Medicare wages and tips), and, if the withholding threshold is met, line 5d (Taxable wages and tips subject to Additional Medicare Tax withholding). Include as a negative adjustment on line 9 the total uncollected employee share of the social security and Medicare taxes.

Specific Instructions:

Part 1: Answer These Questions for This Quarter

1. Number of Employees Who Received Wages, Tips, or Other Compensation

Enter the number of employees on your payroll for the pay period including March 12, June 12, September 12, or December 12, for the quarter indicated at the top of Form 941. Don't include:
- Household employees,
- Employees in nonpay status for the pay period,
- Farm employees,
- Pensioners, or
- Active members of the Armed Forces.

 For purposes of these instructions, all references to "sick pay" mean ordinary sick pay, not "qualified sick leave wages" that are reported on line 5a(i).

2. Wages, Tips, and Other Compensation

Enter amounts on line 2 that would also be included in box 1 of your employees' Forms W-2. See *Box 1—Wages, tips, other compensation* in the General Instructions for Forms W-2 and W-3 for details. Include sick pay paid by your agent. Also include sick pay paid by a third party that isn't your agent (for example, an insurance company) if you were given timely notice of the payments and the third party transferred liability for the employer's taxes to you.

If you're a third-party payer of sick pay and not an agent of the employer, don't include sick pay that you paid to policyholders' employees here if you gave the policyholders timely notice of the payments. See section 6 of Pub. 15-A for more information about sick pay reporting and the procedures for transferring the liability to the employer.

3. Federal Income Tax Withheld From Wages, Tips, and Other Compensation

Enter the federal income tax you withheld (or were required to withhold) from your employees on this quarter's wages, including qualified sick leave wages, qualified family leave wages, and qualified wages (excluding qualified health plan expenses) for the employee retention credit; tips; taxable fringe benefits; and supplemental unemployment compensation benefits. Don't include any income tax withheld by a third-party payer of sick pay even if you reported it on Forms W-2. You will reconcile this difference on Form W-3. Also include here any excise taxes you were required to withhold on golden parachute payments (section 4999). For information on the employment tax treatment of fringe benefits, see Pub. 15-B, Employer's Tax Guide to Fringe Benefits. For information about supplemental unemployment compensation benefits and golden parachute payments, see section 5 of Pub. 15-A.

If you're a third-party payer of sick pay, enter the federal income tax you withheld (or were required to withhold) on third-party sick pay here.

Form 941 Instructions (Page 10)

4. If No Wages, Tips, and Other Compensation Are Subject to Social Security or Medicare Tax . . .

If no wages, tips, and other compensation on line 2 are subject to social security or Medicare tax, check the box on line 4. If this question doesn't apply to you, leave the box blank. For more information about exempt wages, see section 15 of Pub. 15. For religious exemptions, see section 4 of Pub. 15-A.

⚠️ **CAUTION** *If you're a government employer, wages you pay aren't automatically exempt from social security and Medicare taxes. Your employees may be covered by law or by a voluntary Section 218 Agreement with the SSA. For more information, see Pub. 963, Federal-State Reference Guide.*

5a–5e. Taxable Social Security and Medicare Wages and Tips

5a. Taxable social security wages. Enter the total wages, including qualified wages (other than qualified health plan expenses) for the employee retention credit; sick pay; and taxable fringe benefits subject to social security taxes you paid to your employees during the quarter. Don't include the qualified sick leave wages reported on line 5a(i) or qualified family leave wages reported on line 5a(ii). For this purpose, sick pay includes payments made by an insurance company to your employees for which you received timely notice from the insurance company. See section 6 of Pub. 15-A for more information about sick pay reporting. See the instructions for line 8 for an adjustment that you may need to make on Form 941 for sick pay.

Enter the amount before payroll deductions. Don't include tips on this line. For information on types of wages subject to social security taxes, see section 5 of Pub. 15.

For 2021, the rate of social security tax on taxable wages, except for qualified sick leave wages and qualified family leave wages, is 6.2% (0.062) each for the employer and employee or 12.4% (0.124) for both. Stop paying social security tax on and entering an employee's wages on line 5a when the employee's taxable wages, including qualified sick leave wages, qualified family leave wages, and tips, reach $142,800 for the year. However, continue to withhold income and Medicare taxes for the whole year on all wages, including qualified sick leave wages, qualified family leave wages, and tips, even when the social security wage base of $142,800 has been reached.

$$\begin{array}{r} \text{line 5a (column 1)} \\ \times \quad 0.124 \\ \hline \text{line 5a (column 2)} \end{array}$$

5a(i). Qualified sick leave wages. Enter the qualified taxable sick leave wages you paid to your employees during the quarter. Qualified sick leave wages aren't subject to the employer share of social security tax; therefore, the tax rate on these wages is 6.2% (0.062). Stop paying social security tax on and entering an employee's wages on line 5a(i) when the employee's taxable wages, including wages reported on line 5a, qualified sick leave wages, qualified family leave wages, and tips, reach $142,800 for the year. See the instructions for line 5c for reporting Medicare tax on qualified

sick leave wages, including the portion above the social security wage base.

For purposes of the credit for qualified sick and family leave wages, qualified sick leave wages are wages for social security and Medicare tax purposes, determined without regard to the exclusions from the definition of employment under section 3121(b), that an employer pays that otherwise meet the requirements of the Emergency Paid Sick Leave Act (EPSLA), as enacted under the FFCRA and amended by the COVID-related Tax Relief Act of 2020. However, don't include any wages otherwise excluded under section 3121(b) when reporting qualified sick leave wages on lines 5a(i), 5c, and, if applicable, 5d. See the instructions for line 11b for information about the credit for qualified sick and family leave wages.

$$\begin{array}{r} \text{line 5a(i) (column 1)} \\ \times \quad 0.062 \\ \hline \text{line 5a(i) (column 2)} \end{array}$$

EPSLA. For 2021, certain employers with fewer than 500 employees are entitled to credits under the FFCRA, as amended by the COVID-related Tax Relief Act of 2020, if they provide paid sick leave to employees that otherwise meets the requirements of the EPSLA. Under the EPSLA, wages are qualified sick leave wages if paid to employees that are unable to work or telework after March 31, 2020, and before April 1, 2021, because the employee:

1. Is subject to a federal, state, or local quarantine or isolation order related to COVID-19;

2. Has been advised by a health care provider to self-quarantine due to concerns related to COVID-19;

3. Is experiencing symptoms of COVID-19 and seeking a medical diagnosis;

4. Is caring for an individual subject to an order described in (1) or who has been advised as described in (2);

5. Is caring for a son or daughter because the school or place of care for that child has been closed, or the childcare provider for that child is unavailable, due to COVID-19 precautions; or

6. Is experiencing any other substantially similar condition specified by the U.S. Department of Health and Human Services.

Son or daughter. A son or daughter must generally have been under 18 years of age or incapable of self-care because of a mental or physical disability. A son or daughter includes a biological child, adopted child, stepchild, foster child, legal ward, or a child for whom the employee assumes parental status and carries out the obligations of a parent. For more information about who is a son or daughter under the FFCRA, see *DOL.gov/agencies/whd/pandemic.*

💡 **TIP** *Government employers aren't eligible for the credit for qualified sick and family leave wages; however, as with any employer, government employers aren't liable for the employer share of the social security tax on the qualified sick leave wages paid to employees.*

Limits on qualified sick leave wages. The EPSLA provides different limitations for different circumstances under which qualified sick leave wages are paid. For paid sick leave qualifying under (1), (2), or (3) above, the amount of qualified sick leave wages is determined at the employee's

Form 941 Instructions (Page 11)

regular rate of pay, but the wages may not exceed $511 for any day (or portion of a day) for which the individual is paid sick leave. For paid sick leave qualifying under (4), (5), or (6), earlier, the amount of qualified sick leave wages is determined at two-thirds the employee's regular rate of pay, but the wages may not exceed $200 for any day (or portion of a day) for which the individual is paid sick leave. The EPSLA also limits each individual to a maximum of up to 80 hours of paid sick leave. Therefore, the maximum amount of paid sick leave wages paid to one employee can't exceed $5,110 for an employee for leave under (1), (2), or (3), and it can't exceed $2,000 for an employee for leave under (4), (5), or (6). For more information from the Department of Labor on these requirements and limits, see *DOL.gov/agencies/whd/pandemic*.

For more information about qualified sick leave wages, go to *IRS.gov/PLC*.

5a(ii). Qualified family leave wages. Enter the qualified taxable family leave wages you paid to your employees during the quarter. Qualified family leave wages aren't subject to the employer share of social security tax; therefore, the tax rate on these wages is 6.2% (0.062). Stop paying social security tax on and entering an employee's wages on line 5a(ii) when the employee's taxable wages, including wages reported on line 5a, qualified sick leave wages, qualified family leave wages, and tips, reach $142,800 for the year. See the instructions for line 5c for reporting Medicare tax on qualified family leave wages, including the portion above the social security wage base.

For purposes of the credit for qualified sick and family leave wages, qualified family leave wages are wages for social security and Medicare tax purposes, determined without regard to the exclusions from the definition of employment under section 3121(b), that an employer pays that otherwise meet the requirements of the Emergency Family and Medical Leave Expansion Act (Expanded FMLA), as enacted under the FFCRA and amended by the COVID-related Tax Relief Act of 2020. However, don't include any wages otherwise excluded under section 3121(b) when reporting qualified family leave wages on lines 5a(ii), 5c, and, if applicable, 5d. See the instructions for line 11b for information about the credit for qualified sick and family leave wages.

line 5a(ii) (column 1)

x   0.062

line 5a(ii) (column 2)

Expanded FMLA. For 2021, certain employers with fewer than 500 employees are entitled to credits under the FFCRA, as amended by the COVID-related Tax Relief Act of 2020, if they provide paid family leave to employees that otherwise meets the requirements of the Expanded FMLA. Under the Expanded FMLA, wages are qualified family leave wages if paid to an employee who has been employed for at least 30 calendar days when an employee is unable to work or telework due to the need to care for a son or daughter under 18 years of age or incapable of self-care because of a mental or physical disability because the school or place of care for that child has been closed, or the childcare provider for that child is unavailable, due to a public health emergency. See *Son or daughter*, earlier, for more information.

The first 10 days for which an employee takes leave may be unpaid. During this period, employees may use other forms of paid leave, such as qualified sick leave, accrued sick leave, annual leave, or other paid time off. After an employee takes leave for 10 days, the employer must provide the employee paid leave (that is, qualified family leave wages) for up to 10 weeks. For more information from the Department of Labor on these requirements, possible exceptions, and the limitations discussed below, see *DOL.gov/agencies/whd/pandemic*.

TIP *Government employers aren't eligible for the credit for qualified sick and family leave wages; however, as with any employer, government employers aren't liable for the employer share of the social security tax on the qualified family leave wages paid to employees.*

Rate of pay and limit on wages. The rate of pay must be at least two-thirds of the employee's regular rate of pay (as determined under the Fair Labor Standards Act of 1938), multiplied by the number of hours the employee otherwise would have been scheduled to work. The qualified family leave wages can't exceed $200 per day or $10,000 in the aggregate per employee.

For more information about qualified family leave wages, go to *IRS.gov/PLC*.

5b. Taxable social security tips. Enter all tips your employees reported to you during the quarter until the total of the tips and taxable wages, including qualified sick leave wages and qualified family leave wages, for an employee reach $142,800 for the year. Include all tips your employee reported to you even if you were unable to withhold the employee tax of 6.2%. You will reduce your total taxes by the amount of any uncollected employee share of social security and Medicare taxes on tips later on line 9; see *Current quarter's adjustments for tips and group-term life insurance*, later. Don't include service charges on line 5b. For details about the difference between tips and service charges, see Rev. Rul. 2012-18, 2012-26 I.R.B. 1032, available at *IRS.gov/irb/2012-26_IRB#RR-2012-18*.

Your employee must report cash tips to you by the 10th day of the month after the month the tips are received. Cash tips include tips paid by cash, check, debit card, and credit card. The report should include charged tips (for example, credit and debit card charges) you paid over to the employee for charge customers, tips the employee received directly from customers, and tips received from other employees under any tip-sharing arrangement. Both directly and indirectly tipped employees must report tips to you. No report is required for months when tips are less than $20. Employees may use Form 4070 (available only in Pub. 1244), or submit a written statement or electronic tip record.

Don't include allocated tips (described in section 6 of Pub. 15) on this line. Instead, report them on Form 8027. Allocated tips aren't reportable on Form 941 and aren't subject to withholding of federal income, social security, or Medicare taxes.

line 5b (column 1)

x   0.124

line 5b (column 2)

5c. Taxable Medicare wages & tips. Enter all wages, including qualified sick leave wages, qualified family leave wages, and qualified wages (excluding qualified health plan

Form 941 Instructions (Page 12)

expenses) for the employee retention credit; tips; sick pay; and taxable fringe benefits that are subject to Medicare tax. Unlike social security wages, there is no limit on the amount of wages subject to Medicare tax.

The rate of Medicare tax is 1.45% (0.0145) each for the employer and employee or 2.9% (0.029) for both. Include all tips your employees reported during the quarter, even if you were unable to withhold the employee tax of 1.45%.

$$
\begin{array}{r}
\text{line 5c } \text{(column 1)} \\
\times \quad 0.029 \\
\hline
\text{line 5c } \text{(column 2)}
\end{array}
$$

For more information on tips, see section 6 of Pub. 15. See the instructions for line 8 for an adjustment that you may need to make on Form 941 for sick pay.

5d. Taxable wages & tips subject to Additional Medicare Tax withholding. Enter all wages, including qualified sick leave wages, qualified family leave wages, and qualified wages (excluding qualified health plan expenses) for the employee retention credit; tips; sick pay; and taxable fringe benefits that are subject to Additional Medicare Tax withholding. You're required to begin withholding Additional Medicare Tax in the pay period in which you pay wages in excess of $200,000 to an employee and continue to withhold it each pay period until the end of the calendar year. Additional Medicare Tax is only imposed on the employee. There is no employer share of Additional Medicare Tax. All wages that are subject to Medicare tax are subject to Additional Medicare Tax withholding if paid in excess of the $200,000 withholding threshold.

For more information on what wages are subject to Medicare tax, see the chart, *Special Rules for Various Types of Services and Payments*, in section 15 of Pub. 15. For more information on Additional Medicare Tax, go to *IRS.gov/ADMT*. See the instructions for line 8 for an adjustment that you may need to make on Form 941 for sick pay.

Once wages and tips exceed the $200,000 withholding threshold, include all tips your employees reported during the quarter, even if you were unable to withhold the employee tax of 0.9%.

$$
\begin{array}{r}
\text{line 5d } \text{(column 1)} \\
\times \quad 0.009 \\
\hline
\text{line 5d } \text{(column 2)}
\end{array}
$$

5e. Total social security and Medicare taxes. Add the column 2 amounts on lines 5a–5d. Enter the result on line 5e.

5f. Section 3121(q) Notice and Demand—Tax Due on Unreported Tips

Enter the tax due from your Section 3121(q) Notice and Demand on line 5f. The IRS issues a Section 3121(q) Notice and Demand to advise an employer of the amount of tips received by employees who failed to report or underreported tips to the employer. An employer isn't liable for the employer share of the social security and Medicare taxes on unreported tips until notice and demand for the taxes is made to the employer by the IRS in a Section 3121(q) Notice and Demand. The tax due may have been determined from tips reported to the IRS on employees' Forms 4137, Social Security and Medicare Tax on Unreported Tip Income, or

other tips that weren't reported to their employer as determined by the IRS during an examination. For additional information, see Rev. Rul. 2012-18, 2012-26 I.R.B. 1032, available at *IRS.gov/irb/2012-26_IRB#RR-2012-18*.

Deposit the tax within the time period required under your deposit schedule to avoid any possible deposit penalty. The tax is treated as accumulated by the employer on the "Date of Notice and Demand" as printed on the Section 3121(q) Notice and Demand. The employer must include this amount on the appropriate line of the record of federal tax liability (Part 2 of Form 941 for a monthly schedule depositor or Schedule B (Form 941) for a semiweekly schedule depositor).

6. Total Taxes Before Adjustments

Add the total federal income tax withheld from wages, tips, and other compensation (line 3); the total social security and Medicare taxes before adjustments (line 5e); and any tax due under a Section 3121(q) Notice and Demand (line 5f). Enter the result on line 6.

7–9. Tax Adjustments

Enter tax amounts on lines 7–9 that result from current quarter adjustments. Use a minus sign (if possible) to show an adjustment that decreases the total taxes shown on line 6 instead of parentheses. Doing so enhances the accuracy of our scanning software. For example, enter "-10.59" instead of "(10.59)." However, if your software only allows for parentheses in entering negative amounts, you may use them.

Current quarter's adjustments. In certain cases, you must adjust the amounts you entered as social security and Medicare taxes in column 2 of lines 5a–5d to figure your correct tax liability for this quarter's Form 941. See section 13 of Pub. 15.

7. Current quarter's adjustment for fractions of cents. Enter adjustments for fractions of cents (due to rounding) relating to the employee share of social security and Medicare taxes withheld. The employee share of amounts shown in column 2 of lines 5a–5d may differ slightly from amounts actually withheld from employees' pay due to the rounding of social security and Medicare taxes based on statutory rates. This adjustment may be a positive or a negative adjustment.

8. Current quarter's adjustment for sick pay. If your third-party payer of sick pay that isn't your agent (for example, an insurance company) transfers the liability for the employer share of the social security and Medicare taxes to you, enter a negative adjustment on line 8 for the employee share of social security and Medicare taxes that were withheld and deposited by your third-party sick pay payer on the sick pay. If you're the third-party sick pay payer and you transferred the liability for the employer share of the social security and Medicare taxes to the employer, enter a negative adjustment on line 8 for any employer share of these taxes required to be paid by the employer. The sick pay should be included on line 5a, line 5c, and, if the withholding threshold is met, line 5d.

No adjustment is reported on line 8 for sick pay that is paid through a third party as an employer's agent. An employer's agent bears no insurance risk and is reimbursed on a cost-plus-fee basis for payment of sick pay and similar amounts. If an employer uses an agent to pay sick pay, the employer reports the wages on line 5a, line 5c, and, if the withholding threshold is met, line 5d, unless the employer

Form 941 Instructions (Page 13)

has an agency agreement with the third-party payer that requires the third-party payer to do the collecting, reporting, and/or paying or depositing employment taxes on the sick pay. See section 6 of Pub. 15-A for more information about sick pay reporting.

9. Current quarter's adjustments for tips and group-term life insurance. Enter a negative adjustment for:
• Any uncollected employee share of social security and Medicare taxes on tips, and
• The uncollected employee share of social security and Medicare taxes on group-term life insurance premiums paid for former employees.

See the General Instructions for Forms W-2 and W-3 for information on how to report the uncollected employee share of social security and Medicare taxes on tips and group-term life insurance on Form W-2.

Prior quarter's adjustments. If you need to correct any adjustment reported on a previously filed Form 941, complete and file Form 941-X. Form 941-X is an adjusted return or claim for refund and is filed separately from Form 941. See section 13 of Pub. 15.

10. Total Taxes After Adjustments

Combine the amounts shown on lines 6–9 and enter the result on line 10.

11a. Qualified Small Business Payroll Tax Credit for Increasing Research Activities

Enter the amount of the credit from Form 8974, line 12.

⚠ CAUTION *If you enter an amount on line 11a, you must attach Form 8974. The December 2017 revision of Form 8974 instructs you to enter the amount from Form 8974, line 12, on Form 941, line 11. Instead, the amount from Form 8974, line 12, should be entered on Form 941, line 11a.*

11b. Nonrefundable Portion of Credit for Qualified Sick and Family Leave Wages From Worksheet 1

TIP *Form 941 and these instructions use the terms "nonrefundable" and "refundable" when discussing credits. The term "nonrefundable" means the portion of the credit which is limited by law to the amount of the employer share of social security tax. The term "refundable" means the portion of the credit which is in excess of the employer share of social security tax.*

Businesses and tax-exempt organizations with fewer than 500 employees that provide paid sick leave under the EPSLA and/or provide paid family leave under the Expanded FMLA are eligible to claim the credit for qualified sick and family leave wages for the period after March 31, 2020, and before April 1, 2021. For purposes of this credit, qualified sick leave wages and qualified family leave wages are wages for social security and Medicare tax purposes, determined without regard to the exclusions from the definition of employment under section 3121(b), that an employer pays that otherwise meet the requirements of the EPSLA or Expanded FMLA. Enter the nonrefundable portion of the credit for qualified sick and family leave wages from Worksheet 1, Step 2, line 2j. The credit for qualified sick and family leave wages consists of the qualified sick leave wages, the qualified family leave wages, the qualified health plan expenses allocable to those wages, and the employer share of Medicare tax allocable to

those wages. The nonrefundable portion of the credit is limited to the employer share of social security tax reported on Form 941, lines 5a and 5b, after that share is first reduced by any credit claimed on Form 8974 for the qualified small business payroll tax credit for increasing research activities, any credit to be claimed on Form 5884-C for the work opportunity credit for qualified tax-exempt organizations hiring qualified veterans, and/or any credit to be claimed on Form 5884-D for the disaster credit for qualified tax-exempt organizations.

⚠ CAUTION *If you're a third-party payer of sick pay that isn't an agent (for example, an insurance company) and you're claiming the credit for qualified sick and family leave wages for amounts paid to your own employees, the amount of the employer share of social security tax reported on line 5a must be reduced by any adjustment you make on line 8 for the employer share of social security tax transferred to your client. If you received a Section 3121(q) Notice and Demand for tax due on unreported tips (Letter 3263 or Letter 4520) during the quarter, you report the amount for the employer share of social security tax and Medicare tax on Form 941, line 5f. Letter 3263 or Letter 4520 includes an attachment that shows the employer share of social security tax. This amount of the employer share of social security tax can also be reduced by the nonrefundable portion of the credit. See Worksheet 1 to figure your credit.*

Any credit in excess of the remaining amount of the employer share of social security tax is refundable and reported on Form 941, line 13c. For more information on the credit for qualified sick and family leave wages, go to IRS.gov/PLC.

Qualified health plan expenses allocable to qualified sick leave and family leave wages. The credit for qualified sick leave wages and qualified family leave wages is increased to cover the qualified health plan expenses that are properly allocable to the qualified leave wages for which the credit is allowed. These qualified health plan expenses are amounts paid or incurred by the employer to provide and maintain a group health plan but only to the extent such amounts are excluded from the employees' income as coverage under an accident or health plan. The amount of qualified health plan expenses generally includes both the portion of the cost paid by the employer and the portion of the cost paid by the employee with pre-tax salary reduction contributions. However, qualified health plan expenses don't include amounts that the employee paid for with after-tax contributions. For more information, go to IRS.gov/PLC.

TIP *You must include the full amount (both the nonrefundable and refundable portions) of the credit for qualified sick and family leave wages in your gross income for the tax year that includes the last day of any calendar quarter in which a credit is allowed. You can't use the same wages for the employee retention credit and the credits for paid sick and family leave.*

Instructions for Form 941 (Rev. 3-2021)   -13-

Form 941 Instructions (Page 14)

11c. Nonrefundable Portion of Employee Retention Credit From Worksheet 1

TIP *Certain government entities are entitled to the credit for calendar quarters in 2021, including (1) federal instrumentalities described in section 501(c)(1) and exempt from tax under section 501(a), and (2) any government, agency, or instrumentality that is a college or university or the principal purpose or function of the entity is providing medical or hospital care.*

Enter the nonrefundable portion of the employee retention credit from <u>Worksheet 1</u>, Step 3, line 3h. The employee retention credit is 70% of the qualified wages you paid to your employees in the quarter. Qualified wages include <u>qualified health plan expenses for the employee retention credit</u>. The nonrefundable portion of the credit is limited to the employer share of social security tax reported on Form 941, lines 5a and 5b, after that share is first reduced by any credit claimed on Form 8974 for the qualified small business payroll tax credit for increasing research activities, any credit to be claimed on Form 5884-C for the work opportunity credit for qualified tax-exempt organizations hiring qualified veterans, any credit to be claimed on Form 5884-D for the disaster credit for qualified tax-exempt organizations, and/or any credit claimed for the nonrefundable portion of the credit for qualified sick and family leave wages.

CAUTION *If you're a third-party payer of sick pay that isn't an agent (for example, an insurance company) and you're claiming the employee retention credit for amounts paid to your own employees, the amount of the employer share of social security tax reported on line 5a must be reduced by any adjustment you make on line 8 for the employer share of social security tax transferred to your client. If you received a Section 3121(q) Notice and Demand for tax due on unreported tips (Letter 3263 or Letter 4520) during the quarter, you report the amount for the employer share of social security tax and Medicare tax on Form 941, line 5f. Letter 3263 or Letter 4520 includes an attachment that shows the employer share of social security tax. This amount of the employer share of social security tax can also be reduced by the nonrefundable portion of the credit. See <u>Worksheet 1</u> to figure your credit.*

Any credit in excess of the remaining amount of the employer share of social security tax is refundable and reported on Form 941, line 13d. For more information on the employee retention credit, go to *IRS.gov/ERC*.

Qualified wages for the employee retention credit. The tax credit is equal to 70% of qualified wages paid to employees after December 31, 2020, and before July 1, 2021. Qualified wages, including qualified health plan expenses, are limited to a maximum of $10,000 for each employee for the quarter. Qualified wages are wages for social security and Medicare tax purposes paid to certain employees during any period in a quarter in which your business operations are fully or partially suspended due to a government order or during a quarter in which your gross receipts (within the meaning of section 448(c) or, if you're a tax-exempt organization, section 6033) are less than 80% of the gross receipts for the same calendar quarter in calendar year 2019.

The wages and qualified health plan expenses considered in calculating your credit depend on the size of your workforce. Eligible employers that had an average number of 500 or fewer full-time employees during 2019 count wages paid to all their employees and the qualified health plan expenses paid or incurred for all employees during any period in the quarter in which business operations are fully or partially suspended due to a government order or during a quarter in which gross receipts are less than 80% of the gross receipts for the same calendar quarter in calendar year 2019. Eligible employers that had an average number of more than 500 full-time employees in 2019 may count only wages paid to employees for time that the employees weren't providing services, and qualified health plan expenses paid or incurred by the employer allocable to the time those employees weren't providing services, due to the suspension or decline in gross receipts.

Qualified wages don't include wages for which the employer receives a credit for sick or family leave under the FFCRA. Employers can receive both a Small Business Interruption Loan under the Paycheck Protection Program (PPP) and the employee retention credit; however, employers can't receive both loan forgiveness and a credit for the same wages. Any wages taken into account in determining the employee retention credit can't be taken into account as wages for purposes of the credits under sections 41, 45A, 45P, 45S, 51, and 1396. For more information about the employee retention credit, including rules for new employers, an optional election to determine the gross receipts test based on a prior quarter, and rules that allow certain governmental employers to claim the credit for 2021, go to *IRS.gov/ERC*.

Qualified health plan expenses for the employee retention credit. Qualified wages for the employee retention credit include qualified health plan expenses. Qualified health plan expenses are amounts paid or incurred by the employer to provide and maintain a group health plan but only to the extent such amounts are excluded from the employees' income as coverage under an accident or health plan. The amount of qualified health plan expenses taken into account in determining the amount of qualified wages generally includes both the portion of the cost paid by the employer and the portion of the cost paid by the employee with pre-tax salary reduction contributions. However, the qualified health plan expenses shouldn't include amounts that the employee paid for with after-tax contributions. Generally, qualified health plan expenses are those which are allocable to an employee (and to a period) in which your business operations are fully or partially suspended due to a government order or experience a decline in gross receipts. The allocation will be treated as proper if made on the basis of being pro rata among periods of coverage. For more information, see the frequently asked questions for qualified health plan expenses at *IRS.gov/ERC*.

11d. Total Nonrefundable Credits

Add lines 11a, 11b, and 11c. Enter the total on line 11d.

12. Total Taxes After Adjustments and Nonrefundable Credits

Subtract line 11d from line 10 and enter the result on line 12.

• **If line 12 is less than $2,500 or line 12 on the prior quarterly return was less than $2,500, and you didn't incur a $100,000 next-day deposit obligation during the current quarter.** You may pay the amount with Form 941 or you may deposit the amount. To avoid a penalty, you must pay any amount you owe in full with a timely filed return or you must deposit any amount you owe before the due date of

Form 941 Instructions (Page 15)

the return. For more information on paying with a timely filed return, see the instructions for line 14, later.

• **If line 12 is $2,500 or more and line 12 on the prior quarterly return was $2,500 or more, or if you incurred a $100,000 next-day deposit obligation during the current quarter.** You must make required deposits according to your deposit schedule. See *Notice 2020-22* for information about the reduction of certain deposits. The amount shown on line 12 must equal the "Total liability for quarter" shown on line 16 or the "Total liability for the quarter" shown on Schedule B (Form 941). For more information, see the line 16 instructions, later.

For more information and rules about federal tax deposits, see *Depositing Your Taxes*, earlier, and section 11 of Pub. 15.

If you're a semiweekly schedule depositor, you must complete Schedule B (Form 941). If you fail to complete and submit Schedule B (Form 941), the IRS may assert deposit penalties based on available information.

13a. Total Deposits for This Quarter

Enter your deposits for this quarter, including any overpayment from a prior quarter that you applied to this return. Also include in the amount shown any overpayment that you applied from filing Form 941-X, 941-X (PR), 944-X, or 944-X (SP) in the current quarter. Don't include any amount that you didn't deposit because you reduced your deposits in anticipation of the credit for qualified sick and family leave wages and/or the employee retention credit, as discussed in *Notice 2020-22*.

13c. Refundable Portion of Credit for Qualified Sick and Family Leave Wages From Worksheet 1

Businesses and tax-exempt organizations with fewer than 500 employees that provide paid sick leave under the EPSLA and/or provide paid family leave under the Expanded FMLA are eligible to claim the credit for qualified sick and family leave wages. Enter the refundable portion of the credit for qualified sick and family leave wages from Worksheet 1, Step 2, line 2k. The credit for qualified sick and family leave wages consists of the qualified sick leave wages, the qualified family leave wages, the qualified health plan expenses allocable to those wages, and the employer share of Medicare tax allocable to those wages. The refundable portion of the credit is allowed after the employer share of social security tax is reduced to zero by nonrefundable credits.

13d. Refundable Portion of Employee Retention Credit From Worksheet 1

Enter the refundable portion of the employee retention credit from Worksheet 1, Step 3, line 3i. The employee retention credit is 70% of the qualified wages you paid to your employees in the quarter. The refundable portion of the credit is allowed after the employer share of social security tax is reduced to zero by nonrefundable credits.

13e. Total Deposits and Refundable Credits

Add lines 13a, 13c, and 13d. Enter the total on line 13e.

13f. Total Advances Received From Filing Form(s) 7200 for the Quarter

Enter the total advances received from filing Form(s) 7200 for the quarter. If you filed a Form 7200 for the quarter but you haven't received the advance before filing Form 941, don't include on line 13f the amount of the advance requested. Employers were eligible to file Form 7200 for the quarter if they paid qualified sick leave wages, qualified family leave wages, and/or qualified wages for the employee retention credit and the amount of employment tax deposits they retained wasn't sufficient to cover the cost of qualified sick and family leave wages and the employee retention credit.

 Form 7200 may be filed for a quarter up to the earlier of the end of the month after the end of each quarter or filing of Form 941 for the quarter. However, if you file Form 7200 after the end of the quarter, it's possible that it may not be processed prior to the processing of the filed Form 941. Advance payment requests on Form 7200 for a quarter won't be paid after your Form 941 is processed for that quarter. When the IRS processes Form 941, we will correct the amount reported on line 13f to match the amount of advance payments issued or contact you to reconcile the difference before we finish processing Form 941.

13g. Total Deposits and Refundable Credits Less Advances

Subtract line 13f from line 13e. Enter the result on line 13g.

14. Balance Due

If line 12 is more than line 13g, enter the difference on line 14. Otherwise, see *Overpayment*, later.

Never make an entry on both lines 14 and 15.

You don't have to pay if line 14 is under $1. Generally, you should have a balance due only if your total taxes after adjustments and nonrefundable credits (line 12) for the current quarter or prior quarter are less than $2,500, and you didn't incur a $100,000 next-day deposit obligation during the current quarter. However, see section 11 of Pub. 15 for information about payments made under the accuracy of deposits rule.

If you were required to make federal tax deposits, pay the amount shown on line 14 by EFT. If you weren't required to make federal tax deposits (see *Must You Deposit Your Taxes*, earlier) or you're a monthly schedule depositor making a payment under the accuracy of deposits rule, you may pay the amount shown on line 14 by EFT, credit card, debit card, check, money order, or EFW. For more information on electronic payment options, go to *IRS.gov/ Payments*.

If you pay by EFT, credit card, or debit card, file your return using the *Without a payment* address under *Where Should You File*, earlier, and don't file Form 941-V, Payment Voucher.

If you pay by check or money order, make it payable to "United States Treasury." Enter your EIN, "Form 941," and the tax period ("1st Quarter 2021," "2nd Quarter 2021," "3rd Quarter 2021," or "4th Quarter 2021") on your check or money order. Complete Form 941-V and enclose with Form 941.

If line 12 is $2,500 or more on both your prior and current quarter Form 941, and you've deposited all taxes when due, the balance due on line 14 should be zero.

Instructions for Form 941 (Rev. 3-2021)   -15-

Form 941 Instructions (Page 16)

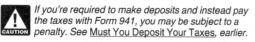 *If you're required to make deposits and instead pay the taxes with Form 941, you may be subject to a penalty. See* <u>Must You Deposit Your Taxes</u>, *earlier.*

What if you can't pay in full? If you can't pay the full amount of tax you owe, you can apply for an installment agreement online. You can apply for an installment agreement online if:
- You can't pay the full amount shown on line 14,
- The total amount you owe is $25,000 or less, and
- You can pay the liability in full in 24 months.

To apply using the Online Payment Agreement Application, go to *IRS.gov/OPA*.

Under an installment agreement, you can pay what you owe in monthly installments. There are certain conditions you must meet to enter into and maintain an installment agreement, such as paying the liability within 24 months, and making all required deposits and timely filing tax returns during the length of the agreement.

If your installment agreement is accepted, you will be charged a fee and you will be subject to penalties and interest on the amount of tax not paid by the due date of the return.

15. Overpayment
If line 13g is more than line 12, enter the difference on line 15.

Never make an entry on both lines 14 and 15.

If you deposited more than the correct amount for the quarter, you can choose to have the IRS either refund the overpayment or apply it to your next return. Check only one box on line 15. If you don't check either box or if you check both boxes, we will generally apply the overpayment to your next return. Regardless of any boxes you check or don't check on line 15, we may apply your overpayment to any past due tax account that is shown in our records under your EIN.

If line 15 is under $1, we will send a refund or apply it to your next return only if you ask us in writing to do so.

Part 2: Tell Us About Your Deposit Schedule and Tax Liability for This Quarter

16. Tax Liability for the Quarter
Check one of the boxes on line 16. Follow the instructions for each box to determine if you need to enter your monthly tax liability on Form 941 or your daily tax liability on Schedule B (Form 941).

De minimis exception. If line 12 is less than $2,500 or line 12 on the prior quarterly return was less than $2,500, and you didn't incur a $100,000 next-day deposit obligation during the current quarter, check the first box on line 16 and go to Part 3.

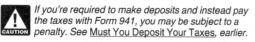 *If you meet the de minimis exception based on the prior quarter and line 12 for the current quarter is $100,000 or more, you must provide a record of your federal tax liability. If you're a monthly schedule depositor, complete the deposit schedule on line 16. If you're a semiweekly schedule depositor, attach Schedule B (Form 941).*

Monthly schedule depositor. If you reported $50,000 or less in taxes during the lookback period, you're a monthly schedule depositor unless the $100,000 Next-Day Deposit Rule discussed in section 11 of Pub. 15 applies. Check the second box on line 16 and enter your tax liability for each month in the quarter. Enter your tax liabilities in the month that corresponds to the dates you paid wages to your employees, not the date payroll liabilities were accrued or deposits were made. Add the amounts for each month. Enter the result in the "Total liability for quarter" box.

Note that your total tax liability for the quarter must equal your total taxes shown on line 12. If it doesn't, your tax deposits and payments may not be counted as timely. Don't reduce your total liability reported on line 16 by the refundable portion of the credit for qualified sick and family leave wages or the refundable portion of the employee retention credit. Don't change your tax liability on line 16 by adjustments reported on any Forms 941-X.

You're a monthly schedule depositor for the calendar year if the amount of your Form 941 taxes reported for the lookback period is $50,000 or less. The lookback period is the 4 consecutive quarters ending on June 30 of the prior year. For 2021, the lookback period begins July 1, 2019, and ends June 30, 2020. For details on the deposit rules, see section 11 of Pub. 15. If you filed Form 944 in either 2019 or 2020, your lookback period is the 2019 calendar year.

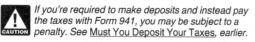 *The amounts entered on line 16 are a summary of your monthly tax liability, not a summary of deposits you made. If you don't properly report your liabilities when required or if you're a semiweekly schedule depositor and enter your liabilities on line 16 instead of on Schedule B (Form 941), you may be assessed an "averaged" FTD penalty. See* Deposit Penalties *in section 11 of Pub. 15 for more information.*

Reporting adjustments from lines 7–9 on line 16. If your net adjustment during a month is negative and it exceeds your total tax liability for the month, don't enter a negative amount for the month. Instead, enter "-0-" for the month and carry over the unused portion of the adjustment to the next month.

Semiweekly schedule depositor. If you reported more than $50,000 of taxes for the lookback period, you're a semiweekly schedule depositor. Check the third box on line 16.

You must complete Schedule B (Form 941) and submit it with your Form 941. Don't file Schedule B (Form 941) with your Form 941 if you're a monthly schedule depositor.

Don't change your tax liability on Schedule B (Form 941) by adjustments reported on any Forms 941-X.

Adjusting tax liability for nonrefundable credits claimed on lines 11a, 11b, and 11c. Monthly schedule depositors and semiweekly schedule depositors must account for nonrefundable credits claimed on lines 11a, 11b, and 11c when reporting their tax liabilities on line 16 or Schedule B (Form 941). The total tax liability for the quarter must equal the amount reported on line 12. Failure to account for the nonrefundable credits on line 16 or Schedule B (Form 941) may cause line 16 or Schedule B (Form 941) to report more than the total tax liability reported on line 12. Don't reduce your monthly tax liability reported on line 16 or your daily tax liability reported on Schedule B (Form 941) below zero.

Qualified small business payroll tax credit for increasing research activities (line 11a). The qualified

Form 941 Instructions (Page 17)

small business payroll tax credit for increasing research activities is limited to the employer share of social security tax on wages paid in the quarter that begins after the income tax return electing the credit has been filed. In completing line 16 or Schedule B (Form 941), you take into account the payroll tax credit against the liability for the employer share of social security tax starting with the first payroll payment of the quarter that includes payments of wages subject to social security tax to your employees. The credit may be taken to the extent of the employer share of social security tax on wages associated with the first payroll payment, and then to the extent of the employer share of social security tax associated with succeeding payroll payments in the quarter until the credit is used. Consistent with the entries on line 16 or Schedule B (Form 941), the payroll tax credit should be taken into account in making deposits of employment tax. If any payroll tax credit is remaining at the end of the quarter that hasn't been used completely because it exceeds the employer share of social security tax for the quarter, the excess credit may be carried forward to the succeeding quarter and allowed as a payroll tax credit for the succeeding quarter. The payroll tax credit may not be taken as a credit against income tax withholding, Medicare tax, or the employee share of social security tax. Also, the remaining payroll tax credit may not be carried back and taken as a credit against wages paid from preceding quarters.

Example. Rose Co. is an employer with a calendar tax year that filed its timely income tax return on April 15, 2021. Rose Co. elected to take the qualified small business payroll tax credit for increasing research activities on Form 6765. The third quarter of 2021 is the first quarter that begins after Rose Co. filed the income tax return making the payroll tax credit election. Therefore, the payroll tax credit applies against Rose Co.'s share of social security tax on wages paid to employees in the third quarter of 2021. Rose Co. is a semiweekly schedule depositor. Rose Co. completes Schedule B (Form 941) by reducing the amount of liability entered for the first payroll payment in the third quarter of 2021 that includes wages subject to social security tax by the lesser of (1) its share of social security tax on the wages, or (2) the available payroll tax credit. If the payroll tax credit elected is more than Rose Co.'s share of social security tax on the first payroll payment of the quarter, the excess payroll tax credit would be carried forward to succeeding payroll payments in the third quarter until it is used. If the amount of the payroll tax credit exceeds Rose Co.'s share of social security tax on wages paid to its employees in the third quarter, the excess credit would be treated as a payroll tax credit against its share of social security tax on wages paid in the fourth quarter. If the amount of the payroll tax credit remaining exceeded Rose Co.'s share of social security tax on wages paid in the fourth quarter, it could be carried forward and treated as a payroll tax credit for the first quarter of 2022.

Nonrefundable portion of credit for qualified sick and family leave wages (line 11b). The nonrefundable portion of the credit for qualified sick and family leave wages is limited to the employer share of social security tax on wages paid in the quarter that is remaining after that share is first reduced by any credit claimed on Form 941, line 11a, for the qualified small business payroll tax credit for increasing research activities; any credit to be claimed on Form 5884-C, line 11, for the work opportunity credit for qualified tax-exempt organizations hiring qualified veterans; and/or any credit to be claimed on Form 5884-D for the disaster credit for qualified tax-exempt organizations. In completing line 16 or Schedule B (Form 941), you take into account the entire quarter's nonrefundable portion of the credit for sick and family leave wages (including the qualified health plan expenses and employer share of Medicare tax allocable to those wages) against the liability for the first payroll payment of the quarter, but not below zero. Then reduce the liability for each successive payroll payment in the quarter until the nonrefundable portion of the credit is used. Any credit for qualified sick and family leave wages that is remaining at the end of the quarter because it exceeds the employer share of social security tax for the quarter is claimed on line 13c as a refundable credit. The refundable portion of the credit doesn't reduce the liability reported on line 16 or Schedule B (Form 941).

Example. Maple Co. is a semiweekly schedule depositor that pays employees every other Friday. In the first quarter of 2021, Maple Co. had pay dates of January 8, January 22, February 5, February 19, March 5, and March 19. Maple Co. paid qualified sick and family leave wages on February 5 and February 19. The nonrefundable portion of the credit for qualified sick and family leave wages for the quarter is $10,000. On Schedule B (Form 941), Maple Co. will use the $10,000 to reduce the liability for the January 8 pay date, but not below zero. If any nonrefundable portion of the credit remains, Maple Co. applies it to the liability for the January 22 pay date, then the February 5 pay date, and so forth until the entire $10,000 is used.

Nonrefundable portion of employee retention credit (line 11c). The nonrefundable portion of the employee retention credit is limited to the employer share of social security tax on wages paid in the quarter that is remaining after that share is first reduced by any credit claimed on Form 941, line 11a, for the qualified small business payroll tax credit for increasing research activities; any credit to be claimed on Form 5884-C, line 11, for the work opportunity credit for qualified tax-exempt organizations hiring qualified veterans; any credit to be claimed on Form 5884-D for the disaster credit for qualified tax-exempt organizations; and/or any credit claimed on Form 941, line 11b, for the nonrefundable portion of the credit for qualified sick and family leave wages. In completing line 16 or Schedule B (Form 941), you take into account the entire quarter's nonrefundable portion of the employee retention credit against the liability for the first payroll payment of the quarter, but not below zero. Then reduce the liability for each successive payroll payment in the quarter until the nonrefundable portion of the credit is used. Any employee retention credit that is remaining at the end of the quarter because it exceeds the employer share of social security tax for the quarter is claimed on line 13d as a refundable credit. The refundable portion of the credit doesn't reduce the liability reported on line 16 or Schedule B (Form 941).

Example. Maple Co. is a semiweekly schedule depositor that pays employees every other Friday. In the first quarter of 2021, Maple Co. had pay dates of January 8, January 22, February 5, February 19, March 5, and March 19. Maple Co. paid qualified wages for the employee retention credit on February 5 and February 19. The nonrefundable portion of the employee retention credit for the quarter is $10,000. On Schedule B (Form 941), Maple Co. will use the $10,000 to reduce the liability for the January 8 pay date, but not below zero. If any nonrefundable portion of the credit remains, Maple Co. applies it to the liability for the January 22 pay date, then the February 5 pay date, and so forth until the entire $10,000 is used.

Instructions for Form 941 (Rev. 3-2021) -17-

Form 941 Instructions (Page 18)

 You may reduce your deposits by the amount of the nonrefundable and refundable portions of the credit for qualified sick and family leave wages, and the nonrefundable and refundable portions of the employee retention credit, as discussed earlier under Reducing your deposits for COVID-19 credits.

Part 3: Tell Us About Your Business

In Part 3, answer only those questions that apply to your business. If the questions don't apply, leave them blank and go to Part 4.

17. If Your Business Has Closed . . .

If you go out of business or stop paying wages, you must file a final return. To tell the IRS that a particular Form 941 is your final return, check the box on line 17 and enter the final date you paid wages in the space provided. For additional filing requirements, including information about attaching a statement to your final return, see *If Your Business Has Closed*, earlier.

18. If You're a Seasonal Employer . . .

If you hire employees seasonally—such as for summer or winter only—check the box on line 18. Checking the box tells the IRS not to expect four Forms 941 from you throughout the year because you haven't paid wages regularly.

Generally, we won't ask about unfiled returns if at least one taxable return is filed each year. However, you must check the box on line 18 on every Form 941 you file. Otherwise, the IRS will expect a return to be filed for each quarter.

Also, when you complete Form 941, be sure to check the box on the top of the form that corresponds to the quarter reported.

⚠ **CAUTION** *The amounts entered on lines 19 through 23 are amounts that you use on Worksheet 1 to figure the credit for qualified sick and family leave wages and the employee retention credit. If you're claiming these credits, you must enter the applicable amounts.*

19. Qualified Health Plan Expenses Allocable to Qualified Sick Leave Wages

Enter the qualified health plan expenses allocable to qualified sick leave wages. This amount is also entered on Worksheet 1, Step 2, line 2b.

20. Qualified Health Plan Expenses Allocable to Qualified Family Leave Wages

Enter the qualified health plan expenses allocable to qualified family leave wages. This amount is also entered on Worksheet 1, Step 2, line 2f.

21. Qualified Wages for the Employee Retention Credit

Enter the qualified wages for the employee retention credit (excluding the amount of any qualified health plan expenses). This amount is also entered on Worksheet 1, Step 3, line 3a.

22. Qualified Health Plan Expenses Allocable to Wages Reported on Line 21

Enter the qualified health plan expenses for the employee retention credit. These expenses are generally those which are allocable to an employee (and to a period) in which your business operations are fully or partially suspended due to a government order or experience a decline in gross receipts. The allocation will be treated as proper if made on the basis of being pro rata among periods of coverage. For more information, go to *IRS.gov/ERC*. The amount from line 22 is also entered on Worksheet 1, Step 3, line 3b.

23. Credit From Form 5884-C, Line 11, for This Quarter

If applicable, enter the credit to be claimed on line 11 of Form 5884-C for the work opportunity credit for qualified tax-exempt organizations hiring qualified veterans for this quarter. Entering an amount here doesn't change your requirement to file Form 5884-C separately from Form 941. You're entering the amount here to notify us that you will file Form 5884-C for the quarter and therefore reduce the amount of the employer share of social security tax that is available to be reduced by the nonrefundable portion of the credit for qualified sick and family leave wages and the nonrefundable portion of the employee retention credit.

Part 4: May We Speak With Your Third-Party Designee?

If you want to allow an employee, a paid tax preparer, or another person to discuss your Form 941 with the IRS, check the "Yes" box in Part 4. Enter the name, phone number, and the five-digit personal identification number (PIN) of the specific person to speak with—not the name of the firm that prepared your tax return. The designee may choose any five numbers as his or her PIN.

By checking "Yes," you authorize the IRS to talk to the person you named (your designee) about any questions we may have while we process your return. You also authorize your designee to do all of the following.
• Give us any information that is missing from your return.
• Call us for information about processing your return.
• Respond to certain IRS notices that you've shared with your designee about math errors and return preparation. The IRS won't send notices to your designee.

You're not authorizing your designee to bind you to anything (including additional tax liability) or to otherwise represent you before the IRS. If you want to expand your designee's authorization, see Pub. 947.

The authorization will automatically expire 1 year from the due date (without regard to extensions) for filing your Form 941. If you or your designee wants to terminate the authorization, write to the IRS office for your location using the *Without a payment* address under *Where Should You File*, earlier.

Part 5: Sign Here (Approved Roles)

Complete all information and sign Form 941. The following persons are authorized to sign the return for each type of business entity.
• **Sole proprietorship**—The individual who owns the business.

Instructions for Form 941 (Rev. 3-2021)

Form 941 Instructions (Page 19)

• **Corporation (including a limited liability company (LLC) treated as a corporation)**—The president, vice president, or other principal officer duly authorized to sign.
• **Partnership (including an LLC treated as a partnership) or unincorporated organization**—A responsible and duly authorized partner, member, or officer having knowledge of its affairs.
• **Single-member LLC treated as a disregarded entity for federal income tax purposes**—The owner of the LLC or a principal officer duly authorized to sign.
• **Trust or estate**—The fiduciary.

Form 941 may be signed by a duly authorized agent of the taxpayer if a valid power of attorney has been filed.

Alternative signature method. Corporate officers or duly authorized agents may sign Form 941 by rubber stamp, mechanical device, or computer software program. For details and required documentation, see Rev. Proc. 2005-39, 2005-28 I.R.B. 82, available at *IRS.gov/irb/ 2005-28_IRB#RP-2005-39*.

Paid Preparer Use Only

A paid preparer must sign Form 941 and provide the information in the *Paid Preparer Use Only* section of Part 5 if the preparer was paid to prepare Form 941 and isn't an employee of the filing entity. Paid preparers must sign paper returns with a manual signature. The preparer must give you a copy of the return in addition to the copy to be filed with the IRS.

If you're a paid preparer, enter your Preparer Tax Identification Number (PTIN) in the space provided. Include your complete address. If you work for a firm, enter the firm's name and the EIN of the firm. You can apply for a PTIN online or by filing Form W-12. For more information about applying for a PTIN online, go to *IRS.gov/PTIN*. You can't use your PTIN in place of the EIN of the tax preparation firm.

Generally, don't complete this section if you're filing the return as a reporting agent and have a valid Form 8655 on file with the IRS. However, a reporting agent must complete this section if the reporting agent offered legal advice, for example, advising the client on determining whether its workers are employees or independent contractors for federal tax purposes.

How To Get Forms, Instructions, and Publications

 You can view, download, or print most of the forms, instructions, and publications you may need at *IRS.gov/Forms*. Otherwise, you can go to *IRS.gov/ OrderForms* to place an order and have them mailed to you. The IRS will process your order for forms and publications as soon as possible. Don't resubmit requests you've already sent us. You can get forms and publications faster online.

Form 941 Instructions (Page 20)

Worksheet 1. Credit for Qualified Sick and Family Leave Wages and the Employee Retention Credit

Keep for Your Records

Determine how you will complete this worksheet

If you paid both qualified sick and family leave wages and qualified wages for purposes of the employee retention credit this quarter, complete Step 1, Step 2, and Step 3. If you paid qualified sick and family leave wages this quarter but you didn't pay any qualified wages for purposes of the employee retention credit this quarter, complete Step 1 and Step 2. If you paid qualified wages for purposes of the employee retention credit this quarter but you didn't pay any qualified sick and family leave wages this quarter, complete Step 1 and Step 3.

Step 1. **Determine the employer share of social security tax this quarter after it is reduced by any credit claimed on Form 8974 and any credit to be claimed on Form 5884-C and/or Form 5884-D**

1a	Enter the amount of social security tax from Form 941, Part 1, line 5a, column 2	1a _____
1b	Enter the amount of social security tax from Form 941, Part 1, line 5b, column 2	1b _____
1c	Add lines 1a and 1b	1c _____
1d	Multiply line 1c by 50% (0.50)	1d _____
1e	If you're a third-party payer of sick pay that isn't an agent and you're claiming credits for amounts paid to your employees, enter the employer share of social security tax included on Form 941, Part 1, line 8 (enter as a positive number)	1e _____
1f	Subtract line 1e from line 1d	1f _____
1g	If you received a Section 3121(q) Notice and Demand during the quarter, enter the amount of the employer share of social security tax from the notice	1g _____
1h	**Employer share of social security tax.** Add lines 1f and 1g	1h _____
1i	Enter the amount from Form 941, Part 1, line 11a (credit from Form 8974)	1i _____
1j	Enter the amount to be claimed on Form 5884-C, line 11, for this quarter	1j _____
1j(i)	Enter the amount to be claimed on Form 5884-D, line 12, for this quarter	1j(i) _____
1k	**Total nonrefundable credits already used against the employer share of social security tax.** Add lines 1i, 1j, and 1j(i)	1k _____
1l	**Employer share of social security tax remaining.** Subtract line 1k from line 1h	1l _____

Step 2. **Figure the sick and family leave credit**

2a	Qualified sick leave wages reported on Form 941, Part 1, line 5a(i), column 1	2a _____
2a(i)	Qualified sick leave wages included on Form 941, Part 1, line 5c, but not included on Form 941, Part 1, line 5a(i), column 1, because the wages reported on that line were limited by the social security wage base	2a(i) _____
2a(ii)	Total qualified sick leave wages. Add lines 2a and 2a(i)	2a(ii) _____
2a(iii)	Qualified sick leave wages excluded from the definition of employment under section 3121(b)	2a(iii) _____
2b	Qualified health plan expenses allocable to qualified sick leave wages (Form 941, Part 3, line 19)	2b _____
2c	Employer share of Medicare tax on qualified sick leave wages. Multiply line 2a(ii) by 1.45% (0.0145)	2c _____
2d	**Credit for qualified sick leave wages.** Add lines 2a(ii), 2a(iii), 2b, and 2c	2d _____
2e	Qualified family leave wages reported on Form 941, Part 1, line 5a(ii), column 1	2e _____
2e(i)	Qualified family leave wages included on Form 941, Part 1, line 5c, but not included on Form 941, Part 1, line 5a(ii), column 1, because the wages reported on that line were limited by the social security wage base	2e(i) _____
2e(ii)	Total qualified family leave wages. Add lines 2e and 2e(i)	2e(ii) _____
2e(iii)	Qualified family leave wages excluded from the definition of employment under section 3121(b)	2e(iii) _____
2f	Qualified health plan expenses allocable to qualified family leave wages (Form 941, Part 3, line 20)	2f _____
2g	Employer share of Medicare tax on qualified family leave wages. Multiply line 2e(ii) by 1.45% (0.0145)	2g _____
2h	**Credit for qualified family leave wages.** Add lines 2e(ii), 2e(iii), 2f, and 2g	2h _____
2i	**Credit for qualified sick and family leave wages.** Add lines 2d and 2h	2i _____
2j	**Nonrefundable portion of credit for qualified sick and family leave wages.** Enter the smaller of line 1l or line 2i. Enter this amount on Form 941, Part 1, line 11b	2j _____
2k	**Refundable portion of credit for qualified sick and family leave wages.** Subtract line 2j from line 2i and enter this amount on Form 941, Part 1, line 13c	2k _____

Step 3. **Figure the employee retention credit**

3a	Qualified wages (excluding qualified health plan expenses) for the employee retention credit (Form 941, Part 3, line 21)	3a _____
3b	Qualified health plan expenses allocable to qualified wages for the employee retention credit (Form 941, Part 3, line 22)	3b _____
3c	Add lines 3a and 3b	3c _____
3d	**Retention credit.** Multiply line 3c by 70% (0.70)	3d _____
3e	Enter the amount of the employer share of social security tax from Step 1, line 1l	3e _____
3f	Enter the amount of the nonrefundable portion of the credit for qualified sick and family leave wages from Step 2, line 2j	3f _____
3g	Subtract line 3f from line 3e	3g _____
3h	**Nonrefundable portion of employee retention credit.** Enter the smaller of line 3d or line 3g. Enter this amount on Form 941, Part 1, line 11c	3h _____
3i	**Refundable portion of employee retention credit.** Subtract line 3h from line 3d and enter this amount on Form 941, Part 1, line 13d	3i _____

Instructions for Form 941 (Rev. 3-2021)

Form 941 Schedule B

Schedule B (Form 941):
Report of Tax Liability for Semiweekly Schedule Depositors

(Rev. January 2017)   Department of the Treasury — Internal Revenue Service

960311

OMB No. 1545-0029

Employer identification number (EIN) ☐☐ – ☐☐☐☐☐☐☐

Name *(not your trade name)*

Calendar year ☐☐☐☐   (Also check quarter)

Report for this Quarter...
(Check one.)

☐ 1: January, February, March
☐ 2: April, May, June
☐ 3: July, August, September
☐ 4: October, November, December

Use this schedule to show your TAX LIABILITY for the quarter; don't use it to show your deposits. When you file this form with Form 941 or Form 941-SS, don't change your tax liability by adjustments reported on any Forms 941-X or 944-X. You must fill out this form and attach it to Form 941 or Form 941-SS if you're a semiweekly schedule depositor or became one because your accumulated tax liability on any day was $100,000 or more. Write your daily tax liability on the numbered space that corresponds to the date wages were paid. See Section 11 in Pub. 15 for details.

Month 1

Days 1–31 entry boxes.

Tax liability for Month 1

Month 2

Days 1–31 entry boxes.

Tax liability for Month 2

Month 3

Days 1–31 entry boxes.

Tax liability for Month 3

Fill in your total liability for the quarter (Month 1 + Month 2 + Month 3) ▶

Total must equal line 12 on Form 941 or Form 941-SS.

Total liability for the quarter

For Paperwork Reduction Act Notice, see separate instructions.   IRS.gov/form941   Cat. No. 11967Q   Schedule B (Form 941) (Rev. 1-2017)

Instructions for Schedule B (Form 941)

Department of the Treasury
Internal Revenue Service

(Rev. March 2021)

Use with the January 2017 revision of Schedule B (Form 941)

Report of Tax Liability for Semiweekly Schedule Depositors

Section references are to the Internal Revenue Code unless otherwise noted.

Future Developments

For the latest information about developments related to Schedule B and its instructions, such as legislation enacted after they were published, go to *IRS.gov/ Form941*.

What's New

Deferral of social security tax expired. The deferral of the deposit and payment of the employer share of social security tax for deposits and payments due on or after March 27, 2020, and before January 1, 2021, as well as the deferral of the withholding, deposit, and payment of the employee share of social security tax on wages paid September 1, 2020, through December 31, 2020, have expired. Any references to these deferrals have been removed from these instructions. For more information about these deferrals, including information on paying the deferrals, see the Instructions for Form 941 or the Instructions for Form 941-SS.

New payroll tax credit for certain tax-exempt organi- zations affected by qualified disasters. Section 303(d) of the Taxpayer Certainty and Disaster Tax Relief Act of 2020 allows for a new payroll tax credit for certain tax-exempt organizations affected by certain qualified disasters **not** related to COVID-19. This credit may still be available to certain tax-exempt organizations during the first and second quarters of 2021. This new credit will be claimed on new Form 5884-D (not on Form 941). Form 5884-D is filed after the Form 941 for the quarter for which the credit is being claimed has been filed. If you will claim this credit on Form 5884-D for a calendar quarter of 2021 and you're also claiming a credit for qualified sick and family leave wages and/or the employee retention credit in that quarter, you must include any credit that will be claimed on Form 5884-D on Worksheet 1 for the Form 941 for that quarter. For more information about this credit, go to *IRS.gov/Form5884D*.

Reminders

Schedule B is filed with Form 941 or Form 941-SS. References to Form 941 in these instructions also apply to Form 941-SS, Employer's QUARTERLY Federal Tax Return (American Samoa, Guam, the Commonwealth of the Northern Mariana Islands, and the U.S. Virgin Islands), unless otherwise noted.

Adjusting tax liability for nonrefundable credits claimed on Form 941, lines 11a, 11b, and 11c. See *Adjusting Tax Liability for Nonrefundable Credits Claimed on Form 941, Lines 11a, 11b, and 11c*, later, for updated instructions on how to report on Schedule B adjustments to your tax liabilities for the qualified small business payroll tax credit for increasing research activities, the credit for qualified sick and family leave wages, and the employee retention credit.

Reporting prior period adjustments. Prior period adjustments are reported on Form 941-X, Adjusted Employer's QUARTERLY Federal Tax Return or Claim for Refund, or Form 944-X, Adjusted Employer's ANNUAL Federal Tax Return or Claim for Refund, and aren't taken into account when figuring the tax liability for the current quarter.

When you file Schedule B with your Form 941, Employer's QUARTERLY Federal Tax Return, don't change your current quarter tax liability by adjustments reported on any Form 941-X or 944-X.

Amended Schedule B. If you have been assessed a failure-to-deposit (FTD) penalty, you may be able to file an amended Schedule B. See *Correcting Previously Reported Tax Liability*, later.

General Instructions

Purpose of Schedule B

These instructions tell you about Schedule B. To determine if you're a semiweekly schedule depositor, see section 11 of Pub. 15, Employer's Tax Guide, or section 8 of Pub. 80, Federal Tax Guide for Employers in the U.S. Virgin Islands, Guam, American Samoa, and the Commonwealth of the Northern Mariana Islands.

Federal law requires you, as an employer, to withhold certain taxes from your employees' pay. Each time you pay wages, you must withhold—or take out of your employees' pay—certain amounts for federal income tax, social security tax, and Medicare tax. You must also withhold Additional Medicare Tax from wages you pay to an employee in excess of $200,000 in a calendar year. Under the withholding system, taxes withheld from your employees are credited to your employees in payment of their tax liabilities.

Federal law also requires employers to pay any liability for the employer share of social security and Medicare taxes. This share of social security and Medicare taxes isn't withheld from employees.

Mar 09, 2021   Cat. No. 38683X

Form 941 Schedule B Instructions (Page 2)

On Schedule B, list your tax liability for each day. Your tax liability is based on the dates wages were paid. Your liability includes:
- The federal income tax you withheld from your employees' pay, and
- Both the employer and employee share of social security and Medicare taxes.

Don't use Schedule B to show federal tax deposits. The IRS gets deposit data from electronic funds transfers.

 The IRS uses Schedule B to determine if you've deposited your federal employment tax liabilities on time. If you're a semiweekly schedule depositor and you don't properly complete and file your Schedule B with Form 941, the IRS may propose an "averaged" FTD penalty. See Deposit Penalties *in section 11 of Pub. 15 or section 8 of Pub. 80 for more information.*

Who Must File?

File Schedule B if you're a semiweekly schedule depositor. You're a semiweekly schedule depositor if you reported more than $50,000 of employment taxes in the lookback period or accumulated a tax liability of $100,000 or more on any given day in the current or prior calendar year. If you became a semiweekly schedule depositor during the quarter, you must complete Schedule B for the entire quarter. See section 11 of Pub. 15 or section 8 of Pub. 80 for more information. The $100,000 tax liability threshold requiring a next-day deposit is determined before you consider any reduction of your liability for nonrefundable credits. For more information, including an example, see frequently asked question 17 at *IRS.gov/ETD*.

 Don't complete Schedule B if you have a tax liability on Form 941, line 12, that is less than $2,500 during the quarter.

When Must You File?

Schedule B is filed with Form 941. Therefore, the due date of Schedule B is the same as the due date for the applicable Form 941. In some situations, Schedule B may be filed with Form 941-X. See *Form 941-X*, later, for details.

Don't file Schedule B as an attachment to Form 944, Employer's ANNUAL Federal Tax Return. Instead, if you're a semiweekly schedule depositor that is required to file a report of tax liability with Form 944, use Form 945-A, Annual Record of Federal Tax Liability.

Specific Instructions
Completing Schedule B

Enter Your Business Information

Carefully enter your employer identification number (EIN) and name at the top of the schedule. Make sure that they exactly match the name of your business and the EIN that the IRS assigned to your business and also agree with the name and EIN shown on the attached Form 941 or Form 941-X.

Calendar Year

Enter the calendar year that applies to the quarter checked.

Check the Box for the Quarter

Under *Report for this Quarter* at the top of Schedule B, check the appropriate box of the quarter for which you're filing this schedule. Make sure the quarter checked on the top of the Schedule B matches the quarter checked on your Form 941 or Form 941-X.

Enter Your Tax Liability by Month

Schedule B is divided into the 3 months that make up a quarter of a year. Each month has 31 numbered spaces that correspond to the dates of a typical month. Enter your tax liabilities in the spaces that correspond to the dates you paid wages to your employees, not the date payroll liabilities were accrued or deposits were made.

For example, if your payroll period ended on December 31, 2020, and you paid the wages for that period on January 6, 2021, you would:
- Go to Month 1 (because January is the first month of the quarter), and
- Enter your tax liability on line 6 (because line 6 represents the sixth day of the month).

 Make sure you have checked the appropriate box in Part 2 of Form 941 to show that you're a semiweekly schedule depositor.

Example 1. Cedar Co. is a semiweekly schedule depositor that pays wages for each month on the last day of the month. On December 24, 2020, Cedar Co. also paid its employees year-end bonuses (subject to employment taxes). Cedar Co. must report employment tax liabilities on Schedule B for the fourth quarter (October, November, December) as follows.

Month	Lines for dates wages were paid
1 (October)	line 31 (pay day, last day of the month)
2 (November)	line 30 (pay day, last day of the month)
3 (December)	line 24 (bonus paid December 24, 2020)
3 (December)	line 31 (pay day, last day of the month)

Example 2. Fir Co. is a semiweekly schedule depositor that pays employees every other Friday. Fir Co. accumulated a $20,000 employment tax liability on each of these pay dates: January 1, 2021; January 15, 2021; January 29, 2021; February 12, 2021; February 26, 2021; March 12, 2021; and March 26, 2021. Fir Co. must report employment tax liabilities on Schedule B as follows.

Month	Lines for dates wages were paid
1 (January)	lines 1, 15, and 29
2 (February)	lines 12 and 26
3 (March)	lines 12 and 26

Example 3. Elm Co. is a new business and monthly schedule depositor for 2021. Elm Co. paid wages every Friday and accumulated a $2,000 employment tax liability on January 15, 2021. On January 22, 2021, and on every subsequent Friday during 2021, Elm Co. accumulated a

-2-   **Instructions for Schedule B (Form 941) (Rev. 3-2021)**

Form 941 Schedule B Instructions (Page 3)

$110,000 employment tax liability. Under the deposit rules, employers become semiweekly schedule depositors on the day after any day they accumulate $100,000 or more of employment tax liability in a deposit period. Elm Co. became a semiweekly schedule depositor on January 23, 2021, because Elm Co. had a total accumulated employment tax liability of $112,000 on January 22, 2021. For more information, see section 11 of Pub. 15 or section 8 of Pub. 80.

Elm Co. must complete Schedule B as shown next and file it with Form 941. Don't check the second box on Form 941, line 16, even though Elm Co. was a monthly schedule depositor until January 23, 2021.

Month	Lines for dates wages were paid	Amount to report
1 (January)	line 15	$2,000
1 (January)	lines 22 and 29	$110,000
2 (February)	lines 5, 12, 19, and 26	$110,000
3 (March)	lines 5, 12, 19, and 26	$110,000

Total Liability for the Quarter

To find your total liability for the quarter, add your monthly tax liabilities.

```
  Tax Liability for Month 1
+ Tax Liability for Month 2
+ Tax Liability for Month 3
  Total Liability for the Quarter
```

⚠ **CAUTION** *Your total liability for the quarter must equal line 12 on Form 941; therefore, don't reduce your total liability reported on Schedule B by the refundable portion of the credit for qualified sick and family leave wages or the refundable portion of the employee retention credit.*

Adjusting Tax Liability for Nonrefundable Credits Claimed on Form 941, Lines 11a, 11b, and 11c

Semiweekly schedule depositors must account for nonrefundable credits claimed on Form 941, lines 11a, 11b, and 11c, when reporting their tax liabilities on Schedule B. The total tax liability for the quarter must equal the amount reported on Form 941, line 12. Failure to account for the nonrefundable credits on Schedule B may cause Schedule B to report more than the total tax liability reported on Form 941, line 12. Don't reduce your daily tax liability reported on Schedule B below zero.

Qualified small business payroll tax credit for increasing research activities (Form 941, line 11a). The qualified small business payroll tax credit for increasing research activities is limited to the employer share of social security tax on wages paid in the quarter that begins after the income tax return electing the credit has been filed. In completing Schedule B, you take into account the payroll tax credit against the liability for the employer share of social security tax starting with the first payroll payment of the quarter that includes payments of wages subject to social security tax to your employees.

The credit may be taken to the extent of the employer share of social security tax on wages associated with the first payroll payment, and then to the extent of the employer share of social security tax associated with succeeding payroll payments in the quarter until the credit is used. Consistent with the entries on Schedule B, the payroll tax credit should be taken into account in making deposits of employment tax. If any payroll tax credit is remaining at the end of the quarter that hasn't been used completely because it exceeds the employer share of social security tax for the quarter, the excess credit may be carried forward to the succeeding quarter and allowed as a payroll tax credit for the succeeding quarter. The payroll tax credit may not be taken as a credit against income tax withholding, Medicare tax, or the employee share of social security tax. Also, the remaining payroll tax credit may not be carried back and taken as a credit against wages paid from preceding quarters. For more information about the payroll tax credit, go to *IRS.gov/ ResearchPayrollTC*.

Example. Rose Co. is an employer with a calendar tax year that filed its timely income tax return on April 15, 2021. Rose Co. elected to take the qualified small business payroll tax credit for increasing research activities on Form 6765. The third quarter of 2021 is the first quarter that begins after Rose Co. filed the income tax return making the payroll tax credit election. Therefore, the payroll tax credit applies against Rose Co.'s share of social security tax on wages paid to employees in the third quarter of 2021. Rose Co. is a semiweekly schedule depositor. Rose Co. completes Schedule B by reducing the amount of liability entered for the first payroll payment in the third quarter of 2021 that includes wages subject to social security tax by the lesser of (1) its share of social security tax on the wages, or (2) the available payroll tax credit. If the payroll tax credit elected is more than Rose Co.'s share of social security tax on the first payroll payment of the quarter, the excess payroll tax credit would be carried forward to succeeding payroll payments in the third quarter until it is used. If the amount of the payroll tax credit exceeds Rose Co.'s share of social security tax on wages paid to its employees in the third quarter, the excess credit would be treated as a payroll tax credit against its share of social security tax on wages paid in the fourth quarter. If the amount of the payroll tax credit remaining exceeded Rose Co.'s share of social security tax on wages paid in the fourth quarter, it could be carried forward and treated as a payroll tax credit for the first quarter of 2022.

Nonrefundable portion of credit for qualified sick and family leave wages (Form 941, line 11b). The nonrefundable portion of the credit for qualified sick and family leave wages is limited to the employer share of social security tax on wages paid in the quarter that is remaining after that share is first reduced by any credit claimed on Form 941, line 11a, for the qualified small business payroll tax credit for increasing research activities; any credit to be claimed on Form 5884-C, line 11, for the work opportunity credit for qualified tax-exempt organizations hiring qualified veterans; and/or any credit to be claimed on Form 5884-D for the disaster credit for qualified tax-exempt organizations. In completing Schedule B, you take into account the entire

Form 941 Schedule B Instructions (Page 4)

quarter's nonrefundable portion of the credit for sick and family leave wages (including the qualified health plan expenses and employer share of Medicare tax allocable to those wages) against the liability for the first payroll payment of the quarter, but not below zero. Then reduce the liability for each successive payroll payment in the quarter until the nonrefundable portion of the credit is used. Any credit for qualified sick and family leave wages that is remaining at the end of the quarter because it exceeds the employer share of social security tax for the quarter is claimed on Form 941, line 13c, as a refundable credit. The refundable portion of the credit doesn't reduce the liability reported on Schedule B. For more information about the credit for qualified sick and family leave wages, including the dates for which the credit may be claimed, go to *IRS.gov/PLC*.

Example. Maple Co. is a semiweekly schedule depositor that pays employees every other Friday. In the first quarter of 2021, Maple Co. had pay dates of January 8, January 22, February 5, February 19, March 5, and March 19. Maple Co. paid qualified sick and family leave wages on February 5 and February 19. The nonrefundable portion of the credit for qualified sick and family leave wages for the quarter is $10,000. On Schedule B, Maple Co. will use the $10,000 to reduce the liability for the January 8 pay date, but not below zero. If any nonrefundable portion of the credit remains, Maple Co. applies it to the liability for the January 22 pay date, then the February 5 pay date, and so forth until the entire $10,000 is used.

Nonrefundable portion of employee retention credit (Form 941, line 11c). The nonrefundable portion of the employee retention credit is limited to the employer share of social security tax on wages paid in the quarter that is remaining after that share is first reduced by any credit claimed on Form 941, line 11a, for the qualified small business payroll tax credit for increasing research activities; any credit to be claimed on Form 5884-C, line 11, for the work opportunity credit for qualified tax-exempt organizations hiring qualified veterans; any credit to be claimed on Form 5884-D for the disaster credit for qualified tax-exempt organizations; and/or any credit claimed on Form 941, line 11b, for the nonrefundable portion of the credit for qualified sick and family leave wages. In completing Schedule B, you take into account the entire quarter's nonrefundable portion of the employee retention credit against the liability for the first payroll payment of the quarter, but not below zero. Then reduce the liability for each successive payroll payment in the quarter until the nonrefundable portion of the credit is used. Any employee retention credit that is remaining at the end of the quarter because it exceeds the employer share of social security tax for the quarter is claimed on Form 941, line 13d, as a refundable credit. The refundable portion of the credit doesn't reduce the liability reported on Schedule B. For more information about the employee retention credit, including the dates for which the credit may be claimed, go to *IRS.gov/ERC*.

Example. Maple Co. is a semiweekly schedule depositor that pays employees every other Friday. In the first quarter of 2021, Maple Co. had pay dates of January 8, January 22, February 5, February 19, March 5, and

March 19. Maple Co. paid qualified wages for the employee retention credit on February 5 and February 19. The nonrefundable portion of the employee retention credit for the quarter is $10,000. On Schedule B, Maple Co. will use the $10,000 to reduce the liability for the January 8 pay date, but not below zero. If any nonrefundable portion of the credit remains, Maple Co. applies it to the liability for the January 22 pay date, then the February 5 pay date, and so forth until the entire $10,000 is used.

TIP *You may reduce your deposits by the amount of the nonrefundable and refundable portions of the credit for qualified sick and family leave wages, and the nonrefundable and refundable portions of the employee retention credit. For more information on reducing deposits, see Notice 2020-22, 2020-17 I.R.B. 664, available at IRS.gov/irb/2020-17_IRB#NOT-2020-22. Also see IRS.gov/ERC and IRS.gov/PLC for more information, including examples, about reducing deposits.*

Correcting Previously Reported Tax Liability

Semiweekly schedule depositors. If you've been assessed an FTD penalty for a quarter and you made an error on Schedule B and the correction won't change the total liability for the quarter you reported on Schedule B, you may be able to reduce your penalty by filing an amended Schedule B.

Example. You reported a liability of $3,000 on day 1 of month 1. However, the liability was actually for month 3. Prepare an amended Schedule B showing the $3,000 liability on day 1 of month 3. Also, you must enter the liabilities previously reported for the quarter that didn't change. Write "Amended" at the top of Schedule B. The IRS will refigure the penalty and notify you of any change in the penalty.

Monthly schedule depositors. You can file a Schedule B if you have been assessed an FTD penalty for a quarter and you made an error on the monthly tax liability section of Form 941. When completing Schedule B for this situation, only enter the monthly totals. The daily entries aren't required.

Where to file. File your amended Schedule B, or, for monthly schedule depositors, your original Schedule B at the address provided in the penalty notice you received. If you're filing an amended Schedule B, you don't have to submit your original Schedule B.

Form 941-X

You may need to file an amended Schedule B with Form 941-X to avoid or reduce an FTD penalty.

Tax decrease. If you're filing Form 941-X for a quarter, you can file an amended Schedule B with Form 941-X if both of the following apply.

1. You have a tax decrease.
2. You were assessed an FTD penalty.

File your amended Schedule B with Form 941-X. The total liability for the quarter reported on your amended Schedule B must equal the corrected amount of tax reported on Form 941-X. If your penalty is decreased, the

Form 941 Schedule B Instructions (Page 5)

IRS will include the penalty decrease with your tax decrease.

Tax increase—Form 941-X filed timely. If you're filing a timely Form 941-X showing a tax increase, don't file an amended Schedule B, unless you were assessed an FTD penalty caused by an incorrect, incomplete, or missing Schedule B. If you're filing an amended Schedule B, don't include the tax increase reported on Form 941-X.

Tax increase—Form 941-X filed late. If you owe tax and are filing a late Form 941-X, that is, after the due date of the return for the return period in which you discovered the error, you must file an amended Schedule B with Form 941-X. Otherwise, the IRS may assess an "averaged" FTD penalty.

The total tax reported on the "Total liability for the quarter" line of the amended Schedule B must match the corrected tax (Form 941, line 12, combined with any correction reported on Form 941-X, line 23) for the quarter, less any previous abatements and interest-free tax assessments.

Paperwork Reduction Act Notice. We ask for the information on Schedule B to carry out the Internal Revenue laws of the United States. You're required to give us the information. We need it to ensure that you're complying with these laws and to allow us to figure and collect the right amount of tax.

You're not required to provide the information requested on a form that is subject to the Paperwork Reduction Act unless the form displays a valid OMB control number. Books or records relating to a form or its instructions must be retained as long as their contents may become material in the administration of any Internal Revenue law. Generally, tax returns and return information are confidential, as required by Code section 6103.

The time needed to complete and file Schedule B will vary depending on individual circumstances. The estimated average time is 2 hours, 53 minutes.

If you have comments concerning the accuracy of this time estimate or suggestions for making Schedule B simpler, we would be happy to hear from you. You can send us comments from *IRS.gov/FormComments*. Or you can send your comments to Internal Revenue Service, Tax Forms and Publications Division, 1111 Constitution Ave. NW, IR-6526, Washington, DC 20224. Don't send Schedule B to this address. Instead, see *Where Should You File?* in the Form 941 instructions.

Instructions for Schedule B (Form 941) (Rev. 3-2021)   -5-

Form 941-X (Page 1)

Form 941-X: (Rev. October 2020)

Adjusted Employer's QUARTERLY Federal Tax Return or Claim for Refund

Department of the Treasury — Internal Revenue Service

OMB No. 1545-0029

Employer identification number (EIN) ☐☐ – ☐☐☐☐☐☐☐

Name (not your trade name)

Trade name (if any)

Address

Number   Street   Suite or room number

City   State   ZIP code

Foreign country name   Foreign province/county   Foreign postal code

Return You're Correcting...

Check the type of return you're correcting.

☐ 941

☐ 941-SS

Check the ONE quarter you're correcting.

☐ **1:** January, February, March

☐ **2:** April, May, June

☐ **3:** July, August, September

☐ **4:** October, November, December

Enter the calendar year of the quarter you're correcting.

☐☐☐☐ (YYYY)

Enter the date you discovered errors.

☐☐ / ☐☐ / ☐☐☐☐

(MM / DD / YYYY)

Read the separate instructions before completing this form. Use this form to correct errors you made on Form 941 or 941-SS. Use a separate Form 941-X for each quarter that needs correction. Type or print within the boxes. You MUST complete all four pages. Don't attach this form to Form 941 or 941-SS unless you're reclassifying workers; see the instructions for line 36.

Part 1: Select ONLY one process. See page 5 for additional guidance.

☐ **1. Adjusted employment tax return.** Check this box if you underreported amounts. Also check this box if you overreported amounts and you would like to use the adjustment process to correct the errors. You must check this box if you're correcting both underreported and overreported amounts on this form. The amount shown on line 27, if less than zero, may only be applied as a credit to your Form 941, Form 941-SS, or Form 944 for the tax period in which you're filing this form.

☐ **2. Claim.** Check this box if you overreported amounts only and you would like to use the claim process to ask for a refund or abatement of the amount shown on line 27. Don't check this box if you're correcting ANY underreported amounts on this form.

Part 2: Complete the certifications.

☐ **3.** I certify that I've filed or will file Forms W-2, Wage and Tax Statement, or Forms W-2c, Corrected Wage and Tax Statement, as required.

Note: If you're correcting underreported amounts only, go to Part 3 on page 2 and skip lines 4 and 5. If you're correcting overreported amounts, for purposes of the certifications on lines 4 and 5, Medicare tax doesn't include Additional Medicare Tax. Form 941-X can't be used to correct overreported amounts of Additional Medicare Tax unless the amounts weren't withheld from employee wages or an adjustment is being made for the current year.

4. If you checked line 1 because you're adjusting overreported federal income tax, social security tax, Medicare tax, or Additional Medicare Tax, check all that apply. You must check at least one box.
I certify that:

☐ **a.** I repaid or reimbursed each affected employee for the overcollected federal income tax or Additional Medicare Tax for the current year and the overcollected social security tax and Medicare tax for current and prior years. For adjustments of employee social security tax and Medicare tax overcollected in prior years, I have a written statement from each affected employee stating that he or she hasn't claimed (or the claim was rejected) and won't claim a refund or credit for the overcollection.

☐ **b.** The adjustments of social security tax and Medicare tax are for the employer's share only. I couldn't find the affected employees or each affected employee didn't give me a written statement that he or she hasn't claimed (or the claim was rejected) and won't claim a refund or credit for the overcollection.

☐ **c.** The adjustment is for federal income tax, social security tax, Medicare tax, or Additional Medicare Tax that I didn't withhold from employee wages.

5. If you checked line 2 because you're claiming a refund or abatement of overreported federal income tax, social security tax, Medicare tax, or Additional Medicare Tax, check all that apply. You must check at least one box.
I certify that:

☐ **a.** I repaid or reimbursed each affected employee for the overcollected social security tax and Medicare tax. For claims of employee social security tax and Medicare tax overcollected in prior years, I have a written statement from each affected employee stating that he or she hasn't claimed (or the claim was rejected) and won't claim a refund or credit for the overcollection.

☐ **b.** I have a written consent from each affected employee stating that I may file this claim for the employee's share of social security tax and Medicare tax. For refunds of employee social security tax and Medicare tax overcollected in prior years, I also have a written statement from each affected employee stating that he or she hasn't claimed (or the claim was rejected) and won't claim a refund or credit for the overcollection.

☐ **c.** The claim for social security tax and Medicare tax is for the employer's share only. I couldn't find the affected employees, or each affected employee didn't give me a written consent to file a claim for the employee's share of social security tax and Medicare tax, or each affected employee didn't give me a written statement that he or she hasn't claimed (or the claim was rejected) and won't claim a refund or credit for the overcollection.

☐ **d.** The claim is for federal income tax, social security tax, Medicare tax, or Additional Medicare Tax that I didn't withhold from employee wages.

Next ▶

For Paperwork Reduction Act Notice, see the separate instructions.   www.irs.gov/Form941X   Cat. No. 17025J   Form **941-X** (Rev. 10-2020)

Form 941-X (Page 2)

Name *(not your trade name)*	Employer identification number (EIN)	Correcting quarter (1, 2, 3, 4)
		Correcting calendar year (YYYY)

Part 3: Enter the corrections for this quarter. If any line doesn't apply, leave it blank.

		Column 1		Column 2		Column 3		Column 4
		Total corrected amount (for ALL employees)	−	Amount originally reported or as previously corrected (for ALL employees)	=	Difference (If this amount is a negative number, use a minus sign.)		Tax correction

6. **Wages, tips, and other compensation** (Form 941, line 2)
Column 1 [.   ] − Column 2 [.   ] = Column 3 [.   ] | Use the amount in Column 1 when you prepare your Forms W-2 or Forms W-2c.

7. **Federal income tax withheld from wages, tips, and other compensation** (Form 941, line 3)
Column 1 [.   ] − Column 2 [.   ] = Column 3 [.   ] | Copy Column 3 here ▶ Column 4 [.   ]

8. **Taxable social security wages** (Form 941 or 941-SS, line 5a, Column 1)
Column 1 [.   ] − Column 2 [.   ] = Column 3 [.   ] × 0.124* = Column 4 [.   ]
* If you're correcting your employer share only, use 0.062. See instructions.

9. **Qualified sick leave wages** (Form 941 or 941-SS, line 5a(i), Column 1)
Column 1 [.   ] − Column 2 [.   ] = Column 3 [.   ] × 0.062 = Column 4 [.   ]

10. **Qualified family leave wages** (Form 941 or 941-SS, line 5a(ii), Column 1)
Column 1 [.   ] − Column 2 [.   ] = Column 3 [.   ] × 0.062 = Column 4 [.   ]

11. **Taxable social security tips** (Form 941 or 941-SS, line 5b, Column 1)
Column 1 [.   ] − Column 2 [.   ] = Column 3 [.   ] × 0.124* = Column 4 [.   ]
* If you're correcting your employer share only, use 0.062. See instructions.

12. **Taxable Medicare wages & tips** (Form 941 or 941-SS, line 5c, Column 1)
Column 1 [.   ] − Column 2 [.   ] = Column 3 [.   ] × 0.029* = Column 4 [.   ]
* If you're correcting your employer share only, use 0.0145. See instructions.

13. **Taxable wages & tips subject to Additional Medicare Tax withholding** (Form 941 or 941-SS, line 5d)
Column 1 [.   ] − Column 2 [.   ] = Column 3 [.   ] × 0.009* = Column 4 [.   ]
* Certain wages and tips reported in Column 3 shouldn't be multiplied by 0.009. See instructions.

14. **Section 3121(q) Notice and Demand—Tax due on unreported tips** (Form 941 or 941-SS, line 5f)
Column 1 [.   ] − Column 2 [.   ] = Column 3 [.   ] | Copy Column 3 here ▶ Column 4 [.   ]

15. **Tax adjustments** (Form 941 or 941-SS, lines 7 through 9)
Column 1 [.   ] − Column 2 [.   ] = Column 3 [.   ] | Copy Column 3 here ▶ Column 4 [.   ]

16. **Qualified small business payroll tax credit for increasing research activities** (Form 941 or 941-SS, line 11a; you must attach Form 8974)
Column 1 [.   ] − Column 2 [.   ] = Column 3 [.   ] | See instructions Column 4 [.   ]

17. **Nonrefundable portion of credit for qualified sick and family leave wages** (Form 941 or 941-SS, line 11b)
Column 1 [.   ] − Column 2 [.   ] = Column 3 [.   ] | See instructions Column 4 [.   ]

18. **Nonrefundable portion of employee retention credit** (Form 941 or 941-SS, line 11c)
Column 1 [.   ] − Column 2 [.   ] = Column 3 [.   ] | See instructions Column 4 [.   ]

19. **Special addition to wages for federal income tax**
Column 1 [.   ] − Column 2 [.   ] = Column 3 [.   ] | See instructions Column 4 [.   ]

20. **Special addition to wages for social security taxes**
Column 1 [.   ] − Column 2 [.   ] = Column 3 [.   ] | See instructions Column 4 [.   ]

21. **Special addition to wages for Medicare taxes**
Column 1 [.   ] − Column 2 [.   ] = Column 3 [.   ] | See instructions Column 4 [.   ]

22. **Special addition to wages for Additional Medicare Tax**
Column 1 [.   ] − Column 2 [.   ] = Column 3 [.   ] | See instructions Column 4 [.   ]

23. Combine the amounts on lines 7 through 22 of Column 4 . . . . Column 4 [.   ]

24. **Deferred amount of social security tax*** (Form 941 or 941-SS, line 13b)
Column 1 [.   ] − Column 2 [.   ] = Column 3 [.   ] | See instructions Column 4 [.   ]
* Use this line to correct the employer deferral for the second quarter of 2020 and the employer and employee deferral for the third and fourth quarters of 2020.

25. **Refundable portion of credit for qualified sick and family leave wages** (Form 941 or 941-SS, line 13c)
Column 1 [.   ] − Column 2 [.   ] = Column 3 [.   ] | See instructions Column 4 [.   ]

Next ▶

Form **941-X** (Rev. 10-2020)

Form 941-X (Page 3)

Name *(not your trade name)*	Employer identification number (EIN)	Correcting quarter (1, 2, 3, 4)
		Correcting calendar year (YYYY)

Part 3: Enter the corrections for this quarter. If any line doesn't apply, leave it blank. *(continued)*

	Column 1	Column 2	Column 3	Column 4
	Total corrected amount (for ALL employees)	*Amount originally reported or as previously corrected (for ALL employees)*	*Difference (If this amount is a negative number, use a minus sign.)*	*Tax correction*

26. Refundable portion of employee retention credit (Form 941 or 941-SS, line 13d)   [.] − [.] = [.]   See instructions   [.]

27. **Total.** Combine the amounts on lines 23 through 26 of Column 4 . . . .   [.]

  If line 27 is less than zero:

  • If you checked line 1, this is the amount you want applied as a credit to your Form 941 or 941-SS for the tax period in which you're filing this form. (If you're currently filing a Form 944, Employer's ANNUAL Federal Tax Return, see the instructions.)

  • If you checked line 2, this is the amount you want refunded or abated.

  If line 27 is more than zero, this is the amount you owe. Pay this amount by the time you file this return. For information on how to pay, see *Amount you owe* in the instructions.

28. Qualified health plan expenses allocable to qualified sick leave wages (Form 941 or 941-SS, line 19)   [.] − [.] = [.]

29. Qualified health plan expenses allocable to qualified family leave wages (Form 941 or 941-SS, line 20)   [.] − [.] = [.]

30. Qualified wages for the employee retention credit (Form 941 or 941-SS, line 21)   [.] − [.] = [.]

31. Qualified health plan expenses allocable to wages reported on Form 941 or 941-SS, line 21 (Form 941 or 941-SS, line 22)   [.] − [.] = [.]

32. Credit from Form 5884-C, line 11, for this quarter (Form 941 or 941-SS, line 23)   [.] − [.] = [.]

33a. Qualified wages paid March 13 through March 31, 2020, for the employee retention credit (use this line to correct only the second quarter of 2020) (Form 941 or 941-SS, line 24)   [.] − [.] = [.]

33b. Deferred amount of the employee share of social security tax included on Form 941 or 941-SS, line 13b (use this line to correct only the third and fourth quarters of 2020) (Form 941 or 941-SS, line 24)   [.] − [.] = [.]

34. Qualified health plan expenses allocable to wages reported on Form 941 or 941-SS, line 24 (use this line to correct only the second quarter of 2020) (Form 941 or 941-SS, line 25)   [.] − [.] = [.]

Next ▶

Form 941-X (Page 4)

Name *(not your trade name)*	Employer identification number (EIN)	Correcting quarter (1, 2, 3, 4)
		Correcting calendar year (YYYY)

Part 4: Explain your corrections for this quarter.

☐ **35.** **Check here if any corrections you entered on a line include both underreported and overreported amounts.** Explain both your underreported and overreported amounts on line 37.

☐ **36.** **Check here if any corrections involve reclassified workers.** Explain on line 37.

37. **You must give us a detailed explanation of how you determined your corrections.** See the instructions.

Part 5: Sign here. You must complete all four pages of this form and sign it.

Under penalties of perjury, I declare that I have filed an original Form 941 or Form 941-SS and that I have examined this adjusted return or claim, including accompanying schedules and statements, and to the best of my knowledge and belief, it is true, correct, and complete. Declaration of preparer (other than taxpayer) is based on all information of which preparer has any knowledge.

X **Sign your name here**

Print your name here _____

Print your title here _____

Date __/__/__

Best daytime phone _____

Paid Preparer Use Only

Check if you're self-employed . . . ☐

Preparer's name		PTIN	
Preparer's signature		Date	__/__/__
Firm's name (or yours if self-employed)		EIN	
Address		Phone	
City	State	ZIP code	

Page **4**

Form **941-X** (Rev. 10-2020)

Form 941-X (Page 5)

Form 941-X: Which process should you use?

Type of errors you're correcting			
Underreported amounts ONLY	**Use the adjustment process** to correct underreported amounts. • Check the box on line 1. • Pay the amount you owe from line 27 by the time you file Form 941-X.		
Overreported amounts ONLY	The process you use depends on **when** you file Form 941-X.	**If you're filing Form 941-X MORE THAN 90 days before the period of limitations on credit or refund for Form 941 or Form 941-SS expires...**	Choose either the adjustment process or the claim process to correct the overreported amounts. **Choose the adjustment process** if you want the amount shown on line 27 credited to your Form 941, Form 941-SS, or Form 944 for the period in which you file Form 941-X. Check the box on line 1. OR **Choose the claim process** if you want the amount shown on line 27 refunded to you or abated. Check the box on line 2.
		If you're filing Form 941-X WITHIN 90 days of the expiration of the period of limitations on credit or refund for Form 941 or Form 941-SS...	You must use the **claim process** to correct the overreported amounts. Check the box on line 2.
BOTH underreported and overreported amounts	The process you use depends on **when** you file Form 941-X.	**If you're filing Form 941-X MORE THAN 90 days before the period of limitations on credit or refund for Form 941 or Form 941-SS expires...**	Choose either the adjustment process or both the adjustment process and the claim process when you correct both underreported and overreported amounts. **Choose the adjustment process** if combining your underreported amounts and overreported amounts results in a balance due or creates a credit that you want applied to Form 941, Form 941-SS, or Form 944. • File one Form 941-X, and • Check the box on line 1 and follow the instructions on line 27. OR **Choose both the adjustment process and the claim process** if you want the overreported amount refunded to you or abated. File two separate forms. 1. **For the adjustment process,** file one Form 941-X to correct the underreported amounts. Check the box on line 1. Pay the amount you owe from line 27 by the time you file Form 941-X. 2. **For the claim process,** file a second Form 941-X to correct the overreported amounts. Check the box on line 2.
		If you're filing Form 941-X WITHIN 90 days of the expiration of the period of limitations on credit or refund for Form 941 or Form 941-SS...	You must **use both the adjustment process and the claim process.** File two separate forms. 1. **For the adjustment process,** file one Form 941-X to correct the underreported amounts. Check the box on line 1. Pay the amount you owe from line 27 by the time you file Form 941-X. 2. **For the claim process,** file a second Form 941-X to correct the overreported amounts. Check the box on line 2.

Page **5**

Form **941-X** (Rev. 10-2020)

Instructions for Form 941-X

Department of the Treasury
Internal Revenue Service

(Rev. October 2020)

Adjusted Employer's QUARTERLY Federal Tax Return or Claim for Refund

Section references are to the Internal Revenue Code unless otherwise noted.

Future Developments

For the latest information about developments related to Form 941-X and its instructions, such as legislation enacted after they were published, go to *IRS.gov/Form941X*.

TIP *The October 2020 revision of Form 941-X updates Form 941-X to allow it to be used to make corrections to the deferred amount of the employee share of social security tax for the third and fourth quarters of 2020.*

What's New

Changes to Form 941-X (Rev. October 2020) for coronavirus (COVID-19) related tax relief. Form 941-X has been revised to allow for correcting the deferred amount of the employee share of social security tax on wages paid on or after September 1, 2020, and before January 1, 2021. Form 941-X, line 24, is now used to correct the deferral of the employer and employee share of social security tax for the third and fourth quarters of 2020. For the second quarter of 2020, Form 941-X, line 24, is used to correct only the deferral of the employer share of social security tax. Form 941-X, line 33, has been renumbered to line 33a, and new line 33b is used to correct the portion of the deferred amount of the employee share of social security tax for the third and fourth quarters of 2020 included on Form 941, line 13b. For more information about the deferral of the employee share of social security tax, see Notice 2020-65, 2020-38 I.R.B. 567, available at *IRS.gov/irb/2020-38_IRB#NOT-2020-65*.

Reminders

Previous changes to Form 941-X for COVID-19 related employment tax credits and other tax relief. The following significant changes were made to Form 941-X to allow for correcting COVID-19 related employment tax credits and other tax relief reported on Form 941.
• Corrections to amounts reported on Form 941, lines 5a(i), 5a(ii), 11b, 13c, 19, and 20, for the credit for qualified sick and family leave wages are reported on Form 941-X, lines 9, 10, 17, 25, 28, and 29, respectively. For more information about the credit for qualified sick and family leave wages, including the dates for which the credit may be claimed, go to *IRS.gov/PLC*.
• Corrections to amounts reported on Form 941, lines 11c, 13d, 21, and 22, for the employee retention credit are reported on Form 941-X, lines 18, 26, 30, and 31, respectively. Corrections to Form 941, lines 24 and 25, are reported on Form 941-X, lines 33a and 34, respectively (these lines are only used for the second quarter of 2020). For more information about the

employee retention credit, including the dates for which the credit may be claimed, go to *IRS.gov/ERC*.
• Corrections to the deferred amount of the employer share of social security tax reported on Form 941, line 13b, are reported on Form 941-X, line 24, for the second quarter of 2020. For the third and fourth quarters of 2020, corrections to both the deferred amount of the employer and employee share of social security tax are reported on Form 941-X, line 24. For more information about the deferral of employment tax deposits, including the dates that deposits may be deferred and when they must be paid, go to *IRS.gov/ETD*.

   Note. If a line on Form 941-X doesn't apply to you, leave it blank. If you're correcting a quarter that began before April 1, 2020, you must leave blank the new lines 9, 10, 17, 18, 24, 25, 26, 28, 29, 30, 31, 32, 33a, 33b, and 34.

! **CAUTION** *If you claimed the credit for qualified sick and family leave wages and/or the employee retention credit on your original Form 941 for the quarter, and you make any corrections on Form 941-X for the quarter to amounts used to figure these credits, you will need to refigure the amount of these credits using Worksheet 1, later. You will also use this worksheet to figure these credits if you're claiming them for the first time on Form 941-X.*

COBRA premium assistance credit. The COBRA premium assistance credit lines are no longer on Form 941-X. The COBRA premium assistance credit was available to an employer for premiums paid on behalf of employees who were involuntarily terminated from employment between September 1, 2008, and May 31, 2010. The COBRA premium assistance credit isn't available for individuals who were involuntarily terminated after May 31, 2010. The IRS previously kept these lines available on Form 941-X because, in rare circumstances, such as instances where COBRA eligibility was delayed as a result of employer-provided health insurance coverage following termination, the credit was still available. It is extremely unlikely that any employers would still be providing health insurance coverage for an employee terminated between September 1, 2008, and May 31, 2010. Therefore, the IRS is no longer accepting claims for the COBRA premium assistance credit. However, if you need to correct a previously claimed COBRA premium assistance credit for a quarter in which the statute of limitations on corrections hasn't expired, you can file the April 2017 revision of Form 941-X and make the corrections on lines 20a and 20b.

Form 941-X is filed to correct Form 941 or Form 941-SS. References to Form 941 on Form 941-X and in these instructions also apply to Form 941-SS, Employer's QUARTERLY Federal Tax Return (American Samoa, Guam, the Commonwealth of the Northern Mariana

Nov 04, 2020   Cat. No. 20331U

Form 941-X Instructions (Page 2)

Islands, and the U.S. Virgin Islands), unless otherwise noted.

Employee consents to support a claim for refund. Rev. Proc. 2017-28, 2017-14 I.R.B. 1061, available at *IRS.gov/irb/2017-14_IRB#RP-2017-28*, provides guidance to employers on the requirements for employee consents used by an employer to support a claim for refund of overcollected social security tax and Medicare tax. The revenue procedure clarifies the basic requirements for both a request for employee consent and for the employee consent, and permits a consent to be requested, furnished, and retained in an electronic format as an alternative to a paper format. The revenue procedure also contains guidance concerning when an employer may claim a refund of only the employer share of overcollected social security tax and Medicare tax. The revenue procedure requires that any request for consent include an Additional Medicare Tax notice indicating that any claim on the employee's behalf won't include a claim for overpaid Additional Medicare Tax.

Qualified small business payroll tax credit for increasing research activities. For tax years beginning after 2015, a qualified small business may elect to claim up to $250,000 of its credit for increasing research activities as a payroll tax credit against the employer share of social security tax. The payroll tax credit election must be made on or before the due date of the originally filed income tax return (including extensions). Any election to take the payroll tax credit may be revoked only with the consent of the IRS. The portion of the credit used against the employer share of social security tax is allowed in the first calendar quarter beginning after the date that the qualified small business filed its income tax return. The election and determination of the credit amount that will be used against the employer share of social security tax is made on Form 6765, Credit for Increasing Research Activities. The amount from Form 6765, line 44, must then be reported on Form 8974, Qualified Small Business Payroll Tax Credit for Increasing Research Activities. Form 8974 is used to determine the amount of the credit that can be used in the current quarter. The amount from Form 8974, line 12, is reported on Form 941, line 11a (line 11 for quarters beginning before April 1, 2020). Any corrections to Form 941, line 11a (line 11 for quarters beginning before April 1, 2020), are reported on Form 941-X, line 16. If you make a correction on Form 941-X, line 16, you must attach a corrected Form 8974. For more information about the payroll tax credit, go to *IRS.gov/ResearchPayrollTC*.

Correcting federal income tax withheld. Generally, you may correct federal income tax withholding errors only if you discovered the errors in the same calendar year you paid the wages. In addition, for an overcollection, you may correct federal income tax withholding only if you also repaid or reimbursed the employees in the same year.

For prior years, you may only correct administrative errors to federal income tax withholding (that is, errors in which the amount reported on Form 941, line 3, isn't the amount you actually withheld from an employee's wages) and errors for which section 3509 rates apply. See section 13 of Pub. 15, Employer's Tax Guide, for more information

about corrections during the calendar year and about administrative errors. See section 2 of Pub. 15 for more information about section 3509. If section 3509 rates apply, see the instructions for lines 19–22, later.

 Only transposition or math errors involving the inaccurate reporting of the amount withheld are "administrative errors."

You can't file a Form 941-X to correct federal income tax withholding for prior years for nonadministrative errors. In other words, you can't correct federal income tax actually withheld from an employee in a prior year if you discover that you didn't withhold the right amount. For example, you can't correct federal income tax withheld in a prior year because you used the wrong income tax withholding table or you didn't treat a payment correctly as taxable or nontaxable. Similarly, if you paid federal income tax in a prior year on behalf of your employee, rather than deducting it from the employee's pay (which resulted in additional wages subject to tax), and in a subsequent year you determine that you incorrectly calculated the amount of tax, you can't correct the federal income tax withholding. However, you must still correct the amount of wages you reported on Form 941 and Form W-2, Wage and Tax Statement, for a prior year by filing Form 941-X and Form W-2c, Corrected Wage and Tax Statement. You will report the correct wages on Form 941-X, line 6, column 1.

TIP *The amount actually withheld is reflected on payroll information or on Form W-2 which can be used by the employee to claim a credit for withholding for individual income tax return purposes.*

Correcting Additional Medicare Tax withholding and wages and tips subject to Additional Medicare Tax withholding. Wages and tips subject to Additional Medicare Tax withholding are reported on Form 941, line 5d. Certain errors discovered on a previously filed Form 941 are corrected on Form 941-X, line 13. However, you can't file a Form 941-X to correct the wrong amount of Additional Medicare Tax actually withheld from an employee in a prior year, including any amount you paid on behalf of your employee rather than deducting it from the employee's pay (which resulted in additional wages subject to tax). See the instructions for line 13, later, for more information on the types of errors that can be corrected and how the correction is reported on Form 941-X. For more information about Additional Medicare Tax withholding, see the Instructions for Form 941 or go to *IRS.gov/ADMT*.

You may need to attach Schedule R (Form 941) to your Form 941-X. If you were required to file Schedule R (Form 941), Allocation Schedule for Aggregate Form 941 Filers, when you filed Form 941, you must complete Schedule R (Form 941) when correcting an aggregate Form 941. Schedule R (Form 941) is completed only for those clients and customers who have corrections reported on Form 941-X. Schedule R (Form 941) is filed as an attachment to Form 941-X.

Approved section 3504 agents and certified professional employer organizations (CPEOs) must complete and file Schedule R (Form 941) when filing an

Instructions for Form 941-X (Rev. 10-2020)

Form 941-X Instructions (Page 3)

aggregate Form 941. Aggregate Forms 941 are filed by agents approved by the IRS under section 3504. To request approval to act as an agent for an employer, the agent files Form 2678 with the IRS. Aggregate Forms 941 are also filed by CPEOs approved by the IRS under section 7705. To become a CPEO, the organization must apply through the IRS Online Registration System at *IRS.gov/CPEO*. CPEOs file Form 8973, Certified Professional Employer Organization/Customer Reporting Agreement, to notify the IRS that they started or ended a service contract with a customer.

Other third-party payers that file aggregate Forms 941, such as non-certified PEOs, must complete and file Schedule R (Form 941) if they have clients that are claiming the qualified small business payroll tax credit for increasing research activities, the credit for qualified sick and family leave wages, or the employee retention credit, or clients deferring the employer or the employee share of social security tax. If you're an other third-party payer that didn't file Schedule R (Form 941) with Form 941 because you didn't meet these requirements, but are now filing Form 941-X to report these credits or the deferral of the employer or the employee share of social security tax for your clients, then you must now file Schedule R (Form 941) and attach it to Form 941-X.

General Instructions: Understanding Form 941-X

What Is the Purpose of Form 941-X?

Use Form 941-X to correct errors on a Form 941 that you previously filed. Use Form 941-X to correct:
* Wages, tips, and other compensation;
* Income tax withheld from wages, tips, and other compensation;
* Taxable social security wages;
* Taxable social security tips;
* Taxable Medicare wages and tips;
* Taxable wages and tips subject to Additional Medicare Tax withholding;
* Deferred amount of the employer share of social security tax;
* Deferred amount of the employee share of social security tax;
* Qualified small business payroll tax credit for increasing research activities;
* Amounts reported on Form 941 for the credit for qualified sick and family leave wages, including adjustments to Form 941, lines 5a(i), 5a(ii), 11b, 13c, 19, and 20; and
* Amounts reported on Form 941 for the employee retention credit, including adjustments to Form 941, lines 11c, 13d, 21, and 22, (for the second quarter of 2020, also Form 941, lines 24 and 25).

Use Form 843, Claim for Refund and Request for Abatement, to request a refund or abatement of assessed interest or penalties. Don't request a refund or abatement of assessed interest or penalties on Form 941 or Form 941-X.

TIP *We use the terms "correct" and "corrections" on Form 941-X and in these instructions to include interest-free adjustments under sections 6205 and 6413 and claims for refund and abatement under sections 6402, 6414, and 6404. See Rev. Rul. 2009-39 for examples of how the interest-free adjustment and claim for refund rules apply in 10 different situations. You can find Rev. Rul. 2009-39, 2009-52 I.R.B. 951, at IRS.gov/irb/ 2009-52_IRB#RR-2009-39.*

When you discover an error on a previously filed Form 941, you must:
* Correct that error using Form 941-X;
* File a separate Form 941-X for each Form 941 that you're correcting; and
* Generally, file Form 941-X separately. Don't file Form 941-X with Form 941. However, if you didn't previously file Form 941 because you mistakenly treated your employees as nonemployees, you may have to file Form 941-X with Form 941. See the instructions for line 36, later.

If you didn't file a Form 941 for one or more quarters, don't use Form 941-X. Instead, file Form 941 for each of those quarters. See also *When Should You File Form 941-X*, later. However, if you didn't file Forms 941 because you improperly treated workers as independent contractors or nonemployees and are now reclassifying them as employees, see the instructions for line 36, later.

Report the correction of underreported and overreported amounts for the same tax period on a single Form 941-X, unless you're requesting a refund or abatement. If you're requesting a refund or abatement and are correcting both underreported and overreported amounts, file one Form 941-X correcting the underreported amounts only and a second Form 941-X correcting the overreported amounts.

You'll use the adjustment process if you underreported employment taxes and are making a payment, or if you overreported employment taxes and will be applying the credit to Form 941 for the period during which you file Form 941-X. However, see the *Caution* under *Is There a Deadline for Filing Form 941-X*, later, if you're correcting overreported amounts during the last 90 days of a period of limitations. You'll use the claim process if you overreported employment taxes and are requesting a refund or abatement of the overreported amount. Follow the chart on page 5 of Form 941-X for help in choosing whether to use the adjustment process or the claim process. Be sure to give us a detailed explanation on line 37 for each correction that you show on Form 941-X.

Continue to report current quarter fractions of cents, third-party sick pay, tips, and group-term life insurance on Form 941, lines 7–9.

You have additional requirements to complete when filing Form 941-X, such as certifying that you filed (or will file) all applicable Forms W-2 and Forms W-2c with the Social Security Administration (SSA). For corrections of overreported federal income tax, social security tax, Medicare tax, or Additional Medicare Tax, you must make any certifications that apply to your situation.

Instructions for Form 941-X (Rev. 10-2020) -3-

Form 941-X Instructions (Page 4)

 Don't use Form 941-X to correct Form CT-1, 943, 944, or 945. Instead, use the "X" form that corresponds to those forms (Form CT-1 X, 943-X, 944-X, or 945-X).

Where Can You Get Help?

For help filing Form 941-X or for questions about federal employment taxes and tax corrections, you can:
• Go to *IRS.gov/EmploymentTaxes* and *IRS.gov/ CorrectingEmploymentTaxes*;
• See Pub. 15 for correcting Form 941, or Pub. 80, Federal Tax Guide for Employers in the U.S. Virgin Islands, Guam, American Samoa, and the Commonwealth of the Northern Mariana Islands, for correcting Form 941-SS; or
• Call the IRS Business and Specialty Tax Line at 800-829-4933 or 800-829-4059 (TDD/TTY for persons who are deaf, hard of hearing, or have a speech disability), Monday–Friday from 7:00 a.m. to 7:00 p.m. local time (Alaska and Hawaii follow Pacific time).

See also *How Can You Get Forms, Instructions, and Publications From the IRS*, later.

When Should You File Form 941-X?

File Form 941-X when you discover an error on a previously filed Form 941.

However, if your only errors on Form 941 relate to the number of employees who received wages (Form 941, line 1) or to federal tax liabilities reported on Form 941, Part 2, or on Schedule B (Form 941), Report of Tax Liability for Semiweekly Schedule Depositors, don't file Form 941-X. For more information about correcting federal tax liabilities reported on Form 941, Part 2, or on Schedule B (Form 941), see the Instructions for Schedule B (Form 941).

Due dates. The due date for filing Form 941-X depends on when you discover an error and if you underreported or overreported tax. If you underreported tax, see *Underreported tax*, later. For overreported amounts, you may choose to either make an interest-free adjustment or file a claim for refund or abatement. If you're correcting overreported amounts, see *Overreported tax—Adjustment process* or *Overreported tax—Claim process*, later.

If any due date falls on a Saturday, Sunday, or legal holiday, you may file Form 941-X on the next business day. If we receive Form 941-X after the due date, we will treat Form 941-X as filed on time if the envelope containing Form 941-X is properly addressed, contains sufficient postage, and is postmarked by the U.S. Postal Service on or before the due date, or sent by an IRS-designated private delivery service (PDS) on or before the due date. If you don't follow these guidelines, we will consider Form 941-X filed when it is actually received. See Pub. 15 or Pub. 80 for more information on legal holidays. For more information about PDSs, see *Where Should You File Form 941-X*, later.

Underreported tax. If you're correcting underreported tax, you must file Form 941-X by the due date of the return for the return period in which you discovered the error and

pay the amount you owe **by the time you file**. Doing so will generally ensure that your correction is interest free and not subject to failure-to-pay (FTP) or failure-to-deposit (FTD) penalties. See *What About Penalties and Interest*, later. For details on how to make a payment, see the instructions for line 27, later.

If Form 941-X is filed late (after the due date of the return for the return period in which you discovered the error), you must attach an amended Schedule B (Form 941) to Form 941-X. Otherwise, the IRS may assess an "averaged" FTD penalty. See *"Averaged" FTD penalty* in section 11 of Pub. 15 or section 8 of Pub. 80 for more information about "averaged" FTD penalties. The total tax reported on the "Total liability for the quarter" line of Schedule B (Form 941) must match the corrected tax (Form 941, line 12, combined with any correction entered on Form 941-X, line 23) for the quarter, less any previous abatements and interest-free tax assessments.

If you discover an error in . . .	Form 941-X is due . . .
1. January, February, March	April 30
2. April, May, June	July 31
3. July, August, September	October 31
4. October, November, December	January 31

The dates shown in the table above apply only to corrections of underreported amounts. If any due date falls on a Saturday, Sunday, or legal holiday, you may file Form 941-X on the next business day.

Example—You owe tax. On April 10, 2020, you discovered that you underreported $10,000 of social security and Medicare wages on your 2019 first quarter Form 941. File Form 941-X and pay the amount you owe by July 31, 2020, because you discovered the error in the second quarter of 2020, and July 31, 2020, is the due date for that quarter. If you file Form 941-X before July 31, 2020, pay the amount you owe by the time you file.

TIP *The due date for filing the adjusted return is determined by the type of return (Form 941 or Form 944) being corrected, without regard to your current filing requirements. Therefore, if you're currently filing Form 941 and you're correcting a previously filed Form 944, you must file Form 944-X by January 31 of the year following the year you discover the error.*

Overreported tax—Adjustment process. If you overreported tax on Form 941 and choose to apply the credit to Form 941 or Form 944, file an adjusted return on Form 941-X soon after you discover the error but more than 90 days before the period of limitations on the credit or refund for Form 941 expires. See *Is There a Deadline for Filing Form 941-X*, later.

Overreported tax—Claim process. If you overreported tax on Form 941, you may choose to file a claim for refund or abatement on Form 941-X any time before the period of limitations on credit or refund expires on Form 941. If you also need to correct any underreported amounts, you must file another Form 941-X reporting only corrections to

-4-   Instructions for Form 941-X (Rev. 10-2020)

Form 941-X Instructions (Page 5)

the underreported amounts. See *Is There a Deadline for Filing Form 941-X?* next.

 You may not file a refund claim to correct federal income tax or Additional Medicare Tax actually withheld from employees.

Is There a Deadline for Filing Form 941-X?

Generally, you may correct overreported taxes on a previously filed Form 941 if you file Form 941-X within 3 years of the date Form 941 was filed or 2 years from the date you paid the tax reported on Form 941, whichever is later. You may correct underreported taxes on a previously filed Form 941 if you file Form 941-X within 3 years of the date the Form 941 was filed. We call each of these time frames a "period of limitations." For purposes of the period of limitations, Forms 941 for a calendar year are considered filed on April 15 of the succeeding year if filed before that date.

Example. You filed your 2018 fourth quarter Form 941 on January 28, 2019, and payments were timely made. The IRS treats the return as if it were filed on April 15, 2019. On January 20, 2022, you discovered that you overreported social security and Medicare wages on that form by $350. To correct the error, you must file Form 941-X by April 18, 2022, which is the end of the period of limitations for Form 941, and use the claim process.

 If you file Form 941-X to correct overreported amounts in the last 90 days of a period of limitations, you must use the claim process. You can't use the adjustment process. If you're also correcting underreported amounts, you must file another Form 941-X to correct the underreported amounts using the adjustment process and pay any tax due.

Where Should You File Form 941-X?

Send your completed Form 941-X to the address shown next.

IF you're in . . .	THEN use this address . . .
Connecticut, Delaware, District of Columbia, Florida, Georgia, Illinois, Indiana, Kentucky, Maine, Maryland, Massachusetts, Michigan, New Hampshire, New Jersey, New York, North Carolina, Ohio, Pennsylvania, Rhode Island, South Carolina, Tennessee, Vermont, Virginia, West Virginia, Wisconsin	Department of the Treasury Internal Revenue Service Cincinnati, OH 45999-0005
Alabama, Alaska, Arizona, Arkansas, California, Colorado, Hawaii, Idaho, Iowa, Kansas, Louisiana, Minnesota, Mississippi, Missouri, Montana, Nebraska, Nevada, New Mexico, North Dakota, Oklahoma, Oregon, South Dakota, Texas, Utah, Washington, Wyoming	Department of the Treasury Internal Revenue Service Ogden, UT 84201-0005
No legal residence or principal place of business in any state	Internal Revenue Service P.O. Box 409101 Ogden, UT 84409
Special filing address for exempt organizations; federal, state, and local governmental entities; and Indian tribal governmental entities, regardless of location	Department of the Treasury Internal Revenue Service Ogden, UT 84201-0005

PDSs can't deliver to P.O. boxes. You must use the U.S. Postal Service to mail an item to a P.O. box address. Go to *IRS.gov/PDS* for the current list of PDSs. If you file Form 941-X using a PDS, send it to the following address.

Ogden - Internal Revenue Submission Processing Center
1973 Rulon White Blvd.
Ogden, UT 84201

Use this address even if your business is located in a state that files in Cincinnati.

How Should You Complete Form 941-X?

Use a Separate Form 941-X for Each Quarter You're Correcting

Use a separate Form 941-X for each Form 941 that you're correcting. For example, if you found errors on your Forms 941 for the third and fourth quarters of 2019, file one Form 941-X to correct the 2019 third quarter Form 941. File a second Form 941-X to correct the 2019 fourth quarter Form 941.

Employer Identification Number (EIN), Name, and Address

Enter your EIN, name, and address in the spaces provided. Also enter your name and EIN on the top of pages 2, 3, and 4, and on any attachments. If your address has changed since you filed your Form 941, enter the corrected information and the IRS will update your address of record. Be sure to write your name, EIN, "Form

Form 941-X Instructions (Page 6)

941-X," the calendar quarter you're correcting (for example, "Quarter 2"), and the calendar year of the quarter you're correcting on the top of any attachments.

Return You're Correcting

In the box at the top of page 1, check the type of return (Form 941 or Form 941-SS) you're correcting. Check the appropriate box for the one quarter you're correcting. Enter the calendar year of the Form 941 you're correcting. Enter the quarter and calendar year on pages 2, 3, and 4.

Enter the Date You Discovered Errors

You **must** enter the date you discovered errors. You discover an error when you have enough information to be able to correct it. If you're reporting several errors that you discovered at different times, enter the earliest date you discovered them here. Report any subsequent dates and related errors on line 37.

Must You Make an Entry on Each Line?

You must provide all of the information requested at the top of page 1 of Form 941-X. You must check one box (but not both) in Part 1. In Part 2, you must check the box on line 3 and any applicable boxes on lines 4 and 5. In Part 3, if any line doesn't apply, leave it blank. Complete Parts 4 and 5 as instructed.

How Should You Report Negative Amounts?

Form 941-X uses negative numbers to show reductions in tax (credits) and positive numbers to show additional tax (amounts you owe).

When reporting a negative amount in columns 3 and 4, use a minus sign instead of parentheses. For example, enter "-10.59" instead of "(10.59)." However, if you're completing the return on your computer and your software only allows you to use parentheses to report negative amounts, you may use them.

How Should You Make Entries on Form 941-X?

You can help the IRS process Form 941-X timely and accurately if you follow these guidelines.
* Type or print your entries.
* Use Courier font (if possible) for all typed or computer-generated entries.
* Omit dollar signs. You may use commas and decimal points, if desired. Enter dollar amounts to the left of any preprinted decimal point and cents to the right of it.
* Always show an amount for cents, even if it is zero. Don't round entries to whole dollars.
* Complete all four pages and sign Form 941-X on page 4.
* Staple multiple sheets in the upper-left corner.

What About Penalties and Interest?

Generally, your correction of an underreported amount won't be subject to an FTP penalty, FTD penalty, or interest if you:
* File on time (by the due date of Form 941 for the quarter in which you discover the error),
* **Pay** the amount shown on line 27 **by the time you file** Form 941-X, and
* Enter the date you discovered the error, and

* Explain in detail the grounds and facts relied on to support the correction.

No correction will be eligible for interest-free treatment if any of the following apply.
* The amounts underreported relate to an issue that was raised in an examination of a prior period.
* You knowingly underreported your employment tax liability.
* You received a notice and demand for payment.
* You received a notice of determination under section 7436.

If you receive a notice about a penalty after you file this return, reply to the notice with an explanation and we will determine if you meet the reasonable-cause criteria. Don't attach an explanation when you file your return.

Overview of the Process

To correct a previously filed Form 941, use Form 941-X to file either an adjusted employment tax return or a claim for refund or abatement. The adjustment process and the claim process are outlined below.

If you underreported the tax. If you underreported the tax on a previously filed Form 941, check the box on line 1 and **pay** any additional amount you owe **by the time you file** Form 941-X. For details on how to make a payment, see the instructions for line 27, later.

Example—You underreported employment taxes. On January 15, 2021, you discover an error that results in additional tax on your 2020 third quarter Form 941. File Form 941-X by April 30, 2021, and pay the amount you owe by the time you file. See *When Should You File Form 941-X*, earlier. Don't attach Form 941-X to your 2021 first quarter Form 941.

If you overreported the tax. If you overreported the tax on a previously filed Form 941, you may **choose** one of the following options.
* *Use the adjustment process.* Check the box on line 1 to apply any credit (negative amount) from line 27 to Form 941 for the quarter during which you file Form 941-X.
* *Use the claim process.* Check the box on line 2 to file a claim on Form 941-X requesting a refund or abatement of the amount shown on line 27.

 *To ensure that the IRS has enough time to process a credit for an **overreporting adjustment** in the quarter during which you file Form 941-X, you're encouraged to file Form 941-X correcting the overreported amount in the first 2 months of a quarter. For example, if you discover an overreported amount in March, June, September, or December, you may want to file Form 941-X in the first 2 months of the next quarter. However, there must be 90 days remaining on the period of limitations when you file Form 941-X. See the Caution under Is There a Deadline for Filing Form 941-X, earlier. This should ensure that the IRS will have enough time to process Form 941-X so the credit will be posted before you file Form 941, thus avoiding an erroneous balance due notice from the IRS. See the example below.*

Example—You want your overreported tax applied as a credit to Form 941. On September 18, 2020, you

-6-   **Instructions for Form 941-X (Rev. 10-2020)**

Form 941-X Instructions (Page 7)

discover you overreported your tax on your 2019 fourth quarter Form 941 and want to choose the adjustment process. To allow the IRS enough time to process the credit, you file Form 941-X on October 2, 2020, and take the credit on your fourth quarter 2020 Form 941.

 If you currently file Form 944 and you're making a correction to a previously filed Form 941 that will be claimed as a credit on Form 944, file Form 941-X before December in any year before the expiration of the period of limitations for the previously filed Form 941. In the year that the period of limitations for the previously filed Form 941 expires, file Form 941-X at least 90 days before the expiration date.

Specific Instructions:

Part 1: Select ONLY One Process

Because Form 941-X may be used to file either an adjusted employment tax return or a claim for refund or abatement, you **must** check one box on either line 1 or line 2. Don't check both boxes.

1. Adjusted Employment Tax Return

Check the box on line 1 if you're correcting underreported amounts or overreported amounts and you would like to use the adjustment process to correct the errors.

If you're correcting both underreported amounts and overreported amounts on this form, you **must** check this box. If you check this box, any negative amount shown on line 27 will be applied as a credit (tax deposit) to your Form 941 or Form 944 for the period in which you're filing this form. See *Example—You want your overreported tax applied as a credit to Form 941*, earlier.

If you owe tax. **Pay** the amount shown on line 27 **by the time you file** Form 941-X. Generally, you won't be charged interest if you file on time, pay on time, enter the date you discovered the error, and explain the correction on line 37.

If you have a credit. You overreported employment taxes (you have a negative amount on line 27) and want the IRS to apply the credit to Form 941 or Form 944 for the period during which you filed Form 941-X. The IRS will apply your credit on the first day of the Form 941 or Form 944 period during which you filed Form 941-X. However, the credit you show on Form 941-X, line 27, may not be fully available on your Form 941 or Form 944 if the IRS corrects it during processing or you owe other taxes, penalties, or interest. The IRS will notify you if your claimed credit changes or if the amount available as a credit on Form 941 or Form 944 was reduced because of unpaid taxes, penalties, or interest.

 Don't check the box on line 1 if you're correcting overreported amounts and the period of limitations on credit or refund for Form 941 will expire within 90 days of the date you file Form 941-X. See Is There a Deadline for Filing Form 941-X, *earlier.*

2. Claim

Check the box on line 2 to use the claim process if you're correcting **overreported amounts only** and you're claiming a refund or abatement for the negative amount (credit) shown on line 27. Don't check this box if you're correcting any underreported amounts on this form.

You must check the box on line 2 if you have a credit and the period of limitations on credit or refund for Form 941 will expire within 90 days of the date you file Form 941-X. See *Is There a Deadline for Filing Form 941-X*, earlier.

The IRS usually processes claims shortly after they are filed. The IRS will notify you if your claim is denied, accepted as filed, or selected to be examined. See Pub. 556, Examination of Returns, Appeal Rights, and Claims for Refund, for more information.

Unless the IRS corrects Form 941-X during processing or you owe other taxes, penalties, or interest, the IRS will refund the amount shown on line 27, plus any interest that applies.

 You may not file a refund claim to correct federal income tax or Additional Medicare Tax actually withheld from employees.

Part 2: Complete the Certifications

You must complete all certifications that apply by checking the appropriate boxes. If all of your corrections relate to underreported amounts, complete line 3 only; skip lines 4 and 5 and go to Part 3. If your corrections relate to overreported amounts, you have a duty to ensure that your employees' rights to recover overpaid employee social security and Medicare taxes that you withheld are protected. The certifications on lines 4 and 5 address the requirement to:
• Repay or reimburse your employees for the overcollection of employee social security and Medicare taxes, or
• Obtain consents from your employees to file a claim on their behalf. See *Rev. Proc. 2017-28* for guidance on the requirements for both a request for employee consent and for the employee consent.

3. Filing Forms W-2 or Forms W-2c

Check the box on line 3 to certify that you filed or will file Forms W-2 or Forms W-2c with the SSA, as required, showing your employees' correct wage and tax amounts. See the General Instructions for Forms W-2 and W-3 for detailed information about filing requirements. References to Form W-2 on Form 941-X and in these instructions also apply to Forms W-2AS, W-2CM, W-2GU, and W-2VI unless otherwise noted.

You must check the box on line 3 to certify that you filed Forms W-2 or Forms W-2c even if your corrections on Form 941-X don't change amounts shown on those forms. For example, if your only correction to Form 941 involves misstated tax adjustments, which don't impact the amounts reported on your employee's Forms W-2 (see the instructions for line 15, later), check the box on line 3 to certify that you already filed all required Forms W-2 and W-2c with the SSA. In this situation, you're certifying that

Form 941-X Instructions (Page 8)

you don't need to file Form W-2c because you already filed a correct Form W-2.

4. Certifying Overreporting Adjustments

If you overreported federal income tax, social security tax, Medicare tax, or Additional Medicare Tax and checked the box on line 1, check the appropriate box on line 4. You may need to check more than one box. If you obtained written statements from some employees but you couldn't locate employees or secure the statements of the remaining employees, check all applicable boxes. Provide a summary on line 37 of the amount of the corrections both for the employees who provided written statements and for those who didn't.

4a. Check the box on line 4a if your overreported amount includes each affected employee share of overcollected taxes. You're certifying that you repaid or reimbursed the employee share of current and prior year taxes and you received written statements from the employees stating that they didn't and won't receive a refund or credit for the prior year taxes. You're certifying that you adjusted federal income tax or Additional Medicare Tax withheld from employees for the current calendar year only. Don't send these statements to the IRS. Keep them for your records. Generally, all employment tax records must be kept for at least 4 years. Copies must be submitted to the IRS if requested.

4b. Check the box on line 4b to certify that your overreported amount is only for the employer share of taxes on those employees who you were unable to find or those who didn't give you a statement described on line 4a.

4c. Check the box on line 4c to certify that your overreported amount is only for federal income tax, social security tax, Medicare tax, or Additional Medicare Tax that you didn't withhold from your employees.

5. Certifying Claims

If you're filing a claim for refund or abatement of overreported federal income tax, social security tax, Medicare tax, or Additional Medicare Tax and checked the box on line 2, check the appropriate box on line 5. You may need to check more than one box. If you obtained written statements or consents from some employees but you couldn't locate employees or secure the statements or consents of the remaining employees, check all applicable boxes. Provide a summary on line 37 of the amount of the corrections for both the employees who provided statements or consents and for those who didn't.

⚠️ **CAUTION** *You can't file a refund claim to correct the incorrect amount of federal income tax or Additional Medicare Tax actually withheld from employees in a prior year. If you request their consent to file a claim for social security tax or Medicare tax, you must tell your employees that you can't claim a refund of any Additional Medicare Tax on their behalf. See Rev. Proc. 2017-28 for sample language to use in your request.*

5a. Check the box on line 5a if your overreported tax includes each affected employee share of social security and Medicare taxes. You're certifying that you repaid or reimbursed to the employees their share of social security

and Medicare taxes. For refunds of employee social security and Medicare taxes overcollected in prior years, you're certifying that you received written statements from those employees stating that they didn't and won't receive a refund or credit for the prior year taxes. Don't send these statements to the IRS. Keep them for your records. Generally, all employment tax records must be kept for at least 4 years. Copies must be submitted to the IRS if requested.

5b. Check the box on line 5b if your overreported tax includes each affected employee share of social security and Medicare taxes and you haven't yet repaid or reimbursed the employee share of taxes. You're certifying that you received consent from each affected employee to file a claim on the employee share of those taxes and you received written statements from those employees stating that they didn't and won't receive a refund or credit for the prior year taxes.

An employee consent must:
- Contain the name, address, and social security number (or truncated taxpayer identification number, when appropriate) of the employee;
- Contain the name, address, and EIN of the employer;
- Contain the tax period(s), type of tax, and the amount of tax for which the consent is provided;
- Affirmatively state that the employee authorizes the employer to claim a refund for the overpayment of the employee share of tax;
- For amounts collected in a prior year, include the employee's written statement certifying that the employee hasn't made any previous claims (or the claims were rejected) and won't make any future claims for refund or credit of the amount of the overcollection;
- Identify the basis of the claim; and
- Be dated and contain the employee's signature under penalties of perjury. The penalties of perjury statement should be located immediately above the required signature.

Don't send these statements and consents to the IRS. Keep them for your records. Generally, all employment tax records must be kept for at least 4 years. Copies must be submitted to the IRS if requested.

In certain situations, you may not have repaid or reimbursed your employees or obtained their consents prior to filing a claim, such as in cases where the period of limitations on credit or refund is about to expire. In those situations, file Form 941-X, but don't check a box on line 5. Tell us on line 37 that you haven't repaid or reimbursed employees or obtained consents at the time you file the claim. However, you must repay or reimburse your employees and certify that you've done so before the IRS can allow the claim.

5c. Check the box on line 5c to certify that your overreported tax is only for the employer share of social security and Medicare taxes. This applies when affected employees didn't give you consent to file a claim for refund for the employee share of social security and Medicare taxes, they couldn't be found, or they didn't give you a statement described on line 5b.

5d. Check the box on line 5d to certify that your overreported amount is only for federal income tax, social

-8-   **Instructions for Form 941-X (Rev. 10-2020)**

Mastering Payroll II

Form 941-X Instructions (Page 9)

security tax, Medicare tax, or Additional Medicare Tax that you didn't withhold from your employees.

Part 3: Enter the Corrections for This Quarter

What Amounts Should You Report in Part 3?

On lines 6–13, columns 1 and 2, for each line you're correcting, show amounts for **all** of your employees, not just for those employees whose amounts you're correcting.

If a correction that you report in column 4 includes both underreported and overreported amounts (see the instructions for line 35, later), give us details for each error on line 37.

Because special circumstances apply for lines 14–22, 24–26, and 28–34, read the instructions for each line carefully before entering amounts in the columns.

If any line doesn't apply to you, leave it blank.

If you previously adjusted or amended Form 941 by using Form 941-X or because of an IRS examination change, show amounts in column 2 that include those previously reported corrections.

6. Wages, Tips, and Other Compensation

If you're correcting the wages, tips, and other compensation you reported on Form 941, line 2, enter the total corrected amount for **all** employees in column 1. In column 2, enter the amount you originally reported or as previously corrected. In column 3, enter the difference between columns 1 and 2. This line doesn't apply to Form 941-SS.

If you or the IRS previously corrected the amount reported on Form 941, line 2, enter in column 2 the amount after any previous corrections.

```
   line 6 (column 1)
 - line 6 (column 2)
   _____
   line 6 (column 3)    If the amount in column 2 is larger than the
                        amount in column 1, use a minus sign in
                        column 3.
```

Example—Wages, tips, and other compensation increased. You reported $9,000 as total wages, tips, and other compensation on line 2 of your 2020 first quarter Form 941. In May of 2020, you discovered that you had overlooked $1,000 in tips for one of your employees. To correct the error, figure the difference on Form 941-X as shown.

Column 1 (corrected amount)	10,000.00
Column 2 (Form 941, line 2)	- 9,000.00
Column 3 (difference)	1,000.00

Example—Wages, tips, and other compensation decreased. You reported $9,000 as wages, tips, and other compensation on line 2 of your 2020 first quarter Form 941. In May of 2020, you discovered that you

included $2,000 in wages for one of your employees twice. To correct the error, figure the difference on Form 941-X as shown.

Column 1 (corrected amount)	7,000.00
Column 2 (Form 941, line 2)	- 9,000.00
Column 3 (difference)	- 2,000.00

Example—Auto allowance; wages, tips, and other compensation increased. You paid one of your employees a $500 monthly auto allowance from October through December 2019, and didn't treat the payments as taxable wages. In February 2020, you realized that the payments were wages because they weren't reimbursements of deductible business expenses that were substantiated and paid under an accountable plan. You correct the error by treating the auto allowance as wages subject to income, social security, and Medicare taxes. Report the additional $1,500 of wages on Form 941-X, lines 6, 8, 12, and, if applicable, line 13.

Be sure to explain the reasons for the corrections on line 37.

 The quarterly amount on line 6, column 1, should be used to figure the annual amount to report on your Forms W-2 or Forms W-2c. This amount should also generally be used for any business expense deduction on your income tax return (or amended return) for wages paid.

7. Federal Income Tax Withheld From Wages, Tips, and Other Compensation

If you're correcting the federal income tax withheld from wages, tips, and other compensation you reported on Form 941, line 3, enter the total corrected amount in column 1. In column 2, enter the amount you originally reported or as previously corrected. In column 3, enter the difference between columns 1 and 2. This line doesn't apply to Form 941-SS.

```
   line 7 (column 1)
 - line 7 (column 2)
   _____
   line 7 (column 3)    If the amount in column 2 is larger than the
                        amount in column 1, use a minus sign in
                        column 3.
```

Copy the amount in column 3 to column 4. Include any minus sign shown in column 3.

Generally, you may correct federal income tax withholding errors only if you discovered the errors in the same calendar year you paid the wages. In addition, for an overcollection, you may correct federal income tax withholding only if you also repaid or reimbursed the employees in the same year. For prior years, you may only correct administrative errors to federal income tax withholding (that is, errors in which the amount reported on Form 941, line 3, isn't the amount you actually withheld from an employee's wages) and errors for which section 3509 rates apply. Only transposition or math errors involving the inaccurate reporting of the

Instructions for Form 941-X (Rev. 10-2020)   -9-

266

Form 941-X Instructions (Page 10)

amount withheld are "administrative errors." See section 13 of Pub. 15 for more information about corrections during the calendar year and about administrative errors. See section 2 of Pub. 15 for more information about section 3509. If section 3509 rates apply, see the instructions for lines 19–22, later.

You can't file a Form 941-X to correct federal income tax withholding for prior years for nonadministrative errors. In other words, you can't correct federal income tax actually withheld from an employee in a prior year if you discover that you didn't withhold the right amount. For example, you can't correct federal income tax withheld in a prior year because you used the wrong income tax withholding table or you didn't treat a payment correctly as taxable or nontaxable. Similarly, if you paid federal income tax in a prior year on behalf of your employee, rather than deducting it from the employee's pay (which resulted in additional wages subject to tax), and in a subsequent year you determine that you incorrectly calculated the amount of tax, you can't correct the federal income tax withholding.

Example—Prior year nonadministrative error (failure to withhold federal income tax when required). You were required to withhold $400 of federal income tax from an employee's bonus that was paid in December of 2019 but you withheld nothing. You discovered the error on March 16, 2020. You can't file Form 941-X to correct federal income tax withheld reported on your 2019 fourth quarter Form 941 because the error involves a previous year and the amount previously reported for the employee represents the actual amount withheld from the employee during 2019.

Example—Prior year administrative error (incorrectly reported amount of federal income tax actually withheld). You had three employees. In the fourth quarter of 2019, you withheld $1,000 of federal income tax from Xavier Black, $2,000 from Sophie Rose, and $6,000 from Leo Wood. The total amount of federal income tax you withheld was $9,000. You mistakenly reported $6,000 on line 3 of your 2019 fourth quarter Form 941. You discovered the error on March 13, 2020. This is an example of an administrative error that may be corrected in a later calendar year because the amount actually withheld from the employees' wages isn't the amount reported on Form 941. Use Form 941-X to correct the error. Enter $9,000 in column 1 and $6,000 in column 2. Subtract the amount in column 2 from the amount in column 1.

Column 1 (corrected amount)	9,000.00
Column 2 (Form 941, line 3)	- 6,000.00
Column 3 (difference)	3,000.00

Report the $3,000 as a tax correction in column 4.

Be sure to explain the reasons for this correction on line 37.

Example—Nonadministrative error reporting federal income tax because of repayment of wages paid in prior year. You prepaid Jack Brown $4,000 of wages for 2 months of work in September 2019. You

withheld $400 of federal income tax at the time you paid Jack. These amounts were reported on your 2019 third quarter Form 941. Jack left employment in October 2019 (after only 1 month of service). In January 2020, Jack repaid $2,000 to you for the 1 month he didn't work. You can't file Form 941-X to reduce the federal income tax withheld because you actually withheld the federal income tax from wages. You also can't file Form 941-X to reduce wages because the wages were income to Jack for the prior year. These amounts were correctly reported on Form 941.

8. Taxable Social Security Wages

If you're correcting the taxable social security wages you reported on Form 941, line 5a, column 1, enter the total corrected amount in column 1. In column 2, enter the amount you originally reported or as previously corrected. In column 3, enter the difference between columns 1 and 2.

line 8 (column 1)	
- line 8 (column 2)	
line 8 (column 3)	If the amount in column 2 is larger than the amount in column 1, use a minus sign in column 3.

Multiply the amount in column 3 by 0.124 and enter that result in column 4.

line 8 (column 3)	
x 0.124	
line 8 (column 4)	If the amount in column 3 used a minus sign, also use a minus sign in column 4.

Note. If you checked the box on Form 941-X, line 4b or line 5c, because you're correcting only the employer share of tax on a decrease to social security wages, use 0.062 (6.2%) when multiplying the amount shown in column 3. If you're correcting both shares of tax for some employees and only the employer share for other employees, enter the properly calculated amount in column 4. Be sure to show your calculations on line 37.

Example—Social security wages decreased. Following *Example—Wages, tips, and other compensation decreased* in the instructions for line 6, the wages that you counted twice were also taxable social security wages. To correct the error, figure the difference on Form 941-X as shown.

Column 1 (corrected amount)	7,000.00
Column 2 (Form 941, line 5a, column 1)	- 9,000.00
Column 3 (difference)	- 2,000.00

Use the difference in column 3 to determine your tax correction.

Instructions for Form 941-X (Rev. 10-2020)

Form 941-X Instructions (Page 11)

Column 3 (difference)	- 2,000.00	line 9 (column 3)	
Tax rate (12.4%)	x 0.124	x 0.062	
Column 4 (tax correction)	- 248.00	line 9 (column 4)	If the amount in column 3 used a minus sign, also use a minus sign in column 4.

Be sure to explain the reasons for this correction on line 37.

9. Qualified Sick Leave Wages

TIP *Adjustments to the social security tax on qualified sick leave wages and qualified family leave wages are reported on Form 941-X, lines 9 and 10, respectively. Adjustments to the nonrefundable portion of the credit for qualified sick and family leave wages are reported on Form 941-X, line 17, and adjustments to the refundable portion of the credit are reported on Form 941-X, line 25. Adjustments to qualified health plan expenses allocable to qualified sick leave wages and to qualified family leave wages are reported on Form 941-X, lines 28 and 29, respectively. Qualified sick and family leave wages and the related credits for qualified sick and family leave wages are only reported on Form 941 with respect to wages paid for leave taken in quarters beginning after March 31, 2020, and before January 1, 2021, unless extended by future legislation (check IRS.gov/Form941X for updates). If you're correcting a quarter beginning before April 1, 2020, don't enter any amounts on lines 9, 10, 17, 25, 28, and 29. If you paid qualified sick and family leave wages in 2021 for 2020 leave, you will claim the credit on your 2021 Form 941. If you claimed the credit for qualified sick and family leave wages on your original Form 941 for the quarter, and you make any corrections on Form 941-X for the quarter to amounts used to figure this credit, you will need to refigure the amount of this credit using Worksheet 1, later. You will also use this worksheet to figure this credit if you're claiming the credit for the first time on Form 941-X. For more information about the credit for qualified sick and family leave wages, go to IRS.gov/PLC.*

Qualified sick leave wages aren't subject to the employer share of social security tax; therefore, the tax rate on these wages is 6.2% (0.062). For more information about qualified sick leave wages, go to *IRS.gov/PLC*. If you're correcting the qualified sick leave wages you reported on Form 941, line 5a(i), column 1, enter the total corrected amount in column 1. In column 2, enter the amount you originally reported or as previously corrected. In column 3, enter the difference between columns 1 and 2.

line 9 (column 1)	
- line 9 (column 2)	
line 9 (column 3)	If the amount in column 2 is larger than the amount in column 1, use a minus sign in column 3.

Multiply the amount in column 3 by 0.062 and enter that result in column 4.

Note. If you erroneously reported qualified sick leave wages on Form 941, line 5a, instead of on line 5a(i), you will need to make a correction on Form 941-X, lines 8 and 9, and enter the properly calculated amount in column 4 for each line.

Example—Qualified sick leave wages increased. You paid $2,000 of qualified sick leave wages to only one of your employees in the second quarter of 2020. In September 2020, you discover that you only reported $1,000 of qualified sick leave wages on Form 941 for the second quarter. To correct the error, figure the difference on Form 941-X as shown.

Column 1 (corrected amount)	2,000.00
Column 2 (Form 941, line 5a(i), column 1)	- 1,000.00
Column 3 (difference)	1,000.00

Use the difference in column 3 to determine your tax correction.

Column 3 (difference)	1,000.00
Tax rate (6.2%)	x 0.062
Column 4 (tax correction)	62.00

Be sure to explain the reasons for this correction on line 37.

10. Qualified Family Leave Wages

Qualified family leave wages aren't subject to the employer share of social security tax; therefore, the tax rate on these wages is 6.2% (0.062). For more information about qualified family leave wages, go to *IRS.gov/PLC*. If you're correcting the qualified family leave wages you reported on Form 941, line 5a(ii), column 1, enter the total corrected amount in column 1. In column 2, enter the amount you originally reported or as previously corrected. In column 3, enter the difference between columns 1 and 2.

line 10 (column 1)	
- line 10 (column 2)	
line 10 (column 3)	If the amount in column 2 is larger than the amount in column 1, use a minus sign in column 3.

Multiply the amount in column 3 by 0.062 and enter that result in column 4.

Form 941-X Instructions (Page 12)

line 10 (column 3)

x 0.062
_____

line 10 (column 4)   If the amount in column 3 used a minus sign, also use a minus sign in column 4.

Note. If you erroneously reported qualified family leave wages on Form 941, line 5a, instead of on line 5a(ii), you will need to make a correction on Form 941-X, lines 8 and 10, and enter the properly calculated amount in column 4 for each line.

Example—Qualified family leave wages decreased. You paid $1,000 of qualified family leave wages to only one of your employees in the second quarter of 2020. In September 2020, you discover that you erroneously reported $3,000 of qualified family leave wages on Form 941 for the second quarter. To correct the error, figure the difference on Form 941-X as shown.

Column 1 (corrected amount)	1,000.00
Column 2 (Form 941, line 5a(ii), column 1)	- 3,000.00
Column 3 (difference)	- 2,000.00

Use the difference in column 3 to determine your tax correction.

Column 3 (difference)	- 2,000.00
Tax rate (6.2%)	x 0.062
Column 4 (tax correction)	- 124.00

Be sure to explain the reasons for this correction on line 37.

11. Taxable Social Security Tips

If you're correcting the taxable social security tips you reported on Form 941, line 5b, column 1, enter the total corrected amount in column 1. In column 2, enter the amount you originally reported or as previously corrected. In column 3, enter the difference between columns 1 and 2.

line 11 (column 1)
- line 11 (column 2)
_____

line 11 (column 3)   If the amount in column 2 is larger than the amount in column 1, use a minus sign in column 3.

Multiply the amount in column 3 by 0.124 and report that result in column 4.

line 11 (column 3)

x 0.124
_____

line 11 (column 4)   If the amount in column 3 used a minus sign, also use a minus sign in column 4.

Note. If you checked the box on Form 941-X, line 4b or line 5c, because you're correcting only the employer

share of tax on a decrease to social security tips, use 0.062 (6.2%) when multiplying the amount shown in column 3. If you're correcting both shares of tax for some employees and only the employer share for other employees, report the properly calculated amount in column 4. Be sure to show your calculations on line 37.

Example—Social security tips increased. Following *Example—Wages, tips, and other compensation increased* in the instructions for line 6, the tips that you overlooked were also taxable social security tips. To correct the error, figure the difference on Form 941-X as shown.

Column 1 (corrected amount)	10,000.00
Column 2 (Form 941, line 5b, column 1)	- 9,000.00
Column 3 (difference)	1,000.00

Use the difference in column 3 to determine your tax correction.

Column 3 (difference)	1,000.00
Tax rate (12.4%)	x 0.124
Column 4 (tax correction)	124.00

Be sure to explain the reasons for this correction on line 37.

12. Taxable Medicare Wages & Tips

If you're correcting the taxable Medicare wages and tips you reported on Form 941, line 5c, column 1, enter the total corrected amount in column 1. In column 2, enter the amount you originally reported or as previously corrected. In column 3, enter the difference between columns 1 and 2.

line 12 (column 1)
- line 12 (column 2)
_____

line 12 (column 3)   If the amount in column 2 is larger than the amount in column 1, use a minus sign in column 3.

Multiply the amount in column 3 by 0.029 (2.9% tax rate) and enter that result in column 4.

line 12 (column 3)

x 0.029
_____

line 12 (column 4)   If the amount in column 3 used a minus sign, also use a minus sign in column 4.

Note. If you checked the box on Form 941-X, line 4b or line 5c, because you're correcting only the employer share of tax on a decrease to Medicare wages and tips, use 0.0145 (1.45%) when multiplying the amount in column 3. If you're correcting both shares of tax for some employees and only the employer share for other employees, enter the properly calculated amount in column 4. Be sure to explain your calculations on line 37.

Form 941-X Instructions (Page 13)

Example—Medicare wages and tips decreased.
Following *Example—Wages, tips, and other compensation decreased* in the instructions for line 6, the wages that you counted twice were also taxable Medicare wages and tips. To correct the error, figure the difference on Form 941-X as shown.

Column 1 (corrected amount)	7,000.00
Column 2 (Form 941, line 5c, column 1)	- 9,000.00
Column 3 (difference)	- 2,000.00

Use the difference in column 3 to determine your tax correction.

Column 3 (difference)	- 2,000.00
Tax rate (2.9%)	x 0.029
Column 4 (tax correction)	- 58.00

Be sure to explain the reasons for this correction on line 37.

13. Taxable Wages & Tips Subject to Additional Medicare Tax Withholding

Generally, you may correct errors to Additional Medicare Tax withholding **only** if you discovered the errors in the same calendar year the wages and tips were paid to employees. However, you may correct errors to Additional Medicare Tax withholding for prior years if the amount reported on Form 941, line 5d, column 2, isn't the amount you actually withheld, including any amount you paid on behalf of your employee rather than deducting it from the employee's pay (which resulted in additional wages subject to tax). This type of error is an administrative error. The administrative error adjustment corrects the amount reported on Form 941 to agree with the amount actually withheld from employees.

You may also correct errors to Additional Medicare Tax withholding for prior years if section 3509 rates apply. If section 3509 rates apply, see the instructions for lines 19–22, later.

If a prior year error was a nonadministrative error, you may correct only the **wages and tips** subject to Additional Medicare Tax withholding that were originally reported on Form 941, line 5d, column 1, or previously corrected on Form 941-X. You can't correct the tax reported on Form 941, line 5d, column 2.

Errors discovered in the same calendar year or prior year administrative errors. If you're correcting the taxable wages and tips subject to Additional Medicare Tax withholding that you reported on Form 941, line 5d, column 1, enter the total corrected amount in column 1. In column 2, enter the amount you originally reported or as previously corrected. In column 3, enter the difference between columns 1 and 2.

line 13 (column 1)	
- line 13 (column 2)	
line 13 (column 3)	If the amount in column 2 is larger than the amount in column 1, use a minus sign in column 3.

Multiply the amount in column 3 by 0.009 (0.9% tax rate) and enter that result in column 4.

line 13 (column 3)	
x 0.009	
line 13 (column 4)	If the amount in column 3 used a minus sign, also use a minus sign in column 4.

Example—Prior year administrative error (incorrectly reported amount of Additional Medicare Tax actually withheld). Xavier Black's wages exceeded the $200,000 withholding threshold for Additional Medicare Tax in November 2019. The total wages paid to Xavier for 2019 were $230,000. You withheld $270 ($30,000 x 0.009) from Xavier's wages. However, on your fourth quarter 2019 Form 941, you mistakenly reported $3,000 on line 5d, column 1, and Additional Medicare Tax withheld of $27 on line 5d, column 2. You discover the error on March 16, 2020. This is an example of an administrative error that may be corrected in a later calendar year because the amount actually withheld isn't the amount reported on your fourth quarter 2019 Form 941. Use Form 941-X, line 13, to correct the error as shown below.

Column 1 (corrected amount)	30,000.00
Column 2 (Form 941, line 5d, column 1)	- 3,000.00
Column 3 (difference)	27,000.00

Use the difference in column 3 to determine your tax correction.

Column 3 (difference)	27,000.00
Tax rate (0.9%)	x 0.009
Column 4 (tax correction)	243.00

Be sure to explain the reasons for this correction on line 37.

Prior year nonadministrative errors. You may correct **only** the taxable wages and tips subject to Additional Medicare Tax withholding that you reported on Form 941, line 5d, column 1. Enter the total corrected amount in column 1. In column 2, enter the amount you originally reported or as previously corrected. In column 3, enter the difference between columns 1 and 2.

Form 941-X Instructions (Page 14)

line 13 (column 1)
- line 13 (column 2)

line 13 (column 3) If the amount in column 2 is larger than the amount in column 1, use a minus sign in column 3.

Don't multiply the amount in column 3 by 0.009 (0.9% tax rate). Leave column 4 blank and explain the reasons for this correction on line 37.

Example—Prior year nonadministrative error (failure to withhold Additional Medicare Tax when required). Sophie Rose's wages exceeded the $200,000 withholding threshold for Additional Medicare Tax in December 2019. The total wages paid to Sophie for 2019 were $220,000. You were required to withhold $180 ($20,000 x 0.009) but you withheld nothing and didn't report an amount on line 5d of your fourth quarter 2019 Form 941. You discover the error on March 16, 2020. File Form 941-X to correct wages and tips subject to Additional Medicare Tax withholding for your 2019 fourth quarter Form 941, but you may not correct the Additional Medicare Tax withheld (column 4) because the error involves a previous year and the amount previously reported for Sophie represents the actual amount withheld from Sophie during 2019.

Combination of prior year administrative and nonadministrative errors. If you're reporting both administrative errors and nonadministrative errors for the same quarter of a prior year, enter the total corrected amount in column 1. In column 2, enter the amount you originally reported or as previously corrected. In column 3, enter the difference between columns 1 and 2. However, multiply only the amount of wages and tips reported in column 3 that are related to administrative errors by 0.009 (0.9% tax rate). Don't multiply any wages and tips reported in column 3 that are related to nonadministrative errors by 0.009 (0.9% tax rate). Use line 37 to explain in detail your corrections. The explanation must include the reasons for the corrections and a breakdown of the amount reported in column 3 into the amounts related to administrative errors and nonadministrative errors.

Example—Combination of prior year administrative and nonadministrative errors. Xavier Black's wages exceeded the $200,000 withholding threshold for Additional Medicare Tax in November 2019. The total wages paid to Xavier for 2019 were $230,000. You withheld $270 ($30,000 x 0.009) from Xavier's wages. However, on your fourth quarter 2019 Form 941, you mistakenly reported $3,000 on line 5d, column 1, and Additional Medicare Tax withheld of $27 on line 5d, column 2. The difference in wages subject to Additional Medicare Tax related to this administrative error is $27,000 ($30,000 - $3,000).

Sophie Rose's wages exceeded the $200,000 withholding threshold for Additional Medicare Tax in December 2019. The total wages paid to Sophie for 2019 were $220,000. You were required to withhold $180 ($20,000 x 0.009) but you withheld nothing and didn't report Sophie's $20,000 in wages subject to Additional Medicare Tax withholding on line 5d of your fourth quarter 2019 Form 941.

You discover both errors on March 16, 2020. Use Form 941-X, line 13, to correct the errors as shown below.

Column 1 (corrected amount)	50,000.00
Column 2 (Form 941, line 5d, column 1)	- 3,000.00
Column 3 (difference)	47,000.00

Determine the portion of wages and tips reported in column 3 that is related to the administrative error ($47,000 - $20,000 (nonadministrative error) = $27,000 (administrative error)). Multiply this portion of column 3 by 0.009 (0.9% tax rate) to determine your tax correction.

Difference related to administrative error	27,000.00
Tax rate (0.9%)	x 0.009
Column 4 (tax correction)	243.00

Be sure to explain the reasons for these corrections on line 37. You must also report that $20,000 of the amount shown in column 3 was related to the correction of a prior year nonadministrative error and $27,000 of the amount shown in column 3 was related to the correction of an administrative error.

14. Section 3121(q) Notice and Demand—Tax on Unreported Tips

Enter on line 14 any corrections to amounts reported on Form 941, line 5f, for the tax due from a Section 3121(q) Notice and Demand. The IRS issues a Section 3121(q) Notice and Demand to advise an employer of the amount of tips received by employees who failed to report or underreported tips to the employer. An employer isn't liable for the employer share of the social security and Medicare taxes on unreported tips until a Section 3121(q) Notice and Demand for the taxes is made to the employer by the IRS.

Be sure to explain the reasons for any corrections on line 37.

15. Tax Adjustments

Use line 15 to correct any adjustments reported on Form 941, lines 7–9. Enter in column 1 the total corrected amount for Form 941, lines 7–9.

Enter in column 2 the total originally reported or previously corrected amounts from Form 941, lines 7–9. In column 3, enter the difference between columns 1 and 2.

line 15 (column 1)
- line 15 (column 2)

line 15 (column 3)

TIP *You may need to report negative numbers in any column. Make sure that the difference you enter in column 3 accurately represents the change to adjustments originally reported or previously corrected on Form 941, lines 7–9.*

Copy the amount in column 3 to column 4. Include any minus sign shown in column 3.

Form 941-X Instructions (Page 15)

On line 37, describe what you misreported on Form 941. Tell us if your adjustment is for fractions of cents, third-party sick pay, tips, or group-term life insurance.

Example—Current quarter's third-party sick pay underreported. You reported $6,900 (shown as "-6,900.00") as a third-party sick pay adjustment (reduction to tax) on line 8 of your 2019 second quarter Form 941. You didn't report any amounts on lines 7 and 9. Your third-party sick pay adjustment should've been $9,600 (shown as "-9,600.00") because your third-party sick pay payer withheld that amount of social security and Medicare taxes from your employees. You discovered the error in April of 2020. To correct the error, figure the difference on Form 941-X as shown.

Column 1 (corrected amount)	- 9,600.00
Column 2 (Form 941, line 8)	- (6,900.00)
Column 3 (difference)	- 2,700.00

Here is how you would enter the numbers on Form 941-X.

Column 1 (corrected amount)	Column 2 (Form 941, line 8)	Column 3 (difference)
-9,600.00	-6,900.00	-2,700.00

Report "-2,700.00" as your correction in column 4.

In this example, you're claiming a credit for $2,700 in overreported tax for your 2019 second quarter Form 941. Always enter the same amount in column 4 (including any minus sign) that you enter in column 3.

Be sure to explain the reasons for this correction on line 37.

16. Qualified Small Business Payroll Tax Credit for Increasing Research Activities

If you're correcting the qualified small business payroll tax credit for increasing research activities that you reported on Form 941, line 11a (line 11 for quarters beginning before April 1, 2020), enter the total corrected amount in column 1. In column 2, enter the amount you originally reported or as previously corrected. In column 3, enter the difference between columns 1 and 2.

Copy the amount in column 3 to column 4. However, to properly show the amount as a credit or balance due item, enter a positive number in column 3 as a negative number in column 4 or a negative number in column 3 as a positive number in column 4.

You must attach a corrected Form 8974 and explain the reasons for this correction on line 37.

CAUTION *The payroll tax credit election must be made on or before the due date of the originally filed income tax return (including extensions). Any election to take the payroll tax credit may be revoked only with the consent of the IRS.*

17. Nonrefundable Portion of Credit for Qualified Sick and Family Leave Wages

 TIP *Form 941-X and these instructions use the terms "nonrefundable" and "refundable" when discussing credits. The term "nonrefundable" means the portion of the credit which is limited by law to the amount of the employer share of social security tax. The term "refundable" means the portion of the credit which is in excess of the employer share of social security tax.*

If you're correcting the nonrefundable portion of the credit for qualified sick and family leave wages that you reported on Form 941, line 11b, enter the total corrected amount from Worksheet 1, Step 2, line 2j, in column 1. In column 2, enter the amount you originally reported or as previously corrected. In column 3, enter the difference between columns 1 and 2. For more information about the credit for qualified sick and family leave wages, go to *IRS.gov/PLC*.

Copy the amount in column 3 to column 4. However, to properly show the amount as a credit or balance due item, enter a positive number in column 3 as a negative number in column 4 or a negative number in column 3 as a positive number in column 4.

The credit for qualified sick and family leave wages is only available for wages paid with respect to leave taken for quarters beginning after March 31, 2020, and before January 1, 2021, unless extended by future legislation (check *IRS.gov/Form941X* for updates). If you paid qualified sick and family leave wages in 2021 for 2020 leave, you will claim the credit on your 2021 Form 941. If you're correcting a quarter beginning before April 1, 2020, don't enter any amount on line 17.

Example—Nonrefundable portion of credit for qualified sick and family leave wages increased. Following *Example—Qualified sick leave wages increased* in the instructions for line 9, you originally reported a $1,000 nonrefundable portion of credit for qualified sick and family leave wages on Form 941, line 11b, for the second quarter of 2020. You use Worksheet 1 to refigure the correct nonrefundable portion of the credit for qualified sick and family leave wages and you determine that the correct credit is now $2,000. To correct the error, figure the difference on Form 941-X as shown.

Column 1 (corrected amount)	2,000.00
Column 2 (Form 941, line 11b)	-1,000.00
Column 3 (difference)	1,000.00

To properly show the credit increase as a reduction to your tax balance, enter the positive number in column 3 as a negative number in column 4. Here is how you would enter the numbers on Form 941-X, line 17.

Form 941-X Instructions (Page 16)

Column 1 (corrected amount)	Column 2 (Form 941, line 11b)	Column 3 (difference)	Column 4 (tax correction)
2,000.00	1,000.00	1,000.00	-1,000.00

Be sure to explain the reasons for this correction on line 37.

18. Nonrefundable Portion of Employee Retention Credit

If you're correcting the nonrefundable portion of the employee retention credit that you reported on Form 941, line 11c, enter the total corrected amount from Worksheet 1, Step 3, line 3j, in column 1. In column 2, enter the amount you originally reported or as previously corrected. In column 3, enter the difference between columns 1 and 2. For more information about the employee retention credit, go to *IRS.gov/ERC*.

Copy the amount in column 3 to column 4. However, to properly show the amount as a credit or balance due item, enter a positive number in column 3 as a negative number in column 4 or a negative number in column 3 as a positive number in column 4.

Be sure to explain the reasons for this correction on line 37.

TIP *Adjustments to the nonrefundable portion of the employee retention credit are reported on Form 941-X, line 18, and adjustments to the refundable portion of the credit are reported on Form 941-X, line 26. Adjustments to qualified wages for the employee retention credit are reported on Form 941-X, line 30. Adjustments to qualified health plan expenses allocable to the employee retention credit are reported on Form 941-X, line 31. Adjustments to qualified wages paid March 13, 2020, through March 31, 2020, for the employee retention credit are reported on Form 941-X, line 33a, and adjustments to qualified health plan expenses allocable to these wages are reported on Form 941-X, line 34. The employee retention credit may only be claimed on Form 941 filed for quarters beginning after March 31, 2020, and before January 1, 2021, unless extended by future legislation (check IRS.gov/Form941X for updates). If you're correcting a quarter beginning before April 1, 2020, don't enter any amounts on lines 18, 26, 30, 31, 33a, and 34. The employee retention credit for wages paid March 13, 2020, through March 31, 2020, is claimed on Form 941 for the second quarter of 2020; therefore, any corrections to the employee retention credit for the period from March 13, 2020, through March 31, 2020, should be reported on Form 941-X filed for the second quarter of 2020. Don't file Form 941-X for the first quarter of 2020 to report these amounts. If you claimed the employee retention credit on your original Form 941 for the quarter, and you make any corrections on Form 941-X for the quarter to amounts used to figure this credit, you will need to refigure the amount of the credit using Worksheet 1, later. You will also use this worksheet to figure this credit if you're claiming the credit for the first time on Form 941-X. For more information about the employee retention credit, go to IRS.gov/ERC.*

19–22. Special Additions to Wages for Federal Income Tax, Social Security Taxes, Medicare Taxes, and Additional Medicare Tax

Section 3509 provides special rates for the employee share of federal income tax, social security tax, Medicare tax, and Additional Medicare Tax withholding when workers are reclassified as employees in certain circumstances. The applicable rate depends on whether you filed required information returns. An employer can't recover any tax paid under this provision from the employees. The full employer share of social security tax and Medicare tax is due for all reclassifications.

Note. Section 3509 rates aren't available if you intentionally disregarded the requirements to withhold taxes from the employee, or if you withheld federal income tax but didn't withhold social security and Medicare taxes. Section 3509 rates are also not available for certain statutory employees.

On lines 19–22, enter **only** corrections to wages resulting from reclassifying certain workers as employees when section 3509 rates are used to calculate the taxes.

If the employer issued the required information returns, use the section 3509 rates as follows.
- For social security taxes, use the employer rate of 6.2% plus 20% of the employee rate of 6.2%, for a total rate of 7.44% of wages.
- For Medicare taxes, use the employer rate of 1.45% plus 20% of the employee rate of 1.45%, for a total rate of 1.74% of wages.
- For Additional Medicare Tax, 0.18% (20% of the employee rate of 0.9%) of wages subject to Additional Medicare Tax.
- For federal income tax withholding, the rate is 1.5% of wages.

If the employer didn't issue the required information returns, use the section 3509 rates as follows.
- For social security taxes, use the employer rate of 6.2% plus 40% of the employee rate of 6.2%, for a total rate of 8.68% of wages.
- For Medicare taxes, use the employer rate of 1.45% plus 40% of the employee rate of 1.45%, for a total rate of 2.03% of wages.
- For Additional Medicare Tax, 0.36% (40% of the employee rate of 0.9%) of wages subject to Additional Medicare Tax.
- For federal income tax withholding, the rate is 3.0% of wages.

Unlike some other lines on Form 941-X, enter in column 1 only the corrected wages for workers being reclassified, not the amount paid to **all** employees. Enter in column 2 previously reported wages (if any) to reclassified employees. To get the amount for column 4, use the applicable section 3509 rates. If you filed the required information returns for some employees but didn't file them for other employees, be sure to use the applicable rates for each employee when calculating the amounts in column 4 and show your calculations on line 37. The tax correction in column 4 will be a positive number if you increased the amount of wages you previously reported. See the instructions for line 36, later, for more information.

Mastering Payroll II

Form 941-X Instructions (Page 17)

23. Subtotal

Combine the amounts from column 4 on lines 7–22 and enter the result on line 23.

Example. You entered "1,400.00" in column 4 on line 7, "-500.00" in column 4 on line 8, and "-100.00" in column 4 on line 12. Combine these amounts and enter "800.00" in column 4 on line 23.

Line 7	1,400.00
Line 8	- 500.00
Line 12	- 100.00
Line 23	800.00

24. Deferred Amount of Social Security Tax

Use Form 941-X, line 24, if you need to correct the deferred amount of the employer share of social security tax for the second, third, or fourth quarter of 2020, and/or the deferred amount of the employee share of social security tax for the third or fourth quarter of 2020, that you reported on Form 941, line 13b. Enter the total corrected amount in column 1. In column 2, enter the amount you originally reported or as previously corrected by you or the IRS. In column 3, enter the difference between columns 1 and 2.

Copy the amount in column 3 to column 4. However, because an increase to the deferred amount of the employer and/or the employee share of social security tax defers the payment due, to properly show the amount as a deferral of payment, enter a positive number in column 3 as a negative number in column 4. A decrease to the deferred amount of the employer and/or the employee share of social security tax decreases the payment you can defer and must be shown as a balance due item; therefore, to properly show the amount as a balance due item, enter a negative number in column 3 as a positive number in column 4. If you make any corrections to the deferred amount of the employee share of social security tax on Form 941-X, line 24, you may also need to make a correction on Form 941-X, line 33b.

Be sure to explain the reasons for any corrections on line 37.

Deferred amount of the employer share of social security tax. If you're filing Form 941-X to increase the amount of social security wages paid on or after March 27, 2020, and before January 1, 2021, so that there is an additional amount of social security tax that hasn't yet been paid, and hasn't yet been deferred, then you may use Form 941-X to increase the amount of the deferred employer share of social security tax originally reported on Form 941, line 13b. If you're filing Form 941-X to decrease the amount of social security wages paid on or after March 27, 2020, and before January 1, 2021, so that there is a decrease in the amount of social security tax that is eligible for deferral, then you must use Form 941-X to decrease the amount of the deferred employer share of social security tax originally reported on Form 941, line 13b, if the decrease in wages causes the amount you originally deferred to exceed the amount that is now eligible for deferral. Otherwise, you may only correct the amount of the deferred employer share of social security

tax if the amount originally reported on Form 941, line 13b, isn't the amount you actually deferred (for example, you incorrectly reported the amount that you actually deferred). If you already paid the correct amount of the employer's share of social security tax for a calendar quarter during the payroll tax deferral period, you may not subsequently defer the payment by filing Form 941-X. See *IRS.gov/ETD* for more information about the interaction of credits and the deferral of employment tax deposits and payments.

The deferred amount of the employer share of social security tax is only available for deposits and payments due on or after March 27, 2020, and before January 1, 2021, as well as deposits and payments due after January 1, 2021, that are required for wages paid during the quarter ending on December 31, 2020. Check *IRS.gov/Form941X* to see if future legislation extends these dates. Generally, 50% of the deferred amounts must be paid by December 31, 2021, and the other 50% must be paid by December 31, 2022. For more information about the deferral of employment tax deposits and payments, including when the deferral must be paid, go to *IRS.gov/ETD*.

Deferred amount of the employee share of social security tax. You may only correct the amount of the deferred employee share of social security tax if the amount originally reported on Form 941, line 13b, isn't the amount you actually deferred (for example, you incorrectly reported the amount that you actually deferred). If you already paid the correct amount of the employee's share of social security tax, you may not subsequently defer the payment by filing Form 941-X.

The deferred amount of the employee share of social security tax is only available for social security wages of less than $4,000 paid to an employee in any biweekly pay period (or the equivalent threshold amount for other pay periods) paid on a pay date during the period beginning on September 1, 2020, and ending on December 31, 2020. The due date for withholding and payment of the deferred employee share of social security tax is postponed until the period beginning on January 1, 2021, and ending on April 30, 2021. For more information about the deferral of the employee share of social security tax, see *Notice 2020-65* and the Instructions for Form 941.

25. Refundable Portion of Credit for Qualified Sick and Family Leave Wages

If you're correcting the refundable portion of the credit for qualified sick and family leave wages that you reported on Form 941, line 13c, enter the total corrected amount from Worksheet 1, Step 2, line 2k, in column 1. In column 2, enter the amount you originally reported or as previously corrected. In column 3, enter the difference between columns 1 and 2. For more information about the credit for qualified sick and family leave wages, go to *IRS.gov/PLC*.

Copy the amount in column 3 to column 4. However, to properly show the amount as a credit or balance due item, enter a positive number in column 3 as a negative number in column 4 or a negative number in column 3 as a positive number in column 4.

Be sure to explain the reasons for this correction on line 37.

Instructions for Form 941-X (Rev. 10-2020)   -17-

Form 941-X Instructions (Page 18)

26. Refundable Portion of Employee Retention Credit

If you're correcting the refundable portion of the employee retention credit that you reported on Form 941, line 13d, enter the total corrected amount from Worksheet 1, Step 3, line 3k, in column 1. In column 2, enter the amount you originally reported or as previously corrected. In column 3, enter the difference between columns 1 and 2. For more information about the employee retention credit, go to IRS.gov/ERC.

Copy the amount in column 3 to column 4. However, to properly show the amount as a credit or balance due item, enter a positive number in column 3 as a negative number in column 4 or a negative number in column 3 as a positive number in column 4.

Be sure to explain the reasons for this correction on line 37.

Corrections to Form 941, Line 13f

Form 941-X doesn't include a line to correct amounts reported on Form 941, line 13f, for the total advances received from filing Form(s) 7200 for the quarter. If a discrepancy exists between the amount reported on Form 941 and the amount of advance payments issued, the IRS will generally correct the amount reported on Form 941, line 13f, to match the amount of advance payments issued. However, aggregate filers may need to correct the amount reported on Form 941, line 13f, to reflect the correct advance payments received by their clients or customers. If you're an aggregate filer that needs to correct the amount reported on Form 941, line 13f, include any increase or decrease to the amount in the "Total" reported on Form 941-X, line 27; write "Correction to line 13f" on the dotted line to the left of the entry box on line 27; explain your correction on line 37; and attach Schedule R (Form 941) to Form 941-X to show corrections for your clients or customers.

27. Total

Combine the amounts from column 4 on lines 23–26 and enter the result on line 27.

Your credit. If the amount entered on line 27 is less than zero, for example, "-115.00," you have a credit because you overreported your federal employment taxes.
• If you checked the box on line 1, include this amount on the "Total deposits" line of Form 941 for the quarter during which you filed Form 941-X. If you currently file Form 944 because your filing requirement changed, include this amount on the "Total deposits" line of Form 944 for the year during which you filed Form 941-X. Don't make any changes to your record of federal tax liability reported on Form 941, line 16, or Schedule B (Form 941) if your Form 941-X is filed timely. The amounts reported on the record should reflect your actual tax liability for the period.
• If you checked the box on line 2, you're filing a claim for refund or abatement of the amount shown.

If your credit is less than $1, we will send a refund or apply it only if you ask us in writing to do so.

Amount you owe. If the amount on line 27 is a positive number, you must **pay** the amount you owe **by the time you file** Form 941-X. You may not use any credit that you show on another Form 941-X to pay the amount you owe, even if you filed for the amount you owe and the credit at the same time.

If you owe tax and are filing a timely Form 941-X, don't file an amended Schedule B (Form 941) unless you were assessed an FTD penalty caused by an incorrect, incomplete, or missing Schedule B (Form 941). Don't include the tax increase reported on Form 941-X on any amended Schedule B (Form 941) you file.

If you owe tax and are filing a late Form 941-X, that is, after the due date for Form 941 for the quarter in which you discovered the error, you must file an amended Schedule B (Form 941) with the Form 941-X. Otherwise, the IRS may assess an "averaged" FTD penalty. The total tax reported on the "Total liability for the quarter" line of Schedule B (Form 941) must match the corrected tax (Form 941, line 12, combined with any correction reported on Form 941-X, line 23) for the quarter, less any previous abatements and interest-free tax assessments.

Payment methods. You may pay the amount you owe on line 27 electronically using the Electronic Federal Tax Payment System (EFTPS), by credit or debit card, or by a check or money order.
• The preferred method of payment is EFTPS. For more information, go to EFTPS.gov, or call EFTPS Customer Service at 800-555-4477 or 800-733-4829 (TDD) toll free. Additional information about EFTPS is also available in Pub. 966.
• To pay by credit or debit card, go to IRS.gov/PayByCard. Your payment will be processed by a payment processor who will charge a processing fee.
• If you pay by check or money order, make it payable to "United States Treasury." On your check or money order, be sure to write your EIN, "Form 941-X," the calendar quarter you corrected (for example, "Quarter 2"), and the calendar year of the quarter you corrected.

You don't have to pay if the amount you owe is less than $1.

Previously assessed FTD penalty. If line 27 reflects overreported tax and the IRS previously assessed an FTD penalty, you may be able to reduce the penalty. For more information, see the Instructions for Schedule B (Form 941).

Lines 28–34

For lines 28–34, you will only enter amounts in columns 1, 2, and 3. These lines don't have an entry space for column 4 because these adjustments don't directly result in an increase or decrease to your tax. The amounts entered on lines 28–33a, and on line 34, are amounts that you use on Worksheet 1 to figure the credit for qualified sick and family leave wages and the employee retention credit. If you reported an incorrect amount on lines 19–25 on your original Form 941, then you will use lines 28–34 of Form 941-X to report the correction. Use Worksheet 1 to refigure the credit for qualified sick and family leave wages and/or the employee retention credit based on the corrected amounts reported in column 1. Be sure to explain the reasons for your corrections to lines 28–34 on line 37.

Form 941-X Instructions (Page 19)

28. Qualified Health Plan Expenses Allocable to Qualified Sick Leave Wages

If you're correcting the qualified health plan expenses allocable to qualified sick leave wages that you reported on Form 941, line 19, enter the total corrected amount for all employees in column 1. In column 2, enter the amount you originally reported or as previously corrected. In column 3, enter the difference between columns 1 and 2. Enter the corrected amount from column 1 on Worksheet 1, Step 2, line 2b.

29. Qualified Health Plan Expenses Allocable to Qualified Family Leave Wages

If you're correcting the qualified health plan expenses allocable to qualified family leave wages that you reported on Form 941, line 20, enter the total corrected amount for all employees in column 1. In column 2, enter the amount you originally reported or as previously corrected. In column 3, enter the difference between columns 1 and 2. Enter the corrected amount from column 1 on Worksheet 1, Step 2, line 2f.

30. Qualified Wages for the Employee Retention Credit

If you're correcting the qualified wages for the employee retention credit that you reported on Form 941, line 21, enter the total corrected amount for all employees in column 1. In column 2, enter the amount you originally reported or as previously corrected. In column 3, enter the difference between columns 1 and 2. Enter the corrected amount from column 1 on Worksheet 1, Step 3, line 3a.

31. Qualified Health Plan Expenses Allocable to Wages Reported on Form 941, Line 21

If you're correcting the qualified health plan expenses allocable to wages reported on Form 941, line 21, that you reported on Form 941, line 22, enter the total corrected amount for all employees in column 1. In column 2, enter the amount you originally reported or as previously corrected. In column 3, enter the difference between columns 1 and 2. Enter the corrected amount from column 1 on Worksheet 1, Step 3, line 3b.

32. Credit From Form 5884-C, Line 11, for This Quarter

If you're correcting the credit from Form 5884-C, line 11, for this quarter, that you reported on Form 941, line 23, enter the total corrected amount in column 1. In column 2, enter the amount you originally reported or as previously corrected. In column 3, enter the difference between columns 1 and 2. Enter the corrected amount from column 1 on Worksheet 1, Step 1, line 1j. Entering an amount here is strictly for purposes of figuring the credit for qualified sick and family wages and/or the employee retention credit on Worksheet 1. Reporting a correction on this line doesn't correct the credit claimed on Form 5884-C.

33a. Qualified Wages Paid March 13 Through March 31, 2020, for the Employee Retention Credit (Use This Line To Correct Only the Second Quarter of 2020)

If you're correcting the qualified wages paid March 13, 2020, through March 31, 2020, for the employee retention credit that you reported on Form 941, line 24, for the second quarter of 2020, enter the total corrected amount for all employees in column 1. In column 2, enter the amount you originally reported or as previously corrected. In column 3, enter the difference between columns 1 and 2. Enter the corrected amount from column 1 on Worksheet 1, Step 3, line 3c.

33b. Deferred Amount of the Employee Share of Social Security Tax Included on Form 941, Line 13b (Use This Line To Correct Only the Third and Fourth Quarters of 2020)

If you're correcting the deferred amount of the employee share of social security tax (for the third and fourth quarters of 2020) that you reported on Form 941, line 24, enter the total corrected amount for all employees in column 1. In column 2, enter the amount you originally reported or as previously corrected. In column 3, enter the difference between columns 1 and 2.

34. Qualified Health Plan Expenses Allocable to Wages Reported on Form 941, Line 24 (Use This Line To Correct Only the Second Quarter of 2020)

If you're correcting the qualified health plan expenses allocable to wages reported on Form 941, line 24, that you reported on Form 941, line 25, for the second quarter of 2020, enter the total corrected amount for all employees in column 1. In column 2, enter the amount you originally reported or as previously corrected. In column 3, enter the difference between columns 1 and 2. Enter the corrected amount from column 1 on Worksheet 1, Step 3, line 3d.

Part 4: Explain Your Corrections for This Quarter

35. Corrections of Both Underreported and Overreported Amounts

Check the box on line 35 if any corrections you entered on lines 7–26, or lines 28–34, column 3, reflect both underreported and overreported amounts.

Example. If you had an increase to social security wages of $15,000 for Xavier Black and a decrease to social security wages of $5,000 for Sophie Rose, you would enter $10,000 on line 8, column 3. That $10,000 represents the net change from corrections.

On line 37, you must explain the reason for both the $15,000 increase and the $5,000 decrease.

36. Did You Reclassify Any Workers?

Check the box on line 36 if you reclassified any workers to be independent contractors or nonemployees. Also check this box if the IRS (or you) determined that workers you treated as independent contractors or nonemployees

Form 941-X Instructions (Page 20)

should be classified as employees. On line 37, give us a detailed reason why any worker was reclassified and, if you used section 3509 rates on lines 19–22 for any worker reclassified as an employee, explain why section 3509 rates apply and what rates you used.

Return not filed because you didn't treat any workers as employees. If you didn't previously file Form 941 because you mistakenly treated all workers as independent contractors or as nonemployees, file a Form 941 for each delinquent quarter.

On each Form 941 for which you're entitled to use section 3509 rates, complete the following steps.
• Write **"Misclassified Employees"** in **bold** letters across the top margin of page 1.
• Enter a zero on line 12.
• Complete the signature area.
• Attach a completed Form 941-X (see instructions next).

On each Form 941-X, complete the following steps.
• Complete the top of Form 941-X, including the date you discovered the error.
• Enter the wage amounts on lines 19–22, column 1.
• Enter zeros on lines 19–22, column 2.
• Complete columns 3 and 4 as instructed in Part 3.
• Provide a detailed statement on line 37.
• Complete the signature area.

If you can't use section 3509 rates (for example, because the workers you treated as nonemployees were certain statutory employees), file a Form 941 for each delinquent quarter. Write "Misclassified Employees" in bold letters across the top margin of page 1 of each Form 941. Complete Form 941 using the Instructions for Form 941. Attach a Form 941-X to each Form 941. Complete the top of Form 941-X, including the date you discovered the error, and provide a detailed explanation on line 37.

37. Explain Your Corrections

Treasury regulations require you to explain in detail the grounds and facts relied upon to support each correction. On line 37, describe in detail each correction you entered in column 4 on lines 7–22, and lines 24–26. Also use line 37 to describe corrections made on line 6 and lines 28–34. If you need more space, attach additional sheets, but be sure to write your name, EIN, "Form 941-X," the quarter you're correcting (for example, "Quarter 2"), and the calendar year of the quarter you're correcting on the top of each sheet.

You must describe the events that caused the underreported or overreported amounts. Explanations such as "social security and Medicare wages were overstated" or "administrative/payroll errors were discovered" or "taxes were not withheld" are insufficient and may delay processing your Form 941-X because the IRS may need to ask for a more complete explanation.

Provide the following information in your explanation for each correction.
• Form 941-X line number(s) affected.
• Date you discovered the error.
• Difference (amount of the error).
• Cause of the error.

You may report the information in paragraph form. The following paragraph is an example.

"The $1,000 difference shown in column 3 on lines 6, 8, and 12 was discovered on May 15, 2020, during an internal payroll audit. We discovered that we included $1,000 of wages for one of our employees twice. This correction removes the reported wages that were never paid."

For corrections shown on lines 19–22, explain why the correction was necessary and attach any notice you received from the IRS.

Part 5: Sign Here

You must complete all four pages of Form 941-X and sign it on page 4. If you don't sign, processing of Form 941-X will be delayed.

Who must sign the Form 941-X? The following persons are authorized to sign the return for each type of business entity.
• **Sole proprietorship**—The individual who owns the business.
• **Corporation (including a limited liability company (LLC) treated as a corporation)**—The president, vice president, or other principal officer duly authorized to sign.
• **Partnership (including an LLC treated as a partnership) or unincorporated organization**—A responsible and duly authorized member, partner, or officer having knowledge of its affairs.
• **Single-member LLC treated as a disregarded entity for federal income tax purposes**—The owner of the LLC or a principal officer duly authorized to sign.
• **Trust or estate**—The fiduciary.

Form 941-X may also be signed by a duly authorized agent of the taxpayer if a valid power of attorney has been filed.

Alternative signature method. Corporate officers or duly authorized agents may sign Form 941-X by rubber stamp, mechanical device, or computer software program. For details and required documentation, see Rev. Proc. 2005-39. You can find Rev. Proc. 2005-39, 2005-28 I.R.B. 82, at *IRS.gov/irb/2005-28_IRB#RP-2005-39*.

Paid Preparer Use Only

A paid preparer must sign Form 941-X and provide the information in the *Paid Preparer Use Only* section of Part 5 if the preparer was paid to prepare Form 941-X and isn't an employee of the filing entity. Paid preparers must sign paper returns with a manual signature. The preparer must give you a copy of the return in addition to the copy to be filed with the IRS.

If you're a paid preparer, enter your Preparer Tax Identification Number (PTIN) in the space provided. Include your complete address. If you work for a firm, enter the firm's name and the EIN of the firm. You can apply for a PTIN online or by filing Form W-12. For more information about applying for a PTIN online, visit the IRS website at *IRS.gov/PTIN*. You can't use your PTIN in place of the EIN of the tax preparation firm.

Generally, you're not required to complete this section if you're filing the return as a reporting agent and have a

Instructions for Form 941-X (Rev. 10-2020)

Form 941-X Instructions (Page 21)

valid Form 8655 on file with the IRS. However, a reporting agent must complete this section if the reporting agent offered legal advice, for example, advising the client on determining whether its workers are employees or independent contractors for federal tax purposes.

Form 941-X Instructions (Page 22)

Worksheet 1. Adjusted Credit for Qualified Sick and Family Leave Wages and the Employee Retention Credit

Keep for Your Records

You must use this worksheet if you claimed the credit for qualified sick and family leave wages and/or the employee retention credit on your original Form 941 for the quarter and you correct any amounts used to figure these credits on Form 941-X. You will also use this worksheet to figure these credits if you're claiming them for the first time on Form 941-X.

Step 1. **Determine the corrected employer share of social security tax this quarter after it is reduced by any credit claimed on Form 8974 and any credit from Form 5884-C**

1a Enter the amount of social security wages from Form 941, line 5a, column 1, or, if corrected, enter the amount from Form 941-X, line 8, column 1 . . . . 1a _____

1b Enter the amount of social security tips from Form 941, line 5b, column 1, or, if corrected, from Form 941-X, line 11, column 1 . . . . 1b _____

1c Add lines 1a and 1b . . . . 1c _____

1d Multiply line 1c by 6.2% (0.062) . . . . 1d _____

1e If you're a third-party payer of sick pay that isn't an agent and you're claiming credits for amounts paid to your employees, enter the employer share of social security tax required to be paid by the employer that you included on Form 941, Part 1, line 8, or, if corrected, the amount of employer social security tax on sick pay that you included on Form 941-X, line 15, column 1 (enter as a **negative** number) . . . . 1e _____

1f Employer share of social security tax included on Form 941-X, line 20, column 4 . . . . 1f _____

1g If you received a Section 3121(q) Notice and Demand during the quarter, enter the amount of the employer share of social security tax from the notice . . . . . . 1g _____

1h **Employer share of social security tax.** Combine lines 1d, 1e, 1f, and 1g . . . . 1h _____

1i Enter the amount from Form 941, Part 1, line 11a, or, if corrected, the amount from Form 941-X, line 16, column 1 (credit from Form 8974) . . . . 1i _____

1j Enter the amount from Form 941, Part 3, line 23, or, if corrected, the amount from Form 941-X, line 32, column 1 (credit from Form 5884-C) . . . . 1j _____

1k **Total nonrefundable credits already used against the employer share of social security tax.** Add lines 1i and 1j . . . . 1k _____

1l **Employer share of social security tax remaining.** Subtract line 1k from line 1h . . . . 1l _____

Step 2. **Figure the sick and family leave credit**

2a Qualified sick leave wages reported on Form 941, Part 1, line 5a(i), column 1, or, if corrected, the amount from Form 941-X, line 9, column 1 . . . . 2a _____

2a(i) Qualified sick leave wages included on Form 941, Part 1, line 5c, or, if corrected, Form 941-X, line 12, column 1, but not included on Form 941, Part 1, line 5a(i), column 1, or Form 941-X, line 9, column 1, because the wages reported on that line were limited by the social security wage base . . . . 2a(i) _____

2a(ii) Total qualified sick leave wages. Add lines 2a and 2a(i) . . . . 2a(ii) _____

2b Qualified health plan expenses allocable to qualified sick leave wages (Form 941, Part 3, line 19, or, if corrected, Form 941-X, line 28, column 1) . . . . 2b _____

2c Employer share of Medicare tax on qualified sick leave wages. Multiply line 2a(ii) by 1.45% (0.0145) . . . . 2c _____

2d **Credit for qualified sick leave wages.** Add lines 2a(ii), 2b, and 2c . . . . 2d _____

2e Qualified family leave wages reported on Form 941, Part 1, line 5a(ii), column 1, or, if corrected, the amount from Form 941-X, line 10, column 1 . . . . 2e _____

2e(i) Qualified family leave wages included on Form 941, Part 1, line 5c, or, if corrected, Form 941-X, line 12, column 1, but not included on Form 941, Part 1, line 5a(ii), column 1, or Form 941-X, line 10, column 1, because the wages reported on that line were limited by the social security wage base . . . . 2e(i) _____

2e(ii) Total qualified family leave wages. Add lines 2e and 2e(i) . . . . 2e(ii) _____

2f Qualified health plan expenses allocable to qualified family leave wages (Form 941, Part 3, line 20, or, if corrected, Form 941-X, line 29, column 1) . . . . 2f _____

2g Employer share of Medicare tax on qualified family leave wages. Multiply line 2e(ii) by 1.45% (0.0145) . . . . 2g _____

2h **Credit for qualified family leave wages.** Add lines 2e(ii), 2f, and 2g . . . . 2h _____

2i **Credit for qualified sick and family leave wages.** Add lines 2d and 2h . . . . 2i _____

2j **Nonrefundable portion of credit for qualified sick and family leave wages.** Enter the smaller of line 1l or line 2i. Enter this amount on Form 941-X, line 17, column 1 . . . . 2j _____

2k **Refundable portion of credit for qualified sick and family leave wages.** Subtract line 2j from line 2i and enter this amount on Form 941-X, line 25, column 1 . . . . 2k _____

Worksheet 1 continues on the next page.

-22-   Instructions for Form 941-X (Rev. 10-2020)

Form 941-X Instructions (Page 23)

Worksheet 1. Adjusted Credit for Qualified Sick and Family Leave Wages and the Employee Retention Credit—*(continued)*

Step 3.		Figure the employee retention credit		
	3a	Qualified wages (excluding qualified health plan expenses) for the employee retention credit (Form 941, Part 3, line 21, or, if corrected, Form 941-X, line 30, column 1)	3a	_____
	3b	Qualified health plan expenses allocable to qualified wages for the employee retention credit (Form 941, Part 3, line 22, or, if corrected, Form 941-X, line 31, column 1)	3b	_____
	3c	Qualified wages (excluding qualified health plan expenses) paid March 13, 2020, through March 31, 2020, for the employee retention credit (Form 941, Part 3, line 24, or, if corrected, Form 941-X, line 33a, column 1). Enter an amount here only for the second quarter Form 941-X	3c	_____
	3d	Qualified health plan expenses allocable to qualified wages paid March 13, 2020, through March 31, 2020, for the employee retention credit (Form 941, Part 3, line 25, or, if corrected, Form 941-X, line 34, column 1). Enter an amount here only for the second quarter Form 941-X	3d	_____
	3e	Add lines 3a, 3b, 3c, and 3d	3e	_____
	3f	**Retention credit.** Multiply line 3e by 50% (0.50)	3f	_____
	3g	Enter the amount of the employer share of social security tax from Step 1, line 1l	3g	_____
	3h	Enter the amount of the nonrefundable portion of the credit for qualified sick and family leave wages from Step 2, line 2j	3h	_____
	3i	Subtract line 3h from line 3g	3i	_____
	3j	**Nonrefundable portion of employee retention credit.** Enter the smaller of line 3f or line 3i. Enter this amount on Form 941-X, line 18, column 1	3j	_____
	3k	**Refundable portion of employee retention credit.** Subtract line 3j from line 3f and enter this amount on Form 941-X, line 26, column 1	3k	_____

Caution:
Only complete lines 3c and 3d for your second quarter 2020 Form 941-X.

How Can You Get Forms, Instructions, and Publications From the IRS?

You can view, download, or print most of the forms, instructions, and publications you may need at *IRS.gov/Forms*. Otherwise, you can go to *IRS.gov/OrderForms* to place an order and have them mailed to you.

Paperwork Reduction Act Notice. We ask for the information on Form 941-X to carry out the Internal Revenue laws of the United States. We need it to figure and collect the right amount of tax. Subtitle C, Employment Taxes, of the Internal Revenue Code imposes employment taxes, including federal income tax withholding, on wages. This form is used to determine the amount of taxes that you owe. Section 6011 requires you to provide the requested information if the tax is applicable to you.

You're not required to provide the information requested on a form that is subject to the Paperwork Reduction Act unless the form displays a valid OMB control number. Books and records relating to a form or instructions must be retained as long as their contents may become material in the administration of any Internal Revenue law.

The time needed to complete and file Form 941-X will vary depending on individual circumstances. The estimated average time is:

Recordkeeping	28 hr., 27 min.
Learning about the law or the form	35 min.
Preparing and sending the form to the IRS	1 hr., 5 min.

If you have comments concerning the accuracy of these time estimates or suggestions for making Form 941-X simpler, we would be happy to hear from you. You can send us comments from *IRS.gov/FormComments*. Or you can send your comments to: Internal Revenue Service, Tax Forms and Publications Division, 1111 Constitution Ave. NW, IR-6526, Washington, DC 20224. Don't send Form 941-X to this address. Instead, see *Where Should You File Form 941-X*, earlier.

Instructions for Form 941-X (Rev. 10-2020) -23-

Form 944 (Page 1)

Form **944 for 2020:** **Employer's ANNUAL Federal Tax Return**

Department of the Treasury — Internal Revenue Service

OMB No. 1545-2007

Employer identification number (EIN) ☐☐ – ☐☐☐☐☐☐☐

Name *(not your trade name)*

Trade name *(if any)*

Address

Number	Street	Suite or room number

City	State	ZIP code

Foreign country name	Foreign province/county	Foreign postal code

Who Must File Form 944

You must file annual Form 944 instead of filing quarterly Forms 941 **only if the IRS notified you in writing.**

Go to *www.irs.gov/Form944* for instructions and the latest information.

Read the separate instructions before you complete Form 944. Type or print within the boxes.

Part 1: Answer these questions for this year. Employers in American Samoa, Guam, the Commonwealth of the Northern Mariana Islands, the U.S. Virgin Islands, and Puerto Rico can skip lines 1 and 2, unless you have employees who are subject to U.S. income tax withholding.

1 Wages, tips, and other compensation . . . . **1** ☐

2 Federal income tax withheld from wages, tips, and other compensation . . . . . . **2** ☐

3 If no wages, tips, and other compensation are subject to social security or Medicare tax **3** ☐ Check and go to line 5.

4 Taxable social security and Medicare wages and tips:

	Column 1		Column 2
4a Taxable social security wages	☐	× 0.124 =	☐
4a (i) Qualified sick leave wages	☐	× 0.062 =	☐
4a (ii) Qualified family leave wages	☐	× 0.062 =	☐
4b Taxable social security tips	☐	× 0.124 =	☐
4c Taxable Medicare wages & tips	☐	× 0.029 =	☐
4d Taxable wages & tips subject to Additional Medicare Tax withholding	☐	× 0.009 =	☐

4e Total social security and Medicare taxes. Add Column 2 from lines 4a, 4a(i), 4a(ii), 4b, 4c, and 4d **4e** ☐

5 Total taxes before adjustments. Add lines 2 and 4e . . . . **5** ☐

6 Current year's adjustments (see instructions) . . . . **6** ☐

7 Total taxes after adjustments. Combine lines 5 and 6 . . . . **7** ☐

8a Qualified small business payroll tax credit for increasing research activities. Attach Form 8974 **8a** ☐

8b Nonrefundable portion of credit for qualified sick and family leave wages from Worksheet 1 **8b** ☐

8c Nonrefundable portion of employee retention credit from Worksheet 1 . . . . . . **8c** ☐

8d Total nonrefundable credits. Add lines 8a, 8b, and 8c . . . . **8d** ☐

▶ You MUST complete all three pages of Form 944 and SIGN it.

Next ▶

For Privacy Act and Paperwork Reduction Act Notice, see the back of the Payment Voucher.

Cat. No. 39316N

Form **944** (2020)

Form 944 (Page 2)

Name *(not your trade name)*	Employer identification number (EIN)

Part 1:   **Answer these questions for this year.** *(continued)*

9   **Total taxes after adjustments and nonrefundable credits.** Subtract line 8d from line 7   .   .   **9** [.]

10a   Total deposits for this year, including overpayment applied from a prior year and overpayments applied from Form 944-X, 944-X (SP), 941-X, or 941-X (PR)   .   .   .   .   .   **10a** [.]

10b   Deferred amount of the employer share of social security tax   .   .   .   .   .   .   **10b** [.]

10c   Deferred amount of the employee share of social security tax   .   .   .   .   .   .   **10c** [.]

10d   Refundable portion of credit for qualified sick and family leave wages from Worksheet 1   **10d** [.]

10e   Refundable portion of employee retention credit from Worksheet 1   .   .   .   .   .   **10e** [.]

10f   **Total deposits, deferrals, and refundable credits.** Add lines 10a, 10b, 10c, 10d, and 10e   .   **10f** [.]

10g   Total advances received from filing Form(s) 7200 for the year   .   .   .   .   .   .   **10g** [.]

10h   **Total deposits, deferrals, and refundable credits less advances.** Subtract line 10g from line 10f   .   .   .   .   **10h** [.]

11   **Balance due.** If line 9 is more than line 10h, enter the difference and see instructions   .   .   .   **11** [.]

12   **Overpayment.** If line 10h is more than line 9, enter the difference [.]   Check one: ☐ Apply to next return.   ☐ Send a refund.

Part 2:   **Tell us about your deposit schedule and tax liability for this year.**

13   Check one: ☐   Line 9 is less than $2,500. Go to Part 3.

           ☐   Line 9 is $2,500 or more. Enter your tax liability for each month. If you're a semiweekly schedule depositor or you became one because you accumulated $100,000 or more of liability on any day during a deposit period, you must complete Form 945-A instead of the boxes below.

	Jan.		Apr.		July		Oct.
13a [.]		**13d** [.]		**13g** [.]		**13j** [.]	
	Feb.		May		Aug.		Nov.
13b [.]		**13e** [.]		**13h** [.]		**13k** [.]	
	Mar.		June		Sept.		Dec.
13c [.]		**13f** [.]		**13i** [.]		**13l** [.]	

           Total liability for year. Add lines 13a through 13l. Total must equal line 9.   **13m** [.]

▶ You MUST complete all three pages of Form 944 and SIGN it.

           [Next ▶]

         Form **944** (2020)

Form 944 (Page 3)

Name *(not your trade name)*	Employer identification number (EIN)

Part 3: Tell us about your business. If any question does NOT apply to your business, leave it blank.

14　If your business has closed or you stopped paying wages . . . . ☐ Check here, and

　　enter the final date you paid wages 　 / 　 / 　 ; also attach a statement to your return. See instructions.

15　Qualified health plan expenses allocable to qualified sick leave wages . . . . . . 　**15**　_____ .

16　Qualified health plan expenses allocable to qualified family leave wages . . . . . . 　**16**　_____ .

17　Qualified wages for the employee retention credit . . . . 　**17**　_____ .

18　Qualified health plan expenses allocable to wages reported on line 17 . . . . . . 　**18**　_____ .

19　Credit from Form 5884-C, line 11, for the year . . . . 　**19**　_____ .

Part 4: May we speak with your third-party designee?

Do you want to allow an employee, a paid tax preparer, or another person to discuss this return with the IRS? See the instructions for details.

☐ Yes. Designee's name and phone number _____　_____

　　　　　　Select a 5-digit personal identification number (PIN) to use when talking to the IRS. ☐ ☐ ☐ ☐ ☐

☐ No.

Part 5: Sign here. You MUST complete all three pages of Form 944 and SIGN it.

Under penalties of perjury, I declare that I have examined this return, including accompanying schedules and statements, and to the best of my knowledge and belief, it is true, correct, and complete. Declaration of preparer (other than taxpayer) is based on all information of which preparer has any knowledge.

X **Sign your name here** _____　　Print your name here _____

　　　　　　　　　　　　　　　　　　Print your title here _____

　　　　　Date _____　　Best daytime phone _____

Paid Preparer Use Only

Check if you're self-employed ☐

Preparer's name	_____	PTIN	_____
Preparer's signature	_____	Date	_____
Firm's name (or yours if self-employed)	_____	EIN	_____
Address	_____	Phone	_____
City	_____ State ____	ZIP code	_____

Form 944 (Page 4)

Form 944-V,
Payment Voucher

Purpose of Form

Complete Form 944-V if you're making a payment with Form 944. We will use the completed voucher to credit your payment more promptly and accurately, and to improve our service to you.

Making Payments With Form 944

To avoid a penalty, make your payment with your 2020 Form 944 **only if** one of the following applies.

• Your net taxes for the year (Form 944, line 9) are less than $2,500 and you're paying in full with a timely filed return.

• Your net taxes for the year (Form 944, line 9) are $2,500 or more and you already deposited the taxes you owed for the first, second, and third quarters of 2020; your net taxes for the fourth quarter are less than $2,500; and you're paying, in full, the tax you owe for the fourth quarter of 2020 with a timely filed return.

• You're a monthly schedule depositor making a payment in accordance with the Accuracy of Deposits Rule. See section 11 of Pub. 15, section 8 of Pub. 80, or section 11 of Pub. 179 for details. In this case, the amount of your payment may be $2,500 or more.

Otherwise, you must make deposits by electronic funds transfer. See section 11 of Pub. 15, section 8 of Pub. 80, or section 11 of Pub. 179 for deposit instructions. Don't use Form 944-V to make federal tax deposits.

 Use Form 944-V when making any payment with Form 944. However, if you pay an amount with Form 944 that should've been deposited, you may be subject to a penalty. See section 11 of Pub. 15, section 8 of Pub. 80, or section 11 of Pub. 179 for details.

Specific Instructions

Box 1—Employer identification number (EIN). If you don't have an EIN, you may apply for one online by visiting the IRS website at *www.irs.gov/EIN*. You may also apply for an EIN by faxing or mailing Form SS-4 to the IRS. If you haven't received your EIN by the due date of Form 944, write "Applied For" and the date you applied in this entry space.

Box 2—Amount paid. Enter the amount paid with Form 944.

Box 3—Name and address. Enter your name and address as shown on Form 944.

• Enclose your check or money order made payable to "United States Treasury." Be sure to enter your EIN, "Form 944," and "2020" on your check or money order. Don't send cash. Don't staple Form 944-V or your payment to Form 944 (or to each other).

• Detach Form 944-V and send it with your payment and Form 944 to the address provided in the Instructions for Form 944.

Note: You must also complete the entity information above Part 1 on Form 944.

Detach Here and Mail With Your Payment and Form 944.

Form **944-V**	**Payment Voucher**	OMB No. 1545-2007
Department of the Treasury Internal Revenue Service	▶ **Don't staple this voucher or your payment to Form 944.**	2020

1 Enter your employer identification number (EIN).	2 **Enter the amount of your payment.** ▶ Make your check or money order payable to "**United States Treasury**"	Dollars	Cents
	3 Enter your business name (individual name if sole proprietor).		
	Enter your address.		
	Enter your city, state, and ZIP code; or your city, foreign country name, foreign province/county, and foreign postal code.		

Form 944 Instructions (Page 1)

20**20**

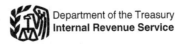

Department of the Treasury
Internal Revenue Service

Instructions for Form 944

Employer's ANNUAL Federal Tax Return

Section references are to the Internal Revenue Code unless otherwise noted.

Future Developments

For the latest information about developments related to Form 944 and its instructions, such as legislation enacted after they were published, go to *IRS.gov/Form944*.

What's New

Changes to Form 944 for coronavirus (COVID-19) related employment tax credits and other tax relief. The following significant changes have been made to Form 944 to allow for the reporting of new employment tax credits and other tax relief related to COVID-19.

• The new credit for qualified sick and family leave wages is reported on line 8b and, if applicable, line 10d. The employee share of social security tax on qualified sick and family leave wages is reported on lines 4a(i) and 4a(ii). Qualified sick and family leave wages aren't subject to the employer share of social security tax. Qualified sick and family leave wages not included on lines 4a(i) and 4a(ii) because the wages reported on that line are limited by the social security wage base are included on line 4c. Qualified health plan expenses allocable to qualified sick and family leave wages are reported on lines 15 and 16. See the instructions for line 8b for information about the new credit for qualified sick and family leave wages.

• The new employee retention credit is reported on line 8c and, if applicable, line 10e. Qualified wages (excluding qualified health plan expenses) for the employee retention credit are reported on line 17 (these amounts should also be included as wages on lines 4a and 4c, and, if applicable, line 4d). Qualified health plan expenses allocable to the qualified wages for the employee retention credit are reported on line 18. See the instructions for line 8c for information about the new employee retention credit.

• Employers, including government employers, can defer the deposit of the employer share of social security tax due on or after March 27, 2020, and before January 1, 2021, as well as payment due for the employer share of social security tax for wages paid on or after March 27, 2020, and before January 1, 2021. The amount of deferral is reported on line 10b. See the instructions for line 10b for more information.

• Employers could defer the withholding and payment of the employee share of social security tax on wages paid on or after September 1, 2020, and before January 1, 2021, but only if the amount of wages for a biweekly pay period were less than $4,000 (or an equivalent amount for other pay periods). The amount of deferral is reported on line 10c. See the instructions for line 10c for more information.

• Employers that requested an advance of the sick and family leave credit and/or the employee retention credit would have filed Form 7200, Advance Payment of Employer Credits Due to COVID-19. The amount of all advances received from Forms 7200 filed for the year is reported on line 10g. See the instructions for line 10g for more information.

• The credit for qualified sick and family leave wages (reported on lines 8b and 10d) and the employee retention credit (reported on lines 8c and 10e) are figured on Worksheet 1.

New filing addresses. The filing addresses have changed for some employers. See *Where Should You File*, later, before filing your return.

Social security and Medicare tax for 2020. The rate of social security tax on taxable wages, except for qualified sick leave wages and qualified family leave wages, is 6.2% (0.062) each for the employer and employee or 12.4% (0.124) for both. Qualified sick leave wages and qualified family leave wages aren't subject to the employer share of social security tax; therefore, the tax rate on these wages is 6.2% (0.062). The social security wage base limit is $137,700.

The Medicare tax rate is 1.45% (0.0145) each for the employee and employer, unchanged from 2019. There is no wage base limit for Medicare tax.

Social security and Medicare taxes apply to the wages of household workers you pay $2,200 or more in cash wages in 2020. Social security and Medicare taxes apply to election workers who are paid $1,900 or more in cash or an equivalent form of compensation in 2020.

Reminders

Qualified small business payroll tax credit for increasing research activities. For tax years beginning after 2015, a qualified small business may elect to claim up to $250,000 of its credit for increasing research activities as a payroll tax credit against the employer share of social security tax. The payroll tax credit election must be made on or before the due date of the originally filed income tax return (including extensions). The portion of the credit used against the employer share of social security tax is allowed in the first calendar quarter beginning after the date that the qualified small business filed its income tax return. The first Form 944 that you could claim this credit on was Form 944 filed for calendar year 2017. The election and determination of the credit amount that will be used against the employer share of social security tax are made on Form 6765, Credit for Increasing Research Activities. The amount from Form 6765, line 44, must then be reported on Form 8974, Qualified Small Business Payroll Tax Credit for Increasing Research Activities. Form 8974 is used to determine the amount of the credit that can be used in the current year. The amount from Form 8974, line 12, is reported on Form

Nov 20, 2020   Cat. No. 39820A

Form 944 Instructions (Page 2)

944, line 8a. If you're claiming the research payroll tax credit on your Form 944, you must attach Form 8974 to Form 944. For more information about the payroll tax credit, see Notice 2017-23, 2017-16 I.R.B. 1100, available at *IRS.gov/irb/2017-16_IRB#NOT-2017-23*, and *IRS.gov/ResearchPayrollTC*. Also see *Adjusting tax liability for nonrefundable credits claimed on lines 8a, 8b, and 8c*, later.

Work opportunity tax credit for qualified tax-exempt organizations hiring qualified veterans. Qualified tax-exempt organizations that hire eligible unemployed veterans may be able to claim the work opportunity tax credit against their payroll tax liability using Form 5884-C. For more information, go to *IRS.gov/WOTC*.

Employers can request to file Forms 941, 941-SS, or 941-PR instead of Form 944. Employers required to file Form 944, who want to file Forms 941, 941-SS, or 941-PR instead, must contact the IRS to request to file quarterly Forms 941, 941-SS, or 941-PR and opt out of filing Form 944. See *What if You Want To File Forms 941, 941-SS, or 941-PR Instead of Form 944*, later.

Correcting a previously filed Form 944. If you discover an error on a previously filed Form 944, make the correction using Form 944-X. Form 944-X is filed separately from Form 944. For more information, see the Instructions for Form 944-X, section 13 of Pub. 15, or go to *IRS.gov/CorrectingEmploymentTaxes*.

Federal tax deposits must be made by electronic funds transfer (EFT). You must use EFT to make all federal tax deposits. Generally, an EFT is made using the Electronic Federal Tax Payment System (EFTPS). If you don't want to use EFTPS, you can arrange for your tax professional, financial institution, payroll service, or other trusted third party to make electronic deposits on your behalf. Also, you may arrange for your financial institution to initiate a same-day wire payment on your behalf. EFTPS is a free service provided by the Department of the Treasury. Services provided by your tax professional, financial institution, payroll service, or other third party may have a fee.

For more information on making federal tax deposits, see section 11 of Pub. 15; section 8 of Pub. 80, Federal Tax Guide for Employers in the U.S. Virgin Islands, Guam, American Samoa, and the Commonwealth of the Northern Mariana Islands; or section 11 of Pub. 179, Guía Contributiva Federal para Patronos Puertorriqueños. To get more information about EFTPS or to enroll in EFTPS, go to *EFTPS.gov* or call one of the following numbers.
- 800-555-4477
- 800-733-4829 (TDD)
- 800-244-4829 (Spanish)
- 303-967-5916 if you're outside the United States (toll call)

Additional information about EFTPS is also available in Pub. 966 or Pub. 966 (SP).

⚠️ **CAUTION** *For an EFTPS deposit to be on time, you must submit the deposit by 8 p.m. Eastern time the day before the date the deposit is due.*

Same-day wire payment option. If you fail to submit a deposit transaction on EFTPS by 8 p.m. Eastern time the day before the date a deposit is due, you can still make your deposit on time by using the Federal Tax Collection Service (FTCS) to make a same-day wire payment. To use the same-day wire payment method, you will need to make arrangements with your financial institution ahead of time. Please check with your financial institution regarding availability, deadlines, and costs. Your financial institution may charge you a fee for payments made this way. To learn more about the information you will need to give your financial institution to make a same-day wire payment, go to *IRS.gov/SameDayWire*.

Timeliness of federal tax deposits. If a deposit is required to be made on a day that isn't a business day, the deposit is considered timely if it is made by the close of the next business day. A business day is any day other than a Saturday, Sunday, or legal holiday. The term "legal holiday" for deposit purposes includes only those legal holidays in the District of Columbia. Legal holidays in the District of Columbia are provided in Pub. 15, Pub. 80, and Pub. 179.

Electronic filing and payment. Businesses can enjoy the benefits of filing tax returns and paying their federal taxes electronically. Whether you rely on a tax professional or handle your own taxes, the IRS offers you convenient programs to make filing and paying easier. Spend less time worrying about taxes and more time running your business. Use e-file and EFTPS to your benefit.
- For e-file, go to *IRS.gov/EmploymentEfile* for more information. A fee may be charged to file electronically.
- For EFTPS, go to *EFTPS.gov* or call EFTPS at one of the numbers provided under *Federal tax deposits must be made by electronic funds transfer (EFT)*, earlier.
- For electronic filing of Forms W-2, Wage and Tax Statement, go to *SSA.gov/employer*. You may be required to file Forms W-2 electronically. For details, see the General Instructions for Forms W-2 and W-3.

⚠️ **CAUTION** *If you're filing your tax return or paying your federal taxes electronically, a valid employer identification number (EIN) is required at the time the return is filed or the payment is made. If a valid EIN isn't provided, the return or payment won't be processed. This may result in penalties. See* Employer identification number (EIN)*, later, for information about applying for an EIN.*

Electronic funds withdrawal (EFW). If you file Form 944 electronically, you can e-file and use EFW to pay the balance due in a single step using tax preparation software or through a tax professional. However, don't use EFW to make federal tax deposits. For more information on paying your taxes using EFW, go to *IRS.gov/EFW*.

Credit or debit card payments. You can pay the balance due shown on Form 944 by credit or debit card. Your payment will be processed by a payment processor who will charge a processing fee. Don't use a credit or debit card to make federal tax deposits. For more information on paying your taxes with a credit or debit card, go to *IRS.gov/PayByCard*.

Online payment agreement. You may be eligible to apply for an installment agreement online if you can't pay the full amount of tax you owe when you file your return.

Form 944 Instructions (Page 3)

For more information, see *What if you can't pay in full*, later.

Paid preparers. If you use a paid preparer to complete Form 944, the paid preparer must complete and sign the paid preparer's section of the form.

Outsourcing payroll duties. You're responsible to ensure that tax returns are filed and deposits and payments are made, even if you contract with a third party to perform these acts. You remain responsible if the third party fails to perform any required action. Before you choose to outsource any of your payroll and related tax duties (that is, withholding, reporting, and paying over social security, Medicare, FUTA, and income taxes) to a third-party payer, such as a payroll service provider or reporting agent, go to *IRS.gov/OutsourcingPayrollDuties* for helpful information on this topic. For more information on the different types of third-party payer arrangements, see section 16 of Pub. 15.

Where can you get telephone help? For answers to your questions about completing Form 944 or tax deposit rules, call the IRS at one of the numbers listed below.
• 800-829-4933 (Business and Specialty Tax Line) or 800-829-4059 (TDD/TTY for persons who are deaf, hard of hearing, or have a speech disability), Monday–Friday from 7:00 a.m. to 7:00 p.m. local time (Alaska and Hawaii follow Pacific time; employers in Puerto Rico receive service from 8:00 a.m. to 8:00 p.m. local time).
• 267-941-1000 if you're outside the United States (toll call), Monday–Friday from 6:00 a.m. to 11:00 p.m. Eastern time.

Photographs of missing children. The IRS is a proud partner with the *National Center for Missing & Exploited Children® (NCMEC)*. Photographs of missing children selected by the Center may appear in instructions on pages that would otherwise be blank. You can help bring these children home by looking at the photographs and calling 1-800-THE-LOST (1-800-843-5678) if you recognize a child.

General Instructions

Purpose of Form 944

Form 944 is designed so the smallest employers (those whose annual liability for social security, Medicare, and withheld federal income taxes is $1,000 or less) will file and pay these taxes only once a year instead of every quarter. These instructions give you some background information about Form 944. They tell you who must file Form 944, how to complete it line by line, and when and where to file it.

If you want more in-depth information about payroll tax topics relating to Form 944, see Pub. 15, Pub. 80, Pub. 179, or go to *IRS.gov/EmploymentTaxes*.

Federal law requires you, as an employer, to withhold certain taxes from your employees' pay. Each time you pay wages, you must withhold—or take out of your employees' pay—certain amounts for federal income tax, social security tax, and Medicare tax. You must also withhold Additional Medicare Tax from wages you pay to an employee in excess of $200,000 in a calendar year.

Under the withholding system, taxes withheld from your employees are credited to your employees in payment of their tax liabilities.

⚠ **CAUTION** *References to federal income tax withholding don't apply to employers in American Samoa, Guam, the Commonwealth of the Northern Mariana Islands, the U.S. Virgin Islands, and Puerto Rico, unless you have employees who are subject to U.S. income tax withholding.*

Federal law also requires you to pay any liability for the employer share of social security tax and Medicare tax. This share of social security tax and Medicare tax isn't withheld from employees.

For more information about annual employment tax filing and tax deposit rules, see Treasury Decision 9566, 2012-8 I.R.B. 389, at *IRS.gov/irb/2012-08_IRB#TD-9566*.

Who Must File Form 944?

In general, if the IRS has notified you to file Form 944, you must file Form 944 instead of Forms 941, 941-SS, or 941-PR to report the following amounts.

• Wages you have paid.
• Tips your employees reported to you.
• Federal income tax you withheld.
• Both the employer and the employee share of social security and Medicare taxes.
• Additional Medicare Tax withheld from employees.
• Current year's adjustments to social security and Medicare taxes for fractions of cents, sick pay, tips, and group-term life insurance.
• Deferred amount of the employer share of social security tax.
• Deferred amount of the employee share of social security tax.
• Qualified small business payroll tax credit for increasing research activities.
• Credit for qualified sick and family leave wages.
• Employee retention credit.

If you received notification to file Form 944, you must file Form 944 to report your social security, Medicare, and withheld federal income taxes for the 2020 calendar year unless you called the IRS between January 1, 2020, and April 1, 2020, or sent a written request postmarked between January 1, 2020, and March 16, 2020, to request to file Forms 941, 941-SS, or 941-PR quarterly instead and received written confirmation that your filing requirement was changed. You must file Form 944 even if you have no taxes to report (or you have taxes in excess of $1,000 to report) unless you filed a final return for the prior year. See *If Your Business Has Closed...*, later. Also see *What if You Want To File Forms 941, 941-SS, or 941-PR Instead of Form 944*, later.

⚠ **CAUTION** *If the IRS notified you in writing to file Form 944, you must file Form 944 (and not Forms 941, 941-SS, or 941-PR) even if your tax liability for 2020 exceeds $1,000. Once your annual tax liability exceeds $1,000, the IRS will notify you that you're no longer eligible to file Form 944 in future years and that you must file Form 941, 941-SS, or 941-PR quarterly. However, until you receive the notice, continue to file*

Form 944 Instructions (Page 4)

Form 944 annually. If you're unsure of your current filing requirement, call 800-829-4933. If you're outside the United States, call 267-941-1000 (toll call).

What if You Want To File Form 944 in Future Years Instead of Forms 941, 941-SS, or 941-PR?

If you haven't received notification to file Form 944 for 2021 but estimate your employment tax liability for calendar year 2021 will be $1,000 or less and would like to file Form 944 instead of Forms 941, 941-SS, or 941-PR, you can contact the IRS to request to file Form 944 for 2021. To file Form 944 for calendar year 2021, you must call the IRS at 800-829-4933 (267-941-1000 (toll call) if you're outside the United States) between January 1, 2021, and April 1, 2021, or send a written request postmarked between January 1, 2021, and March 15, 2021. The mailing addresses for written requests are provided under *What if You Want To File Forms 941, 941-SS, or 941-PR Instead of Form 944*, later. The IRS will send you a written notice that your filing requirement has been changed to Form 944. If you don't receive this notice, you must file Forms 941, 941-SS, or 941-PR for calendar year 2021.

New Employers

New employers are also eligible to file Form 944 if they will meet the eligibility requirements. New employers filing Form SS-4, Application for Employer Identification Number, or Form SS-4PR, Solicitud de Número de Identificación Patronal (*EIN*), must complete line 13 of Form SS-4 or SS-4PR, indicating the highest number of employees expected in the next 12 months, and must check the box on line 14 of Form SS-4 or SS-4PR to indicate whether they expect to have $1,000 or less in employment tax liability for the calendar year and would like to file Form 944. Based on current tax rates, if you pay $5,000 or less in wages subject to social security and Medicare taxes and federal income tax withholding during the calendar year, you're generally likely to pay $1,000 or less in employment taxes. Generally, if you're an employer in Puerto Rico, American Samoa, Guam, the Commonwealth of the Northern Mariana Islands, or the U.S. Virgin Islands and you pay $6,536 or less in wages subject to social security and Medicare taxes during the calendar year, you're likely to pay $1,000 or less in employment taxes. New employers are advised of their employment tax filing requirement when they are issued their EIN.

What if You Want To File Forms 941, 941-SS, or 941-PR Instead of Form 944?

You must file Form 944 if the IRS has notified you to do so, unless the IRS notifies you to file quarterly Forms 941, 941-SS, or 941-PR instead, or you contact the IRS to request to file those forms. To request to file quarterly Forms 941, 941-SS, or 941-PR to report your social security, Medicare, and withheld federal income taxes for the 2021 calendar year, call the IRS at 800-829-4933 (267-941-1000 (toll call) if you're outside the United States) between January 1, 2021, and April 1, 2021, or send a written request postmarked between January 1,

2021, and March 15, 2021. Written requests should be sent to:

Department of the Treasury Internal Revenue Service Ogden, UT 84201-0038	or	Department of the Treasury Internal Revenue Service Cincinnati, OH 45999-0038

If you would mail your return filed without a payment to Ogden, as shown under *Where Should You File*, later, send your request to the Ogden address shown above. If you would mail your return filed without a payment to Kansas City, send your request to the address for Cincinnati shown above. After you contact the IRS, the IRS will send you a written notice that your filing requirement has been changed. If you don't receive this notice, you must file Form 944 for calendar year 2021. For more information about these procedures, see Rev. Proc. 2009-51, 2009-45 I.R.B. 625, available at *IRS.gov/irb/2009-45_IRB#RP-2009-51*.

Who Can't File Form 944?

The following employers can't file Form 944.

- **Employers who aren't notified.** If the IRS doesn't notify you to file Form 944, don't file Form 944. If you would like to file Form 944 instead of Forms 941, 941-SS, or 941-PR, see *What if You Want To File Form 944 in Future Years Instead of Forms 941, 941-SS, or 941-PR*, earlier.
- **Household employers.** If you employ only household employees, don't file Form 944. For more information, see Pub. 926 and Schedule H (Form 1040), or Pub. 179 and Schedule H-PR.
- **Agricultural employers.** If you employ only agricultural employees, don't file Form 944. For more information, see Pub. 51 and Form 943, or Pub. 179 and Form 943-PR.

What if You Reorganize or Close Your Business?

If You Sell or Transfer Your Business...

If you sell or transfer your business during the year, you and the new owner must each file a Form 944, 941, 941-SS, or 941-PR, whichever is required, for the year in which the transfer occurred. Report only the wages you paid.

When two businesses merge, the continuing firm must file a return for the year in which the change took place and the other firm should file a final return.

Changing from one form of business to another—such as from a sole proprietorship to a partnership or corporation—is considered a transfer. If a transfer occurs, you may need a new EIN. See Pub. 1635 and section 1 of Pub. 15 for more information.

Attach a statement to your return with all the following information.

- The new owner's name (or the new name of the business).

-4-

Form 944 Instructions (Page 5)

• Whether the business is now a sole proprietorship, partnership, or corporation.
• The kind of change that occurred (a sale or transfer).
• The date of the change.
• The name of the person keeping the payroll records and the address where those records will be kept.

If Your Business Has Closed...

If you permanently go out of business or stop paying wages to your employees, you must file a final return. To tell the IRS that Form 944 for a particular year is your final return, check the box on line 14 and enter the final date you paid wages. Also attach a statement to your return showing the name of the person keeping the payroll records and the address where those records will be kept.

If you participated in a statutory merger or consolidation, or qualify for predecessor-successor status due to an acquisition, you should generally file Schedule D (Form 941), Report of Discrepancies Caused by Acquisitions, Statutory Mergers, or Consolidations. See the Instructions for Schedule D (Form 941) to determine whether you should file Schedule D (Form 941) and when you should file it.

When Must You File?

For 2020, file Form 944 by February 1, 2021. However, if you made deposits on time in full payment of the taxes due for the year, you may file the return by February 10, 2021.

File Form 944 only once for each calendar year. If you filed Form 944 electronically, don't file a paper Form 944. For more information about filing Form 944 electronically, see *Electronic filing and payment*, earlier.

If we receive Form 944 after the due date, we will treat Form 944 as filed on time if the envelope containing Form 944 is properly addressed, contains sufficient postage, and is postmarked by the U.S. Postal Service on or before the due date, or sent by an IRS-designated private delivery service (PDS) on or before the due date. If you don't follow these guidelines, we will generally consider Form 944 filed when it is actually received. For more information about PDSs, see *Where Should You File*, later.

How Should You Complete Form 944?

Enter your EIN, name, and address in the spaces provided. Also enter your name and EIN at the top of pages 2 and 3. Don't use your social security number (SSN) or individual taxpayer identification number (ITIN). Generally, enter the business (legal) name that you used when you applied for your EIN. For example, if you're a sole proprietor, enter "Tyler Smith" on the *Name* line and "Tyler's Cycles" on the *Trade name* line. Leave the *Trade name* line blank if it is the same as your *Name* line.

If you use a tax preparer to complete Form 944, make sure the preparer uses your correct business name and EIN.

Employer identification number (EIN). To make sure that businesses comply with federal tax laws, the IRS monitors tax filings and payments by using a numerical system to identify taxpayers. A unique nine-digit EIN is assigned to all corporations, partnerships, and some sole proprietors. Businesses needing an EIN must apply for a number and use it throughout the life of the business on all tax returns, payments, and reports.

Your business should have only one EIN. If you have more than one and aren't sure which one to use, write to the IRS office where you file your returns (using the *Without a payment* address under *Where Should You File*, later) or call the IRS at 800-829-4933. If you're outside the United States, call 267-941-1000 (toll call).

If you don't have an EIN, you may apply for one online by visiting *IRS.gov/EIN*. You may also apply for an EIN by faxing or mailing Form SS-4 or SS-4PR to the IRS. If the principal business was created or organized outside of the United States or U.S. territories, you may also apply for an EIN by calling 267-941-1099 (toll call). If you have applied for an EIN but don't have your EIN by the time a return is due, file a paper return and write "Applied For" and the date you applied in the space shown for the number.

 If you're filing your tax return electronically, a valid EIN is required at the time the return is filed. If a valid EIN isn't provided, the return won't be accepted. This may result in penalties.

 Always be sure the EIN on the form you file exactly matches the EIN the IRS assigned to your business. Don't use your SSN or ITIN on forms that ask for an EIN. Filing a Form 944 with an incorrect EIN or using another business's EIN may result in penalties and delays in processing your return.

If you change your business name, business address, or responsible party. Notify the IRS immediately if you change your business name, business address, or responsible party.
• Write to the IRS office where you file your returns (using the *Without a payment* address under *Where Should You File*, later) to notify the IRS of any business name change. See Pub. 1635 to see if you need to apply for a new EIN.
• Complete and mail Form 8822-B to notify the IRS of a business address or responsible party change. Don't mail Form 8822-B with your Form 944. For a definition of "responsible party," see the Instructions for Form SS-4.

Completing and Filing Form 944

Make entries on Form 944 as follows to enable accurate processing.

• Use 12-point Courier font (if possible) for all entries if you're typing or using a computer to complete Form 944. Portable Document Format (PDF) forms on IRS.gov have fillable fields with acceptable font specifications.
• Don't enter dollar signs and decimal points. Commas are optional. Report dollars to the left of the preprinted decimal point and cents to the right of it. Don't round entries to whole dollars. Always show an amount for cents, even if it is zero.
• Leave blank any data field with a value of zero (except line 9).
• Enter negative amounts using a minus sign (if possible). Otherwise, use parentheses.

Instructions for Form 944 (2020)   -5-

Form 944 Instructions (Page 6)

- Enter your name and EIN on all pages.
- Enter your name, EIN, "Form 944," and tax period on all attachments.
- Staple multiple sheets in the upper left corner when filing.

Complete all three pages. You must complete all three pages of Form 944 and sign on page 3. Failure to do so may delay processing of your return.

Required Notice to Employees About the Earned Income Credit (EIC)

To notify employees about the EIC, employers in the United States must give the employees one of the following items.
- Form W-2 which has the required information about the EIC on the back of Copy B.
- A substitute Form W-2 with the same EIC information on the back of the employee's copy that is on the back of Copy B of the IRS Form W-2.
- Notice 797, Possible Federal Tax Refund Due to the Earned Income Credit (EIC).
- Your written statement with the same wording as Notice 797.

For more information, see section 10 of Pub. 15, Pub. 596, and *IRS.gov/EIC*.

Reconciling Form 944 and Form W-3, W-3SS, or W-3PR

The IRS matches amounts reported on your Form 944 with Form W-2, W-2AS, W-2GU, W-2CM, W-2VI, or Form 499R-2/W-2PR amounts totaled on your Form W-3 or W-3SS, Transmittal of Wage and Tax Statements, or Form W-3PR, Informe de Comprobantes de Retención. If the amounts don't agree, you may be contacted by the IRS or the SSA. The following amounts are reconciled.

- Federal income tax withholding, if applicable.
- Social security wages.
- Social security tips.
- Medicare wages and tips.

For more information, see section 12 of Pub. 15.

Where Should You File?

You're encouraged to file Form 944 electronically. Go to *IRS.gov/EmploymentEfile* for more information on electronic filing. If you file a paper return, where you file depends on whether you include a payment with Form 944. Mail your return to the address listed for your location in the table that follows.

PDSs can't deliver to P.O. boxes. You must use the U.S. Postal Service to mail an item to a P.O. box address. Go to *IRS.gov/PDS* for the current list of PDSs. For the IRS mailing address to use if you're using a PDS, go to *IRS.gov/PDSstreetAddresses*. Select the mailing address listed on the webpage that is in the same state as the address to which you would mail returns filed without a payment, as shown next.

Mailing Addresses for Form 944

If you're in . . .	Without a payment . . .	With a payment . . .
Connecticut, Delaware, District of Columbia, Georgia, Illinois, Indiana, Kentucky, Maine, Maryland, Massachusetts, Michigan, New Hampshire, New Jersey, New York, North Carolina, Ohio, Pennsylvania, Rhode Island, South Carolina, Tennessee, Vermont, Virginia, West Virginia, Wisconsin	Department of the Treasury Internal Revenue Service Kansas City, MO 64999-0044	Internal Revenue Service P.O. Box 806532 Cincinnati, OH 45280-6532
Alabama, Alaska, Arizona, Arkansas, California, Colorado, Florida, Hawaii, Idaho, Iowa, Kansas, Louisiana, Minnesota, Mississippi, Missouri, Montana, Nebraska, Nevada, New Mexico, North Dakota, Oklahoma, Oregon, South Dakota, Texas, Utah, Washington, Wyoming	Department of the Treasury Internal Revenue Service Ogden, UT 84201-0044	Internal Revenue Service P.O. Box 932100 Louisville, KY 40293-2100
No legal residence or principal place of business in any state	Internal Revenue Service P.O. Box 409101 Ogden, UT 84409	Internal Revenue Service P.O. Box 932100 Louisville, KY 40293-2100
Special filing address for exempt organizations; federal, state, and local governmental entities; and Indian tribal governmental entities, regardless of location	Department of the Treasury Internal Revenue Service Ogden, UT 84201-0044	Internal Revenue Service P.O. Box 932100 Louisville, KY 40293-2100

⚠️ **CAUTION** *Your filing address may have changed from that used to file your employment tax return in prior years. Don't send Form 944 or any payments to the Social Security Administration (SSA).*

Must You Deposit Your Taxes?

If your liability for withheld federal income tax and social security and Medicare taxes (Form 944, line 9) is less than $2,500 for the year, you can pay the taxes with your return. To avoid a penalty, you should pay in full and file on time. You don't have to deposit the taxes. However, you may choose to make deposits of these taxes even if your liability is less than $2,500. If your liability for these taxes is $2,500 or more, you're generally required to deposit the taxes instead of paying them when you file Form 944. See the *Federal Tax Deposit Requirements for Form 944 Filers* chart, later. If you don't deposit the taxes when required, you may be subject to penalties and interest.

-6-

Form 944 Instructions (Page 7)

The $2,500 threshold at which federal tax deposits must be made is different from the amount of annual tax liability ($1,000 or less) that makes an employer eligible to file Form 944. Form 944 filers whose businesses grow during the year may be required to make federal tax deposits (see chart next), but they will still file Form 944 for the year.

Federal Tax Deposit Requirements for Form 944 Filers

If Your Tax Liability is:	Your Deposit Requirement is:
Less than $2,500 for the year	No deposit required. You may pay the tax with your return. If you're unsure that your tax liability for the year will be less than $2,500, deposit under the rules below.
$2,500 or more for the year, but less than $2,500 for the quarter	You can deposit by the last day of the month after the end of a quarter. However, if your fourth quarter tax liability is less than $2,500, you may pay the fourth quarter's tax liability with Form 944.
$2,500 or more for the quarter	You must deposit monthly or semiweekly depending on your deposit schedule. But, if you accumulate $100,000 or more of taxes on any day, you must deposit the tax by the next business day. See section 11 of Pub. 15, section 8 of Pub. 80, or section 11 of Pub. 179.

See section 11 of Pub. 15, section 8 of Pub. 80, or section 11 of Pub. 179 for information about payments made under the accuracy of deposits rule.

Note. When you make deposits depends on your deposit schedule, which is either monthly or semiweekly, depending on the amount of your tax liability during the lookback period. The lookback period for Form 944 filers is different from the lookback period for Form 941, 941-SS, and 941-PR filers, so your deposit schedule may have changed. For more information, see section 11 of Pub. 15, section 8 of Pub. 80, or section 11 of Pub. 179. The $100,000 tax liability threshold requiring a next-day deposit is determined before you consider any reduction of your liability for nonrefundable credits. See *IRS.gov/ETD* for more information.

Deferring your deposits. Employers can defer the deposit of the employer share of social security tax due on or after March 27, 2020, and before January 1, 2021, as well as payment due for the employer share of social security tax for wages paid on or after March 27, 2020, and before January 1, 2021. The deferral applies before any of the nonrefundable credits claimed on line 8a, 8b, or 8c. However, the deferral doesn't reduce the amount of the employer share of social security tax used to figure those nonrefundable credits. See the instructions for line 10b for more information about the deferral of the employer share of social security tax. Employers could also defer the withholding and payment of the employee

share of social security tax on wages paid on or after September 1, 2020, and on or before December 31, 2020, but only if the amount of social security wages for a biweekly pay period was less than $4,000 (or an equivalent amount for other pay periods). The amount of the employee deferral is reported on line 10c. See the instructions for line 10c for more information.

Reducing your deposits for COVID-19 credits. Employers eligible to claim the credit for qualified sick and family leave wages and/or the employee retention credit can reduce their deposits by the amount of their anticipated credits. Employers won't be subject to a failure-to-deposit (FTD) penalty for reducing their deposits if certain conditions are met. See the instructions for line 8b and line 8c for more information on these credits. This reduction in deposits is in addition to the ability employers have to reduce their deposits by the amount of the employer share of social security tax they defer. For more information on reducing deposits, see Notice 2020-22, 2020-17 I.R.B. 664, available at *IRS.gov/irb/2020-17_IRB#NOT-2020-22*, and *IRS.gov/ETD*. Also see *IRS.gov/ERC* and *IRS.gov/PLC* for more information, including examples, about reducing deposits. See the instructions for line 13, later, for instructions on how to adjust your tax liabilities reported on line 13 or Form 945-A for nonrefundable credits.

What About Penalties and Interest?

Avoiding Penalties and Interest

You can avoid paying penalties and interest if you do all of the following.

- Deposit or pay your taxes when they are due, unless you meet the requirements discussed in *Notice 2020-22* or *IRS.gov/ETD*, or you have chosen to use the relief provided in Notice 2020-65, 2020-38 I.R.B. 567, available at *IRS.gov/irb/2020-38_IRB#NOT-2020-65*.
- File your fully completed Form 944 on time.
- Report your tax liability accurately.
- Submit valid checks for tax payments.
- Give accurate Forms W-2, W-2AS, W-2GU, W-2CM, W-2VI, or Form 499R-2/W-2PR to employees.
- File Form W-3, W-3SS, or W-3PR and Copies A of Forms W-2, W-2AS, W-2GU, W-2CM, W-2VI, or Form 499R-2/W-2PR with the SSA on time and accurately. Go to *SSA.gov/employer* for information on how to file Forms W-2 electronically.

Penalties and interest are charged on taxes paid late and returns filed late at a rate set by law. See sections 11 and 12 of Pub. 15, section 8 of Pub. 80, or section 11 of Pub. 179 for details. Use Form 843 to request abatement of assessed penalties or interest. Don't request abatement of assessed penalties or interest on Form 944, 944-X, 944-X (SP), 941-X, or 941-X (PR).

If you receive a notice about a penalty after you file your return, reply to the notice with an explanation and we will determine if you meet reasonable-cause criteria. Don't include an explanation when you file your return.

 If federal income, social security, and Medicare taxes that must be withheld (that is, trust fund taxes) aren't withheld or aren't deposited or paid

Form 944 Instructions (Page 8)

to the United States Treasury, the trust fund recovery penalty may apply. The penalty is 100% of the unpaid trust fund tax. If these unpaid taxes can't be immediately collected from the employer or business, the trust fund recovery penalty may be imposed on all persons who are determined by the IRS to be responsible for collecting, accounting for, or paying over these taxes, and who acted willfully in not doing so. For more information, see section 11 of Pub. 15, section 8 of Pub. 80, or section 11 of Pub. 179. The trust fund recovery penalty won't apply to any amount of trust fund taxes an employer holds back in anticipation of any credits they are entitled to. It also won't apply to applicable taxes properly deferred under Notice 2020-65 before May 1, 2021.

Specific Instructions

Part 1: Answer These Questions for This Year

 TIP *Employers in American Samoa, Guam, the Commonwealth of the Northern Mariana Islands, the U.S. Virgin Islands, and Puerto Rico may skip lines 1 and 2, unless you have employees who are subject to U.S. income tax withholding.*

TIP *For purposes of these instructions, all references to "sick pay" mean ordinary sick pay, not "qualified sick leave wages" that are reported on line 4a(i).*

1. Wages, Tips, and Other Compensation

Enter amounts on line 1 that would also be included in box 1 of your employees' Forms W-2. See *Box 1—Wages, tips, other compensation* in the General Instructions for Forms W-2 and W-3 for details. Include sick pay paid by your agent. Also include sick pay paid by a third party that isn't your agent (for example, an insurance company) if you were given timely notice of the payments and the third party transferred liability for the employer's taxes to you.

If you're a third-party payer of sick pay and not an agent of the employer, don't include sick pay that you paid to policyholders' employees here if you gave the policyholders timely notice of the payments. See section 6 of Pub. 15-A, Employer's Supplemental Tax Guide, for more information about sick pay reporting and the procedures for transferring the liability to the employer.

2. Federal Income Tax Withheld From Wages, Tips, and Other Compensation

Enter the federal income tax that you withheld (or were required to withhold) from your employees on this year's wages, including qualified sick leave wages, qualified family leave wages, and qualified wages (excluding qualified health plan expenses) for the employee retention credit; tips; taxable fringe benefits; and supplemental unemployment compensation benefits. Don't include any income tax withheld by a third-party payer of sick pay even if you reported it on Forms W-2. You will reconcile this difference on Form W-3. For information on the employment tax treatment of fringe benefits, see Pub.

15-B, Employer's Tax Guide to Fringe Benefits. For information about supplemental unemployment compensation benefits, see section 5 of Pub. 15-A.

If you're a third-party payer of sick pay, enter the federal income tax you withheld (or were required to withhold) on third-party sick pay here.

! **CAUTION** *References to federal income tax withholding don't apply to employers in American Samoa, Guam, the Commonwealth of the Northern Mariana Islands, the U.S. Virgin Islands, and Puerto Rico, unless you have employees who are subject to U.S. income tax withholding.*

3. If No Wages, Tips, and Other Compensation Are Subject to Social Security or Medicare Tax . . .

If no wages, tips, and other compensation on line 1 are subject to social security or Medicare tax, check the box on line 3 and go to line 5. If this question doesn't apply to you, leave the box blank. For more information about exempt wages, see section 15 of Pub. 15, section 12 of Pub. 80, or section 15 of Pub. 179. For religious exemptions, see section 4 of Pub. 15-A. For information on the employment tax treatment of fringe benefits, see Pub. 15-B.

4a–4e. Taxable Social Security and Medicare Wages and Tips

! **CAUTION** *Don't reduce your social security tax reported in column 2 by the deferred amount of the employer or employee share of social security tax reported on line 10b or 10c.*

4a. Taxable social security wages. Enter the total wages, including qualified wages (other than qualified health plan expenses) for the employee retention credit; sick pay; and taxable fringe benefits subject to social security taxes that you paid to your employees during the year. Don't include the qualified sick leave wages reported on line 4a(i) or qualified family leave wages reported on line 4a(ii). For this purpose, sick pay includes payments made by an insurance company to your employees for which you received timely notice from the insurance company. See section 6 of Pub. 15-A for more information about sick pay reporting. See the instructions for line 6 for an adjustment that you may need to make on Form 944 for sick pay.

Enter the amount before payroll deductions. Don't include tips on this line. For information on types of wages subject to social security taxes, see section 5 of Pub. 15, section 4 of Pub. 80, or section 5 of Pub. 179.

For 2020, the rate of social security tax on taxable wages, except for qualified sick leave wages and qualified family leave wages, is 6.2% (0.062) each for the employer and employee or 12.4% (0.124) for both. Stop paying social security tax on and entering an employee's wages on line 4a when the employee's taxable wages, including qualified sick leave wages, qualified family leave wages, and tips, reach $137,700 for the year. However, continue to withhold income and Medicare taxes for the whole year on all wages, including qualified sick leave wages,

-8-

Instructions for Form 944 (2020)

Form 944 Instructions (Page 9)

qualified family leave wages, and tips, even when the social security wage base of $137,700 has been reached.

$$\frac{\text{line 4a (column 1)}}{\text{x} \quad 0.124}$$
$$\text{line 4a (column 2)}$$

4a(i). Qualified sick leave wages. Enter the qualified taxable sick leave wages you paid to your employees during the year. Qualified sick leave wages aren't subject to the employer share of social security tax; therefore, the tax rate on these wages is 6.2% (0.062). Stop paying social security tax on and entering an employee's wages on line 4a(i) when the employee's taxable wages, including wages reported on line 4a, qualified sick leave wages, qualified family leave wages, and tips, reach $137,700 for the year. See the instructions for line 4c for reporting Medicare tax on qualified sick leave wages, including the portion above the social security wage base.

Qualified sick leave wages are wages for social security and Medicare tax purposes required to be paid under the Emergency Paid Sick Leave Act (EPSLA) as enacted under the *Families First Coronavirus Response Act* (FFCRA). See the instructions for line 8b for information about the credit for qualified sick and family leave wages.

$$\frac{\text{line 4a(i) (column 1)}}{\text{x} \quad 0.062}$$
$$\text{line 4a(i) (column 2)}$$

Emergency Paid Sick Leave Act (EPSLA). The EPSLA requires certain government employers and private employers with fewer than 500 employees to provide paid sick leave to employees unable to work or telework after March 31, 2020, and before January 1, 2021, because the employee:

1. Is subject to a federal, state, or local quarantine or isolation order related to COVID-19;

2. Has been advised by a health care provider to self-quarantine due to concerns related to COVID-19;

3. Is experiencing symptoms of COVID-19 and seeking a medical diagnosis;

4. Is caring for an individual subject to an order described in (1) or who has been advised as described in (2);

5. Is caring for a child if the school or place of care has been closed, or the childcare provider is unavailable, due to COVID-19 precautions; or

6. Is experiencing any other substantially similar condition specified by the U.S. Department of Health and Human Services.

 Government employers aren't eligible for the credit for qualified sick and family leave wages; however, as with any employer, government employers aren't liable for the employer share of the social security tax on the qualified sick leave wages paid to employees.

Limits on qualified sick leave wages. The EPSLA provides different limitations for different circumstances under which qualified sick leave wages are paid. For paid sick leave qualifying under (1), (2), or (3) above, the amount of qualified sick leave wages is determined at the employee's regular rate of pay, but the wages may not exceed $511 for any day (or portion of a day) for which the individual is paid sick leave. For paid sick leave qualifying under (4), (5), or (6) above, the amount of qualified sick leave wages is determined at two-thirds the employee's regular rate of pay, but the wages may not exceed $200 for any day (or portion of a day) for which the individual is paid sick leave. The EPSLA also limits each individual to a maximum of up to 80 hours of paid sick leave for the year. Therefore, the maximum amount of paid sick leave wages for the year can't exceed $5,110 for an employee for leave under (1), (2), or (3), and it can't exceed $2,000 for an employee for leave under (4), (5), or (6). For more information from the Department of Labor on these requirements and limits, see *DOL.gov/agencies/whd/pandemic*.

For more information about qualified sick and family leave wages, go to *IRS.gov/PLC*.

4a(ii). Qualified family leave wages. Enter the qualified taxable family leave wages you paid to your employees during the year. Qualified family leave wages aren't subject to the employer share of social security tax; therefore, the tax rate on these wages is 6.2% (0.062). Stop paying social security tax on and entering an employee's wages on line 4a(ii) when the employee's taxable wages, including wages reported on line 4a, qualified sick leave wages, qualified family leave wages, and tips, reach $137,700 for the year. See the instructions for line 4c for reporting Medicare tax on qualified family leave wages, including the portion above the social security wage base.

Qualified family leave wages are wages for social security and Medicare tax purposes required to be paid under the Emergency Family and Medical Leave Expansion Act as enacted under the FFCRA. See the instructions for line 8b for information about the credit for qualified sick and family leave wages.

$$\frac{\text{line 4a(ii) (column 1)}}{\text{x} \quad 0.062}$$
$$\text{line 4a(ii) (column 2)}$$

Emergency Family and Medical Leave Expansion Act. The Emergency Family and Medical Leave Expansion Act requires certain government employers and private employers with fewer than 500 employees to provide paid family leave under the Family and Medical Leave Act of 1993 to an employee who has been employed for at least 30 calendar days. The requirement to provide leave generally applies when an employee is unable to work or telework after March 31, 2020, and before January 1, 2021, due to the need to care for a child because the school or place of care has been closed, or the childcare provider is unavailable, due to COVID-19 related reasons. The first 10 days for which an employee takes leave may be unpaid. During this period, employees may use other forms of paid leave, such as qualified sick

Instructions for Form 944 (2020)   -9-

Form 944 Instructions (Page 10)

leave, accrued sick leave, annual leave, or other paid time off. After an employee takes leave for 10 days, the employer must provide the employee paid leave (that is, qualified family leave wages) for up to 10 weeks. For more information from the Department of Labor on these requirements, possible exceptions, and the limitations discussed below, see *DOL.gov/agencies/whd/pandemic*.

TIP *Government employers aren't eligible for the credit for qualified sick and family leave wages; however, as with any employer, government employers aren't liable for the employer share of the social security tax on the qualified family leave wages paid to employees.*

Rate of pay and limit on wages. The rate of pay must be at least two-thirds of the employee's regular rate of pay (as determined under the Fair Labor Standards Act of 1938), multiplied by the number of hours the employee otherwise would have been scheduled to work. The qualified family leave wages can't exceed $200 per day or $10,000 in the aggregate per employee for the year.

For more information about qualified sick and family leave wages, go to *IRS.gov/PLC*.

4b. Taxable social security tips. Enter all tips your employees reported to you during the year until the total of the tips and taxable wages, including qualified sick leave wages and qualified family leave wages, for an employee reach $137,700 for the year. Include all tips your employees reported to you even if you were unable to withhold the 6.2% employee share of social security tax. You will reduce your total taxes by the amount of any uncollected employee share of social security and Medicare taxes on tips later on line 6; see *Adjustments for tips and group-term life insurance*, later. Don't include service charges on line 4b. For details about the difference between tips and service charges, see Rev. Rul. 2012-18, 2012-26 I.R.B. 1032, available at *IRS.gov/irb/2012-26_IRB#RR-2012-18*.

Your employee must report cash tips to you by the 10th day of the month after the month the tips are received. Cash tips include tips paid by cash, check, debit card, and credit card. The report should include charged tips (for example, credit and debit card charges) you paid over to the employee for charge customers, tips the employee received directly from customers, and tips received from other employees under any tip-sharing arrangement. Both directly and indirectly tipped employees must report tips to you. No report is required for months when tips are less than $20. Employees may use Form 4070 (available only in Pub. 1244) or Form 4070-PR (available only in Pub. 1244-PR), or submit a written statement or electronic tip record.

line 4b (column 1)
x   0.124
line 4b (column 2)

For more information on tips, see section 6 of Pub. 15, section 5 of Pub. 80, or section 6 of Pub. 179.

4c. Taxable Medicare wages and tips. Enter all wages, including qualified sick leave wages, qualified family leave wages, and qualified wages (excluding

qualified health plan expenses) for the employee retention credit; tips; sick pay; and taxable fringe benefits that are subject to Medicare tax. Unlike social security wages, there is no limit on the amount of wages subject to Medicare tax. See the instructions for line 6 for an adjustment that you may need to make on Form 944 for sick pay.

The rate of Medicare tax is 1.45% (0.0145) each for the employer and employee or 2.9% (0.029) for both. Include all tips your employees reported during the year, even if you were unable to withhold the employee tax of 1.45%.

line 4c (column 1)
x   0.029
line 4c (column 2)

4d. Taxable wages & tips subject to Additional Medicare Tax withholding. Enter all wages, including qualified sick leave wages, qualified family leave wages, and qualified wages (excluding qualified health plan expenses) for the employee retention credit; tips; sick pay; and taxable fringe benefits that are subject to Additional Medicare Tax withholding. You're required to begin withholding Additional Medicare Tax in the pay period in which you pay wages in excess of $200,000 to an employee and continue to withhold it each pay period until the end of the calendar year. Additional Medicare Tax is only imposed on the employee. There is no employer share of Additional Medicare Tax. All wages that are subject to Medicare tax are subject to Additional Medicare Tax withholding if paid in excess of the $200,000 withholding threshold.

For more information on what wages are subject to Medicare tax, see the chart, *Special Rules for Various Types of Services and Payments,* in section 15 of Pub. 15. For more information on Additional Medicare Tax, go to *IRS.gov/ADMT*. See the instructions for line 6 for an adjustment that you may need to make on Form 944 for sick pay.

Once wages and tips exceed the $200,000 withholding threshold, include all tips your employees reported during the year, even if you were unable to withhold the employee tax of 0.9%.

line 4d (column 1)
x   0.009
line 4d (column 2)

4e. Total social security and Medicare taxes. Add the column 2 amounts on lines 4a–4d. Enter the result on line 4e.

5. Total Taxes Before Adjustments

Add the total federal income tax withheld from wages, tips, and other compensation from line 2 and the total social security and Medicare taxes before adjustments from line 4e. Enter the result on line 5.

6. Current Year's Adjustments

Enter tax amounts that result from current period adjustments. Use a minus sign (if possible) to show an

-10-   **Instructions for Form 944 (2020)**

Form 944 Instructions (Page 11)

adjustment that decreases the total taxes shown on line 5. Otherwise, use parentheses.

In certain cases, you must adjust the amounts you entered as social security and Medicare taxes in column 2 of lines 4a–4d to figure your correct tax liability for this year's Form 944. See section 13 of Pub. 15, section 9 of Pub. 80, or section 12 of Pub. 179.

Adjustment for fractions of cents. Enter adjustments for fractions of cents (due to rounding) relating to the employee share of social security and Medicare taxes withheld. The employee share of amounts shown in column 2 of lines 4a–4d may differ slightly from amounts actually withheld from employees' pay due to rounding social security and Medicare taxes based on statutory rates. This adjustment may be a positive or a negative adjustment.

Adjustment for sick pay. If your third-party payer of sick pay that isn't your agent (for example, an insurance company) transfers the liability for the employer share of the social security and Medicare taxes to you, enter a negative adjustment on line 6 for the employee share of social security and Medicare taxes that were withheld and deposited by your third-party sick pay payer on the sick pay. If you're the third-party sick pay payer and you transferred the liability for the employer share of the social security and Medicare taxes to the employer, enter a negative adjustment on line 6 for any employer share of these taxes required to be paid by the employer. The sick pay should be included on line 4a, line 4c, and, if the withholding threshold is met, line 4d.

No adjustment is reported on line 6 for sick pay that is paid through a third party as an employer's agent. An employer's agent bears no insurance risk and is reimbursed on a cost-plus-fee basis for payment of sick pay and similar amounts. If an employer uses an agent to pay sick pay, the employer reports the wages on line 4a, line 4c, and, if the withholding threshold is met, line 4d, unless the employer has an agency agreement with the third-party payer that requires the third-party payer to do the collecting, reporting, and/or paying or depositing employment taxes on the sick pay. See section 6 of Pub. 15-A for more information about sick pay reporting.

Adjustments for tips and group-term life insurance. Enter a negative adjustment for:

• Any uncollected employee share of social security and Medicare taxes on tips, and
• The uncollected employee share of social security and Medicare taxes on group-term life insurance premiums paid for former employees.

See the General Instructions for Forms W-2 and W-3 for information on how to report the uncollected employee share of social security and Medicare taxes on tips and group-term life insurance on Form W-2.

Prior year's adjustments. If you need to adjust any amount reported on line 6 from a previously filed Form 944, complete and file Form 944-X. Form 944-X is an adjusted return or claim for refund and is filed separately from Form 944. See section 13 of Pub. 15 or section 9 of Pub. 80.

7. Total Taxes After Adjustments

Combine the amounts shown on lines 5 and 6 and enter the result on line 7.

8a. Qualified Small Business Payroll Tax Credit for Increasing Research Activities

Enter the total amount of the credit from Form 8974, line 12.

If you enter an amount on line 8a, you must attach Form 8974. The December 2017 revision of Form 8974 instructs you to enter the amount from Form 8974, line 12, on Form 944, line 8. For 2020, the amount from Form 8974, line 12, should be entered on Form 944, line 8a.

8b. Nonrefundable Portion of Credit for Qualified Sick and Family Leave Wages From Worksheet 1

Form 944 and these instructions use the terms "nonrefundable" and "refundable" when discussing credits. The term "nonrefundable" means the portion of the credit which is limited by law to the amount of the employer share of social security tax. The term "refundable" means the portion of the credit which is in excess of the employer share of social security tax.

Businesses and tax-exempt organizations with fewer than 500 employees that are required to provide paid sick leave under the EPSLA and/or to provide paid family leave under the Emergency Family and Medical Leave Expansion Act are eligible to claim the credit for qualified sick and family leave wages for the period after March 31, 2020, and before January 1, 2021. Enter the nonrefundable portion of the credit for qualified sick and family leave wages from Worksheet 1, Step 2, line 2j. The credit for qualified sick and family leave wages consists of the qualified sick leave wages, the qualified family leave wages, and the qualified health plan expenses and employer share of Medicare tax allocable to those wages. The nonrefundable portion of the credit is limited to the employer share of social security tax reported on Form 944, lines 4a and 4b, after that share is first reduced by any credit claimed on Form 8974 for the qualified small business payroll tax credit for increasing research activities, or any credit to be claimed on Form 5884-C for the work opportunity credit for qualified tax-exempt organizations hiring qualified veterans.

If you're a third-party payer of sick pay that isn't an agent (for example, an insurance company) and you're claiming the credit for qualified sick and family leave wages for amounts paid to your own employees, the amount of the employer share of social security tax reported on line 4a must be reduced by any adjustment you make on line 6 for the employer share of social security tax transferred to your client. See Worksheet 1 to figure your credit.

Any credit in excess of the remaining amount of the employer share of social security tax is refundable and reported on Form 944, line 10d. For more information on

Form 944 Instructions (Page 12)

the credit for qualified sick and family leave wages, go to *IRS.gov/PLC*.

Qualified health plan expenses allocable to qualified sick leave and family leave wages. The credit for qualified sick leave wages and qualified family leave wages is increased to cover the qualified health plan expenses that are properly allocable to the qualified leave wages for which the credit is allowed. These qualified health plan expenses are amounts paid or incurred by the employer to provide and maintain a group health plan but only to the extent such amounts are excluded from the employees' income as coverage under an accident or health plan. The amount of qualified health plan expenses generally includes both the portion of the cost paid by the employer and the portion of the cost paid by the employee with pre-tax salary reduction contributions. However, qualified health plan expenses don't include amounts that the employee paid for with after-tax contributions. For more information, go to *IRS.gov/PLC*.

TIP *You must include the full amount (both the nonrefundable and refundable portions) of the credit for qualified sick and family leave wages in your gross income for the tax year that includes the last day of any calendar quarter in which a credit is allowed. You can't use the same wages for the employee retention credit and the credits for paid sick and family leave.*

8c. Nonrefundable Portion of Employee Retention Credit From Worksheet 1

CAUTION *An employer may not claim the employee retention credit if the employer receives a Small Business Interruption Loan under the Paycheck Protection Program (PPP) that is authorized under the Coronavirus Aid, Relief, and Economic Security (CARES) Act ("Paycheck Protection Loan"). An employer that receives a Paycheck Protection Loan shouldn't claim an employee retention credit. An employer that applied for a Paycheck Protection Loan, received payment, and repaid the loan by May 18, 2020, will be treated as though the employer had not received a covered loan under the PPP for purposes of the employee retention credit.*

Enter the nonrefundable portion of the employee retention credit from Worksheet 1, Step 3, line 3h. The employee retention credit is 50% of the qualified wages you paid to your employees between March 13, 2020, and December 31, 2020. Qualified wages include qualified health plan expenses for the employee retention credit. The nonrefundable portion of the credit is limited to the employer share of social security tax reported on Form 944, lines 4a and 4b, after that share is first reduced by any credit claimed on Form 8974 for the qualified small business payroll tax credit for increasing research activities, or any credit to be claimed on Form 5884-C for the work opportunity credit for qualified tax-exempt organizations hiring qualified veterans, and/or any credit claimed for the nonrefundable portion of the credit for qualified sick and family leave wages.

CAUTION *If you're a third-party payer of sick pay that isn't an agent (for example, an insurance company) and you're claiming the employee retention credit for amounts paid to your own employees, the amount of the* employer share of social security tax reported on line 4a must be reduced by any adjustment you make on line 6 for the employer share of social security tax transferred to your client. See Worksheet 1 to figure your credit.

Any credit in excess of the remaining amount of the employer share of social security tax is refundable and reported on Form 944, line 10e. For more information on the employee retention credit, go to *IRS.gov/ERC*.

Qualified wages for the employee retention credit. The tax credit is equal to 50% of qualified wages paid to employees between March 13, 2020, and December 31, 2020. Qualified wages, including qualified health plan expenses, are limited to a maximum of $10,000 for each employee for the year. Qualified wages are wages for social security and Medicare tax purposes paid to certain employees during any period in a quarter in which your operations are fully or partially suspended due to a government order or during a quarter in which you have had a significant decline in gross receipts. The law provides that the significant decline in gross receipts is the period beginning with any quarter in which your gross receipts are less than 50% of what they were in the same calendar quarter in 2019 and ending with the quarter that follows the first quarter beginning after the quarter in which your gross receipts were greater than 80% of what they were in the same calendar quarter in 2019.

The wages and qualified health plan expenses considered in calculating your credit depend on the size of your workforce. Eligible employers that had an average number of 100 or fewer full-time employees during 2019 count wages paid to all their employees and the qualified health plan expenses paid or incurred for all employees during any period in the quarter in which operations are fully or partially suspended due to a government order or during a quarter in which there has been a significant decline in gross receipts. Eligible employers that had an average number of more than 100 full-time employees in 2019 may count only wages paid to employees for time that the employees weren't working, and qualified health plan expenses paid or incurred by the employer allocable to the time those employees weren't working, due to the suspension or significant decline in gross receipts; these eligible employers can count only wages that don't exceed what the employer would have paid that employee for working for the same amount of time during the prior 30 days. More information on the employee retention credit is available at *IRS.gov/ERC*.

Qualified health plan expenses for the employee retention credit. Qualified wages for the employee retention credit include qualified health plan expenses. Qualified health plan expenses are amounts paid or incurred by the employer to provide and maintain a group health plan but only to the extent such amounts are excluded from the employees' income as coverage under an accident or health plan. The amount of qualified health plan expenses taken into account in determining the amount of qualified wages generally includes both the portion of the cost paid by the employer and the portion of the cost paid by the employee with pre-tax salary reduction contributions. However, the qualified health plan expenses shouldn't include amounts that the employee paid for with after-tax contributions. Generally, the

-12-

Form 944 Instructions (Page 13)

qualified health plan expense is the amount that is allocable to the hours for which the employees receive qualified wages for the employee retention credit. However, qualified health plan expenses for purposes of the employee retention credit may include health plan expenses allocable to the applicable periods even if the employer isn't paying any qualified wages to the employee. For more information, see the frequently asked questions for qualified health plan expenses at *IRS.gov/ ERC*.

8d. Total Nonrefundable Credits

Add lines 8a, 8b, and 8c. Enter the total on line 8d.

9. Total Taxes After Adjustments and Nonrefundable Credits

Subtract line 8d from line 7 and enter the result on line 9.

- **If line 9 is less than $2,500,** you may pay the amount with Form 944 or you may deposit the amount.
- **If line 9 is $2,500 or more,** you must generally deposit your tax liabilities by EFT. However, if you deposited all taxes accumulated in the first 3 quarters of the year and your fourth quarter liability is less than $2,500, you may pay taxes accumulated during the fourth quarter with Form 944. Also see section 11 of Pub. 15, section 8 of Pub. 80, or section 11 of Pub. 179 for information about payments made under the accuracy of deposits rule. The amount shown on line 9 must equal the amount shown on line 13m or the "Total tax liability for the year" shown on line M of Form 945-A, Annual Record of Federal Tax Liability. For more information, see the line 13 instructions, later.

For more information and rules about federal tax deposits, see *Must You Deposit Your Taxes*, earlier, and section 11 of Pub. 15, section 8 of Pub. 80, or section 11 of Pub. 179. See *Notice 2020-22*, *Notice 2020-65*, and *IRS.gov/ETD* for information about the reduction and deferral of certain deposits.

 If you're a semiweekly schedule depositor, you must complete Form 945-A. If you fail to complete and submit Form 945-A, the IRS may assert deposit penalties based on available information.

10a. Total Deposits for This Year

Enter your deposits for this year, including any overpayment that you applied from filing Form 944-X, 944-X (SP), 941-X, or 941-X (PR) in the current year. Also include in the amount shown any overpayment from a previous period that you applied to this return. Don't include any amount that you didn't deposit because you chose to defer the employer or employee share of social security tax. For more information about the deferrals, see the line 10b and line 10c instructions next. Also, don't include any amount you didn't deposit because you reduced your deposits in anticipation of the credit for qualified sick and family leave wages or the employee retention credit, as discussed in *Notice 2020-22*.

10b. Deferred Amount of the Employer Share of Social Security Tax

Enter the amount of the employer share of social security tax that you're deferring. Employers, including government employers, can defer the deposit of the employer share of social security tax due on or after March 27, 2020, and before January 1, 2021, as well as payment due for the employer share of social security tax for wages paid on or after March 27, 2020, and before January 1, 2021. The employer share of social security tax is included on lines 4a and 4b along with the employee share of social security tax. However, you determine the amount of the employer share of social security tax that can be deferred by only considering social security tax on wages related to deposits and payments due on or after March 27, 2020. Don't include the employee social security tax reported on lines 4a(i) and 4a(ii) as part of the deferred amount of the employer share of social security tax. If you're a third-party payer of sick pay that isn't an agent (for example, an insurance company), you must consider any adjustment that you make on line 6 for the employer share of social security tax transferred to your client before deciding the employer share of social security tax that can be deferred. Don't reduce the amount reported on line 10b by any credits claimed on line 8a, 8b, or 8c or any credit to be claimed on Form 5884-C, line 11, for the work opportunity credit for qualified tax-exempt organizations hiring qualified veterans. However, you can't defer tax that you have already paid; therefore, the maximum amount of social security tax (both the employer and employee share of social security tax) that can be deferred for the year is the lesser of (1) the total of the employer and employee share of social security tax, or (2) the **excess** of (a) line 7 (reduced by the amount, if any, on line 8a) **over** (b) line 10a. For more information about the deferral of employment tax deposits, including limitations on the maximum amount you can defer, go to *IRS.gov/ETD*.

 The deferred amount of the employer share of social security tax is a deferral of deposits and payments, not a deferral of liability. You won't receive a refund or credit of any amount of the employer share of social security tax already deposited or paid for the year. However, in determining whether any amount of the employer share of social security tax was already deposited for this purpose, you can consider prior deposits on or after March 27, 2020, as first being deposited for employment taxes other than the employer share of social security tax. Although employers depositing taxes using EFTPS identify the subcategory of separate deposits for the different employment taxes (for example, social security tax and Medicare tax), those entries are for informational purposes only. The IRS doesn't use that information in comparing liabilities reported on the employment tax return and the total deposits made.

Paying the deferred amount of the employer share of social security tax. One-half of the employer share of social security tax is due by December 31, 2021, and the remainder is due by December 31, 2022. Any payments or deposits you make before December 31, 2021, are first applied against your payment due on December 31, 2021,

Form 944 Instructions (Page 14)

and then applied against your payment due on December 31, 2022. For example, if your employer share of social security tax for 2020 is $20,000 and you deposited $5,000 of the $20,000 during 2020 and defer $15,000 on line 10b, then you must pay $5,000 by December 31, 2021, and $10,000 by December 31, 2022. However, if your employer share of social security tax for 2020 was $20,000 and you deposited $15,000 of the $20,000 during 2020 and defer $5,000 on line 10b, then you don't need to pay any deferred amount by December 31, 2021, because 50% of the amount that could have been deferred ($10,000) has already been paid and is first applied against your payment that would be due on December 31, 2021. Accordingly, you must pay the $5,000 deferral by December 31, 2022.

If you initially deferred (that is, didn't deposit) the employer share of social security tax and later decided to pay or deposit it in 2020, see *Adjusting tax liability for the deferred amount of social security tax that you pay or deposit in 2020*, later. For additional information, go to *IRS.gov/ETD*.

How to pay the deferred amount of social security tax. You may pay the amount you owe electronically using EFTPS, by credit or debit card, or by a check or money order. The preferred method of payment is EFTPS. For more information, visit *EFTPS.gov*, or call 800-555-4477 or 800-733-4829 (TDD). To pay the deferred amount using EFTPS, select Form 944 and the option for payment due on an IRS notice.

To pay by credit or debit card, go to *IRS.gov/ PayByCard*. If you pay by check or money order, include a 2020 Form 944-V, Payment Voucher. Make the check or money order payable to "United States Treasury." Enter your EIN, "Form 944," and "2020" on your check or money order.

Where to send payments. Payments should be sent to:

Department of the Treasury	or	Department of the Treasury
Internal Revenue Service		Internal Revenue Service
Ogden, UT 84201-0030		Kansas City, MO 64999-0030

Send your payment to the address above that is in the same state as the address to which you would mail returns filed without a payment, as shown under *Where Should You File*, earlier.

10c. Deferred Amount of the Employee Share of Social Security Tax

Enter the amount of the employee share of social security tax that you're deferring for the year. On August 8, 2020, the President issued a Presidential Memorandum directing the Secretary of the Treasury to use his authority pursuant to section 7508A of the Internal Revenue Code to defer the withholding, deposit, and payment of certain payroll tax obligations. In *Notice 2020-65*, the Secretary made relief available under section 7508A to employers required to withhold social security taxes from wages paid to employees. Specifically, under the notice, the due date for withholding and payment of the employee share of social security tax on applicable wages is postponed until

the period beginning on January 1, 2021, and ending on April 30, 2021. Applicable wages are social security wages of less than $4,000 in any biweekly pay period (or the equivalent threshold amount for other pay periods), paid on a pay date during the period beginning on September 1, 2020, and ending on December 31, 2020. The determination of whether the deferral of withholding or payment of the employee share of social security tax is available is made on a pay period-by-pay period basis. Nothing prohibits employers from getting employee input on whether to apply the relief to postpone the due date for the withholding and payment of the employee share of social security tax on applicable wages paid to the employee.

You can't defer tax that you have already paid; therefore, the maximum amount of social security tax (both the employer and employee share of social security tax) that can be deferred for the year is the lesser of (1) the total of the employer and employee share of social security tax, or (2) the **excess** of (a) line 7 (reduced by the amount, if any, on line 8a) **over** (b) line 10a.

TIP *If you paid an employee supplemental wages (for example, a bonus or commission) and included the supplemental wages with the employee's regular wages in a single payment (that is, in a single paycheck) for a pay period, but you didn't specifically identify the amount of each, then the entire amount of the payment must be below $4,000 (or equivalent amount for pay periods other than a biweekly pay period) to be eligible for the deferral of the withholding and payment of the employee share of social security tax on the wages. If the entire amount is below $4,000, then you may defer the withholding and payment of the employee share of social security tax on the entire payment of the wages. If you paid the supplemental wages separately from the employee's regular wages (that is, in a separate check), or you combined the wages in a single payment but you specifically identified the amount of each, then the supplemental wages are disregarded for purposes of determining whether the regular wages are below $4,000 (or equivalent amount), but the supplemental wages aren't eligible for the deferral of the withholding and payment of the employee share of social security tax.*

Paying the deferred amount of the employee share of social security tax. The due date for the withholding and payment of the employee share of social security tax is postponed until the period beginning on January 1, 2021, and ending on April 30, 2021. The employer must withhold and pay the total deferred employee share of social security tax ratably from wages paid to the employee between January 1, 2021, and April 30, 2021. If necessary, the employer may make arrangements to otherwise collect the total deferred taxes from the employee. The employer is liable to pay the deferred taxes to the IRS and must do so before May 1, 2021, to avoid interest, penalties, and additions to tax on those amounts. For more information about the deferral of the employee share of social security tax, see *Notice 2020-65*. For information on paying the deferred social security tax, see *How to pay the deferred amount of social security tax*, earlier.

Form 944 Instructions (Page 15)

If you initially deferred (that is, didn't deposit) the employee share of social security tax and later decide to pay or deposit it in 2020, see *Adjusting tax liability for the deferred amount of social security tax that you pay or deposit in 2020*, later.

 For information about how to report the deferred amount of the employee share of social security tax on Form W-2 and Form W-2c for 2020, see IRS.gov/FormW2 and the 2021 General Instructions for Forms W-2 and W-3 (available in early 2021).

10d. Refundable Portion of Credit for Qualified Sick and Family Leave Wages From Worksheet 1

Businesses and tax-exempt organizations with fewer than 500 employees that are required to provide paid sick leave under the EPSLA and/or to provide paid family leave under the Emergency Family and Medical Leave Expansion Act are eligible to claim the credit for qualified sick and family leave wages. Enter the refundable portion of the credit for qualified sick and family leave wages from Worksheet 1, Step 2, line 2k. The credit for qualified sick and family leave wages consists of the qualified sick leave wages, the qualified family leave wages, the allocable qualified health plan expenses, and the employer share of Medicare tax allocable to those wages. The refundable portion of the credit is allowed after the employer share of social security tax is reduced to zero by nonrefundable credits.

10e. Refundable Portion of Employee Retention Credit From Worksheet 1

Enter the refundable portion of the employee retention credit from Worksheet 1, Step 3, line 3i. The employee retention credit is 50% of the qualified wages you paid to your employees between March 13, 2020, and December 31, 2020. The refundable portion of the credit is allowed after the employer share of social security tax is reduced to zero by nonrefundable credits.

10f. Total Deposits, Deferrals, and Refundable Credits

Add lines 10a, 10b, 10c, 10d, and 10e. Enter the total on line 10f.

10g. Total Advances Received From Filing Form(s) 7200 for the Year

Enter the total advances received from filing Form(s) 7200 for the year. If you filed Form 7200 but you haven't received the advance before filing Form 944, don't include that amount. Employers were eligible to file Form 7200 if they paid qualified sick leave wages, qualified family leave wages, and/or qualified wages for the employee retention credit and the amount of employment tax deposits they retained wasn't sufficient to cover the cost of qualified sick and family leave wages and the employee retention credit.

 Form 7200 may be filed up to the earlier of February 1, 2021, or the filing of Form 944 for the year. However, if you file Form 7200 after the end of the year, it's possible that it may not be processed prior to the processing of the filed Form 944. Advance payment

requests on Form 7200 won't be paid after your Form 944 is processed. When the IRS processes Form 944, we will correct the amount reported on line 10g to match the amount of advance payments issued or contact you to reconcile the difference before we finish processing Form 944.

10h. Total Deposits, Deferrals, and Refundable Credits Less Advances

Subtract line 10g from line 10f. Enter the result on line 10h.

11. Balance Due

If line 9 is more than line 10h, enter the difference on line 11. Otherwise, see *Overpayment*, later. **Never make an entry on both lines 11 and 12.**

You don't have to pay if line 11 is less than $1. Generally, you should have a balance due only if your total taxes after adjustments and nonrefundable credits (line 9) are less than $2,500. However, see *If line 9 is $2,500 or more*, earlier, for exceptions.

If you were required to make federal tax deposits, pay the amount shown on line 11 by EFT. If you weren't required to make federal tax deposits (see the *Federal Tax Deposit Requirements for Form 944 Filers* chart, earlier) or you're a monthly schedule depositor making a payment under the accuracy of deposits rule, you may pay the amount shown on line 11 by EFT, credit card, debit card, check, money order, or EFW. For more information on electronic payment options, go to *IRS.gov/ Payments*.

If you pay by EFT, credit card, or debit card, file your return using the *Without a payment* address under *Where Should You File*, earlier. Don't file Form 944-V, Payment Voucher.

If you pay by check or money order, make it payable to "United States Treasury." Enter your EIN, "Form 944," and the tax period on your check or money order. Complete Form 944-V and enclose it with Form 944.

⚠️ **CAUTION** *If you're required to make deposits and instead pay the taxes with Form 944, you may be subject to a penalty.*

What if you can't pay in full? If you can't pay the full amount of tax you owe, you can apply for an installment agreement online. You can apply for an installment agreement online if:
- You can't pay the full amount shown on line 11,
- The total amount you owe is $25,000 or less, and
- You can pay the liability in full in 24 months.

To apply using the Online Payment Agreement Application, go to *IRS.gov/OPA*.

Under an installment agreement, you can pay what you owe in monthly installments. There are certain conditions you must meet to enter into and maintain an installment agreement, such as paying the liability within 24 months, and making all required deposits and timely filing tax returns during the length of the agreement.

If your installment agreement is accepted, you will be charged a fee and you will be subject to penalties and

Form 944 Instructions (Page 16)

interest on the amount of tax not paid by the due date of the return.

12. Overpayment

If line 10h is more than line 9, enter the amount on line 12. **Never make an entry on both lines 11 and 12.**

If you deposited more than the correct amount for the year, you can choose to have the IRS either refund the overpayment or apply it to your next return. Check only one box on line 12. If you don't check either box or if you check both boxes, we will generally apply the overpayment to your next return. Regardless of any boxes you check or don't check on line 12, we may apply your overpayment to any past due tax account that is shown in our records under your EIN.

If line 12 is less than $1, we will send a refund or apply it to your next return only if you ask us in writing to do so.

Part 2: Tell Us About Your Deposit Schedule and Tax Liability for This Year

13. Check One

If line 9 is less than $2,500, check the first box on line 13 and go to line 14.

If line 9 is $2,500 or more, check the second box on line 13. If you're a monthly schedule depositor, enter your tax liability for each month and figure the total liability for the year. The amounts entered on line 13 are a summary of your monthly tax liabilities, not a summary of deposits you made. The IRS gets deposit data from EFTs. Enter your tax liabilities in the month that corresponds to the dates you paid wages to your employees, not the date payroll liabilities were accrued or deposits were made. If you don't enter your tax liability for each month, the IRS won't know when you should have made deposits and may assess an "averaged" FTD penalty. See section 11 of Pub. 15, section 8 of Pub. 80, or section 11 of Pub. 179. If your tax liability for any month is negative after accounting for your adjustments reported on line 6, don't enter a negative amount for the month. Instead, enter zero for the month and subtract that negative amount from your tax liability for the next month.

⚠️ **CAUTION** *The amount shown on line 13m must equal the amount shown on line 9. If it doesn't, your tax deposits and payments may not be counted as timely. Don't reduce your total liability reported on line 13 by the deferred amount of the employer or employee share of social security tax, the refundable portion of the credit for qualified sick and family leave wages, or the refundable portion of the employee retention credit. The deferred amount of the employer or employee share of social security tax reported on line 10b and 10c doesn't reflect deferred liabilities, but instead postponed due dates for payment. Don't change your current year tax liability reported on line 13 by adjustments reported on any Forms 944-X.*

If you're a semiweekly schedule depositor or if you became one because you accumulated $100,000 or more in tax liability on any day in a deposit period, you must complete Form 945-A and file it with Form 944. See *$100,000 Next-Day Deposit Rule* in section 11 of Pub. 15, section 8 of Pub. 80, or section 11 of Pub. 179. Don't complete lines 13a–13m if you file Form 945-A.

Adjusting tax liability for nonrefundable credits claimed on lines 8a, 8b, and 8c. Monthly schedule depositors and semiweekly schedule depositors must account for nonrefundable credits claimed on lines 8a, 8b, and 8c when reporting their tax liabilities on line 13 or Form 945-A. The total tax liability for the year must equal the amount reported on line 9. Failure to account for the nonrefundable credits on line 13 or Form 945-A may cause line 13 or Form 945-A to report more than the total tax liability reported on line 9. Don't reduce your monthly tax liability reported on lines 13a through 13l or your daily tax liability reported on Form 945-A below zero.

Qualified small business payroll tax credit for increasing research activities (line 8a). The qualified small business payroll tax credit for increasing research activities is limited to the employer share of social security tax on wages paid in the quarter that begins after the income tax return electing the credit has been filed. In completing line 13 or Form 945-A, you take into account the payroll tax credit against your liability for the employer share of social security tax starting with the first payroll payment of the quarter that includes payments of wages to your employees subject to social security tax. The credit may be taken to the extent of the employer share of social security tax on wages associated with the first payroll payment, and then to the extent of the employer share of social security tax associated with succeeding payroll payments in the quarter until the credit is used. Consistent with the entries on line 13 or Form 945-A, the payroll tax credit should be taken into account in making deposits of employment tax. If any payroll tax credit is remaining at the end of the quarter that has not been used completely because it exceeds the employer share of social security tax for the quarter, the excess credit may be carried forward to the succeeding quarter and allowed as a payroll tax credit for the succeeding quarter. The payroll tax credit may not be taken as a credit against income tax withholding, Medicare tax, or the employee share of social security tax.

Also, the remaining payroll tax credit may not be carried back and taken as a credit against wages paid from preceding quarters that are reported on the same Form 944 or on Forms 944 for preceding years. If an amount of payroll tax credit is unused at the end of the calendar year because it is in excess of the employer share of social security tax on wages paid during the applicable quarters in the calendar year, the remaining payroll tax credit may be carried forward to the first quarter of the succeeding calendar year as a payroll tax credit against the employer share of social security tax on wages paid in that quarter.

Example. Rose Co. is an employer with a calendar tax year that filed its timely income tax return on April 15, 2020. Rose Co. elected to take the qualified small business payroll tax credit for increasing research activities on Form 6765. The third quarter of 2020 is the first quarter that begins after Rose Co. filed the income tax return making the payroll tax credit election. Therefore,

-16-

Form 944 Instructions (Page 17)

the payroll tax credit applies against Rose Co.'s share of social security tax on wages paid to employees in the third quarter of 2020. Rose Co. is a semiweekly schedule depositor. Rose Co. completes Form 945-A by reducing the amount of liability entered for the first payroll payment in the third quarter of 2020 that includes wages subject to social security tax by the lesser of (1) its share of social security tax on the wages or (2) the available payroll tax credit. If the payroll tax credit elected is more than Rose Co.'s share of social security tax on the first payroll payment of the quarter, the excess payroll tax credit would be carried forward to succeeding payroll payments in the third quarter until it is used. If the amount of the payroll tax credit exceeds Rose Co.'s share of social security tax on wages paid to its employees in the third quarter, the excess credit would be treated as a payroll tax credit against its share of social security tax on wages paid in the fourth quarter. If the amount of the payroll tax credit remaining exceeded Rose Co.'s share of social security tax on wages paid in the fourth quarter, it could be carried forward and treated as a payroll tax credit for the first quarter of 2021.

Nonrefundable portion of credit for qualified sick and family leave wages (line 8b). The nonrefundable portion of the credit for qualified sick and family leave wages is limited to the employer share of social security tax on wages paid in the year that is remaining after that share is first reduced by any credit claimed on Form 944, line 8a, for the qualified small business payroll tax credit for increasing research activities, and/or any credit to be claimed on Form 5884-C, line 11, for the work opportunity credit for qualified tax-exempt organizations hiring qualified veterans. In completing line 13 or Form 945-A, you take into account the nonrefundable portion of the credit for qualified sick and family leave wages (including the qualified health plan expenses and employer share of Medicare tax allocable to those wages) against the liability for the first payroll payment of the year, but not below zero. Then reduce the liability for each successive payroll payment of the year until the nonrefundable portion of the credit is used. Any credit for qualified sick and family leave wages that is remaining at the end of the year because it exceeds the employer share of social security tax is claimed on line 10d as a refundable credit. The refundable portion of the credit doesn't reduce the liability reported on line 13 or Form 945-A.

Example. Maple Co. is a monthly schedule depositor that pays employees every Friday. In 2020, Maple Co. had pay dates every Friday of 2020 starting January 3, 2020. Maple Co. paid qualified sick and family leave wages on May 1 and May 8. The nonrefundable portion of the credit for qualified sick and family leave wages for the year is $300. On line 13, Maple Co. will use the $300 to reduce the liability for the January 3 pay date, but not below zero. If any nonrefundable portion of the credit remains, Maple Co. applies it to the liability for the January 10 pay date, then the January 17 pay date, and so forth until the entire $300 is used.

Nonrefundable portion of employee retention credit (line 8c). The nonrefundable portion of the employee retention credit is limited to the employer share of social security tax on wages paid in the year that is remaining after that share is first reduced by any credit

claimed on Form 944, line 8a, for the qualified small business payroll tax credit for increasing research activities; any credit to be claimed on Form 5884-C, line 11, for the work opportunity credit for qualified tax-exempt organizations hiring qualified veterans; and/or any credit claimed on Form 944, line 8b, for the nonrefundable portion of the credit for qualified sick and family leave wages. In completing line 13 or Form 945-A, you take into account the nonrefundable portion of the employee retention credit against the liability for the first payroll payment of the year, but not below zero. Then reduce the liability for each successive payroll payment of the year until the nonrefundable portion of the credit is used. Any employee retention credit that is remaining at the end of the year because it exceeds the employer share of social security tax is claimed on line 10e as a refundable credit. The refundable portion of the credit doesn't reduce the liability reported on line 13 or Form 945-A.

Example. Maple Co. is a monthly schedule depositor that pays employees every Friday. In 2020, Maple Co. had pay dates every Friday of 2020 starting January 3, 2020. Maple Co. paid qualified wages for the employee retention credit on May 1 and May 8. The nonrefundable portion of the employee retention credit for the year is $300. On line 13, Maple Co. will use the $300 to reduce the liability for the January 3 pay date, but not below zero. If any nonrefundable portion of the credit remains, Maple Co. applies it to the liability for the January 10 pay date, then the January 17 pay date, and so forth until the entire $300 is used.

 You may reduce your deposits by the amount of the nonrefundable and refundable portions of the credit for qualified sick and family leave wages, the nonrefundable and refundable portions of the employee retention credit, and any deferred employment taxes, as discussed earlier under Reducing your deposits for COVID-19 credits.

Adjusting tax liability for the deferred amount of social security tax that you pay or deposit in 2020. If you defer the employer and/or employee share of social security tax and subsequently pay or deposit that deferred amount during 2020, you should report the amount of the payment or deposit on Form 944, line 13, or Form 945-A on the date of the payment or deposit and not the date of liability. You shouldn't include any portion of the deferred amount of social security taxes already paid or deposited by December 31, 2020, on Form 944, line 10b or 10c.

For example, if you're a monthly schedule depositor that has an employment tax liability of $50 every month in 2020 and you defer $10 of the employer share of social security tax from your June liability, but deposit your deferred amount of $10 together with your $50 deposit for your November tax liability, you would report $40 for your June tax liability ($50 minus $10) and $60 for your November liability ($50 plus $10) on line 13. Don't include the $10 deferral on Form 944, line 10b.

Instructions for Form 944 (2020)   -17-

Form 944 Instructions (Page 18)

Part 3: Tell Us About Your Business

In Part 3, answer question 14 only if it applies to your business. If it doesn't apply, leave it blank and go to Part 4.

14. If Your Business Has Closed...

If you permanently go out of business or stop paying wages, you must file a final return. To tell the IRS that a particular Form 944 is your final return, check the box on line 14 and enter the date you last paid wages in the space provided. For additional filing requirements, including information about attaching a statement to your final return, see *If Your Business Has Closed...*, earlier.

Lines 15 Through 19

 The amounts entered on lines 15 through 19 are amounts that you use on Worksheet 1 to figure the credit for qualified sick and family leave wages and the employee retention credit. If you're claiming these credits, you must enter the applicable amounts.

15. Qualified Health Plan Expenses Allocable to Qualified Sick Leave Wages

Enter the qualified health plan expenses allocable to qualified sick leave wages. This amount is also entered on Worksheet 1, Step 2, line 2b.

16. Qualified Health Plan Expenses Allocable to Qualified Family Leave Wages

Enter the qualified health plan expenses allocable to qualified family leave wages. This amount is also entered on Worksheet 1, Step 2, line 2f.

17. Qualified Wages for the Employee Retention Credit

Enter the qualified wages for the employee retention credit (excluding the amount of any qualified health plan expenses allocable to these wages). This amount is also entered on Worksheet 1, Step 3, line 3a.

18. Qualified Health Plan Expenses Allocable to Wages Reported on Line 17

Enter the qualified health plan expenses for the employee retention credit. These expenses are generally allocable to the wages reported on Form 944, Part 3, line 17. However, in some circumstances, qualified health plan expenses for purposes of the employee retention credit are treated as allocable to qualified wages for the employee retention credit even if no wages are paid to the employees during the applicable period (for example, when you furlough an employee because your operations are fully or partially suspended due to a government order but you continue to pay qualified health plan expenses). For more information, go to *IRS.gov/ERC*. The amount from line 18 is also entered on Worksheet 1, Step 3, line 3b.

19. Credit From Form 5884-C, Line 11, for the Year

If applicable, enter the credit to be claimed on line 11 of Form 5884-C for the work opportunity credit for qualified tax-exempt organizations hiring qualified veterans for 2020. Entering an amount here doesn't change your requirement to file Form 5884-C separately from Form 944. You're entering the amount here to notify us that you will file Form 5884-C for the year and therefore reduce the amount of the employer share of social security tax that is available to be reduced by the nonrefundable portion of the credit for qualified sick and family leave wages and the nonrefundable portion of the employee retention credit.

Part 4: May We Speak With Your Third-Party Designee?

If you want to allow an employee, a paid tax preparer, or another person to discuss your Form 944 with the IRS, check the "Yes" box in Part 4. Enter the name, phone number, and the five-digit personal identification number (PIN) of the specific person to speak with—not the name of the firm that prepared your tax return. The designee may choose any five numbers as his or her PIN.

By checking "Yes," you authorize the IRS to talk to the person you named (your designee) about any questions we may have while we process your return. You also authorize your designee to do all of the following.

- Give us any information that is missing from your return.
- Call us for information about processing your return.
- Respond to certain IRS notices that you have shared with your designee about math errors and return preparation. The IRS won't send notices to your designee.

You're not authorizing your designee to bind you to anything (including additional tax liability) or to otherwise represent you before the IRS. If you want to expand your designee's authorization, see Pub. 947.

The authorization will automatically expire 1 year after the due date (without regard to extensions) for filing your Form 944. If you or your designee wants to terminate the authorization, write to the IRS office for your location using the *Without a payment* address under *Where Should You File*, earlier.

Part 5: Sign Here (Approved Roles)

Complete all information and sign Form 944. The following persons are authorized to sign the return for each type of business entity.
- **Sole proprietorship**—The individual who owns the business.
- **Corporation (including a limited liability company (LLC) treated as a corporation)**—The president, vice president, or other principal officer duly authorized to sign.
- **Partnership (including an LLC treated as a partnership) or unincorporated organization**—A responsible and duly authorized partner, member, or officer having knowledge of its affairs.
- **Single-member LLC treated as a disregarded entity for federal income tax purposes**—The owner of the LLC or a principal officer duly authorized to sign.
- **Trust or estate**—The fiduciary.

-18-   Instructions for Form 944 (2020)

Form 944 Instructions (Page 19)

Form 944 may be signed by a duly authorized agent of the taxpayer if a valid power of attorney has been filed.

Alternative signature method. Corporate officers or duly authorized agents may sign Form 944 by rubber stamp, mechanical device, or computer software program. For details and required documentation, see Rev. Proc. 2005-39, 2005-28 I.R.B. 82, available at *IRS.gov/irb/2005-28_IRB#RP-2005-39*.

Paid Preparer Use Only

A paid preparer must sign Form 944 and provide the information in the *Paid Preparer Use Only* section of Part 5 if the preparer was paid to prepare Form 944 and isn't an employee of the filing entity. Paid preparers must sign paper returns with a manual signature. The preparer must give you a copy of the return in addition to the copy to be filed with the IRS.

If you're a paid preparer, enter your Preparer Tax Identification Number (PTIN) in the space provided. Include your complete address. If you work for a firm, enter the firm's name and the EIN of the firm. You can apply for a PTIN online or by filing Form W-12. For more information about applying for a PTIN online, go to *IRS.gov/PTIN*. You can't use your PTIN in place of the EIN of the tax preparation firm.

Generally, don't complete this section if you're filing the return as a reporting agent and have a valid Form 8655 on file with the IRS. However, a reporting agent must complete this section if the reporting agent offered legal advice, for example, advising the client on determining whether its workers are employees or independent contractors for federal tax purposes.

How To Get Forms, Instructions, and Publications

You can view, download, or print most of the forms, instructions, and publications you may need at *IRS.gov/Forms*. Otherwise, you can go to *IRS.gov/OrderForms* to place an order and have forms mailed to you.

Form 944 Instructions (Page 20)

Worksheet 1. Credit for Qualified Sick and Family Leave Wages and the Employee Retention Credit

Keep for Your Records

Determine how you will complete this worksheet

If you paid both qualified sick and family leave wages and qualified wages for purposes of the employee retention credit this year, complete Step 1, Step 2, and Step 3. If you paid qualified sick and family leave wages this year but you didn't pay any qualified wages for purposes of the employee retention credit this year, complete Step 1 and Step 2. If you paid qualified wages for purposes of the employee retention credit this year but you didn't pay any qualified sick and family leave wages this year, complete Step 1 and Step 3.

Step 1. **Determine the employer share of social security tax this year after it is reduced by any credit claimed on Form 8974 and any credit to be claimed on Form 5884-C**

1a   Enter the amount of social security tax from Form 944, Part 1, line 4a, column 2 . . . .   1a _____

1b   Enter the amount of social security tax from Form 944, Part 1, line 4b, column 2 . . . .   1b _____

1c   Add lines 1a and 1b . . . .   1c _____

1d   Multiply line 1c by 50% (0.50) . . . .   1d _____

1e   If you're a third-party payer of sick pay that isn't an agent and you're claiming credits for amounts paid to your employees, enter the employer share of social security tax included on Form 944, Part 1, line 6 (enter as a positive number) . . . .   1e _____

1f   **Employer share of social security tax.** Subtract line 1e from line 1d . . . .   1f _____

1g   Enter the amount from Form 944, Part 1, line 8a (credit from Form 8974) . . . .   1g _____

1h   Enter the amount to be claimed on Form 5884-C, line 11, for this year . . . .   1h _____

1i   **Total nonrefundable credits already used against the employer share of social security tax.** Add lines 1g and 1h . . . .   1i _____

1j   **Employer share of social security tax remaining.** Subtract line 1i from line 1f . . . .   1j _____

Step 2. **Figure the sick and family leave credit**

2a   Qualified sick leave wages reported on Form 944, Part 1, line 4a(i), column 1 . . . . . .   2a _____

2a(i)   Qualified sick leave wages included on Form 944, Part 1, line 4c, but not included on Form 944, Part 1, line 4a(i), column 1, because the wages reported on that line were limited by the social security wage base . . . .   2a(i) _____

2a(ii)   Total qualified sick leave wages. Add lines 2a and 2a(i) . . . .   2a(ii) _____

2b   Qualified health plan expenses allocable to qualified sick leave wages (Form 944, Part 3, line 15) . . . .   2b _____

2c   Employer share of Medicare tax on qualified sick leave wages. Multiply line 2a(ii) by 1.45% (0.0145) . . . .   2c _____

2d   **Credit for qualified sick leave wages.** Add lines 2a(ii), 2b, and 2c . . . .   2d _____

2e   Qualified family leave wages reported on Form 944, Part 1, line 4a(ii), column 1 . . . .   2e _____

2e(i)   Qualified family leave wages included on Form 944, Part 1, line 4c, but not included on Form 944, Part 1, line 4a(ii), column 1, because the wages reported on that line were limited by the social security wage base . . . .   2e(i) _____

2e(ii)   Total qualified family leave wages. Add lines 2e and 2e(i) . . . .   2e(ii) _____

2f   Qualified health plan expenses allocable to qualified family leave wages (Form 944, Part 3, line 16) . . . .   2f _____

2g   Employer share of Medicare tax on qualified family leave wages. Multiply line 2e(ii) by 1.45% (0.0145) . . . .   2g _____

2h   **Credit for qualified family leave wages.** Add lines 2e(ii), 2f, and 2g . . . .   2h _____

2i   **Credit for qualified sick and family leave wages.** Add lines 2d and 2h . . . . . .   2i _____

2j   **Nonrefundable portion of credit for qualified sick and family leave wages.** Enter the smaller of line 1j or line 2i. Enter this amount on Form 944, Part 1, line 8b . . . .   2j _____

2k   **Refundable portion of credit for qualified sick and family leave wages.** Subtract line 2j from line 2i and enter this amount on Form 944, Part 1, line 10d . . . .   2k _____

Step 3. **Figure the employee retention credit**

3a   Qualified wages (excluding qualified health plan expenses) for the employee retention credit (Form 944, Part 3, line 17) . . . .   3a _____

3b   Qualified health plan expenses allocable to qualified wages for the employee retention credit (Form 944, Part 3, line 18) . . . .   3b _____

3c   Add lines 3a and 3b . . . .   3c _____

3d   **Retention credit.** Multiply line 3c by 50% (0.50) . . . .   3d _____

3e   Enter the amount of the employer share of social security tax from Step 1, line 1j . . . .   3e _____

3f   Enter the amount of the nonrefundable portion of the credit for qualified sick and family leave wages from Step 2, line 2j . . . .   3f _____

3g   Subtract line 3f from line 3e . . . .   3g _____

3h   **Nonrefundable portion of employee retention credit.** Enter the smaller of line 3d or line 3g. Enter this amount on Form 944, Part 1, line 8c . . . .   3h _____

3i   **Refundable portion of employee retention credit.** Subtract line 3h from line 3d and enter this amount on Form 944, Part 1, line 10e . . . .   3i _____

Form 945 (Page 1)

Form **945**

Department of the Treasury
Internal Revenue Service

Annual Return of Withheld Federal Income Tax

▶ For withholding reported on Forms 1099 and W-2G.
▶ For more information on income tax withholding, see Pub. 15 and Pub. 15-A.
▶ Go to *www.irs.gov/Form945* for instructions and the latest information.

OMB No. 1545-1430

20**20**

Type or Print

Name (as distinguished from trade name)	Employer identification number (EIN)
Trade name, if any	If address is different from prior return, check here. ▶ ☐
Address (number and street)	
City or town, state or province, country, and ZIP or foreign postal code	

A If you don't have to file returns in the future, check here ▶ ☐ and enter date final payments made. ▶ ------------------------

1	Federal income tax withheld from pensions, annuities, IRAs, gambling winnings, etc.	**1**	
2	Backup withholding	**2**	
3	**Total taxes.** If $2,500 or more, this must equal line 7M below or Form 945-A, line M	**3**	
4	Total deposits for 2020, including overpayment applied from a prior year and overpayment applied from Form 945-X	**4**	
5	**Balance due.** If line 3 is more than line 4, enter the difference and see the separate instructions .	**5**	

6 **Overpayment.** If line 4 is more than line 3, enter the difference ▶ $ _____

Check one: ☐ Apply to next return.   ☐ Send a refund.

- **All filers:** If line 3 is less than $2,500, **don't** complete line 7 or Form 945-A.
- **Semiweekly schedule depositors:** Complete Form 945-A and check here . . . . ▶ ☐
- **Monthly schedule depositors:** Complete line 7, entries A through M, and check here . . . . ▶ ☐

7   **Monthly Summary of Federal Tax Liability.** (**Don't** complete if you were a semiweekly schedule depositor.)

	Tax liability for month			Tax liability for month			Tax liability for month
A January . . .		**F** June		**K** November . .	
B February . .		**G** July		**L** December . .	
C March . . .		**H** August		**M** Total liability for	
D April		**I** September . . .		year (add lines **A**	
E May		**J** October		through **L**) . .	

Third-Party Designee

Do you want to allow another person to discuss this return with the IRS? See separate instructions.   ☐ Yes. Complete the following.   ☐ No.

Designee's name ▶	Phone no. ▶	Personal identification number (PIN) ▶	

Sign Here

Under penalties of perjury, I declare that I have examined this return, including accompanying schedules and statements, and to the best of my knowledge and belief, it is true, correct, and complete. Declaration of preparer (other than taxpayer) is based on all information of which preparer has any knowledge.

Signature ▶   Print Your Name and Title ▶   Date ▶

Paid Preparer Use Only

Print/Type preparer's name	Preparer's signature	Date	Check ☐ if self-employed	PTIN
Firm's name ▶			Firm's EIN ▶	
Firm's address ▶			Phone no.	

For Privacy Act and Paperwork Reduction Act Notice, see the separate instructions.   Cat. No. 14584B   Form **945** (2020)

Form 945 (Page 2)

your identification number. If you fail to provide this information in a timely manner, or provide false or fraudulent information, you may be subject to penalties.

You're not required to provide the information requested on a form that is subject to the Paperwork Reduction Act unless the form displays a valid OMB control number. Books or records relating to a form or instructions must be retained as long as their contents may become material in the administration of any Internal Revenue law.

Generally, tax returns and return information are confidential, as required by section 6103. However, section 6103 allows or requires the IRS to disclose or give the information shown on your tax return to others described in the Code. For example, we may disclose your tax information to the Department of Justice for civil and criminal litigation, and to cities, states, the District of Columbia, and U.S. commonwealths and possessions for use in administering their tax laws. We may also disclose

this information to other countries under a tax treaty, to federal and state agencies to enforce federal nontax criminal laws, or to federal law enforcement and intelligence agencies to combat terrorism.

The time needed to complete and file Form 945 will vary depending on individual circumstances. The estimated average time is: **Recordkeeping,** 5 hr., 58 min.; **Learning about the law or the form,** 24 min.; and **Preparing and sending the form to the IRS,** 30 min. If you have comments concerning the accuracy of these time estimates or suggestions for making Form 945 simpler, we would be happy to hear from you. You can send us comments from *IRS.gov/FormComments*. Or you can send your comments to the Internal Revenue Service, Tax Forms and Publications Division, 1111 Constitution Ave. NW, IR-6526, Washington, DC 20224. Don't send Form 945 to this address. Instead, see *Where To File*, earlier.

Instructions for Form 945 (2020)   -7-

20**20**

Instructions for Form 945

Department of the Treasury
Internal Revenue Service

Annual Return of Withheld Federal Income Tax

Section references are to the Internal Revenue Code unless otherwise noted.

Future Developments

For the latest information about developments related to Form 945 and its instructions, such as legislation enacted after they were published, go to *IRS.gov/Form945*.

What's New

New Form 1099-NEC. There is a new Form 1099-NEC to report nonemployee compensation paid in 2020 and any backup withholding on the compensation.

New filing addresses. The filing addresses have changed for some filers. See *Where To File*, later, before filing your return.

Reminders

Correcting a previously filed Form 945. If you discover an error on a previously filed Form 945, make the correction using Form 945-X, Adjusted Annual Return of Withheld Federal Income Tax or Claim for Refund. Form 945-X is filed separately from Form 945. For more information, see the Instructions for Form 945-X or go to *IRS.gov/CorrectingEmploymentTaxes*.

Federal tax deposits must be made by electronic funds transfer (EFT). You must use EFT to make all federal tax deposits. Generally, an EFT is made using the Electronic Federal Tax Payment System (EFTPS). If you don't want to use EFTPS, you can arrange for your tax professional, financial institution, payroll service, or other trusted third party to make electronic deposits on your behalf. Also, you may arrange for your financial institution to initiate a same-day wire payment on your behalf. EFTPS is a free service provided by the Department of the Treasury. Services provided by your tax professional, financial institution, payroll service, or other third party may have a fee.

For more information on making federal tax deposits, see section 11 of Pub. 15. To get more information about EFTPS or to enroll in EFTPS, go to *EFTPS.gov*, or call 800-555-4477 or 800-733-4829 (TDD). Additional information about EFTPS is also available in Pub. 966.

 For an EFTPS deposit to be on time, you must submit the deposit by 8 p.m. Eastern time the day before the date the deposit is due.

Same-day wire payment option. If you fail to submit a deposit transaction on EFTPS by 8 p.m. Eastern time the day before the date a deposit is due, you can still make your deposit on time by using the Federal Tax Collection Service (FTCS) to make a same-day wire payment. To use the same-day wire payment method, you will need to make arrangements with your financial institution ahead of time. Please check with your financial institution regarding availability, deadlines, and costs. Your financial institution may charge you a fee for payments made this way. To learn more about the information you will need to give your financial institution to make a same-day wire payment, go to *IRS.gov/SameDayWire*.

Timeliness of federal tax deposits. If a deposit is required to be made on a day that isn't a business day, the deposit is considered timely if it is made by the close of the next business day. A business day is any day other than a Saturday, Sunday, or legal holiday. The term "legal holiday" for deposit purposes includes only those legal holidays in the District of Columbia. Legal holidays in the District of Columbia are provided in section 11 of Pub. 15.

Electronic filing and payment. Businesses can enjoy the benefits of filing tax returns and paying their federal taxes electronically. Whether you rely on a tax professional or handle your own taxes, the IRS offers you convenient programs to make filing and paying easier. Spend less time worrying about taxes and more time running your business. Use *e-file* and EFTPS to your benefit.
• For *e-file*, go to *IRS.gov/EmploymentEfile* for additional information. A fee may be charged to file electronically.
• For EFTPS, go to *EFTPS.gov* or call EFTPS Customer Service at 800-555-4477 or 800-733-4829 (TDD) for additional information.

⚠ *If you're filing your tax return or paying your federal taxes electronically, a valid employer identification number (EIN) is required at the time the return is filed or the payment is made. If a valid EIN isn't provided, the return or payment won't be processed. This may result in penalties. See* Employer Identification Number (EIN), *later, for more information about applying for an EIN.*

Electronic funds withdrawal (EFW). If you file Form 945 electronically, you can *e-file* and use EFW to pay the balance due in a single step using tax preparation software or through a tax professional. However, don't use EFW to make federal tax deposits. For more information on paying your taxes using EFW, go to *IRS.gov/EFW*.

Credit or debit card payments. You can pay the balance due shown on Form 945 by credit or debit card. Your payment will be processed by a payment processor who will charge a processing fee. Don't use a credit or debit card to make federal tax deposits. For more information on paying your taxes with a credit or debit card, go to *IRS.gov/PayByCard*.

Online payment agreement. You may be eligible to apply for an installment agreement online if you can't pay the full amount of tax you owe when you file your return. For more information, see *What if you can't pay in full*, later.

Sep 28, 2020

Cat. No. 20534D

Form 945 Instructions (Page 2)

Paid preparers. If you use a paid preparer to complete Form 945, the paid preparer must complete and sign the paid preparer's section of the form.

Outsourcing your tax duties. You're responsible to ensure that tax returns are filed and deposits and payments are made, even if you contract with a third party to perform these acts. You remain responsible if the third party fails to perform any required action. Before you choose to outsource any of your tax duties (that is, withholding, reporting, and paying over federal income tax) to a third-party payer, such as a payroll service provider or reporting agent, go to *IRS.gov/ OutsourcingPayrollDuties* for helpful information on this topic. For more information on the different types of third-party payer arrangements, see section 16 in Pub. 15.

How to get forms and publications. You can download or print some of the forms and publications you may need on *IRS.gov/Forms*. Otherwise, you can go to *IRS.gov/ OrderForms* to place an order and have forms mailed to you. You should receive your order within 10 business days.

Where can you get telephone help? For answers to your questions about completing Form 945 or tax deposit rules, you can call the IRS at 800-829-4933 (Business and Specialty Tax Line) or 800-829-4059 (TDD/TTY for persons who are deaf, hard of hearing, or have a speech disability) Monday–Friday from 7:00 a.m. to 7:00 p.m. local time (Alaska and Hawaii follow Pacific time).

Photographs of missing children. The IRS is a proud partner with the *National Center for Missing & Exploited Children® (NCMEC)*. Photographs of missing children selected by the Center may appear in instructions on pages that would otherwise be blank. You can help bring these children home by looking at the photographs and calling 1-800-THE-LOST (1-800-843-5678) if you recognize a child.

General Instructions

Purpose of Form 945

These instructions give you some background information about Form 945. They tell you who must file Form 945, how to complete it line by line, and when and where to file it.

Use Form 945 to report federal income tax withheld (or required to be withheld) from nonpayroll payments. Nonpayroll payments include:

• Pensions (including distributions from tax-favored retirement plans, for example, section 401(k), section 403(b), and governmental section 457(b) plans), annuities, and IRA distributions;
• Military retirement;
• Gambling winnings;
• Indian gaming profits;
• Certain government payments on which the recipient elected voluntary income tax withholding;
• Dividends and other distributions by an Alaska Native Corporation (ANC) on which the recipient elected voluntary income tax withholding; and
• Payments subject to backup withholding.

Report all federal income tax withholding from nonpayroll payments or distributions annually on one Form 945. Don't file more than one Form 945 for any calendar year.

All federal income tax withholding reported on Forms 1099 (for example, Form 1099-R, Distributions From Pensions, Annuities, Retirement or Profit-Sharing Plans, IRAs, Insurance Contracts, etc.; Form 1099-MISC, Miscellaneous Income; or Form 1099-NEC, Nonemployee Compensation) or Form W-2G, Certain Gambling Winnings, must be reported on Form 945.

Don't report federal income tax withholding from wages on Form 945. All federal income tax withholding and employment taxes reported on Form W-2, Wage and Tax Statement, must be reported on Form 941, Employer's QUARTERLY Federal Tax Return; Form 943, Employer's Annual Federal Tax Return for Agricultural Employees; Form 944, Employer's ANNUAL Federal Tax Return; Schedule H (Form 1040), Household Employment Taxes; or Form CT-1, Employer's Annual Railroad Retirement Tax Return, as appropriate.

Don't report on Form 945 federal income tax withheld on distributions to participants from nonqualified pension plans (including nongovernmental section 457(b) plans) and some other deferred compensation arrangements that are treated as wages and are reported on Form W-2. Report such withholding on Form 941 or Form 944. See *Distributions from nonqualified pension plans and deferred compensation plans* in the *Reminders* section of Pub. 15 for more information.

Compensation paid to H-2A visa holders. Generally, report compensation of $600 or more paid to foreign agricultural workers who entered the country on H-2A visas on Form W-2 and Form 943. However, if an H-2A visa worker didn't provide the employer with a taxpayer identification number, the employee is subject to backup withholding. The employer must report the wages and backup withholding on Form 1099-MISC. The employer must also report the backup withholding on Form 945, line 2. For more information on foreign agricultural workers on H-2A visas, go to *IRS.gov/H2A*.

Who Must File

If you withhold or are required to withhold federal income tax (including backup withholding) from nonpayroll payments, you must file Form 945. See *Purpose of Form 945*, earlier. You don't have to file Form 945 for those years in which you don't have a nonpayroll tax liability. Don't report on Form 945 withholding that is required to be reported on Form 1042, Annual Withholding Tax Return for U.S. Source Income of Foreign Persons.

If you file Form 945, you may also be required to file Form 945-A, Annual Record of Federal Tax Liability. See the line 7 instructions for details.

When To File

For 2020, file Form 945 by February 1, 2021. However, if you made deposits on time in full payment of the taxes for the year, you may file the return by February 10, 2021.

If we receive your return after the due date, we will treat your return as filed on time if the envelope containing your

-2-

Form 945 Instructions (Page 3)

return is properly addressed, contains sufficient postage, and is postmarked by the U.S. Postal Service on or before the due date, or sent by an IRS-designated private delivery service (PDS) on or before the due date. However, if you don't follow these guidelines, we will consider your return filed when it is actually received.

Where To File

You're encouraged to file Form 945 electronically. Go to *IRS.gov/EmploymentEfile* for more information on electronic filing. If you file a paper return, where you file depends on whether you include a payment with Form

945. Mail your return to the address listed for your location in the table below.

PDSs can't deliver to P.O. boxes. You must use the U.S. Postal Service to mail an item to a P.O. box address. Go to *IRS.gov/PDS* for the current list of PDSs. For the IRS mailing address to use if you're using a PDS, go to *IRS.gov/PDSstreetAddresses*. Select the mailing address listed on the webpage that is in the same state as the address to which you would mail returns filed without a payment, as shown in the table below.

Mailing Addresses for Form 945

If you're in . . .	Without a payment . . .	With a payment . . .
Connecticut, Delaware, District of Columbia, Georgia, Illinois, Indiana, Kentucky, Maine, Maryland, Massachusetts, Michigan, New Hampshire, New Jersey, New York, North Carolina, Ohio, Pennsylvania, Rhode Island, South Carolina, Tennessee, Vermont, Virginia, West Virginia, Wisconsin	Department of the Treasury Internal Revenue Service Kansas City, MO 64999-0042	Internal Revenue Service P.O. Box 806534 Cincinnati, OH 45280-6534
Alabama, Alaska, Arizona, Arkansas, California, Colorado, Florida, Hawaii, Idaho, Iowa, Kansas, Louisiana, Minnesota, Mississippi, Missouri, Montana, Nebraska, Nevada, New Mexico, North Dakota, Oklahoma, Oregon, South Dakota, Texas, Utah, Washington, Wyoming	Department of the Treasury Internal Revenue Service Ogden, UT 84201-0042	Internal Revenue Service P.O. Box 932300 Louisville, KY 40293-2300
No legal residence or principal place of business in any state	Internal Revenue Service P.O. Box 409101 Ogden, UT 84409	Internal Revenue Service P.O. Box 932300 Louisville, KY 40293-2300
Special filing address for exempt organizations; federal, state, and local governmental entities; and Indian tribal governmental entities, regardless of location	Department of the Treasury Internal Revenue Service Ogden, UT 84201-0042	Internal Revenue Service P.O. Box 932300 Louisville, KY 40293-2300

Employer Identification Number (EIN)

If you don't have an EIN, you may apply for one online by visiting *IRS.gov/EIN*. If the principal business was created or organized outside of the United States or U.S. territories, you may also apply for an EIN by calling 267-941-1099 (toll call).

You may also apply for an EIN by faxing or mailing Form SS-4 to the IRS. If you haven't received your EIN by the due date of Form 945, file a paper return and write "Applied For" and the date you applied in this entry space.

 If you're filing your tax return electronically, a valid EIN is required at the time the return is filed. If a valid EIN isn't provided, the return won't be accepted. This may result in penalties.

TIP *Always be sure the EIN on the form you file exactly matches the EIN the IRS assigned to your business. Don't use your social security number (SSN) or individual taxpayer identification number (ITIN) on forms that ask for an EIN. The name and EIN on Form 945 must match the name and EIN on your information returns where federal income tax withholding is reported (for example, backup withholding reported on Form 1099-NEC). Filing a Form 945 with an incorrect EIN or using another business's EIN may result in penalties and delays in processing your return.*

If You Change Your Business Name, Business Address, or Responsible Party

Notify the IRS immediately if you change your business name, business address, or responsible party.
• Write to the IRS office where you file your returns (using the *Without a payment* address under *Where To File*, earlier) to notify the IRS of any business name change. See Pub. 1635 to see if you need to apply for a new EIN.
• Complete and mail Form 8822-B to notify the IRS of a business address or responsible party change. Don't mail Form 8822-B with your Form 945. For a definition of "responsible party," see the Instructions for Form SS-4.

Penalties and Interest

There are penalties for filing Form 945 late and for paying or depositing taxes late, unless filing and/or paying late is due to reasonable cause and not due to willful neglect. See section 11 of Pub. 15 for more information on deposit penalties. Interest is charged on taxes paid late at a rate set by law. There are also penalties for failure to file information returns (for example, Forms 1099-MISC, 1099-NEC, 1099-R, or W-2G) and for failure to furnish payee statements to payees.

If you receive a notice about a penalty after you file this return, reply to the notice with an explanation and we will determine if you meet reasonable-cause criteria. Don't attach an explanation when you file your return.

Instructions for Form 945 (2020)   -3-

Form 945 Instructions (Page 4)

Use Form 843 to request abatement of assessed penalties or interest. Don't request abatement of assessed penalties or interest on Form 945 or Form 945-X.

 If taxes that must be withheld (that is, trust fund taxes) aren't withheld or aren't deposited or paid to the United States Treasury, the trust fund recovery penalty may apply. The penalty is 100% of the unpaid trust fund tax. If these unpaid taxes can't be immediately collected from the employer or business, the penalty may be imposed on all persons who are determined by the IRS to be responsible for collecting, accounting for, or paying over these taxes, and who acted willfully in not doing so. For more information, see section 11 of Pub. 15.

Voluntary Income Tax Withholding

States must allow unemployment compensation recipients to elect to have federal income tax withheld at a 10% rate. Recipients paid under the Railroad Unemployment Insurance Act may also elect withholding at a 10% rate.

Recipients of any of the following payments may request federal income tax withholding at a rate of 7%, 10%, 12%, or 22%.
• Social security and Tier 1 railroad retirement benefits.
• Certain crop disaster payments.
• Commodity Credit Corporation loans.
• Dividends and other distributions by an ANC.

The payee may request voluntary withholding on Form W-4V or you may develop your own substitute form. Any voluntary withholding on these payments must be reported on Form 945 (and on the required information return—Form 1099-DIV, Form 1099-G, Form SSA-1099, or Form RRB-1099) and is subject to the deposit rules.

Additional Information About Nonpayroll Payments

• Pub. 15-A includes information on federal income tax withholding from pensions and annuities (section 8).
• Pub. 15-T includes information on federal income tax withholding from Indian gaming profits.
• The Instructions for Forms 1099-R and 5498 provide information about pensions, annuities, IRAs, and military retirement.
• The Instructions for Forms W-2G and 5754 provide information on withholding from gambling winnings.
• Part N in the General Instructions for Certain Information Returns provides information on backup withholding.
• For more information about dividends and other distributions by an ANC, see Notice 2013-77, 2013-50 I.R.B. 632, available at *IRS.gov/irb/ 2013-50_IRB#NOT-2013-77*.
• Go to *IRS.gov/EmploymentTaxes* for additional information about employment taxes.

Depositing Withheld Taxes

Deposit all nonpayroll (Form 945) withheld federal income tax, including backup withholding, by EFT. Combine all Form 945 taxes for deposit purposes. Don't combine deposits for Forms 941, 943, 944, or Form CT-1 with deposits for Form 945. Also, don't combine Form 945 taxes with taxes for Forms 941, 943, 944, or Form CT-1 for purposes of determining any of the deposit rules discussed next, such as whether the $2,500 threshold is applicable, whether you're a monthly or semiweekly schedule depositor, or whether the $100,000 next-day deposit rule applies.

Generally, the deposit rules that apply to Form 941 also apply to Form 945. However, because Form 945 is an annual return, the rules for determining your deposit schedule (discussed below) are different from those for Form 941. See section 11 of Pub. 15 for a detailed discussion of the deposit rules.

TIP *If the total amount of tax for 2020 is less than $2,500, you're not required to make deposits during the year.*

Determining Your Deposit Schedule

There are two deposit schedules—**monthly** or **semiweekly**—for determining when you must deposit withheld federal income tax. These schedules tell you when a deposit is due after a tax liability arises (that is, you make a payment subject to federal income tax withholding, including backup withholding). Before the beginning of each calendar year, you must determine which of the two deposit schedules you must use.

For 2021, you're a monthly schedule depositor for Form 945 if the total tax reported on your 2019 Form 945 (line 3) was $50,000 or less. If the total tax reported for 2019 was more than $50,000, you're a semiweekly schedule depositor.

 If you're a monthly schedule depositor and accumulate a $100,000 liability or more on any day during a calendar month, your deposit schedule changes on the next day to semiweekly for the remainder of the year and for the following year. For more information, see the $100,000 Next-Day Deposit Rule in section 11 of Pub. 15.

Specific Instructions

Line A. Final Return

If you go out of business or end operations and you won't have to file Form 945 in the future, file a final return. Be sure to check the box on line A and enter the date that final nonpayroll payments were made. Also, attach a statement to your return showing the name of the person keeping the payment records and the address where those records will be kept.

If you sell or transfer your business during the year, you and the new owner must each file a Form 945 for the year in which the transfer occurred. Report only the taxes you withheld.

When two businesses merge, the continuing firm must file a return for the year in which the change took place and the other firm should file a final return.

Changing from one form of business to another, such as from a sole proprietorship to a partnership or

-4-

Form 945 Instructions (Page 5)

corporation, is considered a transfer. If a transfer occurs, you may need a new EIN. See Pub. 1635 and section 1 of Pub. 15 for more information.

Attach a statement to your return with all the following information.
• The new owner's name (or the new name of the business).
• Whether the business is now a sole proprietorship, partnership, or corporation.
• The kind of change that occurred (a sale or transfer).
• The date of the change.
• The name of the person keeping the payroll records and the address where those records will be kept.

If no sale or transfer occurred, or you don't know the name of the person to whom the business was sold or transferred, that fact should be included in the statement.

Completing Form 945

Enter dollars to the left of the preprinted line and cents to the right of it. Don't round entries to whole dollars. Always show an amount for cents, even if it is zero.

Line 1. Federal Income Tax Withheld

Enter the federal income tax that you withheld (or were required to withhold) from pensions (including distributions from tax-favored retirement plans, for example, section 401(k), section 403(b), and governmental section 457(b) plans), annuities, IRA distributions, military retirement, Indian gaming profits, and gambling winnings (regular gambling withholding only; backup withholding on gambling winnings is reported on line 2). Also, enter any voluntary amount that you withheld on certain government payments, and on dividends and other distributions by an ANC.

 Federal income tax withholding reported on Form W-2 must be reported on Form 941, Form 943, Form 944, or Schedule H (Form 1040), as appropriate.

Line 2. Backup Withholding

Enter any backup withholding that you withheld (or were required to withhold), including backup withholding on gambling winnings. See part N in the General Instructions for Certain Information Returns for more information on backup withholding.

Regulated investment companies (RICs) and real estate investment trusts (REITs) must report any backup withholding on Form 945 in the year that the dividends are actually paid. This includes January payments of dividends declared during October, November, and December of the prior year. See the Instructions for Form 1099-DIV for special reporting requirements.

Line 3. Total Taxes

Add lines 1 and 2. If total taxes are $2,500 or more, the amount reported on line 3 must equal the total liability for the year reported on line 7M of the Monthly Summary of Federal Tax Liability, or line M of Form 945-A.

Line 4. Total Deposits

Enter your total Form 945 deposits for the year, including any overpayment that you applied from filing Form 945-X

in 2020, and any overpayment that you applied from your 2019 return.

Line 5. Balance Due

If line 3 is more than line 4, enter the difference on line 5. Otherwise, see *Overpayment*, later. You don't have to pay if line 5 is under $1. Generally, you should have a balance due only if your total taxes for the year (line 3) are less than $2,500. If you made payments under the accuracy of deposits rule, see section 11 of Pub. 15.

If you were required to make federal tax deposits, pay the amount shown on line 5 by EFT. If you weren't required to make federal tax deposits or you're a monthly schedule depositor making a payment under the accuracy of deposits rule (see section 11 of Pub. 15), you may pay the amount shown on line 5 by EFT, credit card, debit card, check, money order, or EFW. For more information on electronic payment options, go to *IRS.gov/Payments*.

If you pay by EFT, credit card, or debit card, file your return using the *Without a payment* address under *Where To File*, earlier. Don't file Form 945-V, Payment Voucher. If you pay by check or money order, make it payable to "United States Treasury." Enter your EIN, "Form 945," and "2020" on your check or money order. Complete Form 945-V and enclose with Form 945.

If line 3 is $2,500 or more and you deposited all taxes when due, the amount on line 5 should be zero.

 If you didn't make deposits as required and instead pay the taxes with Form 945, you may be subject to a penalty.

What if you can't pay in full? If you can't pay the full amount of tax you owe, you can apply for an installment agreement online.

You can apply for an installment agreement online if:
• You can't pay the full amount shown on line 5,
• The total amount you owe is $25,000 or less, and
• You can pay the liability in full in 24 months.

To apply using the Online Payment Agreement Application, go to *IRS.gov/OPA*.

Under an installment agreement, you can pay what you owe in monthly installments. There are certain conditions you must meet to enter into and maintain an installment agreement, such as paying the liability within 24 months, and making all required deposits and timely filing tax returns during the length of the agreement.

If your installment agreement is accepted, you will be charged a fee and you will be subject to penalties and interest on the amount of tax not paid by the due date of the return.

Line 6. Overpayment

If line 4 is more than line 3, enter the difference on line 6. **Never make an entry on both lines 5 and 6.**

If you deposited more than the correct amount for the year, you can have the overpayment refunded or applied to your next return by checking the appropriate box. Check only one box below line 6. If you don't check either box or if you check both boxes, generally we will apply the overpayment to your next return. Regardless of any box

Form 945 Instructions (Page 6)

you check or don't check on line 6, we may apply your overpayment to any past due tax account that is shown in our records under your EIN.

If line 6 is under $1, we will send a refund or apply it to your next return only if you ask us in writing to do so.

Line 7. Monthly Summary of Federal Tax Liability

 This is a summary of your monthly tax liability, not a summary of deposits made. If line 3 is less than $2,500, don't complete line 7 or Form 945-A.

Complete line 7 only if you were a **monthly schedule depositor** for the entire year and line 3 is $2,500 or more. See *Determining Your Deposit Schedule*, earlier.

 The amount entered on line 7M must equal the amount reported on line 3.

Report your liabilities on Form 945-A instead of on line 7 if either of the following applies.
• You were a **semiweekly schedule depositor** during 2020. Don't complete entries A through M of line 7. Instead, complete and file Form 945-A with Form 945.
• You were a **monthly schedule depositor** for 2020 and during any month you accumulated nonpayroll taxes of $100,000 or more. Because this converted you to a semiweekly schedule depositor for the remainder of 2020 (and for 2021), you must report your liabilities on Form 945-A for the entire year. Don't complete entries A through M of line 7. For more information, see the *$100,000 Next-Day Deposit Rule* in section 11 of Pub. 15.

Third-Party Designee

If you want to allow an employee, a paid tax preparer, or another person to discuss your Form 945 with the IRS, check the "Yes" box in the *Third-Party Designee* section of Form 945. Enter the name, phone number, and five-digit personal identification number (PIN) of the specific person to speak with—not the name of the firm that prepared your return. The designee may choose any five numbers as his or her PIN.

By checking "Yes," you authorize the IRS to talk to the person you named (your designee) about any questions we may have while we process your return. You also authorize your designee to do all of the following.
• Give us any information that is missing from your return.
• Call us for information about the processing of your return.
• Respond to certain IRS notices that you have shared with your designee about math errors and return preparation. The IRS won't send notices to your designee.

You're not authorizing your designee to bind you to anything (including additional tax liability) or to otherwise represent you before the IRS. If you want to expand the designee's authorization, see Pub. 947.

The authorization will automatically expire 1 year from the due date (without regard to extensions) for filing your Form 945. If you or your designee wants to terminate the authorization, write to the IRS office for your location using the *Without a payment* address under *Where To File*, earlier.

Who Must Sign (Approved Roles)

The following persons are authorized to sign the return for each type of business entity.
• **Sole proprietorship**—The individual who owns the business.
• **Corporation (including a limited liability company (LLC) treated as a corporation)**—The president, vice president, or other principal officer duly authorized to sign.
• **Partnership (including an LLC treated as a partnership) or unincorporated organization**—A responsible and duly authorized partner, member, or officer having knowledge of its affairs.
• **Single-member LLC treated as a disregarded entity for federal tax purposes**—The owner of the LLC or a principal officer duly authorized to sign.
• **Trust or estate**—The fiduciary.

Form 945 may also be signed by a duly authorized agent of the taxpayer if a valid power of attorney has been filed.

Alternative signature method. Corporate officers or duly authorized agents may sign Form 945 by rubber stamp, mechanical device, or computer software program. For details and required documentation, see Rev. Proc. 2005-39, 2005-28 I.R.B. 82, available at *IRS.gov/irb/2005-28_IRB#RP-2005-39*.

Paid Preparer Use Only

A paid preparer must sign Form 945 and provide the information in the *Paid Preparer Use Only* section if the preparer was paid to prepare Form 945 and isn't an employee of the filing entity. Paid preparers must sign paper returns with a manual signature. The preparer must give you a copy of the return in addition to the copy to be filed with the IRS.

If you're a paid preparer, enter your Preparer Tax Identification Number (PTIN) in the space provided. Include your complete address. If you work for a firm, enter the firm's name and the EIN of the firm. You can apply for a PTIN online or by filing Form W-12. For more information about applying for a PTIN online, go to *IRS.gov/PTIN*. You can't use your PTIN in place of the EIN of the tax preparation firm.

Generally, don't complete this section if you're filing the return as a reporting agent and have a valid Form 8655 on file with the IRS. However, a reporting agent must complete this section if the reporting agent offered legal advice, for example, advising the client on determining whether federal income tax withholding is required on certain payments.

Privacy Act and Paperwork Reduction Act Notice. We ask for the information on Form 945 to carry out the Internal Revenue laws of the United States. We need it to figure and collect the right amount of tax. Sections 3402, 3405, and 3406 of the Internal Revenue Code require taxpayers to pay over to the IRS federal income tax withheld from certain nonpayroll payments and distributions, including backup withholding. Form 945 is used to report these withholdings. Section 6011 requires you to provide the requested information if the tax is applicable to you. Section 6109 requires you to provide

-6-   **Instructions for Form 945 (2020)**

Form 945 Instructions (Page 7)

your identification number. If you fail to provide this information in a timely manner, or provide false or fraudulent information, you may be subject to penalties.

You're not required to provide the information requested on a form that is subject to the Paperwork Reduction Act unless the form displays a valid OMB control number. Books or records relating to a form or instructions must be retained as long as their contents may become material in the administration of any Internal Revenue law.

Generally, tax returns and return information are confidential, as required by section 6103. However, section 6103 allows or requires the IRS to disclose or give the information shown on your tax return to others described in the Code. For example, we may disclose your tax information to the Department of Justice for civil and criminal litigation, and to cities, states, the District of Columbia, and U.S. commonwealths and possessions for use in administering their tax laws. We may also disclose this information to other countries under a tax treaty, to federal and state agencies to enforce federal nontax criminal laws, or to federal law enforcement and intelligence agencies to combat terrorism.

The time needed to complete and file Form 945 will vary depending on individual circumstances. The estimated average time is: **Recordkeeping,** 5 hr., 58 min.; **Learning about the law or the form,** 24 min.; and **Preparing and sending the form to the IRS,** 30 min. If you have comments concerning the accuracy of these time estimates or suggestions for making Form 945 simpler, we would be happy to hear from you. You can send us comments from *IRS.gov/FormComments*. Or you can send your comments to the Internal Revenue Service, Tax Forms and Publications Division, 1111 Constitution Ave. NW, IR-6526, Washington, DC 20224. Don't send Form 945 to this address. Instead, see *Where To File*, earlier.

Form 945-A (Page 1)

Form **945-A**	**Annual Record of Federal Tax Liability**	OMB No. 1545-1430

(Rev. December 2020)
Department of the Treasury
Internal Revenue Service

► Go to *www.irs.gov/Form945A* for instructions and the latest information.
► File with Form 945, 945-X, CT-1, CT-1 X, 944, or 944-X.

Calendar Year

Name (as shown on Form 945, 945-X, CT-1, CT-1 X, 944, or 944-X)   Employer identification number (EIN)

You must complete this form if you're a semiweekly schedule depositor or became one because your accumulated tax liability during any month was $100,000 or more. Show tax liability here, not deposits. (The IRS gets deposit data from electronic funds transfers.) Don't change your current year tax liability by adjustments reported on any Form 945-X, CT-1 X, or 944-X.

	January Tax Liability				February Tax Liability				March Tax Liability	
1		17		1		17		1		17
2		18		2		18		2		18
3		19		3		19		3		19
4		20		4		20		4		20
5		21		5		21		5		21
6		22		6		22		6		22
7		23		7		23		7		23
8		24		8		24		8		24
9		25		9		25		9		25
10		26		10		26		10		26
11		27		11		27		11		27
12		28		12		28		12		28
13		29		13		29		13		29
14		30		14				14		30
15		31		15				15		31
16				16				16		
A Total for month ►				B Total for month ►				C Total for month ►		

	April Tax Liability				May Tax Liability				June Tax Liability	
1		17		1		17		1		17
2		18		2		18		2		18
3		19		3		19		3		19
4		20		4		20		4		20
5		21		5		21		5		21
6		22		6		22		6		22
7		23		7		23		7		23
8		24		8		24		8		24
9		25		9		25		9		25
10		26		10		26		10		26
11		27		11		27		11		27
12		28		12		28		12		28
13		29		13		29		13		29
14		30		14		30		14		30
15				15		31		15		
16				16				16		
D Total for month ►				E Total for month ►				F Total for month ►		

For Paperwork Reduction Act Notice, see the separate instructions.   Cat. No. 14733M   Form **945-A** (Rev. 12-2020)

Form 945-A (Page 2)

Form 945-A (Rev. 12-2020)

July Tax Liability				August Tax Liability				September Tax Liability			
1		17		1		17		1		17	
2		18		2		18		2		18	
3		19		3		19		3		19	
4		20		4		20		4		20	
5		21		5		21		5		21	
6		22		6		22		6		22	
7		23		7		23		7		23	
8		24		8		24		8		24	
9		25		9		25		9		25	
10		26		10		26		10		26	
11		27		11		27		11		27	
12		28		12		28		12		28	
13		29		13		29		13		29	
14		30		14		30		14		30	
15		31		15		31		15			
16				16				16			
G Total for month ▶				H Total for month ▶				I Total for month ▶			

October Tax Liability				November Tax Liability				December Tax Liability			
1		17		1		17		1		17	
2		18		2		18		2		18	
3		19		3		19		3		19	
4		20		4		20		4		20	
5		21		5		21		5		21	
6		22		6		22		6		22	
7		23		7		23		7		23	
8		24		8		24		8		24	
9		25		9		25		9		25	
10		26		10		26		10		26	
11		27		11		27		11		27	
12		28		12		28		12		28	
13		29		13		29		13		29	
14		30		14		30		14		30	
15		31		15				15		31	
16				16				16			
J Total for month ▶				K Total for month ▶				L Total for month ▶			

M Total tax liability for the year (add lines **A** through **L**). This must equal line 3 on Form 945 (line 19 on Form CT-1, line 9 on Form 944). . . . . ▶

Form **945-A** (Rev. 12-2020)

Instructions for Form 945-A

Department of the Treasury
Internal Revenue Service

(December 2020)

Annual Record of Federal Tax Liability

Section references are to the Internal Revenue Code unless otherwise noted.

Future Developments

For the latest information about developments related to Form 945-A and its instructions, such as legislation enacted after they were published, go to *IRS.gov/ Form945A*.

What's New

Adjusting tax liability for nonrefundable credits claimed on Form CT-1, lines 16 and 17, or Form 944, lines 8a, 8b, and 8c. See *Adjusting Tax Liability for Nonrefundable Credits Claimed on Form CT-1, Lines 16 and 17, or Form 944, Lines 8a, 8b, and 8c*, later, for instructions on how to report on Form 945-A adjustments to your tax liabilities for the qualified small business payroll tax credit for increasing research activities (Form 944 only), the credit for qualified sick and family leave wages (compensation), and the employee retention credit.

Adjusting tax liability for the deferred amount of social security tax (Tier 1 Employer tax and/or Tier 1 Employee tax) that you pay or deposit in 2020. See *Adjusting tax liability for the deferred amount of social security tax (Tier 1 Employer tax and/or Tier 1 Employee tax) that you pay or deposit in 2020*, later, for instructions on how to report your tax liabilities on Form 945-A if you defer social security tax (Tier 1 Employer tax and/or Tier 1 Employee tax) and subsequently pay or deposit that deferred amount in the same year it was deferred.

Reminders

Reporting prior period adjustments. Prior period adjustments are reported on Form 945-X, Adjusted Annual Return of Withheld Federal Income Tax or Claim for Refund; Form CT-1 X, Adjusted Employer's Annual Railroad Retirement Tax Return or Claim for Refund; or Form 944-X, Adjusted Employer's ANNUAL Federal Tax Return or Claim for Refund, and aren't taken into account when figuring the tax liability for the current year.

When you file Form 945-A with your Form 945, CT-1, or 944, don't change your current year tax liability by adjustments reported on any Form 945-X, CT-1 X, or 944-X.

Amended Form 945-A. If you have been assessed a failure-to-deposit (FTD) penalty, you may be able to file an amended Form 945-A. See *Correcting Previously Reported Tax Liability*, later.

General Instructions

Purpose of Form 945-A

Use Form 945-A to report your federal tax liability (based on the dates payments were made or wages were paid) for the following tax returns.

• Forms 945 and 945-X for federal income tax withholding on nonpayroll payments. Nonpayroll withholding includes backup withholding and federal income tax withholding on pensions, annuities, IRAs, Indian gaming profits, gambling winnings, military retirement, certain government payments on which the recipient elected voluntary income tax withholding, and dividends and other distributions by an Alaska Native Corporation on which the recipient elected voluntary income tax withholding.
• Forms CT-1 and CT-1 X for both employee and employer share of Tier 1 and Tier 2 taxes.
• Forms 944 and 944-X for federal income tax withheld plus both employee and employer share of social security and Medicare taxes.

Don't reduce your liability reported on Form 945-A for Form 944 by the deferred amount of any employer share of social security tax reported on Form 944, line 10b, or by the deferred amount of any employee share of social security tax reported on Form 944, line 10c. Don't reduce your liability reported on Form 945-A for Form CT-1 by the deferred amount of the Tier 1 Employer tax reported on Form CT-1, line 21, or by the deferred amount of any Tier 1 Employee tax reported on Form CT-1, line 22. See the *Caution* under *Enter Your Tax Liability by Month*, later. Don't use Form 945-A to show federal tax deposits. The IRS gets deposit data from electronic funds transfers.

Forms 944(SP) and 944-X (SP)

If you're a semiweekly schedule depositor who files Formulario 944(SP), Declaración Federal ANUAL de Impuestos del Patrono o Empleador, you should use Formulario 943A-PR, Registro de la Obligación Contributiva Federal del Patrono Agrícola, to report your tax liability. You should also file Form 943A-PR if you file Form 944-X (SP) and you need to amend a previously filed Form 943A-PR.

> ⚠ *The IRS uses Form 945-A to match the tax liability you reported on the returns indicated earlier with your deposits. The IRS also uses Form 945-A to determine if you have deposited your tax liabilities on time. Unless Form 945-A is properly completed and filed (if applicable) with your tax return, the IRS may propose an "averaged" FTD penalty. See* Deposit Penalties *in section 11 of Pub. 15,* Employer's Tax Guide, *for more information.*

Dec 16, 2020   Cat. No. 74488U

Form 945-A Instructions (Page 2)

Who Must File?

Semiweekly schedule depositors must complete and file Form 945-A with their tax return. Don't file Form 945-A if your net tax liability for the return period is less than $2,500. Don't file this form if you're a monthly schedule depositor unless you accumulated a tax liability of $100,000 during any month of the year. Monthly schedule depositors who accumulate $100,000 or more of tax liability on any day of a calendar month become semiweekly schedule depositors on the next day and remain so for at least the remainder of the year and for the next year, and must also complete and file Form 945-A for the entire year. The $100,000 tax liability threshold requiring a next-day deposit is determined before you consider any reduction of your liability for nonrefundable credits. See *IRS.gov/ETD* for more information.

The deposit rules, including the $100,000 Next-Day Deposit Rule, are explained in section 11 of Pub. 15 and in the instructions for your tax return.

When Must You File?

File Form 945-A with your Form 945, CT-1, or 944 every year when Form 945, CT-1, or 944 is due. See the instructions for these forms for their due dates.

Specific Instructions

Completing Form 945-A

Enter Your Business Information

Carefully enter your employer identification number (EIN) and name at the top of the form. Make sure that they exactly match the name of your business and the EIN that the IRS assigned to your business and also agree with the name and EIN shown on the attached Form 945, 945-X, CT-1, CT-1 X, 944, or 944-X.

Calendar Year

Enter the calendar year of the Form 945, 945-X, CT-1, CT-1 X, 944, or 944-X to which Form 945-A is attached.

Form 945 Filers

Don't complete entries A through M of the Monthly Summary of Federal Tax Liability (Form 945, line 7). Be sure to mark the semiweekly schedule depositor checkbox above line 7 on Form 945.

Form CT-1 Filers

Don't complete the Monthly Summary of Railroad Retirement Tax Liability (Part II of Form CT-1).

Form 944 Filers

On Form 944, check the box for "Line 9 is $2,500 or more" at line 13, and leave lines 13a through 13m blank.

Enter Your Tax Liability by Month

Each numbered space on Form 945-A corresponds to a date during the year. Enter your tax liabilities in the spaces that correspond to the dates you paid wages to your employees or made nonpayroll payments, not the date liabilities were accrued or deposits were made. The total

tax liability for the year (line M) must equal net taxes on Form 945, line 3; Form CT-1, line 19 (line 15 for years before 2020); or Form 944, line 9. Enter the monthly totals on lines A, B, C, D, E, F, G, H, I, J, K, and L. Enter the total for the year on line M.

For example, if you're a Form 945 filer, and you became liable for a pension distribution on December 31, 2019, but didn't make the distribution until January 7, 2020, you would:
• Go to January on Form 945-A filed with your 2020 return, and
• Enter your tax liability on line 7 because line 7 represents the seventh day of the month.

Example 1. Cedar Co., which has a semiweekly deposit schedule, makes periodic payments on gambling winnings on the 15th day of each month. On December 24, 2020, in addition to its periodic payments, it withheld from a payment on gambling winnings under the backup withholding rules. Since Cedar Co. is a semiweekly schedule depositor, it must record these nonpayroll withholding liabilities on Form 945-A. It must report tax liabilities on line 15 for each month and line 24 for December.

Cedar Co. enters the monthly totals on lines A through L. It adds these monthly subtotals and enters the total tax liability for the year on line M. The amount on line M should equal Form 945, line 3.

Example 2. Fir Co. is a semiweekly schedule depositor. During January, it withheld federal income tax on pension distributions as follows: $52,000 on January 10 and $35,000 on January 24. Since Fir Co. is a semiweekly schedule depositor, it must record its federal income tax withholding liabilities on Form 945-A. It must record $52,000 on line 10 and $35,000 on line 24 for January.

Example 3. Elm Co. is a new business and monthly schedule depositor for 2020. During January, it withheld federal income tax on nonpayroll payments as follows: $2,000 on January 10 and $99,000 on January 24. The deposit rules require that a monthly schedule depositor begin depositing on a semiweekly deposit schedule when a $100,000 or more tax liability is accumulated on any day within a month (see section 11 of Pub. 15 for details). Since Elm Co. accumulated $101,000 ($2,000 + $99,000) on January 24, 2020, it became a semiweekly schedule depositor on January 25, 2020. Elm Co. must complete Form 945-A and file it with Form 945. It must record $2,000 on line 10 and $99,000 on line 24 for January. No entries should be made on Form 945, line 7, even though Elm Co. was a monthly schedule depositor until January 25.

⚠️ **CAUTION** *Form 944 filers. Your total liability for the year must equal line 9 on Form 944; therefore, don't reduce your total liability reported on Form 945-A by the deferred amount of the employer or employee share of social security tax, the refundable portion of the credit for qualified sick and family leave wages, or the refundable portion of the employee retention credit. The deferred amount of the employer share of social security tax reported on Form 944, line 10b, and the deferred amount of the employee share of social security tax reported on Form 944, line 10c, don't reflect deferred*

Form 945-A Instructions (Page 3)

liabilities, but instead postponed due dates for payment. See the Instructions for Form 944 for more information.

⚠ **CAUTION** *Form CT-1 filers.* Your total liability for the year must equal line 19 on Form CT-1; therefore, don't reduce your total liability reported on Form 945-A by the deferred amount of the Tier 1 Employer tax and/or Tier 1 Employee tax, the refundable portion of the credit for qualified sick and family leave compensation, or the refundable portion of the employee retention credit. The deferred amount of the Tier 1 Employer tax reported on Form CT-1, line 21, and the deferred amount of the Tier 1 Employee tax reported on Form CT-1, line 22, don't reflect deferred liabilities, but instead postponed due dates for payment. See the Instructions for Form CT-1 for more information.

Adjusting Tax Liability for Nonrefundable Credits Claimed on Form CT-1, Lines 16 and 17, or Form 944, Lines 8a, 8b, and 8c

💡 **TIP** *The credits discussed in this section aren't available on Form 945. The qualified small business payroll tax credit for increasing research activities is available only on Form 944.*

Semiweekly schedule depositors must account for nonrefundable credits claimed on Form CT-1, lines 16 and 17, or Form 944, lines 8a, 8b, and 8c, when reporting their tax liabilities on Form 945-A. The total tax liability for the year must equal the amount reported on Form CT-1, line 19, or Form 944, line 9. Failure to account for the nonrefundable credits on Form 945-A may cause Form 945-A to report more than the total tax liability reported on Form CT-1, line 19, or Form 944, line 9. Don't reduce your daily tax liability reported on Form 945-A below zero.

Qualified small business payroll tax credit for increasing research activities (Form 944, line 8a). The qualified small business payroll tax credit for increasing research activities is limited to the employer share of social security tax on wages paid in the quarter that begins after the income tax return electing the credit has been filed. In completing Form 945-A, you take into account the payroll tax credit against the liability for the employer share of social security tax starting with the first payroll payment of the quarter that includes payments of wages subject to social security tax to your employees. The credit may be taken to the extent of the employer share of social security tax on wages associated with the first payroll payment, and then to the extent of the employer share of social security tax associated with succeeding payroll payments in the quarter until the credit is used. Consistent with the entries on Form 945-A, the payroll tax credit should be taken into account in making deposits of employment tax. If any payroll tax credit is remaining at the end of the quarter that has not been completely used because it exceeds the employer share of social security tax for the quarter, the excess credit may be carried forward to the succeeding quarter and allowed as a payroll tax credit for the succeeding quarter. The payroll tax credit may not be taken as a credit against income tax withholding, Medicare tax, or the employee share of social security tax. Also, the remaining payroll tax

credit may not be carried back and taken as a credit against wages paid from preceding quarters that are reported on the same Form 944 or on Forms 944 for preceding years. If an amount of payroll tax credit is unused at the end of the calendar year because it is in excess of the employer share of social security tax on wages paid during the applicable quarters in the calendar year, the remaining payroll tax credit may be carried forward to the first quarter of the succeeding calendar year as a payroll tax credit against the employer share of social security tax on wages paid in that quarter. For more information about the payroll tax credit, go to *IRS.gov/ ResearchPayrollTC*.

Example. Rose Co. is an employer with a calendar tax year that filed its timely income tax return on April 15, 2020. Rose Co. elected to take the qualified small business payroll tax credit for increasing research activities on Form 6765. The third quarter of 2020 is the first quarter that begins after Rose Co. filed the income tax return making the payroll tax credit election. Therefore, the payroll tax credit applies against Rose Co.'s share of social security tax on wages paid to employees in the third quarter of 2020. Rose Co. is a semiweekly schedule depositor. Rose Co. completes Form 945-A by reducing the amount of liability entered for the first payroll payment in the third quarter of 2020 that includes wages subject to social security tax by the lesser of (1) its share of social security tax on the wages, or (2) the available payroll tax credit. If the payroll tax credit elected is more than Rose Co.'s share of social security tax on the first payroll payment of the quarter, the excess payroll tax credit would be carried forward to succeeding payroll payments in the third quarter until it is used. If the amount of the payroll tax credit exceeds Rose Co.'s share of social security tax on wages paid to its employees in the third quarter, the excess credit would be treated as a payroll tax credit against its share of social security tax on wages paid in the fourth quarter. If the amount of the payroll tax credit remaining exceeded Rose Co.'s share of social security tax on wages paid in the fourth quarter, it could be carried forward and treated as a payroll tax credit for the first quarter of 2021.

Nonrefundable portion of credit for qualified sick and family leave compensation (Form CT-1, line 16). Follow the instructions under *Part II. Record of Railroad Retirement Tax Liability* in the Instructions for Form CT-1 to adjust your tax liability on Form 945-A.

Nonrefundable portion of credit for qualified sick and family leave wages (Form 944, line 8b). The nonrefundable portion of the credit for qualified sick and family leave wages is limited to the employer share of social security tax on wages paid in the year that is remaining after that share is first reduced by any credit claimed on Form 944, line 8a, for the qualified small business payroll tax credit for increasing research activities, and/or any credit to be claimed on Form 5884-C, line 11, for the work opportunity credit for qualified tax-exempt organizations hiring qualified veterans. In completing Form 945-A, you take into account the nonrefundable portion of the credit for qualified sick and family leave wages (including the qualified health plan expenses and employer share of Medicare tax allocable

Form 945-A Instructions (Page 4)

to those wages) against the liability for the first payroll payment of the year, but not below zero. Then reduce the liability for each successive payroll payment in the year until the nonrefundable portion of the credit is used. Any credit for qualified sick and family leave wages that is remaining at the end of the year because it exceeds the employer share of social security tax is claimed on Form 944, line 10d, as a refundable credit. The refundable portion of the credit doesn't reduce the liability reported on Form 945-A. For more information about the credit for qualified sick and family leave wages, including the dates for which the credit may be claimed, go to *IRS.gov/PLC*.

Example. Maple Co. is a semiweekly schedule depositor that pays employees every Friday. Maple Co. had pay dates every Friday of 2020 starting January 3, 2020. Maple Co. paid qualified sick and family leave wages on May 1 and May 8. The nonrefundable portion of the credit for qualified sick and family leave wages for the year is $10,000. On Form 945-A, Maple Co. will use the $10,000 to reduce the liability for the January 3 pay date, but not below zero. If any nonrefundable portion of the credit remains, Maple Co. applies it to the liability for the January 10 pay date, then the January 17 pay date, and so forth until the entire $10,000 is used.

Nonrefundable portion of employee retention credit (Form CT-1, line 17). Follow the instructions under *Part II. Record of Railroad Retirement Tax Liability* in the Instructions for Form CT-1 to adjust your tax liability on Form 945-A.

Nonrefundable portion of employee retention credit (Form 944, line 8c). The nonrefundable portion of the employee retention credit is limited to the employer share of social security tax on wages paid in the year that is remaining after that share is first reduced by any credit claimed on Form 944, line 8a, for the qualified small business payroll tax credit for increasing research activities; or any credit to be claimed on Form 5884-C, line 11, for the work opportunity credit for qualified tax-exempt organizations hiring qualified veterans; and/or any credit claimed on Form 944, line 8b, for the nonrefundable portion of the credit for qualified sick and family leave wages. In completing Form 945-A, you take into account the nonrefundable portion of the employee retention credit against the liability for the first payroll payment of the year, but not below zero. Then reduce the liability for each successive payroll payment in the year until the nonrefundable portion of the credit is used. Any employee retention credit that is remaining at the end of the year because it exceeds the employer share of social security tax is claimed on Form 944, line 10e, as a refundable credit. The refundable portion of the credit doesn't reduce the liability reported on Form 945-A. For more information about the employee retention credit, including the dates for which the credit may be claimed, go to *IRS.gov/ERC*.

Example. Maple Co. is a semiweekly schedule depositor that pays employees every Friday. Maple Co. had pay dates every Friday of 2020 starting January 3, 2020. Maple Co. paid qualified wages for the employee retention credit on May 1 and May 8. The nonrefundable portion of the employee retention credit for the year is $10,000. On Form 945-A, Maple Co. will use the $10,000 to reduce the liability for the January 3 pay date, but not

below zero. If any nonrefundable portion of the credit remains, Maple Co. applies it to the liability for the January 10 pay date, then the January 17 pay date, and so forth until the entire $10,000 is used.

TIP *You may reduce your deposits by the amount of the nonrefundable and refundable portions of the credit for qualified sick and family leave wages (compensation), the nonrefundable and refundable portions of the employee retention credit, and any deferred employment taxes. For more information on reducing deposits, see Notice 2020-22, 2020-17 I.R.B. 664, available at IRS.gov/irb/2020-17_IRB#NOT-2022-22; Notice 2020-65, 2020-38 I.R.B. 567, available at IRS.gov/irb/2020-38_IRB#NOT-2020-65; and IRS.gov/ETD. Also see IRS.gov/ERC and IRS.gov/PLC for more information, including examples, about reducing deposits.*

Adjusting tax liability for the deferred amount of social security tax (Tier 1 Employer tax and/or Tier 1 Employee tax) that you pay or deposit in 2020. If you defer the employer and/or employee share of social security tax (Tier 1 Employer tax and/or Tier 1 Employee tax) and subsequently pay or deposit that deferred amount during 2020, you should report the amount of the payment or deposit on Form 945-A on the date of the payment or deposit and not the date of liability. You shouldn't include any portion of the deferred amount of social security taxes (Tier 1 Employer tax and/or Tier 1 Employee tax) already paid or deposited by December 31, 2020, on Form 944, line 10b or 10c (or Form CT-1, line 21 or 22).

Example. If you're a semiweekly schedule depositor that has an employment tax liability of $10,000 every 2 weeks and you defer $2,000 of the employer share of social security tax from your August 26, 2020, deposit for the August 19, 2020, pay date, but you deposit your deferred amount of $2,000 together with your deposit of $10,000 on September 23, 2020, for the September 16, 2020, pay date, you would report $8,000 for your August 19, 2020, tax liability ($10,000 minus $2,000) and $12,000 for your September 16, 2020, tax liability ($10,000 plus $2,000) on Form 945-A.

For more information about the deferral of the employer and employee share of social security tax (Tier 1 Employer tax and/or Tier 1 Employee tax), including the dates the payment may be deferred, see the Instructions for Form CT-1, the Instructions for Form 944, and *IRS.gov/ETD*.

Correcting Previously Reported Tax Liability

Semiweekly schedule depositors. If you have been assessed an FTD penalty and you made an error on Form 945-A and the correction won't change the total liability you reported on Form 945-A, you may be able to reduce your penalty by filing an amended Form 945-A.

Example. You reported a tax liability of $3,000 on January 1. However, the liability was actually for March. Prepare an amended Form 945-A showing the $3,000 liability on March 1. Also, you must enter the liabilities previously reported for the year that didn't change. Write "Amended" at the top of Form 945-A. The IRS will refigure the penalty and notify you of any change in the penalty.

Instructions for Form 945-A (12-2020)

Form 945-A Instructions (Page 5)

Monthly schedule depositors. You can file Form 945-A if you have been assessed an FTD penalty and you made an error on the monthly tax liability section of Form 945, CT-1, or 944. When completing Form 945-A for this situation, only enter the monthly totals. The daily entries aren't required.

Where to file. File your amended Form 945-A, or, for monthly schedule depositors, your original Form 945-A at the address provided in the penalty notice you received. If you're filing an amended Form 945-A, you don't have to submit your original Form 945-A.

Forms 945-X, CT-1 X, and 944-X

You may need to file an amended Form 945-A with Forms 945-X, CT-1 X, or 944-X to avoid or reduce an FTD penalty.

Tax decrease. If you're filing Form 945-X, CT-1 X, or 944-X, you can file an amended Form 945-A with the form if both of the following apply.

1. You have a tax decrease.

2. You were assessed an FTD penalty.

File your amended Form 945-A with Form 945-X, CT-1 X, or 944-X. The total liability reported on your amended Form 945-A must equal the corrected amount of tax reported on Form 945-X, CT-1 X, or 944-X. If your penalty is decreased, the IRS will include the penalty decrease with your tax decrease.

Tax increase—Form 945-X, CT-1 X, or 944-X filed timely. If you're filing a timely Form 945-X, CT-1 X, or 944-X showing a tax increase, don't file an amended Form 945-A, unless you were assessed an FTD penalty caused by an incorrect, incomplete, or missing Form 945-A. Don't include the tax increase reported on Form 945-X, CT-1 X, or 944-X on an amended Form 945-A you file.

Tax increase—Form 945-X, CT-1 X, or 944-X filed late. If you owe tax and are filing late, that is, after the due date of the return for the filing period in which you discovered the error, you must file the form with an amended Form 945-A. Otherwise, the IRS may assess an "averaged" FTD penalty.

The total tax reported on line M of Form 945-A must match the corrected tax (Form 945, line 3; Form 944, line 9; Form CT-1, line 19 (line 15 for years before 2020)), combined with any correction reported on Form 945-X,

line 5; Form 944-X, line 18; or Form CT-1 X, line 19, for the year, less any previous abatements and interest-free tax assessments.

⚠ *Form CT-1 X will be revised in March 2021 and Form 944-X will be revised in February 2021. If* **CAUTION** *you're using the March 2021 revision of Form CT-1 X or the February 2021 revision of Form 944-X, the total tax reported on the "Total liability for the year" line of the amended Form 945-A must match the corrected tax (Form CT-1, line 19 (line 15 for years before 2020), combined with any correction reported on Form CT-1 X, line 21; or Form 944, line 9, combined with any correction reported on Form 944-X, line 22) for the year, less any previous abatements and interest-free assessments.*

Paperwork Reduction Act Notice. We ask for the information on this form to carry out the Internal Revenue laws of the United States. You're required to give us the information. We need it to ensure that you're complying with these laws and to allow us to figure and collect the right amount of tax.

You're not required to provide the information requested on a form that is subject to the Paperwork Reduction Act unless the form displays a valid OMB control number. Books or records relating to a form or its instructions must be retained as long as their contents may become material in the administration of any Internal Revenue law. Generally, tax returns and return information are confidential, as required by Code section 6103.

The time needed to complete and file this form will vary depending on individual circumstances. The estimated average time is:

Recordkeeping	6 hr., 27min.
Learning about the law or the form	6 min.
Preparing and sending the form to the IRS . .	12 min.

If you have comments concerning the accuracy of these time estimates or suggestions for making this form simpler, we would be happy to hear from you. You can write to the IRS at the address listed in the Privacy Act Notice for your tax return.

Instructions for Form 945-A (12-2020)   -5-

Form W-2 (Page 1)

22222	VOID ☐	a Employee's social security number	For Official Use Only ▶ OMB No. 1545-0008	

b Employer identification number (EIN)

	1 Wages, tips, other compensation	2 Federal income tax withheld

c Employer's name, address, and ZIP code

3 Social security wages	4 Social security tax withheld
5 Medicare wages and tips	6 Medicare tax withheld
7 Social security tips	8 Allocated tips

d Control number

9	10 Dependent care benefits

e Employee's first name and initial | Last name | Suff.

11 Nonqualified plans	12a See instructions for box 12
13 Statutory employee ☐ Retirement plan ☐ Third-party sick pay ☐	12b
14 Other	12c
	12d

f Employee's address and ZIP code

15 State Employer's state ID number	16 State wages, tips, etc.	17 State income tax	18 Local wages, tips, etc.	19 Local income tax	20 Locality name

Form **W-2** Wage and Tax Statement **2021** Department of the Treasury—Internal Revenue Service

Copy A—For Social Security Administration. Send this entire page with Form W-3 to the Social Security Administration; photocopies are **not** acceptable.

For Privacy Act and Paperwork Reduction Act Notice, see the separate instructions.

Cat. No. 10134D

Do Not Cut, Fold, or Staple Forms on This Page

Form W-2 (Page 2)

Notice to Employee

Do you have to file? Refer to the Instructions for Forms 1040 and 1040-SR to determine if you are required to file a tax return. Even if you don't have to file a tax return, you may be eligible for a refund if box 2 shows an amount or if you are eligible for any credit.

Earned income credit (EIC). You may be able to take the EIC for 2021 if your adjusted gross income (AGI) is less than a certain amount. The amount of the credit is based on income and family size. Workers without children could qualify for a smaller credit. You and any qualifying children must have valid social security numbers (SSNs). You can't take the EIC if your investment income is more than the specified amount for 2021 or if income is earned for services provided while you were an inmate at a penal institution. For 2021 income limits and more information, visit *www.irs.gov/EITC*. See also Pub. 596, Earned Income Credit. **Any EIC that is more than your tax liability is refunded to you, but only if you file a tax return.**

Employee's social security number (SSN). For your protection, this form may show only the last four digits of your SSN. However, your employer has reported your complete SSN to the IRS and SSA.

Clergy and religious workers. If you aren't subject to social security and Medicare taxes, see Pub. 517, Social Security and Other Information for Members of the Clergy and Religious Workers.

Corrections. If your name, SSN, or address is incorrect, correct Copies B, C, and 2 and ask your employer to correct your employment record. Be sure to ask the employer to file Form W-2c, Corrected Wage and Tax Statement, with the Social Security Administration (SSA) to correct any name, SSN, or money amount error reported to the SSA on Form W-2. Be sure to get your copies of Form W-2c from your employer for all corrections made so you may file them with your tax return. If your name and SSN are correct but aren't the same as shown on your social security card, you should ask for a new card that displays your correct name at any SSA office or by calling 800-772-1213. You may also visit the SSA website at *www.SSA.gov*.

Cost of employer-sponsored health coverage (if such cost is provided by the employer). The reporting in box 12, using code DD, of the cost of employer-sponsored health coverage is for your information only. **The amount reported with code DD is not taxable.**

Credit for excess taxes. If you had more than one employer in 2021 and more than $8,853.60 in social security and/or Tier 1 railroad retirement (RRTA) taxes were withheld, you may be able to claim a credit for the excess against your federal income tax. If you had more than one railroad employer and more than $5,203.80 in Tier 2 RRTA tax was withheld, you may also be able to claim a credit. See the Instructions for Forms 1040 and 1040-SR and Pub. 505, Tax Withholding and Estimated Tax.

(See also *Instructions for Employee* on the back of Copy C.)

Form W-2 (Pages 3 and 4)

Instructions for Employee

(See also *Notice to Employee* on the back of Copy B.)

Box 1. Enter this amount on the wages line of your tax return.

Box 2. Enter this amount on the federal income tax withheld line of your tax return.

Box 5. You may be required to report this amount on Form 8959, Additional Medicare Tax. See the Instructions for Forms 1040 and 1040-SR to determine if you are required to complete Form 8959.

Box 6. This amount includes the 1.45% Medicare Tax withheld on all Medicare wages and tips shown in box 5, as well as the 0.9% Additional Medicare Tax on any of those Medicare wages and tips above $200,000.

Box 8. This amount is **not** included in box 1, 3, 5, or 7. For information on how to report tips on your tax return, see the Instructions for Forms 1040 and 1040-SR.

You must file Form 4137, Social Security and Medicare Tax on Unreported Tip Income, with your income tax return to report at least the allocated tip amount unless you can prove with adequate records that you received a smaller amount. If you have records that show the actual amount of tips you received, report that amount even if it is more or less than the allocated tips. Use Form 4137 to figure the social security and Medicare tax owed on tips you didn't report to your employer. Enter this amount on the wages line of your tax return. By filing Form 4137, your social security tips will be credited to your social security record (used to figure your benefits).

Box 10. This amount includes the total dependent care benefits that your employer paid to you or incurred on your behalf (including amounts from a section 125 (cafeteria) plan). Any amount over $5,000 is also included in box 1. Complete Form 2441, Child and Dependent Care Expenses, to figure any taxable and nontaxable amounts.

Box 11. This amount is (a) reported in box 1 if it is a distribution made to you from a nonqualified deferred compensation or nongovernmental section 457(b) plan, or (b) included in box 3 and/or box 5 if it is a prior year deferral under a nonqualified or section 457(b) plan that became taxable for social security and Medicare taxes this year because there is no longer a substantial risk of forfeiture of your right to the deferred amount. This box shouldn't be used if you had a deferral and a

distribution in the same calendar year. If you made a deferral and received a distribution in the same calendar year, and you are or will be age 62 by the end of the calendar year, your employer should file Form SSA-131, Employer Report of Special Wage Payments, with the Social Security Administration and give you a copy.

Box 12. The following list explains the codes shown in box 12. You may need this information to complete your tax return. Elective deferrals (codes D, E, F, and S) and designated Roth contributions (codes AA, BB, and EE) under all plans are generally limited to a total of $19,500 ($13,500 if you only have SIMPLE plans; $22,500 for section 403(b) plans if you qualify for the 15-year rule explained in Pub. 571). Deferrals under code G are limited to $19,500. Deferrals under code H are limited to $7,000.

However, if you were at least age 50 in 2021, your employer may have allowed an additional deferral of up to $6,500 ($3,000 for section 401(k)(11) and 408(p) SIMPLE plans). This additional deferral amount is not subject to the overall limit on elective deferrals. For code G, the limit on elective deferrals may be higher for the last 3 years before you reach retirement age. Contact your plan administrator for more information. Amounts in excess of the overall elective deferral limit must be included in income. See the Instructions for Forms 1040 and 1040-SR.

Note: If a year follows code D through H, S, Y, AA, BB, or EE, you made a make-up pension contribution for a prior year(s) when you were in military service. To figure whether you made excess deferrals, consider these amounts for the year shown, not the current year. If no year is shown, the contributions are for the current year.

A—Uncollected social security or RRTA tax on tips. Include this tax on Form 1040 or 1040-SR. See the Instructions for Forms 1040 and 1040-SR.

B—Uncollected Medicare tax on tips. Include this tax on Form 1040 or 1040-SR. See the Instructions for Forms 1040 and 1040-SR.

C—Taxable cost of group-term life insurance over $50,000 (included in boxes 1, 3 (up to the social security wage base), and 5)

D—Elective deferrals to a section 401(k) cash or deferred arrangement. Also includes deferrals under a SIMPLE retirement account that is part of a section 401(k) arrangement.

E—Elective deferrals under a section 403(b) salary reduction agreement

(continued on back of Copy 2)

Instructions for Employee *(continued from back of Copy C)*

Box 12 *(continued)*

F—Elective deferrals under a section 408(k)(6) salary reduction SEP

G—Elective deferrals and employer contributions (including nonelective deferrals) to a section 457(b) deferred compensation plan

H—Elective deferrals to a section 501(c)(18)(D) tax-exempt organization plan. See the Instructions for Forms 1040 and 1040-SR for how to deduct.

J—Nontaxable sick pay (information only, not included in box 1, 3, or 5)

K—20% excise tax on excess golden parachute payments. See the Instructions for Forms 1040 and 1040-SR.

L—Substantiated employee business expense reimbursements (nontaxable)

M—Uncollected social security or RRTA tax on taxable cost of group-term life insurance over $50,000 (former employees only). See the Instructions for Forms 1040 and 1040-SR.

N—Uncollected Medicare tax on taxable cost of group-term life insurance over $50,000 (former employees only). See the Instructions for Forms 1040 and 1040-SR.

P—Excludable moving expense reimbursements paid directly to a member of the U.S. Armed Forces (not included in box 1, 3, or 5)

Q—Nontaxable combat pay. See the Instructions for Forms 1040 and 1040-SR for details on reporting this amount.

R—Employer contributions to your Archer MSA. Report on Form 8853, Archer MSAs and Long-Term Care Insurance Contracts.

S—Employee salary reduction contributions under a section 408(p) SIMPLE plan (not included in box 1)

T—Adoption benefits (not included in box 1). Complete Form 8839, Qualified Adoption Expenses, to figure any taxable and nontaxable amounts.

V—Income from exercise of nonstatutory stock option(s) (included in boxes 1, 3 (up to the social security wage base), and 5). See Pub. 525, Taxable and Nontaxable Income, for reporting requirements.

W—Employer contributions (including amounts the employee elected to contribute using a section 125 (cafeteria) plan) to your health savings account. Report on Form 8889, Health Savings Accounts (HSAs).

Y—Deferrals under a section 409A nonqualified deferred compensation plan

Z—Income under a nonqualified deferred compensation plan that fails to satisfy section 409A. This amount is also included in box 1. It is subject to an additional 20% tax plus interest. See the Instructions for Forms 1040 and 1040-SR.

AA—Designated Roth contributions under a section 401(k) plan

BB—Designated Roth contributions under a section 403(b) plan

DD—Cost of employer-sponsored health coverage. **The amount reported with code DD is not taxable.**

EE—Designated Roth contributions under a governmental section 457(b) plan. This amount does not apply to contributions under a tax-exempt organization section 457(b) plan.

FF—Permitted benefits under a qualified small employer health reimbursement arrangement

GG—Income from qualified equity grants under section 83(i)

HH—Aggregate deferrals under section 83(i) elections as of the close of the calendar year

Box 13. If the "Retirement plan" box is checked, special limits may apply to the amount of traditional IRA contributions you may deduct. See Pub. 590-A, Contributions to Individual Retirement Arrangements (IRAs).

Box 14. Employers may use this box to report information such as state disability insurance taxes withheld, union dues, uniform payments, health insurance premiums deducted, nontaxable income, educational assistance payments, or a member of the clergy's parsonage allowance and utilities. Railroad employers use this box to report railroad retirement (RRTA) compensation, Tier 1 tax, Tier 2 tax, Medicare tax, and Additional Medicare Tax. Include tips reported by the employee to the employer in railroad retirement (RRTA) compensation.

Note: Keep **Copy C** of Form W-2 for at least 3 years after the due date for filing your income tax return. However, to help **protect your social security benefits,** keep Copy C until you begin receiving social security benefits, just in case there is a question about your work record and/or earnings in a particular year.

Form W-2 (Page 5)

Employers, Please Note—

Specific information needed to complete Form W-2 is available in a separate booklet titled the 2021 General Instructions for Forms W-2 and W-3. You can order these instructions and additional forms at *www.irs.gov/OrderForms*.

Caution: Do not send the SSA Forms W-2 and W-3 that you have printed from IRS.gov. The SSA is unable to process these forms. Instead, you can create and submit them online. See *E-filing,* later.

Due dates. By January 31, 2022, furnish Copies B, C, and 2 to each person who was your employee during 2021. Mail or electronically file Copy A of Form(s) W-2 and W-3 with the SSA by January 31, 2022. See the separate instructions.

Need help? If you have questions about reporting on Form W-2, call the information reporting customer service site toll free at 866-455-7438 or 304-263-8700 (not toll free). For TTY/TDD equipment for persons who are deaf, hard of hearing, or have a speech disability, call 304-579-4827 (not toll free).

E-filing. See the 2021 General Instructions for Forms W-2 and W-3 for information on when you're required to file electronically. Even if you aren't required to file electronically, doing so can save you time and effort. Employers may now use the SSA's W-2 Online service to create, save, print, and submit up to 50 Form(s) W-2 at a time over the Internet. When you *e-file* with the SSA, no separate Form W-3 filing is required. An electronic Form W-3 will be created for you by the W-2 Online service. For information, visit the SSA's Employer W-2 Filing Instructions & Information website at *www.SSA.gov/employer*.

Future developments. Information about any future developments affecting Form W-2 and its instructions (such as legislation enacted after we release them) will be posted at *www.irs.gov/FormW2*.

Forms W-2/ W-3 and W-2c/W3-c Instructions (Page 1)

2021

Department of the Treasury
Internal Revenue Service

General Instructions for Forms W-2 and W-3

(Including Forms W-2AS, W-2CM, W-2GU, W-2VI, W-3SS, W-2c, and W-3c)

Section references are to the Internal Revenue Code unless otherwise noted.

Future Developments

For the latest information about developments related to Forms W-2 and W-3 and their instructions, such as legislation enacted after they were published, go to *IRS.gov/FormW2*.

What's New

Discrepancies when reconciling Forms W-2 and W-3 with Forms 941, 941-SS, 943, 944, CT-1, and Schedule H (Form 1040) due to Coronavirus (COVID-19) related employment tax credits and other tax relief. You may have a discrepancy when reconciling Forms W-2 and W-3 to Forms 941, 941-SS, 943, 944, CT-1, and Schedule H (Form 1040), if you utilized any of the COVID-19 tax relief for 2020. See Pub. 15 or Pub. 51, the instructions for your respective employment tax form, and the *Caution* under *Reconciling Forms W-2, W-3, 941, 941-SS, 943, 944, CT-1, and Schedule H (Form 1040)*, for more information.

Form W-2c reporting of employee social security tax and railroad retirement tax act (RRTA) deferred in 2020. If you deferred the employee portion of social security or RRTA tax under Notice 2020-65, see *Reporting of employee social security and RRTA tax*

deferred in 2020, later, for more information on how to report the deferrals. Also see Notice 2020-65, 2020-38 I.R.B. 567, available at *IRS.gov/irb/2020-38_IRB#NOT-2020-65*. Notice 2021-11, available at *IRS.gov/pub/irs-drop/N-21-11*, modifies Notice 2020-65 to extend the period in 2021 over which you are to withhold and pay the deferred taxes. The notice reflects P.L. 116-260, Division N (the COVID-related Tax Relief Act of 2020), section 274, which extends the withholding period in Notice 2020-65 from April 30, 2021, to December 31, 2021. See Form W-2 Reporting of Employee Social Security Tax Deferred under Notice 2020-65, available at *IRS.gov/Forms-Pubs/Form-W-2-Reporting-of-Employee-Social-Security-Tax-Deferred-Under-Notice-2020-65*.

Disaster tax relief. Disaster tax relief is available for those affected by recent disasters. For more information about disaster relief, go to *IRS.gov/DisasterTaxRelief*.

Penalties increased. Failure to file and failure to furnish penalties, and penalties for intentional disregard of filing and payee statement requirements, have increased due to adjustments for inflation. The higher penalty amounts apply to returns required to be filed after December 31, 2021. See *Penalties* for more information.

Reminders

Due date for filing with SSA. The due date for filing 2021 Forms W-2, W-2AS, W-2CM, W-2GU, W-2VI, W-3, and W-3SS with the SSA is January 31, 2022, whether you file using paper forms or electronically.

Extensions of time to file. Extensions of time to file Form W-2 with the SSA are not automatic. You may request one 30-day extension to file Form W-2 by submitting a complete application on Form 8809, Application for Extension of Time To File Information Returns, indicating that at least one of the criteria on the form and instructions for granting an extension applies, and signing under penalties of perjury. The IRS will only grant the extension in extraordinary circumstances or catastrophe. See *Extension of time to file Forms W-2 with the SSA* for more information. This does not affect extensions of time to furnish Forms W-2 to employees. See *Extension of time to furnish Forms W-2 to employees* for more information.

Get it done faster...
E-file your Forms W-2 and W-2c with the SSA. See E-filing.

Rejected wage reports from the Social Security Administration (SSA). The SSA will reject Form W-2 electronic and paper wage reports under the following conditions.

Jan 29, 2021   Cat. No. 25979S

Forms W-2/ W-3 and W-2c/W3-c Instructions (Page 2)

- Medicare wages and tips are less than the sum of social security wages and social security tips;
- Social security tax is greater than zero; social security wages and social security tips are equal to zero; and
- Medicare tax is greater than zero; Medicare wages and tips are equal to zero.

Additionally, Forms W-2 and W-2c electronic and paper wage reports for household employers will be rejected under the following conditions.
- The sum of social security wages and social security tips is less than the minimum yearly earnings subject to social security and Medicare tax withholding for a household employee, and
- The Medicare wages and tips are less than the minimum yearly earnings subject to social security and Medicare tax withholding for a household employee.

If the above conditions occur in an electronic wage report, the SSA will notify the submitter by email or postal mail to correct the report and resubmit it to the SSA. If the above conditions occur in a paper wage report, the SSA will notify the employer by email or postal mail to correct the report and resubmit it to the SSA.

Note. Do not write "corrected" or "amended" on any resubmitted reports.

Household employers, see Pub. 926, Household Employer's Tax Guide.

Social security numbers. Employers may now truncate the employee's SSN on employee copies of Forms W-2. Do **not** truncate the employees' SSN on Copy A of Forms W-2, W-2c, W-2AS, W-2GU, and W-2VI. See *Taxpayer identification numbers (TINs)*, later. Also see Regulations section 31.6051-1(a)(1)(i)(B) and 31.6051-2(a). To truncate where allowed, replace the first 5 digits of the 9-digit number with asterisks (*) or Xs (for example, an SSN xxx-xx-1234 would appear on the employee copies as ***-**-1234 or XXX-XX-1234). Truncation of SSNs on employee copies of Form W-2 is voluntary. You are not required to truncate SSNs on employee copies of Form W-2. Check with your state, local, territorial, or possession governments to determine whether you are permitted to truncate SSNs on copies of Form W-2 submitted to the government.

An employer's EIN may not be truncated on any form. See Regulations section 31.6051-1(a)(1)(i)(A) and 301.6109-4(b)(2)(iv).

Limit on health flexible spending arrangement (FSA). For 2021, a cafeteria plan may not allow an employee to request salary reduction contributions for a health FSA in excess of $2,750. The salary reduction contribution limitation of $2,750 does not include any amount carried over from a previous year. For 2020 and 2021, there isn't a limitation on the amount that can be carried over from a previous year, if you so provide in your plan. Any unused benefits or contributions remaining in 2020 may be applied to plan year 2021. For more information, see *Health flexible spending arrangement (FSA)*.

Additional Medicare Tax. In addition to withholding Medicare tax at 1.45%, an employer is required to withhold a 0.9% Additional Medicare Tax on any Federal Insurance Contributions Act (FICA) wages or Railroad Retirement Tax Act (RRTA) compensation it pays to an

employee in excess of $200,000 in a calendar year. An employer is required to begin withholding Additional Medicare Tax in the pay period in which it pays wages or compensation in excess of $200,000 to an employee and continue to withhold it until the end of the calendar year. Additional Medicare Tax is imposed only on the employee. There is no employer share of Additional Medicare Tax. All wages and compensation that are subject to Medicare tax are subject to Additional Medicare Tax withholding if paid in excess of the $200,000 withholding threshold.

For more information on Additional Medicare Tax, go to *IRS.gov/ADMT*.

Unless otherwise noted, references to Medicare tax include Additional Medicare Tax.

Medicaid waiver payments. Notice 2014-7 provides that certain Medicaid waiver payments may be excluded from income for federal income tax purposes. See Notice 2014-7, 2014-4 I.R.B. 445, available at *IRS.gov/irb/ 2014-4 IRB#NOT-2014-7*. Also see *IRS.gov/ MedicaidWaiverPayments* for questions and answers on the notice.

Business Services Online (BSO). The SSA has enhanced its secure BSO website to make it easier to register and navigate. Use BSO's online fill-in forms to create, save, and submit Forms W-2 and W-2c to the SSA electronically. BSO lets you print copies of these forms to file with state or local governments, distribute to your employees, and keep for your records. BSO generates Form W-3 automatically based on your Forms W-2. You can also use BSO to upload wage files to the SSA, check on the status of previously submitted wage reports, and take advantage of other convenient services for employers and businesses. Visit the SSA's Employer W-2 Filing Instructions & Information website at *SSA.gov/ employer* for more information about using BSO to save time for your organization. Here you will also find forms and publications used for wage reporting, information about verifying employee social security numbers online, how to reach an SSA employer services representative for your region, and more.

 Preview BSO by viewing a brief online tutorial. Go to SSA.gov/employer/bsotut.htm.

Correcting wage reports. You can use BSO to create, save, print, and submit Forms W-2c, Corrected Wage and Tax Statement, online for the current year as well as for prior years. After logging into BSO, navigate to the Electronic Wage Reporting home page and click on the "Forms W-2c/W-3c Online" tab. Also see *E-filing* and *E-filing Forms W-2c and W-3c*.

Tax relief for victims of terrorist attacks. Disability payments for injuries incurred as a direct result of a terrorist attack directed against the United States (or its allies) are not included in income. Because federal income tax withholding is required only when a payment is includable in income, no federal income tax should be withheld from these payments.

Distributions from governmental section 457(b) plans of state and local agencies. Generally, report

General Instructions for Forms W-2 and W-3 (2021)

Forms W-2/ W-3 and W-2c/W3-c Instructions (Page 3)

distributions from section 457(b) plans of state and local agencies on Form 1099-R, Distributions From Pensions, Annuities, Retirement or Profit-Sharing Plans, IRAs, Insurance Contracts, etc. See Notice 2003-20 on page 894 of Internal Revenue Bulletin 2003-19 at *IRS.gov/pub/irs-irbs/irb03-19.pdf*.

Earned income credit (EIC) notice (not applicable to Forms W-2AS, W-2CM, W-2GU, and W-2VI). You must notify employees who have no income tax withheld that they may be able to claim an income tax refund because of the EIC. You can do this by using the official Internal Revenue Service (IRS) Form W-2 with the EIC notice on the back of Copy B or a substitute Form W-2 with the same statement. You must give your employee Notice 797, Possible Federal Tax Refund Due to the Earned Income Credit (EIC), or your own statement that contains the same wording if (a) you use a substitute Form W-2 that does not contain the EIC notice, (b) you are not required to furnish Form W-2, or (c) you do not furnish a timely Form W-2 to your employee. For more information, see section 10 in Pub. 15 (Circular E), Employer's Tax Guide.

Electronic statements for employees. Furnishing Copies B, C, and 2 of Forms W-2 to your employees electronically may save you time and effort. See *Furnishing Form W-2 to employees electronically* in Pub. 15-A, Employer's Supplemental Tax Guide, for additional information.

E-filing. The SSA encourages all employers to *e-file*. E-filing can save you time and effort and helps ensure accuracy. You must *e-file* if you are required to file 250 or more Forms W-2 or W-2c. If you are required to *e-file* but fail to do so, you may incur a penalty.

 The Taxpayer First Act of 2019, enacted July 1, 2019, authorized the Department of the Treasury and the IRS to issue regulations that reduce the 250 return requirement for 2021 tax returns. If those regulations are issued and effective for 2021 tax returns required to be filed in 2022, we will post an article at IRS.gov/FormW2 explaining the change. Until regulations are issued, however, the number remains at 250, as reflected in these instructions.

The SSA's BSO website makes e-filing easy by providing two ways to submit your Forms W-2 or W-2c Copy A and Forms W-3 or W-3c information.
• If you need to file 50 or fewer Forms W-2 or 25 or fewer Forms W-2c at a time, you can use BSO to create them online. BSO guides you through the process of creating Forms W-2 or W-2c, saving and printing them, and submitting them to the SSA when you are ready. You do not have to wait until you have submitted Forms W-2 or W-2c to the SSA before printing copies for your employees. BSO generates Form W-3 or W-3c automatically based on your Forms W-2 or W-2c.
• If you need to file more than 50 Forms W-2 or more than 25 Forms W-2c, BSO's "file upload" feature might be the best e-filing method for your business or organization. To obtain file format specifications, visit the SSA's website at *SSA.gov/employer/EFW2&EFW2C.htm*, and select the appropriate document. This information is also available

by calling the SSA's Employer Reporting Service Center at 800-772-6270 (toll free).

⚠ CAUTION *If you e-file, do not file the same returns using paper forms.*

For more information about e-filing Forms W-2 or W-2c and a link to the BSO website, visit the SSA's Employer W-2 Filing Instructions & Information website at *SSA.gov/employer*.

In a few situations, reporting instructions vary depending on the filing method you choose. For example, you can include every type of box 12 amount in one employee wage record if you upload an electronic file. If you file on paper or create Forms W-2 online, you can include only four box 12 amounts per Form W-2. See the *TIP* for *Box 12—Codes* under *Specific Instructions for Form W-2*.

Waiver from e-filing. If you are required to *e-file*, you can request a waiver from this requirement by filing Form 8508, Request for Waiver From Filing Information Returns Electronically. Submit Form 8508 to the IRS at least 45 days before the due date of Form W-2, or 45 days before you file your first Form W-2c. See Form 8508 for information about filing this form.

Form 944. Use the "944" checkbox in box b of Form W-3 or Form W-3SS if you filed Form 944, Employer's ANNUAL Federal Tax Return. Also use the "944" checkbox if you filed Formulario 944(SP), the Spanish-language version of Form 944.

Forms W-2 for U.S. possessions. In these instructions, reference to Forms W-2 and W-3 includes Forms W-2AS, W-2CM, W-2GU, W-2VI, and W-3SS, unless otherwise noted. These instructions are not applicable to wage and tax statements for Puerto Rico. Form W-2AS is used to report American Samoa wages paid by American Samoa employers, Form W-2CM is used to report the Commonwealth of the Northern Mariana Islands (CNMI) wages paid by CNMI employers, Form W-2GU is used to report Guam wages paid by Guam employers, and Form W-2VI is used to report U.S. Virgin Islands (USVI) wages paid by USVI employers. Do not use these forms to report wages subject to U.S. income tax withholding. Instead, use Form W-2 to show U.S. income tax withheld.

Military Spouses Residency Relief Act (MSRRA). You may be required to report wages and taxes on a form different from the form you generally use if an employee claims residence or domicile under MSRRA in a different jurisdiction in one of the 50 states, the District of Columbia, American Samoa, the Commonwealth of the Northern Mariana Islands, Guam, Puerto Rico, or the U.S. Virgin Islands.

Under MSRRA, the spouse of an active duty servicemember (civilian spouse) may keep his or her prior residence or domicile for tax purposes (tax residence) when accompanying the servicemember spouse, who is relocating under military orders, to a new military duty station in one of the 50 states, the District of Columbia, or a U.S. possession. Before relocating, both spouses must have had the same tax residence.

For example, if a civilian spouse is working in Guam but properly claims tax residence in one of the 50 states

General Instructions for Forms W-2 and W-3 (2021)   -3-

Forms W-2/ W-3 and W-2c/W3-c Instructions (Page 4)

under MSRRA, his or her income from services would not be taxable income for Guam tax purposes. Federal income taxes should be withheld and remitted to the IRS. State and local income taxes may need to be withheld and remitted to state and local tax authorities. You should consult with state, local, or U.S. possession tax authorities regarding your withholding obligations under MSRRA.

However, for any taxable year of the marriage, the civilian spouse may elect to use the same residence for purposes of taxation as the servicemember regardless of the date on which the marriage of the spouse and the servicemember occurred.

In the previous example, the spouse would be allowed to elect to use the same residence as the servicemember.

Nonqualified deferred compensation plans. You are not required to complete box 12 with code Y (Deferrals under a section 409A nonqualified deferred compensation plan). Section 409A provides that all amounts deferred under a nonqualified deferred compensation (NQDC) plan for all tax years are includible in gross income unless certain requirements are satisfied. See *Nonqualified deferred compensation plans* under *Special Reporting Situations for Form W-2* and the *Nonqualified Deferred Compensation Reporting Example Chart*.

Reporting the cost of group health insurance coverage. You must report the cost of employer-sponsored health coverage in box 12 using code DD. However, transitional relief applies to certain employers and certain types of plans. For more information, see *Box 12—Codes* for *Code DD—Cost of employer-sponsored health coverage*.

Severance payments. Severance payments are wages subject to social security and Medicare taxes. As noted in section 15 of Pub. 15 (Circular E), severance payments are also subject to income tax withholding and FUTA tax.

Substitute forms. You may use an acceptable substitute form instead of an official IRS form.

Form W-2. If you are not using the official IRS form to furnish Form W-2 to employees or to file with the SSA, you may use an acceptable substitute form that complies with the rules in Pub. 1141, General Rules and Specifications for Substitute Forms W-2 and W-3. Pub. 1141 is a revenue procedure that explains the requirements for format and content of substitute Forms W-2 and W-3. Your substitute forms must comply with the requirements in Pub. 1141.

Pub. 1141 prohibits advertising on Form W-2. You must not include advertising on any copy of Form W-2, including coupons providing discounts on tax preparation services attached to the employee copies. See Pub. 1141 for further information.

Form W-2c. If you are not using the official IRS form to furnish Form W-2c to employees or to file with the SSA, you may use an acceptable substitute form that complies with the rules in Pub. 1223, General Rules and Specifications for Substitute Forms W-2c and W-3c. Pub. 1223 is a revenue procedure that explains the requirements for format and content of substitute Forms W-2c and W-3c. Your substitute forms must comply with the requirements in Pub. 1223.

Pub. 1223 prohibits advertising on Form W-2c. You must not include advertising on any copy of Form W-2c, including coupons providing discounts on tax preparation services attached to the employee copies. See Pub. 1223 for further information.

Need Help?

Help with e-filing. If you have questions about how to register or use BSO, call 800-772-6270 (toll free) to speak with an employer reporting technician at the SSA. The hours of operation are Monday through Friday from 7:00 a.m. to 7:00 p.m. Eastern time. If you experience problems using any of the services within BSO, call 888-772-2970 (toll free) to speak with a systems operator in technical support at the SSA. To speak with the SSA's Employer Services Liaison Officer (ESLO) for the U.S. Virgin Islands, call 212-264-4402 (not a toll-free number). For Guam, the Commonwealth of the Northern Mariana Islands, or American Samoa, call 510-970-8247 (not a toll-free number). For all other employers, contact the ESLO that services your region. For a complete telephone listing, visit the SSA's Employer W-2 Filing Instructions & Information website at *SSA.gov/employer/ wage_reporting_specialists.htm*.

Information reporting customer service site. The IRS operates a centralized customer service site to answer questions about reporting on Forms W-2, W-3, 1099, and other information returns. If you have questions about reporting on these forms, call 866-455-7438 (toll free).

TTY/TDD equipment. Telephone help is available using TTY/TDD equipment for persons who are deaf, hard of hearing, or have a speech disability. If you have questions about reporting on information returns (Forms 1096, 1097, 1098, 1099, 3921, 3922, 5498, W-2, W-2G, and W-3), call 304-579-4827.

Employment tax information. Detailed employment tax information is given in:
• Pub. 15 (Circular E), Employer's Tax Guide;
• Pub. 15-A, Employer's Supplemental Tax Guide;
• Pub. 15-B, Employer's Tax Guide to Fringe Benefits;
• Pub. 15-T, Federal Income Tax Withholding Methods;
• Pub. 51 (Circular A), Agricultural Employer's Tax Guide; and
• Pub. 80 (Circular SS), Federal Tax Guide for Employers in the U.S. Virgin Islands, Guam, American Samoa, and the Commonwealth of the Northern Mariana Islands.

You can also call the IRS with your employment tax questions at 800-829-4933 or go to *IRS.gov/Businesses/ Small-Businesses-Self-Employed/Understanding-Employment-Taxes*.

How To Get Forms and Publications

Internet. You can access IRS.gov 24 hours a day, 7 days a week to:
• Download, view, and order tax forms, instructions, and publications.
• Access commercial tax preparation and *e-file* services.
• Research your tax questions online.
• See answers to frequently asked tax questions.
• Search publications online by topic or keyword.

-4-   General Instructions for Forms W-2 and W-3 (2021)

Forms W-2/ W-3 and W-2c/W3-c Instructions (Page 5)

- View Internal Revenue Bulletins published in the last few years.
- Sign up to receive local and national tax news by email.

You can order forms, instructions, and publications at *IRS.gov/OrderForms*. For any other tax information, go to *IRS.gov/Help/Tax-Law-Questions*.

 Do not print Copy A of Forms W-2, W-3, W-2c, or W-3c from IRS.gov and then file them with the SSA. The SSA accepts only e-filed reports and the official red-ink versions (or approved substitute versions) of these forms. For more information about acceptable substitute versions, see Substitute forms. *For information about e-filing, see* E-filing.

Common Errors on Forms W-2

Forms W-2 provide information to your employees, the SSA, the IRS, and state and local governments. Avoid making the following errors, which cause processing delays.

Do not:
- Download Copy A of Forms W-2, W-2AS, W-2GU, W-2VI, and W-3SS; or Form W-3 from IRS.gov and file with the SSA.
- Omit the decimal point and cents from entries.
- Make entries using ink that is too light. Use only black ink.
- Make entries that are too small or too large. Use 12-point Courier font, if possible.
- Add dollar signs to the money-amount boxes. They have been removed from Copy A and are not required.
- Inappropriately check the "Retirement plan" checkbox in box 13. See *Retirement plan*.
- Misformat the employee's name in box e. Enter the employee's first name and middle initial in the first box, his or her surname in the second box, and his or her suffix (such as "Jr.") in the third box (optional).
- Enter the incorrect employer identification number (EIN) or the employee's SSN for the EIN.
- Cut, fold, or staple Copy A paper forms mailed to SSA.
- Mail any other copy other than Copy A of Form W-2 to the SSA.

General Instructions for Forms W-2 and W-3

Who must file Form W-2. You must file Form(s) W-2 if you have one or more employees to whom you made payments (including noncash payments) for the employees' services in your trade or business during 2021.

Complete and file Form W-2 for each employee for whom any of the following applies (even if the employee is related to you).
- You withheld any income, social security, or Medicare tax from wages regardless of the amount of wages; or
- You would have had to withhold income tax if the employee had claimed no more than one withholding allowance (for 2019 or earlier Forms W-4) or had not claimed exemption from withholding on Form W-4; or

- You paid $600 or more in wages even if you did not withhold any income, social security, or Medicare tax.

Only in very limited situations will you not have to file Form W-2. This may occur if you were not required to withhold any income tax, social security tax, or Medicare tax and you paid the employee less than $600, such as for certain election workers and certain foreign agricultural workers. See *Election workers* and *Foreign agricultural workers*, later.

Unless otherwise noted, references to Medicare tax include Additional Medicare Tax.

If you are required to *e-file* Forms W-2 or want to take advantage of the benefits of e-filing, see *E-filing*.

Who must file Form W-3. Anyone required to file Form W-2 must file Form W-3 to transmit Copy A of Forms W-2. Make a copy of Form W-3; keep it and Copy D (For Employer) of Forms W-2 with your records for 4 years. Be sure to use Form W-3 for the correct year. If you are filing Forms W-2 electronically, also see *E-filing*.

Household employers. Even employers with only one household employee must file Form W-3 to transmit Copy A of Form W-2. On Form W-3, check the "Hshld. emp." checkbox in box b. For more information, see Schedule H (Form 1040), Household Employment Taxes, and its separate instructions. You must have an employer identification number (EIN). See *Box b Employer identification number (EIN)*.

Who may sign Form W-3. A transmitter or sender (including a service bureau, reporting agent, paying agent, or disbursing agent) may sign Form W-3 (or use its PIN to *e-file*) for the employer or payer only if the sender satisfies both of the following.
- It is authorized to sign by an agency agreement (whether oral, written, or implied) that is valid under state law; and
- It writes "For (name of payer)" next to the signature (paper Form W-3 only).

 Use of a reporting agent or other third-party payroll service provider does not relieve an employer of the responsibility to ensure that Forms W-2 are furnished to employees and that Forms W-2 and W-3 are filed with the SSA, correctly and on time. See Penalties *for more information.*

Be sure that the payer's name and EIN on Forms W-2 and W-3 are the same as those used on the Form 941, Employer's QUARTERLY Federal Tax Return; Form 943, Employer's Annual Federal Tax Return for Agricultural Employees; Form 944, Employer's ANNUAL Federal Tax Return; Form CT-1, Employer's Annual Railroad Retirement Tax Return; or Schedule H (Form 1040) filed by or for the payer.

When to file. Mail or electronically file Copy A of Form(s) W-2 and Form W-3 with the SSA by January 31, 2022. You may owe a penalty for each Form W-2 that you file late. See *Penalties*. If you terminate your business, see *Terminating a business*.

Extension of time to file Forms W-2 with the SSA. You may request only one extension of time to file Form W-2 with the SSA by submitting a complete application on Form 8809, Application for Extension of Time To File

Forms W-2/ W-3 and W-2c/W3-c Instructions (Page 6)

Information Returns. When completing the Form 8809, indicate that at least one of the criteria on the form and instructions for granting an extension applies. You must sign the application under penalties of perjury. Send the application to the address shown on Form 8809. You must request the extension before the due date of Forms W-2. If the IRS grants your request for extension, you will have an additional 30 days to file. The IRS will grant extensions to file Forms W-2 only in limited cases for extraordinary circumstances or catastrophe, such as a natural disaster or fire destroying the books and records needed for filing the forms. No additional extension of time to file will be allowed. See Form 8809 for details.

 Even if you request and are granted an extension of time to file Forms W-2, you still must furnish Forms W-2 to your employees by January 31, 2022. But see Extension of time to furnish Forms W-2 to employees.

Where to file paper Forms W-2 and W-3. File Copy A of Form(s) W-2 with Form W-3 at the following address.

> **Social Security Administration**
> **Direct Operations Center**
> **Wilkes-Barre, PA 18769-0001**

TIP *If you use "Certified Mail" to file, change the ZIP code to "18769-0002." If you use an IRS-approved private delivery service, add "Attn: W-2 Process, 1150 E. Mountain Dr." to the address and change the ZIP code to "18702-7997." Go to* IRS.gov/PDS *for a list of IRS-approved private delivery services.*

⚠ CAUTION ***Do not send cash, checks, money orders, or other forms of payment with the Forms W-2 and W-3 that you submit to the SSA.*** *Employment tax forms (for example, Form 941 or Form 943), remittances, and Forms 1099 must be sent to the IRS.*

Copy 1. Send Copy 1 of Form W-2, if required, to your state, city, or local tax department. For more information concerning Copy 1 (including how to complete boxes 15 through 20), contact your state, city, or local tax department.

American Samoa. File Copy 1 of Form W-3SS and Forms W-2AS at the following address.

> **American Samoa Tax Office**
> **Executive Office Building**
> **First Floor**
> **Pago Pago, AS 96799**

Guam. File Copy 1 of Form W-3SS and Forms W-2GU at the following address.

> **Guam Department of Revenue and Taxation**
> **P.O. Box 23607**
> **GMF, GU 96921**

For additional information about Form W-2GU, see GuamTax.com.

U.S. Virgin Islands. File Copy 1 of Form W-3SS and Forms W-2VI at the following address.

> **Virgin Islands Bureau of Internal Revenue**
> **6115 Estate Smith Bay**
> **Suite 225**
> **St. Thomas, VI 00802**

For additional information about Form W-2VI, see BIR.VI.gov.

Commonwealth of the Northern Mariana Islands. File Form OS-3710 and Copy 1 of Forms W-2CM at the following address.

> **Division of Revenue and Taxation**
> **Commonwealth of the Northern Mariana Islands**
> **P.O. Box 5234 CHRB**
> **Saipan, MP 96950**

Forms OS-3710 and W-2CM are not IRS forms. For additional information about Form W-2CM, see Finance.gov/mp/forms.php.

Shipping and mailing. If you file more than one type of employment tax form, group Forms W-2 of the same type with a separate Form W-3 for each type, and send them in separate groups. See the specific instructions for Box b—Kind of Payer and Box b—Kind of Employer in *Specific Instructions for Form W-3*.

Prepare and file Forms W-2 either alphabetically by employees' last names or numerically by employees' social security numbers. Do not staple or tape Form W-3 to the related Forms W-2 or Forms W-2 to each other. These forms are machine read. Staple holes or tears interfere with machine reading. Also do not fold Forms W-2 and W-3. Send the forms to the SSA in a flat mailing.

Furnishing Copies B, C, and 2 to employees. Generally, you must furnish Copies B, C, and 2 of Form W-2 to your employees by January 31, 2022. You will meet the "furnish" requirement if the form is properly addressed and mailed on or before the due date.

If employment ends before December 31, 2021, you may furnish copies to the employee at any time after employment ends, but no later than January 31, 2022. If an employee asks for Form W-2, give him or her the completed copies within 30 days of the request or within 30 days of the final wage payment, whichever is later. However, if you terminate your business, see Terminating a business.

You may furnish Forms W-2 to employees on IRS official forms or on acceptable substitute forms. See Substitute forms. Be sure the Forms W-2 you provide to employees are clear and legible and comply with the requirements in Pub. 1141.

Forms W-2 that include logos, slogans, and advertisements (including advertisements for tax preparation software) may be considered as suspicious or altered Forms W-2 (also known as "questionable Forms W-2"). An employee may not recognize the importance of the employee copy for tax reporting purposes due to the use of logos, slogans, and advertisements. Therefore, the IRS has determined that logos, slogans, and advertising will not be allowed on Forms W-3, Copy A of Forms W-2,

Forms W-2/ W-3 and W-2c/W3-c Instructions (Page 7)

or any employee copies reporting wages paid. Limited exceptions on this prohibition exist with respect to employee copies. See Pub. 1141 for more information.

Extension of time to furnish Forms W-2 to employees. You may request an extension of time to furnish Forms W-2 to employees by faxing a letter to:

Internal Revenue Service
Attn: Extension of Time Coordinator
Fax: 866-477-0572 (International: 304-579-4105)

Fax your letter on or before the due date for furnishing Forms W-2 to employees. It must include:
- Your name and address,
- Your EIN,
- A statement that you are requesting an extension to furnish "Forms W-2" to employees,
- The reason for delay, and
- Your signature or that of your authorized agent.

 Requests for an extension of time to furnish Forms W-2 to employees are not automatically granted. If approved, an extension will generally be granted for no more than 15 days from the due date, unless the need for up to a total of 30 days is clearly shown. See the 2021 General Instructions for Certain Information Returns.

Undeliverable Forms W-2. Keep for 4 years any employee copies of Forms W-2 that you tried to but could not deliver. However, if the undelivered Form W-2 can be produced electronically through April 15th of the fourth year after the year at issue, you do not need to keep undeliverable employee copies. Do not send undeliverable employee copies of Forms W-2 to the Social Security Administration (SSA).

Taxpayer identification numbers (TINs). Employers use an employer identification number (EIN) (XX-XXXXXXX). Employees use a social security number (SSN) (XXX-XX-XXXX). When you list a number, separate the 9-digits properly to show the kind of number.

Do not accept an IRS individual taxpayer identification number (ITIN) in place of an SSN for employee identification or for Form W-2 reporting. An ITIN is available only to resident and nonresident aliens who are not eligible for U.S. employment and need identification for other tax purposes. You can identify an ITIN because it is a 9-digit number formatted like an SSN beginning with the number "9" and with a number in one of the following ranges in the fourth and fifth digits: 50–65, 70–88, 90–92, and 94–99 (for example, 9NN-70-NNNN). Do not auto populate an ITIN into box a, Employee's social security number, on Form W-2. See section 4 of Pub. 15 (Circular E).

 An individual with an ITIN who later becomes eligible to work in the United States must obtain an SSN from the Social Security Administration.

The IRS uses SSNs to check the payments that you report against the amounts shown on employees' tax returns. The SSA uses SSNs to record employees' earnings for future social security and Medicare benefits. When you prepare Form W-2, be sure to show the correct SSN for each employee. You may now truncate the

employee's SSN on employee copies of Forms W-2. Do not truncate an employee's SSN on Copy A of Forms W-2. Go to *Social security numbers*, above, for more information. Also see Regulations section 31.6051-1(a)(1)(i)(B) and 31.6051-2(a). For information about verifying SSNs, see section 4 of Pub. 15 (Circular E) or visit the SSA's Employer W-2 Filing Instructions & Information website at *SSA.gov/employer*.

 Form W-2 e-filed with the SSA must contain the employer's complete EIN and the complete SSN of the employee. Do not truncate EINs or SSNs on Copy A.

Special Reporting Situations for Form W-2

Adoption benefits. Amounts paid or expenses incurred by an employer for qualified adoption expenses under an adoption assistance program are not subject to federal income tax withholding and are not reportable in box 1. However, these amounts (including adoption benefits paid from a section 125 (cafeteria) plan, but not including adoption benefits forfeited from a cafeteria plan) are subject to social security, Medicare, and railroad retirement taxes and must be reported in boxes 3 and 5. (Use box 14 if railroad retirement taxes apply.) Also, the total amount including any amount in excess of the $14,440 exclusion, must be reported in box 12 with code T. For more information on reporting adoption benefits in box 12, see *Code T—Adoption benefits*, later.

For more information on adoption benefits, see Notice 97-9, 1997-1 C.B. 365, which is on page 35 of Internal Revenue Bulletin 1997-2 at *IRS.gov/pub/irs-irbs/irb97-02.pdf*. Advise your employees to see the Instructions for Form 8839, Qualified Adoption Expenses.

Agent reporting. An agent who has an approved Form 2678, Employer/Payer Appointment of Agent, should enter the following in box c of Form W-2.

(Name of agent)
Agent for (name of employer)
Address of agent

Each Form W-2 should reflect the EIN of the agent in box b. An agent files one Form W-3 for all of the Forms W-2 and enters its own information in boxes e, f, and g of Form W-3 as it appears on the agent's related employment tax returns (for example, Form 941). Enter the client-employer's EIN in box h of Form W-3 if the Forms W-2 relate to only one employer (other than the agent); if not, leave box h blank.

If the agent (a) is acting as an agent for two or more employers or is an employer and is acting as an agent for another employer, and (b) pays social security wages to an individual on behalf of more than one employer, the agent should file separate Forms W-2 for the affected employee reflecting the wages paid by each employer.

See Rev. Proc. 2013-39, 2013-52 I.R.B. 830, available at *IRS.gov/irb/2013-52_IRB#RP-2013-39* and the Form 2678 instructions for procedures to be followed in applying to be an agent.

General Instructions for Forms W-2 and W-3 (2021)   **-7-**

Forms W-2/ W-3 and W-2c/W3-c Instructions (Page 8)

TIP *Generally, an agent is not responsible for refunding excess social security or railroad retirement (RRTA) tax withheld from employees. If an employee worked for more than one employer during 2021 and had more than $8,853.60 in social security and Tier 1 RRTA tax withheld, he or she should claim the excess on the appropriate line of Form 1040, 1040-SR, or 1040-NR. If an employee had more than $5,203.80 in Tier 2 RRTA tax withheld from more than one employer, the employee should claim a refund on Form 843, Claim for Refund and Request for Abatement.*

Archer MSA. An employer's contribution to an employee's Archer MSA is not subject to federal income tax withholding or social security, Medicare, or railroad retirement taxes if it is reasonable to believe at the time of the payment that the contribution will be excludable from the employee's income. However, if it is not reasonable to believe at the time of payment that the contribution will be excludable from the employee's income, employer contributions are subject to income tax withholding and social security and Medicare taxes (or railroad retirement taxes, if applicable) and must be reported in boxes 1, 3, and 5. (Use box 14 if railroad retirement taxes apply.)

You must report all employer contributions to an Archer MSA in box 12 of Form W-2 with code R. Employer contributions to an Archer MSA that are not excludable from the income of the employee must also be reported in boxes 1, 3, and 5 (box 14 if railroad retirement taxes apply).

An employee's contributions to an Archer MSA are includible in income as wages and are subject to federal income tax withholding and social security and Medicare taxes (or railroad retirement taxes, if applicable). Employee contributions are deductible, within limits, on the employee's Form 1040 or 1040-SR.

For more information, see Pub. 969, Health Savings Accounts and Other Tax-Favored Health Plans, and Notice 96-53, which is found on page 5 of Internal Revenue Bulletin 1996-51 at *IRS.gov/pub/irs-irbs/irb96-51.pdf*.

Clergy and religious workers. For certain members of the clergy and religious workers who are not subject to social security and Medicare taxes as employees, boxes 3 and 5 of Form W-2 should be left blank. You may include a minister's parsonage and/or utilities allowance in box 14. For information on the rules that apply to ministers and certain other religious workers, see Pub. 517, Social Security and Other Information for Members of the Clergy and Religious Workers and section 4 in Pub. 15-A.

Deceased employee's wages. If an employee dies during the year, you must report the accrued wages, vacation pay, and other compensation paid after the date of death. Also report wages that were available to the employee while he or she was alive, regardless of whether they were actually in the possession of the employee, as well as any other regular wage payment, even if you may have to reissue the payment in the name of the estate or beneficiary.

If you made the payment after the employee's death but in the same year the employee died, you must withhold social security and Medicare taxes on the payment and report the payment on the employee's Form W-2 only as social security and Medicare wages to ensure proper social security and Medicare credit is received. On the employee's Form W-2, show the payment as social security wages (box 3) and Medicare wages and tips (box 5) and the social security and Medicare taxes withheld in boxes 4 and 6. Do not show the payment in box 1.

If you made the payment after the year of death, do not report it on Form W-2, and do not withhold social security and Medicare taxes.

Whether the payment is made in the year of death or after the year of death, you must also report it in box 3 of Form 1099-MISC, Miscellaneous Information, for the payment to the estate or beneficiary. Use the name and taxpayer identification number (TIN) of the payment recipient on Form 1099-MISC. However, if the payment is a reissuance of wages that were constructively received by the deceased individual while he or she was still alive, do not report it on Form 1099-MISC.

Example. Before Employee A's death on June 15, 2021, A was employed by Employer X and received $10,000 in wages on which federal income tax of $1,500 was withheld. When A died, X owed A $2,000 in wages and $1,000 in accrued vacation pay. The total of $3,000 (less the social security and Medicare taxes withheld) was paid to A's estate on July 20, 2021. Because X made the payment during the year of death, X must withhold social security and Medicare taxes on the $3,000 payment and must complete Form W-2 as follows.
- Box a— Employee A's SSN
- Box e— Employee A's name
- Box f— Employee A's address
- Box 1— 10000.00 (does not include the $3,000 accrued wages and vacation pay)
- Box 2— 1500.00
- Box 3— 13000.00 (includes the $3,000 accrued wages and vacation pay)
- Box 4— 806.00 (6.2% of the amount in box 3)
- Box 5— 13000.00 (includes the $3,000 accrued wages and vacation pay)
- Box 6— 188.50 (1.45% of the amount in box 5)

CAUTION *Employer X must also complete Form 1099-MISC as follows.*

- *Boxes for recipient's name, address, and TIN—the estate's or beneficiary's name, address, and TIN.*
- *Box 3: 3000.00 (Even though amounts were withheld for social security and Medicare taxes, the gross amount is reported here.)*

If Employer X made the payment after the year of death, the $3,000 would not be subject to social security and Medicare taxes and would not be shown on Form W-2. However, the employer would still file Form 1099-MISC.

Designated Roth contributions. Under section 402A, a participant in a section 401(k) plan, under a 403(b) salary reduction agreement, or in a governmental 457(b) plan that includes a qualified Roth contribution program, may elect to make designated Roth contributions to the plan or

Forms W-2/ W-3 and W-2c/W3-c Instructions (Page 9)

program in lieu of elective deferrals. Designated Roth contributions are subject to federal income tax withholding and social security and Medicare taxes (and railroad retirement taxes, if applicable) and must be reported in boxes 1, 3, and 5. (Use box 14 if railroad retirement taxes apply.)

Section 402A requires separate reporting of the yearly designated Roth contributions. Designated Roth contributions to 401(k) plans will be reported using code AA in box 12; designated Roth contributions under 403(b) salary reduction agreements will be reported using code BB in box 12; and designated Roth contributions under a governmental section 457(b) plan will be reported using code EE in box 12. For reporting instructions, see the box 12 instructions for *Code AA—Designated Roth contributions under a section 401(k) plan*, *Code BB—Designated Roth contributions under a section 403(b) plan*, and *Code EE—Designated Roth contributions under a governmental section 457(b) plan*.

Educational assistance programs. Employer-provided educational assistance up to a maximum of $5,250 is excludable from an employee's wages only if assistance is provided under an educational assistance program under section 127. See Pub. 970, Tax Benefits for Education, and section 2 of Pub. 15-B for more information. Also see *Box 1—Wages, tips, other compensation*.

Election workers. Report on Form W-2 payments of $600 or more to election workers for services performed in state, county, and municipal elections. File Form W-2 for payments of less than $600 paid to election workers if social security and Medicare taxes were withheld under a section 218 (Social Security Act) agreement. Do not report election worker payments on Form 1099-MISC.

If the election worker is employed in another capacity with the same government entity, see Rev. Rul. 2000-6, which is on page 512 of Internal Revenue Bulletin 2000-6 at *IRS.gov/pub/irs-irbs/irb00-06.pdf*.

Employee business expense reimbursements. Reimbursements to employees for business expenses must be reported as follows.
• Generally, payments made under an accountable plan are excluded from the employee's gross income and are not reported on Form W-2. However, if you pay a per diem or mileage allowance and the amount paid for substantiated miles or days traveled exceeds the amount treated as substantiated under IRS rules, you must report as wages on Form W-2 the amount in excess of the amount treated as substantiated. The excess amount is subject to income tax withholding and social security and Medicare taxes (or railroad retirement taxes, if applicable). Report the amount treated as substantiated (that is, the nontaxable portion) in box 12 using code L. See the box 12 instructions for *Code L—Substantiated employee business expense reimbursements*. (Use box 14 if railroad retirement taxes apply.)
• Payments made under a nonaccountable plan are reported as wages on Form W-2 and are subject to federal income tax withholding and social security and Medicare taxes (or railroad retirement taxes, if

applicable). (Use box 14 if railroad retirement taxes apply.)

For more information on accountable plans, nonaccountable plans, amounts treated as substantiated under a per diem or mileage allowance, the standard mileage rate, the per diem substantiation method, and the high-low substantiation method, see Pub. 463, Travel, Gift, and Car Expenses; and section 5 of Pub. 15 (Circular E).

Employee's social security and Medicare taxes (or railroad retirement taxes, if applicable) paid by employer. If you paid your employee's share of social security and Medicare taxes rather than deducting them from the employee's wages, you must include these payments as wages subject to federal (or American Samoa, CNMI, Guam, or U.S. Virgin Islands) income tax withholding and social security, Medicare, and federal unemployment (FUTA) taxes. If you paid your employee's share of railroad retirement taxes, you must include these amounts as compensation subject to railroad retirement taxes. The amount to include as wages and/or compensation is determined by using the formula contained in the discussion of *Employee's Portion of Taxes Paid by Employer* in section 7 of Pub. 15-A and in Rev. Proc. 83-43, 1983-24 I.R.B. 60.

 This does not apply to household and agricultural employers. If you pay a household or agricultural employee's social security and Medicare taxes, you must include these payments in the employee's wages for income tax withholding purposes. However, the wage increase due to the tax payments is not subject to social security, Medicare, or FUTA taxes. For information on completing Forms W-2 and W-3 in this situation, see the Instructions for Schedule H (Form 1040) and section 4 of Pub. 51 (Circular A).

Federal employers in the CNMI. The U.S. Treasury Department and the CNMI Division of Revenue and Taxation entered into an agreement under 5 U.S.C. 5517 ("5517 agreement") in December 2006. Under this agreement, all federal employers (including the Department of Defense) are required to withhold CNMI income taxes, rather than federal income taxes, and deposit the CNMI taxes with the CNMI Treasury for employees who are subject to CNMI taxes and whose regular place of federal employment is in the CNMI. Federal employers are also required to file quarterly and annual reports with the CNMI Division of Revenue and Taxation. For questions, contact the CNMI Division of Revenue and Taxation.

Federal employers may use Form W-2 (rather than Forms W-2CM or OS-3710) to report income taxes withheld and paid to CNMI, as well as to report social security and Medicare taxes. Use the state boxes 15, 16, and 17 for CNMI income tax reporting. See the instructions for boxes 15, 16, and 17 under *Boxes 15 through 20—State and local income tax information*, later. This rule applies only to income tax reporting. Federal employers should withhold and report social security and Medicare taxes for these employees in the same way as for other federal employees. For more information, go to

General Instructions for Forms W-2 and W-3 (2021)   -9-

Forms W-2/ W-3 and W-2c/W3-c Instructions (Page 10)

IRS.gov/Individuals/International-Taxpayers/Special-Withholding-Rules-for-US-Federal-Agency-Employers-With-Employees-in-CNMI-or-Puerto-Rico.

Foreign agricultural workers. You must report compensation of $600 or more paid in a calendar year to an H-2A visa agricultural worker for agricultural labor. If the H-2A visa agricultural worker furnishes a valid taxpayer identification number, report these payments in box 1 of Form W-2. If the worker does not furnish a valid taxpayer identification number, report the payments on Form 1099-MISC. See *Form 1099-MISC* below.

On Form W-2, no amount should be reported in box 3 or 5. In most cases, you do not need to withhold federal income tax from compensation paid to H-2A visa agricultural workers. Employers should withhold federal income tax only if the H-2A visa agricultural worker and the employer agree to withhold. The H-2A visa agricultural worker must provide a completed Form W-4. If the employer withholds income tax, the employer must report the tax withheld in box 2 of Form W-2 and on line 8 of Form 943. See Pub. 51 (Circular A).

Form 1099-MISC. If the H-2A visa agricultural worker fails to furnish a taxpayer identification number to the employer, and the total annual payments made to the H-2A visa agricultural worker are $600 or more, the employer must begin backup withholding on the payments made until the H-2A visa agricultural worker furnishes a valid taxpayer identification number. Employers must report the compensation paid and any backup withholding on Forms 1099-MISC and Form 945, Annual Return of Withheld Federal Income Tax. See the 2021 Instructions for Form 1099-MISC and 1099-NEC and the 2021 Instructions for Form 945.

For more information, go to *IRS.gov/H2A*.

Fringe benefits. Include all taxable fringe benefits in box 1 of Form W-2 as wages, tips, and other compensation and, if applicable, in boxes 3 and 5 as social security and Medicare wages. Although not required, you may include the total value of fringe benefits in box 14 (or on a separate statement). However, if you provided your employee a vehicle, you must include the value of any personal use in boxes 1, 3, and 5 of Form W-2. You must withhold social security and Medicare tax, but you have the option not to withhold federal income tax *if* you notify the employee and include the value of the benefit in boxes 1, 3, 5, and 14. See Pub. 15-B for more information.

Public Law 115-97, section 11045, does not permit employees to deduct unreimbursed employee business expenses for tax years 2018 through 2025. If you included 100% of the vehicle's annual lease value in the employee's income, the employee will not be able to deduct expenses attributable to the business use of an employer-provided vehicle. See Pub. 15-B.

Golden parachute payments (not applicable to Forms W-2AS, W-2CM, W-2GU, or W-2VI). Include any golden parachute payments in boxes 1, 3, and 5 of Form W-2. Withhold federal income, social security, and Medicare taxes (or railroad retirement taxes, if applicable)

as usual and report them in boxes 2, 4, and 6, respectively. (Use box 14 if railroad retirement taxes apply.) Excess parachute payments are also subject to a 20% excise tax. If the excess payments are considered wages, withhold the 20% excise tax and include it in box 2 as income tax withheld. Also report the excise tax in box 12 with code K. For definitions and additional information, see Regulations section 1.280G-1 and Rev. Proc. 2003-68, 2003-34 I.R.B. 398, available at *IRS.gov/irb/2003-34_IRB#RP-2003-68*.

Government employers. Federal, state, and local governmental agencies have two options for reporting their employees' wages that are subject to only Medicare tax for part of the year and both social security and Medicare taxes for part of the year.

The first option (which the SSA prefers) is to file a single set of Forms W-2 per employee for the entire year, even if only part of the year's wages are subject to both social security and Medicare taxes. Check "941" (or "944") in box b of Form W-3 or check "941-SS" in box b of Form W-3SS. The wages in box 5 of Form W-2 must be equal to or greater than the wages in box 3 of Form W-2.

The second option is to file one set of Forms W-2 for wages subject only to Medicare tax and another set for wages subject to both social security and Medicare taxes. Use a separate Form W-3 to transmit each set of Forms W-2. For the Medicare-only Forms W-2, check "Medicare govt. emp." in box b of Form W-3. For the Forms W-2 showing wages subject to both social security and Medicare taxes, check "941" (or "944") in box b of Form W-3 or check "941-SS" in box b of Form W-3SS. The wages in box 5 of Form W-2 must be equal to or greater than the wages in box 3 of Form W-2.

Group-term life insurance. You must include in boxes 1, 3, and 5 (or 14, if railroad retirement taxes apply) the cost of group-term life insurance that is more than the cost of $50,000 of coverage, reduced by the amount the employee paid toward the insurance. Use Table 2-2 in Pub. 15-B to determine the cost of the insurance. Also show the amount in box 12 with code C. For employees, you must withhold social security and Medicare taxes, but not federal income tax. For coverage provided to former employees, the former employees must pay the employee part of social security and Medicare taxes (or railroad retirement taxes, if applicable) on the taxable cost of group-term life insurance over $50,000 on Form 1040 or 1040-SR. You are not required to collect those taxes. However, you must report the uncollected social security tax (or railroad retirement taxes, if applicable) with code M and the uncollected Medicare tax (or RRTA Medicare tax, if applicable) with code N in box 12 of Form W-2. However, any uncollected Additional Medicare Tax (on the cost of group-term life insurance, which, in combination with other wages, is in excess of $200,000) is not reported with code N in box 12.

Health flexible spending arrangement (FSA). For plan year 2021, a cafeteria plan may not allow an employee to request salary reduction contributions for a health FSA in excess of $2,750 (as indexed for inflation).

If a cafeteria plan timely complies with the written plan requirement limiting health FSA salary reduction

Forms W-2/ W-3 and W-2c/W3-c Instructions (Page 11)

contributions, but one or more employees are erroneously allowed to elect a salary reduction of more than $2,750 for the plan year, the cafeteria plan will continue to be a section 125 cafeteria plan for the plan year if:
• The terms of the plan apply uniformly to all participants,
• The error results from a reasonable mistake by the employer (or the employer's agent) and is not due to willful neglect by the employer (or the employer's agent), and
• Salary reduction contributions in excess of $2,750 are paid to the employee and reported as wages for income tax withholding and employment tax purposes on the employee's Form W-2 (or Form W-2c) for the employee's taxable year in which, or with which, ends the cafeteria plan year in which the correction is made.

 The salary reduction contribution limit of $2,750 does not include any amount (up to $550) carried over from a previous year.

For more information, see Notice 2013-71, 2013-47 I.R.B. 532, available at *IRS.gov/irb/ 2013-47_IRB#NOT-2013-71*.

Health savings account (HSA). An employer's contribution (including an employee's contributions through a cafeteria plan) to an employee's HSA is not subject to federal income tax withholding or social security, Medicare, or railroad retirement taxes (or FUTA tax) if it is reasonable to believe at the time of the payment that the contribution will be excludable from the employee's income. However, if it is not reasonable to believe at the time of payment that the contribution will be excludable from the employee's income, employer contributions are subject to federal income tax withholding, social security and Medicare taxes (or railroad retirement taxes, if applicable), and FUTA tax, and must be reported in boxes 1, 3, and 5 (use box 14 if railroad retirement taxes apply); and on Form 940, Employer's Annual Federal Unemployment (FUTA) Tax Return.

You must report all employer contributions (including an employee's contributions through a cafeteria plan) to an HSA in box 12 of Form W-2 with code W. Employer contributions to an HSA that are not excludable from the income of the employee must also be reported in boxes 1, 3, and 5. (Use box 14 if railroad retirement taxes apply.)

An employee's contributions to an HSA (unless made through a cafeteria plan) are includible in income as wages and are subject to federal income tax withholding and social security and Medicare taxes (or railroad retirement taxes, if applicable). Employee contributions are deductible, within limits, on the employee's Form 1040 or 1040-SR. For more information about HSAs, see Notice 2004-2, Notice 2004-50, and Notice 2008-52. Notice 2004-2, 2004-2 I.R.B. 269, is available at *IRS.gov/irb/2004-02_IRB#NOT-2004-2*. Notice 2004-50, 2004-33 I.R.B. 196, is available at *IRS.gov/irb/ 2004-33_IRB#NOT-2004-50*. Notice 2008-52, 2008-25 I.R.B. 1166, is available at *IRS.gov/irb/ 2008-25_IRB#NOT-2008-52*. Also see Form 8889, Health Savings Accounts (HSAs), and Pub. 969.

Lost Form W-2—Reissued statement. If an employee loses a Form W-2, write "REISSUED STATEMENT" on the new copy and furnish it to the employee. You do not have to add "REISSUED STATEMENT" on Forms W-2 provided to employees electronically. Do not send Copy A of the reissued Form W-2 to the SSA. Employers are not prohibited (by the Internal Revenue Code) from charging a fee for the issuance of a duplicate Form W-2.

Military differential pay. Employers paying their employees while they are on active duty in the U.S. uniformed services should treat these payments as wages. Differential wage payments made to an individual while on active duty for periods scheduled to exceed 30 days are subject to income tax withholding, but are not subject to social security, Medicare, and unemployment taxes. Report differential wage payments in box 1 and any federal income tax withholding in box 2. Differential wage payments made to an individual while on active duty for 30 days or less are subject to income tax withholding, social security, Medicare, and unemployment taxes and are reported in boxes 1, 3, and 5. See Rev. Rul. 2009-11, 2009-18 I.R.B. 896, available at *IRS.gov/irb/ 2009-18_IRB#RR-2009-11*.

Moving expenses. Effective for tax years 2018 through 2025, the exclusion for qualified moving expense reimbursements applies **only** to members of the U.S. Armed Forces on active duty who move pursuant to a military order and incident to a permanent change of station. All other employees have only nonqualified moving expenses and expense reimbursements subject to tax and withholding.

Report qualified moving expenses for members of the Armed Forces as follows.
• Qualified moving expenses that an employer paid to a third party on behalf of the employee (for example, to a moving company), and services that an employer furnished in kind to an employee are not reported on Form W-2.
• Qualified moving expense reimbursements paid directly to an employee by an employer are reported only in box 12 of Form W-2 with code P.

Nonqualified moving expenses and expense reimbursements are reported in boxes 1, 3, and 5 (use box 14 if railroad retirement taxes apply) of Form W-2. These amounts are subject to federal income tax withholding and social security and Medicare taxes (or railroad retirement taxes, if applicable).

Nonqualified deferred compensation plans. Section 409A provides that all amounts deferred under a nonqualified deferred compensation (NQDC) plan for all tax years are currently includible in gross income to the extent not subject to a substantial risk of forfeiture and not previously included in gross income, unless certain requirements are met. Generally, section 409A is effective with respect to amounts deferred in tax years beginning after December 31, 2004, but deferrals made before that year may be subject to section 409A under some circumstances.

It is not necessary to show amounts deferred during the year under an NQDC plan subject to section 409A. If you report section 409A deferrals, show the amount in box 12 using code Y. For more information, see Notice 2008-115,

General Instructions for Forms W-2 and W-3 (2021)   **-11-**

Forms W-2/ W-3 and W-2c/W3-c Instructions (Page 12)

2008-52 I.R.B. 1367, available at *IRS.gov/irb/ 2008-52_IRB#NOT-2008-115*.

Income included under section 409A from an NQDC plan will be reported in box 1 and in box 12 using code Z. This income is also subject to an additional tax of 20% that is reported on Form 1040 or 1040-SR. For more information on amounts includible in gross income and reporting requirements, see Notice 2008-115 available at *IRS.gov/irb/2008-52_IRB#NOT-2008-115*. For information on correcting failures to comply with section 409A and related reporting, see Notice 2008-113, 2008-51 I.R.B. 1305, available at *IRS.gov/irb/ 2008-51_IRB#NOT-2008-113*; Notice 2010-6, 2010-3 I.R.B. 275, available at *IRS.gov/irb/ 2010-03_IRB#NOT-2010-6*; and Notice 2010-80, 2010-51 I.R.B. 853, available at *IRS.gov/irb/ 2010-51_IRB#NOT-2010-80*.

See the *Nonqualified Deferred Compensation Reporting Example Chart*.

Qualified equity grants under section 83(i). Report the amount includible in gross income from qualified equity grants under section 83(i)(1)(A) for the calendar year in box 12 using code GG. This amount is wages for box 1 and you must withhold income tax under section 3401(i) at the rate and manner prescribed in section 3401(t). You must withhold at the maximum rate of tax without regard to the employee's Form W-4. Social security and Medicare taxation of the deferral stock is not affected by these rules. See Notice 2018-97, 2018-52 I.R.B. 1062, available at *IRS.gov/irb/ 2018-52_IRB#NOT-2018-97*.

Qualified small employer health reimbursement arrangement. Use box 12, code FF, to report the total amount of permitted benefits under a qualified small employer health reimbursement arrangement (QSEHRA). QSEHRAs allow eligible employers to pay or reimburse medical care expenses of eligible employees after the employees provide proof of coverage. The maximum reimbursement for an eligible employee under a QSEHRA for 2021 is $5,300 ($10,700 if it also provides reimbursements for family members). For more information about QSEHRAs, see Notice 2017-67, 2017-47 I.R.B. 517, available at *IRS.gov/irb/ 2017-47_IRB#NOT-2017-67* and Pub. 15-B under *Accident and Health Benefits*. For information on employer reporting requirements, see *Code FF—Permitted benefits under a qualified small employer health reimbursement*, later.

Railroad employers (not applicable to Forms W-2AS, W-2CM, W-2GU, or W-2VI). Railroad employers must file Form W-2 to report their employees' wages and income tax withholding in boxes 1 and 2. You must file a separate Form W-3 to transmit the Forms W-2 if you have employees covered under the Federal Insurance Contributions Act (FICA) (social security and Medicare) **and** the Railroad Retirement Tax Act (RRTA).

For employees covered by RRTA tax. Check the "CT-1" checkbox on Form W-3, box b, "Kind of Payer," to transmit Forms W-2 for employees with box 1 wages and box 2 tax withholding. Use Form W-2, box 14, to report total RRTA compensation, Tier 1, Tier 2, Medicare

(excluding Additional Medicare Tax), and any Additional Medicare Tax withheld for each employee covered by RRTA tax. Label them "RRTA compensation," "Tier 1 tax," "Tier 2 tax," "Medicare tax," and "Additional Medicare Tax." Include tips reported by the employee to the employer in "RRTA compensation."

Employers should withhold Tier 1 and Tier 2 RRTA taxes on all money remuneration that stems from the employer-employee relationship, including award payments to employees to compensate for working time lost due to an on-the-job injury and lump-sum payments made to unionized employees upon ratification of collective bargaining agreements.

Employee stock options are not "money remuneration" subject to the RRTA. Railroad employers should not withhold Tier 1 and Tier 2 taxes when employees covered by the RRTA exercise stock options. Employers should still withhold federal income tax on taxable compensation from railroad employees exercising their stock options.

For employees covered by social security and Medicare. Check the "941" checkbox on Form W-3, box b, "Kind of Payer," to transmit Forms W-2 with box 1 wages and box 2 tax withholding for employees covered by social security and Medicare. Use Form W-2, boxes 3, 4, 5, 6, and 7, to report each employee's social security and Medicare wages and taxes, including Additional Medicare Tax. These boxes are **not** to be used to report railroad retirement compensation and taxes.

> ⚠ **CAUTION** *Railroad employers must withhold social security and Medicare taxes from taxable compensation of employees covered by social security and Medicare who are exercising their employee stock options.*

Repayments. If an employee repays you for wages received in error, do not offset the repayments against current year wages unless the repayments are for amounts received in error in the current year. Repayments made in the current year, but related to a prior year or years, must be repaid in gross, not net, and require special tax treatment by employees in some cases. You may advise the employee of the total repayments made during the current year and the amount (if any) related to prior years. This information will help the employee account for such repayments on his or her federal income tax return.

If the repayment was for a prior year, you must file Form W-2c with the SSA to correct only social security and Medicare wages and taxes, and furnish a copy to the employee. Do not correct "Wages, tips, other compensation" in box 1, or "Federal income tax withheld" in box 2, on Form W-2c. Also do not correct any Additional Medicare Tax withheld on the repaid wages (reported with Medicare tax withheld in box 6) on Form W-2c. File the "X" return that is appropriate for the return on which the wages or compensation was originally reported (Forms 941-X, 943-X, 944-X, or CT-1X). Correct the social security and Medicare wages and taxes for the period during which the wages or compensation was originally paid. For information on reporting adjustments to Forms 941, 941-SS, 943, 944, or Form CT-1, see section

Forms W-2/ W-3 and W-2c/W3-c Instructions (Page 13)

13 of Pub. 15 (Circular E), the Instructions for Form CT-1X, or section 9 of Pub. 51 (Circular A).

 Tell your employee that the wages paid in error in a prior year remain taxable to him or her for that year. This is because the employee received and had use of those funds during that year. The employee is not entitled to file an amended return (Form 1040-X) to recover the income tax on these wages. For repayments greater than $3,000, the employee may be entitled to a deduction or credit for the repaid wages on his or her Form 1040 or 1040-SR for the year of repayment. However, the employee is entitled to file an amended return (Form 1040-X) to recover Additional Medicare Tax on these wages, if any. Refer your employee to Repayments in Pub. 525, for additional information.

Scholarship and fellowship grants. Give a Form W-2 to each recipient of a scholarship or fellowship grant only if you are reporting amounts includible in income under section 117(c) (relating to payments for teaching, research, or other services required as a condition for receiving the qualified scholarship). Also see Pub. 15-A and Pub. 970. These payments are subject to federal income tax withholding. However, their taxability for social security and Medicare taxes (or railroad retirement taxes, if applicable) depends on the nature of the employment and the status of the organization. See *Students, scholars, trainees, teachers, etc.,* in section 15 of Pub. 15 (Circular E).

Sick pay. If you had employees who received sick pay in 2021 from an insurance company or other third-party payer and the third party notified you of the amount of sick pay involved, you may be required to report the information on the employees' Forms W-2. If the insurance company or other third-party payer did not notify you in a timely manner about the sick pay payments, it must prepare Forms W-2 and W-3 for your employees showing the sick pay. For specific reporting instructions, see section 6 of Pub. 15-A.

SIMPLE retirement account. An employee's salary reduction contributions to a SIMPLE (savings incentive match plan for employees) retirement account are not subject to federal income tax withholding but are subject to social security, Medicare, and railroad retirement taxes. Do not include an employee's contribution in box 1, but do include it in boxes 3 and 5. (Use box 14 if railroad retirement taxes apply.) An employee's total contribution must also be included in box 12 with code D or S.

An employer's matching or nonelective contribution to an employee's SIMPLE retirement account is not subject to federal income tax withholding or social security, Medicare, or railroad retirement taxes, and is not to be shown on Form W-2.

For more information on SIMPLE retirement accounts, see Notice 98-4, 1998-1 C.B. 269. You can find Notice 98-4 on page 25 of Internal Revenue Bulletin 1998-2 at *IRS.gov/pub/irs-irbs/irb98-02.pdf.*

Successor/predecessor employers. If you buy or sell a business during the year, see Rev. Proc. 2004-53 for information on who must file Forms W-2 and employment

tax returns. Rev. Proc. 2004-53, 2004-34 I.R.B. 320, is available at *IRS.gov/irb/2004-34_IRB#RP-2004-53.*

Terminating a business. If you terminate your business, you must provide Forms W-2 to your employees for the calendar year of termination by the due date of your final Form 941, 944, or 941-SS. You must also file Forms W-2 with the SSA by the due date of your final Form 941, 944, or 941-SS. If filing on paper, make sure you obtain Forms W-2 and W-3 preprinted with the correct year. If e-filing, make sure your software has been updated for the current tax year.

However, if any of your employees are immediately employed by a successor employer, see *Successor/ predecessor employers* above. Also, for information on automatic extensions for furnishing Forms W-2 to employees and filing Forms W-2, see Rev. Proc. 96-57, which is on page 14 of Internal Revenue Bulletin 1996-53 at *IRS.gov/pub/irs-irbs/irb96-53.pdf.*

 Get Schedule D (Form 941), Report of Discrepancies Caused by Acquisitions, Statutory Mergers, or Consolidations, for information on reconciling wages and taxes reported on Forms W-2 with amounts reported on Forms 941, 941-SS, or 944.

Uniformed Services Employment and Reemployment Rights Act of 1994 (USERRA) make-up amounts to a pension plan. If an employee returned to your employment after military service and certain make-up amounts were contributed to a pension plan for a prior year(s) under the USERRA, report the prior year contributions separately in box 12. See the *TIP* above Code D under *Box 12—Codes.* You may also report certain make-up amounts in box 14. See *Box 14—Other* in *Specific Instructions for Form W-2.*

Instead of reporting in box 12 (or box 14), you may choose to provide a separate statement to your employee showing USERRA make-up contributions. The statement must identify the type of plan, the year(s) to which the contributions relate, and the amount contributed for each year.

Virtual currency. For federal tax purposes, virtual currency is treated as property. Bitcoin is an example of virtual currency. Transactions using virtual currency (such as Bitcoin) must be reported in U.S. dollars.

The fair market value (FMV) of virtual currency (such as Bitcoin) paid as wages is income and subject to federal income tax withholding, FICA tax, and FUTA tax and must be reported on Form W-2. For more information about how virtual currency is treated for federal income tax purposes, including W-2 requirements, see Notice 2014-21, 2014-16 I.R.B. 938, available at *IRS.gov/irb/ 2014-16_IRB#NOT-2014-21* and Revenue Ruling 2019-24, available at *IRS.gov/irb/2019-44_IRB#REV- RUL-2019-24* and related FAQs, available at *IRS.gov/ Individuals/International-Taxpayers/Frequently-Asked- Questions-on-Virtual-Currency-Transactions.*

Penalties

The following penalties apply to the person or employer required to file Form W-2. The penalties apply to both paper filers and e-filers.

General Instructions for Forms W-2 and W-3 (2021)   -13-

Forms W-2/ W-3 and W-2c/W3-c Instructions (Page 14)

 Employers are responsible for ensuring that Forms W-2 are furnished to employees and that Forms W-2 and W-3 are filed with the SSA correctly and on time, even if the employer contracts with a third party to perform these acts. The IRS strongly suggests that the employer's address, not the third party's address, be the address on record with the IRS. This will ensure that you remain informed of tax matters involving your business because the IRS will correspond to the employer's address of record if there are any issues with an account. If you choose to outsource any of your payroll and related tax duties (that is, withholding, reporting, and paying over social security, Medicare, FUTA, and income taxes) to a third-party payer, go to IRS.gov/ OutsourcingPayrollDuties for helpful information on this topic.

Failure to file correct information returns by the due date. If you fail to file a correct Form W-2 by the due date and cannot show reasonable cause, you may be subject to a penalty as provided under section 6721. The penalty applies if you:
• Fail to file timely,
• Fail to include all information required to be shown on Form W-2,
• Include incorrect information on Form W-2,
• File on paper forms when you are required to *e-file*,
• Report an incorrect TIN,
• Fail to report a TIN, or
• Fail to file paper Forms W-2 that are machine readable.

The amount of the penalty is based on when you file the correct Form W-2. Penalties are indexed for inflation. The penalty amounts shown below apply to filings due after December 31, 2021. The penalty is:
• $50 per Form W-2 if you correctly file within 30 days of the due date; the maximum penalty is $571,000 per year ($199,500 for small businesses, defined in *Small businesses*).
• $110 per Form W-2 if you correctly file more than 30 days after the due date but by August 1; the maximum penalty is $1,713,000 per year ($571,000 for small businesses).
• $280 per Form W-2 if you file after August 1, do not file corrections, or do not file required Forms W-2; the maximum penalty is $3,426,000 per year ($1,142,000 for small businesses).

 If you do not file corrections and you do not meet any of the exceptions to the penalty, the penalty is $280 per information return. The maximum penalty is $3,426,000 per year ($1,142,000 for small businesses).

Exceptions to the penalty. The following are exceptions to the failure to file correct information returns penalty.

1. The penalty will not apply to any failure that you can show was due to reasonable cause and not to willful neglect. In general, you must be able to show that your failure was due to an event beyond your control or due to significant mitigating factors. You must also be able to show that you acted in a responsible manner and took steps to avoid the failure.

2. An inconsequential error or omission is not considered a failure to include correct information. An inconsequential error or omission is an error that does not prevent or hinder the SSA/IRS from processing the Form W-2, from correlating the information required to be shown on the form with the information shown on the payee's tax return, or from otherwise putting the form to its intended use. Errors and omissions that are never inconsequential are those relating to:
• A TIN,
• A payee's surname, and
• Any money amounts.

3. De minimis rule for corrections. Even though you cannot show reasonable cause, the penalty for failure to file correct Forms W-2 will not apply to a certain number of returns if you:
• Filed those Forms W-2 on or before the required filing date,
• Either failed to include all of the information required on the form or included incorrect information, and
• Filed corrections of these forms by August 1.

If you meet all of the de minimis rule conditions, the penalty for filing incorrect information returns (including Form W-2) will not apply to the greater of 10 information returns (including Form W-2) or one-half of 1% of the total number of information returns (including Form W-2) that you are required to file for the calendar year.

4. Forms W-2 issued with incorrect dollar amounts may fall under a safe harbor for certain de minimis errors. The safe harbor generally applies if no single amount in error differs from the correct amount by more than $100 and no single amount reported for tax withheld differs from the correct amount by more than $25.

If the safe harbor applies, you will not have to correct the Form W-2 to avoid penalties. However, if the payee elects for the safe harbor not to apply, you may have to issue a corrected return to avoid penalties. For more information, see Notice 2017-9, 2017-4 I.R.B. 542, available at *IRS.gov/irb/2017-04_IRB#NOT-2017-09*.

Small businesses. For purposes of the lower maximum penalties shown in *Failure to file correct information returns by the due date*, you are a small business if your average annual gross receipts for the 3 most recent tax years (or for the period that you were in existence, if shorter) ending before the calendar year in which the Forms W-2 were due are $5 million or less.

Intentional disregard of filing requirements. If any failure to timely file a correct Form W-2 is due to intentional disregard of the filing or correct information requirements, the penalty is at least $570 per Form W-2 with no maximum penalty.

Failure to furnish correct payee statements. If you fail to provide correct payee statements (Forms W-2) to your employees and cannot show reasonable cause, you may be subject to a penalty as provided under section 6722. The penalty applies if you fail to provide the statement by January 31, 2022, if you fail to include all information required to be shown on the statement, or if you include incorrect information on the statement.

The amount of the penalty is based on when you furnish the correct payee statement. This penalty is an

-14-   **General Instructions for Forms W-2 and W-3 (2021)**

Forms W-2/ W-3 and W-2c/W3-c Instructions (Page 15)

additional penalty and is applied in the same manner, and with the same amounts, as in *Failure to file correct information returns by the due date*.

Exceptions to the penalty. An inconsequential error or omission is not considered a failure to include correct information. An inconsequential error or omission is an error that cannot reasonably be expected to prevent or hinder the payee from timely receiving correct information and reporting it on his or her income tax return or from otherwise putting the statement to its intended use. Errors and omissions that are never inconsequential are those relating to:
• A dollar amount,
• A significant item in a payee's address, and
• The appropriate form for the information provided, such as whether the form is an acceptable substitute for the official IRS form.

See *Exceptions to the penalty* under *Failure to file correct information returns by the due date*, for additional exceptions to the penalty for failure to furnish correct payee statements.

Intentional disregard of payee statement requirements. If any failure to provide a correct payee statement (Form W-2) to an employee is due to intentional disregard of the requirements to furnish a correct payee statement, the penalty is $570 per Form W-2 with no maximum penalty.

Civil damages for fraudulent filing of Forms W-2. If you willfully file a fraudulent Form W-2 for payments that you claim you made to another person, that person may be able to sue you for damages. If you are found liable, you may have to pay $5,000 or more in damages. You may also be subject to criminal sanctions.

Specific Instructions for Form W-2

How to complete Form W-2. Form W-2 is a multi-part form. Ensure all copies are legible. Do not print Forms W-2 (Copy A) on double-sided paper. Send Copy A to the SSA; Copy 1, if required, to your state, city, or local tax department; and Copies B, C, and 2 to your employee. Keep Copy D, and a copy of Form W-3, with your records for 4 years.

Enter the information on Form W-2 using black ink in 12-point Courier font. Copy A is read by machine and must be typed clearly with no corrections made to the entries and with no entries exceeding the size of the boxes. Entries completed by hand, in script or italic fonts, or in colors other than black cannot be read by the machines. Make all dollar entries on Copy A without the dollar sign and comma but with the decimal point (00000.00). Show the cents portion of the money amounts. If a box does not apply, leave it blank.

Send the whole Copy A page of Form W-2 with Form W-3 to the SSA even if one of the Forms W-2 on the page is blank or void. Do not staple Forms W-2 together or to Form W-3. File Forms W-2 either alphabetically by employees' last names or numerically by employees' SSNs.

Also see the *Caution* under *How To Get Forms and Publications*.

Calendar year basis. The entries on Form W-2 must be based on wages paid during the calendar year. Use Form W-2 for the correct tax year. For example, if the employee worked from December 19, 2021, through January 1, 2022, and the wages for that period were paid on January 4, 2022, include those wages on the 2022 Form W-2.

Multiple forms. If necessary, you can issue more than one Form W-2 to an employee. For example, you may need to report more than four coded items in box 12 or you may want to report other compensation on a second form. If you issue a second Form W-2, complete boxes a, b, c, d, e, and f with the same information as on the first Form W-2. Show any items that were not included on the first Form W-2 in the appropriate boxes.

Do not report the same federal, American Samoa, CNMI, Guam, or U.S. Virgin Islands tax data to the SSA on more than one Copy A.

 For each Form W-2 showing an amount in box 3 or 7, make certain that box 5 equals or exceeds the sum of boxes 3 and 7.

Void. Check this box when an error is made on Form W-2 and you are voiding it because you are going to complete a new Form W-2. Do not include any amounts shown on "Void" forms in the totals you enter on Form W-3. See *Corrections*.

Box a—Employee's social security number. Enter the number shown on the employee's social security card.

If the employee does not have a card, he or she should apply for one by completing Form SS-5, Application for a Social Security Card. The SSA lets you verify employee names and SSNs online. For information about these free services, visit the Employer W-2 Filing Instructions & Information website at *SSA.gov/employer*. If you have questions about using these services, call 800-772-6270 (toll free) to speak with an employer reporting technician at the SSA.

If the employee has applied for a card but the number is not received in time for filing, enter "Applied For" in box a on paper Forms W-2 filed with the SSA. If e-filing, enter zeros (000-00-0000 if creating forms online or 000000000 if uploading a file).

Ask the employee to inform you of the number and name as they are shown on the social security card when it is received. Then correct your previous report by filing Form W-2c showing the employee's SSN. If the employee needs to change his or her name from that shown on the card, the employee should call the SSA at 800-772-1213.

If you do not provide the correct employee name and SSN on Form W-2, you may owe a penalty unless you have reasonable cause. For more information, see Pub. 1586, Reasonable Cause Regulations & Requirements for Missing and Incorrect Name/TINs.

ITINs for aliens. Do not accept an ITIN in place of an SSN for employee identification or for work. An ITIN is only available to resident and nonresident aliens who are not eligible for U.S. employment and need identification for other tax purposes. You can identify an ITIN because it is a 9-digit number formatted like an SSN beginning with the number "9" and with a number in one of the following

Forms W-2/ W-3 and W-2c/W3-c Instructions (Page 16)

ranges in the fourth and fifth digits: 50–65, 70–88, 90–92, and 94–99 (for example, 9NN-70-NNNN). An individual with an ITIN who later becomes eligible to work in the United States must obtain an SSN.

 Do not auto populate an ITIN into box a.

Box b—Employer identification number (EIN). Show the EIN assigned to you by the IRS (00-0000000). This should be the same number that you used on your federal employment tax returns (Forms 941, 941-SS, 943, 944, CT-1, or Schedule H (Form 1040)). Do not truncate your EIN. See Regulations section 31.6051-1(a)(1)(i)(A) and 301.6109-4(b)(2)(iv). Do not use a prior owner's EIN. If you do not have an EIN when filing Forms W-2, enter "Applied For" in box b; do not use your SSN. You can get an EIN by applying online at *IRS.gov/EIN* or by filing Form SS-4, Application for Employer Identification Number. Also see *Agent reporting*.

Box c—Employer's name, address, and ZIP code. This entry should be the same as shown on your Forms 941, 941-SS, 943, 944, CT-1, or Schedule H (Form 1040). The U.S. Postal Service recommends that no commas or periods be used in return addresses. Also see *Agent reporting*.

Box d—Control number. You may use this box to identify individual Forms W-2. You do not have to use this box.

Boxes e and f—Employee's name and address. Enter the name as shown on your employee's social security card (first name, middle initial, last name). If the name does not fit in the space allowed on the form, you may show the first and middle name initials and the full last name. It is especially important to report the exact last name of the employee. If you are unable to determine the correct last name, use of the SSA's Social Security Number Verification System may be helpful.

Separate parts of a compound name with either a hyphen or a blank space. Do not join them into a single word. Include all parts of a compound name in the appropriate name field. For example, for the name "John R Smith-Jones," enter "Smith-Jones" or "Smith Jones" in the last name field.

If the name has changed, the employee must get a corrected social security card from any SSA office. Use the name on the original card until you see the corrected card.

Do not show titles or academic degrees, such as "Dr.," "RN," or "Esq.," at the beginning or end of the employee's name. Generally, do not enter "Jr.," "Sr.," or other suffix in the "Suff." box on Copy A unless the suffix appears on the card. However, the SSA still prefers that you do not enter the suffix on Copy A.

Include in the address the number, street, and apartment or suite number (or P.O. box number if mail is not delivered to a street address). The U.S. Postal Service recommends that no commas or periods be used in delivery addresses. For a foreign address, give the information in the following order: city, province or state,

and country. Follow the country's practice for entering the postal code. Do not abbreviate the country name.

Box 1—Wages, tips, other compensation. Show the total taxable wages, tips, and other compensation that you paid to your employee during the year. However, do not include elective deferrals (such as employee contributions to a section 401(k) or 403(b) plan) except section 501(c) (18) contributions. Include the following.

1. Total wages, bonuses (including signing bonuses), prizes, and awards paid to employees during the year. See *Calendar year basis*.

2. Total noncash payments, including certain fringe benefits. See *Fringe benefits*.

3. Total tips reported by the employee to the employer (not allocated tips).

4. Certain employee business expense reimbursements. See *Employee business expense reimbursements*.

5. The cost of accident and health insurance premiums for 2%-or-more shareholder-employees paid by an S corporation.

6. Taxable benefits from a section 125 (cafeteria) plan if the employee chooses cash.

7. Employee contributions to an Archer MSA.

8. Employer contributions to an Archer MSA if includible in the income of the employee. See *Archer MSA*.

9. Employer contributions for qualified long-term care services to the extent that such coverage is provided through a flexible spending or similar arrangement.

10. Taxable cost of group-term life insurance in excess of $50,000. See *Group-term life insurance*.

11. Unless excludable under *Educational assistance programs*, payments for non-job-related education expenses or for payments under a nonaccountable plan. See Pub. 970.

12. The amount includible as wages because you paid your employee's share of social security and Medicare taxes (or railroad retirement taxes, if applicable). See *Employee's social security and Medicare taxes (or railroad retirement taxes, if applicable) paid by employer*. If you also paid your employee's income tax withholding, treat the grossed-up amount of that withholding as supplemental wages and report those wages in boxes 1, 3, 5, and 7. (Use box 14 if railroad retirement taxes apply.) No exceptions to this treatment apply to household or agricultural wages.

13. Designated Roth contributions made under a section 401(k) plan, a section 403(b) salary reduction agreement, or a governmental section 457(b) plan. See *Designated Roth contributions*.

14. Distributions to an employee or former employee from an NQDC plan (including a rabbi trust) or a nongovernmental section 457(b) plan.

15. Amounts includible in income under section 457(f) because the amounts are no longer subject to a substantial risk of forfeiture.

16. Payments to statutory employees who are subject to social security and Medicare taxes but not subject to

-16-   **General Instructions for Forms W-2 and W-3 (2021)**

Forms W-2/ W-3 and W-2c/W3-c Instructions (Page 17)

federal income tax withholding must be shown in box 1 as other compensation. See *Statutory employee*.

17. Cost of current insurance protection under a compensatory split-dollar life insurance arrangement.

18. Employee contributions to a health savings account (HSA).

19. Employer contributions to an HSA if includible in the income of the employee. See *Health savings account (HSA)*.

20. Amounts includible in income under section 409A from an NQDC because the amounts are no longer subject to a substantial risk of forfeiture and were not previously included in income. See *Nonqualified deferred compensation plans* under *Special Reporting Situations for Form W-2*.

21. Nonqualified moving expenses and expense reimbursements. See *Moving expenses.*

22. Payments made to former employees while they are on active duty in the U.S. Armed Forces or other uniformed services.

23. All other compensation, including certain scholarship and fellowship grants. See *Scholarship and fellowship grants*. Other compensation includes taxable amounts that you paid to your employee from which federal income tax was not withheld. You may show other compensation on a separate Form W-2. See *Multiple forms*.

Box 2—Federal income tax withheld. Show the total federal income tax withheld from the employee's wages for the year. Include the 20% excise tax withheld on excess parachute payments. See *Golden parachute payments*.

For Forms W-2AS, W-2CM, W-2GU, or W-2VI, show the total American Samoa, CNMI, Guam, or U.S. Virgin Islands income tax withheld.

Box 3—Social security wages. Show the total wages paid (before payroll deductions) subject to employee social security tax but not including social security tips and allocated tips. If reporting these amounts in a subsequent year (due to lapse of risk of forfeiture), the amount must be adjusted by any gain or loss. See *Box 7—Social security tips* and *Box 8—Allocated tips*. Generally, noncash payments are considered to be wages. Include employee business expense reimbursements and moving expenses reported in box 1. If you paid the employee's share of social security and Medicare taxes rather than deducting them from wages, see *Employee's social security and Medicare taxes (or railroad retirement taxes, if applicable) paid by employer*. The total of boxes 3 and 7 cannot exceed $142,800 (2021 maximum social security wage base).

Report in box 3 elective deferrals to certain qualified cash or deferred compensation arrangements and to retirement plans described in box 12 (codes D, E, F, G, and S) even though the deferrals are not includible in box 1. Also report in box 3 designated Roth contributions made under a section 401(k) plan, under a section 403(b) salary reduction agreement, or under a governmental section 457(b) plan described in box 12 (codes AA, BB, and EE).

Amounts deferred (plus earnings or less losses) under a section 457(f) or nonqualified plan or nongovernmental section 457(b) plan must be included in boxes 3 and/or 5 as social security and/or Medicare wages as of the later of when the services giving rise to the deferral are performed or when there is no substantial forfeiture risk of the rights to the deferred amount. Include both elective and nonelective deferrals for purposes of nongovernmental section 457(b) plans.

Wages reported in box 3 also include:
• Signing bonuses an employer pays for signing or ratifying an employment contract. See Rev. Rul. 2004-109, 2004-50 I.R.B. 958, available at *IRS.gov/irb/2004-50_IRB#RR-2004-109*.
• Taxable cost of group-term life insurance over $50,000 included in box 1. See *Group-term life insurance*.
• Cost of accident and health insurance premiums for 2%-or-more shareholder-employees paid by an S corporation, but only if not excludable under section 3121(a)(2)(B).
• Employee and nonexcludable employer contributions to an MSA or HSA. However, do not include employee contributions to an HSA that were made through a cafeteria plan. See *Archer MSA* and *Health savings account (HSA)*.
• Employee contributions to a SIMPLE retirement account. See *SIMPLE retirement account*.
• Adoption benefits. See *Adoption benefits*.

Box 4—Social security tax withheld. Show the total employee social security tax (not your share) withheld, including social security tax on tips. For 2021, the amount should not exceed $8,853.60 ($142,800 × 6.2%). Include only taxes withheld (or paid by you for the employee) for 2021 wages and tips. If you paid your employee's share, see *Employee's social security and Medicare taxes (or railroad retirement taxes, if applicable) paid by employer*.

Box 5—Medicare wages and tips. The wages and tips subject to Medicare tax are the same as those subject to social security tax (boxes 3 and 7) except that there is no wage base limit for Medicare tax. Enter the total Medicare wages and tips in box 5. Be sure to enter tips that the employee reported even if you did not have enough employee funds to collect the Medicare tax for those tips. See *Box 3—Social security wages* for payments to report in this box. If you paid your employee's share of taxes, see *Employee's social security and Medicare taxes (or railroad retirement taxes, if applicable) paid by employer*.

If you are a federal, state, or local governmental agency with employees paying only Medicare tax, enter the Medicare wages in this box. See *Government employers*.

Example of how to report social security and Medicare wages. You paid your employee $150,000 in wages. Enter in box 3 (social security wages) 142800.00, but enter in box 5 (Medicare wages and tips) 150000.00. There is no limit on the amount reported in box 5. If the amount of wages paid was $142,800 or less, the amounts entered in boxes 3 and 5 will be the same.

Box 6—Medicare tax withheld. Enter the total employee Medicare tax (including any Additional Medicare Tax) withheld. Do not include your share. Include only tax withheld for 2021 wages and tips. If you

General Instructions for Forms W-2 and W-3 (2021)   -17-

Forms W-2/ W-3 and W-2c/W3-c Instructions (Page 18)

paid your employee's share of the taxes, see *Employee's social security and Medicare taxes (or railroad retirement taxes, if applicable) paid by employer*.

For more information on Additional Medicare Tax, go to *IRS.gov/ADMT*.

Box 7—Social security tips. Show the tips that the employee reported to you even if you did not have enough employee funds to collect the social security tax for the tips. The total of boxes 3 and 7 should not be more than $142,800 (the maximum social security wage base for 2021). Report all tips in box 1 along with wages and other compensation. Also include any tips reported in box 7 in box 5.

Box 8—Allocated tips (not applicable to Forms W-2AS, W-2CM, W-2GU, or W-2VI). If you operate a large food or beverage establishment, show the tips allocated to the employee. See the Instructions for Form 8027, Employer's Annual Information Return of Tip Income and Allocated Tips. Do not include this amount in box 1, 3, 5, or 7.

Box 10—Dependent care benefits (not applicable to Forms W-2AS, W-2CM, W-2GU, or W-2VI). Show the total dependent care benefits under a dependent care assistance program (section 129) paid or incurred by you for your employee. Include the fair market value (FMV) of care in a daycare facility provided or sponsored by you for your employee and amounts paid or incurred for dependent care assistance in a section 125 (cafeteria) plan. Report all amounts paid or incurred (regardless of any employee forfeitures), including those in excess of the $5,000 exclusion. This may include (a) the FMV of benefits provided in kind by the employer, (b) an amount paid directly to a daycare facility by the employer or reimbursed to the employee to subsidize the benefit, or (c) benefits from the pre-tax contributions made by the employee under a section 125 dependent care flexible spending account. Include any amounts over $5,000 in boxes 1, 3, and 5. For more information, see Pub. 15-B.

 An employer that amends its cafeteria plan to provide a grace period for dependent care assistance may continue to rely on Notice 89-111 by reporting in box 10 the salary reduction amount elected by the employee for the year for dependent care assistance (plus any employer matching contributions attributable to dependent care). Also see Notice 2005-42, 2005-23 I.R.B. 1204, available at IRS.gov/irb/ 2005-23_IRB#NOT-2005-42 and Notice 2005-61, 2005-39 I.R.B. 607, available at IRS.gov/node/ 51071#NOT-2005-61.

Box 11—Nonqualified plans. The purpose of box 11 is for the SSA to determine if any part of the amount reported in box 1 or boxes 3 and/or 5 was earned in a prior year. The SSA uses this information to verify that they have properly applied the social security earnings test and paid the correct amount of benefits.

Report distributions to an employee from a nonqualified plan or nongovernmental section 457(b) plan in box 11. Also report these distributions in box 1. Make only one entry in this box. Distributions from governmental section 457(b) plans must be reported on Form 1099-R, not in box 1 of Form W-2.

Under nonqualified plans or nongovernmental 457(b) plans, deferred amounts that are no longer subject to a substantial risk of forfeiture are taxable even if not distributed. Report these amounts in boxes 3 (up to the social security wage base) and 5. Do not report in box 11 deferrals included in boxes 3 and/or 5 and deferrals for current year services (such as those with no risk of forfeiture).

⚠️ **CAUTION** *If you made distributions and are also reporting any deferrals in boxes 3 and/or 5, do not complete box 11. See Pub. 957, Reporting Back Pay and Special Wage Payments to the Social Security Administration, and Form SSA-131, Employer Report of Special Wage Payments, for instructions on reporting these and other kinds of compensation earned in prior years. However, do not file Form SSA-131 if this situation applies and the employee was not 61 years old or more during the tax year for which you are filing Form W-2.*

Unlike qualified plans, NQDC plans do not meet the qualification requirements for tax-favored status for this purpose. NQDC plans include those arrangements traditionally viewed as deferring the receipt of current compensation. Accordingly, welfare benefit plans, stock option plans, and plans providing dismissal pay, termination pay, or early retirement pay are generally not NQDC plans.

Report distributions from NQDC or section 457 plans to beneficiaries of deceased employees on Form 1099-MISC, not on Form W-2.

Military employers must report military retirement payments on Form 1099-R.

 Do not report special wage payments, such as accumulated sick pay or vacation pay, in box 11. For more information on reporting special wage payments, see Pub. 957.

Box 12—Codes. Complete and code this box for all items described below. Note that the codes do not relate to where they should be entered in boxes 12a through 12d on Form W-2. For example, if you are only required to report code D in box 12, you can enter code D and the amount in box 12a of Form W-2. Report in box 12 any items that are listed as codes A through HH. Do not report in box 12 section 414(h)(2) contributions (relating to certain state or local government plans). Instead, use box 14 for these items and any other information that you wish to give to your employee. For example, union dues and uniform payments may be reported in box 14.

💡 **TIP** *On Copy A (Form W-2), do not enter more than four items in box 12. If more than four items need to be reported in box 12, use a separate Form W-2 to report the additional items (but enter no more than four items on each Copy A (Form W-2)). On all other copies of Form W-2 (Copies B, C, etc.), you may enter more than four items in box 12 when using an approved substitute Form W-2. See Multiple forms.*

-18-   **General Instructions for Forms W-2 and W-3 (2021)**

Forms W-2/ W-3 and W-2c/W3-c Instructions (Page 19)

Use the IRS code designated below for the item you are entering, followed by the dollar amount for that item. Even if only one item is entered, you must use the IRS code designated for that item. Enter the code using a capital letter(s). Use decimal points but not dollar signs or commas. For example, if you are reporting $5,300.00 in elective deferrals under a section 401(k) plan, the entry would be D 5300.00 (not A 5300.00 even though it is the first or only entry in this box). Report the IRS code to the left of the vertical line in boxes 12a through 12d and the money amount to the right of the vertical line.

See the *Form W-2 Reference Guide for Box 12 Codes*.

The detailed instructions for each code are next.

Code A—Uncollected social security or RRTA tax on tips. Show the employee social security or Railroad Retirement Tax Act (RRTA) tax on all of the employee's tips that you could not collect because the employee did not have enough funds from which to deduct it. Do not include this amount in box 4.

Code B—Uncollected Medicare tax on tips. Show the employee Medicare tax or RRTA Medicare tax on tips that you could not collect because the employee did not have enough funds from which to deduct it. Do not show any uncollected Additional Medicare Tax. Do not include this amount in box 6.

Code C—Taxable cost of group-term life insurance over $50,000. Show the taxable cost of group-term life insurance coverage over $50,000 provided to your employee (including a former employee). See *Group-term life insurance*. Also include this amount in boxes 1, 3 (up to the social security wage base), and 5. Include the amount in box 14 if you are a railroad employer.

Codes D through H, S, Y, AA, BB, and EE. Use these codes to show elective deferrals and designated Roth contributions made to the plans listed. Do not report amounts for other types of plans. See the example for reporting elective deferrals under a section 401(k) plan, later.

The amount reported as elective deferrals and designated Roth contributions is only the part of the employee's salary (or other compensation) that he or she did not receive because of the deferrals or designated Roth contributions. Only elective deferrals and designated Roth contributions should be reported in box 12 for all coded plans; except, when using code G for section 457(b) plans, include both elective and nonelective deferrals.

For employees who were 50 years of age or older at any time during the year and made elective deferral and/or designated Roth "catch-up" contributions, report the elective deferrals and the elective deferral "catch-up" contributions as a single sum in box 12 using the appropriate code and the designated Roth contributions and designated Roth "catch-up" contributions as a single sum in box 12 using the appropriate code.

TIP *If any elective deferrals, salary reduction amounts, or nonelective contributions under a section 457(b) plan during the year are make-up amounts under the Uniformed Services Employment and Reemployment Rights Act of 1994 (USERRA) for a prior year, you must enter the prior year contributions*

separately. *Beginning with the earliest year, enter the code, the year, and the amount. For example, elective deferrals of $2,250 for 2019 and $1,250 for 2020 under USERRA under a section 401(k) plan are reported in box 12 as follows.*

D 19 2250.00, D 20 1250.00. A 2021 contribution of $7,000 does not require a year designation; enter it as D 7000.00. Report the code (and year for prior year USERRA contributions) to the left of the vertical line in boxes 12a through 12d.

The following are not elective deferrals and may be reported in box 14, but not in box 12.
- Nonelective employer contributions made on behalf of an employee.
- After-tax contributions that are not designated Roth contributions, such as voluntary contributions to a pension plan that are deducted from an employee's pay. See the box 12 instructions for *Code AA—Designated Roth contributions under a section 401(k) plan, Code BB—Designated Roth contributions under a section 403(b) plan*, and *Code EE—Designated Roth contributions under a governmental section 457(b) plan* for reporting designated Roth contributions.
- Required employee contributions.
- Employer matching contributions.

Code D—Elective deferrals under a section 401(k) cash or deferred arrangement (plan). Also show deferrals under a SIMPLE retirement account that is part of a section 401(k) arrangement.

Example of reporting excess elective deferrals and designated Roth contributions under a section 401(k) plan. For 2021, Employee A (age 45) elected to defer $21,500 under a section 401(k) plan. The employee also made a designated Roth contribution to the plan of $1,000, and made a voluntary (non-Roth) after-tax contribution of $600. In addition, the employer, on A's behalf, made a qualified nonelective contribution of $2,000 to the plan and a nonelective profit-sharing employer contribution of $3,000.

Even though the 2021 limit for elective deferrals and designated Roth contributions is $19,500, the employee's total elective deferral amount of $21,500 is reported in box 12 with code D (D 21500.00). The designated Roth contribution is reported in box 12 with code AA (AA 1000.00). The employer must separately report the actual amounts of $21,500 and $1,000 in box 12 with the appropriate codes. The amount deferred in excess of the limit is not reported in box 1. The return of excess elective deferrals and excess designated Roth contributions, including earnings on both, is reported on Form 1099-R.

The $600 voluntary after-tax contribution may be reported in box 14 (this is optional) but not in box 12. The $2,000 qualified nonelective contribution and the $3,000 nonelective profit-sharing employer contribution are not required to be reported on Form W-2, but may be reported in box 14.

Check the "Retirement plan" box in box 13.

Code E—Elective deferrals under a section 403(b) salary reduction agreement.

Code F—Elective deferrals under a section 408(k)(6) salary reduction SEP.

General Instructions for Forms W-2 and W-3 (2021)　　-19-

Forms W-2/ W-3 and W-2c/W3-c Instructions (Page 20)

Code G—Elective deferrals and employer contributions (including nonelective deferrals) to any governmental or nongovernmental section 457(b) deferred compensation plan. Do not report either section 457(b) or section 457(f) amounts that are subject to a substantial risk of forfeiture.

Code H—Elective deferrals under section 501(c)(18)(D) tax-exempt organization plan. Be sure to include this amount in box 1 as wages. The employee will deduct the amount on his or her Form 1040 or 1040-SR.

Code J—Nontaxable sick pay. Show any sick pay that was paid by a third party and was not includible in income (and not shown in boxes 1, 3, and 5) because the employee contributed to the sick pay plan. Do not include nontaxable disability payments made directly by a state.

Code K—20% excise tax on excess golden parachute payments (not applicable to Forms W-2AS, W-2CM, W-2GU, or W-2VI). If you made excess golden parachute payments to certain key corporate employees, report the 20% excise tax on these payments. If the excess payments are considered to be wages, report the 20% excise tax withheld as income tax withheld in box 2.

Code L—Substantiated employee business expense reimbursements. Use this code only if you reimbursed your employee for employee business expenses using a per diem or mileage allowance and the amount that you reimbursed exceeds the amount treated as substantiated under IRS rules. See *Employee business expense reimbursements*.

Report in box 12 only the amount treated as substantiated (such as the nontaxable part). Include in boxes 1, 3 (up to the social security wage base), and 5 the part of the reimbursement that is more than the amount treated as substantiated. Report the unsubstantiated amounts in box 14 if you are a railroad employer.

Code M—Uncollected social security or RRTA tax on taxable cost of group-term life insurance over $50,000 (for former employees). If you provided your former employees (including retirees) more than $50,000 of group-term life insurance coverage for periods during which an employment relationship no longer exists, enter the amount of uncollected social security or RRTA tax on the coverage in box 12. Do not include this amount in box 4. Also see *Group-term life insurance*.

Code N—Uncollected Medicare tax on taxable cost of group-term life insurance over $50,000 (for former employees). If you provided your former employees (including retirees) more than $50,000 of group-term life insurance coverage for periods during which an employment relationship no longer exists, enter the amount of uncollected Medicare tax or RRTA Medicare tax on the coverage in box 12. Do not show any uncollected Additional Medicare Tax. Do not include this amount in box 6. Also see *Group-term life insurance*.

Code P—Excludable moving expense reimbursements paid directly to a member of the U.S. Armed Forces. The exclusion for qualified moving expense reimbursements applies only to members of the U.S. Armed Forces on active duty who move pursuant to a military order and incident to a permanent change of station.

Show the total moving expense reimbursements that you paid directly to your employee for qualified (allowable) moving expenses. See *Moving expenses*.

Code Q—Nontaxable combat pay. If you are a military employer, report any nontaxable combat pay in box 12.

Code R—Employer contributions to an Archer MSA. Show any employer contributions to an Archer MSA. See *Archer MSA*.

Code S—Employee salary reduction contributions under a section 408(p) SIMPLE plan. Show deferrals under a section 408(p) salary reduction SIMPLE retirement account. However, if the SIMPLE plan is part of a section 401(k) arrangement, use code D. If you are reporting prior year contributions under USERRA, see the *TIP* above Code D under *Box 12—Codes*.

Code T—Adoption benefits. Show the total that you paid or reimbursed for qualified adoption expenses furnished to your employee under an adoption assistance program. Also include adoption benefits paid or reimbursed from the pre-tax contributions made by the employee under a section 125 (cafeteria) plan. However, do not include adoption benefits forfeited from a section 125 (cafeteria) plan. Report all amounts including those in excess of the $14,440 exclusion. For more information, see *Adoption benefits*.

Code V—Income from the exercise of nonstatutory stock option(s). Show the spread (that is, the fair market value (FMV) of stock over the exercise price of option(s) granted to your employee with respect to that stock) from your employee's (or former employee's) exercise of nonstatutory stock option(s). Include this amount in boxes 1, 3 (up to the social security wage base), and 5. If you are a railroad employer, do not include this amount in box 14 for railroad employees covered by RRTA. For more information, see *For employees covered by RRTA tax* above.

This reporting requirement does not apply to the exercise of a statutory stock option, or the sale or disposition of stock acquired pursuant to the exercise of a statutory stock option. For more information about the taxability of employee stock options, see Pub. 15-B.

Code W—Employer contributions to a health savings account (HSA). Show any employer contributions (including amounts the employee elected to contribute using a section 125 (cafeteria) plan) to an HSA. See *Health savings account (HSA)*.

Code Y—Deferrals under a section 409A nonqualified deferred compensation plan. It is not necessary to show deferrals in box 12 with code Y. For more information, see Notice 2008-115, 2008-52 I.R.B. 1367, available at *IRS.gov/irb/2008-52_IRB#NOT-2008-115*. However, if you report these deferrals, show current year deferrals, including earnings during the year on current year and prior year deferrals. See *Nonqualified deferred compensation plans* under *Special Reporting Situations for Form W-2*.

Code Z—Income under a nonqualified deferred compensation plan that fails to satisfy section 409A. Enter all amounts deferred (including earnings on amounts deferred) that are includible in income under section 409A because the NQDC plan fails to satisfy the

Forms W-2/ W-3 and W-2c/W3-c Instructions (Page 21)

requirements of section 409A. Do not include amounts properly reported on a Form 1099-MISC, corrected Form 1099-MISC, Form W-2, or Form W-2c for a prior year. Also do not include amounts that are considered to be subject to a substantial risk of forfeiture for purposes of section 409A. For more information, see Regulations sections 1.409A-1, -2, -3, and -6; and Notice 2008-115.

The amount reported in box 12 using code Z is also reported in box 1 and is subject to an additional tax reported on the employee's Form 1040 or 1040-SR. See *Nonqualified deferred compensation plans* under *Special Reporting Situations for Form W-2*.

For information regarding correcting section 409A errors and related reporting, see Notice 2008-113, Notice 2010-6, and Notice 2010-80.

Code AA—Designated Roth contributions under a section 401(k) plan. Use this code to report designated Roth contributions under a section 401(k) plan. Do not use this code to report elective deferrals under code D. See *Designated Roth contributions*.

Code BB—Designated Roth contributions under a section 403(b) plan. Use this code to report designated Roth contributions under a section 403(b) plan. Do not use this code to report elective deferrals under code E. See *Designated Roth contributions*.

Code DD—Cost of employer-sponsored health coverage. Use this code to report the cost of employer-sponsored health coverage. **The amount reported with code DD is not taxable.** Additional reporting guidance, including information about the transitional reporting rules that apply, is available on IRS.gov at *Affordable Care Act (ACA) Tax Provisions*.

Code EE—Designated Roth contributions under a governmental section 457(b) plan. Use this code to report designated Roth contributions under a governmental section 457(b) plan. Do not use this code to report elective deferrals under code G. See *Designated Roth contributions*.

Code FF—Permitted benefits under a qualified small employer health reimbursement arrangement. Use this code to report the total amount of permitted benefits under a QSEHRA. The maximum reimbursement for an eligible employee under a QSEHRA for 2021 is $5,300 ($10,700 if it also provides reimbursements for family members).

Report the amount of payments and reimbursements the employee is entitled to receive under the QSEHRA for the calendar year, not the amount the employee actually receives. For example, a QSEHRA provides a permitted benefit of $3,000. If the employee receives reimbursements of $2,000, report a permitted benefit of $3,000 in box 12 with code FF.

If your QSEHRA provides benefits that vary based on the number of family members covered under the arrangement or their ages and an eligible employee receives no payments or reimbursements and provides no proof of minimum essential coverage (MEC), report the highest value permitted benefits that the QSEHRA provides. If the employee later provides proof of MEC establishing eligibility for a lesser value permitted benefit, report this lesser value permitted benefit on Form W-2.

Do not include carryover amounts from prior years in the permitted benefit.

You may need to calculate a prorated permitted benefit under some circumstances.
- If your QSEHRA provides a permitted benefit prorated by month for employees not eligible for the full year, report the prorated permitted benefit. For example, a QSEHRA provides a permitted benefit of $3,000 prorated by the number of months the employee is eligible. If an employee becomes eligible on May 1, the employee's permitted benefit is $2,000 ($3,000 x 8/12) for the calendar year. The employer reports the permitted benefit of $2,000 for that employee in box 12 using code FF.
- If your QSEHRA is not based on a calendar year, prorate the permitted benefit for each part of the QSEHRA's plan year that falls within the calendar year. Report the sum of the prorated permitted benefits for the two portions of the calendar year. For example, a non-calendar year QSEHRA has a plan year that begins on April 1 and ends on March 31 of the following year. From April 1, 2020, through March 31, 2021, the QSEHRA provides a permitted benefit of $2,000. From April 1, 2021, through March 31, 2022, the QSEHRA provides a permitted benefit of $3,000. The employer reports a permitted benefit of $2,750 (($2,000 x 3/12) + ($3,000 x 9/12)) for calendar year 2021.

You may also have to follow special reporting rules for certain taxable reimbursements.
- If an employee who failed to have MEC for one or more months during the year mistakenly received reimbursements for expenses incurred in one of those months, those reimbursements are taxable to the employee. Report the taxable reimbursement as other compensation in box 1, but not in boxes 3 or 5. The taxable reimbursements are not wages for income, social security, or Medicare tax, so do not withhold these taxes. Report the permitted benefit that you would have reported for the employee as though there was no failure to have MEC. If you discover the lapse in MEC after filing with the SSA, furnish the employee a correction on Form W-2c and file the Form W-2c with the SSA.
- If your QSEHRA provides for taxable reimbursements of either (a) over-the-counter drugs bought without a prescription, or (b) premiums paid on a pre-tax basis for coverage under a group health plan sponsored by the employer of the employee's spouse, include the amount of the taxable reimbursements in boxes 1, 3, and 5 and treat as wages for purposes of income, social security, and Medicare taxes. Report the permitted benefit the employee is entitled to receive under the QSEHRA for the calendar year in box 12 using code FF. Although a part of the permitted benefit is a taxable reimbursement, that does not change the amount you report in box 12 with code FF.

For more details on reporting the total amount of QSEHRA permitted benefits, see Notice 2017-67, Q and A 57 through 63, 2017-47 I.R.B. 517 at *IRS.gov/irb/ 2017-47_IRB#NOT-2017-67*.

Code GG—Income from qualified equity grants under section 83(i). Report the amount includible in gross income from qualified equity grants under section

Forms W-2/ W-3 and W-2c/W3-c Instructions (Page 22)

83(i)(1)(A) for the calendar year. See *Qualified equity grants under section 83(i)* for more information.

Code HH—Aggregate deferrals under section 83(i) elections as of the close of the calendar year. Report the aggregate amount of income deferred under section 83(i) elections as of the close of the calendar year.

Box 13—Checkboxes. Check all boxes that apply.

Statutory employee. Check this box for statutory employees whose earnings are subject to social security and Medicare taxes but not subject to federal income tax withholding. Do not check this box for common-law employees. There are workers who are independent contractors under the common-law rules but are treated by statute as employees. They are called statutory employees.

1. A driver who distributes beverages (other than milk) or meat, vegetable, fruit, or bakery products; or who picks up and delivers laundry or dry cleaning, if the driver is your agent or is paid on commission.

2. A full-time life insurance sales agent whose principal business activity is selling life insurance or annuity contracts, or both, primarily for one life insurance company.

3. An individual who works at home on materials or goods that you supply and that must be returned to you or to a person you name, if you also furnish specifications for the work to be done.

4. A full-time traveling or city salesperson who works on your behalf and turns in orders to you from wholesalers, retailers, contractors, or operators of hotels, restaurants, or other similar establishments. The goods sold must be merchandise for resale or supplies for use in the buyer's business operation. The work performed for you must be the salesperson's principal business activity.

For details on statutory employees and common-law employees, see section 1 in Pub. 15-A.

Retirement plan. Check this box if the employee was an "active participant" (for any part of the year) in any of the following.

1. A qualified pension, profit-sharing, or stock-bonus plan described in section 401(a) (including a 401(k) plan).

2. An annuity plan described in section 403(a).

3. An annuity contract or custodial account described in section 403(b).

4. A simplified employee pension (SEP) plan described in section 408(k).

5. A SIMPLE retirement account described in section 408(p).

6. A trust described in section 501(c)(18).

7. A plan for federal, state, or local government employees or by an agency or instrumentality thereof (other than a section 457(b) plan).

Generally, an employee is an active participant if covered by (a) a defined benefit plan for any tax year that he or she is eligible to participate in, or (b) a defined contribution plan (for example, a section 401(k) plan) for any tax year that employer or employee contributions (or forfeitures) are added to his or her account. For additional information on employees who are eligible to participate in

a plan, contact your plan administrator. For details on the active participant rules, see Notice 87-16, 1987-1 C.B. 446; Notice 98-49, 1998-2 C.B. 365; section 219(g)(5); and Pub. 590-A, Contributions to Individual Retirement Arrangements (IRAs). You can find Notice 98-49 on page 5 of Internal Revenue Bulletin 1998-38 at *IRS.gov/pub/irs-irbs/irb98-38.pdf*.

 Do not check this box for contributions made to a nonqualified or section 457(b) plan.

See the *Form W-2 Box 13 Retirement Plan Checkbox Decision Chart*.

Third-party sick pay. Check this box only if you are a third-party sick pay payer filing a Form W-2 for an insured's employee or are an employer reporting sick pay payments made by a third party. See section 6 of Pub. 15-A.

Box 14—Other. If you included 100% of a vehicle's annual lease value in the employee's income, it must also be reported here or on a separate statement to your employee.

You may also use this box for any other information that you want to give to your employee. Label each item. Examples include state disability insurance taxes withheld, union dues, uniform payments, health insurance premiums deducted, nontaxable income, educational assistance payments, or a minister's parsonage allowance and utilities. In addition, you may enter the following contributions to a pension plan: (a) nonelective employer contributions made on behalf of an employee, (b) voluntary after-tax contributions (but not designated Roth contributions) that are deducted from an employee's pay, (c) required employee contributions, and (d) employer matching contributions.

If you are reporting prior year contributions under USERRA (see the *TIP* above Code D under *Box 12—Codes* and *Uniformed Services Employment and Reemployment Rights Act of 1994 (USERRA) make-up amounts to a pension plan*), you may report in box 14 make-up amounts for nonelective employer contributions, voluntary after-tax contributions, required employee contributions, and employer matching contributions. Report such amounts separately for each year.

Railroad employers, see *Railroad employers* for amounts reportable in box 14.

Boxes 15 through 20—State and local income tax information (not applicable to Forms W-2AS, W-2CM, W-2GU, or W-2VI). Use these boxes to report state and local income tax information. Enter the two-letter abbreviation for the name of the state. The employer's state ID numbers are assigned by the individual states. The state and local information boxes can be used to report wages and taxes for two states and two localities. Keep each state's and locality's information separated by the broken line. If you need to report information for more than two states or localities, prepare a second Form W-2. See *Multiple forms*. Contact your state or locality for specific reporting information.

Federal employers reporting income taxes paid to the CNMI under the 5517 agreement, enter the employer's identification number in box 15. Enter the employee's

Forms W-2/ W-3 and W-2c/W3-c Instructions (Page 23)

CNMI wages in box 16. Enter the income taxes paid to the CNMI in box 17. See *Federal employers in the CNMI*, earlier, for more information.

Specific Instructions for Form W-3

How to complete Form W-3. The instructions under *How to complete Form W-2* generally apply to Form W-3. Use black ink for all entries. Scanners cannot read entries if the type is too light. Be sure to send the entire page of the Form W-3.

TIP *Amounts reported on related employment tax forms (for example, Forms W-2, 941, 941-SS, 943, or 944) should agree with the amounts reported on Form W-3. If there are differences, you may be contacted by the IRS and SSA. Retain your reconciliation information for future reference. See* Reconciling Forms W-2, W-3, 941, 941-SS, 943, 944, CT-1, and Schedule H (Form 1040).

Box a—Control number. This is an optional box that you may use for numbering the whole transmittal.

Box b—Kind of Payer. Check the box that applies to you. Check only one box. If you have more than one type of Form W-2, send each type with a separate Form W-3. **Note.** The "Third-party sick pay" indicator box does not designate a separate kind of payer.

941. Check this box if you file Forms 941 or 941-SS and no other category applies. A church or church organization should check this box even if it is not required to file Forms 941, 941-SS, or 944. If you are a railroad employer sending Forms W-2 for employees covered under the Railroad Retirement Tax Act (RRTA), check the "CT-1" box.

Military. Check this box if you are a military employer sending Forms W-2 for members of the uniformed services.

943. Check this box if you are an agricultural employer and file Form 943 and you are sending Forms W-2 for agricultural employees. For nonagricultural employees, send their Forms W-2 with a separate Form W-3, checking the appropriate box.

944. Check this box if you file Form 944 (or Formulario 944(SP), its Spanish-language version), and no other category applies.

CT-1. Check this box if you are a railroad employer sending Forms W-2 for employees covered under the RRTA. Do not show employee RRTA tax in boxes 3 through 7. These boxes are only for social security and Medicare information. If you also have employees who are subject to social security and Medicare taxes, send that group's Forms W-2 with a separate Form W-3 and check the "941" checkbox on that Form W-3.

Hshld. emp. Check this box if you are a household employer sending Forms W-2 for household employees and you did not include the household employee's taxes on Forms 941, 941-SS, 943, or 944.

Medicare govt. emp. Check this box if you are a U.S., state, or local agency filing Forms W-2 for employees subject only to Medicare tax. See *Government employers*.

Box b—Kind of Employer. Check the box that applies to you. Check only one box unless the second checked box is "Third-party sick pay." See Pub. 557, Tax-Exempt Status for Your Organization, for information about 501(c)(3) tax-exempt organizations.

None apply. Check this box if none of the checkboxes discussed next apply to you.

501c non-govt. Check this box if you are a non-governmental tax-exempt section 501(c) organization. Types of 501(c) non-governmental organizations include private foundations, public charities, social and recreation clubs, and veterans organizations. For additional examples of 501(c) non-governmental organizations, see chapters 3 and 4 of Pub. 557.

State/local non-501c. Check this box if you are a state or local government or instrumentality. This includes cities, townships, counties, special-purpose districts, public school districts, or other publicly owned entities with governmental authority.

State/local 501c. Check this box if you are a state or local government or instrumentality, and you have received a determination letter from the IRS indicating that you are also a tax-exempt organization under section 501(c)(3).

Federal govt. Check this box if you are a federal government entity or instrumentality.

Box b—Third-party sick pay. Check this box if you are a third-party sick pay payer (or are reporting sick pay payments made by a third party) filing Forms W-2 with the "Third-party sick pay" checkbox in box 13 checked. File a single Form W-3 for the regular and "Third-party sick pay" Forms W-2. See *941*.

Box c—Total number of Forms W-2. Show the number of completed individual Forms W-2 that you are transmitting with this Form W-3. Do not count "Void" Forms W-2.

Box d—Establishment number. You may use this box to identify separate establishments in your business. You may file a separate Form W-3, with Forms W-2, for each establishment even if they all have the same EIN; or you may use a single Form W-3 for all Forms W-2 of the same type.

Box e—Employer identification number (EIN). Enter the 9-digit EIN assigned to you by the IRS. The number should be the same as shown on your Forms 941, 941-SS, 943, 944, CT-1, or Schedule H (Form 1040) and in the following format: 00-0000000. Do not truncate your EIN. See Regulations section 31.6051-1(a)(1)(i)(A) and 301.6109-4(b)(2)(iv). Do not use a prior owner's EIN. See *Box h—Other EIN used this year*.

If you do not have an EIN when filing your Form W-3, enter "Applied For" in box e, not your social security number (SSN), and see *Box b—Employer identification number (EIN)*.

Box f—Employer's name. Enter the same name as shown on your Forms 941, 941-SS, 943, 944, CT-1, or Schedule H (Form 1040).

Box g—Employer's address and ZIP code. Enter your address.

Box h—Other EIN used this year. If you have used an EIN (including a prior owner's EIN) on Forms 941, 941-SS, 943, 944, or CT-1 submitted for 2021 that is

Forms W-2/ W-3 and W-2c/W3-c Instructions (Page 24)

different from the EIN reported on Form W-3 in box e, enter the other EIN used. Agents generally report the employer's EIN in box h. See *Agent reporting*.

Employer's contact person, Employer's telephone number, Employer's fax number, and Employer's email address. Include this information for use by the SSA if any questions arise during processing. The SSA will notify the employer by email or postal mail to correct and resubmit reports from the information provided on Form W-3.

 Payroll service providers, enter your client's information for these fields.

 The amounts to enter in boxes 1 through 19, described next, are totals from only the Forms W-2 (excluding any Forms W-2 marked "Void") that you are sending with this Form W-3.

Boxes 1 through 8. Enter the totals reported in boxes 1 through 8 on the Forms W-2.

Box 9. Do not enter an amount in box 9.

Box 10—Dependent care benefits (not applicable to Forms W-2AS, W-2CM, W-2GU, and W-2VI). Enter the total reported in box 10 on Forms W-2.

Box 11—Nonqualified plans. Enter the total reported in box 11 on Forms W-2.

Box 12a—Deferred compensation. Enter the total of all amounts reported with codes D through H, S, Y, AA, BB, and EE in box 12 on Forms W-2. Do not enter a code.

 The total of Form W-2 box 12 amounts reported with codes A through C, J through R, T through W, Z, DD, FF, GG, and HH is not reported on Form W-3.

Box 13—For third-party sick pay use only. Leave this box blank. See Form 8922.

Box 14—Income tax withheld by payer of third-party sick pay. Complete this box only if you are the employer and have employees who had federal income tax withheld on third-party payments of sick pay. Show the total income tax withheld by third-party payers on payments to all of your employees. Although this tax is included in the box 2 total, it must be separately shown here.

Box 15—State/Employer's state ID number (territorial ID number for Forms W-2AS, W-2CM, W-2GU, and W-2VI). Enter the two-letter abbreviation for the name of the state or territory being reported on Form(s) W-2. Also enter your state- or territory-assigned ID number. If the Forms W-2 being submitted with this Form W-3 contain wage and income tax information from more than one state or territory, enter an "X" under "State" and do not enter any state or territory ID number.

Federal employers reporting income taxes paid to the CNMI under the 5517 agreement, enter the employer's identification number in box 15. See *Federal employers in the CNMI*, earlier, for more information.

Boxes 16 through 19 (not applicable to Forms W-2AS, W-2CM, W-2GU, and W-2VI). Enter the total of

state/local wages and income tax shown in their corresponding boxes on the Forms W-2 included with this Form W-3. If the Forms W-2 show amounts from more than one state or locality, report them as one sum in the appropriate box on Form W-3. Verify that the amount reported in each box is an accurate total of the Forms W-2.

Federal employers reporting income taxes paid to the CNMI under the 5517 agreement, enter the total of CNMI wages on the Forms W-2 in box 16. Enter the total of income taxes shown on the Forms W-2 paid to the CNMI in box 17. See *Federal employers in the CNMI*, earlier, for more information.

Reconciling Forms W-2, W-3, 941, 941-SS, 943, 944, CT-1, and Schedule H (Form 1040)

Reconcile the amounts shown in boxes 2, 3, 5, and 7 from all 2021 Forms W-3 with their respective amounts from the 2021 yearly totals from the quarterly Forms 941 or 941-SS or annual Forms 943, 944, CT-1 (box 2 only), and Schedule H (Form 1040). When there are discrepancies between amounts reported on Forms W-2 and W-3 filed with the SSA and on Forms 941, 941-SS, 943, 944, CT-1, or Schedule H (Form 1040) filed with the IRS, you will be contacted to resolve the discrepancies.

 To help reduce discrepancies on Forms W-2:

• Report bonuses as wages and as social security and Medicare wages on Form W-2; and on Forms 941, 941-SS, 943, 944, and Schedule H (Form 1040).
• Report both social security and Medicare wages and taxes separately on Forms W-2 and W-3; and on Forms 941, 941-SS, 943, 944, and Schedule H (Form 1040).
• Report social security taxes withheld on Form W-2 in box 4, not in box 3.
• Report Medicare taxes withheld on Form W-2 in box 6, not in box 5.
• Do not report a nonzero amount in box 4 if boxes 3 and 7 are both zero.
• Do not report a nonzero amount in box 6 if box 5 is zero.
• Do not report an amount in box 5 that is less than the sum of boxes 3 and 7.
• Make sure that the social security wage amount for each employee does not exceed the annual social security wage base limit ($142,800 for 2021).
• Do not report noncash wages that are not subject to social security or Medicare taxes as social security or Medicare wages.
• If you use an EIN on any quarterly Forms 941 or 941-SS for the year (or annual Forms 943, 944, CT-1, or Schedule H (Form 1040)) that is different from the EIN reported in box e on Form W-3, enter the other EIN in box h on Form W-3.

To reduce the discrepancies between amounts reported on Forms W-2 and W-3; and Forms 941, 941-SS, 943, 944, CT-1, and Schedule H (Form 1040):
• Be sure that the amounts on Form W-3 are the total amounts from Forms W-2.
• Reconcile Form W-3 with your four quarterly Forms 941 or 941-SS (or annual Forms 943, 944, CT-1, or

Forms W-2/ W-3 and W-2c/W3-c Instructions (Page 25)

Schedule H (Form 1040)) by comparing amounts reported for:

    1. Income tax withholding (box 2).

    2. Social security wages, Medicare wages and tips, and social security tips (boxes 3, 5, and 7). Form W-3 should include Forms 941 or 941-SS; or Forms 943, 944, or Schedule H (Form 1040) adjustments only for the current year. If the Forms 941, 941-SS, 943, or 944 adjustments include amounts for a prior year, do not report those prior year adjustments on the current year Forms W-2 and W-3.

    3. Social security and Medicare taxes (boxes 4 and 6). The amounts shown on the four quarterly Forms 941 or 941-SS (or annual Forms 943, 944, or Schedule H (Form 1040)), including current year adjustments, should be approximately twice the amounts shown on Form W-3.

Amounts reported on Forms W-2 and W-3; and Forms 941, 941-SS, 943, 944, CT-1, or Schedule H (Form 1040) may not match for valid reasons. If they do not match, you should determine that the reasons are valid. Retain your reconciliation information in case you receive inquiries from the IRS or the SSA.

You may have a discrepancy when reconciling Forms W-2 and W-3 to Forms 941, 941-SS, 943, 944, CT-1, or Schedule H (Form 1040), if you utilized any of the COVID-19 tax relief for 2020. You should consider that paid qualified sick leave wages and qualified family leave wages aren't subject to the employer share of social security tax. Also, the deferred amount of the employee share of social security tax is reported on Forms 941, 941-SS, 943, 944, CT-1, or Schedule H (Form 1040), but isn't reported on original Forms W-2 and W-3. See Pub. 15 or Pub. 51 and the instructions for your respective employment tax form for more information regarding these credits. Also see Notice 2020-65, 2020-38 I.R.B. 567, available at IRS.gov/irb/ 2020-38_IRB#NOT-2020-65. Notice 2021-11, available at IRS.gov/pub/irs-drop/N-21-11, modifies Notice 2020-65 to extend the period in 2021 over which you are to withhold and pay the deferred taxes. The notice reflects P.L. 116-260, Division N (the COVID-related Tax Relief Act of 2020), section 274, which extends the withholding period in Notice 2020-65 from April 30, 2021, to December 31, 2021. See Form W-2 Reporting of Employee Social Security Tax Deferred under Notice 2020-65, available at IRS.gov/Forms-Pubs/Form-W-2-Reporting-of-Employee-Social-Security-Tax-Deferred-Under-Notice-2020-65. You can check the Recent Developments section on IRS.gov for your respective employment tax form to see if future legislation extends the dates these credits may be claimed.

General Instructions for Forms W-2c and W-3c

Applicable forms. Use with the current version of Form W-2c and the current version of Form W-3c.

Purpose of forms. Use Form W-2c to correct errors on Forms W-2, W-2AS, W-2CM, W-2GU, W-2VI, or W-2c filed with the SSA. Also use Form W-2c to provide

corrected Forms W-2, W-2AS, W-2CM, W-2GU, W-2VI, or W-2c to employees.

Corrections reported on Form W-2c may require you to make corrections to your previously filed employment tax returns using the corresponding "X" form, such as Form 941-X, Adjusted Employer's QUARTERLY Federal Tax Return or Claim for Refund; Form 943-X, Adjusted Employer's Annual Federal Tax Return for Agricultural Employees or Claim for Refund; Form 944-X, Adjusted Employer's ANNUAL Federal Tax Return or Claim for Refund; or Form CT-1X, Adjusted Employer's Annual Railroad Retirement Tax Return or Claim for Refund. See section 13 of Pub. 15 (Circular E) and the Instructions for Form CT-1X for more information. If you are making corrections to a previously filed Schedule H (Form 1040) (for 2019, Schedule H (Form 1040 or 1040-SR)), see Pub. 926, Household Employer's Tax Guide. If an employee repaid you for wages received in a prior year, also see *Repayments*.

Do not use Form W-2c to report corrections to back pay. Instead, see Pub. 957, Reporting Back Pay and Special Wage Payments to the Social Security Administration, and Form SSA-131, Employer Report of Special Wage Payments.

Do not use Form W-2c to correct Form W-2G, Certain Gambling Winnings. Instead, see the General Instructions for Certain Information Returns for the current reporting year.

Use Form W-3c to send Copy A of Form W-2c to the SSA. Always file Form W-3c when submitting one or more Forms W-2c.

E-filing Forms W-2c and W-3c. The SSA encourages all employers to *e-file* using its secure BSO website. E-filing can save you time and effort and helps ensure accuracy. See *E-filing*.

Where to file paper Forms W-2c and W-3c. If you use the U.S. Postal Service, send Forms W-2c and W-3c to:

    Social Security Administration
    Direct Operations Center
    P.O. Box 3333
    Wilkes-Barre, PA 18767-3333

If you use a carrier other than the U.S. Postal Service, send Forms W-2c and W-3c to:

    Social Security Administration
    Direct Operations Center
    Attn: W-2c Process
    1150 E. Mountain Drive
    Wilkes-Barre, PA 18702-7997

Go to *IRS.gov/PDS* for a list of IRS-designated private delivery services.

 Do not send Forms W-2, W-2AS, W-2CM, W-2GU, or W-2VI to either of these addresses. Instead, see Where to file paper Forms W-2 and W-3.

Forms W-2/ W-3 and W-2c/W3-c Instructions (Page 26)

When to file. File Forms W-2c and W-3c as soon as possible after you discover an error. Also provide Form W-2c to employees as soon as possible.

How to complete. If you file Forms W-2c and W-3c on paper, make all entries using dark or black ink in 12-point Courier font, if possible, and make sure all copies are legible. See *How to complete Form W-2*.

If any item shows a change in the dollar amount and one of the amounts is zero, enter "-0-." Do not leave the box blank.

Who may sign Form W-3c. Generally, employers must sign Form W-3c. See *Who may sign Form W-3*.

Special Situations for Forms W-2c and W-3c

Undeliverable Forms W-2c. See *Undeliverable Forms W-2*.

Correcting Forms W-2 and W-3

Corrections. Use the current version of Form W-2c to correct errors (such as incorrect name, SSN, or amount) on a previously filed Form W-2 or Form W-2c. File Copy A of Form W-2c with the SSA. To *e-file* your corrections, see *Correcting wage reports*.

If the SSA issues your employee a replacement card after a name change, or a new card with a different social security number after a change in alien work status, file a Form W-2c to correct the name/SSN reported on the most recently filed Form W-2. It is not necessary to correct the prior years if the previous name and number were used for the years prior to the most recently filed Form W-2.

File Form W-3c whenever you file a Form W-2c with the SSA, even if you are only filing a Form W-2c to correct an employee's name or SSN. However, see *Employee's incorrect address on Form W-2*, later, for information on correcting an employee's address. See *Correcting an incorrect tax year and/or EIN incorrectly reported on Form W-2 or Form W-3*, later, if an error was made on a previously filed Form W-3.

If you discover an error on Form W-2 after you issue it to your employee but before you send it to the SSA, check the "Void" box at the top of the incorrect Form W-2 on Copy A. Prepare a new Form W-2 with the correct information, and send Copy A to the SSA. Write "CORRECTED" on the employee's new copies (B, C, and 2), and furnish them to the employee. If the "Void" Form W-2 is on a page with a correct Form W-2, send the entire page to the SSA. The "Void" form will not be processed. Do not write "CORRECTED" on Copy A of Form W-2.

If you are making a correction for previously filed Forms 941, 941-SS, 943, 944, or CT-1, use the corresponding "X" forms, such as Forms 941-X, 943-X, 944-X, or CT-1X for the return period in which you found the error. See section 13 of Pub. 15 (Circular E) and the Instructions for Form CT-1X for more details. If you are making corrections to a previously filed Schedule H (Form 1040) (for 2019, Schedule H (Form 1040 or 1040-SR)), see Pub. 926. Issue the employee a Form W-2c if the error

discovered was for the prior year and Form W-2 was filed with the SSA.

Correcting an employee's name and/or SSN only. If you are correcting only an employee's name and/or SSN, complete Form W-2c boxes d through i. Do not complete boxes 1 through 20. Advise your employee to correct the SSN and/or name on his or her original Form W-2.

If your employee is given a new social security card following an adjustment to his or her resident status that shows a different name or SSN, file a Form W-2c for the most current year only.

Correcting an employee's name and SSN if the SSN was reported as blanks or zeros and the employee name was reported as blanks. If you need to correct an employee's name and SSN, and the SSN was reported as blanks or zeros and the employee's name was reported as blanks, do not use Form W-2c to report the corrections. You must contact the SSA at 800-772-6270 for instructions.

Correcting an incorrect tax year and/or EIN incorrectly reported on Form W-2 or Form W-3. To correct an incorrect tax year and/or EIN on a previously submitted Form W-2 or Form W-3, you must prepare two sets of Forms W-2c and W-3c.
• Prepare one Form W-3c along with a Form W-2c for each affected employee. On the Form W-3c, enter the incorrect tax year in box a and the incorrect EIN originally reported in box h. Enter in the "Previously reported" boxes the money amounts that were on the original Form W-2. In the "Correct information" boxes, enter zeros.
• Prepare a second Form W-3c along with a second Form W-2c for each affected employee. On the Form W-3c, enter the correct tax year in box a and/or the correct EIN in box e. Enter zeros in the "Previously reported" boxes, and enter the correct money amounts in the "Correct information" boxes.

Correcting more than one Form W-2 for an employee. There are two ways to prepare a correction for an employee for whom more than one Form W-2 was filed under the same EIN for the tax year. You can (1) consider all the Forms W-2 when determining the amounts to enter on Form W-2c, or (2) file a single Form W-2c to correct only the incorrect Form W-2.

However, state, local, and federal government employers who are preparing corrections for Medicare Qualified Government Employment (MQGE) employees must also follow the instructions in the *Caution* for state, local, and federal government employers in the *Specific Instructions for Form W-2c*.

Correcting more than one kind of form. You must use a separate Form W-3c for each type of Form W-2 (Forms W-2, W-2AS, W-2CM, W-2GU, W-2VI, or W-2c) being corrected. You must also use a separate Form W-3c for each kind of payer/employer combination in box c. If you are correcting more than one kind of form, please group forms of the same kind of payer/employer combination, and send them in separate groups.

Employee's incorrect address on Form W-2. If you filed a Form W-2 with the SSA that reported an incorrect address for the employee, but all other information on the

General Instructions for Forms W-2 and W-3 (2021)

Forms W-2/ W-3 and W-2c/W3-c Instructions (Page 27)

Form W-2 was correct, do not file Form W-2c with the SSA merely to correct the address.

However, if the address was incorrect on the Form W-2 furnished to the employee, you must do one of the following.
• Issue a new, corrected Form W-2 to the employee that includes the new address. Indicate "REISSUED STATEMENT" on the new copies. Do not send Copy A of Form W-2 to the SSA.
• Issue a Form W-2c to the employee that shows the correct address in box i and all other correct information. Do not send Copy A of Form W-2c to the SSA.
• Reissue the Form W-2 with the incorrect address to the employee in an envelope showing the correct address or otherwise deliver it to the employee.

Two Forms W-2 were filed under the same EIN, but only one should have been filed.

Example. Two Forms W-2 were submitted for Mary Smith under the same EIN for the same tax year. One Form W-2 correctly reported social security wages of $20,000. The other Form W-2 incorrectly reported social security wages of $30,000. There are two ways to correct this situation.
• File a Form W-3c along with one Form W-2c, entering $50,000 in box 3 under "Previously reported" and $20,000 in box 3 under "Correct information"; or
• File a Form W-3c along with one Form W-2c, entering $30,000 in box 3 under "Previously reported" and $0.00 in box 3 under "Correct information."

Two Forms W-2 were filed under the same EIN, but wages on one were incorrect.

Example. Two Forms W-2 were submitted for Mary Smith under the same EIN for the same tax year. One Form W-2 correctly reported social security wages of $20,000. The other Form W-2 incorrectly reported social security wages of $30,000, whereas $25,000 should have been reported. There are two ways to correct this situation.
• File a Form W-3c along with one Form W-2c, entering $50,000 in box 3 under "Previously reported" and $45,000 in box 3 under "Correct information"; or
• File a Form W-3c along with one Form W-2c, entering $30,000 in box 3 under "Previously reported" and $25,000 in box 3 under "Correct information."

Reporting of employee social security and RRTA tax deferred in 2020.
Employee social security tax deferred in 2020 under Notice 2020-65 that is withheld in 2021 and not reported on the 2020 Form W-2 should be reported in box 4 (Social security tax withheld) on Form W-2c. Enter tax year "2020" in box c and adjust the amount previously reported in box 4 of the Form W-2 to include the deferred amounts that were withheld in 2021. All Forms W-2c should be filed with the SSA, along with Form W-3c, as soon as possible after you have finished withholding the deferred amounts.

Employee RRTA tax deferred in 2020 under Notice 2020-65 that is withheld in 2021 and not reported on the 2020 Form W-2 should be reported in box 14 on Form W-2c. Enter tax year "2020" in box c and adjust the amount previously reported as Tier 1 tax in box 14 of the Form W-2 to include the deferred amounts that were withheld in 2021.

See Notice 2020-65, 2020-38 I.R.B. 567, available at *IRS.gov/irb/2020-38_IRB#NOT-2020-65*. Notice 2021-11, available at *IRS.gov/pub/irs-drop/N-21-11*, modifies Notice 2020-65 to extend the period in 2021 over which you are to withhold and pay the deferred taxes. The notice reflects P.L. 116-260, Division N (the COVID-related Tax Relief Act of 2020), section 274, which extends the withholding period in Notice 2020-65 from April 30, 2021, to December 31, 2021. See Form W-2 Reporting of Employee Social Security Tax Deferred under Notice 2020-65, available at *IRS.gov/Forms-Pubs/Form-W-2-Reporting-of-Employee-Social-Security-Tax-Deferred-Under-Notice-2020-65*, for more information.

Specific Instructions for Form W-2c

Box a—Employer's name, address, and ZIP code. This entry should be the same as shown on your Forms 941, 941-SS, 943, 944, CT-1, or Schedule H (Form 1040) (for 2019, Schedule H (Form 1040 or 1040-SR)).

Box b—Employer's Federal EIN. Show the correct 9-digit EIN assigned to you by the IRS in the format 00-0000000. Do not truncate your EIN. See Regulations section 31.6051-1(a)(1)(i)(A) and 301.6109-4(b)(2)(iv).

Box c—Tax year/Form corrected. If you are correcting Form W-2, enter all 4 digits of the year of the form you are correcting. If you are correcting Form W-2AS, W-2CM, W-2GU, W-2VI, or W-2c, enter all 4 digits of the year you are correcting, and also enter "AS," "CM," "GU," "VI," or "c" to designate the form you are correcting. For example, entering "2019" and "GU" indicates that you are correcting a 2019 Form W-2GU.

Box d—Employee's correct SSN. You must enter the employee's correct SSN even if it was correct on the original Form W-2. If you are correcting an employee's SSN, you must also complete boxes e through i.

Box e—Corrected SSN and/or name. Check this box only if you are correcting the employee's SSN, name, or both SSN and name. You must also complete boxes d and f through i.

Box f—Employee's previously reported SSN. Complete this box if you are correcting an employee's previously reported incorrect SSN and/or name. If the previous SSN was reported as blanks or not available, then box f should be all zeroes.

Box g—Employee's previously reported name. Complete this box if you are correcting an employee's previously reported incorrect SSN and/or name. You must enter the employee's previously reported full name in box g exactly as it was previously reported. If the previous reported name was reported as blanks or not available, then box g should be all blanks.

 *For boxes f and g, if both the previous SSN and the previous name were reported as blanks, **do not** use Form W-2c. Contact the SSA at 800-772-6270.*

General Instructions for Forms W-2 and W-3 (2021) -27-

Forms W-2/ W-3 and W-2c/W3-c Instructions (Page 28)

Box h—Employee's first name and initial, Last name, Suff. Always enter the employee's correct name. See *Boxes e and f—Employee's name and address* for name formatting information.

Box i—Employee's address and ZIP code. Always enter the employee's correct address. See *Boxes e and f—Employee's name and address* for address formatting information.

 You must enter the employee's full name in boxes g and h.

Boxes 1 through 20. For the items you are changing, enter under "Previously reported" the amount reported on the original Form W-2 or the amount reported on a previously filed Form W-2c. Enter the correct amount under "Correct information."

Do not make an entry in any of these boxes on Copy A unless you are making a change. However, see the *Caution* for state, local, or federal government employers below.

Box 2—Federal income tax withheld. Use this box only to make corrections because of an administrative error. (An administrative error occurs only if the amount you entered in box 2 of the incorrect Form W-2 was not the amount you actually withheld.) If you are correcting Forms W-2AS, W-2CM, W-2GU, or W-2VI, box 2 is for income tax withheld for the applicable U.S. possession.

Boxes 5 and 6. Complete these boxes to correct Medicare wages and tips and Medicare tax withheld. (Exception—do not correct Additional Medicare Tax withheld unless you need to correct an administrative error. An administrative error occurs only if the amount you entered in box 6 of the incorrect Form W-2 is not the amount you actually withheld.) State, local, or federal government employers should also use these boxes to correct MQGE wages. Box 5 must equal or exceed the sum of boxes 3 and 7.

 A state, local, or federal government employer correcting only social security wages and/or social security tips (boxes 3 and/or 7) for an MQGE employee must also complete Medicare wages and tips in box 5. Enter the total Medicare wages and tips, including MQGE-only wages, even if there is no change to the total Medicare wages and tips previously reported.

Boxes 8, 10, and 11. Use these boxes to correct allocated tips, dependent care benefits, or deferrals and distributions relating to nonqualified plans.

Box 12—Codes. Complete these boxes to correct any of the coded items shown on Forms W-2. Examples include uncollected social security and/or Medicare taxes on tips, taxable cost of group-term life insurance coverage over $50,000, elective deferrals (codes D through H, S, Y, AA, BB, and EE), sick pay not includible as income, and employee business expenses. See *Box 12—Codes* in *Specific Instructions for Form W-2* for the proper format to use in reporting coded items from box 12 of Forms W-2.

Employers should enter both the code and dollar amount for both fields on Form W-2c.

If a single Form W-2c does not provide enough blank spaces for corrections, use additional Forms W-2c.

Box 13. Check the boxes in box 13, under "Previously reported," as they were checked on the original Form W-2. Under "Correct information," check them as they should have been checked. For example, if you checked the "Retirement plan" box on the original Form W-2 by mistake, check the "Retirement plan" checkbox in box 13 under "Previously reported," but do not check the "Retirement plan" checkbox in box 13 under "Correct information."

Box 14. Use this box to correct items reported in box 14 of the original Form W-2 or on a prior Form W-2c. If possible, complete box 14 on Copies B, C, 1, and 2 of Form W-2c only, not on Copy A.

Boxes 15 through 20—State/Local taxes. If your only changes to the original Form W-2 are to state or local data, do not send Copy A of Form W-2c to the SSA. Instead, send Form W-2c to the appropriate state or local agency and furnish copies to your employees.

Correcting state information. Contact your state or locality for specific reporting information.

Specific Instructions for Form W-3c

Do not staple or tape the Forms W-2c to Form W-3c or to each other. File a separate Form W-3c for each tax year, for each type of form, and for each kind of payer/employer combination. (The "Third-party sick pay" indicator box does not designate a separate kind of payer or employer.) Make a copy of Form W-3c for your records.

In the money boxes of Form W-3c, total the amounts from each box and column on the Forms W-2c you are sending.

Box a—Tax year/Form corrected. Enter all 4 digits of the year of the form you are correcting and the type of form you are correcting. For the type of form, enter "2," "2AS," "2CM," "2GU," "2VI," "2c," "3," "3SS," or "3c." For example, entering "2019" and "2" indicates that all the forms being corrected are 2019 Forms W-2.

Box b—Employer's name, address, and ZIP code. This should be the same as shown on your Forms 941, 941-SS, 943, 944, CT-1, or Schedule H (Form 1040) (for 2019, Schedule H (Form 1040 or 1040-SR)). Include the suite, room, or other unit number after the street address. If the post office does not deliver mail to the street address and you use a P.O. box, show the P.O. box number instead of the street address.

 The IRS will not use Form W-3c to update your address of record. If you wish to change your address, file Form 8822 or Form 8822-B.

Box c—Kind of Payer. Check the box that applies to you. Check only one box. If your previous Form W-3 or Form W-3SS was checked incorrectly, report your prior incorrect payer type in the "Explain decreases here" area below boxes 18 and 19.

941/941-SS. Check this box if you file Form 941 or Form 941-SS. If you are a railroad employer sending

Forms W-2/ W-3 and W-2c/W3-c Instructions (Page 29)

Forms W-2c for employees covered under the RRTA, check the "CT-1" checkbox.

Military. Check this box if you are a military employer correcting Forms W-2 for members of the uniformed services.

943. Check this box if you file Form 943 and you are correcting Forms W-2 for agricultural employees. For nonagricultural employees, send Forms W-2c with a separate Form W-3c, generally with the 941/941-SS box checked.

944. Check this box if you file Form 944.

CT-1. Check this box if you are a railroad employer correcting Forms W-2 for employees covered under the RRTA. If you also have to correct forms of employees who are subject to social security and Medicare taxes, complete a separate Form W-3c with the "941/941-SS" box or "944" box checked instead.

Hshld. emp. Check this box if you are a household employer correcting Forms W-2 for household employees and you filed a Schedule H (Form 1040) (for 2019, Schedule H (Form 1040 or 1040-SR)). If you also have to correct forms of employees who are not household employees, complete a separate Form W-3c.

Medicare govt. emp. Check this box if you are a U.S., state, or local agency filing corrections for employees subject only to Medicare taxes.

Box c—Kind of Employer. Check the box that applies to you. Check only one box. If your previous Form W-3 or W-3SS was checked incorrectly, report your prior incorrect employer type in the "Explain decreases here" area below boxes 18 and 19.

None apply. Check this box if none of the checkboxes described next apply to you.

501c non-govt. Check this box if you are a non-governmental tax-exempt 501(c) organization. Types of 501(c) non-governmental organizations include private foundations, public charities, social and recreation clubs, and veterans organizations. For additional examples of 501(c) non-governmental organizations, see chapters 3 and 4 of Pub. 557, Tax-Exempt Status for Your Organization.

State/local non-501c. Check this box if you are a state or local government or instrumentality. This includes cities, townships, counties, special-purpose districts, public school districts, or other publicly owned entities with governmental authority.

State/local 501c. Check this box if you are a state or local government or instrumentality, and you have received a determination letter from the IRS indicating that you are also a tax-exempt organization under section 501(c)(3).

Federal govt. Check this box if you are a federal government entity or instrumentality.

Box c—Third-party sick pay. Check this box if you are a third-party sick pay payer (or are reporting sick pay payments made by a third party) correcting Forms W-2 with the "Third-party sick pay" checkbox in box 13 of Form W-2c under "Correct information" checked. File a separate Form W-3c for each payer/employer combination reporting "Third-party sick pay" on Form W-2c.

Box d—Number of Forms W-2c. Show the number of individual Forms W-2c filed with this Form W-3c or enter "-0-" if you are correcting only a previously filed Form W-3 or Form W-3SS.

Box e—Employer's Federal EIN. Enter the correct number assigned to you by the IRS in the following format: 00-0000000. Do not truncate your EIN. See Regulations section 31.6051-1(a)(1)(i)(A) and 301.6109-4(b)(2)(iv). If you are correcting your EIN, enter the originally reported federal EIN you used in box h.

Box f—Establishment number. You may use this box to identify separate establishments in your business. You may file a separate Form W-3c, with Forms W-2c, for each establishment or you may use a single Form W-3c for all Forms W-2c. You do not have to complete this item; it is optional.

Box g—Employer's state ID number. You are not required to complete this box. This number is assigned by the individual state where your business is located. However, you may want to complete this item if you use copies of this form for your state returns.

Box h—Employer's originally reported Federal EIN. Your correct number must appear in box e. Make an entry here only if the number on the original form was incorrect.

Box i—Incorrect establishment number. You may use this box to correct an establishment number.

Box j—Employer's incorrect state ID number. Use this box to make any corrections to your previously reported state ID number.

Boxes 1 through 8, 10, and 11. Enter the total of amounts reported in boxes 1 through 8, 10, and 11 as "Previously reported" and "Correct information" from Forms W-2c.

Box 12a—Deferred compensation. Enter the total of amounts reported with codes D through H, S, Y, AA, BB, and EE as "Previously reported" and "Correct information" from Forms W-2c.

 The total of Form W-2c box 12 amounts reported with codes A through C, J through R, T through W, Z, DD, FF, GG, and HH is not reported on Form W-3c.

Box 14—Inc. tax w/h by third-party sick pay payer. Enter the amount previously reported and the corrected amount of income tax withheld on third-party payments of sick pay. Although this tax is included in the box 2 amounts, it must be shown separately here.

Boxes 16 through 19. If your only changes to the Forms W-2c and W-3c are to the state and local data, do not send either Copy A of Form W-2c or Form W-3c to the SSA. Instead, send the forms to the appropriate state or local agency and furnish copies of Form W-2c to your employees.

Explain decreases here. Explain any decrease to amounts "Previously reported." Also report here any previous incorrect entry in box c, "Kind of Payer" or "Kind of Employer." Enclose (but do not attach) additional

Forms W-2/ W-3 and W-2c/W3-c Instructions (Page 30)

sheets explaining your decreases, if necessary. Include your name and EIN on any additional sheets.

Signature. Sign and date the form. Also enter your title and employer's contact person, employer's telephone number, employer's fax number, and employer's email address, if available. If you are not the employer, see *Who may sign Form W-3*.

Privacy Act and Paperwork Reduction Act Notice. We ask for the information on Forms W-2 and W-3 to carry out the Internal Revenue laws of the United States. We need it to figure and collect the right amount of tax. Section 6051 and its regulations require you to furnish wage and tax statements to employees, the Social Security Administration, and the Internal Revenue Service. Section 6109 requires you to provide your employer identification number (EIN). Failure to provide this information in a timely manner or providing false or fraudulent information may subject you to penalties.

You are not required to provide the information requested on a form that is subject to the Paperwork Reduction Act unless the form displays a valid OMB control number. Books or records relating to a form or its instructions must be retained as long as their contents may become material in the administration of any Internal Revenue law.

Generally, tax returns and return information are confidential, as required by section 6103. However, section 6103 allows or requires the Internal Revenue Service to disclose or give the information shown on your return to others as described in the Code. For example, we may disclose your tax information to the Department of Justice for civil and/or criminal litigation, and to cities, states, the District of Columbia, and U.S. commonwealths and possessions for use in administering their tax laws. We may also disclose this information to other countries under a tax treaty, to federal and state agencies to enforce federal nontax criminal laws, or to federal law enforcement and intelligence agencies to combat terrorism.

The time needed to complete and file these forms will vary depending on individual circumstances. The estimated average times are: Form W-2—30 minutes; Form W-3—28 minutes; Form W-2c—40 minutes; Form W-3c—51 minutes. If you have comments concerning the accuracy of these time estimates or suggestions for making these forms simpler, we would be happy to hear from you. You can send us comments from *IRS.gov/ FormComments*. Or you can write to the Internal Revenue Service, Tax Forms and Publications Division, 1111 Constitution Ave. NW, IR-6526, Washington, DC 20224. Do not send Forms W-2 and W-3 to this address. Instead, see *Where to file paper Forms W-2 and W-3*.

Form W-2 Reference Guide for Box 12 Codes

A	Uncollected social security or RRTA tax on tips	L	Substantiated employee business expense reimbursements	Y	Deferrals under a section 409A nonqualified deferred compensation plan
B	Uncollected Medicare tax on tips (but not Additional Medicare Tax)	M	Uncollected social security or RRTA tax on taxable cost of group-term life insurance over $50,000 (former employees only)	Z	Income under a nonqualified deferred compensation plan that fails to satisfy section 409A
C	Taxable cost of group-term life insurance over $50,000	N	Uncollected Medicare tax on taxable cost of group-term life insurance over $50,000 (but not Additional Medicare Tax) (former employees only)	AA	Designated Roth contributions under a section 401(k) plan
D	Elective deferrals under a section 401(k) cash or deferred arrangement plan (including a SIMPLE 401(k) arrangement)	P	Excludable moving expense reimbursements paid directly to members of the Armed Forces	BB	Designated Roth contributions under a section 403(b) plan
E	Elective deferrals under a section 403(b) salary reduction agreement	Q	Nontaxable combat pay	DD	Cost of employer-sponsored health coverage
F	Elective deferrals under a section 408(k)(6) salary reduction SEP	R	Employer contributions to an Archer MSA	EE	Designated Roth contributions under a governmental section 457(b) plan
G	Elective deferrals and employer contributions (including nonelective deferrals) to a section 457(b) deferred compensation plan	S	Employee salary reduction contributions under a section 408(p) SIMPLE plan	FF	Permitted benefits under a qualified small employer health reimbursement arrangement
H	Elective deferrals to a section 501(c)(18)(D) tax-exempt organization plan	T	Adoption benefits	GG	Income from qualified equity grants under section 83(i)
J	Nontaxable sick pay	V	Income from exercise of nonstatutory stock option(s)	HH	Aggregate deferrals under section 83(i) elections as of the close of the calendar year
K	20% excise tax on excess golden parachute payments	W	Employer contributions (including employee contributions through a cafeteria plan) to an employee's health savings account (HSA)		

See *Box 12 Codes*.

Forms W-2/ W-3 and W-2c/W3-c Instructions (Page 31)

Form W-2 Box 13 Retirement Plan Checkbox Decision Chart

Type of Plan	Conditions	Check Retirement Plan Box?
Defined benefit plan (for example, a traditional pension plan)	Employee qualifies for employer funding into the plan, due to age/years of service—even though the employee may not be vested or ever collect benefits	Yes
Defined contribution plan (for example, a 401(k) or 403(b) plan, a Roth 401(k) or 403(b) account, but not a 457 plan)	Employee is eligible to contribute but does not elect to contribute any money in this tax year	No
Defined contribution plan (for example, a 401(k) or 403(b) plan, a Roth 401(k) or 403(b) account, but not a 457 plan)	Employee is eligible to contribute and elects to contribute money in this tax year	Yes
Defined contribution plan (for example, a 401(k) or 403(b) plan, a Roth 401(k) or 403(b) account, but not a 457 plan)	Employee is eligible to contribute but does not elect to contribute any money in this tax year, but the employer does contribute funds	Yes
Defined contribution plan (for example, a 401(k) or 403(b) plan, a Roth 401(k) or 403(b) account, but not a 457 plan)	Employee contributed in past years but not during the current tax year under report	No (even if the account value grows due to gains in the investments)
Profit-sharing plan	Plan includes a grace period after the close of the plan year when profit sharing can be added to the participant's account	Yes, unless the employer contribution is purely discretionary and no contribution is made by end of plan year

See _Box 13 Checkboxes_.

Mastering Payroll II

Forms W-2/ W-3 and W-2c/W3-c Instructions (Page 32)

Nonqualified Deferred Compensation Reporting Example Chart

Example	How to report on Form W-2
Example 1—Deferral, immediately vested (no risk of forfeiture). Regular wages: $200 Defer, vested: $20 Employer match, vested: $10	Box 1 = $180 ($200 – $20) Boxes 3 and 5 = $210 ($200 + $10) Box 11 = $0
Example 2—Deferral, delayed vesting (risk of forfeiture) of employee and employer portions. Regular wages: $200 Defer, not vested: $20 Employer match, not vested: $10	Box 1 = $180 ($200 – $20) Boxes 3 and 5 = $180 ($200 – $20) Box 11 = $0
Example 3—Deferral, immediately vested. Prior-year deferrals and employer matches are now vesting. Regular wages: $200 Defer, vested: $20 Vesting of prior-year deferrals and employer matches: $100 + $15 (earnings on $100)	Box 1 = $180 ($200 – $20) Boxes 3 and 5 = $315 ($200 + $100 + $15) Box 11 = $115 ($100 + $15)
Example 4—No deferrals, but there are distributions. No vesting of prior-year deferrals. Regular wages: $100 Distribution: $50	Box 1 = $150 ($100 + $50) Boxes 3 and 5 = $100 Box 11 = $50
Special Rule for W-2 Box 11: Distributions and Deferrals in the Same Year—Form SSA-131	If, in the same year, there are NQDC distributions and deferrals that are reportable in boxes 3 and/or 5 (current or prior-year deferrals), do not complete box 11. Instead, report on Form SSA-131 the total amount the employee earned during the year. Generally, the amount earned by the employee during the tax year for purposes of item 6 of Form SSA-131 is the amount reported in box 1 of Form W-2 plus current-year deferrals that are vested (employee and employer portions) less distributions. Do not consider prior-year deferrals that are vesting in the current year. If there was a plan failure, the box 1 amount in this calculation should be as if there were no plan failure. Submit the Form SSA-131 to the nearest SSA office or give it to the employee.
Example 5—Deferral, immediately vested, and distributions. No vesting of prior-year deferrals. Regular wages: $200 Defer, vested: $20 Employer match, vested: $10 Distribution: $50	Box 1 = $230 ($200 – $20 + $50) Boxes 3 and 5 = $210 ($200 + $10) Box 11 = $0 Form SSA-131 = $210 ($230 (box 1) – $50 (distribution) + $30 (vested employee and employer deferrals))
Example 6—Deferral, delayed vesting, and distributions. No vesting of prior-year deferrals. Regular wages: $200 Defer, not vested: $20 Distribution: $50	Box 1 = $230 ($200 – $20 + $50) Boxes 3 and 5 = $180 ($200 – $20) Box 11 = $50
Example 7—Deferral, immediately vested, and distributions. Prior-year deferrals and employer matches are now vesting. Regular wages: $200 Defer, vested: $20 Distribution: $50 Vesting of prior-year deferrals and employer matches: $100 + $15 (earnings on $100)	Box 1 = $230 ($200 – $20 + $50) Boxes 3 and 5 = $315 ($200 + $100 + $15) Box 11 = $0 Form SSA-131 = $200 ($230 (box 1) – $50 (distribution) + $20 (vested deferral))
Example 8—Deferral, delayed vesting, and distributions. Prior-year deferrals and employer matches are now vesting. Regular wages: $200 Defer, not vested: $20 Distribution: $50 Vesting of prior-year deferrals and employer matches: $100 + $15 (earnings on $100)	Box 1 = $230 ($200 – $20 + $50) Boxes 3 and 5 = $295 ($200 – $20 + $100 + $15) Box 11 = $0 Form SSA-131 = $180 ($230 (box 1) – $50 (distribution))

See *Nonqualified deferred compensation plans*.

Forms W-2/ W-3 and W-2c/W3-c Instructions (Page 33)

Nonqualified Deferred Compensation Reporting Example Chart—(*Continued*)

Example	How to report on Form W-2
Special Rule for Payment of Social Security, Medicare, and Unemployment Taxes If the amount cannot be reasonably ascertained (the employer is unable to calculate an amount for a year by December 31), the employer can use two methods. For example, immediately vested employer contributions to NQDC made late in the year would have no effect on Form W-2, box 1, but they would affect FICA and FUTA taxes.	*Estimated Method* Under the estimated method, an employer may treat a reasonably estimated amount as wages paid on the last day of the calendar year (the "first year"). If the employer underestimates the amount deferred and, thereby, underdeposits social security, Medicare, or FUTA taxes, it can choose to treat the shortfall as wages either in the first year or the first quarter of the next year. The shortfall does not include income credited to the amount deferred after the first year. Conversely, if the amount deferred is overestimated, the employer can claim a refund or credit. If the employer chooses to treat the shortfall as wages in the first year, the employer must issue a Form W-2c. Also, the employer must correct the information on the Form 941 for the last quarter of the first year. In such a case, the shortfall will not be treated as a late deposit subject to penalty if it is deposited by the employer's first regular deposit date following the first quarter of the next year. *Lag Method* Under the lag method, an employer may calculate the end-of-the-year amount on any date in the first quarter of the next calendar year. The amount deferred will be treated as wages on that date, and the amount deferred that would otherwise have been taken into account on the last day of the first year must be increased by income earned on that amount through the date on which the amount is taken into account.
Section 409A NQDC Plan Failure Example 9—Deferral, immediately vested. No distributions. Plan failure. Plan balance on January 1, 2010: $325, vested Regular wages: $100 Defer, vested: $50 Employer match, vested: $25 Plan failure in 2010.	Box 12, code Z = $400 • Amount in the plan account on December 31, 2010, not subject to risk of forfeiture and not included in prior-year income: $400 ($325 + $50 + $25) • Current-year distribution: $0 • $400 ($0 + $400) Box 1 = $450 ($100 – $50 + $400) Boxes 3 and 5 = $125 ($100 + $25) Box 11 = $0 Form SSA-131 = not required
Section 409A NQDC Plan Failure Example 10—Deferral, some delayed vesting, and distributions. Plan failure. Plan balance on January 1, 2010: $250 vested; $75 not vested Regular wages: $100 Defer, vested: $50 Employer match, not vested: $25 Distribution: $200 Plan failure in 2010. Vesting of prior-year deferrals and employer matches: $0	Box 12, code Z = $300 • Amount in the plan account on December 31, 2010, not subject to risk of forfeiture and not included in prior-year income: $100 ($250 + $50 – $200) • Current-year distribution: $200 • $100 + $200 = $300 Box 1 = $350 ($100 – $50 + $300 (code Z amount, which already includes the distribution)) Boxes 3 and 5 = $100 Box 11 = $0 Form SSA-131 = $100 ($250 (what box 1 would have been without plan failure) – $200 (distribution) + $50 (vested deferral))

See *Nonqualified deferred compensation plans*.

General Instructions for Forms W-2 and W-3 (2021)   -33-

Forms W-2/ W-3 and W-2c/W3-c Instructions (Page 34)

Index

-34-

Forms W-2/ W-3 and W-2c/W3-c Instructions (Page 35)

-35-

Form W-2c

44444	For Official Use Only ▶ OMB No. 1545-0008		

DO NOT CUT, FOLD, OR STAPLE THIS FORM

a Employer's name, address, and ZIP code	c Tax year/Form corrected / W-2	d Employee's correct SSN
	e Corrected SSN and/or name (Check this box and complete boxes f and/or g if incorrect on form previously filed.) ☐	
	Complete boxes f and/or g only if incorrect on form **previously filed** ▶	
	f Employee's **previously reported** SSN	
b Employer's Federal EIN	g Employee's **previously reported** name	
	h Employee's first name and initial	Last name	Suff.

Note. Only complete money fields that are being corrected (exception: for corrections involving MQGE, see the General Instructions for Forms W-2 and W-3, under Specific Instructions for Form W-2c, boxes 5 and 6).

i Employee's address and ZIP code

Previously reported	Correct information	Previously reported	Correct information
1 Wages, tips, other compensation	1 Wages, tips, other compensation	2 Federal income tax withheld	2 Federal income tax withheld
3 Social security wages	3 Social security wages	4 Social security tax withheld	4 Social security tax withheld
5 Medicare wages and tips	5 Medicare wages and tips	6 Medicare tax withheld	6 Medicare tax withheld
7 Social security tips	7 Social security tips	8 Allocated tips	8 Allocated tips
9	9	10 Dependent care benefits	10 Dependent care benefits
11 Nonqualified plans	11 Nonqualified plans	12a See instructions for box 12	12a See instructions for box 12
13 Statutory employee / Retirement plan / Third-party sick pay ☐ ☐ ☐	13 Statutory employee / Retirement plan / Third-party sick pay ☐ ☐ ☐	12b	12b
14 Other (see instructions)	14 Other (see instructions)	12c	12c
		12d	12d

State Correction Information

Previously reported	Correct information	Previously reported	Correct information
15 State	15 State	15 State	15 State
Employer's state ID number	Employer's state ID number	Employer's state ID number	Employer's state ID number
16 State wages, tips, etc.	16 State wages, tips, etc.	16 State wages, tips, etc.	16 State wages, tips, etc.
17 State income tax	17 State income tax	17 State income tax	17 State income tax

Locality Correction Information

Previously reported	Correct information	Previously reported	Correct information
18 Local wages, tips, etc.	18 Local wages, tips, etc.	18 Local wages, tips, etc.	18 Local wages, tips, etc.
19 Local income tax	19 Local income tax	19 Local income tax	19 Local income tax
20 Locality name	20 Locality name	20 Locality name	20 Locality name

For Privacy Act and Paperwork Reduction Act Notice, see separate instructions.

Copy A—For Social Security Administration

Form **W-2c** (Rev. 8-2014)   **Corrected Wage and Tax Statement**   Cat. No. 61437D   Department of the Treasury
Internal Revenue Service

Form W-3

DO NOT STAPLE

33333	a Control number	For Official Use Only ▶ OMB No. 1545-0008

b Kind of Payer (Check one): 941 ☐ Military ☐ 943 ☐ 944 ☐ CT-1 ☐ Hshld. emp. ☐ Medicare govt. emp. ☐

Kind of Employer (Check one): None apply ☐ 501c non-govt. ☐ State/local non-501c ☐ State/local 501c ☐ Federal govt. ☐

Third-party sick pay (Check if applicable) ☐

c Total number of Forms W-2	d Establishment number	1 Wages, tips, other compensation	2 Federal income tax withheld
e Employer identification number (EIN)		3 Social security wages	4 Social security tax withheld
f Employer's name		5 Medicare wages and tips	6 Medicare tax withheld
		7 Social security tips	8 Allocated tips
		9	10 Dependent care benefits
		11 Nonqualified plans	12a Deferred compensation
g Employer's address and ZIP code			
h Other EIN used this year		13 For third-party sick pay use only	12b
15 State Employer's state ID number		14 Income tax withheld by payer of third-party sick pay	
16 State wages, tips, etc.	17 State income tax	18 Local wages, tips, etc.	19 Local income tax
Employer's contact person		Employer's telephone number	For Official Use Only
Employer's fax number		Employer's email address	

Under penalties of perjury, I declare that I have examined this return and accompanying documents, and, to the best of my knowledge and belief, they are true, correct, and complete.

Signature ▶   Title ▶   Date ▶

Form **W-3** Transmittal of Wage and Tax Statements **2021** Department of the Treasury Internal Revenue Service

Send this entire page with the entire Copy A page of Form(s) W-2 to the Social Security Administration (SSA). Photocopies are not acceptable. Do not send Form W-3 if you filed electronically with the SSA. Do not send any payment (cash, checks, money orders, etc.) with Forms W-2 and W-3.

Reminder

Separate instructions. See the 2021 General Instructions for Forms W-2 and W-3 for information on completing this form. Do not file Form W-3 for Form(s) W-2 that were submitted electronically to the SSA.

Purpose of Form

Complete a Form W-3 Transmittal only when filing paper Copy A of Form(s) W-2, Wage and Tax Statement. Don't file Form W-3 alone. All paper forms **must** comply with IRS standards and be machine readable. Photocopies are **not** acceptable. Use a Form W-3 even if only one paper Form W-2 is being filed. Make sure both the Form W-3 and Form(s) W-2 show the correct tax year and Employer Identification Number (EIN). Make a copy of this form and keep it with Copy D (For Employer) of Form(s) W-2 for your records. The IRS recommends retaining copies of these forms for 4 years.

E-Filing

The SSA strongly suggests employers report Form W-3 and Forms W-2 Copy A electronically instead of on paper. The SSA provides two free e-filing options on its Business Services Online (BSO) website.

• **W-2 Online.** Use fill-in forms to create, save, print, and submit up to 50 Forms W-2 at a time to the SSA.

• **File Upload.** Upload wage files to the SSA you have created using payroll or tax software that formats the files according to the SSA's *Specifications for Filing Forms W-2 Electronically (EFW2).*

W-2 Online fill-in forms or file uploads will be on time if submitted by **January 31, 2022.** For more information, go to *www.SSA.gov/bso*. First-time filers, select *"Register"*; returning filers, select *"Log In."*

When To File Paper Forms

Mail Form W-3 with Copy A of Form(s) W-2 by **January 31, 2022.**

Where To File Paper Forms

Send this entire page with the entire Copy A page of Form(s) W-2 to:

Social Security Administration Direct Operations Center Wilkes-Barre, PA 18769-0001

Note: If you use "Certified Mail" to file, change the ZIP code to "18769-0002." If you use an IRS-approved private delivery service, add "ATTN: W-2 Process, 1150 E. Mountain Dr." to the address and change the ZIP code to "18702-7997." See Pub. 15 (Circular E), Employer's Tax Guide, for a list of IRS-approved private delivery services.

For Privacy Act and Paperwork Reduction Act Notice, see the separate instructions.

Cat. No. 10159Y

Form W-3c

DO NOT CUT, FOLD, OR STAPLE

55555	a Tax year/Form corrected _____ / W- _____	For Official Use Only ▶ OMB No. 1545-0008	

b Employer's name, address, and ZIP code	c Kind of Payer (Check one)	Kind of Employer (Check one)	Third-party sick pay

c Kind of Payer (Check one)

941/941-SS ☐	Military ☐	943 ☐	944 ☐
CT-1 ☐	Hshld. emp. ☐	Medicare govt. emp. ☐	

Kind of Employer (Check one)

None apply ☐	501c non-govt. ☐
State/local non-501c ☐	State/local 501c ☐	Federal govt. ☐

Third-party sick pay

☐ (Check if applicable)

d Number of Forms W-2c	e Employer's Federal EIN	f Establishment number	g Employer's state ID number

Complete boxes h, i, or j only if incorrect on last form filed.	h Employer's **originally reported** Federal EIN	i **Incorrect** establishment number	j Employer's **incorrect** state ID number

Total of amounts previously reported as shown on enclosed Forms W-2c.	Total of corrected amounts as shown on enclosed Forms W-2c.	Total of amounts previously reported as shown on enclosed Forms W-2c.	Total of corrected amounts as shown on enclosed Forms W-2c.
1 Wages, tips, other compensation	1 Wages, tips, other compensation	2 Federal income tax withheld	2 Federal income tax withheld
3 Social security wages	3 Social security wages	4 Social security tax withheld	4 Social security tax withheld
5 Medicare wages and tips	5 Medicare wages and tips	6 Medicare tax withheld	6 Medicare tax withheld
7 Social security tips	7 Social security tips	8 Allocated tips	8 Allocated tips
9	9	10 Dependent care benefits	10 Dependent care benefits
11 Nonqualified plans	11 Nonqualified plans	12a Deferred compensation	12a Deferred compensation
14 Inc. tax w/h by third-party sick pay payer	14 Inc. tax w/h by third-party sick pay payer	12b	12b
16 State wages, tips, etc.	16 State wages, tips, etc.	17 State income tax	17 State income tax
18 Local wages, tips, etc.	18 Local wages, tips, etc.	19 Local income tax	19 Local income tax

Explain decreases here:

Has an adjustment been made on an employment tax return filed with the Internal Revenue Service? ☐ Yes ☐ No

If "Yes," give date the return was filed ▶

Under penalties of perjury, I declare that I have examined this return, including accompanying documents, and, to the best of my knowledge and belief, it is true, correct, and complete.

Signature ▶   Title ▶   Date ▶

Employer's contact person	Employer's telephone number	For Official Use Only
Employer's fax number	Employer's email address	

Form **W-3c** (Rev. 11-2015) **Transmittal of Corrected Wage and Tax Statements** Department of the Treasury
Internal Revenue Service

Purpose of Form

Use this form to transmit Copy A of the most recent version of **Form(s) W-2c**, Corrected Wage and Tax Statement. Make a copy of Form W-3c and keep it with Copy D (For Employer) of Forms W-2c for your records. File Form W-3c even if only one Form W-2c is being filed or if those Forms W-2c are being filed only to correct an employee's name and social security number (SSN) or the employer identification number (EIN). See the General Instructions for Forms W-2 and W-3 for information on completing this form.

E-Filing

The SSA strongly suggests employers report Form W-3c and Forms W-2c Copy A electronically instead of on paper. The SSA provides two free e-filing options on its Business Services Online (BSO) website:

• **W-2c Online.** Use fill-in forms to create, save, print, and submit up to 25 Forms W-2c at a time to the SSA.

• **File Upload.** Upload wage files to the SSA you have created using payroll or tax software that formats the files according to the SSA's *Specifications for Filing Forms W-2c Electronically (EFW2C)*.

For more information, go to *www.socialsecurity.gov/employer*. First time filers, select *"Go to Register"*; returning filers select *"Go To Log In."*

For Paperwork Reduction Act Notice, see separate instructions.

When To File

File this form and Copy A of Form(s) W-2c with the Social Security Administration as soon as possible after you discover an error on Forms W-2, W-2AS, W-2GU, W-2CM, W-2VI, or W-2c. Provide Copies B, C, and 2 of Form W-2c to your employees as soon as possible.

Where To File

If you use the U.S. Postal Service, send Forms W-2c and W-3c to the following address:

**Social Security Administration
Data Operations Center
P.O. Box 3333
Wilkes-Barre, PA 18767-3333**

If you use a carrier other than the U.S. Postal Service, send Forms W-2c and W-3c to the following address:

**Social Security Administration
Data Operations Center
Attn: W-2c Process
1150 E. Mountain Drive
Wilkes-Barre, PA 18702-7997**

Cat. No. 10164R

Form 1099-MISC

9595 ☐ VOID ☐ CORRECTED		

PAYER'S name, street address, city or town, state or province, country, ZIP or foreign postal code, and telephone no.	**1** Rents $	OMB No. 1545-0115	
	2 Royalties $	20**21** Form **1099-MISC**	**Miscellaneous Information**
	3 Other income $	**4** Federal income tax withheld $	**Copy A** For
PAYER'S TIN / RECIPIENT'S TIN	**5** Fishing boat proceeds $	**6** Medical and health care payments $	**Internal Revenue Service Center** File with Form 1096.
RECIPIENT'S name	**7** Payer made direct sales totaling $5,000 or more of consumer products to recipient for resale ☐	**8** Substitute payments in lieu of dividends or interest $	For Privacy Act and Paperwork Reduction Act Notice, see the
Street address (including apt. no.)	**9** Crop insurance proceeds $	**10** Gross proceeds paid to an attorney $	**2021 General Instructions for Certain Information Returns.**
City or town, state or province, country, and ZIP or foreign postal code	**11** Fish purchased for resale $	**12** Section 409A deferrals $	
Account number (see instructions)	FATCA filing requirement ☐	2nd TIN not. ☐ **13** Excess golden parachute payments $	**14** Nonqualified deferred compensation $	
	15 State tax withheld $ $	**16** State/Payer's state no.	**17** State income $ $

Form **1099-MISC**   Cat. No. 14425J   www.irs.gov/Form1099MISC   Department of the Treasury - Internal Revenue Service

Do Not Cut or Separate Forms on This Page — Do Not Cut or Separate Forms on This Page

Form 1099-NEC

☐ VOID ☐ CORRECTED	

PAYER'S name, street address, city or town, state or province, country, ZIP or foreign postal code, and telephone no.		OMB No. 1545-0116	Nonemployee Compensation
		2021	
		Form **1099-NEC**	

PAYER'S TIN	RECIPIENT'S TIN	**1** Nonemployee compensation $	**Copy 1**
RECIPIENT'S name		**2** Payer made direct sales totaling $5,000 or more of consumer products to recipient for resale ☐	**For State Tax Department**
		3	
Street address (including apt. no.)		**4** Federal income tax withheld $	
City or town, state or province, country, and ZIP or foreign postal code		**5** State tax withheld $	**6** State/Payer's state no.	**7** State income $
Account number (see instructions)		$		$

Form **1099-NEC**   www.irs.gov/Form1099NEC   Department of the Treasury - Internal Revenue Service

Form 1099-MISC Instructions (Page 1)

2021
Instructions for Forms 1099-MISC and 1099-NEC

 Department of the Treasury
Internal Revenue Service

Miscellaneous Information and Nonemployee Compensation

Section references are to the Internal Revenue Code unless otherwise noted.

Future Developments

For the latest information about developments related to Forms 1099-MISC and 1099-NEC and their instructions, such as legislation enacted after they were published, go to *IRS.gov/Form1099MISC* or *IRS.gov/Form1099NEC*.

What's New

Form 1099-MISC title change. The title for Form 1099-MISC has been changed from Miscellaneous Income to Miscellaneous Information.

Form 1099-MISC, box 11. Box 11 includes any reporting under section 6050R, regarding cash payments for the purchase of fish for resale purposes, from an individual or corporation who is engaged in catching fish. For further information, see the instructions for box 11, later.

Form 1099-NEC, box 1. Box 1 will not be used for reporting under section 6050R, regarding cash payments for the purchase of fish for resale purposes.

Form 1099-NEC, box 2. Payers may use either box 2 on Form 1099-NEC or box 7 on Form 1099-MISC to report any sales totaling $5,000 or more of consumer products for resale, on buy-sell, deposit-commission, or any other basis. For further information, see the instructions later for box 2 (Form 1099-NEC) or box 7 (Form 1099-MISC).

Form 1099-NEC resized. We have reduced the height of the form so it can accommodate 3 forms on a page.

Electronic filing of returns. The Taxpayer First Act of 2019, enacted July 1, 2019, authorized the Department of the Treasury and the IRS to issue regulations that reduce the 250-return requirement for 2021 tax returns. If those regulations are issued and effective for 2021 tax returns required to be filed in 2022, we will post an article at *IRS.gov* explaining the change.

Reminders

General instructions. In addition to these specific instructions, you should also use the 2021 General Instructions for Certain Information Returns. Those general instructions include information about the following topics.
• Who must file.
• When and where to file.
• Electronic reporting.
• Corrected and void returns.
• Statements to recipients.
• Taxpayer identification numbers (TINs).

• Backup withholding.
• Penalties.
• The definitions of terms applicable for the purposes of chapter 4 of the Internal Revenue Code that are referenced in these instructions.
• Other general topics.

   You can get the general instructions from *General Instructions for Certain Information Returns* at *IRS.gov/1099GeneralInstructions* or go to *IRS.gov/Form1099MISC* or *IRS.gov/Form1099NEC*.

Online fillable copies. To ease statement furnishing requirements, Copies B, C, 1, and 2 have been made fillable online in a PDF format available at *IRS.gov/Form1099MISC* and *IRS.gov/Form1099NEC*. You can complete these copies online for furnishing statements to recipients and for retaining in your own files.

Filing dates. Section 6071(c) requires you to file Form 1099-NEC on or before January 31, 2022, using either paper or electronic filing procedures. File Form 1099-MISC by February 28, 2022, if you file on paper, or March 31, 2022, if you file electronically.

Specific Instructions for Form 1099-MISC

File Form 1099-MISC, Miscellaneous Information, for each person in the course of your business to whom you have paid the following during the year.
• At least $10 in royalties (see the instructions for box 2) or broker payments in lieu of dividends or tax-exempt interest (see the instructions for box 8).
• At least $600 in:

   1. Rents (box 1);

   2. Prizes and awards (box 3);

   3. Other income payments (box 3);

   4. Generally, the cash paid from a notional principal contract to an individual, partnership, or estate (box 3);

   5. Any fishing boat proceeds (box 5);

   6. Medical and health care payments (box 6);

   7. Crop insurance proceeds (box 9);

   8. Gross proceeds paid to an attorney (box 10) (see *Payments to attorneys*, later);

   9. Section 409A deferrals (box 12); or

   10. Nonqualified deferred compensation (box 14).

   You may either file Form 1099-MISC or Form 1099-NEC to report sales totaling $5,000 or more of consumer products

Nov 17, 2020   Cat. No. 74614G

Form 1099-MISC Instructions (Page 2)

to a person on buy-sell, deposit-commission, or other commission basis for resale.

 If you use Form 1099-NEC to report sales totaling $5,000 or more, then you are required to file Form 1099-NEC with the IRS by January 31.

You must also file Form 1099-MISC for each person from whom you have withheld any federal income tax (report in box 4) under the backup withholding rules regardless of the amount of the payment.

 Be sure to report each payment in the proper box because the IRS uses this information to determine whether the recipient has properly reported the payment.

Trade or business reporting only. Report on Form 1099-MISC only when payments are made in the course of your trade or business. Personal payments are not reportable. You are engaged in a trade or business if you operate for gain or profit. However, nonprofit organizations are considered to be engaged in a trade or business and are subject to these reporting requirements. Other organizations subject to these reporting requirements include trusts of qualified pension or profit-sharing plans of employers, certain organizations exempt from tax under section 501(c) or (d), farmers' cooperatives that are exempt from tax under section 521, and widely held fixed investment trusts. Payments by federal, state, or local government agencies are also reportable.

Reportable payments to corporations. The following payments made to corporations must generally be reported on Form 1099-MISC.
• Cash payments for the purchase of fish for resale reported in box 11.
• Medical and health care payments reported in box 6.
• Substitute payments in lieu of dividends or tax-exempt interest reported in box 8.
• Gross proceeds paid to an attorney reported in box 10.

Payments to attorneys. The term "attorney" includes a law firm or other provider of legal services. Attorneys' fees of $600 or more paid in the course of your trade or business are reportable in box 1 of Form 1099-NEC, under section 6041A(a)(1).

Gross proceeds paid to attorneys. Under section 6045(f), report in box 10 payments that:
• Are made to an attorney in the course of your trade or business in connection with legal services, but not for the attorney's services, for example, as in a settlement agreement;
• Total $600 or more; and
• Are not reportable by you in box 1 of Form 1099-NEC.

Generally, you are not required to report the claimant's attorney's fees. For example, an insurance company pays a claimant's attorney $100,000 to settle a claim. The insurance company reports the payment as gross proceeds of $100,000 in box 10. However, the insurance company does not have a reporting requirement for the claimant's attorney's fees subsequently paid from these funds.

These rules apply whether or not:
• The legal services are provided to the payer;
• The attorney is the exclusive payee (for example, the attorney's and claimant's names are on one check); or

• Other information returns are required for some or all of a payment under another section of the Code, such as section 6041.

For example, a person who, in the course of a trade or business, pays $600 of taxable damages to a claimant by paying that amount to a claimant's attorney is required to:
• Furnish Form 1099-MISC to the claimant, reporting damages pursuant to section 6041, generally in box 3; and
• Furnish Form 1099-MISC to the claimant's attorney, reporting gross proceeds paid pursuant to section 6045(f) in box 10.
For more examples and exceptions relating to payments to attorneys, see Regulations section 1.6045-5.

However, these rules do not apply to wages paid to attorneys that are reportable on Form W-2 or to profits distributed by a partnership to its partners that are reportable on Schedule K-1 (Form 1065), Partner's Share of Income, Deductions, Credits, etc.

Payments to corporations for legal services. The exemption from reporting payments made to corporations does not apply to payments for legal services. Therefore, you must report attorneys' fees (in box 1 of Form 1099-NEC) or gross proceeds (in box 10 of Form 1099-MISC), as described earlier, to corporations that provide legal services.

Taxpayer identification numbers (TINs). To report payments to an attorney on Form 1099-MISC, you must obtain the attorney's TIN. You may use Form W-9, Request for Taxpayer Identification Number and Certification, to obtain the attorney's TIN. An attorney is required to promptly supply its TIN whether it is a corporation or other entity, but the attorney is not required to certify its TIN. If the attorney fails to provide its TIN, the attorney may be subject to a penalty under section 6723 and its regulations, and you must backup withhold on the reportable payments.

Deceased employee's wages. When an employee dies during the year, you must report the accrued wages, vacation pay, and other compensation paid after the date of death. If you made the payment in the same year the employee died, you must withhold social security and Medicare taxes on the payment and report them only as social security and Medicare wages on the employee's Form W-2 to ensure that proper social security and Medicare credit is received. On the Form W-2, show the payment as social security wages (box 3) and Medicare wages and tips (box 5) and the social security and Medicare taxes withheld in boxes 4 and 6; do not show the payment in box 1 of Form W-2.

If you made the payment after the year of death, do not report it on Form W-2 and do not withhold social security and Medicare taxes.

Whether the payment is made in the year of death or after the year of death, you must also report the payment to the estate or beneficiary on Form 1099-MISC. Report the payment in box 3 (rather than as nonemployee compensation). See the *Example* that follows. Enter the name and TIN of the payment recipient on Form 1099-MISC. For example, if the recipient is an individual beneficiary, enter the name and social security number of the individual; if the recipient is the estate, enter the name and employer identification number of the estate. The general backup withholding rules apply to this payment.

Death benefits from nonqualified deferred compensation plans or section 457 plans paid to the estate or beneficiary of a deceased employee are reportable on Form 1099-MISC. Do not report these death benefits on Form 1099-R.

Form 1099-MISC Instructions (Page 3)

However, if the benefits are from a qualified plan, report them on Form 1099-R. See the Instructions for Forms 1099-R and 5498.

Example. Before Employee A's death on June 15, 2021, A was employed by Employer X and received $10,000 in wages on which federal income tax of $1,500 was withheld. When A died, X owed A $2,000 in wages and $1,000 in accrued vacation pay. The total of $3,000 (less the social security and Medicare taxes withheld) was paid to A's estate on July 20, 2021. Because X made the payment during the year of death, X must withhold social security and Medicare taxes on the $3,000 payment and must complete Form W-2 as follows.
• Box 1—10000.00 (does not include the $3,000 accrued wages and vacation pay).
• Box 2—1500.00.
• Box 3—13000.00 (includes the $3,000 accrued wages and vacation pay).
• Box 4—806.00 (social security tax withheld).
• Box 5—13000.00 (includes the $3,000 accrued wages and vacation pay).
• Box 6—188.50 (Medicare tax withheld).

Employer X must also complete Form 1099-MISC as follows.
• Boxes for recipient's name, address, and TIN—The estate's or beneficiary's name, address, and TIN.
• Box 3—3000.00 (Even though amounts were withheld for social security and Medicare taxes, the gross amount is reported here.)

If Employer X made the payment after the year of death, the $3,000 would not be subject to social security and Medicare taxes and would not be shown on Form W-2. However, the employer would still file Form 1099-MISC.

Payments made on behalf of another person. For payments reportable under section 6041, if you make a payment on behalf of another person, who is the source of the funds, you may be responsible for filing Form 1099-MISC. You are the payor for information reporting purposes if you perform management or oversight functions in connection with the payment, or have a significant economic interest in the payment (such as a lien). For example, a bank that provides financing to a real estate developer for a construction project maintains an account from which it makes payments for services in connection with the project. The bank performs management and oversight functions over the payments and is responsible for filing information returns for payments of $600 or more paid to contractors. For more information, see Regulations section 1.6041-1(e).

Indian gaming profits, payments to tribal members. If you make payments to members of Indian tribes from the net revenues of class II or class III gaming activities conducted or licensed by the tribes, you must withhold federal income tax on such payments. File Form 1099-MISC to report the payments and withholding to tribal members. Report the payments in box 3 and the federal income tax withheld in box 4. Pub. 15-A contains the necessary Tables for Withholding on Distributions of Indian Gaming Profits to Tribal Members.

State or local sales taxes. If state or local sales taxes are imposed on the service provider and you (as the buyer) pay them to the service provider, report them on Form 1099-MISC as part of the reportable payment. However, if sales taxes are imposed on you (as the buyer) and collected from you by the service provider, do not report the sales taxes on Form 1099-MISC.

Exceptions

Some payments do not have to be reported on Form 1099-MISC, although they may be taxable to the recipient. Payments for which a Form 1099-MISC is not required include all of the following.
• Generally, payments to a corporation (including a limited liability company (LLC) that is treated as a C or S corporation). However, see *Reportable payments to corporations*, earlier.
• Payments for merchandise, telegrams, telephone, freight, storage, and similar items.
• Payments of rent to real estate agents or property managers. However, the real estate agent or property manager must use Form 1099-MISC to report the rent paid over to the property owner. See Regulations section 1.6041-3(d); Regulations section 1.6041-1(e)(5), Example 5; and the instructions for box 1.
• Wages paid to employees (report on Form W-2, Wage and Tax Statement).
• Military differential wage payments made to employees while they are on active duty in the U.S. Armed Forces or other uniformed services (report on Form W-2).
• Business travel allowances paid to employees (may be reportable on Form W-2).
• Cost of current life insurance protection (report on Form W-2 or Form 1099-R, Distributions From Pensions, Annuities, Retirement or Profit-Sharing Plans, IRAs, Insurance Contracts, etc.).
• Payments to a tax-exempt organization including tax-exempt trusts (IRAs, HSAs, Archer MSAs, Coverdell ESAs, and ABLE (529A) accounts), the United States, a state, the District of Columbia, a U.S. possession or territory, or a foreign government.
• Payments made to or for homeowners from the HFA Hardest Hit Fund or similar state program (report on Form 1098-MA).
• Compensation for injuries or sickness by the Department of Justice as a public safety officer disability or survivor's benefit, or under a state program that provides benefits for surviving dependents of a public safety officer who has died as the direct and proximate result of a personal injury sustained in the line of duty.
• Compensation for wrongful incarceration for any criminal offense for which there was a conviction under federal or state law. See section 139F, Certain amounts received by wrongfully incarcerated individuals.

Form 1099-K. Payments made with a credit card or payment card and certain other types of payments, including third-party network transactions, must be reported on Form 1099-K by the payment settlement entity under section 6050W and are not subject to reporting on Form 1099-MISC. See the separate Instructions for Form 1099-K.

Fees paid to informers. A payment to an informer as an award, fee, or reward for information about criminal activity does not have to be reported if the payment is made by a federal, state, or local government agency, or by a nonprofit organization exempt from tax under section 501(c)(3) that makes the payment to further the charitable purpose of lessening the burdens of government. For more information, see Regulations section 1.6041-3(l).

Scholarships. Do not use Form 1099-MISC to report scholarship or fellowship grants. Scholarship or fellowship

Form 1099-MISC Instructions (Page 4)

grants that are taxable to the recipient because they are paid for teaching, research, or other services as a condition for receiving the grant are considered wages and must be reported on Form W-2. Other taxable scholarship or fellowship payments (to a degree or nondegree candidate) do not have to be reported to the IRS on any form, unless section 6050S requires reporting of such amounts by an educational institution on Form 1098-T, Tuition Statement. See section 117(b)–(d) and Regulations section 1.6041-3(n) for more information.

Canceled debt. A canceled debt is not reportable on Form 1099-MISC. Canceled debts reportable under section 6050P must be reported on Form 1099-C. See the Instructions for Forms 1099-A and 1099-C.

Employee business expense reimbursements. Do not use Form 1099-MISC to report employee business expense reimbursements. Report payments made to employees under a nonaccountable plan as wages on Form W-2. Generally, payments made to employees under an accountable plan are not reportable on Form W-2, except in certain cases when you pay a per diem or mileage allowance. For more information, see the Instructions for Forms W-2 and W-3, and Pub. 463. For information on reporting employee moving expense reimbursements on Form W-2, see the Instructions for Forms W-2 and W-3.

Widely held fixed investment trusts (WHFITs). Trustees and middlemen of WHFITs must report items of gross income attributable to a trust income holder (TIH) on the appropriate Form 1099. A tax information statement that includes the information provided to the IRS on Forms 1099, as well as additional information identified in Regulations section 1.671-5(e), must be furnished to TIHs. For details, see the 2021 General Instructions for Certain Information Returns.

Statements to Recipients

If you are required to file Form 1099-MISC, you must furnish a statement to the recipient. For more information about the requirement to furnish a statement to each recipient, and truncation, see part M in the 2021 General Instructions for Certain Information Returns.

You can furnish each recipient with a single payee statement reporting all Form 1099-MISC payment types. You are required to furnish the payee statements by January 31 and file with the IRS by February 28 (March 31, if filing electronically).

Truncating recipient's TIN on payee statements. Pursuant to Regulations section 301.6109-4, all filers of this form may truncate a recipient's TIN (social security number (SSN), individual taxpayer identification number (ITIN), adoption taxpayer identification number (ATIN), or employer identification number (EIN)) on payee statements. Truncation is not allowed on any documents the filer files with the IRS. A payer's TIN may not be truncated on any form. See part J in the 2021 General Instructions for Certain Information Returns.

Foreign Account Tax Compliance Act (FATCA) Filing Requirement Checkbox

Check the box if you are a U.S. payer that is reporting on Form(s) 1099 (including reporting payments on this Form 1099-MISC) as part of satisfying your requirement to report with respect to a U.S. account for the purposes of chapter 4 of the Internal Revenue Code, as described in Regulations

section 1.1471-4(d)(2)(iii)(A). In addition, check the box if you are a foreign financial institution (FFI) reporting payments to a U.S. account pursuant to an election described in Regulations section 1.1471-4(d)(5)(i)(A). Finally, check the box if you are an FFI making the election described in Regulations section 1.1471-4(d)(5)(i)(A) and are reporting a U.S. account for chapter 4 purposes to which you made no payments during the year that are reportable on any applicable Form 1099 (or are reporting a U.S. account to which you made payments during the year that do not reach the applicable reporting threshold for any applicable Form 1099).

2nd TIN Not.

You may enter an "X" in this box if you were notified by the IRS twice within 3 calendar years that the payee provided an incorrect TIN. If you mark this box, the IRS will not send you any further notices about this account.

However, if you received both IRS notices in the same year, or if you received them in different years but they both related to information returns filed for the same year, do not check the box at this time. For purposes of the two-notices-in-3-years rule, you are considered to have received one notice and you are not required to send a second "B" notice to the taxpayer on receipt of the second notice. See part N in the 2021 General Instructions for Certain Information Returns for more information.

 For information on the TIN Matching System offered by the IRS, see the 2021 General Instructions for Certain Information Returns.

Corrections to Form 1099-MISC

If you need to correct a Form 1099-MISC that you have already sent to the IRS:
• For paper forms, see the 2021 General Instructions for Certain Information Returns, part H; or
• For electronic corrections, see Pub. 1220.

 If you are filing a correction on a paper form, do not check the VOID box on the form. A checked VOID box alerts IRS scanning equipment to ignore the form and proceed to the next one. Your correction will not be entered into IRS records if you check the VOID box.

Recipient's TIN

Enter the recipient's TIN using hyphens in the proper format. SSNs, ITINs, and ATINs should be in the XXX-XX-XXXX format. EINs should be in the XX-XXXXXXX format. You should make every effort to ensure that you have the correct type of number reported in the correct format.

Account Number

The account number is required if you have multiple accounts for a recipient for whom you are filing more than one Form 1099-MISC. The account number is also required if you check the "FATCA filing requirement" box. See *Foreign Account Tax Compliance Act (FATCA) Filing Requirement Checkbox*, earlier. Additionally, the IRS encourages you to designate an account number for all Forms 1099-MISC that you file. See part L in the 2021 General Instructions for Certain Information Returns.

Form 1099-MISC Instructions (Page 5)

Box 1. Rents

Enter amounts of $600 or more for all types of rents, such as any of the following.
• Real estate rentals paid for office space. However, you do not have to report these payments on Form 1099-MISC if you paid them to a real estate agent or property manager. But the real estate agent or property manager must use Form 1099-MISC to report the rent paid over to the property owner. See Regulations section 1.6041-3(d) and Regulations section 1.6041-1(e)(5), Example 5.
• Machine rentals (for example, renting a bulldozer to level your parking lot). If the machine rental is part of a contract that includes both the use of the machine and the operator, prorate the rental between the rent of the machine (report that in box 1) and the operator's charge (report that on Form 1099-NEC in box 1).
• Pasture rentals (for example, farmers paying for the use of grazing land).

Public housing agencies must report in box 1 rental assistance payments made to owners of housing projects. See Rev. Rul. 88-53, 1988-1 C.B. 384.

Coin-operated amusements. If an arrangement between an owner of coin-operated amusements and an owner of a business establishment where the amusements are placed is a lease of the amusements or the amusement space, the owner of the amusements or the owner of the space, whoever makes the payments, must report the lease payments in box 1 of Form 1099-MISC if the payments total at least $600. However, if the arrangement is a joint venture, the joint venture must file a Form 1065, U.S. Return of Partnership Income, and provide each partner with the information necessary to report the partner's share of the taxable income. Coin-operated amusements include video games, pinball machines, jukeboxes, pool tables, slot machines, and other machines and gaming devices operated by coins or tokens inserted into the machines by individual users. For more information, see Rev. Rul. 92-49, 1992-1 C.B. 433.

Box 2. Royalties

Enter gross royalty payments (or similar amounts) of $10 or more. Report royalties from oil, gas, or other mineral properties before reduction for severance and other taxes that may have been withheld and paid. Do not include surface royalties. They should be reported in box 1. Do not report oil or gas payments for a working interest in box 2; report payments for working interests in box 1 of Form 1099-NEC. Do not report timber royalties made under a pay-as-cut contract; report these timber royalties on Form 1099-S, Proceeds From Real Estate Transactions.

Use box 2 to report royalty payments from intangible property such as patents, copyrights, trade names, and trademarks. Report the gross royalties (before reduction for fees, commissions, or expenses) paid by a publisher directly to an author or literary agent, unless the agent is a corporation. The literary agent (whether or not a corporation) that receives the royalty payment on behalf of the author must report the gross amount of royalty payments to the author on Form 1099-MISC whether or not the publisher reported the payment to the agent on its Form 1099-MISC.

Box 3. Other Income

Enter other income of $600 or more required to be reported on Form 1099-MISC that is not reportable in one of the other boxes on the form.

Also enter in box 3 prizes and awards that are not for services performed. Include the fair market value (FMV) of merchandise won on game shows. Also include amounts paid to a winner of a sweepstakes not involving a wager. If a wager is made, report the winnings on Form W-2G.

 If, not later than 60 days after the winner becomes entitled to the prize, the winner can choose the option of a lump sum or an annuity payable over at least 10 years, the payment of winnings is considered made when actually paid. If the winner chooses an annuity, file Form 1099-MISC each year to report the annuity paid during that year.

Do not include prizes and awards paid to your employees. Report these on Form W-2. Do not include in box 3 prizes and awards for services performed by nonemployees, such as an award for the top commission salesperson. Report them in box 1 of Form 1099-NEC.

Prizes and awards received in recognition of past accomplishments in religious, charitable, scientific, artistic, educational, literary, or civic fields are not reportable if:
• The winners are chosen without action on their part,
• The winners are not expected to perform future services, and
• The payer transfers the prize or award to a charitable organization or governmental unit under a designation made by the recipient. See Rev. Proc. 87-54, 1987-2 C.B. 669.

Other items required to be reported in box 3 include the following.

1. Payments as explained earlier under *Deceased employee's wages*.

2. Payments as explained earlier under *Indian gaming profits, payments to tribal members*.

3. A payment or series of payments made to individuals for participating in a medical research study or studies.

4. Termination payments to former self-employed insurance salespeople. These payments are not subject to self-employment tax and are reportable in box 3 (rather than box 1 of Form 1099-NEC) if all the following apply.

a. The payments are received from an insurance company because of services performed as an insurance salesperson for the company.

b. The payments are received after termination of the salesperson's agreement to perform services for the company.

c. The salesperson did not perform any services for the company after termination and before the end of the year.

d. The salesperson enters into a covenant not to compete against the company for at least 1 year after the date of termination.

e. The amount of the payments depends primarily on policies sold by the salesperson or credited to the salesperson's account during the last year of the service agreement or to the extent those policies remain in force for some period after termination, or both.

f. The amount of the payments does not depend at all on length of service or overall earnings from the company (regardless of whether eligibility for payment depends on length of service).

If the termination payments do not meet all these requirements, report them in box 1 of Form 1099-NEC.

Instructions for Forms 1099-MISC and 1099-NEC (2021)   **-5-**

Form 1099-MISC Instructions (Page 6)

5. Generally, all punitive damages, any damages for nonphysical injuries or sickness, and any other taxable damages. Report punitive damages even if they relate to physical injury or physical sickness. Generally, report all compensatory damages for nonphysical injuries or sickness, such as employment discrimination or defamation. However, do not report damages (other than punitive damages):

a. Received on account of personal physical injuries or physical sickness;

b. That do not exceed the amount paid for medical care for emotional distress;

c. Received on account of nonphysical injuries (for example, emotional distress) under a written binding agreement, court decree, or mediation award in effect on or issued by September 13, 1995; or

d. That are for a replacement of capital, such as damages paid to a buyer by a contractor who failed to complete construction of a building.

Damages received on account of emotional distress, including physical symptoms such as insomnia, headaches, and stomach disorders, are not considered received for a physical injury or physical sickness and are reportable unless described in item 5b or 5c above. However, damages received on account of emotional distress due to physical injuries or physical sickness are not reportable.

Also report liquidated damages received under the Age Discrimination in Employment Act of 1967.

 Taxable back pay damages may be wages and reportable on Form W-2. See Pub. 957.

Foreign agricultural workers. Report in box 3 compensation of $600 or more paid in a calendar year to an H-2A visa agricultural worker who did not give you a valid TIN. You must also withhold federal income tax under the backup withholding rules. For more information, go to IRS.gov and enter "foreign agricultural workers" in the search box.

Account reported under FATCA. If you are an FFI reporting pursuant to an election described in Regulations section 1.1471-4(d)(5)(i)(A) a U.S. account required to be reported under chapter 4 to which during the year you made no payments reportable on an applicable Form 1099, enter zero in box 3. In addition, if you are an FFI described in the preceding sentence and, during the year, you made payments to the account required to be reported under chapter 4, but those payments are not reportable on an applicable Form 1099 (for example, because the payment is under the applicable reporting threshold), you must report the account on this Form 1099-MISC and enter zero in box 3.

Box 4. Federal Income Tax Withheld

Enter backup withholding. For example, persons who have not furnished their TINs to you are subject to withholding on payments required to be reported in boxes 1, 2 (net of severance taxes), 3, 5 (only with respect to cash payments to crew members for their share of proceeds from the catch), 6, 8, 9, and 10. For more information on backup withholding, including the rate, see part N in the 2021 General Instructions for Certain Information Returns.

Also enter any income tax withheld from payments to members of Indian tribes from the net revenues of class II or class III gaming activities conducted or licensed by the tribes.

Box 5. Fishing Boat Proceeds

If you are the operator of a fishing boat, enter the individual's share of all proceeds from the sale of a catch or the FMV of a distribution in kind to each crew member of fishing boats with normally fewer than 10 crew members. A fishing boat has normally fewer than 10 crew members if the average size of the operating crew was fewer than 10 on trips during the preceding 4 calendar quarters.

In addition, report cash payments of up to $100 per trip that are contingent on a minimum catch and are paid solely for additional duties (such as mate, engineer, or cook) for which additional cash payments are traditional in the industry. However, do not report on Form 1099-MISC any wages reportable on Form W-2.

Box 6. Medical and Health Care Payments

Enter payments of $600 or more made in the course of your trade or business to each physician or other supplier or provider of medical or health care services. Include payments made by medical and health care insurers under health, accident, and sickness insurance programs. If payment is made to a corporation, list the corporation as the recipient rather than the individual providing the services. Payments to persons providing health care services often include charges for injections, drugs, dentures, and similar items. In these cases, the entire payment is subject to information reporting. You are not required to report payments to pharmacies for prescription drugs.

The exemption from issuing Form 1099-MISC to a corporation does not apply to payments for medical or health care services provided by corporations, including professional corporations. However, you are not required to report payments made to a tax-exempt hospital or extended care facility or to a hospital or extended care facility owned and operated by the United States (or its possessions or territories), a state, the District of Columbia, or any of their political subdivisions, agencies, or instrumentalities.

 Generally, payments made under a flexible spending arrangement (as defined in section 106(c)(2)) or a health reimbursement arrangement which is treated as employer-provided coverage under an accident or health plan for purposes of section 106 are exempt from the reporting requirements of section 6041.

Box 7. Payer Made Direct Sales Totaling $5,000 or More

Enter an "X" in the checkbox for sales by you totaling $5,000 or more of consumer products to a person on a buy-sell, deposit-commission, or other commission basis for resale (by the buyer or any other person) anywhere other than in a permanent retail establishment. Do not enter a dollar amount in this box.

You may either use box 7 on Form 1099-MISC or box 2 on Form 1099-NEC to report the direct sales totaling $5,000 or more. If you use Form 1099-NEC to report these sales, then you are required to file the Form 1099-NEC with the IRS by January 31.

The report you must give to the recipient for these direct sales need not be made on the official form. It may be in the form of a letter showing this information along with commissions, prizes, awards, etc.

Form 1099-MISC Instructions (Page 7)

Box 8. Substitute Payments in Lieu of Dividends or Interest

Enter aggregate payments of at least $10 of substitute payments received by a broker for a customer in lieu of dividends or tax-exempt interest as a result of a loan of a customer's securities. Substitute payment means a payment in lieu of (a) a dividend, or (b) tax-exempt interest to the extent that interest (including original issue discount) has accrued while the securities were on loan. For this purpose, a customer includes an individual, trust, estate, partnership, association, company, or corporation. See Notice 2003-67, which is on page 752 of Internal Revenue Bulletin 2003-40 at *IRS.gov/irb/2003-40_IRB#NOT-2003-67*. It does not include a tax-exempt organization, the United States, any state, the District of Columbia, a U.S. possession or territory, or a foreign government. File Form 1099-MISC with the IRS and furnish a copy to the customer for whom you received the substitute payment.

Box 9. Crop Insurance Proceeds

Enter crop insurance proceeds of $600 or more paid to farmers by insurance companies unless the farmer has informed the insurance company that expenses have been capitalized under section 278, 263A, or 447.

Box 10. Gross Proceeds Paid to an Attorney

Enter gross proceeds of $600 or more paid to an attorney in connection with legal services (regardless of whether the services are performed for the payer). See *Payments to attorneys*, earlier.

Box 11. Fish Purchased for Resale

If you are in the trade or business of purchasing fish for resale, you must report total cash payments of $600 or more paid during the year to any person who is engaged in the trade or business of catching fish. You are required to keep records showing the date and amount of each cash payment made during the year, but you must report only the total amount paid for the year on Form 1099-MISC.

"Fish" means all fish and other forms of aquatic life. "Cash" means U.S. and foreign coin and currency and a cashier's check, bank draft, traveler's check, or money order. Cash does not include a check drawn on your personal or business account.

Box 12. Section 409A Deferrals

You do not have to complete this box. For details, see Notice 2008-115, available at *IRS.gov/irb/2008-52_IRB#NOT-2008-115*.

If you complete this box, enter the total amount deferred during the year of at least $600 for the nonemployee under all nonqualified plans. The deferrals during the year include earnings on the current year and prior year deferrals. For additional information, see Regulations sections 1.409A-1 through 1.409A-6. See the instructions for box 14, later.

For deferrals and earnings under NQDC plans for employees, see the Instructions for Forms W-2 and W-3.

Box 13. Excess Golden Parachute Payments

Enter any excess golden parachute payments. An excess parachute payment is the amount over the base amount (the average annual compensation for services includible in the individual's gross income over the most recent 5 tax years).

See Q/A-38 through Q/A-44 of Regulations section 1.280G-1 for how to compute the excess amount.

See *Golden parachute payments*, later, for more information.

Box 14. Nonqualified Deferred Compensation

Enter all amounts deferred (including earnings on amounts deferred) that are includible in income under section 409A because the nonqualified deferred compensation (NQDC) plan fails to satisfy the requirements of section 409A. Do not include amounts properly reported on a Form 1099-MISC, corrected Form 1099-MISC, Form W-2, or Form W-2c for a prior year. Also, do not include amounts that are considered to be subject to a substantial risk of forfeiture for purposes of section 409A. For additional information, see Regulations sections 1.409A-1 through 1.409A-6; Notice 2008-113, available at *IRS.gov/irb/2008-51_IRB#NOT-2008-113*; Notice 2008-115; Notice 2010-6, available at *IRS.gov/irb/2010-03_IRB#NOT-2010-6*; and Notice 2010-80, available at *IRS.gov/irb/2010-51_IRB#NOT-2010-80*.

Boxes 15–17. State Information

These boxes may be used by payers who participate in the Combined Federal/State Filing Program and/or who are required to file paper copies of this form with a state tax department. See Pub. 1220 for more information regarding the Combined Federal/State Filing Program. They are provided for your convenience only and need not be completed for the IRS. Use the state information boxes to report payments for up to two states. Keep the information for each state separated by the dash line. If you withheld state income tax on this payment, you may enter it in box 15. In box 16, enter the abbreviated name of the state and the payer's state identification number. The state number is the payer's identification number assigned by the individual state. In box 17, you may enter the amount of the state payment.

If a state tax department requires that you send them a paper copy of this form, use Copy 1 to provide information to the state tax department. Give Copy 2 to the recipient for use in filing the recipient's state income tax return.

Specific Instructions for Form 1099-NEC

File Form 1099-NEC, Nonemployee Compensation, for each person in the course of your business to whom you have paid the following during the year.
- At least $600 in:

  1. Services performed by someone who is not your employee (including parts and materials) (box 1); or

  2. Payments to an attorney (box 1). (See *Payments to attorneys*, later.)

File Form 1099-NEC or Form 1099-MISC to report sales totaling $5,000 or more of consumer products to a person on buy-sell, deposit-commission, or other commission basis for resale.

 If you use Form 1099-NEC to report sales totaling $5,000 or more, then you are required to file Form 1099-NEC with the IRS by January 31.

You must also file Form 1099-NEC for each person from whom you have withheld any federal income tax (report in

Form 1099-MISC Instructions (Page 8)

box 4) under the backup withholding rules regardless of the amount of the payment.

> ⚠️ *Be sure to report each payment in the proper box because the IRS uses this information to determine whether the recipient has properly reported the payment.*

Trade or business reporting only. Report on Form 1099-NEC only when payments are made in the course of your trade or business. Personal payments are not reportable. You are engaged in a trade or business if you operate for gain or profit. However, nonprofit organizations are considered to be engaged in a trade or business and are subject to these reporting requirements. Other organizations subject to these reporting requirements include trusts of qualified pension or profit-sharing plans of employers, certain organizations exempt from tax under section 501(c) or 501(d), farmers' cooperatives that are exempt from tax under section 521, and widely held fixed investment trusts. Payments by federal, state, or local government agencies are also reportable.

Reportable payments to corporations. The following payments made to corporations must generally be reported on Form 1099-NEC.
• Attorneys' fees reported in box 1.
• Payments by a federal executive agency for services (vendors) reported in box 1.

> ⚠️ *Federal executive agencies may also have to file Form 8596, Information Return for Federal Contracts, and Form 8596-A, Quarterly Transmittal of Information Returns for Federal Contracts, if a contracted amount for personal services is more than $25,000. See Rev. Rul. 2003-66, which is on page 1115 of Internal Revenue Bulletin 2003-26 at IRS.gov/pub/irs-irbs/irb03-26.pdf for details.*

• Cash payments for the purchase of fish for resale reported in box 2.

Payments to attorneys. The term "attorney" includes a law firm or other provider of legal services. Attorneys' fees of $600 or more paid in the course of your trade or business are reportable in box 1 of Form 1099-NEC, under section 6041A(a)(1).

Gross proceeds paid to attorneys. Gross proceeds are not reportable by you in box 1 of Form 1099-NEC. See the Form 1099-MISC, box 10, instructions, earlier.

Payments to corporations for legal services. The exemption from reporting payments made to corporations does not apply to payments for legal services. Therefore, you must report attorneys' fees (in box 1 of Form 1099-NEC) or gross proceeds (in box 10 of Form 1099-MISC) as described earlier to corporations that provide legal services.

Taxpayer identification numbers (TINs). To report payments to an attorney on Form 1099-NEC, you must obtain the attorney's TIN. You may use Form W-9, Request for Taxpayer Identification Number and Certification, to obtain the attorney's TIN. An attorney is required to promptly supply its TIN whether it is a corporation or other entity, but the attorney is not required to certify its TIN. If the attorney fails to provide its TIN, the attorney may be subject to a penalty under section 6723 and its regulations, and you must backup withhold on the reportable payments.

Independent contractor or employee. Generally, you must report payments to independent contractors on Form 1099-NEC in box 1. See the instructions for box 1.

> *Section 530 of the Revenue Act of 1978 as extended by section 269(c) of P.L. 97-248 deals with the employment tax status of independent contractors and employees. To qualify for relief under section 530, employers must file Form 1099-NEC. Additional requirements for relief are discussed in Rev. Proc. 85-18, 1985-1 C.B. 518. Also see Pub. 15-A for special rules that may apply to technical service specialists and test proctors and room supervisors.*

Transit passes and parking for independent contractors. Although you cannot provide qualified transportation fringes to independent contractors, the working condition and de minimis fringe rules for transit passes and parking apply to independent contractors. Tokens or farecards that enable an independent contractor to commute on a public transit system (not including privately operated van pools) are excludable from the independent contractor's gross income and are not reportable on Form 1099-NEC if their value in any month is $21 or less. However, if the value of a pass provided in a month is greater than $21, the full value is part of the gross income and must be reported on Form 1099-NEC. The value of parking may be excludable from an independent contractor's gross income, and, therefore, not reportable on Form 1099-NEC if certain requirements are met. See Regulations section 1.132-9(b), Q/A-24.

Directors' fees. You must report directors' fees and other remuneration, including payments made after retirement, on Form 1099-NEC in the year paid. Report them in box 1.

Commissions paid to lottery ticket sales agents. A state that has control over and responsibility for online and instant lottery games must file Form 1099-NEC to report commissions paid, whether directly or indirectly, to licensed sales agents. For example, State X retains control over and liability for online and instant lottery games. For online ticket sales, State X pays commissions by allowing an agent to retain 5% of the ticket proceeds the agent remits to State X. For instant ticket sales, State X pays commissions by providing tickets to the agent for 5% less than the proceeds to be obtained by the agent from the sale of those tickets. If the commissions for the year total $600 or more, they must be reported in box 1 of Form 1099-NEC. See Rev. Rul. 92-96, 1992-2 C.B. 281.

Payments made on behalf of another person. For payments reportable under section 6041, if you make a payment on behalf of another person, who is the source of the funds, you may be responsible for filing Form 1099-NEC. You are the payor for information reporting purposes if you perform management or oversight functions in connection with the payment, or have a significant economic interest in the payment (such as a lien). For example, a bank that provides financing to a real estate developer for a construction project maintains an account from which it makes payments for services in connection with the project. The bank performs management and oversight functions over the payments and is responsible for filing information returns for payments of $600 or more paid to contractors. For more information, see Regulations section 1.6041-1(e).

Form 1099-MISC Instructions (Page 9)

Exceptions

Some payments do not have to be reported on Form 1099-NEC, although they may be taxable to the recipient. Payments for which a Form 1099-NEC is not required include all of the following.

• Generally, payments to a corporation (including a limited liability company (LLC) that is treated as a C or S corporation). However, see *Reportable payments to corporations*, earlier.

• Payments for merchandise, telegrams, telephone, freight, storage, and similar items.

• Payments of rent to real estate agents or property managers. However, the real estate agent or property manager must use Form 1099-MISC to report the rent paid over to the property owner. See Regulations section 1.6041-3(d); Regulations section 1.6041-1(e)(5), Example 5; and the instructions for box 1.

• Wages paid to employees (report on Form W-2, Wage and Tax Statement).

• Military differential wage payments made to employees while they are on active duty in the U.S. Armed Forces or other uniformed services (report on Form W-2).

• Business travel allowances paid to employees (may be reportable on Form W-2).

• Cost of current life insurance protection (report on Form W-2 or Form 1099-R, Distributions From Pensions, Annuities, Retirement or Profit-Sharing Plans, IRAs, Insurance Contracts, etc.).

• Payments to a tax-exempt organization including tax-exempt trusts (IRAs, HSAs, Archer MSAs, Coverdell ESAs, and ABLE (529A) accounts), the United States, a state, the District of Columbia, a U.S. possession or territory, or a foreign government.

• Payments made to or for homeowners from the HFA Hardest Hit Fund or similar state program (report on Form 1098-MA).

• Compensation for injuries or sickness by the Department of Justice as a public safety officer disability or survivor's benefit, or under a state program that provides benefits for surviving dependents of a public safety officer who has died as the direct and proximate result of a personal injury sustained in the line of duty.

• Compensation for wrongful incarceration for any criminal offense for which there was a conviction under federal or state law. See section 139F, Certain amounts received by wrongfully incarcerated individuals.

State or local sales taxes. If state or local sales taxes are imposed on the service provider and you (as the buyer) pay them to the service provider, report them on Form 1099-NEC as part of the reportable payment. However, if sales taxes are imposed on you (as the buyer) and collected from you by the service provider, do not report the sales taxes on Form 1099-NEC.

Form 1099-K. Payments made with a credit card or payment card and certain other types of payments, including third-party network transactions, must be reported on Form 1099-K by the payment settlement entity under section 6050W and are not subject to reporting on Form 1099-NEC. See the separate Instructions for Form 1099-K.

Fees paid to informers. A payment to an informer as an award, fee, or reward for information about criminal activity does not have to be reported if the payment is made by a federal, state, or local government agency, or by a nonprofit organization exempt from tax under section 501(c)(3) that makes the payment to further the charitable purpose of lessening the burdens of government. For more information, see Regulations section 1.6041-3(l).

Scholarships. Do not use Form 1099-NEC to report scholarship or fellowship grants. Scholarship or fellowship grants that are taxable to the recipient because they are paid for teaching, research, or other services as a condition for receiving the grant are considered wages and must be reported on Form W-2. Other taxable scholarship or fellowship payments (to a degree or nondegree candidate) do not have to be reported to the IRS on any form, unless section 6050S requires reporting of such amounts by an educational institution on Form 1098-T, Tuition Statement. See section 117(b)–(d) and Regulations section 1.6041-3(n) for more information.

Difficulty-of-care payments. Do not use Form 1099-NEC to report difficulty-of-care payments that are excludable from the recipient's gross income. Difficulty-of-care payments to foster care providers are not reportable if paid for fewer than 11 children under age 19 and fewer than six individuals age 19 or older. See section 131(c). Amounts paid for more than 10 children or more than five other individuals are reportable on Form 1099-NEC.

Certain Medicaid waiver payments may be excludable from income as difficulty-of-care payments. For more information, see Notice 2014-7, available at *IRS.gov/irb/ 2014-4_IRB#NOT-2014-7*, and Medicaid waiver payments frequently asked questions (FAQs), available at *IRS.gov/ Individuals/Certain-Medicaid-Payments-May-Be-Excludable-From-Income*.

Canceled debt. A canceled debt is not reportable on Form 1099-NEC. Canceled debts reportable under section 6050P must be reported on Form 1099-C. See the Instructions for Forms 1099-A and 1099-C.

Employee business expense reimbursements. Do not use Form 1099-NEC to report employee business expense reimbursements. Report payments made to employees under a nonaccountable plan as wages on Form W-2. Generally, payments made to employees under an accountable plan are not reportable on Form W-2, except in certain cases when you pay a per diem or mileage allowance. For more information, see the Instructions for Forms W-2 and W-3, and Pub. 463. For information on reporting employee moving expense reimbursements on Form W-2, see the Instructions for Forms W-2 and W-3.

Statements to Recipients

If you are required to file Form 1099-NEC, you must furnish a statement to the recipient. For more information about the requirement to furnish a statement to each recipient, and truncation, see part M in the 2021 General Instructions for Certain Information Returns.

You can furnish each recipient with a single payee statement reporting all Form 1099-NEC payment types. You are required to furnish the payee statements and file with the IRS by January 31.

Truncating recipient's TIN on payee statements. Pursuant to Regulations section 301.6109-4, all filers of this form may truncate a recipient's TIN (social security number (SSN), individual taxpayer identification number (ITIN), adoption taxpayer identification number (ATIN), or employer identification number (EIN)) on payee statements. Truncation is not allowed on any documents the filer files with the IRS. A payer's TIN may not be truncated on any form. See part J in

Instructions for Forms 1099-MISC and 1099-NEC (2021)   -9-

Form 1099-MISC Instructions (Page 10)

the 2021 General Instructions for Certain Information Returns.

2nd TIN Not.

You may enter an "X" in this box if you were notified by the IRS twice within 3 calendar years that the payee provided an incorrect TIN. If you mark this box, the IRS will not send you any further notices about this account.

However, if you received both IRS notices in the same year, or if you received them in different years but they both related to information returns filed for the same year, do not check the box at this time. For purposes of the two-notices-in-3-years rule, you are considered to have received one notice and you are not required to send a second "B" notice to the taxpayer on receipt of the second notice. See part N in the 2021 General Instructions for Certain Information Returns for more information.

 For information on the TIN Matching System offered by the IRS, see the 2021 General Instructions for Certain Information Returns.

Corrections to Form 1099-NEC

If you need to correct a Form 1099-NEC that you have already sent to the IRS:
• For paper forms, see the 2021 General Instructions for Certain Information Returns, part H; or
• For electronic corrections, see Pub. 1220.

If you are filing a correction on a paper form, do not check the VOID box on the form. A checked VOID box alerts IRS scanning equipment to ignore the form and proceed to the next one. Your correction will not be entered into IRS records if you check the VOID box.

Recipient's TIN

Enter the recipient's TIN using hyphens in the proper format. SSNs, ITINs, and ATINs should be in the XXX-XX-XXXX format. EINs should be in the XX-XXXXXXX format. You should make every effort to ensure that you have the correct type of number reported in the correct format.

Account Number

The account number is required if you have multiple accounts for a recipient for whom you are filing more than one Form 1099-NEC. See part L in the 2021 General Instructions for Certain Information Returns.

Box 1. Nonemployee Compensation

Enter nonemployee compensation (NEC) of $600 or more. Include fees, commissions, prizes and awards for services performed as a nonemployee, and other forms of compensation for services performed for your trade or business by an individual who is not your employee. Include oil and gas payments for a working interest, whether or not services are performed. Also include expenses incurred for the use of an entertainment facility that you treat as compensation to a nonemployee. Federal executive agencies that make payments to vendors for services, including payments to corporations, must report the payments in this box. See Rev. Rul. 2003-66.

What is NEC? If the following four conditions are met, you must generally report a payment as NEC.
• You made the payment to someone who is not your employee.

• You made the payment for services in the course of your trade or business (including government agencies and nonprofit organizations).
• You made the payment to an individual, partnership, estate, or, in some cases, a corporation.
• You made payments to the payee of at least $600 during the year.

Self-employment tax. Generally, amounts paid to individuals that are reportable in box 1 are subject to self-employment tax. If payments to individuals are not subject to this tax, report the payments in box 3 of Form 1099-MISC. However, report section 530 (of the Revenue Act of 1978) worker payments in box 1 of Form 1099-NEC.

Examples. The following are some examples of payments to be reported in box 1.
• Professional service fees, such as fees to attorneys (including corporations), accountants, architects, contractors, engineers, etc.
• Fees paid by one professional to another, such as fee-splitting or referral fees.
• Payments by attorneys to witnesses or experts in legal adjudication.
• Payment for services, including payment for parts or materials used to perform the services if supplying the parts or materials was incidental to providing the service. For example, report the total insurance company payments to an auto repair shop under a repair contract showing an amount for labor and another amount for parts, if furnishing parts was incidental to repairing the auto.
• Commissions paid to nonemployee salespersons that are subject to repayment but not repaid during the calendar year.
• A fee paid to a nonemployee, including an independent contractor, or travel reimbursement for which the nonemployee did not account to the payer, if the fee and reimbursement total at least $600. To help you determine whether someone is an independent contractor or an employee, see Pub. 15-A.
• Payments to nonemployee entertainers for services. Use Form 1042-S, Foreign Person's U.S. Source Income Subject to Withholding, for payments to nonresident aliens.
• Exchanges of services between individuals in the course of their trades or businesses. For example, an attorney represents a painter for nonpayment of business debts in exchange for the painting of the attorney's law offices. The amount reportable by each on Form 1099-NEC is the FMV of his or her own services performed. However, if the attorney represents the painter in a divorce proceeding, this is an activity that is unrelated to the painter's trade or business. The attorney must report on Form 1099-NEC the value of his or her services. But the painter need not report on Form 1099-NEC the value of painting the law offices because the work is in exchange for legal services that are separate from the painter's business.
• Taxable fringe benefits for nonemployees. For information on the valuation of fringe benefits, see Pub. 15-B, Employer's Tax Guide to Fringe Benefits.
• Gross oil and gas payments for a working interest.
• Payments to an insurance salesperson who is not your common law or statutory employee. See Pub. 15-A for the definition of employee. However, for termination payments to former insurance salespeople, see the instructions for box 3 of Form 1099-MISC..
• Directors' fees as explained under *Directors' fees*, earlier.

Form 1099-MISC Instructions (Page 11)

- Commissions paid to licensed lottery ticket sales agents as explained under *Commissions paid to lottery ticket sales agents*, earlier.
- Payments to section 530 (of the Revenue Act of 1978) workers. See the *TIP* under *Independent contractor or employee*, earlier.

Golden parachute payments. A parachute payment is any payment that meets all of the following conditions.

1. The payment is in the nature of compensation.

2. The payment is to, or for the benefit of, a disqualified individual. A disqualified individual is one who at any time during the 12-month period prior to and ending on the date of the change in ownership or control of the corporation (the disqualified individual determination period) was an employee or independent contractor and was, in regard to that corporation, a shareholder, an officer, or a highly compensated individual.

3. The payment is contingent on a change in the ownership of a corporation, the effective control of a corporation, or the ownership of a substantial portion of the assets of a corporation (a change in ownership or control).

4. The payment has (together with other payments described in (1), (2), and (3), above, made to the same individual) an aggregate present value of at least three times the individual's base amount.

For more details, see Regulations section 1.280G-1. Also, see Rev. Proc. 2003-68, which is on page 398 of Internal Revenue Bulletin 2003-34 at *IRS.gov/irb/ 2003-34_IRB#RP-2003-68*, concerning the valuation of stock options for purposes of golden parachute payment rules. For the treatment of unvested shares of restricted stock, see Rev. Rul. 2005-39, available at *IRS.gov/irb/ 2005-27_IRB#RR-2005-39*.

Independent contractor. Enter in box 1 the total compensation, including any golden parachute payment. For excess golden parachute payments, see the instructions for box 13 of Form 1099-MISC.

For employee reporting of these payments, see Pub. 15-A.

Payments not reported in box 1. Do not report in box 1:
- Expense reimbursements paid to volunteers of nonprofit organizations;
- Deceased employee wages paid in the year after death (report in box 3 of Form 1099-MISC) (see *Deceased employee's wages*, earlier);
- Payments more appropriately described as rent (report in box 1 of Form 1099-MISC), royalties (report in box 2 of Form 1099-MISC), other income not subject to self-employment tax (report in box 3 of Form 1099-MISC), interest (use Form 1099-INT);

- The cost of current life insurance protection (report on Form W-2 or Form 1099-R);
- An employee's wages, travel or auto allowance, or bonuses and prizes (report on Form W-2); and
- The cost of group-term life insurance paid on behalf of a former employee (report on Form W-2).

Box 2. Payer Made Direct Sales Totaling $5,000 or More

Enter an "X" in the checkbox for sales by you totaling $5,000 or more of consumer products to a person on a buy-sell, deposit-commission, or other commission basis for resale (by the buyer or any other person) anywhere other than in a permanent retail establishment. Do not enter a dollar amount in this box.

You may either use box 2 on Form 1099-NEC or box 7 on Form 1099-MISC to report the direct sales totaling $5,000 or more. If you use Form 1099-NEC to report these sales, then you are required to file the Form 1099-NEC with the IRS by January 31.

The report you must give to the recipient for these direct sales need not be made on the official form. It may be in the form of a letter showing this information along with commissions, prizes, awards, etc.

Box 4. Federal Income Tax Withheld

Enter backup withholding. For example, persons who have not furnished their TINs to you are subject to withholding on payments required to be reported in box 1. For more information on backup withholding, including the rate, see part N in the 2021 General Instructions for Certain Information Returns.

Boxes 5–7. State Information

These boxes are provided for your convenience only and need not be completed for the IRS. Use the state information boxes to report payments for up to two states. Keep the information for each state separated by the dash line. If you withheld state income tax on this payment, you may enter it in box 5. In box 6, enter the abbreviated name of the state and the payer's state identification number. In box 7, you may enter the amount of the state payment.

If a state tax department requires that you send them a paper copy of this form, use Copy 1 to provide information to the state tax department. Give Copy 2 to the recipient for use in filing the recipient's state income tax return.

Form 1099-MISC Instructions (Page 12)

Illustrated Example

The completed Form 1099-NEC illustrates the following example. Z Builders is a contractor that subcontracts drywall work to Ronald Green, a sole proprietor who does business as Y Drywall. During the year, Z Builders pays Mr. Green $5,500. Z Builders must file Form 1099-NEC because they paid Mr. Green $600.00 or more in the course of their trade or business, and Mr. Green is not a corporation.

```
7171        ☐ VOID      ☐ CORRECTED
```

PAYER'S name, street address, city or town, state or province, country, ZIP or foreign postal code, and telephone no. Z Builders 123 Maple Avenue Oaktown, AL 00000 555-555-1212	OMB No. 1545-0116 20**21** Form **1099-NEC** Nonemployee Compensation

PAYER'S TIN 10-9999999	RECIPIENT'S TIN 123-00-6789	**1** Nonemployee compensation $ 5500.00	**Copy A** For Internal Revenue Service Center
RECIPIENT'S name Ronald Green dba/Y Drywall		**2** Payer made direct sales totaling $5,000 or more of consumer products to recipient for resale ☐	File with Form 1096.
Street address (including apt. no.) 456 Flower Lane		**3**	For Privacy Act and Paperwork Reduction Act Notice, see the **2021 General Instructions for Certain Information Returns.**
City or town, state or province, country, and ZIP or foreign postal code Oaktown, AL 00000		**4** Federal income tax withheld $	
Account number (see instructions)	2nd TIN not. ☐	**5** State tax withheld	**6** State/Payer's state no.	**7** State income
		$ $		$ $

Form **1099-NEC**   Cat. No. 72590N   www.irs.gov/Form1099NEC   Department of the Treasury - Internal Revenue Service

Do Not Cut or Separate Forms on This Page — Do Not Cut or Separate Forms on This Page

Form 1099-MISC Instructions (Page 13)

Index

-13-

 Department of the Treasury
Internal Revenue Service

Notice 1439

(May 2018)

Figuring the Amount Exempt from Levy on Wages, Salary, and Other Income - Forms 668-W, 668-W(ACS) and 668-W(ICS)

On December 22, 2017, as part of the Tax Cut and Jobs Act, Congress added Section 6334(d)(4) to the Internal Revenue Code; exception for determining property exempt from levy when the personal exemption amount is zero. To implement this legislation the instructions below replace the instructions contained on the three versions of levy Form 668-W (revision date 01-2015).

If Money Is Due This Taxpayer

Give the taxpayer Parts 2, 3, 4 and 5, as soon as you receive this levy. Part of the taxpayer's wages, salary, or other income is exempt from levy. To claim exemptions, the taxpayer must complete and sign the Statement of Dependents and Filing Status on Parts 3, 4, and 5 and return Parts 3 and 4 to you within 3 work days after you receive this levy. The taxpayer's instructions for completing the Statement of Dependents and Filing Status are listed below. (Note: The Statement of Exemptions and Filing status is being renamed, Statement of Dependents and Filing Status. An example is provided at the end of these instructions.)

There are three steps in figuring the amount exempt from this levy.

1. When you receive the completed Form 668-W Parts 3 and 4 from the taxpayer, use item 1 of the enclosed table (Publication 1494) to figure how much wages, salary, or other income is exempt from this levy. Find the correct block on the table using the taxpayer's filing status, number of dependents claimed, and pay period. Taxpayers cannot claim themselves as a dependent. If no Social Security Number is provided for a dependent, do not allow that dependent, unless "Less than six months old" is written in the space for that person's Social Security Number. If you don't receive the completed Form 668-W Parts 3 and 4, then the exempt amount is what would be exempt if the taxpayer had returned them indicating married filing separate with no dependents (zero). Don't use the information on the taxpayer's Form W-4, Employee's Withholding Allowance Certificate, to determine the amount that is exempt from this levy. That information can be different from what is filed on the employee's individual income tax return.

2. If the taxpayer, or the taxpayer's spouse, is at least 65 years old and/or blind, an additional amount is exempt from this levy. To claim this, the taxpayer counts one for each of the following: (a) the taxpayer is 65 or older, (b) the taxpayer is blind, (c) the taxpayer's spouse is 65 or older, and (d) the taxpayer's spouse is blind. Then, this total (up to 4) is entered next to "ADDITIONAL STANDARD DEDUCTION" on the Statement of Dependents and Filing Status. If the taxpayer has entered a number in this space, use item 2 of the enclosed table to figure the additional amount exempt from this levy.

3. The amount the taxpayer needs to pay support, established by a court or an administrative order, for minor children is also exempt from the levy, but the court or administrative order must have been made before the date of this levy. These children can't be claimed as dependents on Form 668-W Parts 3, 4, and 5.

If the taxpayer's dependents, filing status, or eligibility for additional standard deduction change while this levy is in effect, the taxpayer may give you a new statement to change the amount that is exempt. You can get more forms from an IRS office. If you are sending payments for this levy next year, the amount that is exempt doesn't change merely because the amount that all taxpayers can deduct for dependents, filing status, and additional standard deductions changes for the new year. However, if the taxpayer asks you to recompute the exempt amount in the new year by submitting a new Statement of Dependents and Filing Status, even though there may be no change from the prior statement, you may use the new year's exemption table. This change applies to levies you already have as well as this one. If you are asked to recompute the exempt amount and you don't have the new year's exemption table, you may order one by calling 1-800-829-3676. Ask for Publication 1494. This publication is also available at our internet site www.irs.gov. The taxpayer submits the information under penalties of perjury, and it is subject to verification by the Internal Revenue Service.

IRS Notice 1439 (Page 2)

Instructions to the Taxpayer

A levy was served on the person named on the front of Form 668-W. The information you provide on Form 668-W will be used by that person to figure the amount of your income that is exempt from levy.

Complete Form 668-W Parts 3, 4, and 5. First, indicate your filing status by checking one of the five blocks on the Statement of Dependents and Filing Status. Then, list each person that you can claim as a dependent on your income tax return not claimed on another Notice of Levy on Wages, Salary, and Other Income. Include each person's relationship to you and Social Security Number. If the person is less than six months old and does not have a number yet, write "Less than six months old" in the Social Security Number column. You can't claim yourself as a dependent. Be sure to complete, sign and date all copies of the statement.

The amount of your income that is exempt from this levy each week can be figured by adding the standard deduction you can claim on your income tax return and the amount you claim on it for dependents. Then, this total is divided by 52.

If you or your spouse is at least 65 years old and/or blind, you can claim the additional standard deduction which increases the amount exempt from this levy. Count one for each of the following: (a) you are 65 or older, (b) you are blind, (c) your spouse is 65 or older, and (d) your spouse is blind. Enter this total (up to 4) to the right of "ADDITIONAL STANDARD DEDUCTION" on Form 668-W Parts 3, 4, and 5.

Also, if you are required by a court or administrative order (made before the date of this levy) to support your minor children, then the amount needed to pay the support established by a court or administrative order is also exempt from the levy, and these minor children can't be listed as dependents.

Keep Form 668-W Parts 2 and 5 for your records. Give Form 668-W Parts 3 and 4 to your employer within 3 work days after you receive them. If you do not give the completed statement to your employer, then your exempt amount will be figured as if your filing status is married filing separate with no dependents (zero), plus the amount for paying child support established by a court or administrative order. If you subsequently submit a Statement of Dependents and Filing Status to your employer, your exempt amount will be adjusted to correspond to your statement.

If the number of your dependents or your filing status change while this levy is in effect, file another Statement of Dependents and Filing Status with the person on whom this levy was served. You can get more forms from an Internal Revenue Service office or the office that issued the Form 668-W.

In addition, if this levy is still in effect next year and if the standard deduction and amount deductible for dependents change in the new year for all taxpayers, you may submit a new Statement of Dependents and Filing Status, even though there may be no change from the prior statement. Submitting a new Statement of Dependents and Filing Status will allow your employer to use the new year's exemption table (Publication 1494).

The information you provide is submitted under penalties of perjury and may be verified by the Internal Revenue Service.

Example of Statement of Dependents and Filing Status

Statement of Dependents and Filing Status *(To be completed by taxpayer; instructions are on the back of Part 5)*

My filing status for my income tax return is *(check one)*

☐ Single   ☐ Married Filing a Joint Return   ☐ Married Filing a Separate Return
☐ Head of Household   ☐ Qualifying Widow(er) with dependent child

Additional Standard Deduction _____ *(Enter amount only if you or your spouse is at least 65 and/or blind)*

I certify that I can claim the people named below as dependents on my income tax return and that none are claimed on another Notice of Levy. No one I have listed is my minor child to whom *(as required by court or administrative order)* I make support payments that are already exempt from levy. I understand the information I have provided may be verified by the Internal Revenue Service. Under penalties of perjury, I declare that this statement of dependents and filing status is true.

Name *(Last, First, Middle Initial)*	Relationship *(Qualifying Child or Qualifying Relative)*	Social Security Number (SSN)

Taxpayer's signature	Title	Date

Publication 1494

2021

1. Tables for Figuring Amount Exempt from Levy on Wages, Salary, and Other Income (Forms 668-W(ACS) and 668-W(ICS))

The tables below show the amount of an individual's income (take home pay) that is exempt from a notice of levy used to collect delinquent tax in 2021.

Filing Status: Single

Pay Period	Number of Dependents Claimed on Statement						
	0	1	2	3	4	5	More Than 5
Daily	48.27	64.81	81.35	97.89	114.43	130.97	48.27 plus 16.54 for each dependent
Weekly	241.35	324.04	406.73	489.42	572.11	654.80	241.35 plus 82.69 for each dependent
Biweekly	482.69	648.07	813.45	978.83	1144.21	1309.59	482.69 plus 165.38 for each dependent
Semimonthly	522.92	702.09	881.26	1060.43	1239.60	1418.77	522.92 plus 179.17 for each dependent
Monthly	1045.83	1404.16	1762.49	2120.82	2479.15	2837.48	1045.83 plus 358.33 for each dependent

Filing Status: Head of Household

Pay Period	Number of Dependents Claimed on Statement						
	0	1	2	3	4	5	More Than 5
Daily	72.31	88.85	105.39	121.93	138.47	155.01	72.31 plus 16.54 for each dependent
Weekly	361.54	444.23	526.92	609.61	692.30	774.99	361.54 plus 82.69 for each dependent
Biweekly	723.08	888.46	1053.84	1219.22	1384.60	1549.98	723.08 plus 165.38 for each dependent
Semimonthly	783.33	962.50	1141.67	1320.84	1500.01	1679.18	783.33 plus 179.17 for each dependent
Monthly	1566.67	1925.00	2283.33	2641.66	2999.99	3358.32	1566.67 plus 358.33 for each dependent

Filing Status: Married Filing Joint Return (and Qualifying Widow(er)s)

Pay Period	Number of Dependents Claimed on Statement						
	0	1	2	3	4	5	More Than 5
Daily	96.54	113.08	129.62	146.16	162.70	179.24	96.54 plus 16.54 for each dependent
Weekly	482.69	565.38	648.07	730.76	813.45	896.14	482.69 plus 82.69 for each dependent
Biweekly	965.38	1130.76	1296.14	1461.52	1626.90	1792.28	965.38 plus 165.38 for each dependent
Semimonthly	1045.83	1225.00	1404.17	1583.34	1762.51	1941.68	1045.83 plus 179.17 for each dependent
Monthly	2091.67	2450.00	2808.33	3166.66	3524.99	3883.32	2091.67 plus 358.33 for each dependent

Filing Status: Married Filing Separate Return

Pay Period	Number of Dependents Claimed on Statement						
	0	1	2	3	4	5	More Than 5
Daily	48.27	64.81	81.35	97.89	114.43	130.97	48.27 plus 16.54 for each dependent
Weekly	241.35	324.04	406.73	489.42	572.11	654.80	241.35 plus 82.69 for each dependent
Biweekly	482.69	648.07	813.45	978.83	1144.21	1309.59	482.69 plus 165.38 for each dependent
Semimonthly	522.92	702.09	881.26	1060.43	1239.60	1418.77	522.92 plus 179.17 for each dependent
Monthly	1045.83	1404.16	1762.49	2120.82	2479.15	2837.48	1045.83 plus 358.33 for each dependent

2. Table for Figuring Additional Exempt Amount for Taxpayers at Least 65 Years Old and/or Blind

Filing Status	*	Additional Exempt Amount				
		Daily	Weekly	Biweekly	Semi-monthly	Monthly
Single or Head of Household	1	6.54	32.69	65.38	70.83	141.67
	2	13.08	65.38	130.77	141.67	283.33
Any Other Filing Status	1	5.19	25.96	51.92	56.25	112.50
	2	10.38	51.92	103.85	112.50	225.00
	3	15.58	77.88	155.77	168.75	337.50
	4	20.77	103.85	207.69	225.00	450.00

* ADDITIONAL STANDARD DEDUCTION claimed on Parts 3,4, and 5 of levy.

Examples

These tables show the amount of take home pay that is exempt each pay period from a levy on wages, salary, and other income.

1. A single taxpayer who is paid weekly and claims three dependents has $489.42 exempt from levy.

2. If the taxpayer in number 1 is over 65 and writes 1 in the ADDITIONAL STANDARD DEDUCTION space on Parts 3, 4, & 5 of the levy, $522.11 is exempt from this levy ($489.42 plus $32.69).

3. A taxpayer who is married, files jointly, is paid bi-weekly, and claims two dependents has $1,296.14 exempt from levy.

4. if the taxpayer in number 3 is over 65 and has a spouse who is blind, this taxpayer should write 2 in the ADDITIONAL STANDARD DEDUCTION space on Parts 3,4, and 5 of the levy. If so, $1,399.99 is exempt from this levy ($1,296.14 plus $103.85).

Publication **1494** (2021)   www.irs.gov   Catalog Number 11439T   Department of Treasury -- **Internal Revenue Service**

Instructions: Detach the Final Examination Answer Sheet on page 391 before beginning your final examination. Select the correct letter for the answer to each multiple choice question below; then fill it in on the Answer Sheet. Allow approximately 2½ hours.

1. George is paid $500 per week in 2021 and claims married with 2 allowances on his 2019 Form W-4. What is his FITW using the percentage method of withholding?

    a. $27.14   b. $47.82   c. $9.90   d. $0

2. Joe's group-term life insurance, valued at $25, is imputed to his gross salary of $725. Joe's employer elects not to withhold FIT from this benefit. Assuming FICA of 7.65% and FITW of 15%, what is his net pay?

    a. $555.43   b. $583.88   c. $558.88   d. $555.13

3. Lorna has gross wages of $600 less FITW and FICA of $135.90 and a deduction of $15 for United Way. What is her disposable pay?

    a. $585.00   b. $600.00   c. $464.10   d. $449.10

4. Which of the following fringe benefits is tax-free up to the first $14,440 for 2021?

    a. educational assistance plan payments
    b. adoption assistance
    c. group-term life insurance
    d. employer-provided dental insurance

5. Under the special accounting rule, benefits received in _____ and _____ of 2021 may be recognized as provided in 2022.

    a. September, December
    b. November, December
    c. October, November
    d. December, January

6. WidgeCo reimburses Jose for one night's stay in San Francisco at a per diem of $327 in May 2021. How much taxable income must be recognized for Jose using the high-low substantiation method assuming that he properly substantiated his expenses?

    a. $200   b. $35   c. $292   d. $327

7. The annual lease value method must be used for cars placed in service in 2021 with a value exceeding . . .

    a. $16,000   b. $50,400   c. $15,900   d. $51,100

8. For 2021, an employee's pretax contributions to a 401(k) may not exceed . . .

    a. $5,000   b. $19,500   c. $19,000   d. $13,500

9. Third-party payers are notified to withhold federal income tax from sick pay on Form . . .

    a. W-4P   b. W-2P   c. 1099R   d. W-4S

10. An employee who will be 40 years old on April 1 receives group-term life insurance coverage of $75,000. How much taxable income must this employee recognize for January 2021?

    a. $2.50   b. $2.75   c. $12.75   d. $4.25

11. Tony's employer imputes taxable income of $33 on his next 2021 paycheck for his personal use of a company-owned car. His gross wages are $735, FICA is 7.65%, and FITW is 15%. The employer has elected not to withhold federal income tax on the imputed amount. What is his net pay?

    a. $594.05   b. $566.00   c. $599.00   d. $561.05

12. Which of the following is a monopolistic state?

    a. Wyoming
    b. California
    c. Indiana
    d. New Jersey

13. Al has gross wages of $800 from which his employer deducts total taxes of $250 and a medical insurance contribution of $35. What is his disposable pay?

    a. $765   b. $550   c. $800   d. $515

14. Using the wage-bracket method of withholding, calculate the 2021 federal income tax due on $540 gross wages paid weekly to an employee claiming single with 1 allowance on his 2019 Form W-4.

    a. $22   b. $13   c. $41   d. $43

15. On May 17, 2020, RelCo receives an IRS levy notice for Pete. How much per week is exempt from levy if Pete claims single with 1 dependent on Form 668-W(c)(DO)?

    a. $321.15   b. $315.39   c. $324.02   d. $75.00

16. Which of the following is an example of a working condition fringe benefit?

    a. a free ticket to a sporting event
    b. free coffee and donuts
    c. reimbursed membership dues to an accounting association
    d. employer-provided medical insurance

17. Which one of these benefits would not be reported in Box 12 of the W-2?

    a. group-term life over $50,000
    b. nontaxable third-party sick pay
    c. employee contributions to a 401(k)
    d. personal use of a company-owned vehicle

18. At what rate-per-mile may an employer reimburse an employee tax-free for use of a personal car for business in January 2021?

    a. $0.200   b. $0.56   c. $0.575   d. $0.055

19. What is the IRS annual lease value of a car with a blue book value of $24,500?

    a. $6,600   b. $6,850   c. $6,350   d. $5,100

20. For 2021, an employee's elective deferral to a SEP is reported on the . . .

    a. W-2, Box 1
    b. 941, Line 2
    c. W-2, Box 10
    d. W-2, Box 3

21. Taxable third-party sick pay received by Jean after the first 6 months of her disability is subject to . . .

    a. FITW
    b. FICA
    c. FICA and FUTA
    d. none of the above

22. Philip, who is 35 years old in 2021, receives group-term life insurance coverage of $75,000 and contributes $25 per year on an after-tax basis toward the premium cost. What is his annual taxable income for this benefit?

    a. $74   b. $99   c. $33   d. $2

23. Which of these states is designated "competitive rated" for workers' compensation insurance?

    a. Wyoming
    b. South Carolina
    c. Montana
    d. Washington

24. Using the wage-bracket method of withholding calculate the 2021 federal income tax due on weekly wages of $600 paid to an employee claiming married with 1 allowance and $5 additional withholding on his 2019 Form W-4.

    a. $5   b. $28   c. $55   d. $33

25. In June 2021, Robert's disposable pay is $545 for the week. What is the maximum deduction for an administrative wage garnishment assuming no other attachments apply to these wages?

    a. $463.25   b. $136.25   c. $54.50   d. $81.75

26. ACME pays $275 wholesale for each tape deck and sells it at retail for $350. What is the maximum tax-free discount that it can offer employees on this item?

    a. $70   b. $75   c. $350   d. $275

27. One example of a benefit reported in Box 14 of the W-2 is . . .

    a. use of a company-provided vehicle
    b. taxable relocation expense reimbursement
    c. employee contributions to a 401(k)
    d. group-term life insurance over $50,000

28. DelCo reimburses Natalie $0.59 per mile for driving her own car for business. In February 2021, she is reimbursed for 65 miles that she substantiated as business related. In which two boxes of the W-2 is this reported, and what amount is reported in each box?

    a. Box 1–$36.40   Box 12–$36.40
    b. Box 1–$ 1.95   Box 12–$36.40
    c. Box 1–$ 1.95   Box 12–$38.35
    d. Box 1–$36.40   Box 12–$ 1.95

29. Under the vehicle cents-per-mile method, an employee who drives 1,500 miles in a company car for personal business during August 2021 would recognize taxable income of . . .

    a. $82.50   b. $0   c. $840.00   d. $862.50

30. In 2021, Andrew earns $450 per week and makes a $50 pretax contribution for medical insurance to his employer's flexible benefit plan. Assuming FITW of 15% and FICA of 7.65%, what is his net pay?

    a. $309.40   b. $359.40   c. $298.08   d. $259.40

31. Dolores pays 100% of her disability insurance premium. She requires major surgery and receives $3,500 in sick pay from the insurance company during the first 2 months of her disability. How much of this $3,500 is subject to FICA?

    a. $0   b. $3,500   c. $1,500   d. $2,000

32. Harold is 53 years old in 2021. In 2021, he receives group-term life insurance coverage of $85,000 and makes an annual pretax contribution toward the premium of $50. What is his annual taxable income for this benefit?

    a. $201.60   b. $96.60   c. $251.60   d. $46.60

33. Roberta is a plant supervisor with office and plant duties. Which workers' compensation code should her employer use?

    a. 8810–office and administrative
    b. the governing class code
    c. 8724–salesperson
    d. 7380–driver

34. The flat supplemental withholding rate may not be used for . . .

    a. commissions
    b. incentive bonuses
    c. holiday pay
    d. severance pay

35. FlowerCo charges its landscaping customers $65 per hour. What is the maximum tax-free discount per hour it may offer its employees for this service?

    a. $13   b. $65   c. $15   d. $0

36. When an employee contributes to an employer SEP, the employer must report the SEP on the W-2 in Box 12 and . . .

    a. Box 1   b. Box 14   c. Box 13   d. Box 10

37. The IRS recommends that travel advances be given to employees no more than _____ before the employee's trip.

    a. 60 days   b. 90 days   c. 120 days   d. 30 days

38. Jane is driven to and from work in a free company van pool in 2021. During the year she takes 85 round trips. What is the fair market value of this van pool under the commuting-valuation method assuming the total miles driven were 1,150?

    a. $644.00   b. $22.10   c. $649.75   d. $255.00

39. Jacob is paid $550 per week. He makes a pretax contribution of $50 to his employer's flexible benefit plan for medical insurance. Assuming FITW of 15% and FICA of 7.65%, what is his weekly net pay?

a. $375.43   b. $382.93   c. $386.75   d. $418.75

40. Rachel requires surgery on April 23 and does not return to work until September 1. While on disability, she receives $1,500 in third-party sick pay. Her employer paid 45% of the disability insurance premium. How much of this payment is subject to FICA and FIT?

a. $825 subject to FICA $ 825 subject to FIT
b. $675 subject to FICA $ 675 subject to FIT
c. $1,500 subject to FICA $1,500 subject to FIT
d. $1,500 subject to FICA $ 675 subject to FIT

41. Group-term life insurance over $50,000 is subject to . . .

a. FICA
b. FUTA
c. FITW
d. all of the above

42. Which of the following generally is excluded when determining a workers' compensation insurance premium?

a. holiday pay
b. sick leave
c. commissions
d. tips

43. Uncollected Social Security tax on group-term life provided to a former employee is reported on Form W-2, Box 12 with the Code . . .

a. A   b. G   c. M   d. N

44. An example of a benefit reported on the 941, Line 2 is:

    a. wages paid in the year after an employee's death
    b. employee contributions to a 401(k)
    c. employee contributions to a SEP
    d. group-term life insurance over $50,000

45. In 2021, an employer elects not to withhold federal income tax from the value of employees' personal use of company-provided vehicles. By what date must the employer notify its employees of this election?

    a. December 31, 2021
    b. January 31, 2022
    c. January 31, 2021
    d. December 31, 2022

46. An example of a wage payment reported on a 1099-MISC is . . .

    a. deceased workers' wages paid in year after death
    b. auto allowance
    c. taxable third-party sick pay
    d. group-term life insurance over $50,000

47. An example of a benefit included as an exempt payment on the 940 is . . .

    a. taxable payment of relocation expenses
    b. group-term life insurance over $50,000
    c. taxable third-party sick pay
    d. personal use of a company-owned vehicle

48. Mark is paid $600 per week and contributes 3% of his gross wages to his employer's SEP plan. Assuming FITW of 15% and FICA of 7.65%, what is his weekly net pay?

    a. $450.18   b. $448.80   c. $466.80   d. $600.00

49. Maureen becomes disabled on March 15 and does not return to work until November 15. She receives $2,500 in third-party sick pay through September and $1,000 in October. If her employer pays 35% of the disability insurance premium, how much of the $3,500 is FIT taxable? How much is FICA taxable?

    a. $875 subject to FICA $1,225 subject to FIT
    b. $1,225 subject to FICA $1,225 subject to FIT
    c. $1,225 subject to FICA $ 875 subject to FIT
    d. $875 subject to FICA $ 875 subject to FIT

50. The method of calculating FITW that most closely approximates an automated system's calculation is:

    a. the percentage method
    b. the wage-bracket method
    c. the alternative flat rate
    d. back-up tax

Final Examination Answer Sheet
MASTERING PAYROLL II

Instructions: Detach this sheet before starting the Final Exam. For each question, check the box beneath the letter of the correct answer. Use a pen or a #2 pencil to make a dark impression. When completed, return to: AIPB Continuing Education, Suite 500, 6001 Montrose Road, Rockville, MD 20852. If you attain a grade of at least 70, you will receive the Institute's *Certificate of Completion*. Answer Sheets are not returned.

Certified Bookkeepers: If you attain a grade of at least 70, you are eligible to register seven (7) Continuing Professional Education Credits (CPECs) toward your CPEC requirements.

	a	b	c	d			a	b	c	d			a	b	c	d			a	b	c	d
1.	☐	☐	☐	☐	14.		☐	☐	☐	☐	27.		☐	☐	☐	☐	39.		☐	☐	☐	☐
2.	☐	☐	☐	☐	15.		☐	☐	☐	☐	28.		☐	☐	☐	☐	40.		☐	☐	☐	☐
3.	☐	☐	☐	☐	16.		☐	☐	☐	☐	29.		☐	☐	☐	☐	41.		☐	☐	☐	☐
4.	☐	☐	☐	☐	17.		☐	☐	☐	☐	30.		☐	☐	☐	☐	42.		☐	☐	☐	☐
5.	☐	☐	☐	☐	18.		☐	☐	☐	☐	31.		☐	☐	☐	☐	43.		☐	☐	☐	☐
6.	☐	☐	☐	☐	19.		☐	☐	☐	☐	32.		☐	☐	☐	☐	44.		☐	☐	☐	☐
7.	☐	☐	☐	☐	20.		☐	☐	☐	☐	33.		☐	☐	☐	☐	45.		☐	☐	☐	☐
8.	☐	☐	☐	☐	21.		☐	☐	☐	☐	34.		☐	☐	☐	☐	46.		☐	☐	☐	☐
9.	☐	☐	☐	☐	22.		☐	☐	☐	☐	35.		☐	☐	☐	☐	47.		☐	☐	☐	☐
10.	☐	☐	☐	☐	23.		☐	☐	☐	☐	36.		☐	☐	☐	☐	48.		☐	☐	☐	☐
11.	☐	☐	☐	☐	24.		☐	☐	☐	☐	37.		☐	☐	☐	☐	49.		☐	☐	☐	☐
12.	☐	☐	☐	☐	25.		☐	☐	☐	☐	38.		☐	☐	☐	☐	50.		☐	☐	☐	☐
13.	☐	☐	☐	☐	26.		☐	☐	☐	☐												

Name _____ Title _____

Company _____ Street Address _____

City _____ State _____ Zip _____ Phone Number _____

Email (Important) Please print clearly. _____

Course Evaluation for
MASTERING PAYROLL II

Please complete and return (even if you do not take the Final Examination) to: AIPB Continuing Education, 6001 Montrose Road, Suite 500, Rockville, MD 20852. **PLEASE PRINT CLEARLY.**

Circle one

1. Did you find the instructions clear?   Yes   No

Comments: _____

2. Did you find the course practical?   Yes   No

Comments_____

3. Is this course what you expected?   Yes   No

Comments_____

4. Would you recommend this course to other accounting professionals?   Yes   No

Comments: _____

5. What did you like most about *Mastering Payroll II*? _____

6. What would have made the course even more helpful? _____

7. May we use your comments and name in advertising for the course?   Yes   No

8. Would you be interested in other courses?   Yes   No

Please indicate what subject areas would be of greatest interest to you:

1. _____   4. _____

2. _____   5. _____

3. _____   6. _____

_____

Name (optional)   Title

_____

Company   Street Address

_____

City   State   Zip   Phone Number